Inclusive Wealth Report 2018

T0361981

The Inclusive Wealth Index provides important insights into long-term economic growth and human well-being. The Index measures the wealth of nations through a comprehensive analysis of a country's productive base and the country's wealth in terms of progress, well-being and long-term sustainability. It measures all assets which human well-being is based upon, in particular, produced, human and natural capital to create and maintain human well-being over time.

Shunsuke Managi is Distinguished Professor at Urban Institute & the Faculty of Engineering, Kyushu University.

Pushpam Kumar is Chief of Ecosystem Services Economics Unit, Division of Environment Programme Implementation, UNEP.

Inclusive Wealth Report 2018

Measuring Progress
Towards Sustainability

Edited by Shunsuke Managi and Pushpam Kumar

Routledge
Taylor & Francis Group

LONDON AND NEW YORK

UN environment
United Nations
Environment Programme

Urban Institute

First published 2018
by Routledge
2 Park Square, Milton Park, Abingdon, Oxon OX14 4RN

and by Routledge
52 Vanderbilt Avenue, New York, NY 10017

First issued in paperback 2020

Routledge is an imprint of the Taylor & Francis Group, an informa business

British Library Cataloguing-in-Publication Data
A catalog record for this book is available from the British Library

Library of Congress Cataloging-in-Publication Data
A catalogue record for this book has been requested

ISBN 13: 978-0-367-58808-3 (pbk)
ISBN 13: 978-1-138-54127-6 (hbk)

Typeset in Galliard
by Apex CoVantage, LLC

Contents

Figures

Tables

Contributors

Director

Shunsuke Managi is Distinguished Professor at Urban Institute & the Faculty of Engineering, Kyushu University.

Science advisory group

Partha Dasgupta is Frank Ramsey Professor Emeritus of Economics at the University of Cambridge, United Kingdom.

Anantha Duraiappah is Director of UNESCO MGIEP.

Barbara M. Fraumeni is Special-term Professor at Central University for Finance and Economics and Hunan University, China and Research Associate of the National Bureau of Economic Research, USA.

Harold Mooney is Paul S. and Billie Achilles Professor of Environmental Biology, Emeritus at the Stanford University, United States.

Hamid Zakri is Science Advisor to the Prime Minister of Malaysia, Malaysia.

Policy advisory board

Stig Johansson is Senior Forestry Specialist, Sustainable Development Network at the World Bank.

Pushpam Kumar is Chief Environmental Economist, UN Environment.

Arico Salvatore is Senior Programme Specialist for Biodiversity Assessments and Inter-Agency Coordination at UNESCO.

Agnès Soucat is Director of Health Systems Governance and Financing, World Health Organization.

Kazuhiko Takeuchi is Senior Visiting Professor, United Nations University Institute for the Advanced Study of Sustainability (UNU-IAS).

Authors

Edward B. Barbier is Professor at the Department of Economics, Colorado State University, USA.

David N. Barton is Senior Research Scientist at Norwegian Institute for Nature Research (NINA), Norway.

Anantha Kumar Duraiappah is Director of UNESCO MGIEP, India.

Barbara M. Fraumeni is Research Associate at National Bureau of Economic Research, USA and Professor at Central University for Finance and Economics, China.

Kristine Grimsrud is Senior Researcher at Statistics Norway, Norway.

Haripriya Gundimeda is Professor at the Department of Humanities and Social Sciences, Indian Institute of Technology Bombay, India.

Pushpam Kumar is Chief Environmental Economist, UN Environment.

Henrik Lindhjem is Head of Research at Menon Centre for Environmental and Resource Economics (MERE), Norway and Adjunct Researcher at Norwegian Institute for Nature Research (NINA), Norway.

Gang Liu is Research Fellow at Statistics Norway, Norway.

Shunsuke Managi is Distinguished Professor at Urban Institute & the Faculty of Engineering, Kyushu University.

Ståle Navrud is at the School of Economics and Business, Norwegian University of Life Sciences, Norway.

Bharath M. Palavalli is Researcher at Fields of View Bangalore, India.

Srijan Sil is Researcher at Fields of View Bangalore, India.

Rodney B W Smith is Professor at the Department of Applied Economics, University of Minnesota, USA.

Review board

Eli Fenichel is Assistant Professor at the Department of Bio-Economics and Ecosystem Management, Yale School of Forestry & Environmental Studies, USA.

George Halkos is Professor at the Department of Economics, University of Thessaly, Greece.

Dale W. Jorgenson is Professor at the Department of Economics, Harvard University, USA.

Ramanan Laxminarayan is Director at the Centre for Disease Dynamics, Economics & Policy, USA.

Nandan Nawn is Associate Professor at the Department of Policy Studies, TERI University, India.

Mary O'Mahony is Professor at the Department of Management, King's College London, UK.

Roy P. Remme is Researcher at Wageningen University, the Netherlands.

Noelle Eckley Selin is Associate Professor at the Department of Earth, Atmospheric and Planetary Sciences, Massachusetts Institute of Technology, USA.

Mesfin Tilahun is Assistant Professor at the Department of Economics, Mekelle University, Ethiopia.

Acknowledgements

The Inclusive Wealth Report (IWR) is the outcome of a cooperative effort. Many individuals and organizations participated in various capacities. The IWR would not have been possible without the numerous contributions from authors, reviewers, the Urban Institute, funding agencies and many others who at one point or another contributed to the initiative. We would like to express our deep gratitude to all of them. We acknowledge and thank them for their dedication, compromise and long hours.

Science advisory board

We would like to begin by extending special thanks to the Chair of the Science Advisory Group, Prof. Sir Partha Dasgupta. Our gratitude also goes to Prof. Barbara M. Fraumeni, Dr. Zakri Abdul Hamid, Prof. Dr. Anantha Duraiappah and Prof. Emeritus Dr. Harold Mooney. We are very grateful for their advice, guidance and support.

Authors

We would like to gratefully acknowledge the authors of this report for taking the time to bring the report to fruition: Shunsuke Managi, Pushpam Kumar, Rodney B W Smith, Barbara M. Fraumeni, Gang Liu, Ed Barbier, Kristine Grimsrud, Henrik Lindhjem, David N. Barton, Ståle Navrud, Haripriya Gundimeda, Bharath M. Palavalli, Srijan Sil and Anantha Kumar Duraiappah.

Reviewers

The IWR benefitted greatly from the comments and suggestions provided by our reviewers. We extend our acknowledgements to Dale W. Jorgenson, Eli Fenichel, Noelle Eckley Selin, George Halkos, Ramanan Laxminarayan, Mary O'Mahony, Nandan Nawn, Roy P. Remme and Mesfin Tilahun.

IWR team

The IWR has involved many people who devoted much time and energy. Shunsuke Managi, Executive Director of Urban Institute, Kyushu University, who updated

IWR 2018 and led as the IWR Director. Pushpam Kumar of UNEP, who coordinated and oversaw scientific inputs to the report, is the IWR's Science Director. Moinul Islam and Rintaro Yamaguchi provided analytical and quantitative support.

Funding bodies

The IWR benefitted from a grant by the United Nations Environment Programme (UNEP). We acknowledge the financial support from the Grant in Aid from the Ministry of Education, Culture, Sports, Science and Technology in Japan (MEXT): Grant in Aid for Specially Promoted Research 26000001. The Urban Institute, Kyushu University also played key roles as funding bodies. We are extremely thankful for their essential contribution to the initiative.

Publisher

Finally, we would like to thank our publisher, Routledge, for the time and flexibility given to us throughout the production and printing of the report.

Abbreviations

CO_2	carbon dioxide
EDF	expected damage function
EIA	Energy Information Administration
EPA	United States Environmental Protection Agency
ESVD	Ecosystem Service Valuation Database
ESW	ecosystem service wealth
EU	European Union
FAO	Food and Agricultural Organization of the United Nations
GDP	gross domestic product
GHG	greenhouse gas
GIS	geographical information systems
GTAP	Global Trade Analysis Project
HC	human capital
HDI	Human Development Index
IEA	International Energy Agency
IW	inclusive wealth
IWI	Inclusive Wealth Index
IWIadj	Adjusted Inclusive Wealth Index
IWR	Inclusive Wealth Report
MA	Millennium Ecosystem Assessment
NAFSA	Association of International Educators
NC	natural capital
NCC	Natural Capital Committee
NDP	net domestic product
NIA	national income account
NPV	net present value
NRC	National Research Council
NTFB	non-timber forest benefits
NTFP	non-timber forest products
OECD	Organization for Economic Cooperation and Development
ONS	Office of National Statistics
PC	produced capital
PCE	personal consumption expenditure

PIM	perpetual inventory method
PLA	physical amount of pastureland area available
PPI	per capita income, adjusted by a private consumption
PPP	purchasing power parity
REDD	Reducing Emissions for Deforestation and Degradation
RICE	Regional Integrated Climate-Economy
RPA	rental price per hectare
SEEA	System of Environmental and Economic Accounts
SEPA	State Environmental Protection Administration
SNA	System of National Accounts
TEEB	The Economics of Ecosystems and Biodiversity
TFP	total factor productivity
UN	United Nations
UN-DESA	United Nations Department of Economic and Social Affairs
UNDP	United Nations Development Programme
UNECE	United Nations Economic Commission for Europe
UNECE	CES United Nations Economic Commission for Europe-Conference of European Statisticians
UNEP	United Nations Environment Programme
UNESCO	United Nations Educational, Scientific and Cultural Organization
UN-OWG	United Nations – Open Working Group
USSR	Union of Soviet Socialist Republics
VARG	The Value at Risk or Gain
VSL	value of a statistical life
VSLY	value of a statistical life year
WAVES	Wealth Accounting and the Valuation of Ecosystem Services
WCL	wealth in cropland
WDR	World Development Report
WHA	wealth per hectare
WPL	wealth in pastureland
WTO	World Trade Organization
WTP	willingness to pay

Foreword

The global growth experience since the end of the Second World War has offered two conflicting messages. On the one hand, if we look at the state of the biosphere (fresh water, ocean fisheries, the atmosphere as a carbon sink – more generally, ecosystems), there is strong evidence that the rates at which we are utilizing them are unsustainable. For example, the rate of biological extinctions globally today is 100–1,000 times the average rate over the past several million years (the "background rate"). The mid-20th century years are acknowledged to have been the beginnings of an era that environmental scientists now call the Anthropocene (Vosen, 2016), massively altering the processes that define the biosphere.[1]

On the other hand, it is argued by many that just as previous generations in the West invested in science and technology, education, and machines and equipment so as to bequeath to us the ability to achieve high living standards, we in turn can make investments that would assure still higher living standards in the future. The years immediately following the Second World War are routinely praised by commentators for being the start of the Golden Age of Capitalism.[2]

We should not be surprised that the Anthropocene and the Golden Age of Capitalism began at about the same time. We should also not be surprised that the conflicting signals of the past 65 years do not receive much airing by economic commentators. That's because contemporary models of economic growth and development in large measure ignore the workings of the biosphere (Helpman, 2004).

Recently a group of economists have studied the tension inherent in the conflicting intuitions by appealing to the idea of "sustainable development," a term coined in the famous Brundtland Report (World Commission on Environment and Development, 1987). By sustainable development the Commission meant "development that meets the needs of the present without compromising the ability of future generations to meet their own needs." In this reading sustainable development requires that, relative to their respective demographic bases each generation should bequeath to its successor at least as large a *productive base* as it had inherited from its predecessor. For if a generation were to follow the prescription, the economic possibilities facing its successor would be no worse than those it faced when inheriting productive assets from its predecessor.

The problem is that the rule leaves open the question of how the productive base is to be measured. We are thus in need of an index whose movements over time track the sustainability of development programmes. The authors of *IWR 2018* show that prominent attempts at constructing ways to assess the sustainability of development programmes have been unsatisfactory because they didn't arrive at their favoured indices from a well-articulated notion of sustainable development (Chapter 1).[3]

In recent years a number of authors have shown that if by sustainable development we are to mean that welfare across the generations should not decline over time, the index that measures an economy's productive base is an inclusive measure of wealth.[4]

The authors of *IWR 2018* follow that line of thought and extend the empirical reach of *IWR 2012* and *IWR 2014*. They develop the idea of *inclusive wealth* and uncover the logic underlying its use in sustainability analysis and then put it to work in tracking the inclusive wealth of nations.

Inclusive wealth is the dynamic version of income. It is the accounting value of an economy's stock of manufactured capital, human capital and natural capital (hence the qualifier "inclusive"). Wealth is a stock, whereas income is a flow. In a stationary economy the two amount to the same thing, but they can point in different directions when an economy is not at a stationary state. The authors of *IWR 2018* find that 44 out of the 140 countries in their sample experienced a decline in (inclusive) wealth per capita since 1998, even though GDP (read, "income") per capita increased in all but a handful of them. The tension I alluded to is expressed quantitatively in the present volume.

In this essay I offer an account of the logic and pertinence of inclusive wealth in both sustainability and policy analysis that parallels the authors' reasoning in this volume. My hope is that the two parallel accounts will give a better flavour of the significance of the exercise undertaken in *IWR 2018*.

Framework for economic evaluation

Assessing the sustainability of economic programmes is different from prescribing policy. Although both evaluate change, they differ as to the type of change. In the former, change corresponds to the passage of time; in the latter, change is initiated at a point in time by choice of policy. In either case the change is a "perturbation" to the economy, so we will often use that term.

Sustainability analysis and policy analysis involve exercises in what is commonly known as economic evaluation. I shall refer to the person engaged in economic evaluation as the *social evaluator* (or *evaluator*, for short). She could be a citizen (thinking about things before casting her vote on political candidates); he could be an ethicist employed to offer guidance to the national government; she could be a member of the local council; he could be the proverbial man on the Clapham Omnibus, reflecting on the state of the world on his way back from work; and so on.

The criterion proposed in the Brundtland Report for sustainability analysis differs from the one that has usually been adopted for policy analysis. The former takes the means for promoting the ends of development as its point of interest (for the Brundtland Report those means are the economy's productive capacity), whereas the latter is based directly on ends (promoting human well-being).[5] In order to bring the two types of analysis in line with each other, we need to reconstruct the idea of sustainable development in terms of ends. When we have done that, we will discover that prescribing policy and assessing sustainability involve the same exercise.

Let us call the ends our social evaluator seeks to advance, *social well-being*. Because our evaluator considers not only the well-being of people who are present but that of future people too, social well-being can also be thought of as *intergenerational well-being*, so I will use the terms interchangeably.

Ends and means

There are two points I want to demonstrate here in intuitive terms:

> (1) Evaluation in terms of social well-being is equivalent to evaluation on the basis of the means that further social well-being. (2) Policy and sustainability analyses amount to the same exercise.

In what follows I give a sketch of the pair of equivalences. The equivalences provide the foundations of economic evaluation. I shall call the pair of equivalences *Proposition*. But because of its centrality in intergenerational ethics, it is useful to first study the intuition behind it.

Ends are, to be sure, antecedent to the means. One can articulate ends even without asking whether they can be realized, but it makes no sense to talk of means if the ends they are meant to advance aren't first articulated. The equivalence between ends and means I am alluding to doesn't deny the antecedence of ends; what *Proposition* says is that if the means to a set of ends have been identified, it doesn't in principle make any difference whether we examine the extent to which the ends have been (or are likely to be) furthered by a perturbation to an economy or whether we estimate the degree to which the means to those ends have been (or are likely to be) bolstered by that perturbation: the two point in the same direction. We should imagine also that the equivalence would hold as tightly in a society where the ends are far from being met owing to mis-allocation of the means or unjustified usurpation of the means, as it would in a society where they are met as far as is possible under the prevailing scarcities of the means. Nor should it make a difference whether the perturbation is caused because of a shift in policy or whether it occurs because of the sheer passage of time; in either case the task is to evaluate the perturbation. Both theory and experience say, however, that it is commonly easier to measure the means to the ends than it is to measure the ends themselves. It will prove useful even here to indicate why.

The items that appear in documents that are put before the social evaluator are goods and services. Feasibility reports on investment projects, for example, contain quantitative estimates of the assets that are required at the investment stage (so many pieces of equipment, so many labourers, so many acres of land to be cleared, and so on), the labour hours and material inputs that are expected to be required each year, and the flow of outputs the authors hope will be forthcoming over the project's life. Similarly, proposals for changes in the rate of taxation contain information about their likely impact on the flow of goods and services, expressed in terms of employment (labour of various skills), savings and investment, and redistribution of incomes. Those items are the "means"; they are not themselves the ends. The social evaluator is expected to make use of that information in order to judge whether the investment project or tax change is socially desirable. In order to do that she has to value the goods and services in terms of the ends. She has to do that because goods and services acquire the status of means only when the ends to which they are the means have been articulated. As in the case of private investment decisions, she would attempt to value the goods and services in units of a suitably chosen commodity, expressed in a monetary currency. Moreover, she would know that the value of a commodity depends on its location, intended use, the date and circumstances in which it is to be used as an input or produced as an output, and the persons affected. But once she asks why a commodity's value depends on those features, she is well on her way to the required analysis.[6]

Development experts have been known to view matters otherwise. Authors of the annual *Human Development Report* of the United Nations Development Programme (beginning in UNDP, 1990) have routinely criticized national governments and international organizations for prescribing policy and assessing economic performance on the basis of quantitative indicators that reflect the means, not the ends. They say that to use GDP and its distribution for those purposes is to confuse means for ends, and they caution against the use of GDP as an index of economic achievement on grounds that it is a measure of a country's opulence, not well-being (UNDP, 1994: 14–15). But I have never read a publication in which GDP was taken by its authors to be an end in itself. Moreover, it isn't a mistake to seek to identify success (or the lack of success) in achieving ends in terms of an index of opulence. That it is not is the message of *Proposition*. The point isn't that opulence misleads, but that we should search for the right measure of opulence. GDP misleads when used in social evaluation not because it is a measure of the means, but because it is not the right measure of the means. Nor is the United Nations' Human Development Index the right measure of the means. *Proposition* tells us why our evaluator should not rely on that either.

We have now identified a reason it is better to evaluate change in terms of the means for achieving the ends than by examining the extent to which the ends are met by the change. It is a reason of convenience, not of principle. Of course, the intuition behind the theoretical equivalence between evaluation in terms of ends and means, respectively, has to be supported by a formal argument, with a pointer at showing the way the means should be valued in terms of the ends. The authors of *IWR 2018* construct approximate ways for doing that for a number of assets, including human capital.

IWR 2018 reveals that the hardest task for the social evaluator is to determine the way the ends are reflected in estimates of the social worth of the means. That's especially hard because the ends include the well-being of future persons, and they include the value of nature as we transform it over time by our activities. The reasoning involved in bringing the interests of people in the distant future into decisions over the deployment of today's means is intricate, often non-intuitive. That is why the social evaluator is often obliged to rely on (informed) conjecture because there are matters on which there *can* be no data.

Inclusive wealth and social well-being

In Chapter 1 of *IWR 2018*, the authors show that if the ends are summarized in the idea of intergenerational well-being, the corresponding measure of the means is the economy's productive capacity, a notion that is central to economic evaluation irrespective of how the ends are reached and interpreted by the social evaluator.

The intuition behind it is this: an economy's productive capacity reflects the opportunities open to its members. So it is a measure of the extent to which social well-being can be furthered. At a practical level, however, the relationship between social well-being and productive capacity isn't immediate. Intergenerational well-being includes not only the well-being of those who are present today, but also the well-being of people in the future. Put another way, it is an aggregate measure of the flow of personal well-beings across time and the generations. In contrast, an economy's productive capacity is specific to the time at which it is measured. *Proposition* says that by an economy's productive capacity we should mean an inclusive measure of its *wealth*.

To better appreciate the notion of wealth that *IWR 2018* advances, imagine someone is asked to estimate their personal wealth. The individual would most likely turn first to financial assets (savings in the bank, stocks and bonds) and the properties he owns (house and belongings, for example). And he would use their market value to compute wealth. If pressed, he would acknowledge that his future earnings at work should be included, and he would estimate that part of his wealth by making a forecast of the flow of his (post-tax) earned incomes and adding them over the working life that is ahead of him, using perhaps a market interest rate to discount future earnings. If he were pressed no further, he would probably stop there and agree that his earned incomes represent returns on the human capital he has accumulated (sociality, education, skills, health). He would also agree that wealth is important to him because it determines the opportunities he has to shape his life – the activities he can engage in, the commodities he can purchase for pleasure and so on. But he would probably overlook that his taxes go to pay for the public infrastructure he uses, and he would almost certainly not mention the natural environment he makes use of daily, free of charge.

The notion of wealth the social evaluator is interested in is far wider than that. For her, wealth is the social worth of the economy's entire stock of assets. Assets are often called by a more generic name, "capital goods," so we may use the terms interchangeably. Assets offer potential streams of goods and services over time; the more durable an asset, the more lasting is the potential stream. Time is built into an asset. That explains why an economy's wealth at a point in time is able to reflect the flow of well-being across time and the generations.

The social value (or accounting price) of an asset is the worth of the stream of goods and services a society is able to obtain from it. A mangrove forest is a habitat for fish populations. It is also a recurrent source of timber for inhabitants, and it protects people from storms and tsunamis. An economy's institutions and politics are factors determining the social value of its assets, because they influence what people are able to enjoy from them. The value of a building is not independent of whether society is at peace.

An asset's accounting price can be very different from its market value. The difference between an asset's accounting price and its market price reflects a distortion in the economy and should be eliminated if possible. To give an example, as the market price of fish in the open seas is zero, fishermen harvesting them ought to be charged for doing so. The charge, or tax, in this case is the accounting price of fish in their natural habitat. It may even be judicious to impose a quota on fishing, but quotas are only an extreme form of taxation (zero tax per unit caught up to the quota, a prohibitive tax beyond it).

An economy's inclusive wealth is the accounting value of its stock of assets. It is useful to confine assets to: (i) manufactured capital (roads, buildings, machines, equipment); (ii) human capital (knowledge, aptitude, education, skills); and (iii) natural capital (forests, agricultural land, rivers and estuaries, the atmosphere and the oceans – ecosystems more generally; subsoil resources).

Capital goods are to be distinguished from an economy's social environment, which is the intangible medium in which goods and services are produced and allocated across persons, time and the generations. The social environment consists of the laws and norms that provide people with incentives to choose one course of action rather than another; it includes the workings of social and economic institutions such as families, firms, communities, charities and government; and it includes the play of politics. The social environment is the seat of mutual trust. A strengthening of trust facilitates enterprise and exchange, thus enhancing personal well-being.

The social environment isn't quantifiable, but as it shapes events, its consequences are often quantifiable. It influences the engagements we undertake, such as the rates at which we consume goods and services, save and invest, borrow and lend, engage in social activities and so on. Political scientists say that economic development co-evolves with the social environment, by which they mean institutions and politics adapt to the state of the economy as surely as the economy responds to its institutions and politics. That's another way of saying that the mix of capital goods co-evolves with the economy's social environment.[7] Seemingly innocuous changes to the geography of voters' constituencies are known to influence political outcomes, which in turn influence the shape of institutions, and thus the policies that are chosen. Small differences in religious sensibilities (small, that is, to the sensibilities of outsiders) can make enormous differences to the development of attitudes and thought, and so on. For any conception of social well-being, an economy's stock of capital assets and its social environment, together with a forecast of things to come, determine the accounting price of each capital good. The accounting value of an economy's stock of capital goods is its inclusive wealth.

Proposition

Assets are stocks, not flows. They offer goods and services to us, which are flows. A tree is a stock; the fruit it bears is an annual flow of goods. Moreover, the carbon dioxide its leaves inhale is a continuous flow of services to us. Output is a flow (so many dollars' worth of goods per year), whereas wealth is a stock (so many dollars' worth of capital goods, period). The pair of equivalences we have been describing can now be summarized in

> *Proposition. Any perturbation to an economy that increases social well-being across the generations raises inclusive wealth as well. Similarly, any perturbation that lowers social well-being across the generations reduces inclusive wealth.*

The simplest way to illustrate *Proposition* is to recognize that investment projects are perturbations to the economy. If a project is accepted, the future trajectory of the economy is different from what it would be if the project were not accepted. The common method for evaluating projects is to estimate the present value of social profits accompanying them. *Proposition* implies that a project's present value of social profits is its contribution to wealth. An economy's assets and social environment, taken together, comprise its productive capacity. Inclusive wealth is a measure of that capacity.

I have stated *Proposition* in its starkest form. We should read "wealth" for "wealth, adjusted for its distribution among people and for population size." IWR 2018 does that and considers a form of intergenerational well-being where inclusive wealth per capita is the correct index for both sustainability and policy analysis.

Proposition says that inclusive wealth and social well-being are linked by an unbreakable bond and can be stated in the reverse order: if inclusive wealth increases (no matter what the cause of the rise happens to be), social well-being (the well-being of contemporary people and the potential well-being of future generations) increases. Similarly, if inclusive wealth declines (no matter what the cause of the fall happens to be), social well-being declines. Being respectively the ends and the means to those ends, social well-being and inclusive wealth are not the same, of course; but they move in tandem.

Because *Proposition* is an "if and only if" statement, it has no empirical content. But it has powerful implications for empirical work and theoretical reasoning. It says for example that governments should instruct their statistical offices to prepare wealth accounts and track movements in wealth through time so as to check whether social well-being has risen under their proposed policies. The change in (inclusive) wealth over a period of time, say a year, is called "net investment"; that is, investment net of the wear and tear of capital assets and the degradation of natural capital. *Proposition* can be read as saying that, controlling for population change and the distribution of assets, economic development is sustainable over a period of time if net investment in the economy's stock of assets is positive during the period. That's net investment *in the aggregate*, which means that even if stocks of some capital goods were to decline (in quantity or quality, or both), net investment would be positive if sufficient investment were made toward the accumulation of the remaining assets. Whether investment in manufactured capital and human capital can be relied upon always to compensate for the degradation and depletion of nature remains a bone of contention between growth economists and environmental scientists. But analysing data from the past to infer what lies ahead can lead us astray with tragic consequences.

Proposition puts into perspective recent controversies over the objects of interest in distributive justice – for example whether they should be personal well-beings or whether they should be resources or opportunities.[8] As I understand it, those controversies arose in response to John Rawls' theory of justice (Rawls, 1972). *Proposition* can be used to show that Rawls was entirely right to frame the principles of justice as fairness in terms of the distribution of primary goods (Rawlsian primary goods are the means to personal well-being; they are not themselves a person's well-being). His philosophical move was to identify the circumstances in which agreement over the basic structure of society is to be reached and be committed to. Rawls saw the circumstances as being those in which each person is shrouded by a thick veil of ignorance of what his life from its earliest stages has in store for him. The objects chosen under the veil were derived in Rawls' theory; they were not given *ab initio*. It can be argued that when they are aggregated in an appropriate way, Rawlsian primary goods read as inclusive wealth.[9]

The practical significance of *Proposition* was lost on the framers of the Sustainable Development Goals (SDGs), which were adopted by the United Nations General Assembly in September 2015. The UN has made a commitment to attain the goals by 2030. Seventeen in number, the goals range from poverty eradication and improvements in education and health, to the protection of global assets that include the oceans and a stable climate. Each is of compelling importance. But neither the SDGs nor their background documents mention the need to move to a system of national accounts that contains estimates of wealth. Without that move, however, there would be no way for governments to check that the economic measures they take to meet the international agreement would not jeopardize the sustainability of those goals. If wealth (adjusted for population and the distribution of wealth) increases as governments try to meet the SDGs, the SDGs will be sustainable; if it declines, the SDGs will be unsustainable. It could be that the goals are reached in the stipulated time period but aren't sustainable because the development paths nations follow erode productive capacities beyond repair. The supporting documents of the United Nations' Sustainable Development Goals don't tell us how to check that the goals are being met in a sustainable way.

The theory-practice divide

Economic evaluation is not for the purist. There would be weaknesses in the evaluator's work no matter how she goes about it. She knows that. She worries that the basis on which she has estimated accounting prices is ethically inadequate, that she has neglected vital features of life; she is conscious of cutting corners when measuring items she is trying to measure. The evaluator also knows that she must justify (to herself at the very least) the approximations she has been forced to make in the act of measurement. Rather than express her estimates as exact figures, she knows she should offer them as bands. She is moreover aware that people would be wary of figures for wealth in the aggregate, derived from a numerical rendering of social well-being. They would want a sensitivity analysis of wealth estimates, based on alternative weighting systems on the items of ethical significance. The evaluator could do that by working with alternative specifications of ethical parameters, which is to say alternative values of accounting prices. What she would arrive at is a menu of figures for wealth, each corresponding to a particular specification of facts, theories and values.

Restricting the ends to the well-being of people across the generations is questionable. The social evaluator will want to respond to the suggestion that nature has a value over and above the services it provides humanity. She will be responsive too to the thought that animal life has a value that isn't based solely on their welfare (to think it does would not account for the special role species conservation plays in our ethical sensibilities), nor on the "rights" animals may be assumed to have. Understandably, *IWR 2018* does not enter such matters. For these are early days in the art and science of economic evaluation, done correctly.

Partha Dasgupta

Chair of the IWR science advisory group and
Frank Ramsey Professor Emeritus of Economics
at the University of Cambridge

Notes

1 See Waters et al. (2016). Ehrlich and Ehrlich (2008) is an excellent account of the rise of human dominance over the biosphere and the speed with which that has come about in comparison to evolutionary time scales.
2 Micklethwait and Wooldridge (2000); Ridley (2010); and Norberg (2016) are a sample of books with that message.
3 *IWR 2018* follows two previous Inclusive Wealth Reports (*IWR 2012*; *IWR 2014*) with the same intent.
4 See Dasgupta and Mäler (2000); Arrow et al. (2004); and Arrow et al. (2012, 2013).
5 Policy prescription as practised in welfare economics has the ends explicitly in sight. See for example Graaff (1962) and Atkinson and Stiglitz (1980).
6 There are goods that serve as both ends and means. Health is a prime example. As the two aspects of health can be kept separate, the dual feature of health doesn't cause a problem for economic evaluation.
7 Putnam (1993); Landes (1998); and Mokyr (2002, 2016).
8 See Dworkin (1981a, 1981b); Cohen (1989); Barry (1990); and Sen (1992, 1999, 2009) among many others.
9 I provide the argument in a book I am preparing under the title, *Time and the Generations*.

References

Arrow, K.J., P. Dasgupta, L.H., Goulder, G. Daily, P.R. Ehrlich, G.M. Heal, S. Levin, K.-G. Mäler, S. Schneider, D.A. Starrett, and B. Walker (2004), "Are We Consuming Too Much?," *Journal of Economic Perspectives*, 18(1), 147–172.

Arrow, K.J., P. Dasgupta, L.H. Goulder, K.J. Mumford, and K. Oleson (2012), "Sustainability and the Measurement of Wealth," *Environment and Development Economics*, 17(3), 317–355.

Arrow, K.J., P. Dasgupta, L.H. Goulder, K.J. Mumford, and K. Oleson (2013), "Sustainability and the Measurement of Wealth: Further Reflections," *Environment and Development Economics*, 18(4), 504–516.

Atkinson, A.B. and J.E. Stiglitz (1980), *Lectures in Public Economics* (New York: McGraw Hill).

Barry, B. (1990), "Introduction," in *Political Argument* (Berkeley, CA: University of California Press), a re-issue of Barry (1965) with a new introduction.

Cohen, G.A. (1989), "On the Currency of Egalitarian Justice," *Ethics*, 99(4), 906–944.

Dasgupta, P. and K.-G. Mäler (2000), "Net National Product, Wealth, and Social Well-Being," *Environment and Development Economics*, 5(1), 69–93.

Dworkin, R. (1981a), "What Is Equality? Part 1: Equality of Welfare," *Philosophy & Public Affairs*, 10(3), 185–246.

Dworkin, R. (1981b), "What Is Equality? Part 2: Equality of Resources," *Philosophy & Public Affairs*, 10(4), 283–345.

Ehrlich, P.R. and A.H. Ehrlich (2008), *The Dominant Animal: Human Evolution and the Environment* (Washington, DC: Island Press).

Graaff, J. de V. (1962), *Theoretical Welfare Economics* (Cambridge: Cambridge University Press).

Helpman, E. (2004), *The Mystery of Economic Growth* (Cambridge, MA: Belknap Press).

Landes, D.S. (1998), *The Wealth and Poverty of Nations* (New York: W.W. Norton).

Micklethwait, J. and A. Wooldridge (2000), *A Future Perfect: The Challenge and Promise of Globalization* (New York: Random House).

Mokyr, J. (2002), *The Gifts of Athena: Historical Origins of the Knowledge Economy* (Princeton, NJ: Princeton University Press).

Mokyr, J. (2016), *The Culture of Growth: The Origins of the Modern Economy* (Princeton, NJ: Princeton University Press).

Norberg, J. (2016), *Progress: Ten Reasons to Look Forward to the Future* (London: One World).

Rawls, J. (1972), *A Theory of Justice* (Oxford: Clarendon Press).

Ridley, M. (2010), *The Rational Optimist: How Prosperity Evolves* (London: 4th Estate).

Sen, A. (1992), *Inequality Reexamined* (Oxford: Clarendon Press).

Sen, A. (1999), *Development as Freedom* (Oxford: Oxford University Press).

Sen, A. (2009), *The Idea of Justice* (Cambridge, MA: Harvard University Press).

UNDP (United Nations Development Programme) (1990, 1994), *Human Development Report* (New York: Oxford University Press).

Vosen, P. (2016), "Anthropocene Pinned Down to Post War Period," *Science*, 353(6302), 852–853.

Waters, C.N., J. Zalasiewicz, C. Summerhayes, A.D. Barnosky, C. Poirier, A. Galuszka, A. Cerreta, M. Edgeworth, E.C. Ellis, C. Jeandel, R. Leinfelder, J.R. McNeill, W. Steffen, J. Syritski, D. Vidas, M. Wagreich, M. Williams, A. Zhisheng, J. Grineveld, E. Odada, N. Oreskes, and A.P. Wolfe (2016), "The Anthropocene Is Functionally and Stratigraphically Distinct from the Holocene," *Science*, 351(6269), and 2622(1–10).

World Commission on Environment and Development: The Brundtland Report (1987), *Our Common Future* (New York: Oxford University Press).

Preface

In the arena of global environmental policy, the past several decades have seen some major accomplishments in setting goals. On the onset of 2016, the United Nations ushered in a very ambitious list of goals to be achieved by 2030. The 17 goals set in the Sustainable Development Goals (SDGs) span from no poverty and hunger, gender equality and reduced inequalities, to peace, justice and institutions and partnerships.

The 13th goal of SDGs is devoted to "take urgent action to combat climate change and its impacts." Accordingly, the Paris Agreement was reached at the COP21 on 12 December 2015, and entered into force in the next year. In particular, the Agreement lays down that all countries put an effort to limit the global temperature rise to well below 2 degrees Celsius at least.

This ambitious target-oriented approach to tackling environment and development challenges is commendable in many ways. It serves to share the status of the topic with a wide audience on the globe. Moreover, the goals may facilitate local regions to "downscale" global goals, leading to local initiatives to complement global solutions.

However, this approach and the aforementioned goals have their own setbacks. Sometimes the stipulated goals may seem too ambitious, either in depth or in width. It is no doubt a daunting task to achieve the Paris Agreement if we look at the current state of affairs. Quite a few may have felt overwhelmed to see the whopping 17 priorities in the SDGs.

We take a different approach in this report. Rather than setting somewhat arbitrary goals, all we do in this report is construct and monitor a single index that covers a productive base of the economies around the globe. An index is but an index; it does not imply any solutions to national issues, let alone global issues. Nevertheless, what we have in mind in the construction of the index is that it is eventually used also for gradually improving the resource allocation mechanisms prevailing in the imperfect economies we live in, in the spirit of the late Kenneth Arrow, Partha Dasgupta and Karl-Göran Mäler.

The debate on green national accounting should date back at least to the beginning of the 20th century when such economists as Irving Fisher, Erik Lindahl and John Hicks discussed the concept of income that is consistent with the non-declining wealth criterion. After the 1970s, the welfare significance of net national product was noted by Martin Weitzman, and positive net investment rule was studied by John Hartwick. Our framework is directly based on welfare economic theory of green national accounting that has progressed since around the turn of the century. In particular, shadow prices – the marginal contribution of a given capital asset to social well-being – are used to attach relative weight to capital assets.

We build on the past achievements of Inclusive Wealth Report (IWR) 2012 and 2014, but extend the analysis both in depth and width. The inaugural report, IWR 2012, performed a pilot study of past developments of the three capitals in 20 countries since 1990. The ensuing report, IWR 2014, drastically enlarged the scope to 140 countries, 1990–2010. Some classes of capital assets, including forest resources, used updated information to reflect recent developments of ecosystem valuation.

In the current edition, we retained the scope of countries and the starting period: 140 countries, from 1990 to 2014. Moreover, we have added fishery to the list of capital assets, an increasingly important class of renewable natural capital. Although its share in natural capital turns out to be still small, the falling stock trend is an alarming one. We also show two approaches of human capital valuation, the frontier approach and conventional approach. In the frontier approach, both education and health components of human capital are employed in the so-called frontier function which is hardly founded on welfare economic theory. The sounder conventional approach is plausibly consistent with previous IWR 2012 and 2014 methodology and is the mainstay of the continuing IWR database.

All in all, we trust that this database will be a founding stone on which to record changes and sustainability of capital assets in the 21st century – and hopefully onward. Of course, no index is immune from the need of improvement. Rather, the current Inclusive Wealth Index should be regarded as an evolving process that gradually moves toward an index to better proxy social well-being. The total nine chapters contained in IWR 2018 are either directly or indirectly employing IWR 2018 dataset, but they are mostly relevant to furthering this ongoing discussion.

On a final note, we stress that ours is not conflicting with a goal-oriented approach. Rather, they actually resonate and complement each other, as some chapters demonstrate. We do hope that the current edition of IWR 2018 will lead to shared understanding of the current state of affairs in view of capital assets – from physical to human and natural – and eventually help solve the global problems laid down by the Sustainable Development Goals and Paris Agreement.

Shunsuke Managi

Report Director to the Inclusive Wealth Project, and
Distinguished Professor and Director of Urban Institute,
Kyushu University, Japan

Part I

What does the data say?

1 Accounting for the inclusive wealth of nations

Key findings of the IWR 2018

Shunsuke Managi

1. Introduction

There has been an elusive quest to determine how we can go beyond gross domestic product (GDP) to attain a true indicator of social well-being. The well-known report by Stiglitz et al. (2009) suggested that GDP faces three challenges: conventional problems, quality of life aspects and sustainability issues. While some have argued that GDP is problematic on many fronts, it does have its uses. It is intended to measure the value added in an economy within a period and thus to act as a proxy for the magnitude of economic activity. Here, it is important to remember that one of the fathers of GDP, Simon Kuznets, originally intended to design an index that represents welfare rather than the value added in an economy (Coyle 2015).

In the vast literature of green national accounting, with reference to the long-term well-being of an economy, an adjusted index of GDP – net domestic product (NDP) – has been shown to represent human well-being fairly well (Weitzman 1976; Asheim and Weitzman 2001). NDP is computed from GDP, accounting for changes in capital assets, such as capital depreciation and natural capital depletion.

It is in this sense that NDP goes some way toward representing human well-being. However, this adjustment is not sufficient for representing intergenerational well-being or the sustainability of an economy. In particular, NDP still includes that portion that is supposed to be allocated to current consumption, which could incur the risk of being excessive. Excluding the value of current consumption from NDP leaves us with investment into produced, human and natural capital – that is, an Inclusive Wealth Index (IWI) (Dasgupta et al. 2015).

What makes our index – and the World Bank's genuine savings – distinct from GDP is obvious.[1] It is calculated from stocks, rather than flows; it measures determinants, rather than constituents, of well-being (Dasgupta 2001). For the latter, it is more of a matter of subjective well-being, i.e. happiness, life satisfaction (Helliwell et al. 2017; Easterlin 2003; Kahneman et al. 2006; Layard 2005) and other objective outcomes of well-being, such as the Better Life Index (OECD 2014). The Human Development Index (United Nations Development Programme 1990–2016) is a composite index of education and health, in addition to GDP, which is a commendable innovation in that it has shifted the focus toward human capital aspects of well-being. Although its original intention was not focused on sustainability, it fails to theoretically associate the index with social well-being; natural capital is also absent, but it is an unarguably crucial component of the long-term sustainability of nations (Managi, 2015a, 2015b).

Another strand of the literature arguing to abandon GDP for a true welfare or well-being indicator is also flourishing. Fleurbaey and Gaulier (2009) ranked OECD countries by accounting for international flows of income, labour, risk of unemployment, healthy life expectancy, household demography and inequalities, along with income. In a similar vein, Jones and Klenow (2016) constructed a welfare index, including consumption, leisure, mortality and inequality fronts, and they found that these data are highly correlated with GDP per capita but also deviate. The aspects that they addressed are by no means dismissible; however, our focus is more on the long-term sustainability of determinants of human well-being, thereby leading to the construction of a capital-based indicator.

Of course, no single index can measure every aspect of human well-being, and IWI is not an exception in this regard. Note, in particular, that our IWI says little about the extent to which *current* well-being is achieved in practice, partly because the score of current capital stocks is not fully consumed by contemporaries and also because IWI is by construction a determinant- or *opportunity*-based indicator. It is not meant to be something that can explain the *outcomes* and constituents of well-being.

In principle, IWI should include a sufficiently broad, ideally exhaustive, but not redundant, score of capital assets that is relevant to current and future human well-being. While classical economics focused on the input trio of (produced) capital, labour and land, neoclassical economics has treated capital and labour in production function. Subsequently, the economics of exhaustible resources included capital and non-renewable resources (Dasgupta and Heal 1974; Solow 1974). In mainstream economics, human capital – the capitalized concept of labour – has also played an important role in how economic growth can be decomposed (Mankiw et al. 1992). Regarding the sustainable development of well-being, natural capital – a broader notion than natural resource stock only – should not be absent. Thus, we have come full circle to attain the ultimate set of capital stocks as productive bases: produced, human and natural capital.

Figure 1.1 shows how these three capitals lead to the ultimate purpose – if any – of an economy: social well-being. The three capitals are inputs into the production system; thus, they are called the *productive base* of the economy. Produced capital is the easiest to imagine: roads, ports, cables, buildings, machines, equipment and other physical infrastructures. Human capital consists of population (size and composition), the knowledge and skills acquired by education, and health (enhancing quality of life, extending life and boosting productivity). For natural capital, the current accounting addresses subsoil non-renewable resources, forests and agricultural land, but it should ideally also include ecosystems in general.

Along with these three familiar capital assets, our first edition (UNU-IHDP and UNEP 2012) noted that knowledge, population, institutions and even time can be conceived as capital assets. Dasgupta (2015) called them *enabling assets* in the sense that they enable the three capital assets to function well to improve social well-being. Formally, they could increase the shadow prices of pillar capital assets. All in all, unconventional capitals include the following:

• Institutions (property rights, firms, government, households);
• Knowledge (natural laws, algorithms, theorems, cultural narratives);
• Social capital (the law, social norms, habitual practices); and
• Time (exogenous changes experienced by society over time).

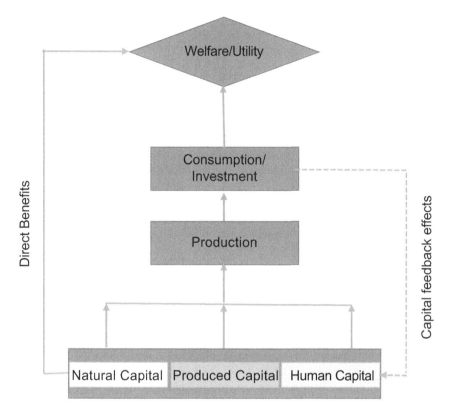

Figure 1.1 A three capital model of wealth creation

While including these capital assets would be commendable, they are at least elusive as they currently stand. Changing institutions reveal themselves in how capital assets are employed to improve social well-being; thus, they could be a determinant of the shadow prices of capital assets. Time as an asset represents the value of waiting, including Solowian technological progress, resource price movements, population changes and other exogenous shocks to the economy in question. The IWR 2014 and our edition of this IWR 2018 address all of these terms in the adjustment of IWI, namely population changes, total factor productivity (TFP), oil capital gains and carbon damage. Thus, time as an asset is already addressed in our framework.

Once we establish relevant capital assets, then the output of this production process is either consumed or invested, as a result of national accounting identity. Current consumption directly improves current well-being, while investment increases the accumulation of productive base, which in turn improves future well-being. This fundamental trade-off between consumption and investment has been a classic problem of optimal saving, dating back at least to Ramsey (1928). However, in our context of sustainable development, economies should strike a balance between consumption and investment, the latter including the degradation – negative investment – of natural capital.[2]

Some studies have suggested that there is a direct effect of capital stocks on utility, circumventing the consumption channel. For example, air pollution or climate change can cause disutility, for which increased consumption cannot be a substitute (Krautkraemer 1985; Xepapadeas 2005; d'Autume and Schubert 2008). It is not uncommon in climate change modelling to assume that climate directly affects utility (van der Ploeg and Withagen 2014). It is for these reasons that we present an alternative route from a productive base to welfare in Figure 1.1.

It is of the utmost importance to note that the absolute value of wealth *per se* does not indicate anything. Only the comparison of wealth across time or space (nations) can have welfare significance. Asheim (2010) showed that net national product (NNP) per capita can be the most appropriate index for the purpose of welfare comparisons across different countries. In any case, we must resist the temptation to compare the absolute value of inclusive wealth (per capita); our interest should lie in the *change* in inclusive wealth per capita over the course of years.

Building on our first and second editions of IWR, this year's report features several advancements and expansions. First, our rich sample continues to track the 140-country sample of IWR 2014, compared with 20 countries (IWR 2012). The dataset now represents the lion's share of world GDP (56,835 billion) and of the global population (6,885 million).

Second, the studied time period is also expanded by five years to a quarter century, expanding our coverage to the period of 1990–2014, which provides us with a picture of the changes in capital assets over almost a generation.

Third, our dataset of natural capital now includes one of the most significant renewable but mobile resources: fisheries. This inclusion adds to our collection of renewable resource natural capital, which already included forest resources and agricultural land in IWR 2012 and 2014. IWR 2012 included some discussion of the fishery resources of no more than four countries for the time period of 1990–2006, based on studies of fishery stock (the RAM Legacy Stock Assessment Database (Ricard et al. 2012)) and shadow prices (SAUP 2011). Our edition boasts a much more refined calculation of fish stocks extended for many countries (Sugiawan et al. 2017).

Fourth, the methodologies for calculating components of human capital are enriched and updated. In particular, we present alternative shadow prices of human capital (education and health), based on a non-parametric methodology called *frontier analysis*. Throughout the report, we call it the *frontier approach*. This approach is contrasted to that adopted in IWR 2012 and 2014, following the literature on pricing human capital using a lifetime income approach.

The remainder of this introductory chapter is organized as follows. In Section 2, the basic idea and methodology behind the Inclusive Wealth Index (IWI) are introduced. Further details regarding the architecture of the index are relegated to a Methodological Annex at the end of the report. Section 3 presents the central results and findings resulting from inclusive wealth calculations, based on non-parametric computation of shadow prices for human capital (education and health). Section 4 shows our parallel results, which employ former methods for human capital (education) calculation, consistent with the traditional interpretation of the rate of return on education and the IWR 2014 results. Section 5 summarizes our results, explains some limitations of the current methodology and addresses some concerns and potential criticisms of IWI in general.

2. Methods

In this section, we outline our underlying framework, which is premised on the body of work in the literature on green accounting, especially under imperfect economies (Arrow et al. 2012). We note that the economy's objective is sustainable development, in the sense that intertemporal well-being at t:

$$V(t) = \int_t^\infty U(C_\tau) e^{-\delta(\tau-t)} d\tau,$$

is not declining. This expression is merely a discounted sum of instantaneous welfare that is depicted in Figure 1.1. A central assumption is that this intertemporal well-being is a function of capital assets in the economy. Thus, denoting produced, human and natural capital as K, H and N, we have the following equivalence between inclusive wealth and well-being:

$$W(K,H,N,t) = V(t) = \int_t^\infty U(C_t) e^{-\delta(\tau-t)} dt,$$

where W is inclusive wealth. Then, sustainable development is equivalent to non-declining inclusive wealth. Formally, we would like to ensure the sign of the temporal change of inclusive wealth:

$$\frac{dW(K,H,N,t)}{dt} = p_K \frac{dK}{dt} + p_H \frac{dH}{dt} + p_N \frac{dN}{dt} + \frac{\partial V}{\partial t},$$

where p_K, p_H and p_K are the marginal shadow prices of produced, human and natural capital, respectively. Note that aside from the three capital channels, we have a direct channel through which only the passing of time directly affects well-being. The shadow prices are essentially marginal contributions to the intertemporal well-being of an additional unit of capital in question. They are formally defined by

$$p_K \equiv \frac{\partial V}{\partial K}, p_H \equiv \frac{\partial V}{\partial H}, p_N \equiv \frac{\partial V}{\partial N},$$

given a forecast of how produced, human and natural capitals, as well as other flow variables, evolve in the future in the economy in question. In practice, shadow prices act as a weight factor attached to each capital, resulting in the measure of wealth, or IWI:

$$IWI = \rho_K K + \rho_H H + \rho_N N.$$

In practice, we can use W and IWI interchangeably.[3] For sustainability analysis, what we need is the change in capital assets or what we can call *inclusive investment*,

$$\frac{dW(K,H,N,t)}{dt} = p_K \frac{dK}{dt} + p_H \frac{dH}{dt} + p_N \frac{dN}{dt} + \frac{\partial V}{\partial t}.$$

In our accounting, barring oil capital gains, which we elaborate on later, we omit the change in the shadow prices for both theoretical and practical reasons. Shadow prices are defined as the marginal changes when there is a hypothetical, small perturbation in capital assets. Thus, for tracking relatively short-term sustainability, it suffices to use fixed, average shadow prices within the studied period. It also makes practical sense in our report since fixing shadow prices will enable us to focus on the quantity changes in inclusive wealth.

In addition, if there is a large perturbation, such as large project implementation, natural disasters or financial crises, we must account for the change in shadow prices even within a short time period. We might consider the price change – capital gains on any capital asset – seriously because we will accumulate our editions of IWR over the course of the years ahead.

One exception of this rule of constant shadow prices assumed over the studied period is oil capital gains. Oil prices, or commodity prices for that matter, are notorious for fluctuations within relatively short periods of time. Even if the physical quantity of an oil-rich nation does not change, a spike in the oil price will translate into better opportunities for the country because the country can cash in its oil wealth on the market for increased consumption and investment into inclusive wealth. This fact is particularly relevant for oil-rich nations in the Middle East, where economic powerhouses other than oil-related industries have long been craved. Nurturing an industry from scratch takes a long time. Conversely, net oil importing countries tend to witness their social well-being being degraded by rising oil prices. We account for this loss of opportunity by allocating global oil capital gains to oil-importing countries according to the current share of oil imports. Formally, if we allow the shadow price of natural capital p_N to change, we have

$$\frac{\partial V}{\partial t} = p_N N \frac{dp_N / dt}{p_N},$$

which represents our capital gain adjustment.

Aside from these oil capital gains, there is another class of adjustment contributed by our enabling assets, as we mentioned earlier. How capital assets are employed and utilized to yield ultimate social well-being can change over time, perhaps as the enhanced productivity of activities, technological progress, or improvement in trust and social capital. In practice, however, all of these factors should be captured by the change in TFP. In so far as social well-being improves (deteriorates) more than the individual contributions of capital assets increase (decrease), this residual should also be considered. Arrow et al. (2012) showed that what needs to be done in accounting is only to add TFP growth rate to inclusive wealth growth rate.

Finally, there is another aspect of the natural environment that need not be dismissed in coming centuries. Increasing carbon emissions are likely to cause climate change, which endangers many lives, as well as other potentially devastating socio-economic damages. It can be conceivably stated that the current economic activity is reducing the carbon sink stock of our planet, which can be accounted for as another capital asset in inclusive wealth. Alternatively, we can tap into the ongoing and increasing research on the social cost of carbon to be employed to value the damage done to social well-being by additional emissions of carbon. In this report, we continue to adopt the latter approach. In particular, the total global emissions of carbon are evaluated using the social cost of carbon, which is then allocated to individual countries according to the share of the global damage done, which is further subtracted from the inclusive wealth of nations.[4]

Figure 1.2 provides our schematic representation of how our three-pillar capital assets, as well as adjustment factors, shape our final index of inclusive wealth. Along with the familiar capital assets that we consider from previous reports (IWR 2012, 2014), this report adds fishery resource stock to the list of natural capital. In the ensuing sections, we report many aspects of the aggregated figures of Inclusive Wealth Index, both before and after adjustments.

To avoid confusion, in Section 3, we focus on inclusive wealth based on the frontier approach, which uses a non-parametric valuing of education- and health-induced human capital. Produced and natural capital are computed in a similar manner as in IWR 2012 and 2014. In Section 4, we extend the conventional approach inherited from IWR 2012 and 2014. For human capital, we account only for the education-induced portion. For further notes on the different methodologies, readers are advised to examine the Methodological Annex.

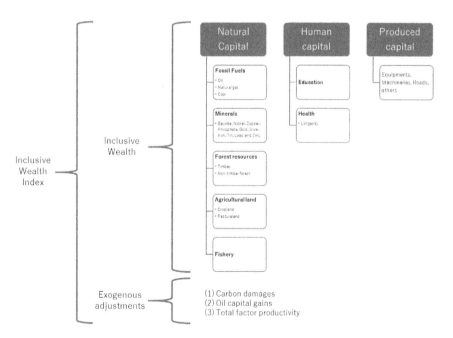

Figure 1.2 Schematic representation of the Inclusive Wealth Index and the Adjusted Inclusive Wealth Index

3. The inclusive wealth of nations

3.1. Measuring performances based on changes in wealth

In this subsection, we evaluate the countries' sustainability conditions over the past 25 years by calculating human capital, including both education and health shadow prices, using the frontier approach. The sustainable growth of the nations is evaluated by analysing changes in IWI. We show the changes in inclusive wealth, both in absolute and per capita forms, for 140 countries over the past few decades. In addition, we discuss how the changes and per capita changes in wealth correlate with other traditional indicators.

The results show that the growth of inclusive wealth of the nations is positive for a considerable number of countries. However, the slower progress of wealth than population growth results in negative per capita growth of wealth for a significant number of countries as well. In addition, some of the negative per capita growth of wealth occurred in countries that experienced absolute gains in wealth. The changes of countries' wealth are calculated by annual average growth rates over the past 25 years, and 1990 is set as a base year.

Our estimation results show that 135 of the 140 countries assessed in the IWR 2017 present growth in inclusive wealth (before adjusted factors) (Figure 1.3a). On a per capita basis, 89 of the 140 countries (64%) show positive growth rates in IWI (Figure 1.3b).

When IWI includes the adjustments of TFP, carbon damages and oil capital gains to evaluate social well-being, 124 of the 140 countries showed positive growth rate (Figure 1.4a). In a per capita analysis, 96 of the 140 countries (69%) experienced positive IWI growth rates after adjustments (Figure 1.4b).

We investigate the IW growth by identifying countries and regions in Figure 1.5a. Three countries can be identified in Quadrant III – Congo, Trinidad and Tobago – and Ukraine experienced negative growth rates in both absolute and per capita terms. Two former Soviet-allied countries – Bulgaria and Moldova – *improved* their performance when population is considered in the index because both countries have had declining populations over time (Quadrant II of Figure 1.5a). The population decreased in these countries, and more resources became available for persons compared to the

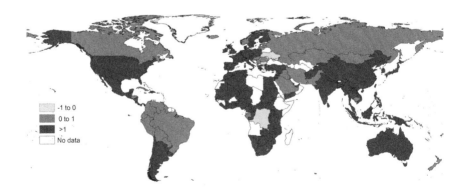

Figure 1.3a Annual average growth rate of Inclusive Wealth Index

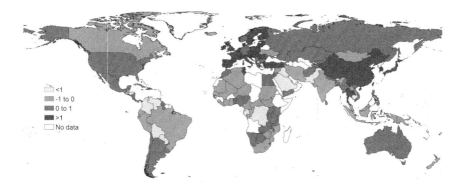

Figure 1.3b Annual average growth rate of Inclusive Wealth Index per capita

Figure 1.3 Annual average growth rate in IWI and IWI per capita before adjustments for 140 countries, annual average for 1990–2014

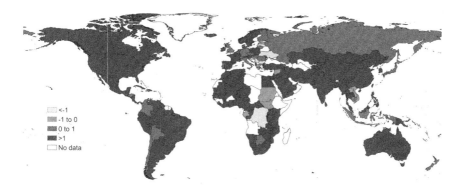

Figure 1.4a Growth in Inclusive Wealth Index (adjusted)

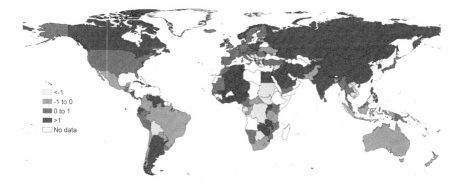

Figure 1.4b Growth in Inclusive Wealth Index per capita (adjusted)

Figure 1.4 Annual average growth rate in IWI and IWI per capita after adjustments for 140 countries assessed in the IWR 2017 during the period of 1990 and 2014

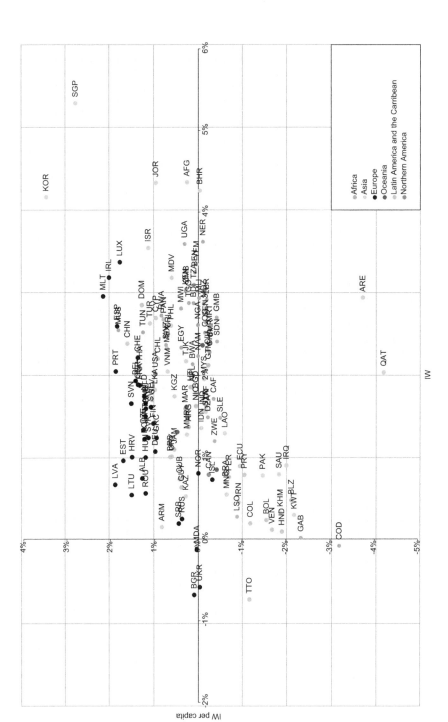

Figure 1.5a Annual average growth rate in IW and IW per capita (unadjusted)

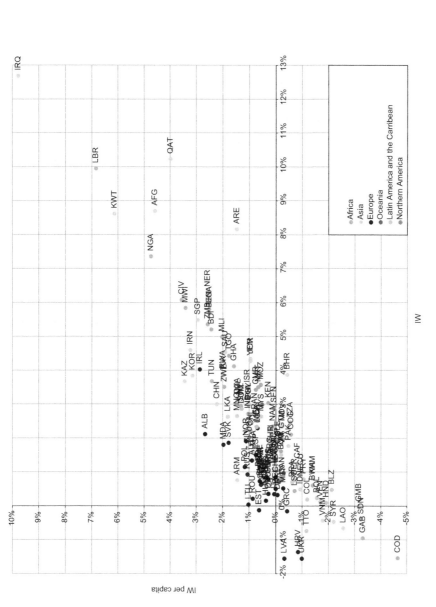

Figure 1.5b Annual average growth rate in IW and IW per capita (adjusted)

Figure 1.5 Annual average growth rate in IW and IW per capita

base year. Of 135 countries with positive absolute growth in wealth (Quadrant I and IV), 87 also experienced per capita growth in wealth as well (Quadrant I). The remaining 48 countries with decreases in wealth on a per capita basis (Quadrant IV) can be regarded as underinvesting in wealth in light of their population growth.

We identify the IW growth rates of countries in addition to the three adjustments of IW in Figure 1.5b. Fifteen countries are assessed as unsustainable by IW per capita adjusted: Bulgaria, Congo, Gabon, Gambia, Greece, Croatia, Haiti, Jamaica, Laos, Latvia, Sudan, Serbia, Syria, Ukraine and Vietnam. Both absolute and per capita terms showed negative growth rates in Quadrant III of Figure 1.5b. Estonia is the only country that improved when population is considered (Quadrant II). Of the 124 countries with positive absolute growth in inclusive wealth adjusted (Quadrant I and IV), 95 countries also experienced growing wealth per capita (Quadrant I). The remaining 29 countries had eroded wealth on a per capita basis.

3.2. *Wealth change compositions*

In this section, we break down inclusive wealth change by the contributions of capital assets. Contributions of natural, human and produced capital to average inclusive wealth growth are shown in Figure 1.6. It should be noted that natural

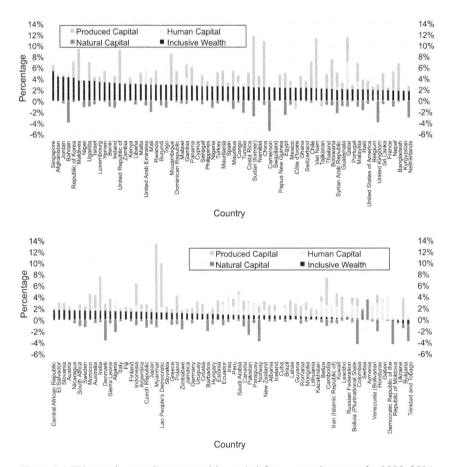

Figure 1.6 IW growth rates disaggregated by capital form, annual average for 1990–2014

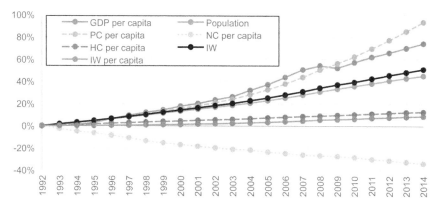

Figure 1.7 Changes in worldwide inclusive wealth per capita and other indicators for 1992–2014

capital is positive for only 31 countries. In contrast, in 133 nations, human capital increased during the period from 1990 to 2014; for produced capital, 136 of the 140 countries gained.

On a per capita front, positive growth in human capital is achieved by 122 countries. Similarly, 120 of the 140 nations experienced growth for produced capital from 1990 to 2014. The contribution of human capital was 59% over 1990–2014, followed by produced capital (21%) and natural capital (20%). For the breakdown of human capital, 33% and 26% come from education and health, respectively.

The global change in inclusive wealth in absolute and per capita terms is critical to evaluate the performance of the global economy. We calculate the changes in inclusive wealth and per capita inclusive wealth in international dollars using purchasing power parity (PPP) exchange rates. These data are the aggregated wealth of all nations for 1992 to 2014, and results are illustrated in Figure 1.7. Changes in global wealth were significantly positive from 1990 to 2014. The major positive changes can be observed for produced capital, followed by human capital. In contrast, natural capital experienced a significant decline from 1992.

3.3. *Wealth composition*

In this section, we discuss the wealth stock of nations by sources. The compositions of the assets of countries are shown in Figure 1.8a–c, representing the relative importance of each capital. Human capital is dominant over the other two capitals for 93 of the 140 countries evaluated. In addition, the majority (77) of these 93 countries owned 50% or a higher share of human capital than natural and produced capital.

Turning to natural capital, it turned out to be the most important source of wealth for 21 countries. Interestingly, 16 of the 21 natural capital-abundant nations are low-income or middle-income economies. South America, Middle Africa and Western Asia are regions where natural capital is an important source of wealth.

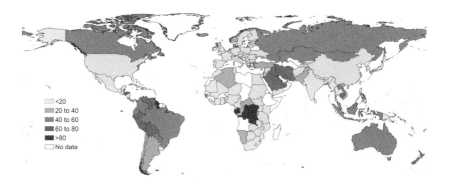

Figure 1.8a Percentage of natural capital in total wealth

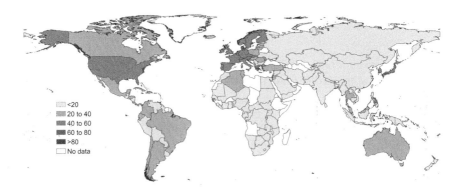

Figure 1.8b Percentage of produced capital in total wealth

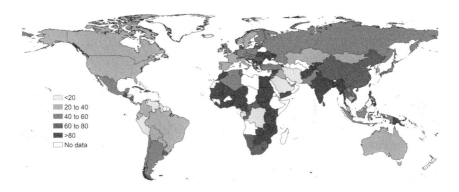

Figure 1.8c Percentage of human capital in total wealth

Figure 1.8 Percentages of human, produced and natural capital in total wealth, annual average for 1990–2014

For 19 countries, produced capital is the main source of capital. Of those nations with a lion's share of produced capital in composition, all are high-income countries and geographically located in Europe, North America and East Asia.

We also explore how overall capital is composed on the global level. The share of human capital clearly demonstrates its importance, with a representation of 59% (Figure 1.9a). Developments of the capitals over time show that, while the average contributions of human and produced capital to the total capital increased, the natural capital share declined, as symbolically expressed in the crossing line of Figure 1.9b.

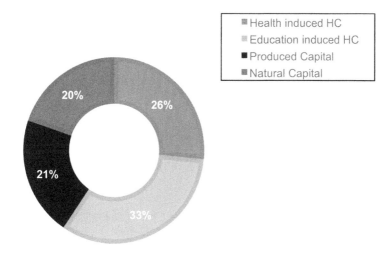

Figure 1.9a Average wealth compositions across countries (mean 1990–2014)

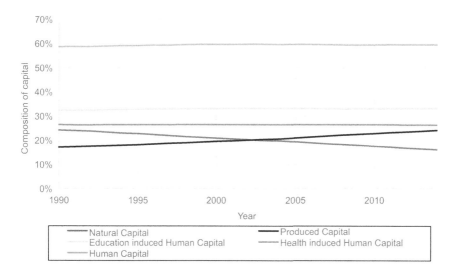

Figure 1.9b Developments in the country average wealth composition

Figure 1.9 Developments in the composition of wealth by capital from 1990–2014

An interesting composition between human and natural capital can be observed in Figure 1.10a: countries with high shares of human capital generally have lower shares of natural capital. As expected, high-income countries also tend to have higher shares of produced capital and lower shares of natural capital (Figure 1.10b). Moreover, high-income countries have a balanced share of human and produced capital (Figure 1.10c). These shares should be interpreted with caution, however, because they only show the worth of one capital in relation to the total wealth of the country.

3.4. IWI *adjusted*

In this subsection, we investigate the performance of IW, after considering three factors.

1   Carbon damage: accounting for damages due to climate change, which are experienced by nations due to increased impacts of carbon concentrations on the atmosphere
2   TFP: explaining the exogenous factors that are missing but that impact economic growth
3   Oil capital gains: capturing the changes in oil price and how the value of the productive base changes

The adjustment factors can affect the IW of nations either positively or negatively. If oil prices increase, oil-producing countries benefit, while oil-importing countries experience loss. TFP can also impact either way; less efficient use of resources will cause negative productivity in the subsequent year (Managi 2015a; Kurniawan and Managi 2017). In Figure 1.11, we show estimates of how each of the adjustment factors contributes to the IW of nations. We plot the adjusted IW in gradually decreasing order to identify the impacts on countries.

In our analysis, Moldova and Trinidad and Tobago are the "gainers" by adjustments; they move from negative to positive IW growth rates. In contrast, 13 countries reported positive growth in IW but turned to negative IW growth after adjustments.[5] In per capita terms before adjustments, 89 countries experienced positive growth in IW; after adjustments, the number of countries with positive growth in IW per capita increased to 98 countries.

We examine the contributions of specific adjustment factors.

Oil capital gains show that 113 of the 140 countries suffered from increasing prices of oil (Figure 1.12a). The remaining 27 countries experienced positive impacts of oil price increases. Six oil-abundant countries, mainly in the Middle East, for instance, gained at least 4% from increasing oil prices: Venezuela, Iraq, Qatar, Kuwait, Saudi Arabia and the United Arab Emirates.

TFP growth rates were positive for 87 countries and negative for 53 countries (Figure 1.12b). The average growth of TFP ranged from +7% to −3% and had significant impacts on several countries. For instance, Malaysia moved to positive growth of per capita IW adjusted, primarily due to positive TFP growth. In contrast, Serbia moved to negative IW per capita adjusted, mainly due to negative changes in TFP.

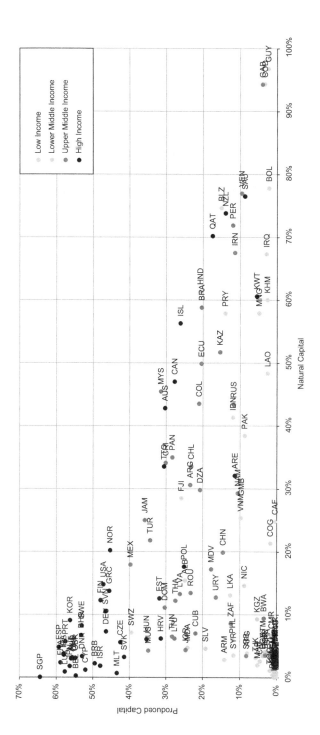

Figure 1.10a Percentage share of human capital and natural capital in total wealth

Figure 1.10 (Continued)

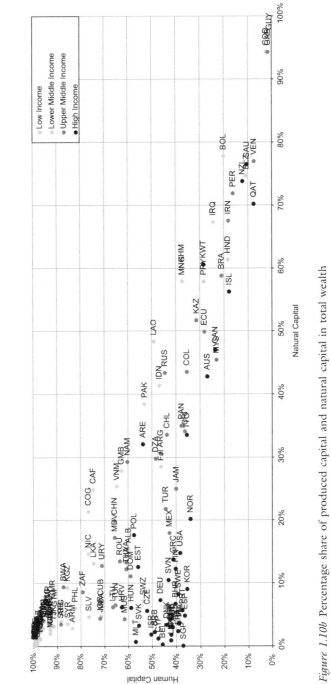

Figure 1.10b Percentage share of produced capital and natural capital in total wealth

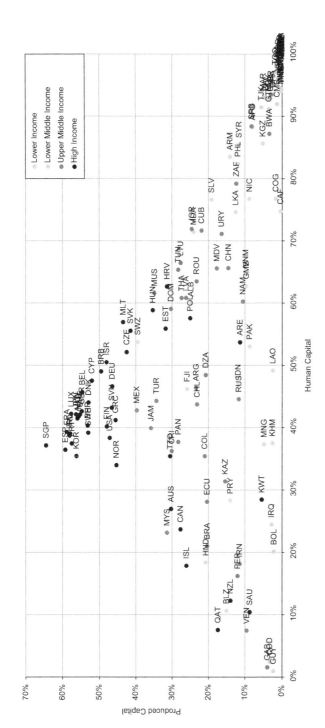

Figure 1.10c Percentage share of produced capital and human capital in total wealth

Figure 1.10 Percentage share of capital in total wealth, average 1990–2014

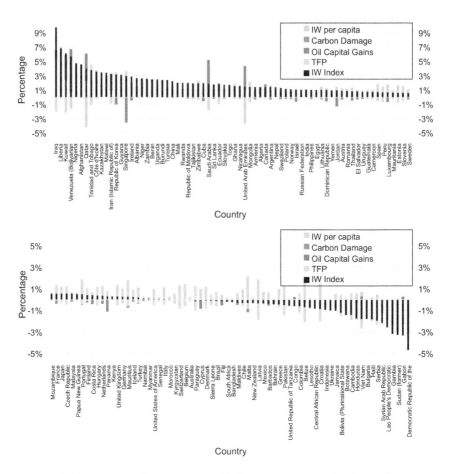

Figure 1.11 Average annual growth rates of IWI disaggregated by the three adjustments

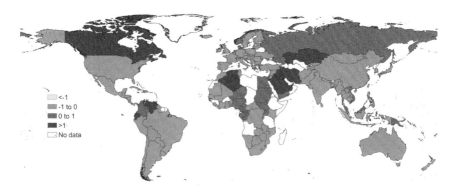

Figure 1.12a Average growth rate of oil capital gains in 1990–2014

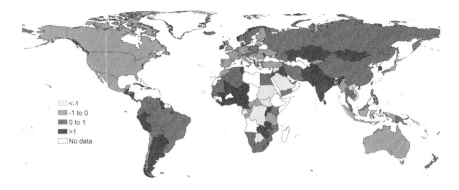

Figure 1.12b Average growth rate of Total Factor Productivity (TFP) in 1990–2014

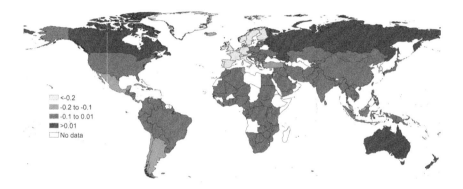

Figure 1.12c Average growth rate of carbon damage in 1990–2014

Figure 1.12 Annual average growth of the adjustment factors in 1990–2014

Regarding carbon damage incurred by climate change, 134 of the 140 countries face negative economic impacts (Figure 1.12c). Only six countries improved their productive base and avoided the adverse impacts of climate change damage. However, its impact is less than 0.5% of IW per capita adjusted, which can be said to be relatively low.

3.5. Measuring economic performance: comparison of inclusive wealth, GDP, HDI and happiness

For evaluating nations' economic and social performance, there exist a number of indicators. Three of the commonly used indicators are gross domestic product (GDP), Human Development Index (HDI) and happiness. GDP is the indicator to measure the market value of final goods and services in an economy over a period. HDI measures the well-being of nations by considering education, life expectancy and

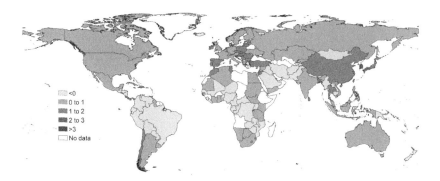

Figure 1.13a IW per capita

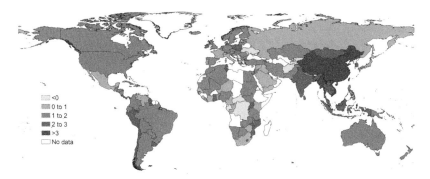

Figure 1.13b GDP per capita

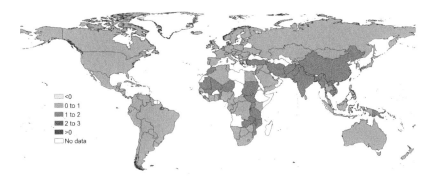

Figure 1.13c HDI

Figure 1.13 Average annual growth rates of IW per capita, GDP per capita and HDI, period 1990–2014

income. Happiness, although measured in many ways, basically evaluates the people's subjective satisfaction by considering freedom, social support, life expectancy and corruption, among other things. Figures 1.13a–c provide an overview of the countries' GDP per capita, HDI and inclusive wealth per capita in terms of annual average growth rate over the period of 1990 to 2014.

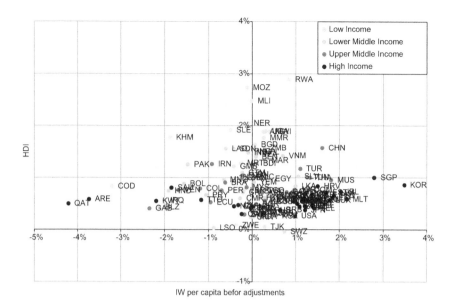

Figure 1.14a HDI vs. IW per capita (unadjusted)

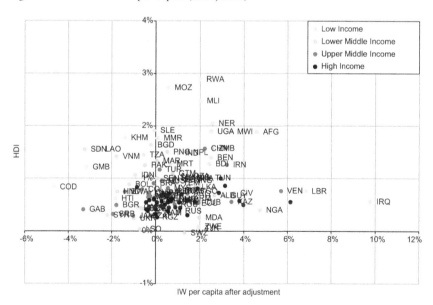

Figure 1.14b HDI vs. IW per capita adjusted

Figure 1.14 HDI vs. IW per capita

Figure 1.14a provides the relationship between the growth of HDI and IW per capita. We find positive growth of IW per capita for 89 countries and negative growth for 51 countries. Figure 1.14b represents the growth of HDI and adjusted IW per capita. We identify positive growth of IW for 97 countries, while in the case of HDI,

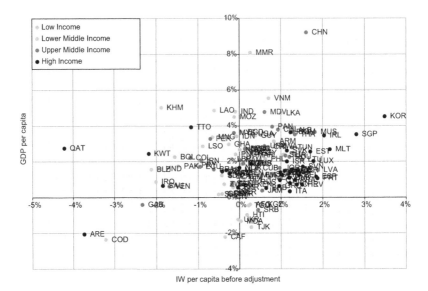

Figure 1.15a GDP per capita vs. IW per capita (unadjusted)

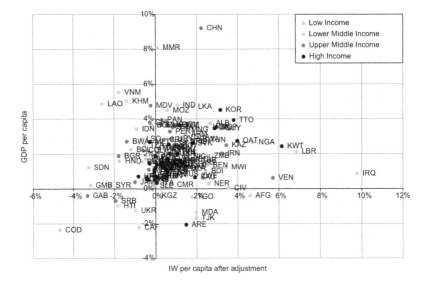

Figure 1.15b GDP per capita vs. IW per capita adjusted

Figure 1.15 GDP per capita vs. IW per capita

139 of 140 countries show positive growth. Thus, the IW per capita shows more a pessimistic picture of progress of nations than HDI. In terms of GDP, 128 of 140 countries indicate positive growth rates over the past 25 years; the remainder are mostly African nations (Figure 1.15a and 1.15b), which is evidently a dissimilar picture from that shown by IWI or even other indicators of sustainability.

Because GDP, HDI and IWI do not represent the same – if not totally different – aspects of human well-being, the evaluation of the countries is not always consistent among the three (Figure 1.16). We note, however, that, when the nations are grouped into high-income or developed economies, all three measures consistently show a positive growth rate. In addition, the measure of happiness also shows a high satisfaction level (not growth) in developed countries (Figure 1.17a and 1.17b).

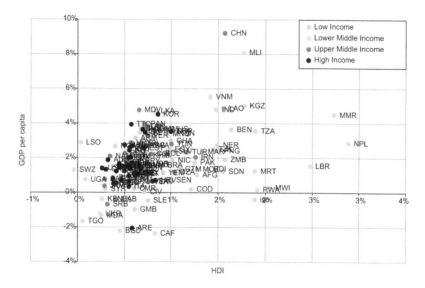

Figure 1.16 GDP per capita vs. HDI

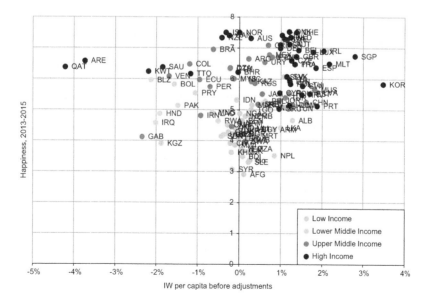

Figure 1.17a Happiness vs. IW per capita (unadjusted)

Figure 1.17 (Continued)

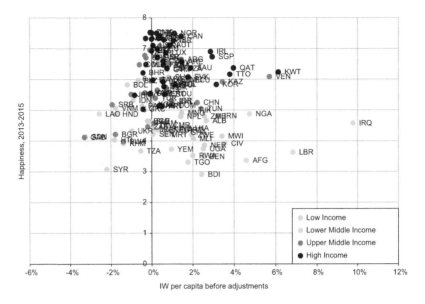

Figure 1.17b Happiness vs. IW per capita adjusted

Figure 1.17 Happiness vs. IW per capita

4. The inclusive wealth of nations: education as human capital

4.1. *Measuring performance based on changes in wealth*

This section shows the inclusive wealth of nations following the approach used in IWR 2012 and 2014, based on the idea of education as human capital and shadow prices following IWR 2012 and 2014, which we henceforth call the *education approach*. The main difference lies in the calculation of human capital: the educational rate of return is used as its shadow price. In line with IWR 2014, health capital is beyond the scope in this method, primarily because it would swamp other capital assets. Additionally, conventional TFP values are used for IW adjusted. We report our results based on this approach, along with the frontier approach in Section 3, because this methodology is in line with the long history of the economics of education and its consistency helps the reader to compare our results with previous editions of IWR in a continuous manner. Needless to say, the question to be asked continues from the previous section: Have nations been maintaining their wealth for the past quarter century? The dataset continues to be all 140 countries from 1990 to 2014.

As the methodology in this subsection inherits from previous reports (IWR 2012 and IWR 2014), it turns out that the basic trend in inclusive wealth also continues to hold for them. In particular, the aggregated accumulation of wealth has been slower than population growth, leading to negative growth rates in inclusive wealth per capita.

According to the total wealth of nations, 133 of the 140 countries (95%) enjoyed positive growth rates in inclusive wealth over the past quarter century (see Figure 1.18a). That the overall wealth has been increasing in the world in aggregate seems to be good news, but conversely, the remaining five countries experienced degradation of their wealth.

If we change the measure from total to *per capita*, 84 of the 140 countries (60%) under study presented positive inclusive wealth per capita (see Figure 1.18b). The worse performance indicates that the simple Malthusian effect on sustainability is negative all worldwide and perhaps more so in developing countries.

Finally, growth in inclusive wealth per capita with adjustments by TFP, carbon damage and oil capital gains (Figure 1.18c) indicates that 81 of the 140 countries (58%) are on a sustainable path.

They can be contrasted with the previous results of IWR 2014: for the studied period of 1990–2010, only 128, 85 and 58 of the 140 countries (compared to 133, 84 and 81 in the current edition) experienced an increase in inclusive wealth in absolute terms, inclusive wealth per capita and inclusive wealth per capita adjusted,

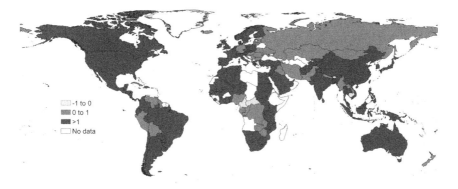

Figure 1.18a Growth in Inclusive Wealth Index (unadjusted), using the education approach

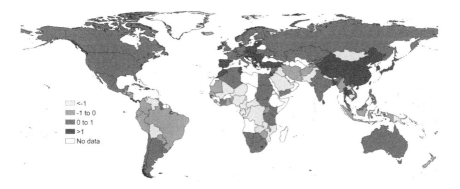

Figure 1.18b Growth in Inclusive Wealth Index per capita (unadjusted), using the education approach

Figure 1.18 (Continued)

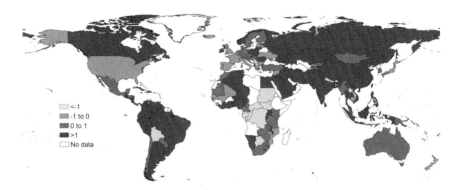

Figure 1.18c Growth in Inclusive Wealth Index per capita adjusted, using the education approach

Figure 1.18 Growth in Inclusive Wealth Index, using the education approach

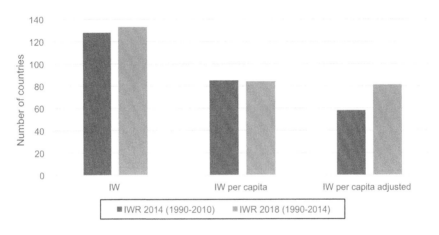

Figure 1.19 Comparison of numbers of countries of positive IW growth, education approach

respectively (see Figure 1.19). Since the sample countries remain unchanged, and the methodology has not changed drastically, this better performance can be trace-able either to expansion of the study period by four recent years (2011–2014) or to the addition of fishery resources to natural capital.

Figure 1.20 shows the relationship with inclusive wealth on an absolute versus per capita basis. Overall, we observe an upward relationship between the two: the larger that the growth in inclusive wealth is, the larger that the growth in inclusive wealth per capita tends to be. Note also that almost all of the European and North American countries fall into Quadrant I: they have experienced increasing wealth in both absolute and *per capita* terms. For the other regions, the results are mixed. Bahrain, the United Arab Emirates and Qatar, all of which are sitting on enormous oil and gas capital, lie somewhat as outliers.

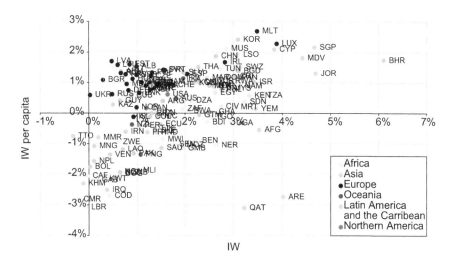

Figure 1.20 Inclusive wealth and inclusive wealth per capita (education approach)

The seven countries with negative inclusive wealth growth include four African nations (Cameroon, the Central African Republic, Liberia and Sudan), Trinidad and Tobago, the Republic of Moldova and Cambodia. It is remarkable that, of these seven countries, only the oil-rich Caribbean nation, Trinidad and Tobago, falls into the high-income category. In absolute terms, the country's natural capital has been eroded by 3.9% per annum. It seems like the country has depleted ample natural capital across the board, from agricultural land to oil and gas, but the extent to which nature has been converted into produced and human capital seems to have been insufficient.

4.2. Wealth change compositions

In this subsection, we take a closer look at the breakdown of the contributions of each capital asset group to total inclusive wealth average growth rates. In particular, Figure 1.21 shows the breakdown of (unadjusted) inclusive wealth growth into produced, natural and human capital groups. We can observe that, even within high inclusive wealth growth countries, the composition of each capital asset varies. For example, oil-rich gulf nations (Bahrain, the United Arab Emirates and Qatar) have converted massive natural capital into other capitals, especially human capital. Other nations, such as Singapore, Tanzania, Bangladesh, South Korea and the Philippines, have been on a sustainable path, primarily by growing their produced capital, with very little rundown of their natural resources, or because they are poorly endowed with these resources in the first place.

Turning to unsustainable or barely sustainable countries in Figure 1.21, despite their sluggish growth in inclusive wealth, it should be noted that human capital has grown by more than 2%, with several exceptions. Therefore, the degradation of

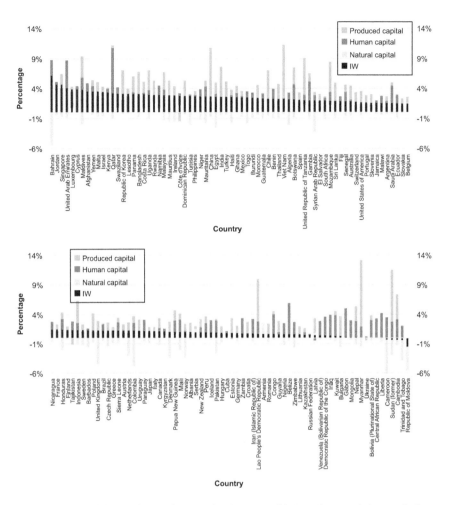

Figure 1.21 Breakdown of growth rates of inclusive wealth into three capital assets before adjustments (education approach)

natural capital and slow growth in produced capital are mainly responsible for their disappointing growth rates of inclusive wealth. Notable exceptions include several former Soviet republics, such as Ukraine, Russia, Kazakhstan, Lithuania and the Republic of Moldova, the populations and, thus, human capital of which have decreased in the latest quarter century. Furthermore, all of these countries have decreased in natural capital, whereas the Republic of Moldova was the only country that eroded in all three capital assets.

We note here that, since the growth rates are expressed in geometric means, the growth rates of each component simply do not add up. Therefore, some ASEAN countries, such as Laos, Myanmar and Cambodia, have recently accumulated produced capital, which does not contribute to high growth rates in inclusive wealth for the studied period.

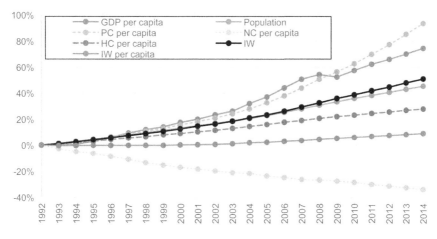

Figure 1.22 Growth rates of inclusive wealth *per capita* and its components, relative to the level of 1992 worldwide (education approach)

What if we aggregate all of the countries all over the world? In other words, has the world been preserving its wealth on the whole? Figure 1.22 shows the global change rates of inclusive wealth and its components on a *per capita* basis, setting 1992 as the reference year.[6] Inclusive wealth per capita has been slightly positive, especially over the last decade. Observe that this trend is a cumulatively large decrease of inclusive wealth in absolute terms. Figure 1.22 also demonstrates vividly that natural capital degradation – which amounts to approximately 35% in a cumulative fashion – has been compensated for by investment in human capital and, to a much greater extent, in produced capital.

Another interesting observation from Figure 1.22 is that all of the growth in capital assets has been linear if we aggregate it across the world, whether these assets have been positive (produced and human) or negative (natural). In contrast, GDP growth has been mostly linearly positive, but the enormous financial crisis caused a drop in this trend in 2008.

4.3. Wealth composition

As we have stated, what matters in sustainability assessment is the change in capital assets over the course of years. However, it is of some interest to also examine the composition of capital assets themselves. Figure 1.23 shows the percentage of three capitals in inclusive wealth, averaged for the period between 1990 and 2014. Panel a of the figure in the following suggests that it accounts for less than 20% of total wealth in many countries. It is relatively more important in some developed nations, such as the USA, the European Union, South Korea and Japan. In contrast, the share of produced capital is alarmingly low in some developing countries; it accounted for less than 5% in some sub-Saharan African countries in 2014. It is difficult to draw normative implications only from this percentage, but investing in produced capital would help some poor countries take off, as history suggests.

Figure 1.23a Percentage of produced capital in total wealth

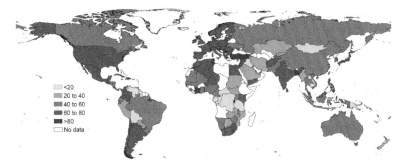

Figure 1.23b Percentage of human capital in total wealth

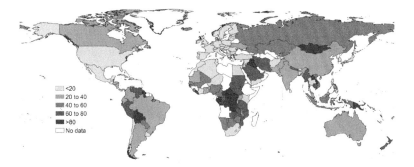

Figure 1.23c Percentage of natural capital in total wealth

Figure 1.23 Percentages of produced, human and natural capital in total wealth, average for 1990–2014, education approach

Figure 1.23b shows the (education-induced) human capital share, annually averaged for 1990–2014 for the whole world. It demonstrates that human capital accounts for the lion's share in many countries. There are, however, several exceptions in the less developed world. As of 2014, it was still less than 20% in Belize, Bolivia, Guyana, the Central African Republic, Laos, Liberia, Mongolia, Papua New Guinea and Tanzania.

Finally, Figure 1.23c represents the natural capital share in inclusive wealth. In contrast to other capital forms, the share of natural capital largely depends on initial endowments, so it is not infrequently very small, whether in low-income or high-income countries. For example, natural capital stands for less than 5% in both Belgium and Bangladesh. It is also worth mentioning that some countries that are presumably rich in natural capital are actually running out of it: less than 1% of wealth was in the form of natural capital in Bahrain and the United Kingdom as of 2014. Both of them might have depleted their oil capital over the last several decades.

What about the wealth composition across the whole world? Figure 1.24a indicates that, on average, human capital is responsible for more than half of inclusive wealth, followed by natural capital, with approximately one quarter of total wealth. Produced capital accounts for the smallest share of inclusive wealth, less than one-fifth of total wealth worldwide. Note, however, that this figure is aggregated both over time and worldwide. To determine the temporal change of this composition, the right panel of Figure 1.24a shows its temporal development. One can see clearly that natural capital has been substituted primarily by produced capital. It is somewhat surprising to see that the shares of natural and produced capital converge at approximately 20%, while the share of human capital continues to account for more than half of total wealth.

However, a different picture emerges when we aggregate in a different manner. In Figure 1.24b, instead of calculating the average of the shares, we first aggregate each capital for a specific year for the whole world to compute each capital share in the right panel. This amount is further averaged for the whole period in the pie chart. According to this calculation, the places of produced and natural capital were changed in the mid-1990s. Furthermore, natural capital only accounts for 15% of total wealth, which is a somewhat sobering figure in light of the time trend.

This replacement of natural capital by produced capital should be examined in further detail. Inclusive Wealth Report 2014 found that the share of produced capital tends to be slightly less than 20% in many countries, and – interestingly – natural and human capital shares tend to be inversely correlated. This tendency continues to hold for our updated data, as shown in Figure 1.24c. This apparently linear relationship between produced and natural capital tempts us to assert that natural capital is being depleted and converted into human capital. Our approximation

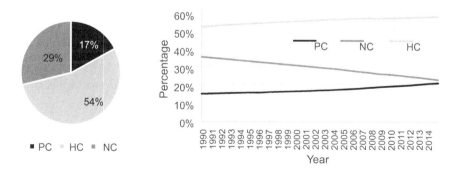

Figure 1.24a Global aggregate wealth composition, mean 1990–2014 and over time, education approach

Note: Shares of each capital are computed for a specific country and year first, and they are then aggregated across countries in the right panel. This amount is further averaged for the whole period, 1990–2014, in the left panel.

Figure 1.24 (Continued)

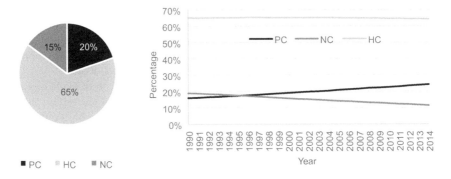

Figure 1.24b Global aggregate wealth composition, mean 1990–2014 and over time, education approach

Note: Each capital is first aggregated across countries for specific years in the right panel. This amount is further averaged for the whole period, 1990–2014, in the left panel.

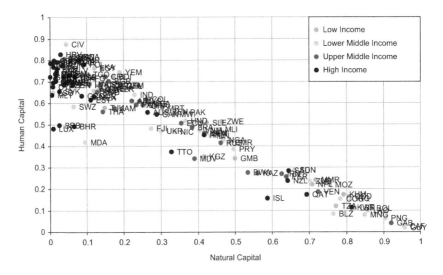

Figure 1.24c Percentage shares of human capital and natural capital in total wealth, average 1990–2014 (education approach)

Figure 1.24 Global aggregate wealth composition, education approach

suggests that, if one starts from the state of natural capital being 100% of wealth, a 20% decrease in natural capital would translate into a 15% increase in human capital, which would be reminiscent of the well-known Hartwick rule, which says that rents of depleted natural capital should be invested into other forms of capital to maintain future consumption and well-being (Hartwick 1977; Dixit et al. 1980). Although this story is easy to comprehend, recall that the apparent relationship in Figure 1.24c only represents that across countries. In other words, the way that capital assets are substituted for each other differs from country to country accord-ing to their historical paths. Moreover, it is important to remember that this correla-tion does not suggest any causation; it could be that, in theory, nations can invest into natural capital, resulting in a lower share of human capital.

In summary, it is confirmed that natural capital has been used to increase produced and, to a lesser extent, human capital. The higher that the share of natural capital is, the lower that the share of human capital tends to be. However, this amount is the global aggregate, and a closer look is always warranted. In particular, the share of natural capital has little to do with the advancement of the economy in question. After all, it is the change in combined wealth that counts.

4.4.   *IWI adjusted*

As we have demonstrated in the methodology section, the increase in inclusive wealth should show the same direction in which social well-being moves. Aside from population growth and its Malthusian effect, there are at least three factors that affect social well-being but that avoid the three capital channels: carbon dam-age, oil capital gains and TFP. Carbon damage erodes a nation's well-being because of its nature as a global public bad; the damage to the economy caused by climate change, which is affected by an aggregate of global carbon emissions, does not necessarily have something to do with its own levels of carbon emission or natural capital changes. Oil capital gains boost the total wealth by an exogenous increase in the price of natural capital. The economy can also enjoy improved social well-being in the presence of an increase in TFP, without any improvement in the quantity of inclusive wealth, representing technological progress in a broad sense across the whole society. Of course, one can think of TFP as another capital asset (Arrow et al. 2012).

Figure 1.25 shows the breakdown of the change in inclusive wealth, adjusted for the three terms. The figure starts from IW per capita and then introduces carbon damage, oil capital gains/losses and TFP to reach IW *per capita* adjusted.

Not surprisingly, carbon damage as a share of inclusive wealth affects small countries more because their inclusive wealth tends not to be sufficiently large enough to absorb such exogenous shocks. In this regard, our measure proves useful because we express carbon damage as a share of inclusive wealth. Per annum, the carbon damage adjustment does not exceed 1% of inclusive wealth, and it proves to be the least contributor to the adjustment terms of inclusive wealth. The largest order of carbon damage with regard to inclusive wealth is seen in Luxembourg (–0.6%), followed by Malta (–0.4%), Maldives (–0.4%), Bahrain (–0.4%) and Barbados (–0.3%). It should be noted that it is the well-known island nations that are most vulnerable to climate change and on the verge of non-existence, some of which lie out of the scope of our 140 studied countries. In absolute terms, however, carbon damage is relatively large in high-income countries such as Germany, France, the United Kingdom and the United States, among others. In per capita terms, carbon damage exceeds USD500 in Austria, Belgium, Switzerland, Germany, Denmark, Finland, France, the United Kingdom, Ireland, Iceland, Italy, Luxembourg, the Netherlands, Norway and Sweden. It is also interesting to note that some countries become *better* off due to climate change: Australia, Canada, Israel, New Zealand, Russia and Singapore actually gained as a

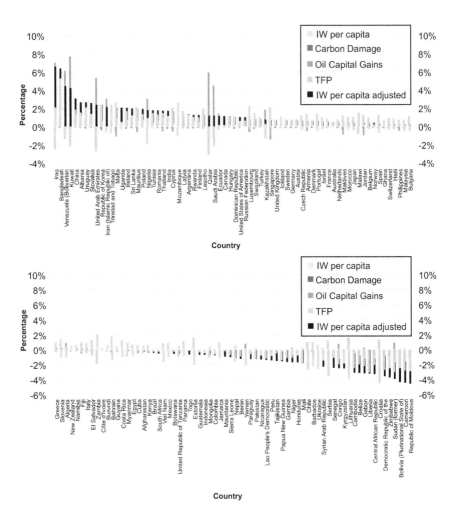

Figure 1.25 Breakdown of growth rates of inclusive wealth adjusted into three adjustment assets (education approach)

result of global carbon emissions. Thus, in these countries, carbon damage is recorded in positive terms in our accounting.

A much larger effect can be observed for oil capital gains and losses. In the current edition, an annual increase of 3% in the rental price of oil is assumed, corresponding to the annual average oil price increase during 1990–2014 (BP 2015), which means that even if no oil is withdrawn, the country in question can enjoy 3% growth in social well-being.[7,8] As shown in Figure 1.26, there has been dramatic volatility in oil prices in the last decade. Over the last quarter century, however, oil capital gain counts for more than 1% annually of inclusive wealth in the following dozen countries: Kuwait (7.7%), Iraq (7.0%), Venezuela (6.1%), Qatar (5.9%), the United Arab Emirates (5.4%), Saudi Arabia (4.5%), Iran (3.1%), Nigeria (3.0%),

Figure 1.26 Crude oil price movements since 1976, USD, with no inflation adjustments

Source: BP (2015), averaged prices of Dubai, Brent, Nigerian Forcados and West Texas Intermediate.

Uganda (2.1%), Kazakhstan (1.8%), Ecuador (1.4%) and Canada (1.1%). They are all countries with enormous reserves of either oil or natural gas, regardless of their income levels. As unconventional fossil fuel such as shale oil and gas comes to the fore, countries endowed with them will gain more if oil prices continue to increase. Among those nations with large oil capital gains, the adjusted IW per capita of the United Arab Emirates ends up at a moderate 2.0%. In other words, had it extracted its oil wealth more moderately, its IW per capita would have been on a par with, for example, United Kingdom.

Conversely, because sources of wealth cannot appear out of this air, there are "losers" in terms of these exogenous oil price movements. For completeness, we record negative numbers for those that faced higher import prices of oil. Those importing countries with negative oil capital gains comprise the majority (113 of 140 countries). The largest oil capital loss appears in Singapore, equivalent to –1.5% per annum of its initial wealth in 1990, followed by smaller nations, such as Malta (–1.1%), Jordan (–1.0%), Maldives (–0.9%) and Panama (–0.8%), because their inclusive wealth is considered to be relatively scarce with regard to importing oil price shocks. In comparison with oil capital gains, the order of magnitude of capital losses for individual countries is smaller, reflecting that oil-importing countries are geographically much more dispersed than exporting ones.

Finally, TFP measures residual GDP growth that the contributions of the three capital assets cannot explain. As Arrow et al. (2012) demonstrated, all we have to do is add the residual TFP growth to the change in inclusive wealth growth. In the education approach of this section, we take a different tack from the frontier approach in Section 3 and instead follow IWR 2012, taking the 25-year average of the TFP growth rates reported by the Conference Board (2017).[9] The only shortcoming of this dataset is the lack of natural capital as an input, which indicates that the TFP values might overestimate the true technical progress. However, this concern is not serious because, with our purpose of sustainability assessment, the final IW per capita adjusted by TFP would be the lowest bar to overcome. The development paths of those countries with negative IW per capita and with somewhat optimistic TFP would not be judged as sustainable even if TFP considering natural capital input were readily available. The top countries in terms of annual average TFP growth rates include Bangladesh, Mozambique, Trinidad and Tobago, Uruguay and Iraq, all surpassing 2%. Less than half of the sample (52 of 140) witnessed positive growth in TFP over the last 25 years.

All things considered, the ultimate IW growth rate, which is adjusted for the three factors along with population growth, can be calculated and shown, as in Figure 1.25. Among the top countries, Iraq, Venezuela, Kuwait and the United Arab Emirates all have experienced negative inclusive wealth per capita because of the depletion of their oil capital. This finding demonstrates how much oil capital gains might have worked as proverbial windfall benefits in terms of the sustainable development of those nations. Bangladesh, China, Albania, Uruguay, Slovakia and South Korea have moderately accumulated inclusive wealth and TFP.

On the opposite end, 59 countries have seen negative growth in adjusted IW per capita. It is remarkable that, aside from Croatia, all ten of the worst performing countries have had both negative inclusive wealth per capita and negative TFP. If they not only continue to lack investment in the usual set of capital assets but are also sluggish in improving the overall efficiency of their economies, their paths to sustainable well-being look far-fetched.

4.5. Comparison with GDP and HDI

In this subsection, we compare our results, based on conventional calculations, with the past performances of other well-known indices. GDP per capita is the most popular index to date for monitoring the progress of nations. Since its launch in the early 1990s, the Human Development Index (HDI) has also been widely cited as an index for tracking the development of nations. HDI is a composite index of human capital (health and education) and income levels (GDP). Happiness, or more generally subjective well-being, has gained attention recently, shedding light on the other side of social well-being, rather than our determinant-based indicator of social well-being. Finally, the closest to our index is the World Bank's genuine savings, formally adjusted net savings, which keeps track of savings (and dissavings) in produced, human and natural capital. For our comparison, we exhibit IWI per capita, both before and after adjustments, because they differ greatly.

4.5.1. GDP per capita

GDP has been criticized for sending an incorrect message regarding the sustainability of social well-being. Their growth can differ from our IWI per capita, as shown in Figures 1.27a and 1.27b. Countries in Quadrant I, which form the majority, have experienced both positive GDP and IWI on per capita terms. This finding is understandable to a certain extent since portions of GDP are directed toward investment in capital assets. More importantly, several dozens of countries still fall into Quadrant II,

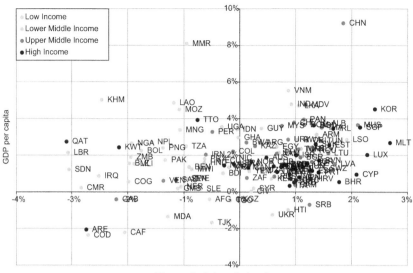

Figure 1.27a Growth rates in IW per capita (before adjustment) (education approach) vs. GDP per capita

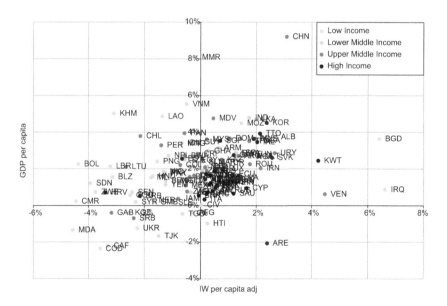

Figure 1.27b Growth rates in IW per capita adjusted (education approach) vs. GDP per capita

Figure 1.27 Growth rates in IW per capita (education approach) vs. GDP per capita

with positive GDP per capita but negative IW per capita, both in non-adjusted and adjusted terms. Note, from Quadrant IV, that the reverse is not true: positive IW per capita is associated with negative GDP per capita for only five countries and two countries, without and with adjustments, respectively. This finding shows that it might be sufficient to monitor IW per capita growth, even for the purpose of tracking GDP growth.

There is a very weak correlation between GDP per capita and IW per capita before adjustment, but there is a weak but positive correlation between GDP per capita and IW per capita after adjusting for all of the income strata. The latter finding is not surprising since one of the adjustment terms, TFP, measures the unaccounted-for contribution of capital assets to GDP.

4.5.2. Growth volatility

Some authors have argued that volatility of resource prices could hurt economic performance (e.g. van der Ploeg and Poelhekke 2009). Although there is no formal theory to prove that volatility of output hampers sustainable development, it would be helpful to have a picture of how these two factors can be placed. Figure 1.28 plots GDP volatility as measured by the standard deviation of the past 25-year output and the natural capital share. In contrast to our predictions, there is almost no relationship between volatility and dependence on natural capital. Although it is not reported, we do not see a clear correlation between volatility and IW per capita growth rate either. Countries that depend highly on natural capital are not necessarily experiencing volatile output growth, although Iraq, Kuwait and Liberia have seen bumpy growth rates.

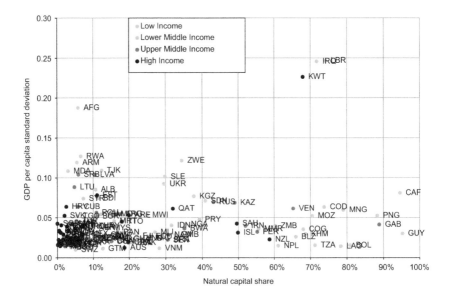

Figure 1.28 Natural capital share in 2014 (education approach) vs. 25-year average GDP per capita variation (standard deviation)

4.5.3.   Human Development Index (HDI)

What about the correlation of IWI and another oft-cited index of development, HDI? Figure 1.29 shows that there is no apparent relationship between the two indices. For lower middle-income countries, it even shows a slightly negative relationship; thus, HDI could send an incorrect message regarding sustainability. However, with a closer look at Figure 1.29b, we could say that the higher that the

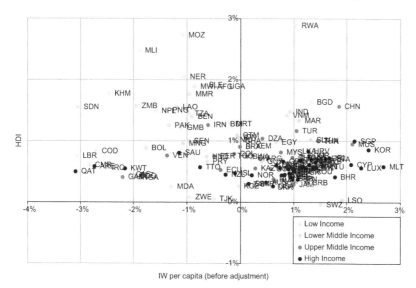

Figure 1.29a Growth rates in IW per capita (before adjustment) (education approach) vs. HDI

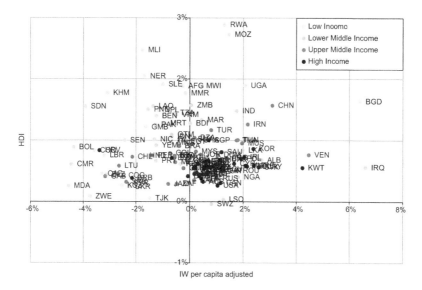

Figure 1.29b Growth rates in IW per capita adjusted (education approach) vs. HDI

Figure 1.29 Growth rates in IW per capita (education approach) vs. HDI

growth IWI per capita adjusted is, the higher that HDI growth is for a limited set of nations, with a slightly weak correlation of $R^2 = 0.17$ for low-income nations and $R^2 = 0.21$ for upper middle-income countries. No such relationship is clearly detected for high or lower middle-income nations. Again, a slightly better fit for IW per capita adjusted can be justified since the economic component of HDI is GDP per capita, which contains TFP, which in turn is used in our adjustment terms to IWI.

4.5.4. Happiness

As we articulated earlier in this chapter, inclusive wealth addresses the determinants of social well-being. Capital assets comprise the productive base of the economy, which in turn becomes the source of utility for further generations. It is not intended, therefore, to address the constituents of well-being (Dasgupta 2001). It is not that the constituents can be ignored; in contrast, they can complement each other to express current and future social well-being.

As depicted in Figure 1.30a and 1.30b, there seems to be almost no correlation between the twin aspects of well-being, at least for our studied sample. Note that the vertical axis represents the status of happiness, instead of the growth rate of happiness. For some income categories, a slightly negative relationship even can be detected. Although we are tempted to cynically state that non-declining inclusive wealth might not be able to buy happiness, this observation is not necessarily bad news; as we have argued, they are totally different aspects of social well-being, emphasizing the need to allow them to complement each other.

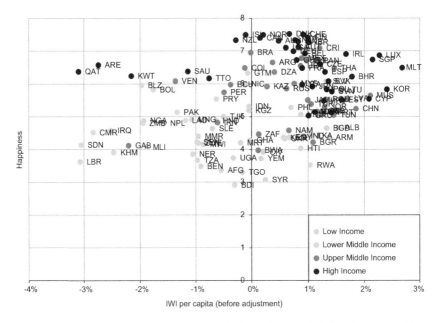

Figure 1.30a Growth rates in IW per capita (before adjustment) (education approach) vs. happiness

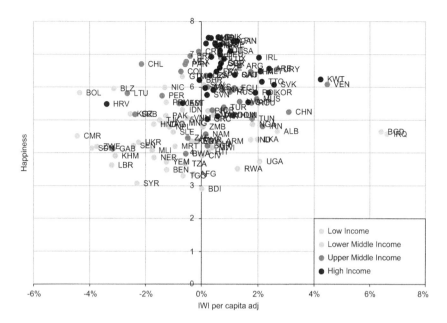

Figure 1.30b Growth rates in IW per capita adjusted (education approach) vs.
happiness

Figure 1.30 Growth rates in IW per capita (education approach) vs. happiness

4.5.5.   Genuine savings

As part of their World Development Indicators database, the World Bank started to
compute the genuine savings of nations as early as 1999. Its composite index is an
affine to our IWI because they both measure the changes in produced, human and
natural capital. However, we differ from the World Bank in many important details.
Most notably, the World Bank does not compute capital assets *per se* annually; what
it accounts for is the change in capital assets. For example, the change in produced
capital corresponds to net national savings. Human capital is recorded as the change
in inputs (i.e. education expenditure) instead of outputs (i.e. return on education).
For natural capital, the World Bank studies fossil fuels, minerals, forests and carbon
damage, but not agricultural land and fisheries. Additionally, its notion of intangible
capital is based on the residual of the net present value of consumption, which cannot be explained by tangible capital assets. It is not our purpose to extensively discuss
the theoretical difference here: for further extensive discussion of the comparison,
see IWR 2012 (UNU-IHDP and UNEP 2012).[10]

In principle, they could look similar, but are they empirically different in the
assessment of sustainability over the years? Figure 1.31a shows correlation of IWI
per capita with genuine savings. It would be best if we could express genuine savings as a share of wealth-like figures, but the World Bank does not publish stock
data annually. We instead use the average genuine savings, excluding particulate

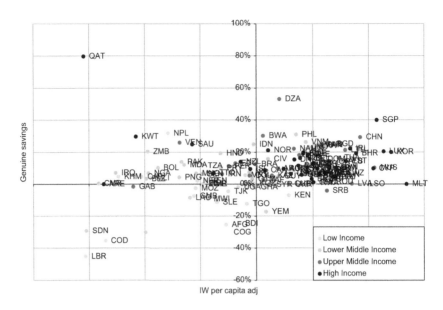

Figure 1.31a Growth rates in IW per capita (before adjustment)(education approach) vs. genuine savings as a share of GNI

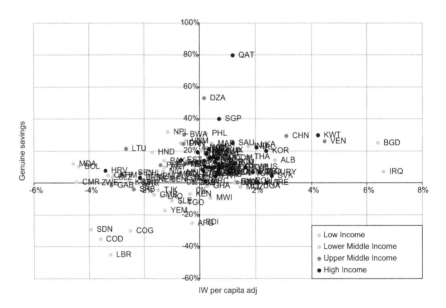

Figure 1.31b Growth rates in IW per capita adjusted (education approach) vs. genuine savings as a share of GNI

Figure 1.31 Growth rates in IW per capita (education approach) vs. genuine savings as a share of GNI

Source: Genuine savings excluding particulate matter emissions are expressed as a share of GNI, taking the average values of 1990–2014.

matter emissions, as part of the average gross national income (GNI). For genuine savings and IW per capita (without adjustment), the two indices do not have an evident relationship. In fact, a negative relationship can be found for high-income countries. However, once IW per capita is adjusted (Figure 1.31b), a mildly positive relationship can be found for all income groups, indicating that both indices tend to produce similar sustainability assessments, although we still have many country samples in Quadrant II. In a similar manner to the relationship with GDP per capita, we observe few countries in Quadrant IV: very few countries with positive IW per capita have negative genuine savings, but not the other way around. In this sense, IW per capita could be a more conservative indicator of sustainability.

5.   Final remarks

Sustainability assessment based on capital stocks seems to be here to stay. However, it should be emphasized that the equivalence between wealth and well-being is the premise from which we all should start. Under such an equivalence, the change in well-being should move in the same direction as the change in wealth. Standing on the shoulders of Inclusive Wealth Report (IWR) 2012 and 2014, we continue our effort to show a truer wealth of nations. As we have stressed, it is the change in capital assets and wealth that counts. The value of wealth itself does not have welfare significance. Nonetheless, the picture of wealth also provides an interesting piece of information.

Specifically, in the current edition of IWR, we show the inclusive wealth of nations, consisting of produced, human and natural capital, based on a non-parametric method, which we call the *frontier approach*. In this approach, shadow prices are determined so that GDP is the output and the three capitals are inputs. As it turns out, 135, 89 and 96 of the 140 countries saw increases compared to their levels in 1990 in inclusive wealth (IW), IW per capita and IW per capita adjusted. The global growth rate was 44%, which is an average growth rate of 1.8% per annum. However, this rate is smaller than the annual average GDP growth rate suggests (3.4%) during the same period. Turning to the breakdown of growth, we find that produced capital increased at an annual average rate of 3.8%, while health- and education-induced human capital growth remained at 2.1%, and natural capital decreased by 0.7%. In short, investment in produced capital has been facilitated; however, health, education and natural capital, in which we see enormous potential for future well-being, either grew modestly or even decreased. On a global scale, the configuration of capital has been as follows: produced (21%), education (26%), health (33%) and natural (20%). It is remarkable that, of the trio of capitals, the value decreased only for natural capital. A natural way to interpret this outcome is that produced capital and, to a lesser extent, human capital have been enhanced at the cost of natural capital.

Since some readers might want to see education as human capital using the IWR 2014 approach, in which the shadow prices of human capital are based on the rate of return on education, as well as conventional TFP (Arrow et al. 2012), we have also shown the results of education computation of capital assets, following IWR 2012 and 2014. According to this approach, for the studied period of 1990–2014, 133, 84 and 81 countries experienced increases in IW in absolute terms, IW per capita and IW per capita adjusted, respectively. Since the number of countries and the methodology are comparable to previous editions of IWR, these numbers can be said to have improved from 128, 85 and 58 of the 140 countries reported in IWR 2014 for the studied period of 1990–2010. Because we do not include health capital in the education approach for practical reasons, frontier and education approaches are not directly comparable because many would be double counted. Having noted this fact, the averages of the shares of capital assets (which is further averaged for the 25-year period) are as follows: produced (17%), human (54%) and natural (29%), with little change from IWR 2014. However, on a different scale, the averages are produced (20%), human (65%) and natural (15%). The last is an alarmingly low number, highlighting the rising scarcity of nature.

We conclude this chapter by alluding to some of the major challenges and potential discussions.

Completing the list of capital assets

By construction, we are asked to account for many capital assets, provided that they affect intertemporal well-being and they do not overlap with existing capital assets. Otherwise, the very premise of an equivalent relationship between wealth and well-being would collapse.[11] We have included fish wealth as an important constituent of natural capital for virtually the first time. Another class of natural capital that comes to mind is water, which is vital to economies and people of all income categories. As was experimentally discussed in UNU-IHDP and UNEP (2012), water poses a challenge in terms of a tricky relationship between flow and stock variables.[12] In addition, the resilience of nature can be added as another essential capital to economies, at least conceptually (Mäler and Li 2010) and locally in practice (Walker et al. 2010). Accounting for resilience in a non-local manner would be difficult, if not impossible.

Furthermore, institutions and social capital are even more challenging classes to consider. Aside from their intangibility, part of the issue arises from the very nature of these assets: they enable other capital assets to function to yield well-being (Dasgupta 2015). Therefore, we should resist the temptation to add, for example, social capital as another capital asset in an ad hoc manner, such as the valuation of social capital through revealed preference. A more promising method would be to account for social capital in a two-stage setup, in which we can see how social capital raises the shadow prices of other capital assets.

Shadow prices

Even in imperfect economies, as we know, the relative weight of capital assets has been shown to be formalized as their marginal contributions to social well-being, given a forecast of an economy (Arrow et al. 2012), as we demonstrated in Section 2. In the current volume of IWR, we have shown results in which non-parametric frontier analysis is used to compute the shadow prices of human capital. This capital comes with its costs: compared to the education approach to human capital shadow prices, GDP is used as the output, corresponding to the three capitals.[13] Inclusive wealth accounting for sustainability assessment is, by construction, founded on intertemporal well-being, so it would be best if we could use the latter as the output. Admittedly, the education approach is also not without faults: the rate of return on education, as well as value of statistical life (VSL) year, is derived from market transactions and thus can deviate from the marginal impact on well-being. Perhaps of more concern to us in the face of looming climate change is the non-linearity of shadow prices. We are required to update our shadow prices, if necessary, once scientific evidence of the scarcity of the components of natural capital is revealed.

Coevolution and interdependence of capital assets

The shadow price of a given capital reflects marginal social value, but it can also be subject to other capital assets. In the language of ecological economists, capital assets co-evolve. For example, we can think of negative externality in health capital. We already have accounted for carbon damage by greenhouse gases in the adjustment terms, but it might also be a good idea to include local air pollution, as is performed for particulate matter in the World Bank's (2016) computation of genuine savings. Indeed, there is ample evidence that local air pollution, both indoor and outdoor, is hazardous to health and poses a hindrance to longevity. Local air pollution acts more like a flow variable rather than a stock, but it could be formalized as a persistent negative natural capital. Even so, care should be taken not to double count health capital because, if the VSL already captures shorter life years caused by air pollution, then it would be redundant to account for its externality to health.

To provide another example, it is not necessarily clear to which capital urban land is allocated; currently, it is implicitly within produced capital in many cases. In its analysis of state-by-state wealth accounting, Chapter 5 of UNU-IHDP and UNEP (2012) has explicitly treated urban land under produced capital. Improving the amenity value of the environment in cities, therefore, could potentially boost the shadow value of urban land. Conversely, natural capital shadow prices could be affected by produced capital investment. However, this question remains open to discussion since it would involve consumers' surplus, which might not exactly match shadow value in inclusive wealth accounting. This consideration would bring us back, like it or not, to the matter of shadow prices.

Notes

1 See UNU-IHDP and UNEP (2012) for what makes the Inclusive Wealth Index distinct from the World Bank's genuine savings. To be more precise, genuine savings are constructed from flow variables, complemented by stock calculations.
2 Hartwick (1977) and Dixit et al. (1980) showed that investing exhaustible resource rents into produced capital yields non-declining consumption, which is another way of defining sustainable development.
3 In theory, W is different from IWI, which is calculated based on constant shadow prices. When reckoning the real W, it is obvious that, for example, the last drop of oil should have a different marginal value than the regular drop when it is not scarce. We compute IWI on the premise that the studied period is relatively short.
4 More specifically, the ratio of carbon damage to inclusive wealth can be deducted from the inclusive wealth growth rate to arrive at the adjusted inclusive wealth growth rate.
5 These countries are Estonia, Gabon, Gambia, Greece, Croatia, Haiti, Jamaica, Laos, Latvia, Sudan, Serbia, Syria and Vietnam.
6 The years 1990 and 1991 are skipped here to avoid missing data in some former Soviet republics.
7 In theory, the value of oil natural capital can remain intact if the decreasing rate of oil quantity can be compensated for by the oil price increase rate when the quantity is fixed.

8 When oil prices are expected to increase in the future for some reason or another, the current list of capital assets could also be adjusted to reflect such a gain in social well-being (Vincent et al. 1997; Hamilton and Bolt 2004; van der Ploeg 2010). We do not consider this possibility since future oil prices are too uncertain, as our recent experience demonstrates.

9 Of the 140 countries sampled, there are 33 countries with TFP data missing in Conference Board (2017), which are complemented by regional averages.

10 The methodology of the World Bank's genuine savings is delineated in World Bank (2011).

11 If our list of capital assets is not complete, wealth could deviate from well-being. On an empirical level, there have been studies to test genuine savings and consumption changes (Ferreira et al. 2008; Greasley et al. 2014), and we recommend similar studies be conducted for inclusive wealth as well.

12 Fenichel et al. (2016) attempted to account for local groundwater in an imperfect economy.

13 One can defend the use of GDP as the output of three capitals by claiming that the value of life expressed as health capital implicitly nests future generations. However, this interpretation of utility function would be very limited, so we do not push this thesis any further.

References

Arrow, K. J., Dasgupta, P., Goulder, L. H., Mumford, K. J., & Oleson, K. (2012). Sustainability and the measurement of wealth. *Environment and Development Economics*, *17*(3), 317–353.

Asheim, G. B. (2010). Global welfare comparisons. *Canadian Journal of Economics*, *43*(4), 1412–1432.

Asheim, G. B., & Weitzman, M. L. (2001). Does NNP growth indicate welfare improvement? *Economics Letters*, *73*(2), 233–239.

BP. (2015). *Statistical Review of World Energy 2015*. https://www.bp.com/content/dam/bp-country/es_es/spain/documents/downloads/PDF/bp-statistical-review-of-world-energy-2015-full-report.pdf.

Conference Board. (2017). *The Conference Board Total Economy Database™ (Adjusted Version)*, May 2017.

Coyle, D. (2015). *GDP: A Brief But Affectionate History*. Princeton, NJ: Princeton University Press.

Dasgupta, P. (2001). *Human Well-Being and the Natural Environment*. Oxford: Oxford University Press.

Dasgupta, P. (2015). Disregarded capitals: What national accounting ignores. *Accounting and Business Research*, *45*(4), 447–464.

Dasgupta, P., Duraiappah, A., Managi, S., Barbier, E., Collins, R., Fraumeni, B., Gundimeda, H., Liu, G., & Mumford, K. J. (2015). How to measure sustainable progress. *Science*, *13*(35), 748.

Dasgupta, P., & Heal, G. (1974). The optimal depletion of exhaustible resources. *Review of Economic Studies*, *41*, 3–28.

d'Autume, A., & Schubert, K. (2008). Hartwick's rule and maximin paths when the exhaustible resource has an amenity value. *Journal of Environmental Economics and Management*, *56*(3), 260–274.

Dixit, A., Hammond, P., & Hoel, M. (1980). On Hartwick's rule for regular maximin paths of capital accumulation and resource depletion. *Review of Economic Studies*, *47*(3), 551–556.

Easterlin, R. A. (2003). Explaining happiness. *Proceedings of the National Academy of Sciences*, *100*(19), 11176–11183.

Fenichel, E. P., Abbott, J. K., Bayham, J., Boone, W., Haacker, E. M., & Pfeiffer, L. (2016). Measuring the value of groundwater and other forms of natural capital. *Proceedings of the National Academy of Sciences*, *113*(9), 2382–2387.

Ferreira, S., Hamilton, K., & Vincent, J. R. (2008). Comprehensive wealth and future consumption: Accounting for population growth. *The World Bank Economic Review*, 22(2), 233–248.

Fleurbaey, M., & Gaulier, G. (2009). International comparisons of living standards by equivalent incomes. *Scandinavian Journal of Economics*, 111(3), 597–624.

Greasley, D., Hanley, N., Kunnas, J., McLaughlin, E., Oxley, L., & Warde, P. (2014). Testing genuine savings as a forward-looking indicator of future well-being over the (very) long-run. *Journal of Environmental Economics and Management*, 67(2), 171–188.

Hamilton, K., & Bolt, K. (2004). Resource price trends and development prospects. *Portuguese Economic Journal*, 3(2), 85–97.

Hartwick, J. M. (1977). Intergenerational equity and the investing of rents from exhaustible resources. *American Economic Review*, 67(5), 972–974.

Helliwell, J., Layard, R., & Sachs, J. (2017). *World Happiness Report 2017*. New York: Sustainable Development Solutions Network.

Jones, C. I., & Klenow, P. J. (2016). Beyond GDP? Welfare across countries and time. *American Economic Review*, 106(9), 2426–2457.

Kahneman, D., Krueger, A. B., Schkade, D., Schwarz, N., & Stone, A. A. (2006). Would you be happier if you were richer? A focusing illusion. *Science* (80). 312, 1908–1910.

Krautkraemer, J. A. (1985). Optimal growth, resource amenities and the preservation of natural environments. *Review of Economic Studies*, 52(1), 153–169.

Kurniawan, R., & Managi, S. (2017). Sustainable development and performance measurement: Global productivity decomposition. *Sustainable Development*, 25, 639–654.

Layard, R. (2005). *Happiness*. London: Penguin Books.

Mäler, K. G., & Li, C. Z. (2010). Measuring sustainability under regime shift uncertainty: A resilience pricing approach. *Environment and Development Economics*, 15(6), 707–719.

Managi, S. (Ed.). (2015a). *The Economics of Green Growth: New Indicators for Sustainable Societies*. New York: Routledge.

Managi, S. (Ed.). (2015b). *The Routledge Handbook of Environmental Economics in Asia*. New York: Routledge.

Mankiw, N. G., Romer, D., & Weil, D. N. (1992). A contribution to the empirics of economic growth. *Quarterly Journal of Economics*, 107(2), 407–437.

OECD. (2014). *Better Life Index*. OECD Better Life Initiative. http://www.oecd betterlifeindex.org/

Ramsey, F. (1928). A mathematical theory of saving. *The Economic Journal*, 38(152), 543–559.

Ricard, D., Minto, C., Jensen, O. P., & Baum, J. K. (2012). Examining the knowledge base and status of commercially exploited marine species with the RAM Legacy Stock Assessment Database. *Fish and Fisheries*, 13(4), 380–398.

SAUP. (2011). *The Sea Around Us Project Database*. Retrieved May, 2011, from www.seaaroundus.org/data/

Solow, R. M. (1974). Intergenerational equity and exhaustible resources. *Review of Economic Studies*, 41, 29–45.

Stiglitz, J., Sen, A., Fitoussi, J.-P. (2009). The measurement of economic performance and social progress revisited. Reflections overview. *Comm. Meas. Econ. Perform. Soc. Progress*, Paris.

Sugiawan, Y., Islam, M., & Managi, S. (2017). Global marine fisheries with economic growth. *Economic Analysis and Policy*, 55, 158–168.

United Nations Development Programme. (1990–2016). *Human Development Report*. http://hdr.undp.org/en/global-reports

UNU-IHDP, & UNEP. (2012). *Inclusive Wealth Report 2012: Measuring Progress toward Sustainability*. Cambridge: Cambridge University Press.

UNU-IHDP, & UNEP. (2014). *Inclusive Wealth Report 2014: Measuring Progress toward Sustainability*. Cambridge: Cambridge University Press.

van der Ploeg, F. (2010). Why do many resource-rich countries have negative genuine saving?: Anticipation of better times or rapacious rent seeking. *Resource and Energy Economics*, *32*(1), 28–44.

van der Ploeg, F., & Poelhekke, S. (2009). Volatility and the natural resource curse. *Oxford Economic Papers*, *61*(4), 727–760.

van der Ploeg, F., & Withagen, C. (2014). Growth, renewables, and the optimal carbon tax. *International Economic Review*, *55*(1), 283–311.

Vincent, J. R., Panayotou, T., & Hartwick, J. M. (1997). Resource depletion and sustainability in small open economies. *Journal of Environmental Economics and Management*, *33*(3), 274–286.

Walker, B., Pearson, L., Harris, M., Maler, K. G., Li, C. Z., Biggs, R., & Baynes, T. (2010). Incorporating resilience in the assessment of inclusive wealth: An example from South East Australia. *Environmental and Resource Economics*, *45*(2), 183–202.

Weitzman, M. L. (1976). On the welfare significance of national product in a dynamic economy. *The Quarterly Journal of Economics*, *90*(1), 156–162.

World Bank. (2011). *The Changing Wealth of Nations: Measuring Sustainable Development in the New Millennium*. Washington, DC. https://openknowledge.worldbank.org/handle/10986/2252

World Bank. (2016). *World Development Indicators Database*. https://data.worldbank.org/products/wdi

Xepapadeas, A. (2005). Economic growth and the environment. *Handbook of Environmental Economics*, *3*, 1219–1271.

2 Inclusive wealth

From theory to practice

Pushpam Kumar and Rodney B W Smith

Introduction

One is unlikely to find a major publicly traded firm that does not conduct asset accounting and balance sheet analysis. The information embedded in such reports provides investors valuable insights into the composition of firm assets and insights into its short and long-run trends. Surprisingly, few nations have a history of preparing annual balance sheets, thus hamstringing the ability of policy analysts and policymakers to understand trends in the composition and status of national wealth, and use such information to inform policy design. Recently, however, the advent of wealth accounting by UN Environment and others is helping fill this information gap – how this information will be used remains to be seen.

Currently, UN Environment measures of wealth are calculated as weighted sums of human, natural and produced capital, with the weighted index called the *Inclusive Wealth Index* (IWI).[1] One can view a nation's wealth as an index of the productive base from which the flow of goods and services (i.e. gross national product, or GDP) is generated. Roughly speaking, if the productive base (per capita) of a country has not fallen over time, and if projections suggest this pattern will continue into the future, we say the country's growth is sustainable. Note that while sustainable growth can accommodate a pattern of increasing (or decreasing) GDP per capita over time, it is not wise to assume that a pattern of increasing GDP over time is consistent with sustainable growth. A simple example in the next section illustrates.

This chapter has four sections. The first section provides an overview of the rationale underlying the claim that – from an intergenerational welfare perspective – linking resource allocation policies to changes in wealth is more appropriate than linking resource allocation policies to changes in gross domestic product (GDP). This second section provides an overview of the basis for wealth estimation and explores how various types of conservation and development policies recognizing the trade-off can be understood better with the help of inclusive wealth. The second section also brings the wealth concept closer to national level policies on selected conservation goals and targets, and shows its comparative advantage over others.

The third section illustrates some of the advantages of estimating wealth in the context of Sustainable Development Goals (SDGs) of the United Nations endorsed in 2015. The chapter examines some of the global policy goals manifested in Agenda 2030 and the Sustainable Development Goals (SDGs). By selecting a few goals and targets, it has been shown how we can achieve greater results for the SDGs if the indicator is orchestrated through wealth index. Finally, the chapter synthesizes the lessons learned including caveats and limitations of wealth in formulating policies of conservation and development at various levels of decision-making units.

1. Gross domestic product, wealth measurement, substitution and sustainability

Gross domestic product and inclusive wealth

Gross domestic product was introduced at the Bretton Woods conference in 1944 and was to serve as an index of the size of a country's economy – an accounting measure of all goods and services produced in a country over a given period of time. Since its inception, however, GDP gradually morphed from simply a measure of market activity, into a measure of a country's overall well-being – per capita GDP – a far cry from its original interpretation in the 1940s.

The shortcomings of GDP as a measure of social well-being are well-known, with the two most germane to this discussion being – GDP ignores: (i) the value of human capital and the non-market values of natural capital; and (ii) the economic value of externalities, both positive and negative. Few will argue that GDP was to serve as a measure of social inclusivity or environmental sustainability.[2] Perhaps this is why, as countries continue to advance economically, one questions the ability of GDP to adequately gauge human well-being and sustainability – this is especially the case when natural resource availability appears to present impediments to economic growth.

Gross domestic product is a measure of the value of service flows generated by an economy's produced (or physical), human and natural capital over a period of time. Wealth – in this case inclusive wealth – is defined as the sum of the value of three types of capital stock: human capital, physical capital and natural capital. The value of each capital is defined as the unit stock value of that capital multiplied by the quantity of that capital. For example, if the unit stock price of physical capital is $1 and the economy is endowed with 5,000,000 units of physical capital, the stock value of physical capital is $5,000,000.

The Inclusive Wealth Index measures the wealth of a country by carrying out a comprehensive analysis of the country's productive base – with the productive base including three types of capital: manufactured or physical, human and natural. Its objective is that of measuring a nation's capacity to create and maintain human well-being over time. A country's inclusive wealth is the social value (as contrasted with market values) of all its capital assets, including natural capital, human capital and produced capital. If a country's IWI is non-decreasing over time, we say its growth is sustainable. The implication being the average household in the future is no worse off than households today.

Manufactured capital is the physical capital produced by humans – automobiles, roads, buildings, etc. Human capital is often defined as the stock of knowledge and skills possessed by a population, and the health status of that population. Investments in education, training and health are called investments in human capital.[3] Natural capital can be viewed as the stocks of natural assets, ranging from soil, water and air, to all living things.

The wide range of services natural capital provide are called ecosystem services, some of which are *provisioning* services like fuel from wood, cooking water from streams and lakes, and food from agricultural production. In developing countries, the poor and other economically vulnerable groups are highly dependent on eco-system services for their livelihoods, with natural capital accounting for 36% of wealth in low-income countries (WAVES, 2012).

In addition to the provisioning service flows that directly support human life, there are less visible ecosystem services that come within the purview of regulat-ing, habitat and supporting, and cultural functions. Although these services can be just as important – in some cases, essential – for human well-being, their contributions typically fall outside the domain of market valuation. An example of regulating services include a forest's contribution to flood control and climate regulation, and its carbon storage services – each of which may be intangible from an economic standpoint, but undeniably valuable to humans, animals and other life forms. Despite the importance of the regulating and sustaining services to human well-being, the value of the services or the natural capital that produce them are seldom measured.

One could argue that, traditionally, economic policymakers focused on efficient production (e.g. eliminating subsidies, curtailing trade barriers) and increasing per capita GDP growth. The thinking was that efficiency and growth would increase the size of the economy, and the larger the economy, the more goods and services available for social consumption. Such productive activities, however, were often accompanied by negative externalities like air and water pollution. As the negative impact of the environmental externalities became more apparent, and documented with verifiable statistics, many countries adjusted their industrial policies to lessen the levels and impact of the externalities. Still, in spite of the efforts to curtail negative outcomes like air pollution, air pollution levels in cities across the globe provide evidence of the continued negative side effects of modern economic production.[4] Furthermore, the impacts of environmental degradation on health and recreational quality have not yet made its way into any well-known economic indices.

We have come to a similar point with natural resource and ecosystem manage-ment: a more clear understanding – and acceptance – of the potential problems associated with natural resource and ecosystem degradation has led to efforts to collect data that eventually should help better manage ecosystems and increasingly scarce natural resources. Data such as water stocks and qualities across nations, soil depth, forested area and carbon sequestration are beginning to enter national account tables via the United Nations' System and Environmental Economic Accounting (SEEA).[5] The hope is to eventually use the natural resource stock levels to calculate natural resource, and possibly ecosystem service, stock and flow value indices.

Why a wealth-based index of sustainability?

Typically, if per capita GDP growth is non-negative, decision makers assume the economy is doing well. The following example, however, illustrates this assumption could be misleading. Table 2.1 presents hypothetical levels of physical, human and natural capital for an (closed) economy, along with unit flow and unit stock prices.

Table 2.1 Productive base – capital quantities, unit flow and stock values, GDP and inclusive wealth

Factor	Quantity	Unit cost	Unit stock value	Flow value	Initial stock value
Physical capital	10,000,000	$0.10	$1.00	$1,000,000	$10,000,000
Human capital	150	$20,000	$400,000	$3,000,000	$60,000,000
Natural capital	1,000,000	$20	$20	$5,000,000	$20,000,000
GDP	–	–	–	$9,000,000	–
Inclusive wealth	–	–	–	–	$90,000,000

For simplicity, assume the economy produces a single final good, and that producing a unit of the final good takes one year, and requires a one unit of natural capital, 40 units of physical capital and 0.006 units of labour.[6] The reader can verify that given the factor endowments in Table 2.1, the maximum amount of the final good the economy can produce over the year is 250,000 units. In such a case, given the unit rental (Flower & Schreve) rates of capital and labour, and assuming the unit cost of the unit price of timber is $20; the economy's GDP is $9,000,000. The initial value of inclusive wealth is equal to the sum of the stock values of physical, human and natural capital: $1 × 10,000,000 + $400,000 × 150 + $20 × 1,000,000 = $90,000,000.

To keep calculations simple, assume physical and human capital do not depreciate, and the economy never replaces the natural capital used over the year. Then GDP in the subsequent year would also be equal to $9,000,000. However, since the economy used 250,000 units of natural capital, its capital stock would be equal to 750,000 and its inclusive wealth equal to $85,000,000. In this simple example, the economy could generate $9,000,000 in GDP for four years. On the other hand, inclusive wealth per capita is falling over time – hence, the economy's growth pattern is not sustainable.

In this simple example, GDP does not change and provides no indication the economy is approaching a cliff. The inclusive wealth measure, however, provides a warning, as inclusive wealth falls each period. As a sustainability index, it appears the Inclusive Wealth Index is superior to GDP (and any current measure of income changes) as a sustainability index. As such, the example illustrates why we might want to focus on wealth-based measures of sustainability. For an elegant mathematical argument underlying the superiority of wealth based sustainability measures, see Dasgupta (2009).

Of course, with no trade, and given the fixed coefficient production structure, the economy would be unable to produce any of the final good in the fifth year. This example, of course, is highly stylized but does show what can happen to a region in a country if an essential natural resource is improperly managed and if one ignores sustainability concerns. An extremely relevant example is the Aral Sea debacle, where water diversions for cotton and rice production caused the surface area of the Aral Sea to fall enough where ships could no longer reach the shores of existing cities – transforming a once economically vibrant water body into one with virtually no economic value.

Substitution and sustainability indices

The GDP and inclusive wealth pattern in the above example occurs because the assumed production technology did not allow input substitution, e.g. did not allow the economy to use more human capital and less natural capital and get the same level of output. If it was possible to produce income without natural capital, or produce the same level of output with less natural capital and more human or physical capital, the economy or region could continue generating income as natural capital levels fell. This issue of substitution possibilities for natural capital is central to an ongoing discourse on policy formulation for sustainable development.

Many economists assume technological advances will offset the potential fall in productivity due to natural capital losses. This view implicitly assumes human and physical capital can serve as substitutes for natural capital. On the other hand, many ecological scientists assume the substitution possibilities between human, physical and natural capital are limited, and that natural capital stocks impose a limit on productivity; this notion borrows from the concept of carrying capacity (Ehrlich & Pringle). The ecologists implicitly assume a shrinking natural capital base implies a decreasing level of potential productivity – maintaining the life support system of the earth is required to ensure sustainability.

Concerns with the substitutability of natural, human and physical capital influence the way we define and measure sustainability indices. Two broad classes of sustainability indices exist. One class assumes human and physical capital are unable to serve as substitutes for natural capital. *Strong sustainability goals* are linked to such restrictions. A sustainability index designed to satisfy strong sustainability goals would likely require the level of natural capital stocks per capita to not fall over time, *and* a separate index of human and physical capital per capita not fall over time.

The other class of sustainability indices accommodates substitution between natural, human and physical capital. *Weak sustainability* goals are linked to these requirements. The Inclusive Wealth Index is a single index composed of the values of human, physical and natural capital and yields a weak sustainability index. By construction, it allows for an increase in inclusive wealth (per capita) in the face of natural capital depreciation – it can increase as long as the decrease in natural capital stocks is offset by enough of an increase in human and physical capital stocks.

Combining, or reconciling, the economists' and ecologists' perspectives should be possible if the context and character of resources are known. More to the point, the ecologists' notion of substitution and sustainability are captured in the example above, where there are no substitution possibilities across human, physical and natural capital. The Aral Sea debacle is a real world example of such a case. An island tourism economy is an example of how substitution could lead to an opposite outcome. Say the island's growth is linked to water recreation activities and, over time, loses natural capital through the degradation of its coral reef system. If the island invests in casinos and associated activities, it is possible the increase in physical and human capital could lead to an outcome where inclusive wealth per capita increases over time.

Some types of natural capital have little to no human or physical capital alternatives. In poor nations the ability of climate conditions to control vector borne diseases may be limited. The regulative services inherent in nutrient cycling, soil formation and bioremediation also likely have few human and physical capital alternatives. The capital underlying these services is referred to as *critical capital*. If one could identify and measure critical capital and monitor the levels and growth of that capital it might be possible to develop a sustainability index of critical capital, but it is unlikely a market value of the capital would enter GDP measures anytime soon.

The Aral Sea, island tourism and critical capital examples suggest the degree of ease with which an economy can substitute human or physical capital for natural capital will determine whether a strong or weak sustainability criteria is appropriate. Initial empirical studies suggest substitution possibilities exist for a wide range of production scenarios (Markandya, 2007, How substitutable is natural capital?).

The Inclusive Wealth Report (IWR) also suggests that, over the past 20 years, for over 100 countries, the negative wealth effects of a decline in natural capital have been offset by growth in human and physical capital. However, the emergence of concepts like *critical natural capital* and *regulating services* of ecosystems and their role in sustaining the extremely impoverished, suggests there remain significant deficiencies in our current crop of sustainability indices. For instance, like GDP, the IWI has very little to say about income distribution and its impact on social welfare.

The Inclusive Wealth Index has the potential to measure a nation's wealth in terms of economic progress and long-term sustainability. It measures the wealth of nations via implementing an analysis of a country's productive base. The value of the productive base provides an index of an economy's production potential: if the IWI increases over time, it signals the economy is making economic progress much the same way that per capita GDP does. If the health and human capital component of the IWI increases, it provides a signal that human well-being is improving as well. An increasing IWI also suggests past and current consumption is not coming at the cost of future generations' consumption potential.

Using the IWI can scale up resource efficiency – by providing policymakers with an overview of changes in the productive base of a country. It provides insights into trends within the capital asset groups, particularly human and natural capital – the central pillars of inclusive wealth that remain underserved by current statistical collection efforts, and economic and policymaking analysis. The IWI can provide insights into whether current growth is sustainable or is based on overexploiting natural capital. This information can help develop policy better suited to sustaining growth while better managing human and natural capital. For example, results from the 2014 Inclusive Wealth Report (IWR) demonstrate that investing in human capital would be most beneficial for countries with the highest rates of population growth. It also demonstrates the multiple benefits of investments in natural capital, in particular agricultural land and forest.

2.   Wealth, income, growth and sustainability

Inclusive wealth and growth accounting

Section 1 provides an overview of the rationale for preferring changes in wealth per capita over GDP per capita as an index of sustainability. Although changes in per capita wealth is the preferred metric of sustainability, we should not assume GDP is devoid of policy relevance. We compared the per capita growth rates of inclusive wealth and GDP for 121 countries and found 47 averaged negative rates of growth in per capita inclusive wealth over the years 1990 through 2010.

Table 2.2 reports the growth rates of the 47 countries and reveals almost all of them are either developing or middle-income countries; ten of the countries

Table 2.2 Countries with negative (average) per capita growth rates* in inclusive wealth: 1990–2015

Country	Per capita growth		Country	Per capita growth		Country	Per capita growth	
	IWI	GDP		IWI	GDP		IWI	GDP
Burundi	-0.6%	-8.0%	Ecuador	-4.6%	6.0%	Nicaragua	-3.0%	7.8%
Cameroon	-8.4%	-1.0%	Ghana	-3.6%	12.5%	Nigeria	-8.6%	15.9%
Central Afr Rep	-9.8%	-1.0%	Guyana	-0.5%	20.4%	Papua New Guinea	-12.8%	9.2%
Congo	-12.5%	-13.9%	Honduras	-3.0%	5.8%	Paraguay	-5.5%	5.3%
Côte d'Ivoire	-2.6%	-4.1%	Indonesia	-0.1%	16.9%	Peru	-2.8%	17.4%
Gabon	-8.1%	-5.7%	Iran	-3.5%	14.7%	Saudi Arabia	-6.5%	1.7%
Niger	-5.1%	-2.1%	Iraq	-13.7%	12.2%	Senegal	-5.0%	4.5%
Tajikistan*	-4.9%	-1.0%	Lao	-7.2%	25.5%	Sierra Leone	-4.2%	0.7%
UA Emirates	-13.9%	-13.8%	Liberia	-14.7%	38.9%	Sudan	-7.5%	18.0%
Zimbabwe	-5.4%	-12.0%	Malawi	-6.2%	8.9%	Tanzania	-10.9%	9.7%
Algeria	-3.6%	6.4%	Mali	-7.7%	10.3%	Trinidad & Tobago	-1.0%	27.5%
Belize	-6.6%	11.4%	Mongolia	-5.8%	12.5%	Uganda	-1.5%	18.5%
Benin	-6.0%	5.6%	Mozambique	-11.5%	26.2%	Venezuela	-5.3%	3.6%
Bolivia	-9.8%	9.9%	Myanmar	-6.3%	50.9%	Yemen	-1.9%	7.7%
Botswana	-0.9%	13.3%	Namibia	-3.8%	10.5%	Zambia	-11.1%	10.1%
Colombia	-0.5%	9.9%	Nepal	-7.5%	13.5%			

Sources: This report and the World Bank Development Indicators.

* Note: Reported averages are five-year averages, e.g. $(\text{GDP}_{1995} - \text{GDP}_{1990})/\text{GDP}_{1990}$.

experienced negative per capita GDP growth over the 20-year period. Almost half of the countries in Table 2.2 are in sub-Saharan Africa. The remaining 74 countries experienced positive rates of growth in both per capita inclusive wealth and per capita GDP (for a list of these countries, see Table 2.6 in the appendix).

Often, macroeconomists use an analytical tool called growth accounting to gain insight into economic growth dynamics. This tool can also be used to understand inclusive wealth dynamics, and albeit growth accounting provides a more clear understanding of what contributes to growth, it does not imply causality. Before writing the growth accounting expression, consider the following definitions: Let A_t denote the value of inclusive wealth at time t – a proxy for the aggregate value of physical capital, human capital and natural capital. Let k_t, H_t and N_t denote the levels of physical capital, human capital and natural capital (respectively) at time t. Let P_K, P_H and P_N denote the (respective) unit prices of physical, human and natural capital – to keep subsequent notation simply, these prices are assumed constant over time. Given this notation, we write inclusive wealth as:

$$A_t = P_K K_t + P_H H_t + P_N N_t$$

Given our Inclusive Wealth Index is defined in per capita terms, divide both sides of this equation by population, which we denote by L_t. Reasonably straightforward algebraic manipulations yield the following inclusive wealth growth accounting expression:[7]

$$\frac{\dot{a}_t}{a_t} = \alpha_{K,t}\left(\frac{\dot{K}_t}{K_t} - \frac{\dot{L}_t}{L_t}\right) + \alpha_{H,t}\left(\frac{\dot{H}_t}{H_t} - \frac{\dot{L}_t}{L_t}\right) + \alpha_{N,t}\left(\frac{\dot{N}_t}{N_t} - \frac{\dot{L}_t}{L_t}\right) \tag{1}$$

Here $\dot{a}_t$ is the (instantaneous) change in the level of inclusive wealth per capita. The remaining "dotted" variables represent the change in that variable given a change in time, e.g. $\dot{K}_t$ is the instantaneous change in the physical capital. The following variables are inclusive wealth *value shares* at time t; $\alpha_{K,t} = P_K K_t / A_t$ is physical capital's share of inclusive wealth; $\alpha_{H,t} = P_H H_t / A_t$ is human capital's share of inclusive wealth; and $\alpha_{N,t} = P_N N_t / A_t$ is natural capital's share of inclusive wealth. The three shares sum to unity. Finally, the term $\dot{a}_t / a_t$ is the (instantaneous) rate of growth in inclusive wealth per capita – analogous definitions extend to the remaining variables, e.g. $\dot{L}_t / l_t$ is the rate of growth in population.

Equation (1) reveals seven sources of Inclusive Wealth Index growth. One source is population growth, which puts downward pressure on the IWI. Between 1990 and 2015, the average annual rate of population growth in sub-Saharan Africa was 2.7%, as compared to less than 1% annual growth in the Organization for Economic Cooperation and Development (OECD) countries. Hence, even if a country did not over-exploit its natural resource base, high population growth rates could explain a large part of a pattern of unsustainable growth.

Changes in physical, human and natural capital account for three more sources of IWI growth. An increase in the stock of physical and human capital occurs when a nation invests enough of its income (GDP) to yield a net increase in physical or human capital. For example, when investment in physical capital is greater than the amount lost through depreciation, then physical capital growth contributes positively to IWI growth. Investments in agricultural extension training can lead to soil conservation and lower levels of natural resource degradation, as could training in forest management – both forms of human capital investment. What we hope is clear is, even if an economy is experiencing a decline in natural resource stocks, the IWI index can increase if the economy reinvests enough of its income to increase its physical and human capital stocks.

The remaining three potential influences on IWI growth are the inclusive wealth asset shares. Consider two countries, both of which are depleting their natural resource base. "All else equal," the country having the larger natural capital share will have the larger fall in its IWI. An implication for development is, arguably, the inclusive wealth share of natural resources in most developing countries will be higher than that for a typical developed country. If this is the case, to support sustainable development a developing country will likely need larger rates of growth in physical (and human) capital stocks than the typical developed country. If the natural resource share in one country is 5% and the physical capital share is 50%, a 10% fall in natural capital stocks can be offset by a 1% increase in physical capital. On the other hand, if the natural resource share in the country is 20% and the physical capital share is 50%, the country would need a 4% increase in the capital stock to offset a 10% fall in natural capital

Returning to Table 2.2, for almost all 47 countries, natural resources serve as an important source of GDP, and one can safely assume that the fall in per capita inclusive wealth is linked directly to natural resource extraction (e.g. minerals and oil) or harvesting (e.g. forest). Also, population growth is high in most of the countries, which further serves to hamper sustainable growth. Finally, at least for the developing countries in the list, natural resource shares are likely quite high. Hence, in spite of the relatively high rates of GDP growth experienced by some of the countries, these factors combine to make sustainable growth a difficult objective to achieve. Table 2.3 provides an example of inclusive wealth growth accounting for Malawi. Note, natural capital accounts for over 50% of Malawi's inclusive wealth in 1990, and falls to 37% by 2010. The rates of growth in human capital are very low relative to the rates of decline in natural capital, as are the rates of growth in

Table 2.3 Malawi inclusive wealth growth accounting

Asset type	2005 US$ per capita					5-year growth			
	1990	*1995*	*2000*	*2005*	*2010*	*1995*	*2000*	*2005*	*2010*
Human	1,505	1,488	1,504	1,571	1,576	−0.011	0.011	0.045	0.003
Physical	889	871	749	671	789	−0.020	−0.140	−0.104	0.176
Natural	2,499	2,287	1,983	1,690	1,414	−0.085	−0.133	−0.148	−0.163
Inclusive wealth	4,893	4,646	4,236	3,932	3,779	−0.050	−0.088	−0.072	−0.039
	Inclusive wealth shares					**Contributions to IWI growth**			
Human	0.308	0.320	0.355	0.400	0.417	−0.003	0.003	0.016	0.001
Physical	0.182	0.187	0.177	0.171	0.209	−0.004	−0.026	−0.018	0.030
Natural	0.511	0.492	0.468	0.430	0.374	−0.043	−0.065	−0.069	−0.070

Table 2.4 China inclusive wealth growth accounting

Asset type	2005 US$ per capita					5-year growth			
	1990	1995	2000	2005	2010	1995	2000	2005	2010
Human	8,043	8,620	9,138	9,504	10,025	0.072	0.060	0.040	0.055
Physical	1,369	1,995	3,123	5,044	8,748	0.457	0.565	0.615	0.734
Natural	6,805	6,355	5,882	5,429	5,061	−0.066	−0.074	−0.077	−0.068
Inclusive wealth	16,217	16,970	18,143	19,977	23,834	0.046	0.069	0.101	0.193
	Inclusive wealth shares					**Contributions to IWI growth**			
Human	0.496	0.508	0.504	0.476	0.421	0.036	0.031	0.020	0.026
Physical	0.084	0.118	0.172	0.252	0.367	0.039	0.066	0.106	0.185
Natural	0.420	0.374	0.324	0.272	0.212	−0.028	−0.028	−0.025	−0.018

physical capital. These factors all contribute to the unsustainable wealth trajectory for the country.

As for the 74 countries in the appendix, even if a country's natural capital stocks are falling, its reinvestment in physical and human capital more than offsets the wealth lost through depleted natural assets – the result being an increase in inclusive wealth, and hence, what appears to be a sustainable growth trajectory. Table 2.4 reports inclusive growth accounting figures for China. China begins with a natural capital share of 42% in 1990, which falls to 21% by 2010. Note, however, the rates of growth in its human and physical capital stocks (relative to its decline in natural capital stocks). This reinvestment in human and physical capital is one of the reasons China's Inclusive Wealth Index has outperformed all other countries.

3.   Wealth and the Sustainable Development Goals (SDGs)

Unlike the Millennium Development Goals, which were more focused on achieving certain development targets for developing nations, the proposed Sustainable Development Goals (SDGs)[8] are truly global in nature. Applicable to all nations, developing or developed, the SDGs emerged from an evolving and collaborative process, representing collective aspirations, while taking into account different national realities, capacities and levels of development. Rooted in the outcome document, *The Future We Want*, from the Rio+20 summit in 2012, the SDGs were promulgated to reflect the pursuit of all three dimensions of sustainable development – social, economic and environmental. Through Rio+20, the Open Working Group was formed with representatives from 70 countries, which by July 2014 published a draft with a set of 17 goals and 169 targets. Assessing and valuing natural capital and the change in per capita inclusive/comprehensive wealth over time has the potential to keep track of progress on most Sustainable Development Goals (SDGs).

IWI is a multi-purpose, multi-target measure of sustainable development. An increase in IWI will suggest poverty eradication (SDG, 1) and an improvement in food security, while promoting sustainable agriculture (SDG 2) and healthy lives and well-being (SDG 3). An increase in IWI will also indicate sustained, but not necessarily inclusive economic growth (SDG 8), and sustainable consumption and production patterns (SDG 12). A decrease in IWI will indicate degradation of natural capital and failure to take steps to combat climate change and its impacts (SGD 13), conserve and sustainably using the oceans, seas and marine resources (SDG 14), protect, restore and promote the sustainable use of terrestrial ecosystems, sustainably manage forests, combat desertification, reverse land degradation and halt biodiversity loss (SDG 15). IWI can measure the strength of the means of implementation for sustainable development (SDG 17).

IWI has a specific role to play in complementing SDG Target 8.1, which is currently measured by GDP growth with a target of 7% per year (a measure of growth in the level of transactions). IWI complements this by emphasizing the growth of wealth – something that is much better aligned with the SDGs as the indicators and targets clearly link the sustainability with the productive base of the economy, water, air, soil and other natural assets.

The environmental dimension of SDGs is very explicit. Most of the targets are directly or indirectly related to the status of natural capital. The overarching message from Agenda 2030 is for nations to keep their natural capital stocks intact. Since GDP does not track natural capital levels, it will most certainly be inadequate for managing these resources.

Figure 2.1 highlights one conclusion we can draw from the chapters in this volume: that natural capital's share (NC_Capital_Share) in inclusive wealth has fallen since 1990, while the share of human capital (HC_Capital_Share) and physical capital (PC_Capital_Share) has steadily increased. Under a weak substitutability criteria, the world has been experiencing sustainable growth. Our guess, however, is the world likely would not satisfy sustainability under a strong substitutability criteria.

One of the core strengths of the Sustainable Development Goals is their recognition of the complex interlinkages that prevail between human well-being, economic

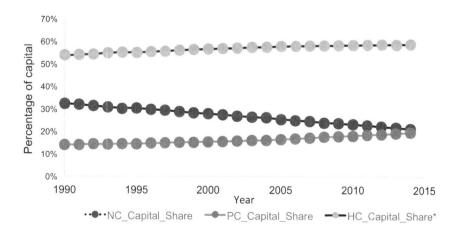

Figure 2.1 Global trend in human (HC), natural (NC) and physical (PC) capital shares

prosperity and a healthy natural habitat. Thus, as we move towards exploring more sustainable ways of developing, we need forms of measure that reflect such objectives. In this regard, an indicator or a bundle of indicators that can reflect such interlinkages, connectivity and causality by recognizing impact on sustainability and inclusivity are key to measuring long-term progress.

Inclusive wealth index – sustainability and inclusivity

By incorporating changes in human and natural capital alongside the existing measures of produced capital, namely GDP, the IWI provides a balance sheet for nations that offers them a more comprehensive view of their asset endowments. Fundamentally, the approach aims to address the major policy gaps that exist on growth and development that fail to address issues of sustainability, natural resource depletion and human well-being.

The 2014 Inclusive Wealth Report assessed data from 140 countries over a span of 20 years and observed changes in produced capital, human capital and natural capital. The aggregate data suggest that GDP and the Human Development Index (HDI) made significant strides over the period, but natural capital declined in 127 of the 140 countries. Such analysis through the IWI enables countries to monitor their comprehensive capital pool and push for greater action and accountability and the pursuit of more sustainable pathways.

Assessing and valuing natural capital and the change in per capita inclusive/ comprehensive wealth over time has the potential to keep track of progress on several Sustainable Development Goals (SDGs). Figure 2.2 illustrates.

IWI has a specific role to play in tracking Sustainable Development Goals and related Targets 1, 2, 3 and 8.1. IWI complements the current target provided by technical work of the Sustainable Development Goals, of 7% per year in GDP (a measure of growth in the level of transactions) as the wealth estimates would keep track of the base from which income is generated. The wealth estimate is much better aligned with the SDGs as they are more reliable about information on the productive base of the economy.

The IWI's key strength lay in its potential to serve as an indicator for guiding sustainable development policy. The wealth can inform planning and investment decisions that promote a low carbon, resource efficient and socially inclusive economy. Wealth estimate organizes information on various types of wealth and trade-off . As the estimates in this volume suggest, a number of countries are recording growth in human capital at the cost of natural capital (unsustainable agriculture and industrialisation leading to better port, roads and infrastructure, at least in the short-run). Unlike GDP, information on wealth can also be used as an instrument in designing more efficient and effective policy reforms and regulation changes that act as a catalyst for sustainable investment and development pathways.

Recognizing natural capital as an important source of wealth to the economy and its contributions to the poor can inform planning and policy decisions that prioritize investing in natural capital as a way of reinvesting in wealth. Inter alia, fighting poverty is conditional on the sustainable management of land. Without managing our natural resources such as agricultural land, forests and fish stocks we will not be able to ensure sustainable economic growth and inclusive green economy (UNEP, 2015).

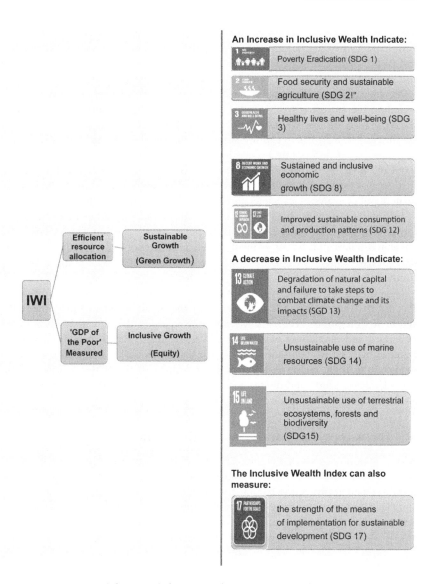

Figure 2.2 Institutional framework for IWI and Sustainable Development Goals (SDGs)

However, in order to monitor progress towards SDGs, we must be equipped with appropriate benchmark data, be capable of assessing progress from one year to the next and have a meaningful way to compare progress across countries. Such analysis through universally accepted indicators and statistical frameworks is key to understanding how the globe is faring. Significant data gaps exist, however, specifically with regards to natural capital measurement. As data is a key building block in the development framework, we must explore: (i) how innovation in information technology and existing data infrastructures can be aligned to produce improved development data; (ii) how participatory mechanisms and qualitative methods and knowledge can strengthen quantitative information to enhance our understanding; and (iii) disaggregating data to enable more nuanced insights into the inequalities and challenges faced by particular groups within an given economy.

Moreover, the new sustainability indicators that emerged over the past decade – including the Inclusive Wealth Index – have pushed the envelope and called for a re-imagination of how we define and measure progress. Although these indicators are the results of efforts to capture the three domains of sustainable development – economic, social and political – it is important to more clearly identify and understand the links, inter-dynamics and causality between these domains. Indeed, this is an area of work not limited to economists or statisticians, but entails the involvement of policy analysts, academics and development practitioners from diverse fields.

In order to support all these initiatives, indices and measurement of SDG performance, there is a fundamental need for policy coherence. Building capacities for integrated policy and data assessment as well as coherence and coordination among strategies to achieve the SDGs can allow for mutual co-benefits and avoid any counterproductive results.

Nonetheless it is important to acknowledge and appreciate the political processes thus far that have led to the culmination of the SDGs. Fundamentally, the SDGs and their widespread acceptance will not only represent the aspirations of both the developed and developing worlds but will reflect their mutual meeting ground. It is imperative that we continue to work past the challenges that may arise and strive to make the three common foundational principles of the SDGs – leave no one behind; ensure equity and dignity for all; and achieve prosperity within Earth's safe and restored operating space (UNEP, 2015) – a reality.

4. Inclusive wealth and conservation policies

A large literature exists that argues the current System of National Accounts (SNA) undervalues natural capital and its contributions to human well-being. In such cases, policies aimed at protecting natural capital will at best be fraught with inefficiencies and likely lead to sub-optimal resource allocations. The inclusive wealth account can serve as a key tool in designing more efficient and effective environmentally sustainable policies that underpin economic and social progress, and overall sustainable development imperatives. This section discusses how the IWR can be used to inform policy decisions related to the conservation of natural capital, with a specific focus on forests, air pollution and fisheries.

Inclusive wealth and forestry policy

As demonstrated in Chapter 6, in many countries, forests comprise a major share of their capital stocks and are a source of a range of vital ecosystem services: provisioning services (e.g. food, fuel and fibre); regulating (e.g. carbon regulation); supporting (e.g. biodiversity conservation); and sustaining cultural services (e.g. recreation and tourism) (MA, 2005). Yet in many countries, the present SNA does not adequately account for the contributions of forest capital to watershed protection, carbon storage, biodiversity conservation as well as the contributions of forest capital as a factor of production to other sectors of an economy.

Under the IWR, the value of forest capital is calculated as the present value of the future net benefits expected over the life of a forest resource. It integrates the contributions of a wide range of forest services, although current data limitations preclude a full accounting of all contributions. The forest capital component of the IWR can serve as an indicator of whether forest resources are being used sustainably for the present and future generations. This information could be used to move resource managers and country authorities towards policy options aimed at: (i) managing trade-offs among competing forest uses; (ii) designing effective and efficient economic policy instruments (e.g. property rights, taxes and subsidies, creating markets for non-market forest services); and (iii) providing the basis for monitoring policy implementation and effectiveness (Lange, 2004).

Lange (2004, 2003) outlines six key policy questions related to managing forest resources or developing cross-sectoral policies that facilitate forest management. These policy questions underlie World Bank initiatives like WAVES (Wealth Accounting and the Valuation of Ecosystem Services). Given that policy uses and management options likely vary from country to country, we do not attempt to provide an exhaustive list of relevant questions and policy options. The remaining section outlines how the IWR and, in particular, the forest account component of the IWR could be used to inform some of these policy questions.

What is the total economic contribution of forests and forest ecosystems, and what are the potential benefits from sustainable management?

The forest capital component of the IWI takes into account a wide range of forest contributions and, therefore, reflects a more accurate approximation of the value of forest resources. Consequently, the value of forest capital is likely to be higher than that typically embedded in GDP calculations. This higher valuation should help forest resources gain wider recognition in macroeconomic policy deliberations: a higher value of forest contributions to GDP could potentially increase the forestry sector's bargaining power for a larger share of national budget for forest management and investment.

How are benefits of forest resources distributed across society?

Presently, inclusive wealth measures provide country level aggregate measures of forestry assets. However, it has been argued that a more robust accounting needs to distinguish the spatial productivity of different forest assets. For instance, it is important to distinguish between forest benefits that accrue to commercial users (e.g. hydroelectric power, municipalities and fisheries) and those that accrue to subsistence users (charcoal for heating and cooking), and between benefits that accrue to direct and indirect beneficiaries. It would also be useful to distinguish between forest benefits to local communities, downstream users, non-local communities and the global community (e.g. biodiversity and carbon storage).

The United Nations Framework for the System of Environmental and Economic Accounting (SEEA) highlights the importance of this information – particularly those regarding optimal forest management aimed at meeting both economic and social objectives (e.g. local community preservation versus increased equity). Policy response may include designing economic instruments like property rights – ensuring that beneficiaries pay for the benefits (e.g. inform of environmental fees) to compensate those who might be sacrificing the benefits. At watershed levels, the value of forest capital can be useful in designing Payment for Ecosystem Services (PES) schemes.

Is economic growth sustainable or is it based on the depletion of forests?

Inclusive wealth can be used for evaluating trade-offs between economic (gross domestic product) growth and forest wealth. This information is a key indicator of whether economic growth across a range of countries for which data are available is sustainable, or if economic growth comes at the expense of declining forest wealth triggered by deforestation and land use change. This information would be useful for re-evaluating existing forestry and economy-wide policy options for example:

1   Which sectors are the key contributors to economic growth?
2   How are these sectors linked to forestry resources, and what are the potential impacts?
3   What are the costs of forest asset depletion?
4   Can available resources be re-allocated across sectors to achieve at least the same level of economic growth with minimal or no damage to the forestry sector?

What are the economic trade-offs among competing users, and how can we optimize forest resource utilization?

Forest accounts from inclusive wealth could help assess the trade-offs among competing users: for example, forestry versus agricultural land use, and commercial logging versus catchment protection. Assessing the level of economic trade-offs could help in the design of appropriate economic instruments to minimize losses tied to these trade-offs – instruments like use fees, compensating payments and property rights.

What are the impacts of other sectors' policies on forests?

Linking forestry values to other sectors and the wider economy would provide a convenient way of integrating forestry policy with national development and monitoring interactions and feedback across different sectors. This would make it possible to measure the winners and losers, and measure pressures on forest capital coming from alternative macroeconomic or development policies. Potential conflicts, for example, between forestry vs. agriculture, are relatively easy to identify – e.g. deforestation and cattle grazing. Policy response would include creating optimal forest management strategies aimed at addressing these conflicts. One set of strategies includes developing economic instruments like fees and compensating payments schemes to influence forest use. Another is to build social capital – for example, facilitate strategic alliances with stakeholders across sectors who are dependent on the forestry sector (agriculture, tourism, electric power and water).

Table 2.5 further illustrates how information from forest accounts can be used to inform these questions and their corresponding policy linkages.

Table 2.5 Selected policy applications of forest accounts

Indicator/measure	Use for policy analysis	Examples of policies and actions taken from policy analysis
1. What is the total economic contribution of forests, and what are the benefits from sustainable management?		
Total value of forests including *non-market* forest goods and services.	More comprehensive, accurate value of forests' contribution to GDP.	Showing a higher value for forest contribution to GDP may increase the forestry sector's ability to request a larger share of national budget for forest management and investment.
Value of forest services to non-forestry sectors.	Measure of the economic importance of forest services to agriculture, electricity, fisheries, tourism, municipal water supply, etc.	Design economic instruments to promote sustainable forest use, for example:
		• Institute conservation fee on water and hydroelectricity tariffs for downstream beneficiaries that can be used for forest management or to compensate local communities.
		• Institute tourism fees for biodiversity conservation for forest management/ compensation of local communities.
		• Negotiate international payments for carbon storage services of forests.
		Build multi-sectorial stakeholder alliances based on mutual benefits.
		Identify institutional weaknesses in forest management, e.g. where one sector benefits but does not pay, or does not have a say in forest management.
Value of forest goods and services used by local communities.	Share of forest goods in rural livelihoods provides measure of dependence on forests of local communities.	Useful for design and implementation of PRSPs.
2. What is the distribution of forest benefits among different groups in society?		
Share of forest benefits accruing to commercial, artisanal and subsistence users of forests	Identify social benefits from preservation of local communities and increased equity.	Identify potential conflicts, e.g. benefits to subsistence users/local communities are low because commercial/downstream users obtain benefits.
Or		Design economic instruments so that beneficiaries pay for the benefits, compensating those who may sacrifice benefits. For example, property rights – some say over how a forest is managed – and fees for environmental services received.
Share accruing to local, downstream and global beneficiaries.		Optimize investment in forests and forest infrastructure that balances social objectives for equity and regional development as well as economic objectives of maximizing national income.

(*Continued*)

Table 2.5 (Continued)

Indicator/measure	Use for policy analysis	Examples of policies and actions taken from policy analysis
3. Is economic growth sustainable or is it based on the depletion of forests?		
Value of forest assets and the cost of deforestation and forest degradation.	Macroeconomic indicators of sustainability (such as NDP, national wealth, asset depletion).	Reassess forest management if deforestation is occurring.
4. What are the trade-offs among competing users of forests?		
Value of forest goods and services under alternative forest management options.	Measure economic linkages between forestry and other sectors of the economy, upstream and downstream.	Optimize forest use and investment in forests and forest infrastructure by considering total economic value of forests, market and non-market, including linkages to non-forestry sectors and impacts on all stakeholders, economy-wide.
	Identify the economic trade-offs among competing sectors.	Identify winners and losers.
		Design appropriate economic instruments to achieve that strategy (fees, compensating payments, property rights, etc.).
5. What are the impacts of non-forestry policies on forest use?		
Analyse economic development scenarios that trace the full chain of causation from macroeconomic policy and/or non-forestry sector policies to their impact on forestry and land use.	Measures the winners and losers, pressures on forests and forest users from alternative development strategies.	Identify winners and losers.
	Identifies potential conflicts between development objectives of forestry and those of other sectors, e.g. commercial logging vs. catchment protection (Ministry of Agriculture, Ministry of Energy, etc.).	Identify optimal forest management strategy, based on addressing conflicts among ministries and within a single ministry.
	Identify conflicts among divisions of the same ministry (Ministry of Agriculture), e.g. pastoralists' use of forest vs. downstream crop farmers.	Design appropriate economic instruments to achieve that strategy (fees, compensating payments, property rights, etc.).

5. Conclusions

It is possible that in various situations the gross domestic product (GDP), usually known as income (GDP at factor cost), correlates strongly with national wealth, but there are many critical information analogous to a balance sheet of the nations, which are revealed by the wealth of the nation. They are central not only to resolve the trade amongst various types of capital (produced for natural, for example) but to provide a better compass to measure progress and sustainability. And hence there is adequate rationale for inclusive national wealth accounts.

One of the key aspects of wealth estimate is robust methodology to value natural capital in the wealth estimate. It goes much beyond the transaction or exchange value which does not capture externality aspects. On the contrary, the shadow pricing method for natural capital is more reliable and scientifically credible. It is well known, though, that the share of natural capital in total wealth of the nation would also depend on how well those assets are maintained as the value of natural capital are directly related to institutions and technological advancement of the nations which is reflected through rent from the natural assets. The shadow pricing method is well equipped to capture these aspects.

There should be a regular estimate of wealth at the national scale natural capital must get a priority, as they are likely to be pushed on the margin, as there is no well-functioning market especially in developing countries to capture their contribution.

Scale, unit and dimension of natural capital must be spelt out up front and each of the conservation policies should be clearly linked with the wealth of the natural capital and how they get affected.

At the institutional level, there should be a natural capital committee in every country to monitor and assess the trend and condition. They should closely work with the Ministry of Finance.

In order to see the impact of trade reform and agricultural policies like subsidies, the ease with which one capital can substitute should be estimated.

In the case of critical natural capital, assessment and monitoring is a must at the national scale.

Every country is in the process of designing means to achieve SDGs, so a detailed mapping of the goals and targets should be done vis a vis natural capital.

Policies on protected areas (marine/terrestrial), forest, land degradation neutrality, climate change and biodiversity have better prospect to be embraced by the public at large if their link with natural capital is delineated properly.

Finally, wealth information can supplement the information of the System of National Accounts (SNA), but eventually all the macroeconomic policies and allocation of resources should be cognizant of status of change in net per capita wealth and that would serve as the key lamp post for sustainability and equity including various targets of the Sustainable Development Goals (SDGs).

Notes

1 The long-run plan is to eventually define quantifiable measures of social and cultural capital, and introduce into future wealth measures.
2 One might have an equally difficult time arguing inclusive wealth is a measure of social inclusivity, too.

3 See www.econlib.org/library/Enc/HumanCapital.html for a short discussion by Becker on human capital.
4 For example, see www.who.int/phe/health_topics/outdoorair/databases/cities/en/ for historical data on air pollution, and https://waqi.info/ for real-time (current) air quality data.
5 For more information, see https://unstats.un.org/unsd/envaccounting/seea.asp.
6 This production structure – one unit of natural capital, 40 units of physical capital and 0.006 units of labour – is often referred to as a *fixed coefficient* or *Leontief* production function.
7 For the empirical exercises conducted in prior chapters, the change in time is a year, not instantaneous as depicted in this section. A rough approximation of equation (1) using discrete time is

$$\Delta a_t = \alpha_{K,t}\left(\frac{\Delta K_t}{K_t} - \frac{\Delta L_t}{L_t}\right) + \alpha_{H,t}\left(\frac{\Delta H_t}{H_t} - \frac{\Delta L_t}{L_t}\right) + \alpha_{N,t}\left(\frac{\Delta N_t}{N_t} - \frac{\Delta L_t}{L_t}\right)$$

8 For a full list of Sustainable Development Goals and Targets, see https://sustainable development.un.org/sdgs

References

Ehrlich, P. R., & Pringle, R. M. (2008). Where does biodiversity go from here? A grim business-as-usual forecast and a hopeful portfolio of partial solutions. *Proc. Natl Acad. Sci. USA*, *105*, 11579–11586.
FAO. Policy Uses of Forest Accounts. Retrieved from www.fao.org/docrep/007/j1972e/J1972E04.htm
Flower, L. O. H., & Schreve, D. C. (2014). An investigation of palaeodietary variability in European Pleistocene canids. *Quaternary Science Reviews*, *96*, 188–203. doi:10.1016/j.quascirev.2014.04.015
Lange, G. (2003). Bringing Forest Ecosystem Services into the National Economic Accounts: An Environmental Accounting Approach. A Paper Presented at the Conference on Ecosystem Services in the Tropics, International Society of Tropical Foresters, Yale University. Retrieved April 4–5, 2003 from
Lange, G. (2004). Manual for Environmental and Economic Accounts for Forestry: A Tool for Cross-Sectoral Policy Analysis. FAO Forestry Department, Policy and Institutions Service, Working Paper. FAO Rome. Retrieved from www.fao.org/docrep/007/j1972e/J1972E04.htm
MA. (2005). *Living beyond our means: Natural assets and human well-being* (Statement from the Board). New York: United Nations. Retrieved from

Appendix

Table 2.6 Countries with negative (average) per capita growth rates* in inclusive wealth: 1990–2015

Country	Per capita growth		Country	Per capita growth		Country	Per capita growth	
	IWI	GDP		IWI	GDP		IWI	GDP
Albania	3.9%	23.1%	Gambia	0.2%	2.4%	Norway	1.5%	10.0%
Argentina	1.6%	15.1%	Germany	7.6%	6.6%	Pakistan	3.2%	8.9%
Armenia	5.3%	25.2%	Greece	5.0%	9.0%	Panama	3.1%	18.7%
Australia	1.6%	9.8%	Guatemala	1.3%	7.1%	Philippines	2.5%	8.9%
Austria	5.8%	8.5%	Iceland	0.1%	8.0%	Poland	5.7%	20.9%
Bahrain	4.1%	4.2%	India	3.8%	26.1%	Portugal	5.2%	8.0%
Bangladesh	7.2%	17.5%	Ireland	7.9%	21.6%	Romania	5.3%	13.1%
Barbados	3.2%	4.0%	Israel	4.4%	10.8%	Russia	0.7%	7.2%
Belgium	5.3%	7.6%	Italy	4.1%	4.0%	Rwanda	3.3%	14.2%
Brazil	0.6%	9.0%	Jamaica	3.4%	2.7%	Singapore	9.7%	20.5%
Bulgaria	4.9%	14.7%	Japan	4.6%	4.1%	South Africa	0.5%	5.3%
Canada	1.4%	6.9%	Jordan	3.5%	11.0%	Spain	9.9%	8.4%
Chile	5.7%	21.5%	Kazakhstan	1.6%	17.5%	Sri Lanka	6.0%	23.7%
China	10.2%	58.4%	Kenya	1.0%	1.2%	Swaziland	1.6%	8.0%
Costa Rica	4.0%	13.7%	Kyrgyzstan	0.8%	0.8%	Sweden	3.2%	8.8%
Cuba	0.6%	11.3%	Lesotho	4.5%	14.6%	Switzerland	2.2%	4.0%
Cyprus	5.0%	10.0%	Luxembourg	7.7%	12.6%	Thailand	6.4%	20.4%
Czech Republic	5.8%	9.5%	Malaysia	2.2%	19.4%	Tunisia	5.7%	16.9%
Denmark	2.5%	7.0%	Malta	8.5%	15.4%	Turkey	4.6%	12.1%
Dom Republic	5.1%	20.8%	Mauritania	1.4%	4.4%	Ukraine	1.9%	0.5%
Egypt	3.3%	13.8%	Mauritius	6.6%	21.3%	UK	4.3%	8.0%
El Salvador	8.1%	12.9%	Mexico	4.6%	5.7%	Uruguay	3.8%	15.3%
Fiji	3.5%	5.8%	Morocco	5.6%	13.6%	USA	3.0%	7.6%
Finland	3.5%	9.0%	Netherlands	4.7%	9.3%	Vietnam	10.0%	31.5%
France	5.5%	5.8%	New Zealand	2.4%	7.6%			

Sources: This report and the World Bank Development Indicators.

* Note: Reported averages are five-year averages, e.g. $(GDP_{1995} - GDP_{1990})/GDP_{1990}$.

Part II
Natural capital

3 More on natural wealth of nations and regions

Shunsuke Managi

Introduction

An economy may satisfy current sustainable development or may have satisfied the criterion in the recent past but might not continue to do so in the near future. Whether an economy can continue sustainable development depends on the scale of the economy (e.g. GDP), and if the scale becomes too large relative to the natural capital (NC) base, the economy will be unable to maintain the inclusive wealth. Therefore, maintaining the NC base for sustainable development is unavoidable.

This chapter focuses on the role and importance of natural capital in measuring the inclusive wealth of nations. The analysis is based on the same dataset used in Chapter 1: a 140-country analysis of inclusive wealth for 25 years (1990 to 2014). Following Arrow et al. (2012) and previous editions of Inclusive Wealth Report, the report expands the scope of NC and accounts for the national wealth to allow for a broader understanding. In this report, NC can be classified into two major categories: (1) renewable resources and (2) non-renewable resources.

As shown in Figure 3.1, renewable resources is further decomposed into (a) forest resources, which consists of timber and non-timber forest benefits; (b) fisheries, which are represented by the catch; and (c) agricultural land, which consists of cropland and pastureland, whereas non-renewable resources can be broken down to (d) fossil fuels (oil, natural gas and coal); and (e) minerals (bauxite, copper, gold, iron, lead, nickel, phosphate, silver, tin and zinc). A relatively common accounting method is used to value these resources. Total natural wealth is estimated by calculating the physical amount available and corresponding shadow prices (rent) of the resources.

As we have illustrated elsewhere in the current report, IWI is a linear index of produced, human and natural capital. In theory, however, shadow prices are defined as the additional contribution to social well-being. This contribution is expected to easily change as natural capital becomes relatively scarce, so shadow prices can also change in the long-term. This is true of produced and human capital as well but is especially relevant to natural capital, whose assumption of absolute substitutability is not a realistic one (UNU-IHDP, 2012).

Natural capital also deserves special attention because it can collapse with no advanced notice in a non-linear manner, which is related to the idea of thresholds and tipping points. Climate change is a prime example of this, which is why negotiations have reached a consensus to set the 2-degree target in the Paris Agreement.

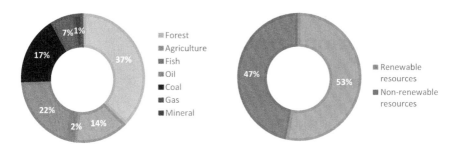

Figure 3.1 Average share of resources, renewables and non-renewables in natural capital from 1990–2014

The non-linearity of natural capital is also observed in local contexts as well (e.g. Walker et al. 2010). This drives Section 3 of this chapter, in which we examine the regional disaggregation of natural capital change for the studied period. It appears to be misleading to talk about natural capital trends without differentiating regional disparities and types of natural capital (non-renewable vs. renewable, etc.).

In Section 4, we explore the interaction between natural capital and natural disasters. Some of the natural capital has been known to help vulnerable regions cope with natural disasters. The use of mangrove trees as a defence against flooding is a prime example (Barbier 2009; UNU-IHDP and UNEP, 2012). The same qualifier suggests that nature can provide benefits many times, while in other times, it could be a threat to human beings. We discuss this interconnectedness, citing recent examples of natural disasters.

In Section 5, we report the fishery capital stock of nations in more detail. We begin with a basis of renewable resource dynamics, on which our methodology of counting stocks is based. This stock trend is contrasted with that of the capture production of fishery. Overall, we show that global fishery capital is on the decline at an alarming rate, whereas capture production continues to rise, especially in Asia. This may be attenuated by investing in aquaculture and sustainable and responsible management of the industry.

Section 6 is devoted to, as far as we are concerned, the first estimate of renewable energy as capital stocks. Although renewable energy has been a focus of attention and massive investment in both developed and emerging economies for greener growth, this has not appeared in the accounting or even a debate of inclusive wealth accounting and sustainability assessment. Section 7 concludes.

The natural capital of nations

Nature is extremely important and different from human and manufactured capital stock: it always operates by its own complex laws and systems. The assumption of strong sustainability, which considers important aspects of natural capital as irreplaceable, is scientifically evident. The concept of environmental sustainability largely addresses the issue of critical natural capital (Ekins et al. 2003). It is important to distinguish between weak and strong sustainability. The maintenance of human well-being is the main purpose of economic activity, as our inclusive wealth framework stresses, but at the same time, there is little doubt of the necessity of natural capital by itself. This motivates this section that peeks at the past increase or decrease of natural capital independently.

Overall, 31 of 140 countries experience positive growth of natural capital. Natural capital indicators, for instance, show that forest resources increase in 55 of 140 countries over 1990–2014. Renewable resources are an important contributor of natural capital, and 39 of 140 countries meaningfully increase their resources. Although natural capital is an important source of resources for developing and less developed countries, if the decreasing trend will continue, it could take its toll on their future development.

The average annual growth rate of wealth and natural capital per capita can be classified into four quadrants in Figure 3.2:

Quadrant 1: growth in wealth and natural capital
Quadrant 2: decline in wealth and growth in natural capital
Quadrant 3: decline in wealth and natural capital
Quadrant 4: growth in wealth and decline in natural capital

Our empirical findings show that most countries (123 of 140) experienced a declining trend of natural capital while achieving an increasing trend of wealth over 1990–2014. A group of seven countries (Albania, Armenia, Estonia, Guyana, Lithuania, Russia and Slovenia) experiences the most desirable situation in terms of experienced growth in wealth and natural capital (quadrant 1, Figure 3.2). These countries can be on a sustainable development path both from strong and weak sustainability perspectives. Additionally, five countries in our sample exhibit a decline in wealth while increasing the natural capital (quadrant 2, Figure 3.2).

For a better understanding of the contribution of natural capital on sustainability, Figure 3.3 intended to reveal the country conditions. We disaggregated the annual average growth rate of the natural capitals of nations per capita, to identify the contribution of agricultural land, forest, fisheries and fossil fuels differently. Countries are ordered according to their growth rate of natural capital per capita from 1990–2014. Discrepancies are major among countries, and the decreasing trend of NC is clearly visible throughout the countries.

Renewable resources

In this section, we present an overview of renewable resources of natural capital, which contains agricultural land, fisheries and forest resources. Both natural capital and renewable resource growth was positive for 25 of the 140 countries. Belgium, Cote d'Ivoire and Tanzania have experienced positive growth in natural capital and renewable resources of over 1% from 1990 to 2014. In particular, 15 countries experienced 1% growth or more in forest over this period, while only six countries achieved 1% growth or more in fisheries. Overall, only seven countries have reported a positive natural capital growth rate of over 1% from 1990 to 2014. Figure 3.4 represents the growth rate of renewable resources from 1990–2014 per capita, which is a gloomier picture than growth in inclusive wealth.

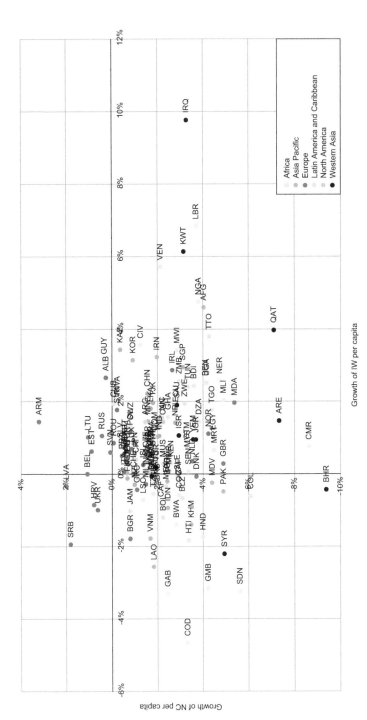

Figure 3.2 Measuring the per capita changes in natural capital and IW: average annual growth rate from 1990 to 2014

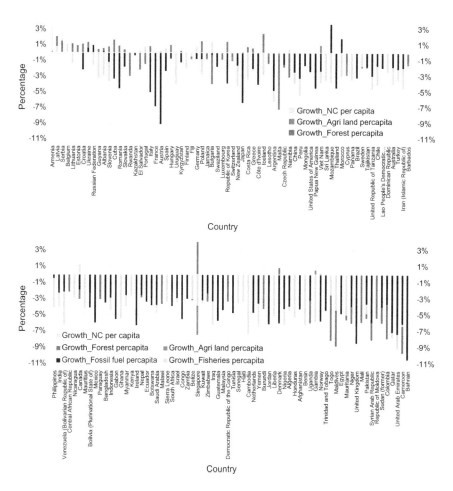

Figure 3.3 Annual average growth rate of natural capital per capita disaggregated by agricultural land, forest, fisheries and fossil fuels

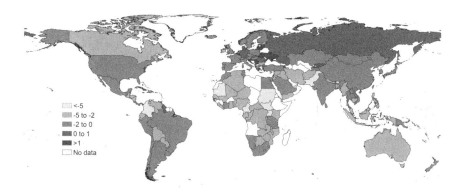

Figure 3.4 Average annual growth rate of renewables per capita from 1990–2014

Agricultural land

As FAO defined, agricultural land comprises cropland and pastureland. Overall, 49 countries have experienced positive growth of cropland, while only 15 countries have a positive growth rate per capita (Figure 3.5). For pastureland, 36 countries reported positive growth and 7 countries identify positive growth per capita (Figure 3.6). However, the way in which these changes affect the natural capital depends on how important these changes are with respect to the total share of the natural capital.

Globally, food security is tremendously important, and available land is in high demand to keep the demand and supply chain balanced. However, the increasing population in developing countries where millions are under-nourished due to food shortages maintains continuous pressure on agricultural land. The demand of agricultural land is directed by population growth, as well as the diet of the population (UNU-IHDP, 2014), and they together have been an obstacle to the achievement of sustainable economic development.

The alternative use of agriculture land is always important to measure food availability and security. For instance, the increased demand of pastureland and biofuel

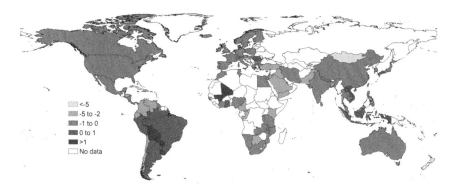

Figure 3.5 Average annual growth rate of cropland per capita from 1990 to 2014

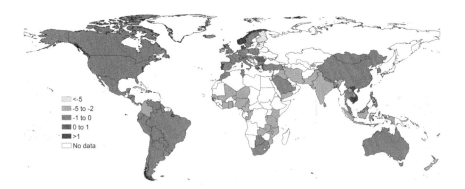

Figure 3.6 Average annual growth rate of pastureland per capita from 1990 to 2014

in Brazil is a significant threat to the Amazon rainforest, which is being destroyed to accommodate continued demand for land. The growth of cropland has been positive in Latin American countries over the last 25 years, which continuously substitutes the other important use of the land.

Forest and fishery

Forest resources consist of timber and non-timber forest resources accessed by the population of the country. Forest sources of timber and non-timber generally move in the same directions because they are directly connected to the total forest surface of a country. The growth of forest resources is positive for European Union (EU) countries, Japan and Russia. On the other hand, the decline of forests in Africa, Latin America, China, India, Brazil, the US and Canada is creating pressure on their sustainable development process.

Forest accounts explain 37% of the natural capital of nations, although with major fluctuations among countries. Only 31 of 140 countries experience positive growth in forest resources per capita, whereas 54 countries reported an overall positive growth rate of forestry (Figure 3.7). Even within high-income countries, Singapore has had 8% growth of forest resources from 1990 to 2014 and has been identified as the foremost country that has also experienced 5% growth of forest resources per capita. In contrast, the United Kingdom has had a 6% reduction of forest resources over this 25-year period.

Fisheries are one of the most important renewable resources that directly relate to the food security of nations. Within each country, there is an enormous variation in fish stock and species. Fisheries are a small but essential part of natural capital, but most nations are experiencing a decreasing trend of the fishery stocks. Fish stock can be managed as a renewable resource by limiting the harvest of endangered species and harvesting abundant species.

Overall, we find that 15 countries have successfully increased the fishery wealth of nations. However, 92 countries reported a negative growth rate of fishery wealth, while 33 countries reported no fishery wealth. Figure 3.8 shows the growth rate of global fishery wealth, where only Canada and some European countries have seen

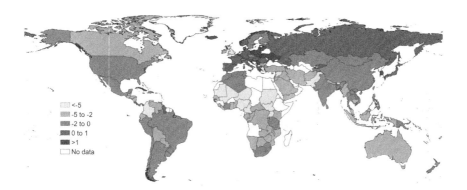

Figure 3.7 Average annual growth rate of forests per capita from 1990 to 2014

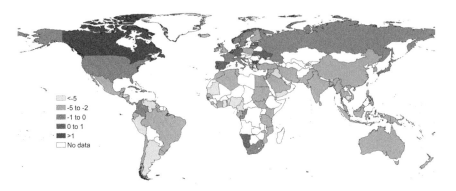

Figure 3.8 Average annual growth rate of fisheries per capita from 1990 to 2014

their fish stock increase in the past 25 years. This is intuitive especially given high population growth in Asian and African countries and recent preferences of more sustainable fishery in western countries.

Fossil fuels

Non-renewable resources of energy are the main inputs for the energy system of most countries. Countries with abundant fossil fuel resources are greatly reducing their stock value over time. In Figure 3.10 and Figure 3.11, the per capita growth of oil and gas is negative for the countries from 1990 to 2014. The background of the reduced availability and production of fossil fuels is clearly visible, which is a good sign for sustainable development. As expounded in Section 5, alternative renewable energy is garnering attention and contributing to sustainable development by substituting fossil fuels.

Oil is considered the most widely used fossil fuel and contributes up to 22% of global natural capital. It is widely considered a carbon-intensive source of energy, and its non-renewable characteristics trivially result in a gradual decline of this resource. Figure 3.10 shows the average annual growth rate of oil per capita from 1990 to 2014.

Natural gas is another important source of energy, which accounts for 7% of global natural capital. Natural gas has a lower carbon content than oil, which improves our carbon damage adjustment in IWI. Its use is also increasing due to its geopolitical diversity. According to Figure 3.12, except Ukraine, all countries have seen reduced growth in coal resources for 25 years.

The rule of the game has been changed in the field of non-renewable resources recently. In particular, after the steep rise in oil prices in the late 2000s, the United States has been aggressive in developing unconventional resources such as shale oil and gas, making North America an important fossil fuel exporter. This could change the future oil and gas in the future, as well as such important adjustments to well-being as oil capital gains and carbon damage.

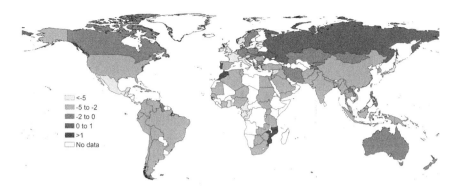

Figure 3.9 Average annual growth rate of non-renewables per capita from 1990–2014

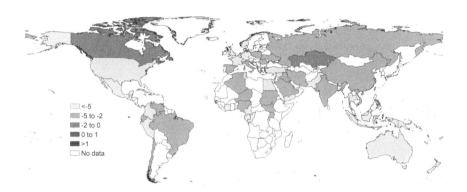

Figure 3.10 Average annual growth rate of oil per capita from 1990 to 2014

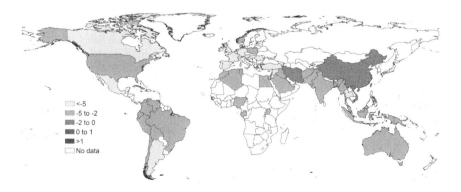

Figure 3.11 Average annual growth rate of natural gas per capita from 1990 to 2014

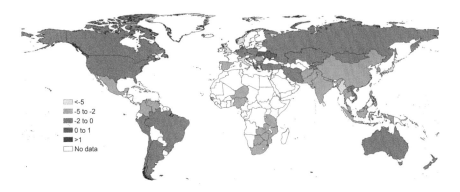

Figure 3.12 Average annual growth rate of coal per capita from 1990 to 2014

Minerals

Non-renewable mineral resources are the smallest contributor of NC for nations (1% of NC) in terms of capital stocks. In Figure 3.13, the decline of minerals is consistent for countries from 1990 to 2014, and this is caused primarily by the downward trend of its mineral stock. In our analysis, 44 countries reported negative growth of mineral wealth from 1990–2014, and, notably, several countries reported mineral depletion that is more than 5%.

Regional natural capital growth and sustainability

This section describes natural capital growth at six regional levels, while an examination of disaggregated resources will provide a better understanding. Asia Pacific, Africa, Europe, Latin America and the Caribbean, West Asia, and North America are representative regions where natural capital and wealth have been observed from 1992 to 2014. Our regional category depends upon UNEP (2016) Global Environment Outlook (GEO-6) Assessment. This regional analysis can evaluate the development and sustainability of the region more specifically.

Asia and the Pacific

Economic growth in Asia and the Pacific no doubt has had a notable impact on increased welfare but also places significant pressure on natural capital. The climate change effect and increasing number of natural disasters is causing major damage in this region. Meanwhile, Asia Pacific countries are also taking action regarding green growth action, and environmental awareness is gradually increasing. Countries are taking initiatives in low carbon green growth and are investing in green technology.

This region is experiencing the fastest rate of urbanization and population growth, which creates significant environmental challenges (UNEP 2016). Stronger institutions, good governance and strict monitoring are important for sustainable development in the Asia and the Pacific region. Greater emphasis on regional and local climate change adaptation for increased resilience is also unavoidable.

Asia and the Pacific countries have decreased their natural capital base as well as population growth. However, this drawdown of natural capital does not necessarily reduce the wealth in this region. No countries in this sample exhibit a decline in

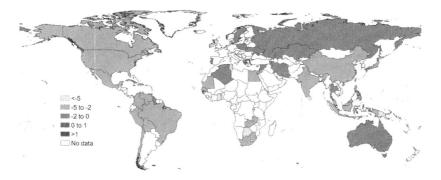

Figure 3.13 Average annual growth rate of minerals per capita from 1990–2014

Table 3.1 Measuring the changes of natural capital in Asia and the Pacific countries: average annual growth rates from 1990–2014

Countries	Natural capital growth (decline)	Population growth (%)	Natural capital per capita (%)	IWI per capita (%)
Australia	−0.6%	1.3%	−1.9%	0.0%
Afghanistan	−0.1%	4.1%	−4.0%	4.6%
Australia	−0.6%	1.3%	−1.9%	0.0%
Bangladesh	−0.8%	1.7%	−2.4%	−0.2%
China	−0.8%	0.8%	−1.6%	2.2%
Fiji	0.1%	0.8%	−0.7%	−0.1%
Indonesia	−1.1%	1.4%	−2.4%	−0.9%
India	−0.4%	1.7%	−2.1%	1.0%
Iran	−0.6%	1.4%	−2.0%	3.2%
Japan	−0.9%	0.1%	−1.0%	0.6%
Cambodia	−1.3%	2.2%	−3.5%	−1.4%
Republic of Korea	−0.3%	0.7%	−0.9%	3.1%
Laos	0.0%	1.9%	−1.8%	−2.6%
Sri Lanka	−0.9%	0.8%	−1.7%	1.8%
Maldives	−1.9%	2.6%	−4.4%	−0.2%
Myanmar	−1.5%	1.0%	−2.5%	0.1%
Mongolia	−0.4%	1.2%	−1.6%	1.5%
Malaysia	−1.3%	2.1%	−3.3%	0.5%
Nepal	−1.1%	1.7%	−2.8%	1.4%
New Zealand	0.3%	1.3%	−1.0%	−0.3%
Pakistan	−2.7%	2.3%	−4.9%	−0.5%
Philippines	−0.1%	2.0%	−2.0%	1.0%
Papua New Guinea	0.8%	2.5%	−1.6%	0.5%
Singapore	−0.7%	2.5%	−3.1%	2.9%
Thailand	−1.0%	0.8%	−1.7%	0.8%
Viet Nam	−0.4%	1.3%	−1.7%	−1.8%

wealth while increasing natural capital in per capita form, as is clear from Table 3.1. Figure 3.14 clearly shows a declining trend of agricultural land, fossil fuel and fishery resources. In contrast, forestry is the only resource that indicates recovery after facing a decline from 1992 to 2010. Specifically, New Zealand and Japan are two

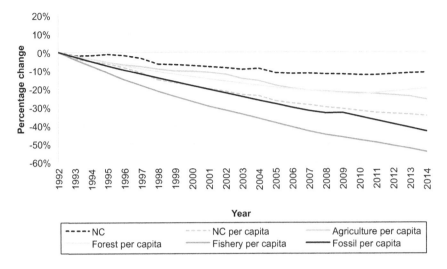

Figure 3.14 Percentage change in natural capital in Asia and the Pacific countries from 1992 to 2014

representative countries in the Asia Pacific that have successfully recovered their forest resources and indicate sustainability.

Africa

Africa faces environmental challenges due to weak environmental governance, climate change, loss of biodiversity and dependence on fossil fuels. Although Africa has large varieties of natural resources, the sustainable management of natural capital is critical, since natural capital accounts for a relatively large portion of natural capital in the region. Cropland and pastureland degradation takes place every year due to soil erosion, salinization, deforestation, etc. In addition, urbanization creates continuous pressure on agriculture, which impacts reduced agricultural productivity.

It is important for Africa to improve land productivity and increase efforts to use renewable energy. Policies to reduce marine and ecosystem degradation and enact inclusive natural capital management should be implemented. Simultaneous economic development and promotion of ecosystem improvement can ensure the welfare of Africa.

Africa is rich in natural resources, but weak resource management reduces the gain from this resource. Most African countries have experienced a decline in natural capital and high growth in the population over 1992–2014. Figure 3.15 shows a clear declining condition of agricultural land, forests and fisheries. Fossil fuels facing decline was dramatic over the 1992–2007 period and started increasing from 2007 to 2009. However, fossil fuels were decreasing from 2009 until 2014.

Table 3.2 shows a high population growth rate in the region, which has a potential to increase human capital. As a result, the decreasing natural resources that impact

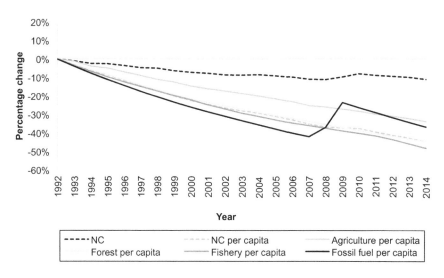

Figure 3.15 Percentage change in natural capital in African countries from 1992 to 2014

Table 3.2 Measuring the changes of natural capital in African countries: average annual growth rates from 1990–2014

Countries	Natural capital growth (decline)	Population growth (%)	Natural capital per capita (%)	IWI per capita (%)
Burundi	−0.9%	2.8%	−3.6%	2.4%
Benin	−1.0%	3.2%	−4.1%	2.5%
Central African Republic	−0.1%	2.1%	−2.1%	−0.8%
Côte d'Ivoire	1.2%	2.5%	−1.3%	3.6%
Cameroon	−6.2%	2.7%	−8.6%	0.7%
Congo D.R	−0.2%	3.2%	−3.3%	−4.7%
Congo	−0.3%	2.7%	−2.9%	−0.6%
Algeria	−2.2%	1.7%	−3.8%	1.4%
Egypt	−2.6%	1.9%	−4.4%	1.0%
Gabon	−0.1%	2.4%	−2.4%	−3.3%
Ghana	0.0%	2.6%	−2.5%	1.6%
Gambia	−1.2%	3.1%	−4.2%	−3.2%
Kenya	0.1%	2.7%	−2.6%	0.3%
Liberia	−0.7%	3.1%	−3.7%	6.8%
Morocco	−0.5%	1.3%	−1.7%	0.0%
Mali	−2.1%	3.0%	−4.9%	2.0%
Mozambique	1.2%	3.0%	−1.7%	0.6%
Mauritania	−1.8%	2.8%	−4.5%	0.7%
Mauritius	−1.5%	0.7%	−2.2%	0.3%
Malawi	−0.5%	2.4%	−2.9%	3.4%

(*Continued*)

Table 3.2 (Continued)

Countries	Natural capital growth (decline)	Population growth (%)	Natural capital per capita (%)	IWI per capita (%)
Niger	−1.2%	3.7%	−4.7%	2.6%
Nigeria	−1.3%	2.6%	−3.8%	4.7%
Rwanda	1.6%	1.9%	−0.2%	2.0%
Sudan (former)	−2.9%	2.9%	−5.6%	−3.2%
Senegal	−0.6%	2.8%	−3.4%	0.1%
Sierra Leone	−0.9%	2.0%	−2.9%	−0.1%
Togo	−1.8%	2.7%	−4.4%	1.8%
Tunisia	−2.1%	1.3%	−3.3%	2.4%
Tanzania	1.1%	3.0%	−1.8%	−0.5%
Uganda	−1.0%	3.3%	−4.2%	2.5%
Zambia	−0.3%	2.8%	−2.9%	2.6%
Zimbabwe	−1.7%	1.6%	−3.2%	1.9%

the growth of wealth is not significant, and many African countries experience growth in inclusive wealth. By enhancing natural resource management, Africa is potentially able to enjoy higher growth in inclusive wealth.

Pan-European

Biodiversity loss, climate change and ecosystem degradation is affecting economic development in the pan-European region. Increased changes in land use and urbanization are some key reasons for biodiversity decline.

Despite the improvement in the environment, air pollution is the greatest health risk of the population. International shipping, transportation and extensive economic activities are responsible for air pollution in this region.

In addition, across the pan-European region, marine biodiversity is poor given that fishery resources have faced decline despite the regulations on fish catches by EU countries. Changing weather conditions and sea level increases may also affect marine biodiversity. This leads to revenue loss from fisheries, tourism, the shipping industry, etc., as well as the well-being of the residents.

The pan-European region has improved the condition of its natural resources, and the growth of natural resources and total wealth are representative of this region. It also leads to a comprehensive growth of wealth across Europe. In Figure 3.16, we note an increase or no change of renewables and a sharp decrease of non-renewables. This is an ideal condition for natural resources and represents sustainability.

Population growth in the Pan-European region is low, and it is remarkable that natural capital growth is positive or slightly negative, both in aggregate and per capita terms. The growth of wealth is not rapid either, partly because human capital is not

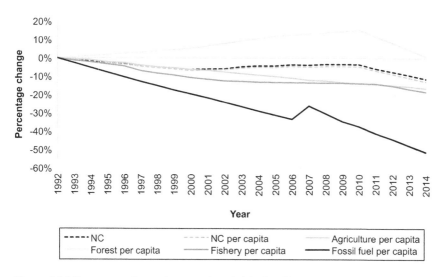

Figure 3.16 Percentage change in natural capital in Pan-European countries from 1992 to 2014

Table 3.3 Measuring the changes of natural capital in Pan-European countries: average annual growth rates from 1990–2014

Countries	Natural capital growth (decline)	Population growth (%)	Natural capital per capita (%)	IWI per capita (%)
Albania	−0.3%	−0.5%	0.3%	2.7%
Austria	−0.1%	0.4%	−0.6%	0.9%
Belgium	1.6%	0.5%	1.1%	0.0%
Bulgaria	−1.6%	−0.8%	−0.8%	−1.8%
Switzerland	−0.1%	0.8%	−0.9%	0.0%
Czech Republic	−1.4%	0.1%	−1.5%	0.6%
Germany	−0.6%	0.1%	−0.7%	0.3%
Denmark	−3.3%	0.4%	−3.7%	−0.1%
Spain	0.2%	0.7%	−0.6%	0.7%
Estonia	0.1%	−0.7%	0.9%	0.6%
Finland	−0.3%	0.4%	−0.7%	0.4%
France	0.0%	0.5%	−0.5%	0.6%
United Kingdom	−4.4%	0.5%	−4.9%	0.3%
Greece	−0.8%	0.3%	−1.1%	−0.4%
Croatia	0.3%	−0.5%	0.8%	−0.9%
Hungary	−0.8%	−0.2%	−0.6%	0.4%
Ireland	−1.5%	1.1%	−2.6%	2.9%
Iceland	−0.3%	1.0%	−1.4%	0.2%
Italy	−0.2%	0.3%	−0.5%	0.1%
Lithuania	0.1%	−1.0%	1.0%	1.0%
Kazakhstan	−0.1%	0.2%	−0.4%	3.4%

(*Continued*)

Table 3.3 (Continued)

Countries	Natural capital growth (decline)	Population growth (%)	Natural capital per capita (%)	IWI per capita (%)
Kyrgyzstan	0.5%	1.2%	−0.7%	0.0%
Luxembourg	0.7%	1.6%	−0.9%	0.7%
Latvia	0.8%	−1.2%	2.0%	−0.3%
Republic of Moldova	−5.5%	−0.2%	−5.4%	2.0%
Malta	−0.7%	0.8%	−1.5%	−0.3%
Netherlands	−3.0%	0.5%	−3.5%	0.3%
Norway	−3.5%	0.8%	−4.2%	1.1%
Poland	−0.8%	0.0%	−0.8%	1.2%
Portugal	−0.3%	0.2%	−0.4%	0.5%
Romania	−0.7%	−0.6%	−0.1%	0.9%
Russian Federation	0.3%	−0.1%	0.4%	1.1%
Serbia	1.5%	−0.3%	1.8%	−1.9%
Slovakia	−0.1%	0.1%	−0.2%	1.8%
Slovenia	0.2%	0.1%	0.1%	0.6%
Sweden	−1.3%	0.5%	−1.8%	0.6%
Tajikistan	0.1%	1.9%	−1.8%	2.0%
Ukraine	0.1%	−0.6%	0.6%	−1.0%

the fastest growing element in this region. Nevertheless, countries manage a positive trend of wealth over 1990–2014 through economic activities.

Latin America and the Caribbean

Latin America and the Caribbean region (LAC) includes some of the most unique eco-regions in the world and provides valuable ecosystem service. However, land degradation is creating major challenges for its ecological zones, resulting in unsustainable land management. Deforestation in the Amazon and other forest ecosystems is a major challenge for LAC resource management. Although culti-vatable land is increasing to maintain the food demand, this extension is not sustainable.

The LAC region is responsible for approximately 25% of fishery catches, and overharvesting is affecting the local ecosystem. This continued marine biodiversity loss in LAC has far-reaching consequences and risks. For instance, the biomass of some species will become extinct in the near future. However, the areas under protection increased over the 1990 to 2014 period.

LAC countries are identified as worrying and persistent through natural capital degradation. In Figure 3.17, there is a clear trend of reduction in all components of natural capital – for instance, agriculture, forest, fishery, fossil fuels, etc. This region is also facing biodiversity loss, climate change and unsustainable production and consumption patterns.

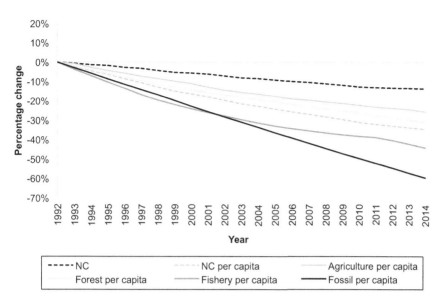

Figure 3.17 Percentage change in natural capital in Latin America and the Caribbean countries from 1992 to 2014

Table 3.4 Measuring the changes of natural capital in Latin America and the Caribbean countries: average annual growth rates from 1990–2014

Countries	Natural capital growth (decline)	Population growth (%)	Natural capital per capita (%)	IWI per capita (%)
Argentina	−0.3%	1.1%	−1.5%	1.4%
Belize	−0.5%	2.7%	−3.1%	−0.7%
Bolivia	−0.5%	1.8%	−2.2%	−1.2%
Brazil	−0.4%	1.3%	−1.7%	−0.1%
Barbados	−1.6%	0.4%	−2.0%	−0.4%
Chile	−0.6%	1.3%	−1.8%	−0.3%
Colombia	−4.8%	1.4%	−6.1%	−0.6%
Costa Rica	0.7%	1.8%	−1.1%	0.4%
Cuba	0.2%	0.3%	−0.1%	1.9%
Dominican Republic	−0.3%	1.6%	−1.9%	1.0%
Ecuador	−1.0%	1.9%	−2.8%	1.8%
Guatemala	−1.0%	2.4%	−3.3%	0.8%
Guyana	0.6%	0.2%	0.3%	3.1%
Honduras	−2.0%	2.0%	−4.0%	−1.7%
Haiti	−1.8%	1.7%	−3.4%	−1.8%
Jamaica	−0.3%	0.5%	−0.8%	−1.0%
Mexico	−0.8%	1.6%	−2.4%	−0.3%

(*Continued*)

Table 3.4 (Continued)

Countries	Natural capital growth (decline)	Population growth (%)	Natural capital per capita (%)	IWI per capita (%)
Nicaragua	−0.7%	1.6%	−2.2%	1.6%
Panama	0.1%	1.9%	−1.7%	0.3%
Peru	−0.1%	1.5%	−1.6%	0.7%
Paraguay	−0.6%	1.9%	−2.4%	0.0%
El Salvador	0.3%	0.6%	−0.4%	0.8%
Trinidad and Tobago	−3.9%	0.4%	−4.3%	3.8%
Uruguay	−0.3%	0.4%	−0.7%	0.8%
Venezuela	−0.3%	1.8%	−2.1%	5.7%

West Asia

West Asia is facing serious risks of deforestation and land degradation. High population growth is placing significant pressure on arable land, fresh water and food. Urbanization, soil salinity, soil erosion and converted wetland to dry land are some reasons for the degradation of the agricultural land. As a result, food security in this area will be at risk.

Biodiversity in West Asia is under threat due to overconsumption based on forestry, fossils and other biological resources. Beyond the biocapacity, continued anthropogenic actions pose a serious risk to natural resources. The exploitation rate of marine resources is also increasing dramatically in West Asia. Modification of the coast in Gulf Cooperation Council (GCC) countries is also responsible for marine biodiversity damage.

West Asian countries are experiencing a slow decline of natural resources but rapid growth of the population. The impact of population growth is clearly visible in Figure 3.18, where the natural capital per capita is sharply declining. Natural resources in this region consist primarily of fossil fuels and are seen as dirty due to its high emission factor of greenhouse gases. Environmental governance, coupled with prudent oil wealth management (Collier et al. 2010), is the process through which West Asia can achieve sustainability.

In Table 3.5, high population growth is contributing to the growth of human capital in the West Asia region, and consequently inclusive wealth is growing significantly. The decline of natural capital is not guiding wealth into these countries. However, a multi-sectoral policy design can improve the resilience in West Asia.

North America

North America has rich biodiversity and diverse ecosystems. Agriculture land is well-managed and provides a sustainable food supply. Moreover, agricultural land is increasing overall. Some Canadian forests are converted to cropland. Despite the recent gains, the loss of forests to cropland can pose risks. Some natural consequences such as wildfire also put pressure on forest resources.

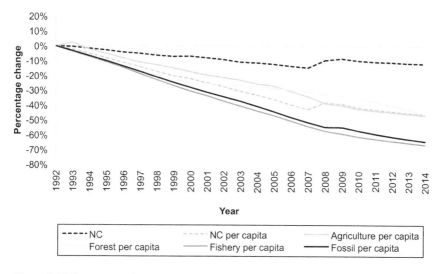

Figure 3.18 Percentage change in natural capital in West Asian countries from 1992 to 2014

Table 3.5 Measuring the changes of natural capital in West Asia: average annual growth rates from 1990–2014

Countries	Natural capital growth (decline)	Population growth (%)	Natural capital per capita (%)	IWI per capita (%)
United Arab Emirates	−0.9%	7.0%	−7.3%	1.5%
Armenia	2.5%	−0.7%	3.2%	1.4%
Bahrain	−5.5%	4.3%	−9.4%	−0.4%
Cyprus	0.0%	1.7%	−1.7%	−0.1%
Iraq	−0.4%	3.0%	−3.3%	9.8%
Israel	−0.6%	2.4%	−2.9%	1.1%
Jordan	−0.5%	3.4%	−3.7%	1.0%
Kuwait	−0.7%	2.5%	−3.2%	6.1%
Qatar	−1.0%	6.5%	−7.1%	4.0%
Saudi Arabia	−0.2%	2.7%	−2.9%	1.9%
Syrian Arab Republic	−3.3%	1.7%	−4.9%	−2.2%
Turkey	−0.5%	1.5%	−1.9%	0.2%
Yemen	−0.4%	3.3%	−3.6%	1.0%

Fisheries in North America and specifically in Canada are growing partly due to sustainable policies adopted by the government. The dependency on fossil fuel is also declining because of renewable energy technology development. Solar energy capacity in North America is increasing, and household use of solar power is becoming increasingly popular.

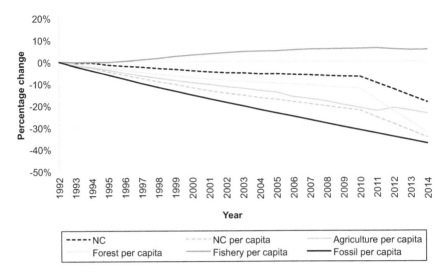

Figure 3.19 Percentage change in natural capital in North America countries from 1992 to 2014

Table 3.6 Measuring the changes of natural capital in North America: average annual growth rates from 1990–2014

Countries	Natural capital growth (decline)	Population growth (%)	Natural capital per capita (%)	IWI per capita (%)
Canada	–1.2%	1.0%	–2.2%	1.4%
United States of America	–0.6%	1.0%	–1.6%	0.1%

North America has been performing relatively well on the natural capital front. In Figure 3.19, the decreasing trend of non-renewable fossil resources and the increasing trend of renewable fishery resources is a snapshot of the improved environmental conditions. However, remaining and emerging environmental challenges could interfere with sustainable growth in the future.

Incorporating natural disaster resilience in the assessment of natural capital

It is a common understanding that the stage of economic development of a nation and its resilience to natural disasters have a positive relationship (Toya and Skidmore 2007). As an easy way to confirm an aspect of this argument, the numbers of deaths, injuries and homeless people are reduced as national incomes rise (Kahn 2005).

We discuss the importance of natural capital and the inclusive wealth of nations in coping with natural disasters. Some forms of natural capital have been known to work as a natural protection against natural disasters. A prime example is the wealth of mangrove trees that have a regulating ecosystem service such as coastal protection (Barbier et al. 2008).

Of course, an abundance of natural capital may not translate into greater public awareness in vulnerable areas, and a stronger social response to disaster risk and management is essential. Governments may be less responsive and less efficient in handling disaster response initiatives in low-income countries.

However, lowering dependence on non-renewable resources is strongly correlated to awareness of climate change and damage from natural disasters. Moreover, we analysed the data on natural disasters from the EM-DAT for every recorded disaster from 140 countries over the 1990–2014 period, and identified that higher inclusive wealth is correlated with more damage reduction policies against natural disasters.

Asia Pacific countries are the most disaster-prone in the world, and most natural disasters that have been reported in this region have occurred over the past 25 years. In the absence of adaptation, hundreds of millions of people will be affected by disasters. What is worrisome is that this region is also continuously losing natural forests, mangroves and croplands. Cumulative climate change and natural resource degradation are threating sustainability in this area.

Africa is also highly vulnerable to natural disasters. Drought, salinity and wildfires are destroying agricultural and wild fauna and flora. This disaster also results in a loss of biodiversity in this region. Climate change-induced challenges are clearly visible in Africa. For instance, 90% of the population in Sub-Saharan Africa is exposed to air pollution and increased greenhouse gas emissions. The poor air quality in Africa is causing severe health problems for the inhabitants.

Climate change across Europe represents one of the largest risk factors and is responsible for extreme weather events. Temperature increases and the coastal sea level rises are affecting many areas in this region. Flash and coastal floods have become more intense, and storms are becoming more frequent. However, the ambitious mitigation policy of the European Union (EU) has reduced emissions from 1990 to 2014.

In the LAC region, the climate change impact on coastal areas is more visible and is causing disasters. Hurricanes, sea level rises, storm surges and coastal flooding have become more frequent and lead to significant damage. However, integrated coastal zone management action may improve the changing conditions in LAC.

Climate change-induced changes in weather are taking place in West Asian countries. Rainfall, temperature and humidity are showing variations. This region also experienced an increase in carbon dioxide emissions due to fossil fuel consumption. The sea level rise will affect the economy, agriculture and tourism in this area.

The impact of climate change is more evident in the North America region. Recent devastating droughts and floods have damaged many parts of the US and Canada. Hurricane Sandy in 2012 and Hurricane Katrina in 2005 were directly responsible for human and economic losses. Canada and the US are taking steps to mitigate and adapt to unavoidable climate change across regions and beyond.

Sustainability and resilience are important for understanding how the growth of the inclusive wealth of a nation is performing. For instance, in addition to agricultural production, groundwater conservation is having a significant impact on regional welfare (Walker et al. 2010). Resilience is the capacity of a system to sustain itself after a shock and the ability to absorb the shock without it being transferred to an alternate system. According to Walker et al. (2004), the more resilient a system is, the more shock it absorbs without shifting. Walker et al. (2010) is an attempt to include resilience as an addition to the list of capital stocks. While intriguing in itself as a case study of the region, their approach poses a challenge when it comes to upscaling to the national level.

Renewable energy as capital stocks

Despite the fact that the shift from non-renewable to renewable energy sources for power plants has been seen as a more sustainable move, what this means in terms of inclusive wealth and sustainability assessment has not been clear. In this subsection, therefore, we aim to clarify how this substitution enters the framework of inclusive wealth as an indicator of sustainable development and to show the magnitude of this power shift in the inclusive wealth of nations.

Investment into renewable energy power plants is recorded as an increase in produced capital. This may feel awkward in a sense, especially when other renewable resources, such as forest, agricultural land and fisheries are counted as part of natural capital in IWI. Indeed, inputs into renewable energy facilities, such as solar, wind, water, geothermal energy, etc., are actually renewable, and tend to substitute conventional natural capital such as oil and natural gas.

However, it is acceptable to count renewable energy plants as produced capital, not only because they are literally manufactured structures but also because they do not meet certain characteristics unique to natural capital – for natural capital differs from produced capital in many important ways. First, the process is sometimes irreversible if its quantity in, for example, an ecosystem has surpassed the (lower bound) threshold level; it could be difficult to restore the system to its original state. This has been found in ecosystems at varied scales, from a non-convex shallow lake that faces phosphorous deposits (Dasgupta and Mäler 2003) to the global climate system (Lemoine and Traeger 2016). Second, some natural capital can be substituted by produced capital to a limited extent, as the strong sustainability argument has stressed. Third, the response and change of natural capital can be unexpected and, more often than not, non-linear. It is non-debatable that renewable energy power plants do not meet these characteristics.

We may come up with at least two approaches to account for shadow prices of renewable energy (RE) capital. Given the current physical capital stock, shadow pricing can be performed based either on past unit cost data or on future income projection. In this illustrative analysis, we focus on the cost-based accounting of RE capital.[1]

Our dataset of past investments into solar and wind relies on BP (2015). We skip hydroelectricity here as it is considered conventional energy production, and the opportunity cost of using water is not necessarily nil, in contrast to solar and wind. We do not consider biofuels either due to its nature of competing use of land with food crops.

Solar energy

Based on the cumulative installed capacity of solar power (photovoltaic), we estimate annual gross investment into this power source. Applying a depreciation rate of 5%

per annum, net investment can be reached. It could be the case that the cumulative installed capacity already is free of decommissioned power plants, in which case the depreciation would be double counted. However, this would only result in a conservative undervaluation of cumulative stock.

To value the actual expenditure of laying out the solar energy power units, one has to assume unit costs. It is well known that the cost of renewable energy, both in terms of instalment and operation, has sharply declined in recent years. The use of past average unit cost would inflate the value of the current capital stock with vintages, although that would be an accurate depiction of the actual expenditure. It can also be considered that the unit cost of construction is lower in a larger capacity due to scale economies. Geographical factors matter as well; the unitary cost of installing solar power units in Japan is double that of Europe, for example. Nevertheless, for brevity and clarity of analysis, we simply assume that the unit cost of installing a plant is USD 2,000 per kW across the board.[2] Note that this treatment tends to overestimate the value of the current stock in Europe and the US and underestimate it in Japan and other less developed countries.

This depreciation adjusted solar energy capital in monetary units in 2014 turned out to be the highest in Germany ($64b), followed by China ($54b), Japan ($43b), the United States ($34b) and Italy ($32b). It is only in 2016 that Asia Pacific surpassed Europe and Eurasia in unadjusted capacity, aided by explosive growth in China afterwards.

In per capita terms, the big picture changes. By far the largest is Germany ($785), followed by Italy ($540), Belgium ($480), Greece ($418) and Japan ($335). These top five countries have adopted some supporting mechanisms for renewable energy, including solar power, typically feed-in systems or quota obligations.

Wind energy

In much the same way as solar power capital, we can estimate wind power capital. Past data on capacity instalment can be used to compute the current stock of wind power plants in terms of kW, which can be converted to social value by using actual expenditures.

More specifically, to convert past investments into capital stock, we need assumptions for unit costs. The cost of wind turbines, which has been decreasing in recent years, makes up for most of the initial capital cost. The initial capital cost varies depending on the country, project, geographical condition and technologies. For example, an offshore wind farm, which is still in its infant stage, is likely to cost more than conventional wind farms provided that they are equipped with related infrastructure such as a subsea distribution network. However, we bypass this heterogeneity as our information is limited, which would yield complexities in accounting. The U.S. DOE (2016) reports that in the US, the average turbine prices reached a low of $800/kW around the turn of the century, increased to $1,600/kW by the end of 2008, and then declined again to approximately $1,000. According to the same report, performance in terms of the capacity factor has improved significantly even within the past several years to 42.5% (those built in 2014 or 2015), compared to an average of 25%–32% for those built around the turn of the century to the 2000s.[3] Considering that our sample period ends in 2014 and the US can be one of the forerunners in the relevant technologies, we have no reason to adopt a number less than this figure. Thus, we assume that the unit cost of wind energy is simply $1,000 per kW for all periods and all countries, which happens to be half of our assumed unit cost of solar power. Again, this will make our estimates in some regions lower than the actual expenditure.

The cost-based capital stock of wind power turns out to have accumulated in China ($84b), the United States ($51b), Germany ($26b), India ($17b) and Spain ($15b). In regional aggregates, Asia Pacific is leading ($109b), followed by Europe and Eurasia ($98b) and North America ($61b). It is interesting to see this in per capita terms as the top countries are focused on Europe, in the order Sweden ($476), Denmark ($433), Ireland ($379), Spain ($328) and Portugal ($325).

Summary

As we argued at the outset of this section, renewable energy output can be considered a joint product of renewable energy-produced capital and natural capital. Renewable energy capital (RE) is produced capital (PC) from a physical perspective, but it can substitute for natural capital (NC), especially non-renewable fossil fuels, such as coal, oil and gas. Thus, in Table 3.7, we show a comparison of our results with produced and natural capital (per capita) in selected countries. As Table 3.7 illustrates, China, Germany, the United States, Japan and Italy are the top five countries in terms of the value of total renewable energy capital (RE) as of 2014. They are a mix of developed and emerging countries. Renewable energy capital per capita (REpc) has accumulated widely in Europe: Germany, Italy, Denmark, Belgium and Greece.

Table 3.7 also reports the share of RE in terms of produced capital, natural capital and inclusive wealth. In the current inclusive wealth framework, RE stocks have already been accounted for in the PC category. Apparently, RE does not account for most PC in any country, but in some Eastern European countries (Bulgaria and Romania), it accounts for 1 to 2% of the total PC. This may be because RE has been aggressively introduced across Europe and PC accumulates less in less developed parts of Europe.

More interesting is the ratio of RE to natural capital (NC), which varies widely since natural capital endowment differs from country to country. In Belgium, for example, the combined RE capital of solar and wind already surpassed the level of natural capital. Other European countries, including United Kingdom and Italy, and Israel already have RE capital, which is more than a 10% equivalent of natural capital of their nations. It could be the case that these countries have depleted their natural capital in exchange for investing in renewable energy. It could also be the case that they have invested in RE because they are poorly endowed with non-renewable resources in the first place. Another possibility is that they are replacing conventional power plants (produced capital) using fossil fuels or nuclear power.

Table 3.7 Renewable energy capital of selected countries, and its ratio compared to other capitals

Countries	Solar	Wind	RE	REpc	RE/PC	RE/NC	RE/IW
Argentina	–	254	254	6	0.000	0.000	0.000
Australia	7,262	3,290	10,551	449	0.003	0.004	0.001
Austria	1,440	1,604	3,044	353	0.002	0.054	0.001
Belgium	5,389	1,636	7,025	626	0.004	1.084	0.001
Bulgaria	1,836	530	2,366	328	0.021	0.043	0.005
Brazil	–	5,503	5,503	27	0.002	0.001	0.000
Canada	3,507	8,162	11,669	328	0.003	0.003	0.001
Switzerland	1,945	–	1,945	236	0.001	0.023	0.000
Chile	434	716	1,150	65	0.002	0.004	0.001
China	53,869	84,342	138,211	99	0.008	0.018	0.003
Costa Rica	–	132	132	28	0.002	0.002	0.000
Czech Republic	3,376	–	3,376	318	0.005	0.059	0.002
Germany	63,930	26,182	90,112	1,106	0.008	0.064	0.002
Denmark	1,112	2,455	3,567	630	0.004	0.104	0.001
Egypt	–	427	427	5	0.001	0.004	0.000
Spain	8,242	15,253	23,496	505	0.005	0.076	0.001
Finland	18	528	546	100	0.001	0.004	0.000
France	10,103	7,461	17,564	274	0.002	0.064	0.000
United Kingdom	10,422	10,762	21,184	326	0.003	0.128	0.001
Greece	4,706	1,444	6,151	546	0.007	0.030	0.002
Honduras	8	–	8	1	0.000	0.000	0.000
Hungary	149	251	400	41	0.001	0.007	0.000
India	5,698	17,081	22,779	18	0.005	0.007	0.001
Ireland	–	1,777	1,777	379	0.002	0.060	0.001
Israel	1,265	–	1,265	159	0.002	0.101	0.001
Italy	32,202	6,560	38,761	651	0.005	0.116	0.001
Japan	42,903	1,945	44,848	350	0.002	0.098	0.001
Morocco	–	693	693	20	0.002	0.009	0.000
Mexico	191	2,216	2,407	19	0.001	0.003	0.000
Malaysia	386	–	386	13	0.001	0.001	0.000
Netherlands	2,091	1,810	3,901	231	0.001	0.052	0.000
Norway	12	666	678	132	0.001	0.003	0.000
New Zealand	–	502	502	110	0.001	0.000	0.000
Pakistan	233	248	481	3	0.001	0.001	0.000
Philippines	38	272	310	3	0.001	0.002	0.000
Poland	–	3,385	3,385	88	0.003	0.008	0.001
Portugal	737	3,407	4,144	396	0.005	0.071	0.001
Romania	2,506	2,667	5,173	259	0.010	0.028	0.003
Slovakia	918	–	918	169	0.004	0.065	0.001
Sweden	144	4,613	4,757	491	0.003	0.031	0.001
Thailand	2,440	208	2,648	39	0.003	0.010	0.001

(Continued)

Table 3.7 (Continued)

Countries	Solar	Wind	RE	REpc	RE/PC	RE/NC	RE/IW
Tunisia	–	203	203	18	0.001	0.012	0.000
Turkey	110	3,189	3,299	43	0.002	0.006	0.000
Ukraine	1,511	–	1,511	34	0.003	0.002	0.001
Uruguay	–	518	518	151	0.007	0.014	0.002
United States of America	33,947	51,095	85,042	268	0.002	0.009	0.000
South Africa	2,012	554	2,566	47	0.003	0.007	0.001

Source: Based on BP (2016); U.S. DOE (2015); UN (2015); and other sources.

Note: See Yamaguchi (2017) for detailed methodology. RE, REpc, PC, NC and IW stand for renewable energy capital, renewable energy capital per capita, produced capital, natural capital and inclusive wealth (in the conventional IWR 2014 approach), respectively. Solar, wind and RE are expressed in million USD, while REpc is in USD.

Fish wealth of nations

Background

Fish and fisheries has long sustained humans – literally for many millennia. Not only has it been a primary source of protein for humans, but it has also had an important place in the food chain of the marine ecosystem. The increasing human population around the world, aided by preferences for health consciousness, has pushed demand for fish and related products. On the supply side, improving technology has given rise to more availability for human consumption. Moreover, aquaculture surpassed conventional capture fishery for human consumption for the first time in 2014 (FAO 2016).

The FAO's assessment of fishery stocks, however, is sobering. Approximately one-third of the total fishery stock was assessed as being "mined" at a biologically unsustainable level in 2013. In the context of the inclusive wealth accounting framework, with such characteristics as contribution to human well-being, thresholds and irreversibility, non-substitutability and non-linearity, fishery is a prime example of natural capital. With poor substitutability for other nutrition, it is imperative to preserve this type of natural capital for the well-being of future generations. As is the case with other natural capital, the abundance of the stock and its management are important for sustainability. Somewhat contrary to other classes of natural capital, fishery resources are prone to yearly volatility. Thus, sustainability should be assessed in from a longer-term perspective.

Against this backdrop, the current edition of IWR is almost the first to estimate fish capital stock as part of renewable natural capital in the context of inclusive wealth accounting. The qualification "almost" refers to the accounting of fisheries in six selected countries in our pilot-inclusive wealth report (UNU-IHDP, 2012). IWR 2012 accounted for varying numbers of fish stocks from four countries in 1990–2008: 12 from Australia, nine from Canada, ten from South Africa and 40 from the United States. The fishery capital stock estimate was based on the available stock of fisheries within these countries' fishing areas from the newly developed

RAM Legacy Stock Assessment Database (Ricard et al. 2012). To attach shadow prices, IWR 2012 derived prices per tonne from the total landing value and quantity of the Sea Around Us Project (SAUP 2011), which were averaged across species. This was finally converted to shadow prices using the fishery rental rate. Although IWR 2012 was commendable for partially including fisheries as part of natural capital, their scope and methodology was admittedly small and limited. In the following section, we illustrate how we attempted to extend our natural capital database to this important class of natural capital.

Methodology

Estimating fish stock is a herculean task, compared to other classes of natural capital, for many reasons. They cannot be estimated based on the habitat area, unlike forest or agricultural land, whose computation can be based on the area. Moreover, the sheer mobility of the resource not only makes the exercise harder but also poses a fundamental question: to what area can a given fishery be attributed, given that a marine fishery habitat is usually not within national borders? In the current exercise, we simplify the matter by assuming that the fish stock belongs to the country where harvest takes place and the resources are loaded. Of course, this is a crude treatment in many ways: just because fishery biomass is loaded to a particular country does not necessarily mean that the fishery belongs to that country. Having acknowledged this shortcoming, we have no alternative sound theory to allocate harvests to countries. In what follows, our estimates of the fishery wealth of nations should be interpreted as capital stocks that exist in the fisheries operating in these countries.

In renewable resource economics, or bioeconomics, there is a long tradition of assuming resource dynamics (Clark 1976/1990). The stock is the population growth net of harvest:

$$\frac{dS_t}{dt} = G(S_t) - H_t,$$

where S_t denotes the renewable resource biomass stock; $G(S_t)$ is the growth function; and H_t is the harvest. The population, whether it is a renewable resource or human beings, is often assumed to follow a logistic growth function:

$$G(S_t) = rS_t\left(1 - \frac{S_t}{k}\right),$$

where r and k are the parameters that represent the intrinsic (relative) growth rate and carrying capacity of the resource stock, respectively. The harvest, in turn, depends on the resource abundance. A simple but empirically supported harvest production function is to assume that it is proportional to the product of effort and stock, i.e.,

$$H_t = qE_tS_t,$$

where q is called the catchability coefficient. E_t stands for the effort put into the production process, which is often proxied by the number of vessels or fishermen's working hours. Combining these two equations, we arrive at a well-known Gordon-Schaeffer model:

$$\frac{dS_t}{dt} = rS_t\left(1 - \frac{S_t}{k}\right) - qE_tS_t.$$

All this means that, to estimate the fishery stock, S_t, we can resort either to the harvest function, (1), or total resource dynamics, (2). Global fish stocks are commonly assessed by examining the trends in catch or harvest data. Although this catch-based assessment method has attracted significant criticism (see, for instance, Daan et al. (2011)) either due to its technical or conceptual flaws, it is still considered the most reliable method for assessing fish stock (Froese et al. 2012; Kleisner et al. 2013). The main reason is simply that the only data available for most fisheries are the weight of fish caught each year (Pauly et al. 2013). If effort and harvest are known data points as well as the catchability coefficient q, then S_t can be estimated solely from the Schaefer production function (Yamaguchi et al. 2016).

However, effort data are sparse worldwide, so we cannot employ this method for inclusive wealth accounting across the globe. Alternatively, we can appeal to resource dynamics. For the lack of reliable data on r and k for most fish stocks, we follow Martell and Froese (2013), who developed an algorithm to randomly generate feasible (r,k) pairs from a uniform distribution function. The likelihood of the generated (r,k) pairs is further evaluated using the Bernoulli distribution to ensure that the estimated stock meets the following assumptions: it never collapsed or exceeded the carrying capacity, and the final stock lies within the assumed range of depletion.

In cases where the values of (r,k) are not feasible, the stocks were simply estimated according to the following rules:

- If the year being studied follows the year of the maximum catch, then the biomass stock is estimated as twice the catch;
- Otherwise, the biomass stock is estimated as twice the maximum catch, net of the catch ($2 \times$ Maximum Catch – Catch).

The time-series data of the catch (tonnage and value) of each country's economic exclusive zone (EEZ), either by domestic or foreign fleets, for the period of 1950–2010 are obtained from the Sea Around Us Project (SAUP 2016). We only evaluate the stock with a catch record of at least 20 years and which has a total catch in a given area of at least 1,000 tonnes over the time span.

The shadow prices of fisheries, like other classes of natural capital, ideally reflect their marginal contribution to social well-being. More specifically, they also represent not only their marginal abundance but the substitution possibilities with other capital forms (Dasgupta 2009). In a case study of predator-prey dynamics in a Baltic Sea commercial fishery, Do Yun et al. (2017) showed that the shadow prices of species are interdependent on relative abundance and scarcity in a multispecies ecosystem-based management context. Applying a similar methodology to our current natural capital estimate would need a much more detailed dataset than ours. Moreover, there is an obvious trade-off between disaggregated, state-dependent shadow prices and clarity of accounting. For example, if we attach shadow prices that differ according to countries, species, cohorts, years, etc., it would be difficult to disaggregate the reason for the change in the value of capital stocks, although this may be resolved by advancing the way the figures are presented. Additionally, the period-average shadow prices, which are adopted elsewhere in IWR, can be shown to be justified as a good approximation, either in a short period of time or the shadow price change is linear in time. Thus, currently, we choose to use a simple unit market rent that reflects a period-average, species-average market price adjusted by the rental rate.

Results and discussion

In Figure 3.20, we show the past trend of catches from the top 10 countries. Asian demand has been on the rise, mostly driven by the increase in China, Indonesia and India. The US has been stable, and Russia and Japan have declined. Peru has been volatile, largely due to anchovy captures. Note that this figure only considers capture production for both marine and inland waters, which accounts for a portion of fishery production. Leading countries in aquaculture include China (59 m tonnes) and India (14 m tonnes). We also exclude aquaculture production, largely because this class of fishery production has more characteristics of produced capital. This is somewhat analogous to classifying cultivated forests as produced capital, not natural capital.

Figure 3.21 shows the capital stock levels in monetary value comparing 1990 and 2014. Among countries affiliated with a large amount of fishery stock, it is only Canada and Spain that increased their level in the period from 1990 to 2014. In other major fishery producing countries, including China, Indonesia, Japan, Malaysia, Peru and Vietnam, capital stocks have decreased. In the US, capital stocks slightly decreased.

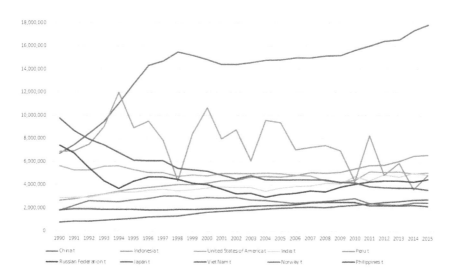

Figure 3.20 Top 10 countries in fishery capture production
Source: FAO – Fishery and Aquaculture Information and Statistics Branch.

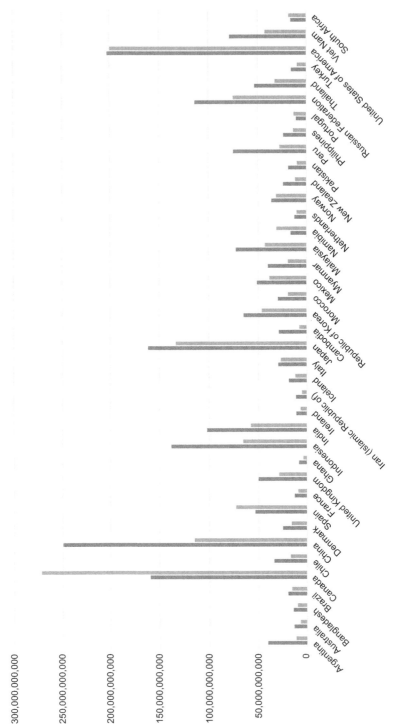

Figure 3.21 The value of fishery stocks of selected nations, 1990 and 2014

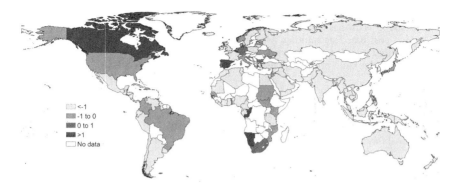

Figure 3.22 Average annual growth rate of fishery from 1990 to 2014

Around the world, the value of fishery stock has decreased from $2,325 billion to $1,713 billion (Figure 3.22). Although the methodology of shadow pricing can be improved, and the absolute figure has no welfare significance,[4] this declining trend is an alarming one *per se*. Given that the capture production is on the increase, the downward pressure of production on the stock appears to remain prevalent.

Part of this problem may have been circumvented in the increase in aquaculture, as we have argued. In addition, there has been an effort to promote policy and management based on Maximum Sustainable Yield (MSY). MSY has its own limitations in that multispecies and ecosystem interactions tend to be absent; however, it is a step in the right direction to modify MSY-based fishery policy. This has just begun, and its effect has yet to be seen, but we hope to have set the base to monitor policy intervention effects on the marine fish capital stock.

Concluding remarks

In this chapter, we took a deeper look at the natural capital of nations from regional perspectives. Data were also used to study the relationship between natural capital and natural disasters.

Some new insights were gained regarding regions and newer classes of natural capital – fishery and renewable energy capital. Admittedly, some challenges remain: shadow prices of fishery and renewable energy capital are still developing. In particular, they have to be estimated in a consistent manner with their addition to social well-being. As IWR 2012 notes, "[w]e will never get shadow prices 'right,' but we can attempt to narrow the range in which they are taken by reasonable people to lie." We believe that this chapter is a step in the right direction.

Notes

1 For a detailed discussion on cost- vs. income-based or backward- and forward-looking accounting of capital assets, and a further discussion and analysis of RE capital, see Yamaguchi (2017).
2 This is slightly more expensive than the cost in Europe in 2014 and is two-thirds of the cost in Japan (METI 2016).

3 In all, "the capacity-weighted average installed project cost stood at nearly \$1,690/kW, down \$640/kW or 27% from the apparent peak in average reported costs in 2009 and 2010." This has declined even more to \$1,590/kW in 2016 (U.S. DOE 2016). In our cost-based accounting, we focus on actual investment expenditure, so the unweighted installed project cost should be used.
4 Note that the same price is applied to the whole stock for simplicity.

References

Arrow, K. J., Dasgupta, P., Goulder, L. H., Mumford, K. J., & Oleson, K. (2012). Sustainability and the measurement of wealth. *Environment and Development Economics*, *17*(3), 317–353.

Barbier, E. B., Koch, E. W., Silliman, B. R., Hacker, S. D., Wolanski, E., Primavera, J., et al. (2008). Coastal ecosystem-based management with nonlinear ecological functions and values. *Science*, *319*(5861), 321–323.

Barbier, E. B. (2009). Ecosystems as natural assets. Found. Trends® Microeconomics *4*, 611–681.

BP Statistical Review of World Energy. (2015). https://www.bp.com/content/dam/bp-country/es_es/spain/documents/downloads/PDF/bp-statistical-review-of-world-energy-2015-full-report.pdf

BP Statistical Review of World Energy. (2016). https://www.bp.com/content/dam/bp/pdf/energy-economics/statistical-review-2016/bp-statistical-review-of-world-energy-2016-full-report.pdf

Clark, C. W. (1976/1990). *Mathematical Bioeconomics: The Optimal Management of Renewable Resources*. New York: Wiley.

Collier, P., van der Ploeg, F., Spence, M., & Venables, A. J. (2010). Managing resource revenues in developing economies. *IMF Staff Papers*, *57*(1), 84–118.

Daan, N., Gislason, H., Pope, J. G., & Rice, J. C. (2011). Apocalypse in world fisheries? The reports of their death are greatly exaggerated. *ICES Journal of Marine Science*, *68*, 1375–1378.

Dasgupta, P. (2007). Measuring sustainable development: Theory and application. *Asian Development Review*, *24*(1), 1.

Dasgupta, P. (2009). The welfare economic theory of green national accounts. *Environmental and Resource Economics*, https://doi.org/10.1007/s10640-008-9223-y

Dasgupta, P., & Mäler, K. G. (2003). The economics of non-convex ecosystems: Introduction. *Environmental and Resource Economics*, *26*(4), 499–525.

Do Yun, S., Hutniczak, B., Abbott, J. K., & Fenichel, E. P. (2017). Ecosystem-based management and the wealth of ecosystems. *Proceedings of National Academy of Sciences*, *114*, 6539–6544.

EM-DAT: The OFDA/CRED International Disaster Database, Université Catholique de Louvain, Brussels, Belgium. Retrieved from www.em-dat.net

Ekins, P., Simon, S., Deutsch, L., Folke, C., & De Groot, R. (2003). A framework for the practical application of the concepts of critical natural capital and strong sustainability. *Ecological Economics*, *44*(2), 165–185.

FAO. (2016). *The State of World Fisheries and Aquaculture 2016: Contributing to Food Security and Nutrition for All*. Rome: FAO.

Froese, R., Zeller, D., Kleisner, K., & Pauly, D. (2012). What catch data can tell us about the status of global fisheries. *Marine Biology*, *159*, 1283–1292.

Kahn, M. (2005). The death toll from natural disasters: The role of income, geography, and institutions. *Review of Economics and Statistics*, *87*, 271–284.

Kleisner, K., Zeller, D., Froese, R., & Pauly, D. (2013). Using global catch data for inferences on the world's marine fisheries. *Fish and Fisheries*, *14*, 293–311.

Lemoine, D., & Traeger, C. P. (2016). Economics of tipping the climate dominoes. *Nature Climate Change, 6*, 514–519.

Martell, S., & Froese, R. (2013). A simple method for estimating MSY from catch and resilience. *Fish and Fisheries, 14*, 504–514.

Ministry of Economy, Trade, and Industry. (2016). Retrieved from www.meti.go.jp/committee/chotatsu_kakaku/pdf/025_01_00.pdf

Pauly, D., Hilborn, R., & Branch, T. A. (2013). Fisheries: does catch reflect abundance? *Nature, 494*, 303–306.

Ricard, D., Minto, C., Jensen, O. P., & Baum, J. K. (2012). Examining the knowledge base and status of commercially exploited marine species with the RAM Legacy Stock Assessment Database. *Fish and Fisheries, 13*(4), 380–398.

SAUP. (2011/2016). *The Sea Around Us Project Database.* Retrieved May, 2011 and December, 2016, from www.seaaroundus.org/data/

Toya, H., & Skidmore, M. (2007). Economic development and the impacts of natural disasters. *Economics Letters, 94*(1), 20–25.

UNEP (2016). *Global Environmental Outlook (GEO) GEO-6 Assessments.*

UN Energy Statistics Yearbook (2015). https://unstats.un.org/unsd/energy/yearbook/default.htm

UNU-IHDP (2012). *Inclusive wealth report 2012: measuring progress toward sustainability.* Cambridge University Press.

UNU-IHDP (2014). *Inclusive wealth report 2014:measuring progress toward sustainability.* Cambridge University Press.

U.S. Department of Energy. (2015). *2015 Wind Technologies Market Report.*

U.S. Department of Energy. (2016). *2016 Wind Technologies Market Report.*

Walker, B., Holling, C. S., Carpenter, S., & Kinzig, A. (2004). Resilience, adaptability and transformability in social–ecological systems. *Ecology and Society, 9*(2).

Walker, B., Pearson, L., Harris, M., Maler, K. G., Li, C. Z., Biggs, R., & Baynes, T. (2010). Incorporating resilience in the assessment of inclusive wealth: An example from South East Australia. *Environmental and Resource Economics, 45*(2), 183–202.

Yamaguchi, R., Sato, M., & Ueta, K. (2016). Measuring regional wealth and assessing sustainable development: A case study of a disaster-torn region in Japan. *Social Indicators Research, 129*(1), 365–389.

Yamaguchi, R. (2017). Wealth and population growth under dynamic average utilitarianism. *Environment and Development Economics*, 1–18.

Appendix

Table 3.8 Growth rate of natural capital and renewable resources from 1990–2014

Country	Growth of natural capital	Growth of renewables	Growth of forest	Growth of fisheries
Afghanistan	−0.1%	0.0%	0.0%	
Albania	−0.3%	−0.1%	0.0%	−3.4%
United Arab Emirates	−0.9%	−2.8%		−2.8%
Argentina	−0.3%	−0.2%	−0.3%	−5.2%
Armenia	2.5%	−0.5%	−0.5%	
Australia	−0.6%	−0.7%	−0.8%	−2.7%
Austria	−0.1%	0.2%	0.5%	
Burundi	−0.9%	−0.9%	−1.6%	
Belgium	1.6%	1.6%	1.5%	1.6%
Benin	−1.0%	−1.0%	−1.0%	−3.3%
Bangladesh	−0.8%	−0.7%	−0.2%	−1.5%
Bulgaria	−1.6%	−3.4%	−4.7%	0.6%
Bahrain	−5.5%	−1.6%	−6.4%	−1.6%
Belize	−0.5%	−0.5%	−0.6%	−0.4%
Bolivia	−0.5%	−0.4%	−0.5%	
Brazil	−0.4%	−0.4%	−0.4%	−0.9%
Barbados	−1.6%	−0.7%	−0.9%	0.2%
Botswana	−0.9%	−0.8%	−0.9%	
Central African Republic	−0.1%	−0.1%	−0.1%	
Canada	−1.2%	−1.6%	−2.0%	2.2%
Switzerland	−0.1%	−0.1%	0.3%	
Chile	−0.6%	−0.3%	0.1%	−2.8%
China	−0.8%	−0.2%	−0.8%	−3.2%
Côte d'Ivoire	1.2%	1.3%	1.7%	−1.3%
Cameroon	−6.2%	−6.4%	−7.3%	−3.8%
Democratic Republic of the Congo	−0.2%	−0.2%	−0.2%	
Congo	−0.3%	0.0%	−0.1%	1.7%
Colombia	−4.8%	−5.9%	−6.6%	−0.3%
Costa Rica	0.7%	0.7%	2.6%	−1.7%

Country	Growth of natural capital	Growth of renewables	Growth of forest	Growth of fisheries
Cuba	0.2%	1.7%	1.9%	−1.2%
Cyprus	0.0%	0.0%	0.3%	
Czech Republic	−1.4%	−1.8%	−1.8%	
Germany	−0.6%	0.3%	0.8%	0.8%
Denmark	−3.3%	−1.4%	1.2%	−1.8%
Dominican Republic	−0.3%	−0.3%	−0.2%	−0.9%
Algeria	−2.2%	−1.1%	−0.3%	−2.8%
Ecuador	−1.0%	−0.6%	−0.6%	−1.3%
Egypt	−2.6%	0.8%		−2.3%
Spain	0.2%	0.4%	1.2%	1.3%
Estonia	0.1%	0.1%	0.2%	−0.7%
Finland	−0.3%	−0.3%	−0.3%	−1.7%
Fiji	0.1%	0.1%	0.0%	0.4%
France	0.0%	0.0%	0.6%	−1.4%
Gabon	−0.1%	0.0%	0.0%	−1.6%
United Kingdom	−4.4%	−1.0%	−5.9%	−2.3%
Ghana	0.0%	0.1%	0.1%	−3.0%
Gambia	−1.2%	−1.2%	0.4%	−2.9%
Greece	−0.8%	−0.5%	0.8%	−2.1%
Guatemala	−1.0%	−1.0%	−0.9%	−2.4%
Guyana	0.6%	0.6%	0.7%	−3.1%
Honduras	−2.0%	−2.0%	−2.3%	−3.4%
Croatia	0.3%	0.5%	0.6%	−0.7%
Haiti	−1.8%	−1.8%	−1.8%	−1.7%
Hungary	−0.8%	−0.6%	0.8%	
Indonesia	−1.1%	−0.8%	−1.2%	−3.0%
India	−0.4%	−0.1%	0.1%	−2.3%
Ireland	−1.5%	−1.4%	−1.3%	−2.1%
Iran	−0.6%	−1.0%	−0.9%	−3.2%
Iraq	−0.4%	−0.2%	0.1%	−3.4%
Iceland	−0.3%	−0.3%	3.5%	−1.8%
Israel	−0.6%	−0.5%	0.5%	−1.1%
Italy	−0.2%	0.0%	1.1%	−0.4%
Jamaica	−0.3%	−0.2%	−0.1%	0.5%
Jordan	−0.5%	−0.1%	0.0%	−0.3%
Japan	−0.9%	−0.7%	0.2%	−0.8%
Kazakhstan	−0.1%	0.1%	0.1%	
Kenya	0.1%	0.1%	0.1%	0.0%
Kyrgyzstan	0.5%	1.4%	1.4%	
Cambodia	−1.3%	−1.3%	−1.3%	−5.3%
Republic of Korea	−0.3%	−0.1%	2.1%	−1.4%
Kuwait	−0.7%	−1.1%		−1.1%
Laos	0.0%	0.0%	−0.1%	

(*Continued*)

Table 3.8 (Continued)

Country	Growth of natural capital	Growth of renewables	Growth of forest	Growth of fisheries
Liberia	−0.7%	−0.7%	−0.7%	−2.2%
Sri Lanka	−0.9%	−0.9%	−0.9%	−2.7%
Lesotho	−0.2%	−0.2%	−0.2%	
Lithuania	0.1%	0.1%	0.2%	−2.3%
Luxembourg	0.7%	0.7%	0.7%	
Latvia	0.8%	0.8%	0.8%	−0.4%
Morocco	−0.5%	−0.5%	0.3%	−1.7%
Republic of Moldova	−5.5%	−5.5%	−5.5%	
Maldives	−1.9%	−1.9%	−6.5%	−2.0%
Mexico	−0.8%	−0.1%	−0.1%	−1.2%
Mali	−2.1%	−2.1%	−3.1%	
Malta	−0.7%	−0.7%	−6.5%	1.0%
Myanmar	−1.5%	−1.5%	−1.3%	−3.0%
Mongolia	−0.4%	−0.4%	−0.3%	
Mozambique	1.2%	−0.4%	−0.5%	−0.8%
Mauritania	−1.8%	−2.4%	−2.9%	−2.3%
Mauritius	−1.5%	−1.5%	−0.5%	−3.4%
Malawi	−0.5%	−0.5%	−1.3%	
Malaysia	−1.3%	−0.5%	−0.1%	−2.2%
Namibia	0.7%	0.5%	−0.9%	2.7%
Niger	−1.2%	−1.4%	−2.5%	
Nigeria	−1.3%	−0.3%	−2.9%	−3.8%
Nicaragua	−0.7%	−0.7%	−1.3%	−1.4%
Netherlands	−3.0%	−0.5%		−0.8%
Norway	−3.5%	0.3%	0.9%	−0.6%
Nepal	−1.1%	−1.1%	−1.2%	
New Zealand	0.3%	0.3%	0.5%	−3.0%
Pakistan	−2.7%	−2.9%	−3.3%	−2.7%
Panama	0.1%	0.1%	0.2%	−1.7%
Peru	−0.1%	0.0%	0.1%	−4.0%
Philippines	−0.1%	−0.1%	0.2%	−2.2%
Papua New Guinea	0.8%	0.9%	1.0%	−2.2%
Poland	−0.8%	−0.9%	1.4%	−2.8%
Portugal	−0.3%	−0.3%	−1.3%	0.9%
Paraguay	−0.6%	−0.6%	−1.2%	
Qatar	−1.0%	−0.5%		−1.8%
Romania	−0.7%	0.0%	0.2%	
Russian Federation	0.3%	0.0%	0.0%	−1.7%
Rwanda	1.6%	−0.4%	−1.1%	
Saudi Arabia	−0.2%	1.7%	0.0%	−2.2%
Sudan (former)	−2.9%	−3.3%	−3.3%	−0.8%
Senegal	−0.6%	−0.6%	−0.6%	−0.8%

Country	Growth of natural capital	Growth of renewables	Growth of forest	Growth of fisheries
Singapore	-0.7%	-0.7%	7.7%	-1.5%
Sierra Leone	-0.9%	-0.9%	-0.9%	-1.4%
El Salvador	0.3%	0.3%	-1.5%	1.0%
Serbia	1.5%	1.2%	1.2%	
Slovakia	-0.1%	0.5%	0.5%	
Slovenia	0.2%	0.9%	0.9%	-3.5%
Sweden	-1.3%	-1.3%	-1.4%	-1.2%
Swaziland	0.8%	1.3%	1.3%	
Syrian Arab Republic	-3.3%	-1.3%	-6.5%	-1.0%
Togo	-1.8%	-1.8%	-5.7%	0.1%
Thailand	-1.0%	-0.3%	0.2%	-2.0%
Tajikistan	0.1%	0.0%	0.0%	
Trinidad and Tobago	-3.9%	-3.1%	-4.0%	-0.3%
Tunisia	-2.1%	-0.1%	-0.5%	-2.3%
Turkey	-0.5%	-0.4%	-0.6%	-2.1%
United Republic of Tanzania	1.1%	1.1%	1.2%	-1.8%
Uganda	-1.0%	-2.9%	-2.9%	
Ukraine	0.1%	0.7%	0.8%	-0.5%
Uruguay	-0.3%	-0.3%	0.3%	-3.6%
United States of America	-0.6%	0.2%	0.3%	-0.1%
Venezuela (Bolivarian Republic of)	-0.3%	-0.2%	-0.3%	-4.5%
Viet Nam	-0.4%	0.0%	0.6%	-2.5%
Yemen	-0.4%	-0.4%	0.0%	-3.3%
South Africa	-1.2%	0.1%	-0.1%	0.5%
Zambia	0.3%	-0.2%	-0.3%	
Zimbabwe	-1.7%	-1.8%	-1.8%	

4 Reconciling inclusive wealth and Piketty

Natural capital and wealth in the 21st century

Edward B. Barbier

Introduction

In his book *Capital in the Twenty-First Century*, Piketty (2014) documents the rise in the wealth-income ratios over 1970 to 2010 for eight high-income economies – the United States, Japan, Germany, France, the United Kingdom, Italy, Canada and Australia. For each of these countries, the wealth-income ratio has increased from 200–400% in 1970 to 400–600% in 2010. In addition, the rise in this ratio has been accompanied by another important trend. Over the past four decades, much of the accumulated capital in rich countries is predominantly private wealth, and it comprises largely financial and industrial capital and urban real estate (i.e. housing). The effect of these trends has contributed to what Piketty (2014, pp. 193–194) describes as the "financialization" of the global economy, and as a result, increasing wealth and income inequality:

> Broadly speaking, the 1970s and 1980s witnessed an extensive "financialization" of the global economy, which altered the structure of wealth in the sense that the total amount of financial assets and liabilities held by various sectors (household, corporations, government agencies) increased more rapidly than net wealth. In most countries, the total amount of financial assets and liabilities in the early 1970s did not exceed four to five years of national income. By 2010, this amount had increased to ten to fifteen years of national income (in the United States, Japan, Germany and France in particular) and to twenty years of national income in Britain, which set an absolute historical record.

To construct these measures of wealth and income for 1970 to 2010, Piketty (2014) uses official national accounts for each country, following the UN System of National Accounts (SNA). Wealth is defined conventionally as market value "national wealth," which can be decomposed into domestic capital (including land and real estate) and net foreign assets.[1] Income is "net-of-depreciation national income," which is the sum of gross domestic product and net foreign income, less any domestic capital depreciation. Similarly, the national saving flow that adds to wealth is also measured net of capital depreciation.

As pointed out by Barbier (2015, 2017), the SNA approach used by Piketty (2014) to estimate wealth, net income and net savings does not include the depreciation in natural resources essential to domestic production and income, such as fossil fuels, minerals and forests. These resources are important sources of "natural" capital, and the value of their net depletion should also be deducted from annual income and savings (Arrow et al. 2012; Hamilton and Clemens 1999; Hartwick 1977, 1990; Solow 1986; Weitzman 1976; World Bank 2011). The rationale is intuitive: if we use up more of energy, mineral and forest resources to produce additional economic output today, then we have less natural capital for production tomorrow; thus, net national income and savings today should also account for any natural capital depreciation.

Accounting for natural capital depletion in wealth accounts is, of course, a key and familiar contribution of the inclusive wealth approach, as highlighted in previous Inclusive Wealth Reports (UNU-IHDP-UNEP 2012, 2014). Barbier (2017) has shown that it is possible to reconcile this approach of accounting for natural capital depreciation with Piketty's method of estimating net national income and saving. Specifically, this leads to two key indicators: the net national saving rate adjusted for natural capital depreciation, and the ratio of this saving rate with respect to the long-run average annual growth in adjusted net national income per capita. Using World Bank data, Barbier (2017) applies these two indicators to examine the impacts of depreciation of key natural resources, such as fossil fuels, minerals and forests, on the accumulation of adjusted net wealth over 1970–2013 for the same eight rich countries analysed by Piketty (2014) and Piketty and Zucman (2014), and for comparison, over 1979–2013 for 95 low and middle-income economies. Whereas in developing economies capital accumulation has largely kept pace with rising natural capital depletion, in the rich countries adjusted net savings have fallen to converge with the rate of natural capital depreciation, suggesting less compensation by net increases in other capital.

In sum, natural capital depreciation clearly matters for wealth accumulation and long-run wealth-income ratios in all economies, including rich countries. Moreover, the result has important implications for Piketty's explanation for growing global inequality. If overall wealth accumulation net of natural capital depreciation is slowing in rich countries, then the "financialization" of economies observed by Piketty (2014) will continue to worsen wealth and income inequality.

The purpose of this chapter is to explore further the implications of reconciling the inclusive wealth approach of Barbier (2017) to adjusting net income and savings for natural capital depreciation with Piketty's method of estimating long-run trends in wealth-income ratios. In addition, the analysis is extended from Piketty's original group of eight rich countries to 30 high-income economies that are members of the Organization for Economic Cooperation and Development (OECD) over 1970 to 2014. Evidence suggests that growing income and wealth inequality has been pervasive in all OECD economies (OECD 2011), and thus determining whether natural capital depreciation impacts long-run wealth accumulation in these economies may be an important factor underlying this trend.

This chapter also extends the analysis by Barbier (2017) of these natural capital depreciation, net income and net savings trends to 113 low and middle-income (developing) economies from 1970 to 2014. For comparison, the sub-group of 26 low-income countries is also analysed separately, which turn out to display different trends over 1970–2014 than either all developing or the rich OECD economies.

The main findings are that, although over the past four decades the rate of natural capital depreciation has been on average five times larger in developing countries than in the rich OECD economies, in low and middle-income economies other forms of capital investments have largely compensated for the rising natural capital depletion that has occurred since the late 1990s. In contrast, in the rich countries, the rate of adjusted net savings has converged to the rate of natural capital depreciation. For low-income economies, adjusted net wealth accumulation fell on average each year at a rate that is four times more than long-run growth, although since 2000 this trend may have been reversing. If this rising trend continues, then low-income countries could experience accumulation in net adjusted wealth at a faster pace than long-run per capita income growth.

Over the past 40 years there may have been substantial accumulation of wealth relative to income in rich economies, but as this accumulation has proceeded, natural capital depreciation is being compensated less and less each year by net increases in other forms of capital. The overall implications are that, given that stocks of natural resources are depleted for current production and wealth accumulation, a measure of national wealth that excludes natural capital depreciation likely exaggerates the actual increase in an economy's wealth over time, especially in those countries where accumulation of other forms of wealth is failing to compensate for diminishing natural capital. This suggests that income and wealth inequality may be worsening in rich countries, and in the global economy generally, as emphasized by Piketty (2014).

Conventional versus adjusted net income accounting

Because official national account statistics do not routinely account for changes in stocks of natural capital – even fossil fuels, minerals, forests and similar natural resources that can be bought and sold on markets – it is difficult to measure directly long-run trends in the natural capital/national income ratio for an economy. However, it is possible to indicate how natural resource depreciation affects wealth accumulation, through extending the approach to measuring national wealth developed by Piketty (2014) and Piketty and Zucman (2014).[2]

The appendix to this chapter outlines how this can be done, which is summarized here. Let W_t denote the market value of national wealth at time t, and Υ_t be conventionally defined net national income (NNI), which is gross national income less any depreciation in domestic capital assets (e.g. factories, machines, equipment, buildings, etc.) that occurs in producing national income each year. Similarly, S_t is conventional net national savings (NNS) at time t, which is gross savings also adjusted for domestic capital depreciation. Consequently, Piketty (2014) and Piketty and Zucman (2014) focus on three important relationships among these conventional indicators:

- Net wealth accumulation: $W_{t+1} - W_t = S_t$
- Net national saving rate: $S_t / \Upsilon_t = s_t$
- Wealth-income ratio: $W_t / \Upsilon_t = \beta_t$.

However, as argued by Barbier (2017), an economy also contains a stock of available natural resources for production, with market value at time t of $\tilde{N}_t \geq 0$. This suggests that the *adjusted net wealth* of the economy is $W_t^* = W_t + \tilde{N}_t$. As wealth now includes an endowment of natural capital, net national income Υ_t and net national savings S_t need to be adjusted for natural capital depreciated through its use in production over t and $t+1$. Let Υ_t^* and S_t^* represent the adjustments to net national income (ANNI) and savings (ANNS) for any natural capital depreciation, respectively. This leads to three additional indicators:

- Adjusted net wealth accumulation: $W_{t+1}^* - W_t^* = S_t^*$
- Adjusted net national saving rate: $S_t^*/\Upsilon_t^* = s_t^*$
- Natural capital depreciation rate: $\left(\tilde{N}_{t+1} - \tilde{N}_t\right)/\Upsilon_t^* = n_t^*$.

Figure 4.1 outlines how the conventional economic indicators of gross and net national income can be adjusted for natural capital depreciation to derive *adjusted net national income* (ANNI). Similarly, Figure 4.2 shows how conventional gross and net savings can be adjusted to determine *adjusted net national savings* (ANNS).

Barbier (2017) also suggests that the savings rate s_t^* can also be expressed as a ratio with respect to the long-run average growth in ANNI per capita, $\bar{g}^*$. This leads to another indicator:

- Saving-ANNI growth ratio: $s_t^*/\bar{g}^*$.

Trends in this ratio indicate how the rate of wealth accumulation over time, $W_{t+1}^* - W_t^*/\Upsilon_t^*$, compares with the long-run growth rate of an economy.

The rest of this chapter explores long-run trends in s_t^*, n_t^* and $s_t^*/\bar{g}^*$ for high-income OECD, developing and low-income economies and the implications of these trends for the wealth and income inequality arguments of Piketty (2014). However, first we show the key trends that lead Piketty to conclude that inequality has been worsening in the major rich countries and the global economy.

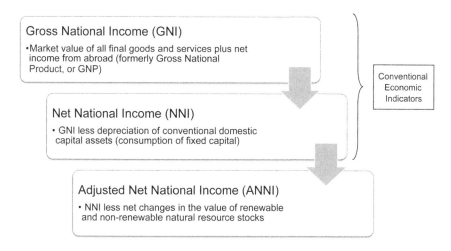

Figure 4.1 Net national income (NNI) adjusted for natural capital depreciation

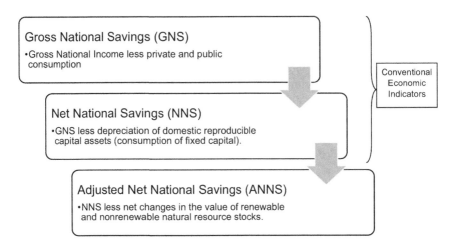

Figure 4.2 Net national savings (NNS) adjusted for natural capital depreciation

Financialization and inequality

Piketty (2014) argues that rising wealth and income inequality is attributed to several important features in the pattern of wealth accumulation in the world economy. First, the ratio of conventionally measured national wealth to income has increased steadily over 1970 to 2010 for the eight richest economies. Figure 4.3 recreates these trends in the wealth-income ratio $W_t/Y_t = \beta_t$ for these countries. For the past four decades the average trend in the wealth-income ratio (dotted line) for this group of wealthy economies has been rising. In 1970, wealth ranged from two to four years (200% to 400%) of national income for these countries, and by 2010 wealth was four to six years (400% to 600%) of income.

Piketty (2014) also notes that national wealth in rich countries is predominantly private wealth, and it comprises largely financial and industrial capital as well as urban real estate (i.e. housing). In contrast, agricultural land is no longer a significant share of wealth in these economies. In particular, the ratio of financial assets to national income has risen markedly, which Piketty calls the extensive "financialization" of rich countries and thus the global economy. Figure 4.4 replicates Piketty's trends in the financial asset-income ratio in rich economies from 1960–2010.[3]

Especially since the 1980s, the financial asset share of national income in all wealthy economies has risen sharply (see Figure 4.4). In 1980, this share amounted to four to nine years (400% to 900%) of income in these countries. By 2010, financial assets accounted for seven years (700%) of national income in Australia, ten to 15 years of income in the United States, Japan and Germany, and 20 years in the United Kingdom. As can be seen from comparing Figures 4.3 and 4.4, the financial asset share of national income has risen much more quickly than the overall wealth-income ratio in rich countries. It is this extensive and rapid "financialization" of the global structure of wealth that Piketty (2014) argues is the main cause of the jump in the growing income and wealth inequality in recent decades. In particular, the

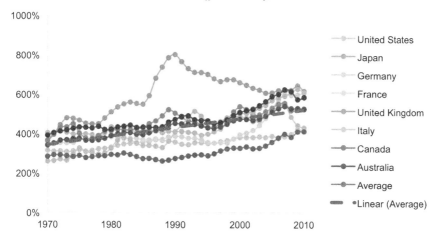

Figure 4.3 Wealth-income ratios in rich countries, 1970–2010

Source: Piketty and Zucman (2014), Appendix Table A1: National wealth-national income ratio 1870–2010 (annual series), available at http://piketty.pse.ens.fr/fr/capitalisback.

Note: Financial assets are the total amount of financial assets and liabilities held by various sectors (household, corporations, government agencies) of an economy.

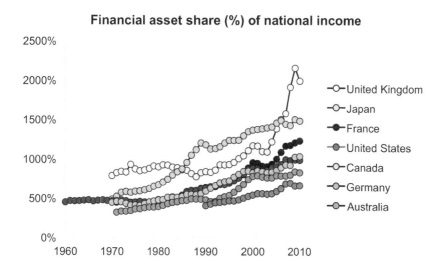

Figure 4.4 Financial asset-income ratios in rich countries, 1960–2010

Source: Piketty and Zucman (2014), Appendix Table A30: Gross financial assets of all domestic sectors 1960–2010 (% of national income), available at http://piketty.pse.ens.fr/fr/capitalisback.

Table 4.1 Increase in wealth of the world's rich, 1987–2013

	Wealth or income in:		Average annual growth (%) 1987–2013
	1980	*2013*	
The richest billionaires[a]	$3.4 billion	$32.3 billion	6.8%
Billionaires[b]	$1.6 billion	$14.0 billion	6.4%
Average world wealth per adult	$26,065	$76,628	2.1%
Average world income per adult	$7,759	$19,187	1.4%
World adult population	2.85 billion	4.68 billion	1.9%
World gross domestic product (GDP)	$22,119 billion	$89,719 billion	3.3%

Source: Thomas Piketty. 2014. *Capital in the Twenty-First Century.* Harvard University Press, Cambridge, MA, Table 12.1 and Supplementary Table S12.3 http://piketty.pse.ens.fr/capital21c.
   All values are in US dollars, and adjusted net of inflation (2.3% per year from 1987 to 2013).
a About 30 adults out of 3 billion in the 1980s, and 45 adults out of 4.5 billion in 2010.
b About 150 adults out of 3 billion in the 1980s, and 225 adults out of 4.5 billion in 2010.

increasing gap between rich and poor is due to the increasing wealth of the world's rich, who benefitted most from the financialization of the world economy.

For example, based on estimates by Piketty (2014) compiled from data on billionaires' wealth in *Forbes* magazine, Table 4.1 indicates how the wealth of the very rich increased from 1987 to 2013 compared to average world wealth per adult. The richest billionaires in the world consisted of 30 adults out of 3 billion people in the 1980s, and their average wealth was US$3.4 billion in 1980. Their accumulated assets grew each year by 6.8% to 2013, totalling US$32.3 billion. Billionaires numbered 150 adults out of 3 billion in the 1980s, and their average wealth grew at 6.4% per year between 1987 and 2013, from US$1.6 billion to US$14.0 billion. In comparison, average world wealth per adult increased by only 2.1% annually from 1987 to 2013, and average income per person by just 1.4%. Thus, the wealth of the global rich appears to be growing much faster than that of the average individual.

Most analysts agree that, although data on long-run trends are available for only a handful of countries, the wealth of the super-rich – the wealthiest 1% of all adults – has been increasing since the early 1970s for some economies and since 1980 for others.[4] More importantly, worldwide:

• The top 1% today account for almost half of the all the wealth in the world,
• The richest 10% own 87% of all assets, and
• The lower half of the global population possess less than 1% of global wealth.[5]

Wealth inequality is not only continuing to rise but also spreading throughout the world economy. Table 4.2 depicts the level of inequality in 46 major economies and

Table 4.2 Trends in wealth inequality across countries, 2000–2014

	Change in wealth share of the top decile, 2000–2014						
	Rapid fall	*Fall*	*Slight fall*	*Flat*	*Slight rise*	*Rise*	*Rapid rise*
Top decile wealth share, 2014							
> 70% Very high inequality (US ca. 1910)		Malaysia Philippines	Switzerland	Peru *South Africa* Thailand *United States*		*Brazil* *Indonesia*	*Argentina* Egypt Hong Kong *India* *Russia* *Turkey*
> 60% High inequality (US ca. 1950)	Poland *Saudi Arabia*	Colombia *Mexico*	Denmark Germany	Austria Norway Sweden	Chile	Czech Republic Israel	*China* *South Korea* Taiwan
> 50% Medium inequality (Europe ca. 1980)		*Canada* *France* New Zealand Singapore		Australia Finland Greece Ireland *Italy* Netherlands Portugal	United Arab Emirates	*United Kingdom*	Spain
< 50% Low inequality			*Japan*	Belgium			

Source: Markus Stierli, Anthony Shorrocks, Jim Davies, Rodrigo Lluberas and Antonios Koutsoukis. 2014. *Global Wealth Report 2014*. Credit Suisse Research Institute, Zurich, Table 1, p. 30 and Table 2, p. 33.

Notes: The top decile is the wealthiest 10% of all adults.
Forty-six countries, with the Group of 20 (G20) countries indicated in italics. The members of the G20 include 19 countries (Argentina, Australia, Brazil, Canada, China, France, Germany, India, Indonesia, Italy, Japan, Mexico, Russia, Saudi Arabia, South Africa, South Korea, Turkey, the UK and the US), plus the European Union.

also indicates whether the level has been rising or falling from 2000 to 2014. Wealth inequality is high or very high in 30 of these countries. Moreover, since 2000, nine countries have experienced a rapid rise in inequality, five have seen a rise and three a slight rise. Of particular concern is that nine of these countries are members of the Group of 20, which comprises the largest and most populous economies. Wealth inequality also appears to be a problem for a number of developing economies, although for most of them it appears to be unchanged or falling.

If natural capital depreciation does matter for long-run wealth accumulation in all economies, including rich countries, then there may be further implications for Piketty's explanation of growing global inequality. Current measures of national wealth, income and saving that excludes natural capital depreciation likely exaggerate the actual increase in an economy's wealth over time, especially in those countries where accumulation of other forms of wealth is failing to compensate for diminishing natural capital. This suggests that income and wealth inequality may be even worse than in the global economy generally, as emphasized by Piketty (2014) and other scholars. To examine whether this is the case, the next section explores long-run trends in s_t^*, n_t^* and $s_t^*/\bar{g}^*$ for high-income OECD, developing and low-income economies.

Measuring adjusted net national income, saving and growth

The World Bank's World Development Indicators contain time-series of the value of net natural resource depletion, net national saving rates and adjusted net national income from 1970 to 2014 for most countries of the world (World Bank 2017). Using these data, it is possible to construct long-run trends in the natural capital depreciation rate n_t^*, the adjusted net savings rate s_t^*, and the saving-ANNI growth ratio $s_t^*/\bar{g}^*$ for high-income OECD, developing and low-income economies.

The World Bank defines the value of net natural resource depletion as the sum of net forest, fossil fuel and mineral depletion.[6] Net forest depletion is unit resource rents times the excess of round wood harvest over natural growth. Energy depletion is the ratio of the value of the stock of energy resources to the remaining reserve lifetime (capped at 25 years). It covers coal, crude oil and natural gas. Mineral depletion is the ratio of the value of the stock of mineral resources to the remaining reserve lifetime (capped at 25 years). It includes tin, gold, lead, zinc, iron, copper, nickel, silver, bauxite and phosphate.

The World Development Indicators (WDI) provide annual estimates over 1970–2014 of the World Bank's aggregate value of net natural resource depletion as a percentage of gross national income (GNI) for the eight high-income countries. Converting this estimate to natural resource depletion as a share of adjusted net national income (constant 2010 $), which is the natural capital depreciation rate n_t^*, involves multiplying the WDI's annual measure of net natural resource depletion as a percentage of gross national income (GNI) by its measure of GNI (constant 2010 $), and then dividing the result by the WDI's annual estimates of adjusted net national income (constant 2010 $).

Annual net national savings, which are gross national savings less the value of consumption of fixed capital, are also calculated as a percentage of GNI in the WDI. To estimate the adjusted net savings rate s_t^* requires first adjusting the annual net national savings rate for natural capital depreciation as a share of GNI, multiplying by GNI (constant 2010 \$), and then dividing by adjusted net national income (constant 2010 \$). Finally, the average annual growth of adjusted net national income per capita over 1970–2014, which is already estimated in the WDI, serves as the measure of $\bar{g}^*$.

OECD high-income countries

Figure 4.5 depicts the estimates over 1970–2014 of n_t^* and s_t^* averaged across 30 high-income countries that are also members of the Organization of Economic Cooperation and Development (OECD). They include the eight countries originally analysed by

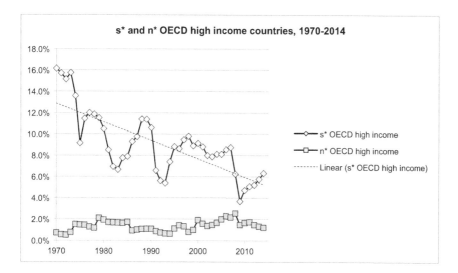

Figure 4.5 Adjusted net savings and natural capital depreciation in OECD high-income countries, 1970–2014

Notes: The 30 OECD high-income countries are Australia, Austria, Belgium Canada, Chile, Czech Republic, Denmark, Estonia, Finland, France, Germany, Greece, Hungary, Ireland, Israel, Italy, Japan, Korea Republic, Netherlands, New Zealand, Norway, Poland, Portugal, Slovak Republic, Slovenia, Spain, Sweden, Switzerland, United Kingdom and United States. High-income economies are those in which 2015 GNI per capita was \$12,476 or more.

The data are based on the World Development Indicators (World Bank 2017). The measure of s^* is gross national savings less the value of consumption of fixed capital and the value of net natural resource depletion as a % of adjusted net national income (constant 2010 US\$); the measure of n^* is annual value of net natural resource depletion as a % of adjusted net national income (constant 2010 US\$).

Over 1970–2014, the average s^* for these eight countries was 9.1%, and average n^* was 1.4%. The margin of error (95% confidence level) associated with the sample mean for s^* and n^* was 1.7 and 1.2, respectively.

Piketty (2014) – the United States, Japan, Germany, France, the United Kingdom, Italy, Canada and Australia.

The adjusted net savings rate for these countries declined considerably during these four decades. It was around 15%–16% in the early 1970s but from the mid-1990s to mid-2000s hovered around 8%–10%. The savings rate fell to below 4% during the Great Recession, but has recovered since to above 6%. On average from 1970 to 2014, s_t^* was 9.1% (see Figure 4.5). In contrast, natural capital depreciation has remained between 1% and 2% of adjusted net national income for most of the past 40 years. Thus, it appears that s_t^* and n_t^* have been converging for the rich economies of the world. The long-run fall in the adjusted net savings rate indicates that, in these economies, there is less accumulation of other forms of capital each year to compensate for ongoing natural capital depreciation. The result is that the overall annual accumulation in adjusted net wealth relative to income has been trending downwards since the 1970s.

Figure 4.6 shows the estimate in the saving-ANNI growth ratio $s_t^*/\bar{g}^*$ averaged for the 30 OECD high-income economies over 1970–2014. For illustrative purposes, the figure also includes the trend in the (conventional) capital-income ratio $\beta_t = W_t/Y_t$ averaged for the eight rich countries over 1970–2010 that was estimated by Piketty and Zucman (2014). Finally, Figure 4.6 also includes the average $s_t^*/\bar{g}^*$ ratio over the four decades.

The trend in β_t depicted in Figure 4.6 confirms Piketty's finding that the capital-income ratio for the eight wealthiest countries has increased steadily over 1970 to 2010. In 1970, their average capital-income ratio was around 340% (i.e. more than three years) of national income, and has risen to 525% (more than five years) of national income in 2010.[7]

In contrast, the saving-ANNI growth ratio for all 30 OECD high-income countries displays a distinctly downward trend. In the early 1970s, this ratio was around 700%, which suggests that the annual rate of adjusted net wealth accumulation was more than seven times the long-run average growth rate for the 30 countries over 1970–2014. But since the mid-2000s, the $s_t^*/\bar{g}^*$ ratio has fallen below 300%, which indicates that the rate of adjusted net wealth accumulation each year has been less than three times the growth rate. On average over 1970–2014, the saving-ANNI growth ratio was 422%, i.e. the rate of adjusted net wealth accumulation each year was four times long-run growth.

The falling trends in s_t^* and $s_t^*/\bar{g}^*$ depicted in Figures 4.5 and 4.6 indicate that the rate of net national saving adjusted for natural capital depreciation has declined even faster than any slowdown in long-run growth in rich economies from 1970 to 2014. This could have implications for long-run adjusted net wealth relative to income in these countries. For example, it is possible that the decline in saving-ANNI growth ratio over the past four decades in OECD high-income countries will continue into future years. If so, the rate of net wealth accumulation relative to growth will continue to fall well below the average rate of 422% over 1970–2014. Verifying this possible long-run trend will require more analysis of these trends in the coming years.

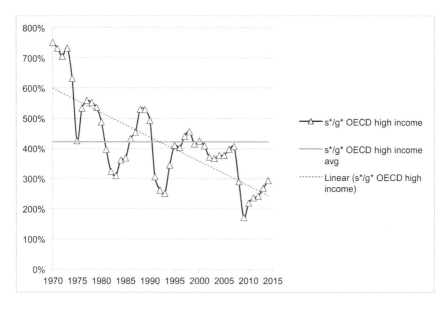

Figure 4.6 Wealth-income accumulation relative to growth in OECD high-income countries, 1970–2014

The 30 OECD high-income countries are Australia, Austria, Belgium Canada, Chile, Czech Republic, Denmark, Estonia, Finland, France, Germany, Greece, Hungary, Ireland, Israel, Italy, Japan, Korea Republic, Netherlands, New Zealand, Norway, Poland, Portugal, Slovak Republic, Slovenia, Spain, Sweden, Switzerland, United Kingdom and United States. High-income economies are those in which 2015 GNI per capita was $12,476 or more.

β is the capital/income ratio averaged for eight countries over 1970–2010, based on the national income-national wealth annual data series in Table A1 of the online technical appendix accompanying Piketty and Zucman (2014), available at http://piketty.pse.ens.fr/en/capitalis-back (Accessed 12 June 2014). The eight countries are the United States, Japan, Germany, France, United Kingdom, Italy, Canada and Australia.

The data for constructing the s^*/g^* ratio are based on the World Development Indicators (World Bank 2017). The measure of s^* is gross national savings less the value of consumption of fixed capital and the value of net natural resource depletion as a % of adjusted net national income (constant 2010 US$); the measure of g^* is average annual growth of net national income per capita adjusted for the value of net natural resource depletion (constant 2010 US$).

Over 1970–2014, the average s^* for these eight countries was 9.1%, and g^* was 2.1%; consequently, the average s^*/g^* ratio for this period was 422%. The margin of error (95% confidence level) associated with the sample mean for s^* and g^* was 1.7 and 0.5, respectively.

Developing countries

In comparison, very different trends in s_t^*, n_t^* and $s_t^*/\bar{g}^*$ have occurred for low and middle-income countries over the past few decades.

Figure 4.7 indicates the average annual rates of adjusted net saving s_t^* and natural capital depreciation n_t^* for 113 developing economies from 1970 to 2014. Both rates

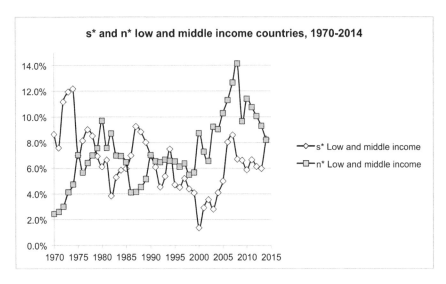

Figure 4.7 Adjusted net saving and natural capital depreciation in developing countries, 1970–2014

Notes: Based on a sample of 113 low and middle-income (or developing) countries, which are economies with 2015 per capita income of $12,475 or less.

The data are based on the World Development Indicators (World Bank 2017). The measure of *s** is gross national savings less the value of consumption of fixed capital and the value of net natural resource depletion as a % of adjusted net national income (constant 2010 US$); the measure of *n** is annual value of net natural resource depletion as a % of adjusted net national income (constant 2010 US$).

Over 1970–2014, the average *s** for these developing countries was 6.5%, and average *n** was 7.3%. The margin of error (95% confidence level) associated with the sample mean for *s** and *n** was 2.1 and 2.8, respectively.

have varied considerably, and there were distinct periods when the adjusted net saving rate has been above then fallen below the rate of natural capital depreciation. For example, in the 1970s the rate of natural capital deprecation was generally below the rate of savings, whereas from the mid-1990s onward the rate of natural capital depreciation has largely exceeded the adjusted net savings rate. One reason is that the natural capital depreciation rate begin rising from around 6% in the 1990s to peak at 14% in 2008, before declining to 8% by 2014. However, since its low point in 2000, the adjusted net savings rate has also increased, and in more recent years has been hovering around 6%–7%. On average from 1970 to 2014, both the rates of natural capital deprecation and adjusted net saving in developing countries were around 6%–7%. These long-run averages, plus the possibly converging trends in the two rates since 2005, indicate that, by and large, increases in other forms of capital may be keeping pace with the large natural capital depreciation occurring in these economies.

Overall, the saving-ANNI growth ratio $s_t^*/\bar{g}^*$ has declined for low and middle-income countries from 1970 to 2014 (Figure 4.8). However, the ratio has been rising since 2000, although in more recent years it has tended to fluctuate around

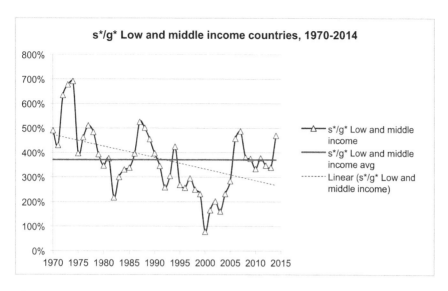

Figure 4.8 Wealth-income accumulation relative to growth in developing countries, 1970–2014

Notes: Based on a sample of 113 low and middle-income (or developing) countries, which are economies with 2015 per capita income of $12,475 or less.

The data for constructing the $s*/g*$ ratio are based on the World Development Indicators (World Bank 2017). The measure of $s*$ is gross national savings less the value of consumption of fixed capital and the value of net natural resource depletion as a % of adjusted net national income (constant 2010 US$); the measure of $g*$ is average annual growth of net national income per capita adjusted for the value of net natural resource depletion (constant 2010 US$).

Over 1970–2014, the average $s*$ for the sample of developing countries was 6.5%, and $g*$ was 1.8%; consequently, the average $s*/g*$ ratio for this period was 371%. The margin of error (95% confidence level) associated with the sample mean for $s*$ and $g*$ was 2.1 and 1.4, respectively.

the long-run average of 371%. This is still slightly lower than the average ratio of 422% over 1970–2014 for the OECD high-income economies (see Figure 4.6). It is unclear whether the long-run average $s_t^*/\bar{g}^*$ ratio for developing countries will rise, as that will require the current trend of accumulating more net wealth relative to increasing income to continue into the future.

Low-income countries

As shown in Figure 4.9, the adjusted net saving rate across 28 low-income economies has averaged 0.1% over 1975–2014, which is much lower than the average rate of 6.5% for s_t^* over 1970–2014 for all 113 developing countries (see Figure 4.7). More-over, for low-income countries, there is still a considerable gap between the long-run adjusted net saving rate and the natural capital depreciation rate, which is 6.9%. Although s_t^* has been rising since 1995 for poor economies, so has n_t^*. The result is that the gap between these two rates is still considerable, and may even be growing.

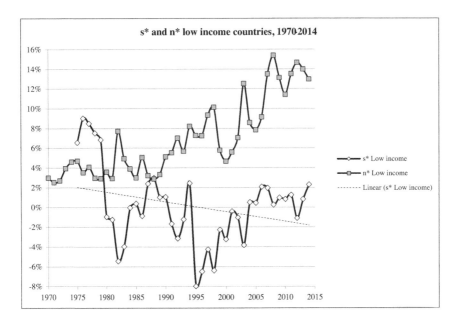

Figure 4.9 Adjusted net saving and natural capital depreciation in low-income countries, 1970–2014

Notes: Based on a sample of 28 low and middle-income (or developing) countries, which are economies with 2015 per capita income of $1,025 or less.

The data are based on the World Development Indicators (World Bank 2017). The measure of *s** is gross national savings less the value of consumption of fixed capital and the value of net natural resource depletion as a % of adjusted net national income (constant 2010 US$); the measure of *n** is annual value of net natural resource depletion as a % of adjusted net national income (constant 2010 US$).

Over 1970–2014, the average *s** for these developing countries was 0.1%, and average *n** was 6.9%. The margin of error (95% confidence level) associated with the sample mean for *s** and *n** was 4.7 and 4.3, respectively.

Since the mid-2000s the adjusted net saving rate for low-income countries has fluctuated between 0% and 2%, whereas the rate of natural capital depreciation has risen from 8%–9% to around 13%–15%.

These trends in s_t^* and n_t^* have important implications for long-run wealth-income accumulation relative to growth in poor economies (Figure 4.10). First, the long-run average growth in ANNI per capita $\bar{g}^*$ was only 0.5% for low-income countries over 1975–2014, which was much lower than the long-run rate for all developing countries of 1.8% (see Figure 4.8). Consequently, the average ratio of adjusted net saving to this growth rate over this period was only 24%, and there have been long stretches over the past four decades when this ratio has been significantly negative (see Figure 4.10). However, since 2000 the $s_t^*/\bar{g}^*$ ratio for the 28 low-income economies has been rising, and over 2005–2014 has averaged 190%. If this positive trend continues, then low-income countries will continue to experience accumulation in net adjusted wealth at a faster pace than long-run per capita income growth.

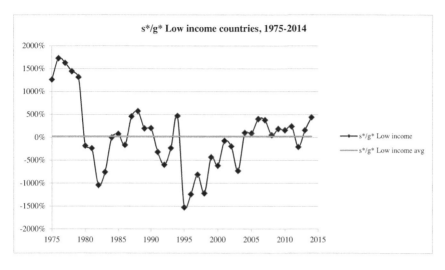

Figure 4.10 Wealth-income accumulation relative to growth in low-income countries, 1975–2014

Notes: Based on a sample of 28 low and middle-income (or developing) countries, which are economies with 2015 per capita income of $1,025 or less.

The data for constructing the s^*/g^* ratio are based on the World Development Indicators (World Bank 2017). The measure of s^* is gross national savings less the value of consumption of fixed capital and the value of net natural resource depletion as a % of adjusted net national income (constant 2010 US$); the measure of g^* is average annual growth of net national income per capita adjusted for the value of net natural resource depletion (constant 2010 US$).

Over 1975–2014, the average s^* for the sample of developing countries was 0.1%, and g^* was 0.5%; consequently, the average s^*/g^* ratio for this period was 24%. The margin of error (95% confidence level) associated with the sample mean for s^* and g^* was 4.7 and 1.0, respectively.

To summarize, the high and rising rate of natural capital depreciation in low-income countries remains a concern. Although the rate of adjusted net saving has been rising since 1995, the fact that it remains very low – less than 2% – implies that in poor countries accumulation of other forms of wealth is not keeping pace with ongoing natural capital depreciation. The increase in wealth-income accumulation relative to growth in poor economies is encouraging, but this is in large part due to the very low growth in ANNI per capita over the long-run (0.1%) in these countries. Reducing natural capital depreciation and increasing accumulation of other forms of capital is essential to improving long-run net wealth accumulation in poor economies over the long-term.

Implications for wealth-income ratios and inequality

As the above analysis indicates, the wealth-income ratios for OECD high-income economies over the past four decades are clearly influenced by the depreciation of key natural resources essential to domestic production, such as fossil fuels, minerals and forests. Although there may have been substantial accumulation of wealth relative to income, natural capital depreciation in this rich economies is being compensated less and less each year by net increases in other forms of capital. This implies that wealth accumulation, net of natural capital depreciation, has declined as a share of national income. As depicted in Figure 4.5, this trend has been steadily falling over the past four decades.

If these trends for rich countries continue into the future, there will be even less net wealth creation relative to growth in these economies. If this is accompanied by increased financialization as observed by Piketty (2014), then the result will be worsening wealth and income inequality. Recall that Piketty finds that national wealth in rich countries is predominantly private wealth, and it comprises largely financial and industrial capital as well as urban real estate (i.e. housing), and it is this concentration of wealth that is the source of much of the inequality in these countries and the global economy. If overall wealth accumulation net of natural capital depreciation as a share of national income is falling while private financial wealth is rising, then the gap between rich and poor will continue to widen in all economies (see Tables 4.1 and 4.2). Not surprising, studies of inequality in OECD countries already suggest that the problem is a serious one for these economies (OECD 2011).

For developing countries, although net wealth accumulation appears to have increased relative to income in recent years (see Figure 4.7), the high rate of natural capital depreciation remains a concern. Over the long-run, the current rate of over 7% across all low and middle-income countries may adversely affect their net wealth accumulation. The overall trend of saving to ANNI growth has also been negative over the past four decades (see Figure 4.8). Finally, as indicated in Table 4.2, wealth inequality appears to be a problem for some developing economies. High rates of natural capital depreciation that reduce net wealth accumulation in low and middle-income countries will only exacerbate this problem.

The high and rising rate of natural capital depreciation in low-income countries is a major concern (see Figure 4.9). The long-run average rate is around 7%, but in recent years it has climbed from 8%–9% to 13%–15%. The gap with the current adjusted net saving rate, which is 0%–2%, is therefore considerable, and indicates that investment in other forms of wealth is failing to compensate for the high rate of natural capital loss in poor economies. Not surprisingly, the long-run average growth in ANNI per capita (0.5%) and net saving relative to this growth (24%) is extremely low for these countries. Although it is difficult to determine the implications for wealth inequality in low-income economies, the lack of progress in net wealth accumulation does not bode well for either fostering sustainable development or reducing any inequality.

Conclusion

This chapter has demonstrated that it is possible to reconcile the inclusive wealth approach with Piketty's efforts to analyse long-run trends in wealth-income ratios and the composition of wealth for major economies. Moreover, given improved data sources, it is feasible to extend such an analysis to a wider set of economies. Here, the approach of adjusting to net national saving, income and growth for natural capital depreciation has been extended to 30 high-income economies that are members of the Organization for Economic Cooperation and Development (OECD) over 1970 to 2014. We have also examined the resulting implications for net wealth accumulation and inequality that have been observed by Piketty (2014) and other studies.

These trends have several important implications. For the OECD high-income countries, the long-run convergence of adjusted net savings rates with natural capital depreciation rates should raise concerns about overall wealth creation and growing inequality in these economies. For these countries, policies to encourage more economy-wide investment in other forms of capital to raise adjusted net saving rates, and especially the long-run rate of net wealth accumulation relative to growth, are urgently needed. Although human capital accumulation is not included in the analysis of this chapter, there is also concern that investments in skills, training and education in these economies are lagging in these economies, both absolutely and relative to natural resource use (Barbier 2015; Goldin and Katz 2008; OECD 2011).

For developing countries, although net wealth accumulation appears to have kept pace with income growth in recent years, the high rate of natural capital depreciation is worrisome, especially in low-income economies where the problem appears to be worsening. Over the long-run, these high rates of depreciation are bound to affect adversely the sustainability of development efforts and to worsen inequality. A key focus of policies should be to improve the efficiency and sustainability of natural resource use so that natural capital depreciation in developing countries is diminished substantially. This could be especially important for low-income countries, where reducing natural capital depreciation may prove instrumental to improving the adjusted net wealth-income ratio of these poorer economies over the long-run.

To verify the long-run trends in net national saving, income and income growth adjusted for natural capital depreciation will require long-term data on natural capital stocks as well as depreciation rates. As we develop better measures of natural capital stocks and depreciation for 70–100 years or even longer, other considerations need to be taken into account, such as the role of demographic transitions, total factor productivity changes, appropriate accounting for long-run natural capital asset and price appreciation, and the economic contributions of ecosystems and other environmental assets beyond fossil fuels, minerals and forests (Arrow et al. 2012; Fenichel and Abbott 2014; Greasley et al. 2014).

Finally, the long-run trends identified here confirm a bigger issue, which is explored by Barbier (2015). Namely, the world economy faces two major threats: increasing natural resource degradation and the growing gap between rich and poor. These two threats are symptomatic of a growing structural imbalance in all economies, which is how nature is exploited to create wealth and how it is shared among the population. As argued by Barbier (2015), the root of this imbalance is that natural capital is underpriced, and hence overly exploited, and the resulting proceeds are insufficiently invested in accumulating other forms of wealth, especially human capital. The long-run trends in net national saving, income and income growth analysed for rich and poor economies in this chapter gives some indication of this structural imbalance. We need further development of such indicators – and perhaps others too – to shed further light on the possible links between growing environmental and natural resource scarcity and inequality in all economies.

Appendix
Adjusting conventional national income and savings for natural capital depreciation

Following the approach developed by Barbier (2017), it is possible to modify the conventional income and savings measures used by Piketty (2014) and Piketty and Zucman (2014) to allow for natural capital depreciation.

Following their approach and notation, let W_t denote the market value of national wealth at time t, and S_t is the net national savings flow between time t and $t+1$. In the absence of any capital gains or losses between t and $t+1$, then wealth accumulation is simply $W_{t+1} - W_t = S_t$. If Y_t is net national income (i.e. national income less domestic capital depreciation) at time t, then the corresponding net national saving rate in the economy is $s_t = S_t/Y_t$ and the ratio of wealth (or capital) to income is $\beta_t = W_t/Y_t$.

Suppose that, in addition to W_t, an economy also contains a stock of available natural resources for production, with market value at time t of $\tilde{N}_t \geq 0$. The total wealth of the economy at time t is therefore $W_t^* = W_t + \tilde{N}_t$. As wealth now includes an endowment of natural capital, both net national income and net national savings in time t should be adjusted for any depreciation of natural capital depletion through its use in production over t and $t+1$, net of any changes in the endowment due to new discoveries over the year and also renewable resource growth. Barbier (2017) refer to this modification of Piketty's definition of wealth W_t^* as *adjusted net wealth*.

Let Y_t^* and S_t^* represent the adjustments to net national income and savings for any natural capital depreciation, respectively. It follows that the accumulation in adjusted net wealth between t and $t+1$ is

$$W_{t+1}^* - W_t^* = S_t^*.$$

Dividing both sides by adjusted net national income Y_t^* yields

$$\frac{W_{t+1}^* - W_t^*}{Y_t^*} = \frac{\Delta W^*}{Y_t^*} = s_t^*, \tag{1}$$

where $s_t^* = S_t^*/Y_t^*$ is the net national saving rate adjusted for natural capital depreciation, or the *adjusted net saving* rate. As equation (1) states, s_t^* is an indicator of the annual change in wealth (inclusive of natural capital) relative to net national income (adjusted for natural capital depreciation).[8]

The saving rate s_t^* can also be expressed as a ratio with respect to the long-run average annual growth in adjusted net national income per capita. For any period of T years, the latter growth rate is $\bar{g}^* = \dfrac{1}{T}\sum_{t=0}^{T-1}\dfrac{\Delta \Upsilon_t^*}{\Upsilon_t^*}$. Consequently,

$$\frac{s_t^*}{\bar{g}^*} = \frac{\Delta W^*/\Upsilon_t^*}{\bar{g}^*}. \tag{2}$$

The ratio indicates how annual changes in adjusted net wealth relative to income compare with the average annual income growth per capita over some defined time period of T years. For example, if this growth rate is 2% per year, and adjusted net saving is 10%, then the rate of adjusted net wealth accumulation each year is 500% of long-run growth. However, if the adjusted net saving rate falls to 4%, then the rate of annual wealth accumulation relative to income is only 200% of $\bar{g}^*$. Thus, this ratio is an important indicator as it depicts, over a defined period of T years, how the annual rate of net wealth accumulation compares to long-run growth over that period. Consequently, if there is a discernible trend in the $s_t^*/\bar{g}^*$ ratio, it indicates whether or not adjusted net wealth is accumulating relative to increases in income in economies over the long-term.

Notes

1 See also Piketty and Zucman (2014) for a more detailed modelling approach and investigation of the 1970–2010 wealth trends analysed by Piketty (2014). Note that both Piketty and Zucman (2014) and Piketty (2014) use the terms "national wealth" and "national capital" interchangeably.

2 See the appendix of Barbier (2017), which shows analytically how the one-good wealth accumulation model of Piketty and Zucman (2014) can be modified to allow for natural capital depreciation in the context of intertemporal optimizing behaviour.

3 Piketty (2014) and Piketty and Zucman (2014) estimate financial assets as the total amount of financial assets and liabilities held by various sectors (household, corporations, government agencies) of an economy. Thus, this estimate of financial assets can exceed their measure of national wealth for some countries in some years.

4 See, for example, Alvaredo et al. (2013) and Stierli et al. (2014). The ten countries with long-term wealth inequality data that are the focus of Stierli et al. (2014) are Australia, Denmark, Finland, France, the Netherlands, Norway, Sweden, Switzerland, the United Kingdom and the United States. Alvaredo et al. (2013) also analyse long-term trends for Canada and Japan, but not Denmark, Finland, the Netherlands, Norway and Switzerland.

5 Stierli et al. (2014, p. 13).

6 Further details on this methodology can be found in World Bank (2011) and in the notes accompanying World Bank (2017). Although the depreciation of key natural resources, such as fisheries and fresh water supplies, are missing from this measure, the net depletion of subsoil assets and forests by economies accounts for much of their natural capital used up in current production and wealth accumulation.

7 However, Jones (2015) shows that, when the value of the capital stock for the United States, France and the United Kingdom calculated by Piketty and Zucman (2014) and Piketty (2014) excludes land and housing, the rise in the capital-output ratios for

each of these three countries in recent decades is more gradual. For example, in France, "the rise in the capital-output ratio since 1950 is to a great extent due to housing, which rises from 85 percent of national income in 1950 to 371 percent in 2010" (Jones 2015, p. 41).

8 As shown in the appendix to Barbier (2017), the adjusted net savings rate is also an indicator of the annual change in adjusted net wealth per capita relative to adjusted net national income per capita $s_t^* = \dfrac{\Delta \hat{W}^*}{\hat{Y}_t^*}$, where η_t represents population growth and a "hat" ($\wedge$) indicates a per capita variable.

References

Alvaredo, Facundo, Anthony B. Atkinson, Thomas Piketty and Emmanuel Saez. 2013. "The Top 1 Percent in International and Historical Perspective." *Journal of Economic Perspectives* 27:3–20.

Arrow, Kenneth J., Partha S. Dasgupta, Lawrence H. Goulder, Kevin J. Mumford and Kirsten Oleson. 2012. "Sustainability and the Measurement of Wealth." *Environment and Development Economics* 17(3):317–353.

Barbier, Edward B. 2015. *Nature and Wealth: Overcoming Environmental Scarcities and Inequality.* Palgrave Macmillan, London and New York.

Barbier, Edward B. 2017. "Natural Capital and Wealth in the 21st Century." *Eastern Economic Journal,* 43(3):391–405.

Fenichel, Eli P. and Joshua K. Abbott. 2014. "Natural Capital: From Metaphor to Measurement." *Journal of the Association of Environmental and Resource Economists* 1:1–27.

Goldin, Claudia and Lawrence F. Katz. 2008. *The Race Between Education and Technology.* Harvard University Press, Cambridge, MA.

Greasley, David, Nick Hanley, Jan Kunnas, Eoin McLaughlin, Les Oxley and Paul Warde. 2014. *Journal of Environmental Economics and Management* 67:171–188.

Hamilton, Kirk and Michael Clemens. 1999. "Genuine Savings Rates in Developing Countries." *World Bank Economic Review* 13(2):333–356.

Hartwick, John M. 1977. "Intergenerational Equity and the Investment of Rents from Exhaustible Resources." *American Economic Review* 67(5):972–974.

Hartwick, John M. 1990. "Natural Resources, National Accounting and Economic Depreciation." *Journal of Public Economics* 43:291–304.

Jones, Charles I. 2015. "Pareto and Piketty: The Macroeconomics of Top Income and Wealth Inequality." *Journal of Economic Perspectives* 29:29–46.

Organization for Economic Cooperation and Development (OECD). 2011. *An Overview of Growing Income Inequalities in OECD Countries: Main Findings: Divided We Stand: Why Inequality Keeps Rising.* OECD, Paris.

Piketty, Thomas. 2014. *Capital in the Twenty-First Century.* Harvard University Press, Cambridge, MA.

Piketty, Thomas and Gabriel Zucman. 2014. "Capital is Back: Wealth-Income Ratios in Rich Countries, 1700–2010." *Quarterly Journal of Economics* 129:1255–1310.

Solow, Robert M. 1986. "On the Intergenerational Allocation of Natural Resources." *Scandinavian Journal of Economics* 88(1):141–149.

Stierli, Markus, Anthony Shorrocks, Jim Davies, Rodrigo Lluberas and Antonios Koutsoukis. 2014. *Global Wealth Report 2014.* Credit Suisse Research Institute, Zurich.

United Nations University (UNU)-International Human Dimensions Programme (IHDP) on Global Environmental Change-United Nations Environment Programme (UNEP). 2012. *Inclusive Wealth Report 2014: Measuring Progress Toward Sustainability.* Cambridge University Press, Cambridge and New York.

United Nations University (UNU)-International Human Dimensions Programme (IHDP) on Global Environmental Change-United Nations Environment Programme (UNEP). 2014. *Inclusive Wealth Report 2014: Measuring Progress Toward Sustainability.* Cambridge University Press, Cambridge and New York.

Weitzman, Martin L. 1976. "On the Welfare Significance of National Product in a Dynamic Economy." *Quarterly Journal of Economics* 90(1):156–162.

World Bank. 2011. *The Changing Wealth of Nations: Measuring Sustainable Development in the New Millenium.* The World Bank, Washington, DC.

World Bank. 2017. *World Development Indicators.* The World Bank, Washington, DC. http://databank.worldbank.org/data/reports.aspx?source=world-development-indicators. Accessed on 02/01/2017.

5 Challenges to ecosystem service valuation for wealth accounting

Kristine Grimsrud, Henrik Lindhjem,
David N. Barton, and Ståle Navrud

1. Introduction

The inclusive wealth framework is a tool to analyse "society's sustainability" (Dasgupta and Duraiappah 2012), which may be interpreted as non-declining human well-being over time. Dasgupta and Duraiappah (2012, p. 22) argues that the best index to track human well-being over time is society's wealth, where "wealth is the social worth of an economy's capital assets". Further, the inclusive wealth framework defines the aggregate wealth as the shadow value (or price) of the stocks of all assets of an economy, and suggests that ecosystems should be included as an important form of "natural capital" in this wealth. Shadow values are a key measure to inclusive wealth. Dasgupta and Duraiappah (2012) define the shadow price/value of a capital asset as the monetary measure of the contribution a marginal unit of that asset is forecast to make to human well-being. The shadow value is thus a more comprehensive measure of value than, for example, (unadjusted) market prices. Shadow prices internalize environmental (and other) externalities and capture the substitutability of the capital assets not just in the present period but also in the future. The inclusive wealth framework can accommodate non-linear processes of natural systems and provide early warnings in the process to avert such thresholds from being reached if the shadow prices are estimated using certain valuation methods (e.g. the so-called production function approach).

The major challenge, however, is to estimate the shadow prices of the natural and ecosystem capital assets. For example, we do not have full knowledge of the production functions of life supporting systems. Dasgupta and Duraiappah (2012) recognize that we may never get the shadow prices "right," instead we can simply try to estimate the range in which they lie. The next best solution, they argue, is to use shadow prices based on willingness to pay measures, while recognizing that these shadow prices may not capture threshold effects of an ecosystem (Farley 2012).

The inclusive wealth accounting framework proposes to expand the net domestic product (NDP), which equals the gross domestic product (GDP) adjusted for appreciation/depreciation of capital, as is currently measured in most national economies, in two ways:

1 The NDP should include the depreciation or appreciation of human and natural capital (i.e. natural resources and ecosystems) as well.
2 The basis for valuing the capital stocks should be shadow prices. Exchange values as is currently used in statistical offices may be used if the exchange values are a good approximation to the shadow prices.

In the System of National Accounts (SNA) goods are valued using exchange values when such values are available. The reason is that national accounts aim to provide a measure of production, not welfare as such, and therefore exclude consumer surplus. While the exchange value often is the market price, it is important to be aware of some slight nuances between the concept of a market price and an exchange value. Market prices depend on level of scarcity and on market conditions. The following definition has been used for market price: "Market prices are the amounts of money that willing purchasers pay to acquire goods, services or assets from willing sellers" (EC et al. 2009, para 3. 119). In national accounting one refers to "exchange values" and not to "market prices" where an exchange value is "the value at which goods, services and assets are exchanged regardless of the prevailing market conditions" (Obst et al. 2016).

The inclusive wealth accounting framework and the System of Environmental Economic Accounting (SEEA) (United Nations et al. 2014a) of the UN have several challenges in common in terms of valuing natural resources and ecosystems. Both accounting frameworks have as a goal to account for the importance of ecosystem and natural capital stocks to society. SEEA aims to better account for the relationships between the economy and the environment and the stock of environmental assets and how environmental assets benefit humanity. The inclusive wealth framework considers the impact of changes in capital stocks on human welfare. A major difference between the two accounting frameworks, is that inclusive wealth requires shadow prices for valuing capital stocks while SEEA requires exchange values in valuing capital stocks. Exchange values are required by the latter to be consistent with the accounting framework of the System of National Accounts (SNA), which countries use to estimate the asset value of produced capital stocks.

Here we focus on the SEEA system for ecosystem accounting, SEEA Experimental Ecosystem Accounting (SEEA EEA) (United Nations et al. 2014b). SEEA EEA has a goal to account for the contribution of ecosystems to production and consumption of economic units including households – where the concept of production and consumption is broader than the standard SNA to include all types of contributions from ecosystems to economic units (Obst 2017, pers. comm.). Both the inclusive wealth framework and the SEEA EEA framework rely on non-market valuation methods for ecosystem assets. SEEA EEA requires that the non-market valuation methods are consistent with the methods used in the field of accounting. The inclusive wealth framework has in past reports drawn more generally on the non-market valuation methods used in environmental economics, and so far, a large number of studies using these methods have been performed. Thus, there is a need to clarify and bridge the gap between the disciplines of accounting and environmental economics when it comes to non-market valuation.

At the same time, there are challenges with the non-market valuation methods that are accepted within both the accounting and the environmental economics communities. Since many of the challenges with using the valuation methods are the same for both accounting frameworks, we will discuss some of the progress that has been made on meeting these challenges in the last version of the SEEA EEA (United Nations 2014b) and the associated draft Technical Recommendations (United Nations 2017).[1] As development and practical implementation and testing of SEEA EEA are moving forward, many of the measurement challenges with valuation of ecosystem services will become better understood and potential solutions are already being discussed. This progress of SEEA EEA is of great relevance for addressing many of the measurement challenges within the inclusive wealth framework (Perrings 2012). A criticism from the accounting community of the various forms of "green accounting" and different indicators proposed to measure macroeconomic welfare in the economic literature, where inclusive wealth is one of several such indicators, has been that they are situated at a very "high level of abstraction without searching any longer for any relationship to actual national accounting measurements" (Vanoli 2005; Obst et al. 2016).

In this chapter we provide an overview of recent progress on the SEEA. In Section 3 we discuss the inclusions of spatially explicit physical and monetary accounts for ecosystems (SEEA EEA). In Section 4 we discuss some key challenges and ways forward for monetary valuation of ecosystem services, benefits and assets within this accounting framework. We use examples from Norway as illustrations. We end the chapter by discussing some limitations of the SEEA accounting framework and future directions.

2.   System of Environmental Economic Accounting (SEEA)

The main goal of the SEEA is to better monitor the interactions between the economy and the state of the environment to inform decision-making, typically at the national level. The SEEA framework is consistent with the System of National Accounts (SNA) to facilitate the integration of environmental and economic statistics and the adoption of the SEEA system by national statistical offices. Compared to SNA, the SEEA framework expands the production boundary with the aim to include the whole biophysical environment and a broader set of ecosystem services. SEEA 2012 (United Nations et al. 2014a) builds upon revisions of SEEA 2003 (discussed in the Inclusive Wealth Report 2012 by Perrings (2012)) and SEEA 1993. SEEA contains the internationally agreed upon concepts for producing internationally comparable statistics on the environment and its relationship with the economy. By 2014, 18% of UN member countries had initiated a programme to enhance Environmental Economic Accounting, and 27% of developing countries and 8% of developed countries had a programme for Environmental Economic Accounting. Thus, the current initiatives of the United Nations Statistical Commission (UNSC) to revise and improve the SEEA system appear to be welcomed by member countries. SEEA consists of three parts:

- The SEEA Central Framework (SEEA CF).
- The SEEA Experimental Ecosystem Accounting (SEEA EEA).
- The SEEA Subsystems for Energy, Water, Fisheries and Agriculture. The "subsystems" are consistent with SEEA, but provide further details on specific topics.

The central framework of SEEA, SEEA CF, accounts for individual resources such as timber resources, land, energy and minerals resources, physical environmental flows (such as water, energy, emissions and waste) and environmentally related transactions within the economy (such as environmental protection expenditure and environmental taxes). The SEEA CF was adopted by UNSC in 2012 as the first international standard for environmental economic accounting. The official version of SEEA CF was published in 2014.

Since the publication of the previous Inclusive Wealth Reports, rapid progress has been made in the effort to develop an accounting system for ecosystem flows and assets both in physical and monetary terms through the work on the SEEA Experimental Ecosystem Accounting (SEEA EEA). In 2013, the UNSC endorsed SEEA EEA for further development and testing, and the accounting framework was published in 2014. The SEEA EEA: Technical Recommendations (SEEA EEA TR) presents information that supports the testing and research on SEEA EEA and is motivated by the practical experiences with the accounting framework and advances in thinking on specific topics since the first SEEA EEA (United Nations 2017). The SEEA EEA TR is under revision, and work has been initiated to revise the SEEA EEA by 2020.

Monetary valuation of ecosystem services in SEEA EEA is motivated by several perspectives: input for wealth accounting, demonstration of the contribution of ecosystems to human welfare, and evaluation of policy alternatives. SEEA EEA provides insight into how ecosystems can be considered a form of capital that can appreciate and depreciate, in the same way as other forms of capital such as human, social and economic capital.

The development of the necessary accounting compatible concepts for a spatially explicit accounting system for ecosystem assets and their services is a challenging task, and currently work is in progress. The concepts and thinking developed and implemented in SEEA EEA to date should be helpful in contributing to improve inclusive wealth accounting of natural capital.

3.   SEEA Experimental Ecosystem Accounting

SEEA EEA contains spatially explicit physical and monetary accounts for ecosystems. As such, compiling the accounts requires a multidisciplinary approach. To determine rates of asset appreciation or depreciation one also needs these accounts to be compiled regularly over time. SEEA EEA is termed experimental because many concepts for such spatially explicit and repeated accounts for ecosystem services and assets are still under testing and development (see e.g. Remme et al. 2015).

As noted above, the work on developing the SEEA EEA accounts is progressing fast. In the experimental phase the focus is generally on policy relevant case studies where concepts are being developed and tested. In this phase, numbers may not be as accurate as one would desire, but several argue that having approximate numbers that map ecosystems and that can demonstrate their importance to the general economy may be better than the current practice of implicitly valuing ecosystems through our decisions concerning maintaining or transforming ecosystems. Bateman et al. (2013, 2011) show, for example, in the context of the UK National Ecosystem Assessment (UK NEA), that taking account of multiple environmental objectives in systematic environmental and economic analysis of the benefits and costs of land use options, fundamentally alters decisions regarding optimal land use.

Figure 5.1 provides an overview of the conceptual thinking for the ecosystem accounting in SEEA EEA. At the basis for the accounting system are ecosystems. In the accounting terminology, individual contiguous ecosystems are considered ecosystem assets (element 1 in Figure 5.1).[2] Ecosystems are characterized by their

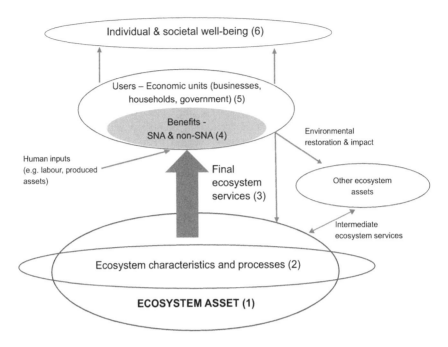

Figure 5.1 Ecosystem accounting framework for SEEA EEA
Source: United Nations (2017).

extent, biotic and abiotic components and their processes. Ecosystem assets may be aggregated into the ecosystem types, for example forests or agricultural ecosystems within the accounting area under study. Ecosystem types are ecosystems with similar ecology and use and are typically not contiguous.

The relevant characteristics and processes describe the ecosystem functioning (element 2). An ecosystem asset delivers ecosystem services, and the focus in SEEA EEA is on final ecosystem services (United Nations et al. 2014b) consistently with Banzhaf and Boyd (2012) and UK NEA (2011) (element 3 in Figure 5.1). Final ecosystem services are either, benefits to users (economic units) directly in themselves or the ecosystem service can be thought of as being an input to production of benefits along with other inputs such as labour and produced assets (e.g. built capital). Both for accounting purposes and for monetary valuation it is important to clarify this distinction between ecosystem services and ecosystem benefits (United Nations et al. 2014b; Banzhaf and Boyd 2012). Making this distinction helps to avoid double counting. The SEEA EEA uses the classification of final ecosystem services into provisioning services (i.e. those relating to the supply of food, fibre, fuel and water); regulating services (i.e. those relating to actions of filtration, purification, regulation and maintenance of air, water, soil, habitat and climate); and cultural services (i.e. those relating to the activities of individuals in, or associated with, nature).

The benefits that are produced by ecosystem services may either be so-called SNA benefits meaning they are already accounted for in SNA (e.g. timber products) or they may be non-SNA benefits, which means they are benefits that are outside the accounting boundary of SNA (e.g. flood protection) (see element 4 in Figure 5.1). It is important to be clear about whether an ecosystem service has already been accounted for in SNA to prevent potential double counting. It is important to make the role of ecosystem services explicit also for those ecosystem services that presently are within the accounting boundary of SNA.

The supply of final ecosystem services is matched with the economic units that receive the benefits (element 5 in Figure 5.1). The economic units are businesses, households and the government. To be consistent with the accounting framework, supply of ecosystem benefits must equal use. The benefits contribute to "individual and societal well-being," the measure of which – according Figure 5.1 – is the ultimate purpose of the accounting framework. As we will discuss, this stated purpose may be misleading because the valuation methods that are consistent with accounting only aim to quantify ecosystems contribution to the economy, not societal well-being or welfare. The accounting system is designed to account for benefits both in terms of physical production and in monetary units where possible.

It should be noted that intermediate ecosystem services are also identified in the framework. Intermediate ecosystem services are those ecosystem services that are inputs to the supply of other ecosystem services. In ecosystem accounting, if one ecosystem produces services that contribute to produce ecosystem services in another ecosystem (e.g. pollination and flood control) these are also considered intermediate (SEEA EEA TR, paragraph 5.40).

Further, the SEEA EEA has five core accounts:

1   Ecosystem extent account – physical terms
2   Ecosystem condition account – physical terms
3   Ecosystem services supply and use account – physical terms
4   Ecosystem services supply and use account – monetary terms
5   Ecosystem monetary asset account – monetary terms

Figure 5.2 describes the relationship between these accounts as a series of physical (a) and monetary (b) steps, arriving at a set of integrated accounts. Even if one may describe this as a sequence of accounts, it should be emphasized that the development of these accounts most often will be iterative permitting one to go back to adjust and make improvements. Hence, an arrow could be drawn from the final step back to the first. Each of the accounts is intended to provide useful information in itself while also being an input into other accounts. Considering the complexity in completing the accounting chain, the identification of 'stand-alone' policy uses of individual accounts is important to motivate further allocation of resources by policymakers to building the system of accounts. In Figure 5.2, ecosystem services supply and use accounts are included as two separate boxes to reflect the iterative process in generating ecosystem services supply and use accounts in physical terms.

SEEA EEA TR includes example tables for all the accounts. These tables are useful illustrations of the accounts but too extensive to include here. The ecosystem extent account maps the area of land in each land use/ecosystem type. Examples of ecosystems here are forests, agriculture, wetlands and urban, although subcategories of these ecosystem types may be deemed necessary depending on the circumstances. For example, natural forest and planted forests for timber production will have quite different characteristics. For each of the ecosystem types, the condition account includes the available and appropriate indicators of the "overall quality of an ecosystem

a. Steps in physical terms

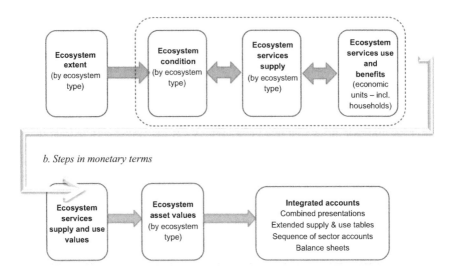

Figure 5.2 Broad steps in ecosystem accounting
Source: United Nations (2017).

asset in terms of its characteristics" (United Nations et al. 2014b, paragraph 2.35). The condition of the ecosystem is the basis for the capacity of the ecosystem to provide ecosystem services in the future, which in turn affects the ecosystem asset value. The ecosystem condition may be evaluated by comparing ecological indicator values now with the ecological indicator values in the reference condition for the ecosystem. What the reference condition should be is discussed in the Technical Recommendations (United Nations 2017) and is part of an ongoing debate, since some ecosystems in some countries have been affected by human beings for such a long time that the ecosystems have evolved to be dependent on human management. One suggestion is to identify the condition that existed when data collection began (United Nations 2017).[3] Depending on the condition of an ecosystem, the ecosystem supplies a basket of ecosystem services, and the ecosystem services use and benefits are further attributed to economic units. Examples of economic units here are households, agriculture, the government and other economic sectors. Again, the subcategories one chooses for the economic units depends on the circumstances, in particular the policy analysis question which accounting should inform. The measurements necessary for the ecosystem condition account, the ecosystem services supply and ecosystem services use may be completed concurrently. This is indicated by the dotted line. Experience with urban ecosystem accounting at high spatial resolution in Oslo has shown that ecosystem extent and condition accounts also need to be determined concurrently, because, depending on the spatial resolution at which land cover is classified, it can also indicate ecosystem condition.

While the first row in Figure 5.2 contains all physical accounts, the second row in Figure 5.2 contains monetary accounts, that we are primarily concerned with here. The first box in the second row is the account for the ecosystem services use and supply values.

In the SEEA EEA TR the ecosystem monetary asset account is defined as accounts that "record the monetary value of opening and closing stocks of all ecosystem assets within an ecosystem accounting area and addition and reductions in those stocks" (United Nations 2017, paragraph 7.5). The motivation for monetary valuation of ecosystem assets in SEEA EEA is twofold. One motivation is that monetary valuation gives a common measurement unit which is – in principle – helpful when comparing alternative uses of ecosystem assets (in practice monetary valuation relies on the completeness of the physical accounts). A second motivation is that monetary valuation permits the ecosystem asset account to be integrated with other accounts for the other capital assets discussed in Chapter 1 of this report. In that sense, compiling the SEEA EEA ecosystem asset accounts and integrating them with the net domestic product could contribute to giving a more complete assessment of a nation's net wealth. As in the inclusive wealth framework, the SEEA EEA framework considers a depreciation of aggregate ecosystem assets a potential sign of unsustainable ecosystem use, but there are some important differences in the view on the meaning and treatment of depreciation in the two frameworks (Obst 2017, pers. comm.).

The thinking regarding the construction of ecosystem asset accounts in SEEA EEA is related but slightly different than the ecosystem capital thinking in the inclusive wealth framework. SEEA EEA is an expansion of the accounting framework in the System of National Accounts. The SNA defines the gross domestic product as a measure of economic performance and states explicitly that GDP is not a measure of human welfare (United Nations et al. 2008). SEEA EEA TR recognizes that there are several perspectives that may be taken when it comes to estimating a nation's wealth in terms of natural and ecosystem capital (United Nations 2017, paragraph 7.1). In the perspective of the inclusive wealth framework, the goal is to maximize intergenerational human welfare derived from all capital stocks. When operationalizing this, the inclusive wealth framework proposes to expand the net domestic product (the depreciation adjusted GDP) to include all types of capital.

SEEA EEA holds that one may account for ecosystem asset, as for any other asset, using a capital theoretic framework. If there is no market for an asset, which is often the case for ecosystem assets, then the monetary value of the asset may be estimated in terms of the present value of the future flow of income attributable to an asset. For an ecosystem asset, estimation of the monetary asset value requires information on:

- The appropriate exchange values now and in the future;
- The expected future ecosystem service supply;
- The appropriate discount rate to calculate the net present value (NPV); and
- The expected life of the asset.

The expected ecosystem service supply should be as close as possible to what one actually expects to be used and the exchange values should be as close as possible to the exchange values one expects for the future.

The final box in Figure 5.2 refers to the integration of ecosystem accounts with the standard national accounts, one of the steps in EEA. Technical guidelines may give the impression that integration of monetary asset accounts with other capital assets is the final purpose of accounting. Further work is needed showing how integrated accounts are a means to the ends of different policy analysis. This may be done in several ways depending on how closely one wants to integrate the accounts. The methods range from combined presentation of only physical data on ecosystem condition and services alongside with presentations of standard national accounts numbers to complete integration where the value of ecosystem assets is incorporated with the values of other capital assets in order to extend the measure of national wealth.

The SEEA EEA offers useful concepts and accounting structures ultimately leading to ecosystem asset accounts. Furthermore, the SEEA EEA provides a framework that is compatible with national accounts and therefore with statistical offices' definitions used in the net domestic product. However, SEEA EEA differs from the theoretical framework of the inclusive wealth model since the latter requires that all the economy's capital assets should be valued at their shadow value.

4.   Valuation challenges for ecosystem services, benefits and assets

As noted above, the meaning of an exchange value is quite different from the meaning of a shadow value in terms of its implications for human welfare. Yet, there are some commonalities in terms of the challenges that one may run into when attempting to determine these values. We now discuss some of these challenges.

4.1.   *Ecosystem service delineation and some fundamental challenges*

The definition of an ecosystem service has been widely discussed in the literature in recent years, and the definition in MEA (2005), for example, has been deemed inappropriate for valuation and accounting purposes both in the inclusive wealth framework and in SEEA EEA (Pearson et al. 2012; United Nations 2017, paragraph 5.35). Instead, the need to focus on final ecosystem services and to separate between ecosystem services and ecosystem benefits to avoid double counting has been recognized in both the previous Inclusive Wealth Reports and in the SEEA EEA (see also discussion in Section 3 above). By making the distinction between benefits (also called goods in the UK NEA) and services it is possible to include several ecosystem services that are inputs in the production function of an ecosystem benefit. For example, while harvested fish is an ecosystem benefit, one must subtract the cost of harvesting to find the contribution of the ecosystem (that is the ecosystem service) to the benefit. Several definitions of ecosystem services and goods exist; for example, Barbier (2012) adopts the definition that "ecosystem services are the direct or indirect contributions that ecosystems make to the well-being of human populations (EPA 2009, p. 12)." Whichever definition one adopts, the literature has reached the conclusion that the definition be such that one avoids double counting, and this is possible by focusing on final ecosystem benefits (indirect) and services (direct).

Before we take a practical and pragmatic approach to estimating monetary values for ecosystem services, benefits and assets, it is necessary to recall that many ecosystems are complex and poorly understood both by scientists, policy-makers and the general population (see e.g. the example of the recently discovered cold water corals in Norway discussed in Aanesen et al. 2015). Barbier (2012, p. 163), for example, states: "There is inadequate knowledge to link changes in ecosystem structure and function to the production of valuable goods and services." Since knowledge of ecosystem processes is never going to be complete or perfect, it is likely better to attempt with available knowledge to demonstrate the potential importance and value of ecosystems for human well-being under different methodological assumptions. Implicit valuation by a limited number of decision makers making policy choices uniformed by information on ecosystem services, is unlikely to reach efficient or welfare optimal choices (as noted above in the context of the UK NEA). This is also the argument made by the international project and process of The Economics and Ecosystems and Biodiversity (TEEB) (Kumar 2010).

In the following, we discuss some important challenges with valuation of ecosystem services and benefits that are market (section 4.2) and non-market (section 4.3), respectively, and the valuation of ecosystem assets (section 4.4). We relate the discussion to the framework of experimental ecosystem accounting (cf. back to Figures 5.1 and 5.2 above) and especially the use of methods for non-market services.

4.2. *Market ecosystem services and benefits*

Many ecosystem services and benefits such as fish, grains, timber and products derived from these have market prices which are relevant exchange values and therefore compatible with national accounting and SEEA EEA. When estimating the contribution of the ecosystem to harvested fish, one estimates the monetary surplus remaining after all costs related to harvesting have been subtracted from the total revenue. This monetary surplus is also denoted as the resource rent. In an accounting framework, it is important to be aware of the impact the institutional arrangement has on the value of the resource rent of many of the provisioning goods. The institutional arrangement may affect both the prices received by fishers and the costs of harvesting, and it is the prices and costs along with the quantity produced that in turn determine the size of the resource rent. For fisheries, examples of institutional arrangements may be open access, quotas or individually tradable quotas, and more. In an open access management regime, the value of the resource rents tends to zero and it is an open question how to value the resource under such circumstances (Hein et al. 2015). But other management regimes can contribute to conceal the resource rent in national accounts even if access to the fishery is limited. Policies that make fishing artificially expensive, for example, may cause the resource rent to be masked in national accounts. For an example of this see Box 5.1. In such cases, there are likely to be other indicators than resources rents

---

Box 5.1 Institutional arrangements affect the estimated contribution of the ecosystem service for fish

Traditionally, export of fish was a major source of income for Norway. Later other natural resource based income, particularly from oil and gas, overtook fish income. Opposition to new oil extraction in areas that are in important breeding grounds for Norwegian fish stocks confirms the fact that many Norwegians consider fisheries an important natural capital asset to preserve for the future.

Entry to Norwegian fishery is currently managed through fishing licenses and quotas and the fish stocks are not considered overharvested. Yet, for many years, the income from fisheries as it appears in national accounts is negative. Thus, according to national accounts numbers, Norwegian fisheries contributed negatively to Norwegian national wealth in the period 1984–2014 with the exception of 2010–2011 (Greaker et al. 2017). Figure 5.3 shows the components of the resource rent for the period 1984–2014.

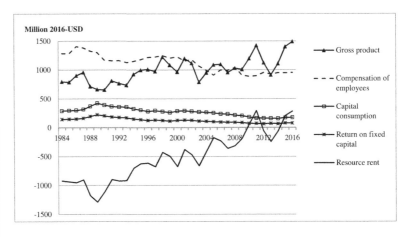

Figure 5.3 Resource rent in the Norwegian fishery 1984–2016

that are of policy importance and which can be monitored, such as employment. In cases where exchange value principles do not provide any additional information, parallel accounts and complementary indicators must be relied upon.

As Figure 5.3 shows, the actual resource rent has generally been on an increasing trend from 1984 to 2016. Norwegian fisheries have in some of the later years had positive resource rent, apart from the period 2012–2014. Factors contributing to the increasing resource rent over time are a year by year reduction in the number of hours worked in the sector reducing total compensation of employees (including compensation to the vessel owner – there are differing views on whether compensation to the vessel owner should be included here). There has also been a year by year reduction in the number of vessels, thus reducing fixed costs and capital consumption, although the gross tonnage has remained fairly constant.

Greaker et al. (2017) hypothesize that the potential value of the fishery resources is higher than what the calculations show in Figure 5.3. The reason is that the values of all parameters entering the calculation of the resource rent are conditional on the existing management regime. This management regime has by law several goals, and one of them is that fisheries should contribute to maintaining viable coastal communities. To help reach this rural development goal, fishing quotas are distributed among fishing vessel with different technologies and geographical locations.

Greaker et al. (2017) explore what the potential resource rent could be in 2011, which was an average year in terms of catch (in the period 2006–2016), without the current distribution of fishing quotas. Using a numerical optimization model, they find that the counter factual resource rent if the 2011 quotas were harvested efficiently with the available technology would be close to 1.6 billion USD. This is 1.20 billion USD more than the observed resource rent.

When decomposing the change in potential resource rent compared to the actual rent into changes in total revenue and total costs, the results show that total revenue falls by about 10%. Simultaneously, total cost falls by around 80%. In 2010 and 2012 the average fish prices were lower. However, if adjusting total revenue and total cost for the national accounts numbers in 2010 and 2012 correspondingly, the potential resource rent is 1.14 and 1.23 billion higher than the one observed in 2010 and 2012, respectively. Even if this is a very simple adjustment, these numbers are not far from the rent dissipation of 1.20 billion USD in 2011. The potential resource rent found here is around 60% of the first-hand value in the fisheries in 2011. This is similar to Wilen's rule of thumb that says that half of the total revenue is resource rent (Wilen 2000).

Some have argued that the ongoing rent dissipation in Norwegian fisheries simply is a way to redistribute income in the fishery sector. But the resource rent could be increased by applying fewer fishers and fewer vessels, and per definition, one is in a situation with resource waste in the fishery sector because well as lower value creation in other sectors because both the fishers and vessels have an alternative value in other industries. However, in cases where the fishers and vessels that are removed from the fisheries have low/zero alternative value in other sectors, the present management system could be described as a more efficient way of financing employment in the fisheries through rent dissipation without leading to lower value creation in other industries as well.

4.3. *Non-market ecosystem services and benefits*

The most significant challenge for valuation of ecosystem services is that so many of them are non-marketed (Barbier 2014). The field of environmental economics has developed a number of methods to value non-market ecosystem services. Barbier (2012) provides an overview of the progress that has been made in environmental

---

Box 5.2 Categories of non-market valuation methods

Stated preference methods: Willingness to pay/or to accept compensation for changes in provision of ecosystem services/benefits are elicited from respondents in surveys using structured questionnaires. Stated preference methods are the only methods that can cover non-use/existence values. Well-known methods include contingent valuation and choice experiments.

Revealed preference methods: Values are "revealed" through studying consumers' choices and the resulting price changes in actual markets that can then be associated with changes in provision of ecosystem services. A well-known method is *hedonic pricing* of property characteristics, i.e. where the impact of environmental quality attributes on prices of properties is distinguished from other factors that affect prices. *Travel cost methods* used to value recreational benefits of ecosystems are often also included in this category.

Production/damage function approaches: A group of methods used to value an ecosystem service, where intermediate ecosystem services are one of several "inputs" to the final service or good enjoyed by people. Ecosystems' marginal contribution to the final service is valued.

Cost-based methods: Assume that expenditures involved in preventing, avoiding ("averting"), mitigating or replacing losses of ecosystem services represent a minimum value estimate of what people are willing to pay for the ecosystem service. In ecosystem accounting a distinction is made between replacement cost (of a particular ecosystem service) and restoration cost (of an ecosystem asset and its bundle of ecosystem services).

Benefits/value transfer methods: Refer to the use of secondary, existing study valuation estimates, from any of the valuation methods mentioned above, transferred to the "policy context" in need of value information. Values can either be transferred using unit value transfer methods or more advanced function-based transfers (e.g. based on meta-analysis of the literature).

Sources: Champ et al. (2017); Barton and Harrison (2017); Johnston et al. (2015); Barbier (2012); and Koetse et al. (2015).

economics on developing methodologies for valuation of non-market ecosystem services, and presents the non-market valuation methods that are currently available along with the ecosystem services for which each of the methods is appropriate. These valuation methods are summarized in Box 5.2.

Even if the coverage of environmental valuation studies may be considered patchy across ecosystem benefits and services (Barbier 2014), a large number of valuation studies for ecosystem benefits and services have been carried out in the last few years using environmental economic methods (e.g. Kumar 2010). The ideal would be to have valuation studies specifically designed for accounting purposes. This is rarely the case. This means that accountants and economists typically must use value or benefit transfer methods (see Box 5.2) based on suitable, existing studies to estimate exchange values with typically relatively large uncertainty (see e.g. Johnston and Wainger 2015).[4]

National accountants also have their set of accounting compatible valuation methods for non-market environmental goods (Vincent 2015). Only a subset of the non-market valuation methods developed in environmental economics are considered directly appropriate in an accounting framework ("accounting compatible"). This is because environmental economics is focused on finding estimates of welfare, and as a consequence, most non-market valuation methods that have been developed produce value estimates that include consumer surplus. SNA-compatible accounting requires exchange values, excluding consumer surplus. At the same time, finding accounting compatible monetary values for all ecosystem services is a significant challenge for SEEA EEA (United Nations 2014b). The SEEA EEA TR therefore offers several suggestions to bridge the gap between accounting and economics when it comes to valuation.

A subset of valuation methods developed in environmental economics does not include consumer surplus and has therefore been deemed appropriate for SEEA EEA. SEEA

EEA TR (United Nations 2017, Table 6.1) provides a list of valuation techniques that are accounting compatible:

- Production, cost and profit function techniques addressing separate provisioning, regulating and cultural ecosystem services;
- Hedonic techniques, which can estimate the marginal contribution of a bundle of ecosystem services/amenity attributes on house prices; and
- Methods that provide information about expenditures such as defensive expenditures and travel cost where information in the methods is used to estimate a market exchange value.

While national accountants typically use cost-based techniques (e.g. replacement cost), such techniques are only supported within the field of environmental economics if, "the alternative considered provides the same services; the alternative is the least cost alternative and if there is substantial evidence that the service would be demanded by society if it were provided by the least-cost alternative" (Barbier 2012, p. 180). These are relatively strict conditions.

Further research is needed to develop and test valuation techniques that reflect exchange values and hence exclude consumer surplus for non-market ecosystem services (Hein et al. 2015). The challenges of valuing ecosystem services without a market price while still being consistent with SNA, and while providing complementary information to support policy assessment, is one of the topics that is under testing and development in SEEA EEA.

Specifically, SEEA EEA TR proposes to develop methods where non-market valuation studies that originally were meant to derive values that include consumer surplus may later be used to derive the demand curve that would have existed if there was a marked for the good in question. Through combining such a demand function with the supply function for the ecosystem service or benefits one may be able to derive the exchange value. In this step, one would also have to make assumptions about the institutional arrangement for the exchange (see also discussion in Box 5.1 above). Here one might have to try to evaluate as realistically as possible what the institutional arrangement would have been had a market existed. Developing such credible provision scenarios is one of the strengths of stated preference methods when they are conducted to state-of-the art standards. This information combined with a supply curve for the ecosystem service could yield information about the exchange value of the ecosystem service or benefit. Caparros et al. (2017) provide an example of how this method may be put into practice.

In Boxes 5.3 and 5.4 below we show how one could use restoration cost and contingent valuation methods, normally considered inappropriate or incompatible with accounting standards, along the lines of the thinking above to arrive at estimates of exchange values that could be decision-relevant and fit for accounting. The first example discusses the restoration costs of city trees as basic of exchange value and how to avoid double counting (Box 5.3). For an application of ecosystem service valuation for ecosystem accounting in a developing country context that includes provisioning, regulating and cultural services, see e.g. Sumarga et al (2015).

Box 5.3 Use of restoration costs for replacing city trees

Restoration cost refers to the estimated cost to restore an ecosystem asset to an earlier, benchmark condition. The SEEA EEA Technical Recommendations suggest that the methods are likely to be inappropriate since they do not determine a price for an individual ecosystem service, but may serve to inform valuation of a basket of services. Accounting incompatibility in this case is due to an increased risk of double counting when ecosystem services cannot be identified separately, and instead are valued as a bundle associated with a specific ecosystem site or green structure. The valuation method is nevertheless useful in municipal policy and can meet accounting requirements under special conditions. For example, in the city of Oslo, restoration costs of city trees are calculated as a basis for a compensation fee to be paid by parties responsible for damaging trees on public land. The replacement cost is adjusted for the age, health and physical qualities of the tree. The compensation cost is in many cases absorbed as a transaction cost of property development when destroying a tree is unavoidable. As such this is an exchange value, although it has been set through regulation rather than the market. Regarding the risk of double counting, this may be avoided by not including municipal trees in other valuation models (e.g. hedonic pricing models).

Source: Barton et al. (2015).

Box 5.4 Use of contingent valuation to assess cost-recovery-based maintenance of city trees

Contingent valuation is based on survey responses to questions about willingness to pay for ecosystem services and is used to estimate economic value for awareness raising purposes, or as input to benefit-cost analysis. The SEEA EEA Technical Recommendations suggest that using values directly from the method is inappropriate since it measures consumer surplus rather than exchange values. However, as the Technical Recommendations suggest, it is possible to estimate a demand curve from stated preference studies, and that this information may be used in forming exchange values for ecosystem services. As an example, the contingent valuation method was used in Oslo to obtain the willingness to pay a municipal fee for maintaining the density of public street trees. Aggregate willingness to pay across Oslo's population was estimated at 60 million NOK/year for maintaining or increasing street trees across the city. By comparison current municipal costs for maintaining trees in municipal parks and streets is only 12 million NOK/year. While these contingent valuation estimates cannot be used directly to estimate the accounting value of current street trees, the information is useful as decision support and for determining a financially feasible level of supply. Municipal utility services such as water and waste management are charged according to the cost recovery principle (i.e. no producer surplus). The contingent valuation estimates could be used to determine the increased level of street tree maintenance possible if the stated amount was actually charged to households following a cost recovery principle. Future increased supply – here increased maintenance of city trees – might be based on the findings from this contingent valuation study. The contingent valuation identifies feasible cost recovery fees per household and the maximum future maintenance costs that are feasible. While not determined by a market transaction, a public utility fee for maintenance costs of street trees should be accounting compatible as it is a service transaction price (although, as in nature, public utilities are rights-based, or technically difficult to withhold even if no payment is forthcoming from the user).

Source: Haavardsholm (2015).

The second example shows how a contingent valuation survey of people's willingness to pay to maintain or increase the density of street trees can be combined with the costs of supply, to arrive at an exchange price that may be deemed acceptable for accounting purposes (Box 5.4).

The SEEA EEA TR further proposes as a way to determine the most suitable valuation method to use for accounting purposes, to identify so-called "channels" (Atkinson and Obst 2017) through which an underlying ecosystem asset provides

Box 5.5 Valuation methods and links to accounting via channels to users

In order to see the relevance of the non-market valuation methods from environmental economics for accounting purposes, it is useful to view the "channels" through which an underlying ecosystem asset ultimately provides benefits to, or affects the well-being of, the users or economic units. SEEA EEA TR (United Nations 2017, Atkinson and Obst 2017) summarizes three such channels:

1 Ecosystem services used as inputs for production (such as pollination for agricultural production).
2 Ecosystem services that act as joint inputs to household final consumption (such as nature recreation that requires time and travel expenditures on part of the household).
3 Ecosystem services that provide household well-being directly. This is an abstract channel that includes non-use values.

These channels have parallels in accounting, in the way GDP is affected either through inputs to existing (economic) production (channel 1) or to final household consumption (channels 2 and 3). The idea is to identify each buyer (producer or household) and seller (ecosystem), and identify valuation methods that can be used to estimate exchange values, under prevailing institutional conditions. Valuation methods can be grouped according to channels in a supply and use context (Freeman et al. 2014). For industry users, for example, provisioning, regulating and cultural services would provide value through channel 1. For households, provisioning services work through channel 1, regulating through channel 2, and cultural through both channels 2 and 3. Once suitable services, channels, users and methods have been identified, the next step is to use the methods to construct an exchange value estimate for the non-market service. There are different ways this can be done, e.g. as illustrated in Boxes 5.3 and 5.4 above.

Sources: Atkinson and Obst (2017), Freeman et al. (2014) and United Nations (2017).

benefits to the users or economic units (see Box 5.5). The next step is then to identify ecosystem services and benefits and respective valuation methods for each service channel and user. Some of the methods will be accounting compatible and some will require adjustments along the lines noted above, to arrive at exchange values.

Even for non-market valuation techniques from environmental economics that are considered accounting compatible, there are still other challenges related to using these methods for valuation.

As spatially explicit accounting frameworks both SEEA EEA and inclusive wealth accounting need spatially explicit valuation of ecosystem benefits and services. There is a lack of studies in general, though in recent years numbers have increased. Many valuation studies are not motivated by policy questions (Laurans et al. 2013). In those cases where valuation addresses policy, some questions tend to come up more often, and some services appear to be more frequently valued than others. Recreation benefits, for example, may be valued more often than some regulating services. This is also due to the complexity of modelling the ecosystems as well as some services and benefits.

Through adopting landscape, or land area, as the basic accounting unit, characterizing the ecosystem as a natural asset is relatively straightforward. To match the accounting units, non-market valuation studies should also be spatially explicit. With increased availability and use of satellite data maps and geographical information systems, and spatially explicit data analysis techniques, the number of valuation studies that are spatially explicit is expected to rise. But at present, SEEA EEA accounting efforts will by necessity rely on benefit transfer based on studies that are rarely spatially explicit in the sense required for accounting purposes. For those valuation results that are available and site specific on some level of spatial resolution, a main challenge, pointed out by Hein et al. (2015), is to transfer values to other sites and scale the estimates to larger areas required for accounting purposes.

To transfer to other sites there must be sufficient ecological and economic correspondence between the study and the policy sites (Johnston et al. 2015; Barbier 2014). The benefit transfer literature offers simple and more advanced (and sometimes more precise) methods for benefit transfer that sometimes use GIS and scaling-up procedures (see e.g. Brander et al. 2012). Meta-analysis requires knowledge of the values of the independent variables for the policy site of interest and assumes that the statistical relationship between the dependent and independent variables is the same between the study and the policy sites. It is not always guaranteed that more advanced methods perform better (Lindhjem and Navrud 2008). It is also important to delineate different ecosystems and services, to avoid double counting (Barbier 2012).

For wealth accounting purposes it is often ideal to have aggregate values of ecosystem services at the regional or national level. If ecosystem services values have been estimated based on case studies at specific sites, one may question whether the target population of such studies will be appropriate for wealth accounting. That is, can the numbers based on a case study in one location be scaled up to a national level? It is not uncommon that local land use preferences differ from the national preferences for land use (see e.g. Lindhjem 2007 on forest services). Differences in preferences for a policy are not unexpected when a policy has a different impact locally than nationally. Local communities which are more affected by a policy may have per capita net benefits that are much greater (lower) than the average per capita net benefits nationally. But the aggregate net benefits at the national level may be much greater (lower) than the local net benefits.

Using a simple physical index of an area, such as hectares, to expand value estimates to another scale may violate basic economic principles such as diminishing marginal utility, changing relative scarcity and substitutability. However, using average per hectare values is often the way scaling-up is done in practice, for lack of information to adjust values for such factors we know from theory and empirical studies should affect values. In some cases average per hectare values for some degree of scaling may work as approximations that in any case are better than no such information.

To track the wealth of a nation the aggregate values of ecosystem services at the regional or national level should ideally be replicated and updated annually. An important use of such information is to track trends over time. But with the scarcity of non-market valuation studies one is forced to use outdated values. Preferences or demand may change over time, for example as incomes increase, people on average tend to prefer to use more cultural ecosystem services. Preferences are shown in some valuation studies to be stable for periods of up to five years, but for periods beyond 20 years this is not the case (Skourtos et al. 2010). Non-market valuation methods have also improved and can hopefully provide more reliable estimates than some older studies.

The current SEEA EEA process is geared towards testing the operationalization of the SEEA EEA TR in practical cases and through increased practice to gather experiences that may help solve some of the challenges in deriving exchange values for accounting. One relatively large-scale implementation of SEEA EEA principles is currently under way in the greater Oslo area in Norway (see Box 5.6). The aim is to test how the SEEA EEA framework can identify the economic contributions that urban ecosystems make to the municipal, household and commercial sectors in greater Oslo.

4.4.   *Accounting for the value of ecosystem assets in SEEA EEA*

In estimating the expected ecosystem services supply it is important to assess possible trade-offs between different ecosystem services in particular policy contexts; for example, there may be a trade-off between forest recreation and production of timber. When valuing ecosystem assets, it requires aggregation of many ecosystem services under the assumption that the prices are independent (Hein et al. 2015).

Box 5.6 Ecosystem accounting at municipal level

Figure 5.4 shows the recommended system of accounts in the SEEA EEA (in grey), placed in the context of different municipal uses of information compiled for accounting. The framework emphasizes the need at the municipal level to base decisions on available information on value of ecosystems. The valuation methods used – whether exchange-based or consumer surplus based – depend on the type of policy question at hand. Information stemming from different valuation and indicator methods is complementary and can be triangulated. This approach has been called integrated or plural valuation (Jacobs et al. 2016), exploring the role of SEEA EEA as a contribution to "considering ecosystems through multiple analytical lenses." Ecosystem accounting within such a plural valuation approach is being tested at the municipal level within the metropolitan area of greater Oslo, Norway. Local and city governments already make use of land use mapping and thematic environmental and socio-cultural indicators to inform impact assessments, municipal planning and zoning. The URBAN EEA project is testing SEEA EEA recommendation on how to identify the economic contributions that urban ecosystems make to the municipal, household and commercial sectors in greater Oslo. Ecosystem accounting offers a complementary set of indicators to municipal government aimed at making fragmented urban nature and blue-green infrastructure more

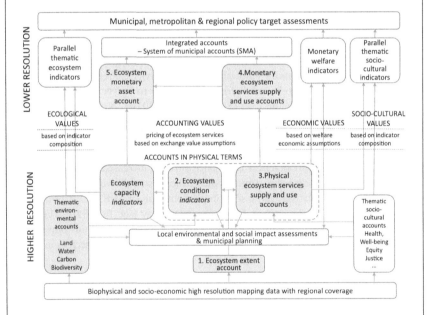

Figure 5.4 Conceptual framework for municipal experimental ecosystem accounting

Source: Based on Barton et al. (2017).

visible in city planning. The project has found that characteristics of urban land-scapes may limit the scope of monetary ecosystem accounts in the assessment of municipal policy targets. Urban green structures can be small and hard to identify in GIS, but still be locally valuable. Remnant and constructed urban nature is highly spatially fragmented, mixed-use density is high and highly localized. This makes it challenging to identify marginal values of particular green space qualities and ecosystem services from transactions in the property market. Municipal utilities such as water supply, rainwater management, sewage treatment and solid waste management operate according to cost recovery, meaning that the residual resource rent attributable to ecosystems is zero. Recreational time use in neighbourhood public spaces is very high relative to travel expenses to use the areas, leaving little trace in market transactions. Given these and other challenges of valuation urban ecosystem services (Gomez-Baggethun and Barton 2013), urban EEA aims to provide municipal government with a suite of spatially explicit indicators of accounting compatible exchange value, as well as parallel indicators of ecological, welfare economic and socio-cultural values that are at stake across a cityscape.

As discussed in the Technical Recommendations, while the link between physical flows and provisioning services is quite tangible, the same may not be the case for regulating and cultural services. The supply of these services depends on factors that often are not stable over time such as vegetation, management regimes and pollution levels. Further, one may have limited information about the capacity of the ecosystem to supply the service over time. Finally, for cultural services such as enjoying biodiversity and aesthetic aspects of nature, it may be difficult to identify and describe in general terms the specific link between the condition of the ecosystem in physical terms and the supply of cultural services. Hence, indicators for cultural services require the most further development at this stage, according to the Technical Recommendations (United Nations 2017, paragraph 7.16).

For integration of ecosystem asset accounts with national accounts, the SEEA EEA TR states that consistency with the exchange value concept in SNA, one also should use the market-based discount rates. Estimating using a variety of discount rates to demonstrate the sensitivity of the estimates is recommended. For a more thorough discussion on the application net present value (NPV) for natural resources see SEEA CF (United Nations 2014a, section 5.4).

The life (duration) of the ecosystem asset depends on how it is being used. If use is sustainable then one can assume an infinite asset life. But some ecosystem asset uses can be unsustainable and this will limit the asset life. But even in cases where the asset life is assumed to be infinite, discounting incomes at a high rate may cause the present value of incomes to be negligible after two or three decades. Thus, the decision about discount rate and asset life are not independent. Since there is no a priori preferred asset life, the SEEA EEA TR highlights the need for sensitivity analyses on the asset life and the discount rate.

In finding NPV values, one must recognize that the expected future flows of ecosystem services for an ecosystem asset is affected by the ecosystem condition, which again is affected by the use of ecosystem services. The nexus between use and condition of an ecosystem leads us to the concept of ecosystem capacity. Hein et al. (2016) define the concept of ecosystem capacity for accounting purposes as "the ability of an ecosystem to generate an ecosystem service under current conditions and uses at the maximum yield or use level that does not negatively affect the future supply of the same or other ecosystem services." Thus, capacity may be thought of as the sustainable use of an ecosystem service for which there is demand, preferably at aggregate scales such as at the landscape level.

The SEEA EEA TR (United Nations 2017) states that "ecosystem capacity is considered a topic of ongoing research but with a very high priority" (paragraph 7.68), and that the "concept of ecosystem capacity is a central one for explaining the ecosystem accounting model and applying the model in practice. This is especially the case in relation to developing information sets that can support the discussion of sustainability" (paragraph 7.33).

Some of the reasons why the concept of ecosystem capacity still is under development is that it involves ecologically complex effects such as threshold effects, resilience, ecosystem dynamics and other non-linear effects. These effects also create challenges for standard valuation (exchange or welfare-based valuations, see e.g. discussion in Farley 2012). In addition, one needs to resolve how to measure capacity in practice.

The SEEA EEA TR discusses issues of the measurement of ecosystem capacity. Ecosystem capacity may be monetized in terms of the NPV of estimates for the future basket of services. To obtain an estimate of ecosystem capacity one needs to have an estimate of the future ecosystem service use that is as close as possible to the actual or revealed patterns of use under the expected legal and institutional arrangements. This implies that the estimated future use does not necessarily reflect sustainable uses. One may then compare the NPV of ecosystem use at capacity to the NPV of the actual use, and determine whether the ecosystem is being used above, below or at capacity. Sustainable ecosystem management ultimately requires managing ecosystems below capacity (safe minimum standards). If the ecosystem is used above capacity, it reduces the opportunity for this and future generations to manage the ecosystem sustainably. A decline in condition of an ecosystem asset as a result of economic and other human activity would in SEEA EEA be considered ecosystem degradation. How to include ecosystem degradation has also to be determined. While ecosystem degradation is clearly related to declining condition, it can be defined more specifically as reflecting either a decline in the ecosystem asset value as measured in relation to the change in the NPV of an ecosystem asset based on the expected flow of services, or in relation to the change in the NPV of an ecosystem asset based on its capacity. For both the concept of ecosystem degradation and for the concept of ecosystem capacity one needs to resolve some practical measurement issues that will also have bearings on how to value ecosystem assets within the SEEA EEA framework.

5.   Discussion, conclusion and future directions

SEEA and its developments are seen as an important step on the road to wealth accounting (Perrings 2012). We have discussed how the accounting framework SEEA EEA is currently moving towards developing operational solutions to important challenges related to monetary valuation as discussed in the SEEA EEA TR (United Nations 2017).

The requirement only to permit exchange values in SEEA EEA is motivated by the goal of compatibility with national accounting. This would later make it possible to consistently estimate the asset value of a nation's total capital stock. However, accounting that only includes exchange values will not fully reflect the importance of ecosystem services to society (Remme et al. 2015). For example, risks may be unaccounted for in the exchange values (Hein et al. 2015). Further, capturing the value of many regulating and cultural services with exchange value methods will remain a challenge. Further research and testing, is necessary in order to integrate values into an ecosystem accounting framework that is useful for policy assessment (e.g. Remme et al. 2015; Hein et al. 2015).

Another challenge with using exchange values for ecosystem services is that a large share of existing estimates of non-market ecosystem services are in the form of willingness to pay, which includes consumer surplus (i.e. a welfare-based approach) and not in the form of exchange values. However, research on how to derive the exchange value from welfare-based studies is ongoing (see e.g. Caparros et al. 2017; Day 2013; United Nations 2017).

Like SEEA EEA, inclusive wealth accounting is mainly constrained by the lack of shadow prices for ecosystem assets, and "there is insufficient experience with the calculation of these shadow prices at the scale required for accounting" (Hein et al. 2015, p. 90; Barbier 2013). Dasgupta and Duraiappah (2012) recognize that we can never get the shadow prices "right." Instead, we can simply try to estimate the range in which they lie. Given these challenges, empirical studies in the inclusive wealth framework have also resorted to using market prices (exchange value) for those ecosystem services/benefits that have market prices. However, research is also ongoing to find better estimates of shadow prices (Fenichel and Abbott 2014). The next best solution, suggested by Dasgupta and Duraiappah (2012, p. 26), is to use "willingness to pay shadow prices," while recognizing that these prices may not capture threshold effects of an ecosystem.

Both for SEEA EEA and the inclusive wealth framework there is increasing interest among researchers to tailor valuation studies for natural and ecosystem capital accounting, as recommended by Tallis et al. (2012). This would be the ideal situation, since the need for and challenges of benefit transfer and scaling-up would be reduced. For both wealth accounting frameworks, it may be difficult to account for non-use values such as existence values and other subtler cultural services/benefits, even though we know from many studies that such benefits can be important for people's welfare (Lindhjem et al. 2015). If the goal is to demonstrate the importance of an ecosystem service, one may have to use other indicators of value (see Box 5.6 and Barbier 2014) when direct valuation of the ecosystem service fails. This could be due to lack of data, difficulty in defining institutional arrangements that mimic exchange values or because accounting compatible values capture only a very small part of welfare (Jacobs et al. 2016).

Inclusive wealth accounting is a developing accounting framework for both human, natural and ecosystem capital with the goal of demonstrating the importance of these types of capital to human well-being. Since the focus is welfare-based one needs shadow values of the capital stocks, and estimates of shadow values are hard to come by. SEEA EEA specializes in ecosystem accounting using a national accounting framework. While the national accounting framework implies some restrictions, such as the use of exchange values, developing ecosystem accounts based on an existing accounting framework may be quite helpful. The SEEA EEA has developed concrete solutions to several accounting challenges and contributed to operationalize measurement. Furthermore, the need to complement the SEEA EEA framework with ecosystem capacity accounts to better track sustainability of ecosystem use has been recognized.

On the other hand, inclusive wealth accounting emphasizes intergenerational welfare and is not restricted by national accounting standards. However, calculating the total value of natural capital for inclusive wealth calculations is also quite difficult and may go beyond what can currently be achieved. A more achievable goal might be to evaluate the marginal value of natural capital, which is how a small change will alter the present value of the flow of services. Further, in order to find the present value of future flows of ecosystem services one will need models to estimate the impact of changes in natural capital on the provision of ecosystem services. One also needs to predict the future prices and determine the appropriate discount rate. Other related challenges include issues related to resilience and thresholds of ecosystems.

Finally, equity is also a crucial part of sustainability. Solely focusing on aggregated numbers at the national level may not be the best way to evaluate sustainability because numbers at the national level might mask the impacts at the local level as well as inequalities among income groups in the current generation, and across generations. Thus, inclusive wealth accounting should also address the spatial and temporal distribution of wealth.

In the end, if attempting to account such complex assets as ecosystem assets, no matter which accounting system one applies, it is important one is aware of the assumptions and the limitations of the accounting framework and the benefits of an accounting framework that can be applied consistently over time.

Notes

1 See also the recent developments on a so-called Integrated system of Natural Capital and ecosystem services Accounting in the EU (KIP INCA) (La Notte et al. 2017). This system aims to work according to the SEEA EEA system and to further develop this based on EU experiences.
2 Note that in the ecosystem accounting framework biodiversity is treated as a component of the ecosystem asset rather than as an ecosystem service in its own right (United Nations 2017). In addition, biodiversity is also included in standalone thematic accounts.
3 Data collection started in many countries when ecosystems were already at a highly modified, depleted state. Hence, this view of the references condition has its problems.
4 It is worth noting that the international database of valuation studies, Environmental Valuation Reference Inventory (EVRI), has just recently been opened for the public: www.evri.ca

References

Aanesen, M. et al. (2015) Willingness to pay for unfamiliar public goods: Preserving cold-water coral in Norway. *Ecological Economics* 112: 53–67.
Atkinson, G. and C. Obst (2017) Prices for Ecosystem Accounting. https://www.wavespartnership.org/sites/waves/files/kc/Prices%20for%20ecosystem%20accounting.pdf
Banzhaf, S. and J. Boyd (2012) The architecture and measurement of an ecosystem services index. *Sustainability* 4: 430–461.

Barbier, E. B. (2012) *Ecosystem services and wealth accounting*, IHDP-UNU/UNEP Inclusive Wealth Report 2012, Cambridge University Press, Cambridge.

Barbier, E. B. (2013) Wealth accounting, ecological capital and ecosystem services. *Environmental and Development Economics* 18: 133–161.

Barbier, E. B. (2014) *Challenges to ecosystem services valuation for wealth accounting*, IHDP-UNU/UNEP Inclusive Wealth Report 2014, Cambridge University Press, Cambridge.

Barton, D. N. et al. (2015) *Economic valuation of ecosystem services for policy: A pilot study on green infrastructure in Oslo*, NINA Report 1114, 77p. Norwegian Institute of Nature Research, Oslo.

Barton, D. N. and P. A. Harrison (eds.) (2017) Integrated valuation of ecosystem services: Guidelines and experiences. European Commission FP7, 2017. EU FP7 OpenNESS Project Deliverable 33–44.

Barton, D. N., S. Jacobs, I. I. Arandia, H. Saarikoski, M. Termansen, M. P. Soba and E. Kelemen (2017) OpenNESS brief no 5 (2017). Available at: www.openness-project. eu/sites/default/files/Policy%20brief%20%235%20Capturing%20diverse%20 nature%20values_Final.pdf. Last accessed Oct. 7, 2017.

Bateman, I., G. M. Mace, C. Fezzi, G. Atkinson and K. Turner (2011) Economic analysis for ecosystem service assessments. *Environmental and Resource Economics* 48: 177–218.

Bateman, I. et al. (2013) Bringing ecosystems services into economic decision-making: Land use in the United Kingdom. *Science* 341: 45–50.

Brander, L. et al. (2012) Using meta-analysis and GIS for value transfer and scaling up: Valuing climate change induced losses of European Wetlands. *Environmental and Resource Economics* 52(3): 395–413.

Caparros, A., J. L. Oviedo et al. (2017) Simulated exchange values and ecosystem accounting: Theory and application to free access recreation. *Ecological Economics* 139: 140–149.

Champ, P. A., K. J. Boyle and T. C. Brown (2017) *A primer on non-market valuation*, 2nd edition, Springer, Netherlands.

Dasgupta, P. and A. Duraiappah (2012) *Well-being and wealth*, IHDP-UNU/UNEP Inclusive Wealth Report 2012, Cambridge University Press, Cambridge.

Day, B. (2013) *An overview of valuation techniques for ecosystem accounting*, School of Environmental Sciences, University of East Anglia, mimeo, East Anglia.

Environmental Protection Agency (EPA) (2009) *Valuing the protection of ecological systems and services*, EPA, Washington, DC.

European Commission, International Monetary Fund, Organsation for Economic Co-operation and Development, World Bank (2009) System of National Accounts 2008. United Nations, New York.

Farley, J. (2012) Ecosystem services: The economics debate. *Ecosystem Services* 1: 40–49.

Fenichel, E. P. and J. K. Abbott (2014) Natural capital: From metaphor to measurement. *Journal of the Association of Environmental and Resource Economists* 1(1/2): 1–27.

Freeman, A. M. III et al. (2014) *The measurement of environmental and resource values: Theory and methods*, 3rd edition, RFF Press, Washington, DC.

Gomez-Baggethun, E. and D. N. Barton (2013) Classifying and valuing ecosystem services for urban planning. *Ecological Economics* 86: 235–245.

Greaker, M., K. M. Grimsrud and L. Lindholt (2017) The potential resource rent from Norwegian fisheries. *Marine Policy* (84): 156–166.

Haavardsholm, O. (2015) *Valuing urban ecosystem services: A contingent valuation study on street trees in Oslo*. M.Sc. University of Oslo, Oslo.

Hein, L., K. Bagstad, B. Edens, C. Obst, Carl, R. de Jong and J. P. Lesschen (2016) Defining ecosystem assets for natural capital accounting. *PloS ONE* 11(11).

Hein, L., C. Obst, B. Edens and R. Remme (2015) Progress and challenges in the development of ecosystem accounting as a tool to analyse ecosystem capital. *Current Opinion in Environmental Sustainability* 14: 86–92.

IHDP-UNU/UNEP (2012) Inclusive Wealth Report 2012, Cambridge University Press, Cambridge.

Jacobs, S. et al. (2016) A new valuation school: Integrating diverse values of nature in resource and land use decisions. *Ecosystem Services* 22 Part B: 213–220.

Johnston, R. J., J. Rolfe, R. S. Rosenberger and R. Brouwer (2015) *Benefit transfer of environmental and resource values: A guide for researchers and practitioners.* Springer, Netherlands.

Johnston, R. J. and L. A. Wainger (2015) Benefit transfer for ecosystem service valuation: An introduction to theory and methods. In Johnston, R. J., J. Rolfe, R. S. Rosenberger and R. Brouwer (eds.) *Benefit transfer of environmental and resource values: A guide for researchers and practitioners.* Springer, Netherlands.

Koetse, M. J., R. Brouwer and B. J. H. van Beukering (2015) Economic valuation methods for ecosystem services. In Bouma, J. and P. van Beukering (eds.) *Ecosystem services: From concept to practice.* Cambridge University Press, Cambridge.

Kumar, P. (ed.) (2010) *The economics of ecosystems and biodiversity ecological and economic foundations.* Earthscan, London and Washington.

La Notte, A., S. Vallecillo, C. Polce, G. Zulian and J. Maes (2017) Implementing an EU system of accounting for ecosystems and their services. Initial proposals for the implementation of ecosystem services accounts, EUR 28681 EN; Publications Office of the European Union, Luxembourg, doi:10.2760/214137, JRC107150.

Laurans, Y. et al. (2013) Use of ecosystem services economic valuation for decision making: Questioning a literature blindspot. *Journal of Environmental Management* 119: 208–219.

Lindhjem, H. (2007) 20 years of stated preference valuation of non-timber benefits from fennoscandian forests: A meta-analysis. *Journal of Forest Economics* 12: 251–277.

Lindhjem, H., K. Grimsrud, S. Navrud and S. O. Kolle (2015) The social benefits and costs of preserving forest biodiversity and ecosystem services. *Journal of Environmental Economics and Policy* 4(2): 202–222.

Lindhjem, H. and S. Navrud (2008) How reliable are meta-analyses for international benefit transfers? *Ecological Economics* 66(2–3): 425–435.

Millennium Ecosystem Assessment (2005) *Ecosystems and human well-being*, Synthesis Report. Island Press, Washington, DC.

Obst, C. (2017) Personal communication. Oct. 6. 2017.

Obst, C., L. Hein and B. Edens (2016) National accounting and the valuation of ecosystem assets and their services. *Environmental and Resource Economics* 64: 1–23.

Pearson, L., P. Munoz and E. Darkey (2012) *The significance of the natural wealth of nations*, IHDP-UNU/UNEP Inclusive Wealth Report 2012, Cambridge University Press, Cambridge.

Perrings, C. (2012) *The road to wealth accounting*, IHDP-UNU/ UNEP (2012) Inclusive Wealth Report 2012, Cambridge University Press, Cambridge.

Remme, R. P., B. Edens, M. Schröter and L. Hein (2015) Monetary accounting of ecosystem services: A test case for Limburg province, the Netherlands. *Ecological Economics* 112: 116–128.

Skourtos, M., A. Kontogianniog and P. A. Harrison (2010) Reviewing the dynamics of economic values and preferences for ecosystem goods and services. *Biodiversity and Conservation* 19(10): 2855–2872.

Sumarga, E., L. Hein, B. Edens and A. Suwarno (2015) Mapping monetary values of ecosystem services in support of developing ecosystem accounts. *Ecosystem Services* 12: 71–83.

Tallis, H., S. Polasky, J. S. Lozano and S. Wolny (2012) *Inclusive wealth accounting for regulating ecosystem services*. IHDP-UNU/ UNEP (2012) Inclusive Wealth Report 2012, Cambridge University Press, Cambridge.

United Nations, European Commission, International Monetary Fund, Organisation for Economic Co-operation and Development, The World Bank (2008) System of National Accounts 2008. United Nations, New York.

United Nations (2017) SEEA Experimental Ecosystem Accounting: Technical Recommendations, Consultation Draft V4.1:6 – March 2017. Draft prepared as part of the joint UNEP/UNSD/CBD project on Advancing Natural Capital Accounting funded by NORAD.

United Nations, European Commission, Food and Agricultural Organization of the United Nations, International Monetary Fund, Organisation for Economic Co-operation and Development, the World Bank (2014a) *System of environmental-economic accounting 2012: Central framework*. United Nations, New York.

United Nations, European Commission, Food and Agricultural Organization of the United Nations, International Monetary Fund, Organisation for Economic Co-Operation and Development, the World Bank (2014b) *System of environmental-economic accounting 2012: Experimental ecosystem accounting*. United Nations, New York.

Vanoli, A. (2005) *A history of national accounting*. IOS Press, Amsterdam.

Vincent, J. R. (2015) *Valuing environmental services in the SNA*, Report prepared for the Policy and Technical Experts Committee (PTEC) of the World Bank's Wealth Accounting and Valuation of Ecosystem Services (WAVES) Program, Washington DC.

Wilen, J. E. (2000) Renewable resource economists and policy: What differences have we made? *Journal of Environmental Economics and Management* 39(3): 306–327.

6 Is economic growth linked with comprehensive wealth? Link to state-level analysis in India

Haripriya Gundimeda

1. Introduction

Economic growth, the goal of all the countries, does not happen in a black box, but depends on the quality of the produced, natural, human and social capital. The skills, knowledge that the humans have is a form of capital and is a prerequisite for growth. The important role played by human capital in driving economic growth is well established (Lucas, 1988, Romer, 1989, Barro, 1991, Schultz, 1961). Human capital stock is important to enhance the productivity of both labour and physical capital, and to drive the innovation and diffusion of technology. Very strong two-way association between economic growth, human capital and life expectancy has been found in the literature.

Natural capital provides necessary and essential substitutable and non-substitutable materials and services (e.g. energy stocks, minerals, forests) for the economy to thrive and survive. For example, wood and coal are substitutes and the solar energy can be a substitute for oil, while the regulatory services (like carbon regulation) cannot be substituted by other forms of capital. Technology can offset some of the functions of resources but there are limits to technological possibilities. Ample but inconclusive evidence exists in the literature, which explored the relation between natural resources and economic growth. There are examples, where natural resources drive the economic growth (Norway, Malaysia, Botswana, Canada) as well as counter factual evidences on how higher natural resource base can lead to slower growth rates, low incomes, weak political institutions etc. Research by Sachs and Warner (1997), Auty (1993), for example, showed that countries which are rich in agricultural and mining capitals grew more slowly during 1970 to 1990 compared to resource poor economies and this phenomenon has been named as natural resource drag. The abundance of natural resources pulls economic growth downwards (called *natural resource drag*). For example, many of the countries in Africa (Congo, Nigeria, Angola) have high poverty rates despite abundance of natural resources.

Some researchers argue that a natural resources curse exists not because the countries are resource rich but due to rent seeking behaviour and abundance of certain types of natural resources (for example energy resources) (see Congleton et al., 2008; Boschini et al., 2007). In countries with abundant natural resources, the rent seeking behaviour by political elites is responsible for the resource curse. Some studies take to the view that natural resource abundance can lead to Dutch disease and crowding out of human and physical capital (Atkinson & Hamilton, 2003; Gylfason & Zoega, 2006). However, no consensus has emerged. Deaton and Rode (2012), Mehlum et al. (2006) opine that the mixed evidence relating to abundance in natural resources and economic growth is because of the quality of the institutions (economic and political) in the countries – emphasizing that natural capital alone cannot explain the counter factual evidence. This aspect of other factors is supported by meta-analysis by Havranek et al. (2016). Havranek et al. (2016) based on a quantitative survey of 605 estimates from 43 studies show that 20 percent of the papers found a positive relationship, 40 percent found no effect and 40 percent of the papers showed a negative effect of natural resources on the economic growth. The study concludes that the interaction between the quality of institutions, extent of natural resource dependence and abundance along with the level of investments impacts the economic growth. Interestingly, the level of natural capital also seems to influence the level of human capital. Gylfason (1999) shows that the school enrolment at all levels is inversely related to the natural resource abundance, as measured by the share of labour force engaged in primary production, across countries. However, social capital has got a role to play in understanding how the resources are invested back in various forms of capital. Norway, for example, despite being rich in energy resources, does not neglect the human capital. The human capital in turn also impacts the better conditions for governance by improving health and equality (Aghion et al., 1999). Thus the social capital provides the enabling conditions for rest of the capitals to thrive and in turn is enabled by other forms of capital.

The viewpoint until the 1990s that manufactured capital is the only productive base of the economy has been contested as the role of other forms of capital has been recognized (UNU and IHDP, 2012; United Nations University International Human Dimensions and Programme, 2015). Higher GDP need not translate into a higher quality of life or imply the well-being of the nation – which is derived from different forms of capital, and not from GDP alone. The GDP does not measure the impact of production activities on the quality of the environment and natural resources and thus on the human well-being. Substituting natural capital to achieve higher growth can impact the health of people which could impact the human capital and thus the produced capital. It is very clear that the capital is not additively separable but is strongly correlative with other forms of capital.

Inclusive wealth is based on measuring the capital stocks which influence the well-being, and thus it is important to track the changes in the value of nations' stocks. As mentioned by Arrow, Dasgupta, Goulder, Munford, and Oleson (2012), the "state's capacity to produce goods and services requires measuring growth in comprehensive wealth and not merely the capital stock formation alone". "As long as the state is on optimal growth path, the growth in net capital formation can be a good measure of growth. If not, an income-based measure like GDP could lead to qualitatively different conclusions about economic growth than a direct measure of the growth of the capital stock". (Arrow et al., 2012).

The objective of this study is to understand the link between economic growth and different forms of capital for the period 2001–2011 using comprehensive wealth as an indicator. To illustrate the arguments, two different forms of natural capital – renewable (forests) and non-renewable (minerals) – were considered along with human capital and the produced capital as a measure of wealth. These are then viewed in the context of other basic tenants of the quality of life measured from the perspective of human development index and health. In Section 2, some perspective on growth and development in India at the state level is discussed, Section 3 discusses the concept of measurement of produced, natural and human capital, and Section 4 links it to the state-level analysis.

2.   Some perspective on growth and the links to development in India at state level

Figure 6.1 gives the contribution of different states considered in the study to the GDP in India. It can be clearly seen that Maharashtra contributes 17% of the income, followed by Tamil Nadu, Uttar Pradesh, Gujarat, West Bengal and Karnataka, which together contribute to 56% of the GDP. A similar trend has been observed in 2001 though the relative contributions differed. Uttar Pradesh, the most populous state in India with a share of 16.9% of population, contributes only 8.7% of the GDP in 2011 and the other populous states in the order Maharashtra (9.4%), Bihar (8.8%), West Bengal (7.64%) and Andhra Pradesh (7.1%) contribute 17.1%, 2.7%, 6.6% and 8.4% to GDP respectively.

In terms of the per capita income (per capita net state domestic product), of the states considered in this study, Goa has the highest per capita income (almost 10 times that of Bihar the poorest state), followed by Sikkim, Haryana, Maharashtra and Tamil Nadu (Delhi has the second highest per capita income after Goa), while the states Bihar, Uttar Pradesh, Assam, Manipur and Madhya Pradesh are the poorest. These five states have approximately 34% of the Indian population.

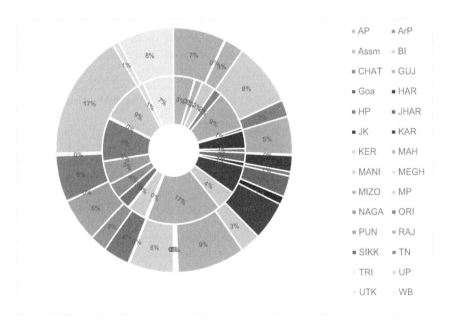

Figure 6.1 States share of GDP and population in 2011

Note: The inner pie represents GDP in 2011.

Source: Figure based on data from http://mospi.nic.in/data, http://censusindia.gov.in/.

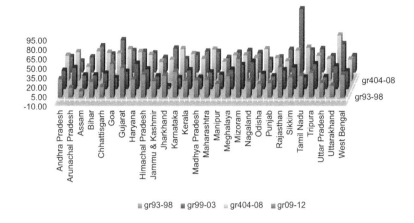

Figure 6.2 Cumulative growth in per capita income during 1993–2012
Source: Figure drawn and data compiled from http://niti.gov.in/.

The growth story presents a different picture. The highest cumulative growth during 2001–2011 occurred in Sikkim, Uttarakhand, Goa, Gujarat and Tamil Nadu while Assam, Manipur, Jammu and Kashmir, West Bengal and Uttar Pradesh had low growth. During the first half of the decade (2001–2006), the states Uttarakhand Gujarat, Maharashtra, Tamil Nadu and Karnataka were the fastest while in the second half of the decade (2006–2011), Sikkim, Uttarakhand, Goa and Bihar grew faster than the other states.

Thus GDP and its decadal growth is influenced not only by the demographic factors and size, but also by the workforce and the quality, along with the investments made in the state. Figure 6.3 presents the indicators on change in output per worker, the work participation rate along with the gross capital formation in these states. It is apparent that these are all related but are not the only factors in the Indian context. The fast-growing state Uttarakhand and Sikkim has very high gross capital formation (data not available for Sikkim) and has seen an increase in work participation rates (an indicator of expansion in economic activity), which explains the growth as well as the increase in gross value added per unit of worker. Some of the slow growing states have suffered from low capital formation as well as have seen a decline in the value of output per worker. Thus the human capital measure can be used to explain the economic growth to an extent.

How are the states faring in terms of the overall development, measured in terms of HDI? HDI has been measured using different approaches. Based on the analysis by Mukherjee et al. (2014), the state of Kerala has been consistently well off the mark. The next in HDI rank are Goa, Himachal Pradesh, Tamil Nadu and Maharashtra. UP, the most populous state, contributing to 8.5% of GDP in India and Bihar,

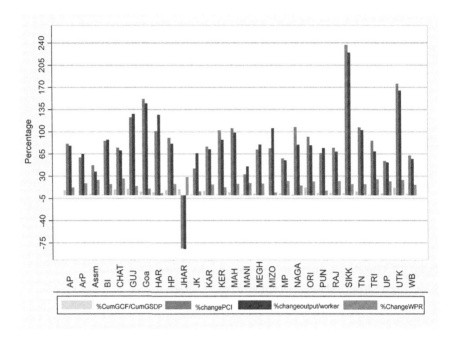

Figure 6.3 Decadal change in per capita income, output per worker, work participation rates and gross capital formation

Source: Figure drawn based on data compiled from different sources from http://niti.gov.in/, http://mospi.nic.in/data, http://censusindia.gov.in/.

rank very low on the Human Development Index. Most of the northeastern states are yet to catch up and have registered low decadal growth as well (with the exception of Sikkim, whose growth has been phenomenal). Uttarakhand has registered significant growth and ranked 11 in terms of HDI, next only to Gujarat. Andhra Pradesh, despite being an economically important state, does not figure in the top 15, and Karnataka does not figure in the top 10.

The study does find some evidence between economic growth and development, but however does not explain the complete story. The initial stock of the state's assets are important as well and thus a capital perspective becomes important. It is useful to understand how different states have used their natural capital and accumulated their produced and human capital. To reiterate Arrow et al. (2012), "the state's capacity to produce goods and services requires a measure of the growth in comprehensive accounting of all forms of capital and not merely the capital stock formation alone. As long as the state is on an optimal growth path, the growth in net capital formation can be a good measure of growth. If not, an income-based measure like GDP could lead to qualitatively different conclusions on economic growth than a direct measure of the growth of the capital stock" (Arrow et al., 2012).

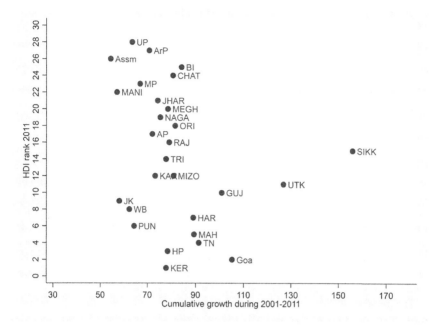

Figure 6.4 Decadal cumulative growth in GDP (2001–2011) vs. HDI 2011
Source: Author's illustration.

3. Methodology for measuring comprehensive wealth and investments of states

The national accounts recognize the importance of capital stock as an important indicator in assessing the growth potential of the economy. However, the capital stock estimates are limited to include produced assets and some non-produced assets (like land) but do not consider the natural capital (renewable and non-renewable) and human capital stocks. Here we give the estimates of natural capital stock and human capital stocks for different states in India for the year 2001, for which the estimates are available consistently across the states. The study considers forest capital and mineral assets – under the categories renewable and non-renewable natural capital. The methodology used in estimating the natural capital stocks and human capital stocks is given below and is extracted from the work carried out by the author earlier.

3.1. Renewable natural capital – forests

Natural capital is an asset and change in natural wealth is akin to capital formation of produced assets. In this paper, the forest capital is included as an example of renewable natural capital. Estimating the value of natural capital formation requires estimating the flow of ecosystem services from forests and valuing them at their shadow process. Based on the summary of earlier studies by the author ((Gundimeda,

Sanyal, Sinha, & Sukhdev, The value of Timber, Carbon and Non-timber forest products in India Monopgraph 1, 2005); (Gundimeda, Sanyal, Sinha, & Sukhdev, The Value of Biodiversity in India's Forests, 2006); (Gundimeda, Sanyal, Sinha, & Sukhdev, 2007); (Gundimeda & Atkinson, Accounting for India's forest wealth, 2006)), the value of forest wealth is obtained as the discounted present value of flows from six forest products for which the estimates are available – timber, fuelwood, non-timber forest products (NTFPs), forest biomass carbon and recreational and genetic services. The data for the stock of forests come from the Forest Survey of India, which documents forest changes every two years based on satellite data and ground verification.

Timber is the most obvious component of forest wealth, which can be directly estimated from the volume of growing timber. To obtain carbon stocks, the volume of forest biomass was first estimated from the growing stock estimates and then converted to carbon, assuming a carbon content of 0.5 Mg C per Mg oven dry biomass (Gundimeda, Estimation of Biomass in Indian Forests, 2000b), (Gundimeda, Carbom Budget of the Indian Forest Ecosystem, 2003)). Since forests cannot be used for timber extraction and carbon sequestration at the same time, reserved forests has been assumed to be used for carbon sequestration and protected forests for timber, fuelwood, non-timber products, etc. Forests also provide erosion control, hydrological services, biodiversity, etc. Changes in these services are more difficult to assess.

The biggest challenge in estimating changes in wealth arises from establishing shadow prices. As Arrow et al. (2012) show, shadow prices reflect contributions to well-being by the direct and indirect use of forest goods and services. Various methods were used to obtain the shadow values of different components of India's forest wealth. The shadow price of timber equals net rent, i.e. price less the cost of extraction. Resource rent is estimated as the average prices of round wood and fuelwood minus the unit costs of extraction (Gundimeda, 2000a, 2001). (Gundimeda, (Gundimeda, Integrating Forest Resources in the System of National Accounts, 2000a), (Gundimeda, Accounting for the Forest Resources in the National Accounts in India, 2001)). Carbon was valued at $20/tC, based on its global market value at that time. The shadow price of NTFPs was computed as the discounted value of products per hectare (Gundimeda, 2000a, 2001). The shadow price of recreation has been estimated using the consumer surplus derived for tourists, estimated using a benefit transfer approach. The biodiversity values of forests were estimated by assessing the value of marginal species for medicinal purposes. Here the approach was to establish the incremental contribution of a species to the probability of making a commercial discovery (Rausser, 2000). Methodological details on shadow values of biodiversity and recreational services are provided in Gundimeda et al. (2006).

3.2.   *Non-reproducible capital – mineral wealth*

"India produces around 89 minerals including four fuel minerals, 52 non-metallic minerals, 11 metallic minerals and 22 minor minerals. The sector's contribution to GDP hovered around 2% to 2.3% during 1979 to 2005. The production statistics of 2004 show that fuels account for about 79%, metallic minerals about 8%, non-metallic minerals around 3% and minor minerals the remaining 10% (IBM, 2004). Among the fuel minerals, petroleum and natural gas contributed to around 43% and coal and lignite 36%. In terms of geographical distribution of mineral resources, the offshore accounted for 29% value of the mineral production while the remaining was accounted for mainly by Andhra Pradesh (9%), Gujarat, Jharkhand (8% each), Chhattisgarh (7%), Orissa, Madhya Pradesh (6% each), Assam (5%), Maharashtra, Rajasthan, Uttar Pradesh (4% each) and West Bengal (3%). With its contribution of about 16% in exports and 20% in imports, the mineral sector is an important component of India's foreign trade. The majority of the exports (75%) are contributed by cut diamond and crude petroleum accounts for 67% of imports. As 85% of the value addition comes from coal, iron ore, oil, natural gas and limestone, only these were included for analysis " (Gundimeda, 2017).

"The value of stock of a natural resource (RV) can be computed as the net present value of the stream of the future resource rents the resources yield till exhaustion. Estimating net present value requires knowledge on (1) the resource rent, (2) rate of extraction of the resource, (3) the life span of the resource and (4) the discount rate. However, NPV approach is complicated due to the uncertainties in future price of the commodity, the technology, the true size of the deposits and the quality of the deposits that are yet to be found. In this study, the estimates of asset prices are based on net price method. The data have been obtained from the Central Statistical Organization and the annual reports of the mining companies " (Gundimeda, 2016).

The physical stock data were obtained from the publication "Indian Minerals Year book" published by Indian Bureau of Mines. What is considered as stock is an important issue worth exploring here. The most commonly used system of classification is McKelvey classification, which classifies mineral resources based on the two combined criteria i.e. the degree of uncertainty (proven, probable or classified as measured, indicated, inferred, potential and speculative) and economic feasibility of extraction (economic, marginally-economic, sub-economic). "Proven" reserves are those where it is known that it is both technically feasible and economically viable to extract the mineral resource. "Probable" includes the reserves that are known to exist but where some doubt exists over whether they are technically or economically viable. "Possible" covers reserves where there is considerable doubt over the technical and or financial viability of extraction. "Potential" reserves are known to exist but thought to be not technically or economically feasible to extract. "Speculative" reserves cover estimates which have not been positively identified but which, based on previous geological experience, it is reasonable to expect in proximity to that already in the "proven" and "probable" categories (Lange & Wright, 2004). For computing the wealth estimates, only proven reserves were considered.

The biggest challenge comes from valuation of the physical stock of minerals. Market prices if available provide a good description of the scarcity. However, these prices are often distorted due to institutional arrangements. If the private parties own the asset, it is possible to get market prices but if the assets are owned by government and are not sold, market prices do not exist. If there are no market prices, (SEEA, 2012) suggests using the cost of extracting the assets as a lower bound on its value. The argument behind using such an approach is that assets would not be extracted unless the benefits obtained were at least as high as the costs.

3.3. Human capital

The following section is an extract from Gundimeda et al. (2007). Human capital is one of the most important assets of a country and a key determinant of a nation's economic performance. Human capital can be defined in many ways, but in this paper we have used the following definition adopted by OECD (Organization for Economic Cooperation and Development) (1998): "The knowledge, skills, competences and other attributes embodied in individuals that are relevant to economic activity." Human capital, in this paper, is captured through returns to education as done by other seminal contributions Becker (1966); Mincer (1974); and Schultz (1961). In the literature we find three different approaches to estimate the value of human capital – the "cost-based approach" (cost-of-production approach), the "income-based approach" (capitalized earnings procedure), and the "educational stock-based approach." In cost-based approach, the human capital is estimated using the depreciated value of the dollar amount spent on an individual. The income-based approach (capitalized earnings procedure) measures the total human capital embodied in an individual who has completed his schooling by the total discounted values of expected future stream of lifetime earnings. The most commonly used measures for "educational stock-based approach" include education-augmented labour input, adult literacy rates, school enrolment ratios and the average years of schooling of the working-age population. As activities like formal education, on-the-job training, specific training and other recognized investments in human capital have an influence on earnings, which also include some costs. Thus, the total amount invested in human capital and the rate of return on this investment can be estimated from using the information on observed earnings and costs of schooling and foregone earnings.

The estimates of human capital are obtained as follows (based on Gundimeda et al. (2007)). The stocks of population categorized by age cohorts, rural and urban, male and female by educational qualifications for different years is obtained from the Census data published by the Government of India. The shadow price on educational capital stock is obtained by first estimating a Mincerian earning function where in the wage of an individual is regressed on the level of schooling, skills possessed, technical qualifications, on-the-job training (job experience used as a proxy) and other socio-economic characteristics that represent the innate abilities of the individual. From the estimated Mincerian function, the predicted wages for different age cohorts by the educational levels has been obtained from the marginal rate of return for different educational qualifications, gender and geographical location. The predicted wage for different educational levels, gender and geographic locations were used to obtain the net present value of the lifetime labour income. The present value of the lifetime labour income of an individual is the discounted value of future income weighted by the probability of survival and the discount rate. For estimating the lifetime labour income two stages were used: (1) work and study stage (age group 15–25) and (2) work only. The total value of the human capital in different Indian states is obtained by multiplying the present value of annualized life income for different educational qualifications for different age cohorts with the population in each educational group in different age cohorts from the Census data.

3.4. Physical capital

Capital stock of a country is broadly referred to as that part of national wealth which is reproducible; it consists of all resources which contribute to the production of goods and services. The United Nations Guidelines in 1977 defined the national wealth as "total of various kinds of net tangible and intangible non-financial assets of residents, plus financial claims on non-residents less financial liabilities to non-residents." "Tangible assets have been further classified into (i) reproducible tangible assets (i.e. capital stock) comprising fixed assets and stocks (i.e. inventories) and (ii) non-reproducible tangible assets comprising, land, timber tracts and forests, subsoil assets and extraction sites, fisheries and historical monuments. The reproducible fixed tangible assets (i.e. fixed assets used for the production of goods and services) commonly known as fixed capital stock comprise assets in the form of residential buildings, non-residential buildings, dams, irrigation and flood control projects, other construction works, transport equipment, machinery and equipment, breeding stock, drought animals, dairy cattle and the like, and capital expenditure on land improvement, plantations, orchard developments and afforestation. These fixed assets include uncompleted construction assets also". However, while net fixed capital stock estimates by type of institution are available from the Central Statistical Organization, the capital stock estimates are not available at the state level in India. The gross fixed capital formation by assets and industry for the public sector are available for some of the states. Thus, in this chapter a comparison is made by gross fixed capital formation alone.

4. Links to state-level analysis and changes in different forms of capital in India

Figure 6.5 gives the share of capital stocks in different states in India. The states Himachal Pradesh, Mizoram, Tripura, West Bengal, Tamil Nadu and Kerala emerge as the wealthiest states in terms of natural capital, and the states Bihar (including

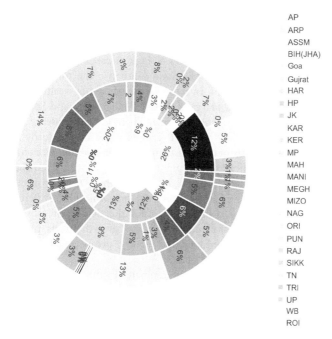

Figure 6.5 Share of forest, subsoil assets and human capital in Indian states

Source: Based on author's estimates.

Jharkhand), Madhya Pradesh (including Chhattisgarh), Karnataka, Rajasthan, Andhra Pradesh and Orissa have rich mineral capital. The states Uttar Pradesh (including Uttarakhand), Maharashtra, Andhra Pradesh, West Bengal and Tamil Nadu have very high human capital.

The data on produced capital stock estimates at the state level are not available, but based on the cumulative gross capital formation in the decade, the states Gujarat, Maharashtra, Tamil Nadu, Karnataka, Andhra Pradesh and Orissa top. So if we take comprehensive wealth (sum of all capitals – produced, human and natural capital) and produced capital proxied by cumulative gross fixed capital formation, together, we see that the states Gujarat, Maharashtra, Tamil Nadu, Karnataka and Uttar Pradesh (including Uttarakhand) emerge the richest in terms of absolute comprehensive wealth. Estimating separate capital stock estimates for these states is required to know their exact ranking. However, viewed in terms of per capita wealth, the states Goa, Gujarat, Himachal, Karnataka, Haryana, Orissa, Maharashtra and Sikkim emerge in the top eight. The data for gross fixed capital formation are not available for Sikkim and despite this, Sikkim is ranked among the top ten richest states. The state has seen an increase in GDP growth and has seen very proactive environmental measures. These are also the states which have high per capita income and have registered above average growth rates during the decade.

5.   Conclusions

Table 6.1 summarises the results. The analysis indicates that the states are at different stages of development but to understand the long-term sustainability of these economies requires a much deeper capital perspective. The economic thinking should embed within it the connections between different forms of capital and their inter-linkages. The states which have registered high decadal growth rates – Sikkim, Uttarakhand, Goa, Gujarat and Tamil Nadu – are also the ones with rich natural capital and comprehensive wealth. In terms of the per capita wealth, the states Goa, Gujarat, Himachal, Karnataka, Haryana, Orissa, Maharashtra and Sikkim emerge in the top eight, in line with per capita income. There is clear evidence that development of a state is not explained by GDP growth alone but is clearly impacted by the interaction between institutions and natural resource abundance along with the level of investments in education and physical capital, as seen from the growth in some of the northeastern states in India. Kerala tops in HDI and natural capital but in terms of per capita income it is among the bottom eight. Different forms of capital can be substitutes or complements, and the degree of substitutability or complementarity should be analysed. Population growth exerts pressure on the natural resources, thereby diminishing the income prospects of the economies if adequate investment does not take place.

The study has certain limitations. The estimates in this study are very conservative. In the mining states, the value of mineral wealth may be severely undervalued because the mining operations are mostly under the control of government regulation. The rents captured by the Indian mining sector are also very low. Moreover, the market is far from perfect because of subsidies, imperfect prices and low cost of labour. Though Indian government levies a number of taxes and fees on its mineral industry, the revenue earned through these levies is not sufficient. For many

Table 6.1 Ranking of states based on HDI, per capita GSDP and investments in comprehensive wealth

HDI	Per capita NSDP	GSDP	Comprehensive wealth	Natural capital	Cumulative gross capital formation	Human capital	Mineral wealth
Kerala	Goa	Maharashtra	Gujarat	Himachal Pradesh	Gujarat	Uttar Pradesh	Bihar
Goa	Sikkim	Tamil Nadu	Maharashtra	Mizoram	Maharashtra	Maharashtra	Madhya Pradesh
Himachal Pradesh	Haryana	UTTAR PRADESH	Tamil Nadu	Tripura	Tamil Nadu	Andhra Pradesh	Karnataka
Tamil Nadu	Maharashtra	GUJARAT	Karnataka	West Bengal	Karnataka	West Bengal	Rajasthan
Maharashtra	Tamil Nadu	WEST BENGAL	Uttar Pradesh (incl Uttarakhand)	Tamil Nadu	Andhra Pradesh	Bihar	Andhra Pradesh
Punjab	Gujarat	Karnataka	Andhra Pradesh	Kerala	Orissa	Tamil Nadu	Orissa
Haryana	KARNATAKA	Rajasthan	Odisha	Karnataka	Uttar Pradesh	Madhya Pradesh	Madhya Pradesh
West Bengal	Uttarakhand	Andhra Pradesh	Madhya Pradesh (Chattisgarh)	Meghalaya	Jharkhand	Karnataka	
Jammu and Kashmir	Himachal Pradesh	Kerala	West Bengal	Nagaland	Haryana	Gujarat	
Gujarat	Nagaland	MADHYA PRADESH	Haryana	Uttar Pradesh (incl. Uttarakhand)	West Bengal	Kerala	
Uttarakhand	Punjab	Haryana	Rajasthan	Orissa	Rajasthan	Rajasthan	
Karnataka	Jharkhand	Punjab	Punjab	Madhya Pradesh (incl. Chattisgarh)	Chattisgarh	Orissa	
Mizoram	Tripura	Bihar	Himachal Pradesh	Andhra Pradesh	Uttarakhand	Punjab	
Tripura	Andhra Pradesh	Orissa	Kerala	Arunachal Pradesh	Punjab	Haryana	
Sikkim	Mizoram	Jharkhand	Assam	Maharashtra	Madhya Pradesh	Assam	

Rajasthan	Arunachal Pradesh	Chattisgarh	Bihar (Jharkhand)	Bihar (incl. Jharkhand)	Himachal Pradesh	Jammu and Kashmir
Andhra Pradesh	Meghalaya	Assam	Goa	Rajasthan	Kerala	Himachal Pradesh
Orissa	West Bengal	Uttarakhand	Jammu and Kashmir	Jammu and Kashmir	Assam	Tripura
Nagaland	Rajasthan	Himachal Pradesh	Meghalaya	Assam	Goa	Nagaland
Meghalaya	Jammu and Kashmir	Jammu and Kashmir	Tripura	Gujarat	Bihar	Manipur
Jharkhand	Madhya Pradesh	Goa	Sikkim	Manipur	Jammu and Kashmir	Goa
Manipur	Chhattisgarh	Tripura	Manipur	Sikkim	Meghalaya	Meghalaya
Madhya Pradesh	Orissa	Meghalaya	Nagaland	Goa	Sikkim	Arunachal Pradesh
Chhattisgarh	Kerala	Nagaland	Mizoram	Punjab	Tripura	Mizoram
Bihar	Manipur	Manipur	Arunachal Pradesh	Haryana	Manipur	Sikkim
Assam	Assam	Arunachal Pradesh	Gujarat	Himachal Pradesh	Nagaland	Uttar Pradesh
Arunachal Pradesh	Uttar Pradesh	Sikkim	Maharashtra	Mizoram		Maharashtra
Uttar Pradesh	Bihar	Mizoram				Orissa

Source: Summary tables based on the analysis in the paper and earlier studies by the author (Gundimeda, How equitable and sustainable is the growth in India, 2016).

minerals, the net rents are negative. All these could result in an underestimate of the value of minerals. It should also be remembered that mining is often involved with significant environmental degradation and health impacts, which are not considered in the study because of lack of data. Similarly, the forests have a lot of unaccounted benefits and they are not properly reflected in the national accounts and thus these values are to be viewed as conservative. The data on produced capital stocks are not available and the data on gross capital formation are not available for all the states, limiting the analysis. These are some of the limitations of this study and more recent estimates of capital stock will be useful and these estimates are being updated by the author and are still under progress.

References

Aghion, P., Caroli, E. & Cecilia-Garcia, P., 1999. Inequality and Economic Growth: The Perspective of the New Growth Theories. *Journal of Economic Literature*, 37(4), pp. 1615–1660.

Arrow, K. et al., 2012. Sustainability and Measurement of Wealth. *Environment and Development Economics*, 17, pp. 317–353.

Atkinson, G. & Hamilton, K., 2003. Savings, Resource Growth and Resource Curse Hypothesis. *World Development*, 31(11), pp. 1793–1807.

Auty, R. M., 1993. *Sustaining Development i Mineral Economies: The Resource Curse Hypothesis*. London: Routledge.

Barro, R., 1991. Economic Growth in a Cross Section of Countries. *The Quarterly Journal of Economics*, 106(2), pp. 407–443.

Boschini, A. D., Pettersson, J. & Roine, J., 2007. Resource Curse o not: A question of appropriability. *Scandinavian Journal of Economics*, 109(3), pp. 593–617.

Central Statistical Organisation, 2012. *National Account Statistics: Sources and Methods*. New Delhi: Ministry of Statistics and Programme Implementation.

Congleton, R. D., Hillan, A. L. & Konrad, K., 2008. Forty Years of Research on Rent Seeking: An Overview. In: R. D. Congleton, A. L. Hillan & K. Konrad, eds. *Forty Years of Research on Renk Seeking*. Berlin: Springer.

Deacon, R. T. & Rode, A., 2012. *Rent Seeking and the Resource Curse*. s.l.: s.n.

Gundimeda, H., 2000a. Integrating Forest Resources in the System of National Accounts. *Environment and Development Economics*, 5, pp. 143–156.

Gundimeda, H., 2000b. Estimation of Biomass in Indian Forests. *Biomass and Bioenergy*, 19(4), pp. 245–258.

Gundimeda, H., 2001. Accounting for the Forest Resources in the National Accounts in India. *Environmental and Resource Economics*, 19(1), pp. 73–95.

Gundimeda, H., 2003. Carbom Budget of the Indian Forest Ecosystem. *Climatic Change*, 56(3), pp. 291–319.

Gundimeda, H., 2016. How Equitable and Sustainable Is the Growth in India. *Sarvekshana*, Volume Special 100th Issue, pp. 22–34.

Gundimeda, H. & Atkinson, G., 2006. Accounting for India's Forest Wealth. *Ecological Economics*, 59(4), pp. 462–476.

Gundimeda, H., Sanyal, S., Sinha, R. & Sukhdev, P., 2005. *The Value of Timber, Carbon and Non-Timber Forest Products in India*. Monograph 1. New Delhi: TERI Press.

Gundimeda, H., Sanyal, S., Sinha, R. & Sukhdev, P., 2006. *The Value of Biodiversity in India's Forests*. Monograph 4 ed. New Delhi: TERI Press.

Gundimeda, H., Sanyal, S., Sinha, R. & Sukhdev, P., 2007. *Estimating the Value of Human Capital Formation in India*. Monograph 5 ed. New Delhi: TERI Press.

Gylfason, T. H. T. Z. G., 1999. A mixed blessing: Natural resources and economic. *Macroeconomic Dynamics*, 3, pp. 204–225.

Gylfason, T. & Zoega, G., 2006. Natural Resources and Economic Growth: The Role of Investment. *The World Economy*, 29(8), pp. 1091–1115.

Havranek, T., Horvath, R. & Zeynalov, A., 2016. Natural Resources and Economic Growth: A Meta Analysis. *World Development*, 88(1), pp. 134–151.

Lange, G.-M. & Wright, M., 2004. Sustainable Development in Mineral Economies: The example of Botswana. *Environment and Development Economics*, 9(4), pp. 485–505.

Lucas, R. E., 1988. On the mechanics of economic development. *Journal of Monetary Economics*, Volume 22, pp. 3–42.

Mehlum, H., Moene, K. & Torvik, R., 2006. Cursed by Resources or Institutions? *The World Economy*, 29(8), pp. 117–1131.

Mukherjee, S., Chakraborty, D. & Sikdar, S., 2014. *Three Decades of Human Development across Indian States: Inclusive Growth or Perpetual Diversity*. New Delhi: National Institute of Public Finance and Policy.

Rausser, G. C. A. S. A. A., 2000. Valuing Research Leads: Bioprospecting and the Conservation of Genetic Resources. *Journal of Political Economy*, 108(1), pp. 173–206.

Romer, P., 1989. *Himan Capital and Growth*, s.l.: National Bureau of Economic Research.

Sachs, J. D. & Warner, A. M., 1997. Fundamental Sources of Long Run Growth. *American Economic Review*, 87(2), pp. 184–88.

Schultz, T. W., 1961. Investments in Human Capital. *American Economic Review*, 51, pp. 1–17.

SEEA, 2012. *System of Environmental Accounting 2012: central Framework*. s.l.:United Nations, European Commission, Food and Agriculture Organisation of the United Nations, Internatioanl Monetary Fund, Organisation for Economic Cooperation and Development, World Bank.

United Nations University International Human Dimensions and Programme, U. N. E., 2015. *Inclusive Wealth Report 2014*. s.l.: Cambridge University Press.

UNU and IHDP, 2012. *Inclusive Wealth Report 2012: Measuring Progress towards Sustainability*. Cambridge, UK: Cambridge University Press.

Part III
New insights

7 Human capital

Educational attainment progress

Barbara M. Fraumeni and Gang Liu

1. Introduction

Human capital is an essential component of individual well-being and vital for a country's sustainability (e.g. OECD, 2013; UNU-IHDP and UNEP, 2014). Arguably more attention around the world has been paid to gross domestic product (GDP) than any other indicators, including human capital. Although GDP is an important macroeconomic construct, it fails to consider environmental and inequality impacts, and the future viability of a country (e.g. Stiglitz et al., 2010).

Human capital and other wealth measures as presented in this report will help to fill the gaps in GDP. This chapter focuses on human capital, particularly on those that are captured in levels and trends in country's educational attainment, with reference to the United Nations' Millennium Project and Sustainable Development education goals.

The UN Millennium Project, an international effort which operated from 2002 through 2006, established eight goals and 18 technical indicators with 48 associated targets to measure progress towards the Millennium Development Goals (MDGs). Two goals relate to education: Goal 2 – Achieve Universal Primary Education and Goal 3 – Promote Gender Equality and Empower Women. The stated objective of Target 3 of Goal 2 is to have all boys and girls complete a full course of primary schooling by 2015. The stated objective of Target 4 of Goal 3 is to eliminate gender disparity in primary and secondary education in the short-run (2005) and in all levels of education in the intermediate run (2015).

However, as stated in the report of the UN Secretary-General, despite progress, the world failed to meet the MDGs of achieving universal primary education by 2015. For instance, in 2013, 59 million children of primary school age were out of school. Estimates show that, among those 59 million children, 1 in 5 of those children had dropped out. In addition, recent trends suggest that 2 in 5 of out-of-school children will never set foot in a classroom (UN, 2016).

In 2015, the United Nations' member states reached agreement on 17 Sustainable Development Goals (SDGs) with 169 associated targets. SDG 4 and SDG 5 are similar to MDG 2 and MDG 3, respectively. SDG 4 calls for inclusive and quality education for all and the promotion of lifelong learning by 2030. SDG 5 calls for gender equality by 2030, noting the importance of education and the elimination of discrimination in jobs, unpaid work and political office in achieving the goal.

Following an indicators-based approach to measuring human capital,[1] human capital developed due to education is frequently proxied by educational attainment, such as average years of schooling. A famous example in this field is the Barro-Lee dataset that has been established through many years' research (see Barro and Lee, 2001, 2013). The previous Inclusive Wealth Reports (IWR) also used the Barro-Lee dataset as one of the primary data sources for calculating monetary estimates of human capital (e.g. IWR, 2012, 2014).

This chapter, by using numerical estimates based mainly on the latest Barro-Lee dataset (Barro and Lee, 2016), tries to investigate educational attainment progress across major regions in the world, and over the time period of 1950–2010. We also investigate what has been achieved during this time period with reference to the educational attainment gender gaps and age differences in different regions. As the quality of education matters as well as the average years of schooling, discussions are also provided around the methods about how the quality side of educational attainment is practically taken into account.

In the next section, the methodology for compiling the Barro-Lee dataset is summarized. This is followed by the section presenting and discussing several numerical results. A subsequent section focuses on the quality of education, where by using the implicit quality-adjustment method, the findings drawn from the progress of primary, secondary and tertiary education are presented and discussed as well. The final section concludes.

2.   Barro-Lee methodology

Barro-Lee average years of schooling estimates enter into the IWR human capital (due to education) calculations in two ways. The IWR uses a country representative adult approach. The representative adult's educational attainment by gender (*Edu*) comes from the Barro-Lee average years of schooling. The minimum age of an adult in a country by gender is determined by *Edu*+5. The total number of adults by gender is equal to the number of individuals in the country who are at least the minimum age. All adult individuals are counted whether or not they perform paid work. A complete description of the IWR human capital measuring methodology is in Annex 2.

The Barro-Lee dataset (2016) is available by gender in five calendar year increments from 1950 through 2010 for five-year age groups from age 15 through 74, and for age 75 and over, for 146 countries. The data used in this chapter by age groups and gender include population, the no school percentage and the average years of total schooling, as well as the average years of primary, secondary and tertiary schooling, respectively.

The Barro-Lee benchmark data are collected from various census and/or survey information and compiled by UNESCO, Eurostat, national statistic agencies and other sources.[2] The Barro-Lee dataset uses a variety of techniques to fill in gaps in observations and educational attainment subcategories, with the purpose to avoid misestimating of average years of schooling.

To fill in missing observations (as benchmarks are not available for all five-year periods), they begin by calculating the distribution of educational attainment among four broad categories: no formal education (h_u), primary (h_p), secondary (h_s) and tertiary education (h_h). Primary and tertiary are further divided into complete and incomplete; secondary is further divided into lower secondary and upper secondary.

Most missing observations are filled in with backward or forward extrapolation with an appropriate time lag. The 13 five-year age groups are referred to by *ag* = 1

(15–19 years old) through to $ag = 13$ (75 years and over). The forward extrapolation method assumes that the educational attainment distribution of the age group ag at time t is identical to that of the age group that was five years younger at time $t - 5$.

Equation 1

$$b_{j,t}^{ag} = b_{j,t-5}^{ag-1},$$

where $j = u, p, s, h$ and $ag = 3$ (25–29 years old), through to $ag = 11$ (65–69 years old).

This forward extrapolation applies to individuals who have completed their schooling by time $t - 5$. As those younger than 25 are potentially still in school, a different methodology is employed.

Similarly, the backward extrapolation assumes that the educational attainment distribution of the age group ag at time t is the same as that of the age group that is five years older at time $t+5$.

Equation 2

$$b_{j,t}^{ag} = b_{j,t+5}^{ag+1},$$

where $j = u, p, s, h,$ and $ag = 2$ (20–24 years old), through to $ag = 10$ (60–64 years old).

As a result, the net effect of this methodology is to hold an individual's educational attainment constant from age 25 through to 64.

For older individuals, the probability of dying is observed to differ by educational attainment level. Accordingly, for the three oldest age groups: $ag = 11$ (65–69 years old), $ag = 12$ (70–74 years old) and $ag = 13$ (75 years and over), survival probabilities are estimated by educational attainment level. Highly educated individuals live, on average, longer than their less educated peers; this correction is necessary to ensure accurate estimations of average educational attainment for older age groups. For all younger age groups ($ag = 10$ (60–64 years old) and below), it is assumed that survival rates do not differ by educational attainment.

The process for creating subcategories of educational attainment (complete and incomplete for primary and higher education; lower and upper for secondary school) depends upon the age level. For primary school, the Barro-Lee dataset uses country and age-specific completion ratio profiles to estimate the subcategories for $ag = 1$ (15–19 years old) and $ag = 2$ (20–24 years old). For $ag = 3$ (25–29 years old), the primary school completion rate is set equal to the ratio of the number of individuals who completed primary school, but did not enter secondary school, to the number of individuals who entered primary school. Backward and forward extrapolation and other methods are used to fill in any missing observations for $ag = 3$ (25–29 years old) and above.

When there are missing observations, secondary school enrollees for $ag = 1$ (15–19 years old) are assumed to be incompletely educated at the secondary level, and higher-school enrollees for $ag = 2$ (20–24 years old) are assumed to be incompletely educated at the higher level.

Other estimation problems arise because some countries do not report the proportion of the population who have no formal education, but do report on the proportion of the educated population who have achieved primary, secondary or tertiary level of education. Alternatively, the proportion of the population with no formal education, or who have achieved at most some level of primary education, is often reported as a single number. The Barro-Lee dataset uses illiteracy rate, primary enrolment ratio and/or data from other census years to resolve such inconsistencies.

Finally, estimations are made for the average number of years of schooling for the population aged 15 and above, and separately for each of the 13 five-year age groups. For those aged 15 and above, the average years of total schooling at time t, S_t, is measured as:

Equation 3

$$S_t = \sum_{ag} l_t^{ag} s_t^{ag},$$

where the summation is over all age groups (i.e. $ag = 1$ (15–19 years old), $ag = 2$ (20–24 years old), . . ., $ag = 13$ (75 years old and over); l_t^{ag} is the population share of the group ag in the total population aged 15 and above; s_t^{ag} is the average number of years of schooling for age group ag.

The average number of years of schooling by age group ag at time t is:

Equation 4

$$S_t^{ag} = \sum_j h_{j,t}^{ag} d_{j,t}^{ag},$$

where the summation is over educational attainment levels $j = p$, s (incomplete, complete), h (incomplete, complete); $h_{j,t}^{ag}$ is the fraction of the group ag with the educational level j; $d_{j,t}^{ag}$ is the corresponding duration of school attendance in years.

3.   Educational attainment, gender gaps and age differences

To examine educational attainment progress in the world and across the different regions, the 146 countries covered by the Barro-Lee dataset are divided first into two broad groups: Advanced and other economies. The Advanced Economies consist of 24 countries, other economies are divided into six regions: East Asia and the Pacific (19 countries or special administrative districts); Europe and Central Asia (20 countries); Latin America and Caribbean (25 countries); Middle East and North Africa (18 countries); South Asia (7 countries); and Sub-Saharan Africa (33 countries).[3]

In Table 7.1, information on the educational attainment (in terms of the average years of total schooling) is presented for the total population aged 15 and above, for both males and females, in all the seven regions over the period covered by Barro and Lee (2013), i.e. 1950–2010. As shown, all regions in the world have made significant progresses in educational attainment during this period.

By 2010, the Europe and Central Asia region has almost caught up with the Advanced Economies, and its average educational attainment levels for both males and females are just slightly lower than those of the latter. Until the most recent period of 2000–2010, the average rate of percentage increase per year for the Europe and Central Asia exceeds that for the Advanced Economies.

Table 7.1 Educational attainment, aged 15 and above, by region and gender

	Average years		Average increase per year (percentage)					
	2010		1950–2010		1950–2000		2000–2010	
	Female	Male	Female	Male	Female	Male	Female	Male
Advanced Economies	11.4	11.7	1.03	0.96	1.04	1.01	1.00	0.71
East Asia and the Pacific	7.6	8.3	3.17	2.21	3.48	2.48	1.67	0.87
Europe and Central Asia	11.2	11.4	1.72	1.35	1.90	1.51	0.82	0.54
Latin America and Caribbean	8.3	8.3	2.04	1.77	2.14	1.85	1.55	1.37
Middle East and North Africa	6.8	7.9	4.75	3.39	5.18	3.80	2.66	1.35
South Asia	4.8	7.3	4.23	2.62	4.68	2.86	2.03	1.41
Sub-Saharan Africa	4.8	5.9	2.81	2.19	2.94	2.40	2.19	1.14

Source: Authors' calculations based on Barro-Lee February 2016 version (www.barrolee.com).

Not surprisingly, the Sub-Saharan Africa region has the lowest average 2010 educational attainment, and for the period as a whole (1950–2010), and in the first subperiod (1950–2000), its average percentage increase per year is not among the highest in all regions. This is also true for males in the second subperiod (2000–2010). Only for females and in the second subperiod has its average percentage increase per year reached the second place among all regions.

For the whole period (1950–2010) and the first subperiod (1950–2000), the Middle East and North Africa region has the highest average percentage increase per year for both males and females, but in the last subperiod (2000–2010), although its average percentage increase per year is still the highest for females, it recedes to the third place for males in all regions. The South Asia region has the second highest average percentage increase per year both for the whole period (1950–2010) and the first subperiod (1950–2000), but in the second subperiod (2000–2010), its average percentage increase per year is the highest for males, while it falls to the third place for females in all regions. For all seven regions, the average percentage increase per year is lower in 2000–2010 than in 1950–2000, regardless of gender.

The slowdown in percentage growth rate of educational attainment progress is quite noticeable in the East Asia and the Pacific, the Europe and Central Asia, the Middle East and North Africa, and the South Asia regions, where the average percentage increase per year in 2000–2010 roughly halved for females, and more than halved for males, compared to the corresponding 1950–2000 percentage rates. For males in the Sub-Saharan Africa region, the average percentage increase per year in 2000–2010 more than halved its 1950–2000 percentage rate.

Average yearly percentage increases tend to fall as the level of educational attainment rises, indicating that advancement relative to existing levels may be significantly easier when educational attainments are low compared to when they are higher.

To answer the question whether the current educational attainment gaps among the regions can be filled up by 2030, a simulation analysis is carried out based on the estimates shown in Table 7.1. Three scenarios are simulated where Scenario M,

Scenario H and Scenario L refer to that all regions, starting from the 2010 educational attainment level, follow the average annual percentage increase rate of 1950–2010, 1950–2000 and 2000–2010, respectively. In other words, Scenario M, H and L represent relatively Middle, High and Low growth scenarios, respectively.

The simulation results are displayed in Figure 7.1, separately for males and females. Using the 2030 educational attainment level in the Advanced Economies as the target, the predicted 2030 levels in the Europe and Central Asia and the Middle East and North Africa regions, for both males and females, will be higher in Scenario M and Scenario H, while lower in Scenario L, than the corresponding levels in the Advanced Economies.

For the East Asia and the Pacific region, the predicted 2030 educational attainment level for females is higher than that in the Advanced Economies in Scenario M and Scenario H, while lower in Scenario L. For males, the predicted 2030 level in this region is lower in all three scenarios. As for the Latin America and Caribbean, the South Asia, and the Sub-Saharan Africa regions, their predicted 2030 educational attainment levels, for both males and females, and regardless of the scenario, are all lower than the corresponding levels in the Advanced Economies.

The situation is even more critical for the last mentioned three regions. For the Latin America and Caribbean region, the predicted 2030 educational attainment level in Scenario L is even lower than the 2010 level in the Advanced Economies. This is also true for the South Asia region; in addition for females in Scenario M, the predicted 2030 educational attainment level is lower than the 2010 level in the Advanced Economies. In the Sub-Saharan Africa region, in all scenarios and regardless of gender, the predicted 2030 levels are significantly lower than the corresponding 2010 levels in the Advanced Economies.

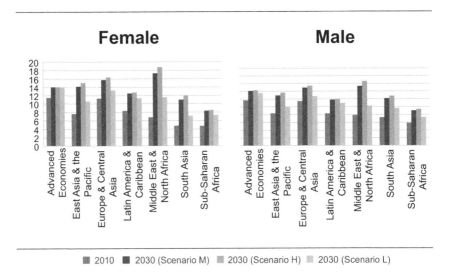

Figure 7.1 Predicted educational attainment in 2030 in different scenarios, by region, gender

Source: Authors' calculations based on Barro-Lee February 2016 version (www.barrolee.com).

Apparently, a variety of external factors in a number of countries may add to the difficulty of realizing educational gains, such as conflicts, poverty and recessions. Since the general state of many countries in the world, especially in the three last mentioned regions, points to the difficulty in attaining MDGs or SDGs educational attainment goals, more efforts are needed in order to catch up in the future.

Both MDGs and SDGs call for gender equity. As also shown in Table 7.1, in all regions, the average educational attainment of females is in general less than that of males in 2010. Only in the Latin America and the Caribbean region is there gender parity. In the Advanced Economies, East Asia and the Pacific, and Europe and Central Asia, the difference is at most 0.7 of a year of total schooling, but in the Middle East and North Africa, the Sub-Saharan Africa and the South Asia regions, it is substantially greater, i.e. 1.1, 1.1 and 2.5 years of total schooling, respectively.

However, for all periods and regions considered, the average percentage increase in educational attainment per year for females is without exception greater than that for males (see Table 7.1). As Table 7.2 shows, for the overall period, the Middle East and North Africa region is the leader in closing the gender gap in education, but the progress is notable for all regions except in the Advanced Economies and in the Latin America and the Caribbean region, which have the smallest average educational gender gaps already in 1950.

Note that the regions which have the largest educational attainment gender gaps in 2010 (the South Asia and the Sub-Saharan Africa regions) as shown in Table 7.2 are also those having lowest average years of total schooling as shown in Table 7.1. For the Sub-Saharan Africa region, the 2010 educational attainment gender gap can almost be filled up by 2030 if following the latest average annual gap reduction, while for the South Asia region, even faster (than that shown in Table 7.2) annual reductions are needed to fill the 2010 gap, which is the largest among all regions in 2010.

Literature review on private returns to schooling has demonstrated that returns to schooling seem to be higher in low or middle-income economies than in high-income economies. Moreover, estimated returns to schooling are higher for females

Table 7.2 The gender educational attainment gap*, aged 15 and above, by region

	Average gap (percentage)			*Average reduction per year (percentage points)*		
	1950	*2000*	*2010*	*1950– 2010*	*1950– 2000*	*2000– 2010*
Advanced Economies	6.5	5.0	2.2	0.07	0.03	0.28
East Asia and the Pacific	48.1	15.6	8.6	0.66	0.65	0.70
Europe and Central Asia	20.8	4.3	1.6	0.32	0.33	0.27
Latin America and Caribbean	15.0	1.6	-0.1	0.25	0.27	0.17
Middle East and North Africa	60.4	23.5	13.0	0.79	0.74	1.05
South Asia	74.2	38.0	34.2	0.67	0.72	0.39
Sub-Saharan Africa	43.4	26.6	18.6	0.41	0.34	0.80

Source: Authors' calculations based on Barro-Lee February 2016 version (www.barrolee.com).

* The gender educational attainment gap in percentage points is defined as (1 – (female educational attainment/male educational attainment)) × 100.

than for males (e.g. Psacharopoulos, 1994; Psacharopoulos and Patrinos, 2004). This conclusion holds both for the world as a whole and for all regions individually (Montenegro and Patrinos, 2014). Therefore, investments in education are more rewarding in these regions than in others, as well as for females than for males.

A comparison of educational attainment of 25–34-year-olds to 55–64-year-olds gives a sense of what the future might look like given current levels of educational attainment of younger potential workers. Because younger workers have longer remaining working years than their elder counterparts, they will contribute more to the future economic growth. Table 7.3 reports on the educational attainment of aged 25–34 relative to those of aged 55–64 by percentage range groups. The individual cells of Table 7.3 show how many countries in each region fall in the five percentage range categories. For example, there are two countries in the Advanced Economies having the calculated percentage points between 50% and 100%, and nine countries in the range of 20% to 50%, etc.

As shown in Table 7.3, clearly the largest concentrations of the Sub-Saharan Africa and the South Asia countries are in the range of greater than 50% to at most 500% category. The largest concentrations of the Latin America and Caribbean and the East Asia and the Pacific countries are in the greater than 20% to at most 100% range category. The largest concentration of the Advanced Economies, however, is in the greater than 0% to at most 50% range category. Finally, the largest concentration of the Europe and Central Asia countries are in the range of 0 or less percent to at most 20% category, while the countries in the Middle East and North Africa regions are more or less evenly distributed over the five percent range categories.

These results in particular point toward the future educational attainment potential gains of the Sub-Saharan Africa countries, and the potential slowdown in

Table 7.3 Country distribution by educational attainment differences of younger (25–34) vs. older (55–64) in 2010

Percentage range (%)	(100–500]	(50–100]	(20–50]	(0–20]	(-∞-0]	No. of countries
Advanced Economies	0	2	9	12	1	24
East Asia and the Pacific	3	7	7	2	0	19
Europe and Central Asia	0	0	1	13	6	20
Latin America and Caribbean	2	9	9	4	1	25
Middle East and North Africa	6	3	4	2	2	17
South Asia	4	2	1	0	0	7
Sub-Saharan Africa	16	11	5	1	0	33
SUM						145

Source: Authors' calculations based on Barro-Lee February 2016 version (www.barrolee.com).

Notes:
1. The educational attainment differences of younger (25–34) vs. elder (55–64) in percentage points are defined as (educational attainment of aged 25–34 – educational attainment of aged 55–64)/ educational attainment of aged 55–64;
2. Yemen (in Middle East & North Africa) is excluded from this table as its educational attainment of 25–34 year olds is approximately 5000% higher than that of 55–64 year olds.
3. The symbol "(" denotes greater than and the symbol "]" denotes less than or equal to.

educational attainment gains in Europe and Central Asia, as well as in Advanced Economies.

A goal of SDG 4 is for all youths to achieve literacy and numeracy by 2030. The facts and figures section of SDG 4 notes that almost half of all children not in school are in the Sub-Saharan Africa region. This comment is also reflected in analysis results based on the Barro-Lee dataset.[4] In 2010, the Sub-Saharan Africa region still has a larger number of countries than other regions with a high share of individuals aged 15–19 who have no years of schooling: 17 of 33 countries with no school percentages over 20%. In contrast, the other regions each have at most three countries with such a high percentage of individuals aged 15–19 with no school.

On the other hand, almost 25% (eight countries) of the Sub-Saharan Africa countries have at most two percent of individuals aged 15–19 without school. For all other regions in the Barro-Lee dataset, this low category of no school contained much larger shares of countries in each region, from a low of about 43% of countries for the South Asia to a high of 85% of countries for the Europe and Central Asia. In many countries of the regions considered, the goal of universal literacy has essentially been accomplished, but in others progress has yet to be made.

4. Quality of education

Up to now, focus has been put solely on the quantitative side of educational attainment, in terms of the average years of total schooling. An obvious fact is that human capital accumulated due to education will be different if the quality of education varies. Since quality education is more explicitly addressed in SDG 4, this section will discuss the quality side of educational attainment progress.

In contrast to the quantity of education, the quality of education is non-observable. It can only be reflected by indicators of outcomes, either directly (such as by test scores) or indirectly (such as by differentials of economic or non-economic benefits),[5] through the use of human capital. But all these direct or indirect outcomes are determined not only by human capital alone, but also by many other environmental factors that will play important roles leading to the occurrence of certain outcomes (see Liu and Fraumeni, 2016).

In order to take into account the qualitative side of the educational attainment, there are in general two ways, either explicitly or implicitly.

4.1. Education quality – treated explicitly

Taking quality *explicitly* is to directly focus on some quality indicators, which are constructed based on various outcomes. For instance, test scores are often used as good indicators of quality of educational attainment (e.g. Hanushek and Kimko, 2000; Angrist et al., 2013; Altinok et al., 2014; Barro and Lee, 2015). In some cases, internationally comparable test scores are even considered to be a direct measure of human capital stock (e.g. Hanushek and Kimko, 2000; Hanushek and Woessmann, 2012).

As mentioned, outcomes are jointly determined by many factors. Thus, one major challenge is how to separate the effects that are attributable to education from those due to other factors. For instance, innate ability is regarded as one of the important determinants of student's test achievements (see Hanushek, 1986; Hanushek and

Woessmann, 2011). Despite one element of human capital in a broad sense (see Liu and Fraumeni, 2014), at least some of the innate ability (such as natural-born talent) is not that type of human capital that is developed solely due to education.

Another difficulty of using test scores lies in translating test scores of different subject matters (e.g. reading, mathematics, science) into an aggregate common metric. The estimated relationship between the test scores (quality) and the average years of schooling (quantity) may depend on how the aggregate test scores are constructed.

In a recent dataset, the aggregate test scores are constructed based on scores for mathematics and science only, with those for reading excluded. It has been shown that the correlation coefficient of the average years of schooling and aggregate test scores for secondary students in 2010 among 146 countries is 0.70 (Barro and Lee, 2015).

However, as shown in Figure 7.2, the PISA aggregate test scores and the average years of schooling for those aged 15–19 in 2010 is not strongly correlated among 57 countries, with the calculated correlation coefficient between the corresponding rankings being just 0.24.[6,7] Note that here the PISA aggregate test scores are an equally weighted average of mean test scores of reading, mathematics and science.[8]

Results have also shown that in two small groups of economies (one group with 15 top-performers in educational attainment quantity, the other with 15 top-performers in secondary aggregate test scores), the correlation coefficient between the quantity (average years of schooling) and the quality (test scores) within each group is negative and low (Barro and Lee, 2015).

Therefore, the empirical results as regards the relationship between the average years of schooling (quantity) and the test scores (quality) drawn from internationally comparable test are mixed, and they depend not only on how the aggregate test scores are constructed, but also on the sample size as well.

To combine both the quantity and the quality side of educational attainment, research has been conducted by using the quality indicators to adjust the educational attainment quantity, the quality indicator including test scores (e.g. Barro and Lee, 2015), labour earnings (e.g. Barro and Lee, 2015) or lifetime income (IWR Reports, 2012, 2014). Since the data sources and the detailed choice of methodologies vary among these studies, findings from these studies may not be directly comparable.

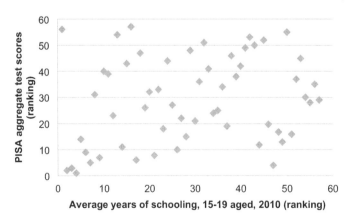

Figure 7.2 PISA aggregate test scores and average years of schooling (aged 15–19) in 2010

Sources: Barro-Lee February 2016 version (www.barrolee.com) and PISA mean test scores

4.2. Education quality – treated implicitly

Taking quality *implicitly* is to stratify quantitative educational attainment (e.g. average years of total schooling) into disaggregate categories (e.g. average years of primary, secondary and tertiary schooling), with the assumption that in terms of quality, all disaggregate categories are considered to be heterogeneous with each other, while homogenous within each single category.

Based on the Barro-Lee dataset, instead of using the average years of *total* schooling as discussed in previous sections, focus now is placed on the educational attainment progress in terms of average years of schooling by different categories, namely, primary, secondary and tertiary levels, across the world major regions and over 1950–2010.

As shown in Figure 7.3, in all regions, all three levels of educational attainment have increased over the observed period of 1950–2010. In particular, compared to

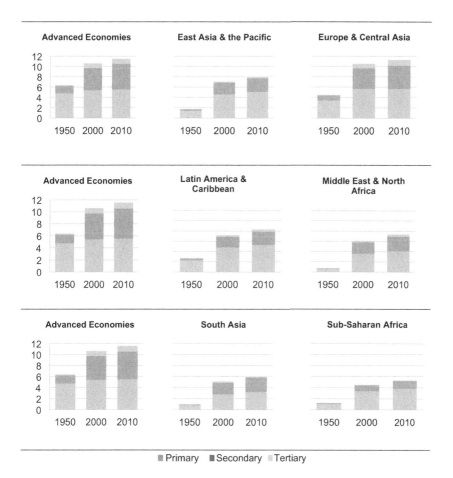

■ Primary ■ Secondary ▪ Tertiary

Figure 7.3 Average years of primary, secondary and tertiary schooling by regions, aged 15 and above, 1950, 2000, 2010

Source: Authors' calculations based on Barro-Lee February 2016 version (www.barrolee.com).

the Advanced Economies, the beginning all levels for other regions were lower in 1950, but progresses made in these regions are significant. For instance, the Europe and Central Asia region has acquired approximately the same corresponding levels as the Advanced Economies in 2010.

The Latin America and Caribbean regions has roughly the same primary educational level as the Advanced Economies in 2010.

Note that Advanced Economies had achieved almost the primary educational level of 2010 already in 2000, so had the Europe and Central Asia region. Using the education levels in 2010 in these two regions as target, the educational gaps are still visible for many other regions. And the secondary and tertiary levels in most of these regions are still lagging behind.

Human capital developed through education is one of the crucial driving forces for modern economic growth (e.g. Lucas, 1988; Romer, 1990a, 1990b), so demand for higher educated and skilled people is bound to be ever increasing in the days to come, both for the developed and for the developing countries as well.

Recent research has found that the private returns to tertiary education are higher than those to either primary or secondary education, in most of the regions considered in this chapter. In addition, among all regions, they are highest with a substantial margin in two regions with the lowest average years of tertiary schooling as shown in Figure 7.3, i.e. the South Asia and the Sub-Saharan Africa regions. These findings also hold for both males and females. Moreover, the returns to tertiary education for females are, without exception, larger than those for males in all regions (Montenegro and Patrinos, 2014).

5. Conclusions

Based on the Barro-Lee dataset, this chapter focuses on the level and trend of educational attainment progress, with reference to the MPGs and SDGs. In terms of the average years of total schooling, educational attainment has made significant progresses in the world and across the regions over 1950–2010. However, in 2010 the distribution of educational attainment is still uneven across the regions considered in the chapter, with some regions significantly lagging behind, if compared with Advanced Economies.

Filling these gaps by 2030 is challenging, especially for the Latin America and Caribbean, the South Asia and the Sub-Saharan Africa regions. Although some of these regions have shown considerable growth rates during the period of 1950–2010, because of low starting levels in 1950, their educational attainment levels in 2010 are still lower than that in Advanced Economies with sizable margins.

Simulation analyses indicate that even in the high growth scenario, the predicted 2030 educational attainment level in these regions (i.e. the Latin America and Caribbean, the South Asia and the Sub-Saharan Africa regions) will be lower than the corresponding level in Advanced Economies. Given that the average growth rate of the last subperiod (2000–2010) is significantly lower, compared to that in the first subperiod (1950–2000), to remove the currently existent gaps, more bolder efforts are needed, beyond the measures undertaken in the past.

MDGs and SDGs strongly support the reduction of gender disparity in education. Over the period of 1950–2010, the observed educational attainment gender gaps have been decreasing. In particular, a significant progress has been achieved in the Middle East and North Africa, and the East Asia and the Pacific regions. However, large gaps are visible in the South Asia and the Sub-Saharan Africa regions in 2010, even though annual reduction of gender gaps in the two regions has accelerated and are the highest among all regions in the last subperiod (2000–2010). Thus, filling these gender gaps by 2030 demands more active actions.

In many regions considered in the chapter, the goal of universal literacy has essentially been accomplished in 2010, reflected by very low share of individuals aged 15–19 who have no years of schooling in the country of these regions. Unfortunately, in other regions, and in particular, in the Sub-Saharan Africa region, there are a large number of countries where the youth aged 15–19 are without school, and thus substantial progress needs to be made for these countries.

The quantity and equity of educational attainment are important, so is the quality. Education quality is more addressed in the SDGs. However, unlike the quantity, the quality of education is non-observable, and can only be proxied by some indicators, which are drawn based on various outcomes, such as test scores and labour earnings.

Research focusing on international comparable test scores and combining them with the quantitative average years of schooling is plentiful. However, due to the differences among the data sources, as well as the detailed methodological choices, results from these studies have yet to be further investigated.

Instead of focusing explicitly on the quality indicators, the chapter, by implicitly taking quality dimension into account, examines the educational attainment progress in terms of the average years of primary, secondary and tertiary schooling. Despite substantial progress in all levels, the secondary and tertiary levels are still significantly lagging behind for many of the regions, compared to Advanced Economies and the Europe and Central Asia region in 2010.

As economic development necessitates wide employment of higher educated people in the future, and research results have shown that private economic returns to the investments in higher education are larger than in primary education, and the returns are highest in the least developed regions, such as the South Asia and the Sub-Saharan Africa regions, more investments in higher education in these regions are therefore rewarding.

Notes

1 For discussions on other approaches to measuring human capital, as well as the strengths and weaknesses associated with each measuring approach, please refer to Liu and Fraumeni (2014).
2 The description of the Barro-Lee methodology draws heavily from Chapter 4 of the 2014 Inclusive Wealth Report (Fraumeni and Liu, 2014), which is the description of the methodology applied in Barro and Lee (2013).
3 The 24 Advanced Economies include: Australia, Austria, Belgium, Canada, Denmark, Finland, France, Germany, Greece, Iceland, Ireland, Italy, Japan, Luxembourg, Netherlands, New Zealand, Norway, Portugal, Spain, Sweden, Switzerland, Turkey, the United Kingdom, and the United States. The 19 East Asia and the Pacific countries or special administrative districts include: Brunei Darussalam, Cambodia, mainland China, China – Hong Kong, China – Macao, Fiji, Indonesia, Lao People's Democratic Republic, Malaysia, Mongolia, Myanmar, Papua New Guinea, Philippines, Republic of Korea, Singapore, Taiwan, Thailand, Tonga and Viet Nam. The 20 Europe and Central Asia countries include: Albania, Armenia, Bulgaria, Croatia, Czech Republic, Estonia, Hungary, Kazakhstan, Kyrgyzstan, Latvia, Lithuania, Poland, Republic of Moldova,

Romania, Russian Federation, Serbia, Slovakia, Slovenia, Tajikistan and Ukraine. The 25 Latin America and Caribbean countries include: Argentina, Barbados, Belize, Bolivia, Brazil, Chile, Columbia, Costa Rica, Cuba, Dominican Republic, Ecuador, El Salvador, Guatemala, Guyana, Haiti, Honduras, Jamaica, Mexico, Nicaragua, Panama, Paraguay, Peru, Trinidad and Tobago, Uruguay and Venezuela. The 18 Middle East and North Africa countries include: Algeria, Bahrain, Cyprus, Egypt, Iran (Islamic Republic of), Iraq, Israel, Jordan, Kuwait, Libyan Arab Jamahiriya, Malta, Morocco, Qatar, Saudi Arabia, Syrian Arab Republic, Tunisia, United Arab Emirates and Yemen. The seven South Asia countries include: Afghanistan, Bangladesh, India, Maldives, Nepal, Pakistan and Sri Lanka. The 33 Sub-Saharan Africa countries include: Benin, Botswana, Burundi, Cameroon, Central African Republic, Congo, Cote d'Ivoire, Democratic Republic of the Congo, Gabon, Gambia, Ghana, Kenya, Lesotho, Liberia, Malawi, Mali, Mauritania, Mauritius, Mozambique, Namibia, Niger, Reunion, Rwanda, Senegal, Sierra Leone, South Africa, Sudan, Swaziland, Togo, Uganda, United Republic of Tanzania, Zambia and Zimbabwe.
4 Detailed analysis and the results are not fully presented here but are available upon request.
5 Here "direct" or "indirect" is a relative concept, with indirect outcomes being further away than direct outcomes from the development/production process of human capital. From direct to indirect outcomes, more and more environmental factors other than human capital itself will play a part giving rise to certain outcomes (see Liu and Fraumeni, 2016).
6 The Programme for International Student Assessment (PISA) is an OECD test of subject matter competencies. The core tests are in reading, mathematics and science for 15–16-year-old students. PISA has been administered every three years, beginning in 2000, through to 2015 (see www.oecd.org/pisa/).
7 The 57 countries include Albania, Argentina, Australia, Austria, Brazil, Bulgaria, Canada, Chile, Colombia, Costa Rica, Croatia, Czech Republic, Denmark, Estonia, Finland, France, Germany, Greece, Hong Kong-China, Hungary, Iceland, Indonesia, Ireland, Israel, Italy, Japan, Jordan, Kazakhstan, Korea, Latvia, Lithuania, Luxembourg, Macao-China, Malaysia, Mexico, Netherlands, New Zealand, Norway, Peru, Poland, Portugal, Qatar, Romania, Russian Federation, Serbia, Singapore, Slovak, Slovenia Republic, Spain, Sweden, Switzerland, Thailand, Tunisia, Turkey, United Kingdom, United States and Uganda.
8 To make it more comparable, the aggregate test scores are an arithmetic average of those for 2006 and 2009, because the average years of schooling refer to those aged 15–19 in 2010.

References

Altinok, N., Diebolt, C., & De Meulemeester, J. L. (2014). A New International Database on Educational Quality: 1965–2010. *Applied Economics*, 46(11), 1212–1247.

Angrist, N., Patrinos, H. A., & Schlotter, M. (2013). An Expansion of a Global Data Set on Education Quality. No. WPS6536, The World Bank Policy Research Working Paper.

Barro, R. & Lee, J. W. (2001). International Data on Educational Attainment: Updates and Implications. *Oxford Economic Papers*, 53(3), 541–563.

Barro, R. & Lee, J. W. (2013). A New Data Set of Educational Attainment in the World. 1950–2010. *Journal of Development Economics*, 104(C), 184–198.

Barro, R. & Lee, J. W. (2015). *Education Matters: Global Schooling Gains from the 19th to the 21st Century*. New York, NY: Oxford University Press.

Barro, R. & Lee, J. W. (2016). Barro-Lee Educational Attainment Data Set. Last updated February 2016. At www.barrolee.com/.

Fraumeni, B. M. & Liu, G. (2014). Human Capital: Country Estimates Using Alternative Approaches. Chapter 4 in UNU-IHDP and UNEP. Inclusive Wealth Report 2014.

Measuring Progress Toward Sustainability. Cambridge: Cambridge University Press, 109–122.

Hanushek, E. A. (1986). The Economics of Schooling: Production and Efficiency in Public Schools. *Journal of Economic Literature*, 24(3), 1141–1177.

Hanushek, E. A. & Kimko, D. D. (2000). Schooling Labor-Force Quality and the Growth of Nations. *American Economic Review*, 90(5), 1184–1208.

Hanushek, E. A. & Woessmann, L. (2011). The Economics of International Differences in Educational Achievement. In E. A. Hanushek, S. Machin, & L. Woessmann (Eds.), *Handbook of the Economics of Education*, Vol. 3. Amsterdam: North Holland, 89–200.

Hanushek, E. A. & Woessmann, L. (2012). Do Better School Lead to More Growth? Cognitive Skills, Economic Outcomes, and Causation. *Journal of Economic Growth*, 17(4), 267–321.

Liu, G. & Fraumeni, B. M. (2014). Human Capital Measurement: A Bird's Eye View. Chapter 3 in UNU-IHDP and UNEP, Inclusive Wealth Report 2014: Measuring Progress Toward Sustainability. Cambridge: Cambridge University Press.

Liu, G. & Fraumeni, B. M. (2016). Human Capital Measurement: Country Experiences and International Initiatives. In D. W. Jorgenson, K. Fukao, & M. P. Timmer (Eds.), *Growth and Stagnation in the World Economy*. Cambridge: Cambridge University Press.

Lucas, R. E., Jr. (1988). On the Mechanics of Economic Development. *Journal of Monetary Economics*, 22(1), 3–42.

Montenegro, C. E. & Patrinos, H. A. (2014). Comparable Estimates of Returns to Schooling Around the World. (No. WPS7020). The World Bank Policy Research Working Paper.

OECD (2013). *How's Life? 2013: Measuring Well-Being*. OECD Publishing. http://dx.doi.org/10.1787/9789264201392-en.

Psacharopoulos, G. (1994). Returns to Education: A Global Update. *World Development*, 22(9), 1325–1343.

Psacharopoulos, G., & Patrinos, H. A. (2004). Returns to Investment in Education: A Further Update. *Education Economics*, 12(2), 111–134.

Romer, P. M. (1990a). Endogenous Technological Change. *Journal of Political Economy*, 98(5), Part 2, 71–102.

Romer, P. M. (1990b) Human Capital and Growth: Theory and Evidence. *Carnegie-Rochester Conference Series on Public Policy*, 32, 251–286.

Stiglitz, J. E., Sen, A. & Fitoussi, J. P. (2010). *Mismeasuring Our Lives: Why GDP Doesn't Add Up*. New York: The New Press.

United Nations (2016). Progress towards the Sustainable Development Goals. Report of the Secretary-General, E/2016/75.

UNU-IHDP & UNEP (2012). Inclusive Wealth Report 2012, Measuring Progress Toward Sustainability. Cambridge: Cambridge University Press.

UNU-IHDP & UNEP (2014). Inclusive Wealth Report 2014, Measuring Progress Toward Sustainability. Cambridge: Cambridge University Press.

8 Operationalizing IWI for policymaking through a learning game

Bharath M. Palavalli, Srijan Sil, and Anantha Kumar Duraiappah

Economics is a simple yet complex subject. Sounds oxymoronic but in many ways correct. A key objective of economics is about finding the most efficient use of limited resources. But the actual decision-making of making the nearly infinite set of choices with different combinations of inputs and outputs makes it a non-trivial task. Economic policymaking is not an exact science. This is especially the case at the macro level where governments need to make decisions on investments for economic growth and ensuring high rates of return of these investments towards the gross domestic product (GDP).

Most governments have traditionally focused on maximizing GDP growth as their prime objective. They understood economic growth measured by income growth as synonymous with improving human well-being (Stiglitz, Sen, & Fitoussi, 2010). The focus, therefore, had been on maximizing income accruing from resources and the question of sustainability was never an issue (Dasgupta, 2009). This has, however, changed over the past few years. The increasing recognition of the finite nature of resources and the increasing attention to negative externalities accruing from economic activities has made it necessary for governments to address the sustainability dimension of economic activities. Equally important has been the recognition that just growth in income or GDP does not automatically contribute to well-being (Dasgupta & Duraiappah, 2012).

There has been increasing recognition that well-being is dependent on a number of constituents and determinants of well-being including subjective and objective notions of well-being as critical for countries to achieve. This has led in many ways a move from seeing economic growth as the key development agenda to a more nuanced and comprehensive agenda that includes sustainability of well-being. This can be seen very clearly of the transition by the global community from the Millennium Development Goals which made the first move from a "one variable" approach to well-being to a multidimensional perspective to well-being. But this was still seen as incomplete and a call for incorporating the sustainability of well-being was growing among the global community.

In 2015, 193 countries signed 17 ambitious goals called the Sustainable Development Goals. Targets and indicators were set for each of these goals and a timeframe of 15 years was established. The key progress was the acknowledgement among countries that these goals were relevant to all countries and not as in the past just directed towards the poorer countries. The universality of the SDGs suggested a need for cooperation among countries to improve the well-being of their societies.

For example, SDG 13 on climate change definitely requires all countries to do their part in curtailing greenhouse gas emissions so as to minimize the global impact of climate change.

The challenge for every government, of course is to find the resources, sometimes financial but also human resources, to achieve these goals. For example, countries wanting to achieve SDG 4 on education would require resources to build schools, train teachers and put in place Information Technology (IT) infrastructure to avail students of the latest pedagogical advances. These resources, unfortunately, are not infinite and the need to find ways and means to use them in the most effective manner is crucial if the achievements are to be sustainable.

The present system of accounts used by governments provides a good starting point. However, these accounts are still incomplete with major gaps in the accounting and tracking of natural and human capital. The development of the inclusive wealth accounts and the corresponding index offers some guidance to evaluate if the achievement of the SDGs is sustainable over the longer-term. The focus of the Index on the productive base of the country offers valuable insights on the efficient use of its resources and the rate of return on each of the assets within the overall productive base for achieving the various SDGs.

This chapter offers insights on economic investment policymaking in the use of the asset/productive base of an economy and demonstrates how students of economics and sustainable development can learn from playing games through scenario role-playing. Section 2 offers some insights on the use of IWI in policymaking and the various factors that should be taken into account when making investment decisions on the use of a country's productive base. This is then followed by a section highlighting the strengths of using games as a learning pedagogy for students of economics and sustainability. The last two sections offer some insights on some preliminary results emerging from the game developed for the IWI followed by ideas for future work to be done.

IWI and policymaking

The SDGs require resources if the targets are to be achieved. Policymakers will need access to the right type of information to make the right decisions. At the present, policymakers rely on the System of National Accounts (SNA) to give them an idea of how much resources their respective countries have at their disposal to meet demands such as achieving literacy rates, reducing malnourishment, providing hospitals and medical support to meet health standards and so forth. In fact, one of the main challenges facing countries post signing the SDG agreement is to fund the ambitious development agenda set out by the SDGs.

This is where a dilemma emerges. Let us illustrate this with an example. A key requirement of the SDG 4 which is on education is to reduce illiteracy rates, provide higher and vocational education, and improve the quality of schools and teachers. This requires funds to build schools, teacher training and technology support among other demands. Governments have to set aside budgets for accomplishing these targets. The question is where are these resources to come from. It does not matter if the funds are sourced within a country or aid is provided by others, the bottom line is that resources have to be used to produce the funds to achieve the SDGs. This key element was not factored within the SDG agenda.

A framework is needed that can provide policymakers the information to make the choices on where to appropriate the resources. The inclusive wealth accounts as illustrated in the earlier chapters offer such a framework. As already demonstrated, a country's asset base, or also called its productive base, is comprised of three main categories of capitals; produced, natural and human capital. In many ways, the state of some of these capitals can be mapped directly to some of the SDG goals. For example, literacy rates are directly reflected in the state of human capital. Education levels are a key variable in the computation of human capital. In similar fashion, schools are reflected in the produced capital asset category.

The IW framework offers policymakers and students of policymaking a framework to look at the following three main issues. These are:

1   Understanding trade-offs across different assets bases and across time when making decisions on sustainability.
2   Understanding interconnected externalities.
3   Understanding the role of population growth.
4   Understanding social prices and market prices and their deviations.

Trade-offs present and in future

The notion of trade-offs is not new. In a world of limited resources with a large set of demands, trade-offs are inevitable. Difficult decisions have to be made when prioritizing goals. The main question on our mind is if we can achieve all the SDGs without having to forego one for the other. For example, will countries have sufficient resources to achieve poverty reduction while at the same time having the resources to build the schools and train teachers at the same time? The issue takes on another level of complexity if the achievements achieved can be maintained across a time span greater than just the 15 years that have been given to achieve the SDGs. So, even if all the SDGs are achieved by 2030, the magic question is if these gains can be maintained and not slip back as resources get exhausted. These are questions that the IW can provide policymakers. It maintains a close track on the state of the country's productive base; a declining asset base implies a non-sustainable trajectory.

Interconnected externalities

One of the most challenging and emerging issues facing present societies is climate change. Let's assume that we accept the consensus of the world scientific community that climate change is being caused by the excessive greenhouse gases emitted by anthropogenic activities by countries across the world, some more than others. The IW framework accounts for these impacts. Damages caused by greenhouse gases have been computed using the latest findings from global model simulations and appropriated across countries. The impacts are not the same across countries. The countries that emit the most greenhouse gases are not necessarily the countries which are impacted the most. The IW framework captures these dichotomies and helps policymakers prepare for the impacts of climate change but also prepare them when they negotiate for reductions in greenhouse gases as well as for compensations accruing from climate change.

Population growth

One variable ignored in the SDGs is population. The world has seen the fastest growth in human population ever witnessed in human history. The impacts of this population growth have not been considered in most policymaking in nearly every country. In fact, many countries seeing a decline in their populations have initiated population boosting policies fearing the demise of a workforce required to maintain economic activity. There are consequences of these types of policies in a world where resources are finite and becoming scarce. Some of the results from previous IW reports have shown conclusively how countries can move from being sustainable when computed in absolute terms and become unstainable when population growth is factored in the computation. Understanding population growth and the impact it has on the productive base is a critical variable that policymakers should begin to factor in their policymaking process. This will have huge implications on the achievement of the SDGs. Population growth was not factored when the SDGs were designed and are based on an assumption of a static world from the perspective of population numbers and their needs.

Social prices and market prices

Many of the assets that are critical for maintaining the productive base are either not priced or are priced at much lower levels than they should rightly be. This is especially true for natural capital and human capital assets. Natural capital assets such as forests and water bodies such as mangroves have only been valued for the products they provide for the market. These include timber and aquatic products such as fish. However, these ecosystems offer a much larger suite of services such as water purification, water regulation and habitat provisioning for species among many others. These are not priced when valuing these assets.

Individual SDGs and sustainability of SDGs

The individual SDGs have fairly well-designed metrics and parameters that a policymaker can deploy in order to ensure that the impact of policies can be measured and course corrections are performed at the right time. The challenge, however, for policymakers stems from the fact that they have limited resources at their disposal to improve "performance" and will have to prioritize between various investment/ improvement options. Therefore, real world changes can render the long-term deployment of SDG oriented development a challenge for policymakers. The game will provide the policymakers a "sandbox" environment with which they will be able to understand long-term deployment of SDG oriented policy planning.

Games as a policy learning tool

Definition of the game

Shubik argues that "games provide a structured, non-confrontational, realistic environment which allows players to immerse themselves in the situation, experience the consequences of their actions, and subsequently learn from them" (Shubik, 1975). In a similar vein, Igor Mayer interprets games as experi(m)ent(i)al, rule-based, interactive environments in which players learn by taking actions and experiencing their effects through feedback mechanisms that are deliberately built into and around the game. Mayer here argues that gaming is based on the assumption that the individual and social learning that emerges in the game can be transferred to the world outside the game and therefore has resonance with reality (Mayer, 2009).

Planning at the country level is a wicked problem (Rittel & Webber, 1973). There are no true or false solutions, rather what we have are a range of options. In order to grapple with wicked problems, we need a space that allows us to explore possible options, understand their implications and learn from that experience. Games have been widely used to understand wicked problems and to explore ways to tackle them. They provide a space for reflection, collaboration and learning. A game places a player or a group of players in a simulated environment to recreate the sensations of the intended scenario. The target persons can then be made to "experience" various situations (Abt, 1987; Breuer & Bente, 2010; Crookall, 2010; Duke & Geurts, 2004; Susi, Johannesson, & Backlund, 2007). The game can be used to understand trade-offs in the policy decisions, which will enable players to then understand consequences and impact of their choices (Duke & Geurts, 2004; Mayer, 2009). In order to understand the complexity of the choices at their disposal, players often have greater incentive to rule out least desirable consequences after having experienced such outcomes (Haug, Huitema, & Wenzler, 2011; Hoysala, Murthy, Palavalli, Subrahmanian, & Meijer, 2013; Palavalli, Krishna, & Hoysala, 2011).

In order to learn concepts in policy planning and analysis, it becomes essential for the policymakers to understand and evaluate various options both qualitatively and quantitatively. Games allow players to weigh various parameters that can be quantified and tangible with those that are often intangible and unquantifiable, thereby determining their next steps. Policymakers need to be equipped to make decisions under uncertainties and to factor changing scenarios into their strategies. Games provide policymakers with the experience to test their hypotheses without the consequences of real world failure but will provide them with the experience. To simulate the uncertainties involved in governing a complex socio-economic system such as a country, the game can provide the players with different events and external factors. It is this process that forms the space for the players to observe and reflect, helping them process the experiences in the game to turn it to learning (Bots & Van Daalen, 2007; Brewer, 1986; Crookall, 2010; Duke, 1982; Fischer & Forester, 1993; Haug, Huitema, & Wenzler, 2011; Roth & Erev, 1995; Wenzler, 1993).

Experiential learning

David Kolb, an American educational theorist, popularised the idea of experiential learning. Kolb's model of experiential learning consists of four elements: concrete experience, observation and reflection, the formation of abstract concepts and testing in new situations (Kolb, 2014). This process itself is a cycle, although learning can begin at any stage. Role-playing also reinforces what has already been learned elsewhere, say a textbook. Games, thus, can be used to complement traditional learning methods used in classrooms. In a game, the player's choices chart the course of the game, which in turn lets the player invest more in the narrative built.

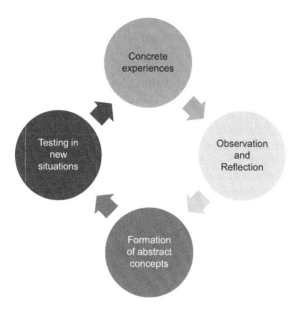

Figure 8.1 Kolb's Experiential Learning Cycle
Source: Derived from Kolb (2014).

With different players interacting with each other, the different narratives build to become a site for experiential learning.

In order to demonstrate the various capabilities and components of IWI, it will be used in a game for a policy design exercise. We propose to incorporate IWI into a *computer supported* game to help demonstrate its use by simulating different scenarios. In a computer supported game, the game is played with the aid of a computer rather than use the computer as the platform. This type of game allows for physical interactions among the players (classroom). A computer based game will also be able to manage data intensive models. The graphical capabilities supported by a computer supported game allows us to provide different views of the underlying models to ease understanding.

Impact of IWI in policymaking through the game

Objectives of and in the game

The broad objectives of the game are to understand (i) the implications of policy decisions, (ii) the relationship between the three capitals (produced, human and natural) and (iii) what it could mean to achieve the sustainable development goals in the future. In order to make policy decisions, it often becomes important that the trade-offs between resources and constraints of policy operationalization are mapped. Often, the challenge that policymakers have is the differences between short-, medium- and long-term impact of policy choices. This often translates into real world challenges such as political stability and the impact of these decisions on continued political stability. The long-term nature (often intergenerational or decadal) of high impact policies is again at odds with the pressure that policymakers face to deliver results in the short-term which is achieved by piecemeal short-term projects. The transition from having targets such as economic growth measured by GDP to including human development, emissions and the use of natural resources requires an understanding of the interlinkages of the various factors that exist between the human, natural and produced capitals. This translates to elements such as making use of natural resources in order to improve economic growth in the short-term, and to understand the impact of growth with high carbon emission on long-term sustainability and climate change. Given the increasing adoption of SDGs and the need to operationalize SDGs, the game will take into account the three SDGs 4, 7 and 13. This decision was based on the parameters that are included in the Inclusive Wealth Index as described in Table 8.5. In order to ensure the data is available (temporal availability and granularity) for the players and to ensure consistency of data (variation in different datasets and statistical significance of new parameters being introduced to IWI), SDG 1 had to be ruled out. The targets on economic growth and development have been incorporated as individual targets. Therefore, SDGs 4, 7 and 13 were shortlisted as specific targets for all players in the game.

Game design

Given the complexity of the subject matter, the game is designed to be used as a classroom teaching aid with multiple students participating simultaneously and not as a standalone single-player game. The target audience for the game will include policymakers; graduate students of sustainability studies, environmental economics, public policy and economics; and mid-career policy professionals. As discussed in the earlier section, testing hypotheses learned in the class by experimenting in the game will allow the players to learn the concepts better. Figure 8.2 presents a conceptual model of each round for every player-group in the proposed game. The different interconnected parameters that underlie a country's social, political and economic context will be modelled based on the parameters and variables available in the Inclusive Wealth Index. The players make changes to the various parameters in the game through specific policy interventions that are either monetary investment in nature or regulatory change or providing subsidies in the game. Examples of such actions are described in the subsequent sections.

Shortlisting of countries

In order to ensure that the players are not overwhelmed by the data in the game and to ensure that players experience the challenges from different perspectives, the number of countries in the playing environment is restricted. In order to decide the countries of interest, the following criteria were used:

1 "Resource Rich" or "Resource Poor" and "Developed" or "Emerging".
2 There must be a significant change in the growth rates of per capita and total GDP and IWI.
3 The country must be subject social, political and environmental shocks.
4 Continental representation and percentage of global population.

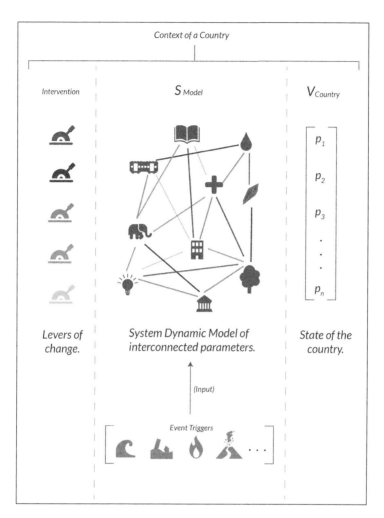

Figure 8.2 Conceptual model of the game

As this "sandbox" environment must allow the player to understand implications of policy choices and the nature of unforeseen circumstances, two additional cycles of filtration were carried out using educational attainment and risk of disasters.

The change in IWI and GDP was factored in first by directionality of change of IWI and GDP (Table 8.1) and then using the significant change in IWI and GDP (Table 8.2). The change is considered significant if the growth rate of GDP/IWI for the given country is above the third quartile of the growth rates of all countries. This gives rise to 16 possible combinations (4 × 4) of countries that are of interest for the game (Table 8.3).

Within each of the groups, the countries were ranked according to their strengths in the following parameters: Total Affected Natural Capital, Total Damage Natural Capital, Total Affected Tech, Total Damage Tech, GDP Per Capita 2005, GDP

Per Capita 2010, Population Density 2005, Population Density 2010, Educational Attainment 2010. The top five countries in each group were first shortlisted based on the above parameters. The countries were further shortlisted based on the value of the damage function. They were ranked in descending order, i.e. the ones with higher damage function values are ranked higher as these are significant from the game design perspective. We then ensured that percentage of the global population and continental representation was accounted for in these countries (point 4). Based on this filtration procedure the final set of countries is presented in Table 8.4.

Table 8.1 Directionality of change between IWI and GDP

	IWI +ve	IWI -ve
GDP +ve		
GDP -ve		

Table 8.2 Significance of change in IWI and GDP

	IWI significant	IWI marginal
GDP significant		
GDP marginal		

Table 8.3 Combinations of change in IWI and GDP, where P = CAGR of per capita IWI and Q = CAGR of per capita GDP

Amount of change/ Directionality of change	G1	G2	G3	G4
T1	P++, Q++	P++, Q+	P+, Q++	P+, Q+
T2	P++, Q –	P++, Q –	P+, Q –	P+, Q –
T3	P –, Q++	P –, Q+	P –, Q++	P –, Q+
T4	P –, Q –	P –, Q –	P –, Q –	P –, Q –

Table 8.4 Shortlisted countries

Group/ Type	G1	G2	G3	G4	Countries added based on the 4th criteria
T1	China	Chile	Indonesia	Japan	United States
	India	Republic of Korea	Peru	Germany	Brazil
T2	Spain	Greece	Italy		Norway
	Luxembourg		United Kingdom		UAE
T3	Myanmar	Iraq	Cambodia	Algeria	Russia
	Mozambique	Saudi Arabia		Ecuador	Australia
T4	Nigeria				

Equations guiding the flow of the game

As discussed earlier, players are given an option to make a monetary investment in key areas of their choice and deciding on the policies that they would like to improve. The monetary investments are defined by the amount of money at their disposal, and for the purpose of the game, it is defined as a function of the produced capital in the country. It is determined by the produced capital as described in the equation below,

$$B_{t,c} = \left[1 + \left(\frac{PC_{t-1,c} - PC_{t-2,c}}{PC_{t-2,c}}\right)\right] * B_{t-1,c} + BS_{t-1,c} + L_{t-1,c}$$

$$B_{t,c} = \left[1 + \left(\frac{PC_{t-1,c} - PC_{t-2,c}}{PC_{t-2,c}}\right)\right] * B_{t-1,c} - BD_{t-1,c} + L_{t-1,c}$$

Where,

$B_{t,c}$ = Annual budget at time t for country c

$B_{t-1,c}$ = Annual budget in previous year for country c

$PC_{t-1,c}$ = Produced capital at time t − 1 or in previous year for country c

$PC_{t-2,c}$ = Produced capital at time t − 2 year for country c

$BS_{t-1,c}$ = Budget surplus in previous year or at time t − 1

$BD_{t-1,c}$ = Budget deficit in previous year or at time t − 1

$L_{t-1,c}$ = Borrowing or Loans for the country c at time t − 1

However, in order to ensure that a certain amount of pedagogical control is available to the facilitator, the deviation of a parameter in the game world from the value in the real world at any given year is bounded in the following manner.

$$|AV_{t,c}| = \left[1 - \left\{\left(\frac{\Delta_{2010} - \Delta_{1990}}{20}\right) * (t - 1990) + \Delta_{1990}\right\}\right] * V_{t,c}$$

$$|AV_{t,c}| = \left[1 + \left\{\left(\frac{\Delta_{2010} - \Delta_{1990}}{20}\right) * (t - 1990) + \Delta_{1990}\right\}\right] * V_{t,c}$$

Where,

Δ = Deviation from the rate being set by the facilitator ($0 <= \Delta <= 1$)

$Av_{t,c}$ = Action variable at time t for country c

In order to help the player to understand the interconnected nature of the parameters, the effect of SDG on the individual parameter is captured in the game. The effect of the player decisions on the sustainable development goal is defined as follows,

$$SDG_{t,c} = \sum \left[P_{SDG,c} * \left(\frac{A_{t-1,c}}{T_c}\right)\right]$$

Where,

$SDG_{t,c}$ = Percentage of SDG achieved at time t for country c

$P_{SDG,c}$ = Priority for SDG for country c and $\sum P_{SDG,c} = 1$

$A_{t-1,c}$ = Achieved value of independent indicator at time t-1
T_c = Targeted value of independent indicator

$$AV_{t,c} = \left\{\alpha * \left(1 + \frac{I_{t,V}\, r_{V,C}}{B_{t,c}}\right) + \beta * SDG_{t,c}\right\} * AV_{t-1,c}$$

Where,
$I_{t,V}$ = Investment at time t for variable V by the player
$r_{V,C}$ = Correlation between the variable V and the corresponding Capital
$\alpha + \beta = 1$ where α and β will be decided by the facilitator based on the weightage given to player's investment to a certain sector and weightage for prioritizing different SDGs.

While the previous equations describe the changes in variables based on player decisions, it is restricted only to the countries chosen by players, i.e. in a classroom size of X (where X is less than 27), then only the parameters of these X countries will change. However, in order to ensure that the game world remains consistent for believability and player experience, we need to show changes in the non-played countries. We ensure that the changes in the other countries are a function of the average change in the other countries in the same year.

$$R_{t-1,c,v} = G_{t-1,c,v} + E_{t-1,c,v}$$
$$R_{t-1,c,v} = -G_{t-1,c,v} - E_{t-1,c,v}$$

Where,
$R_{t-1,c,v}$ = Rate of change of variable V for previous year for country c
$G_{t-1,c,v}$ = Rate of change of variable V for previous year for country c which is not shortlisted for the game
$E_{t-1,c,v}$ = Average rate of change of variable V for previous year for country c which is not shortlisted for the game

$$E_{t-1,c,v} = \frac{1}{n}\sum k_{t-1,c,v}$$

Where,
$k_{t-1,c,v}$ = Rate of change of variable V for previous year for shortlisted country c
n = Number of shortlisted countries c (i.e. n = 26)

$$V_{t,c} = (1 + R_{t-1,c,v}) * V_{t-1,c}$$

Where,
$V_{t,c}$ = Variables at time t or current year for country c which is not shortlisted for the game
$R_{t-1,c,v}$ = Rate of change of variable V for previous year for country c
$V_{t-1,c}$ = Variables at previous year for country c

Preliminary results

The IWI is measured based on the interconnectedness of economic health, human well-being and environmental condition of an economy. The index to measure a country's environmental condition is the wealth of natural capital. The natural capital has been included as an addition to the measurement of gross domestic product (GDP) and Human Development Index (HDI) through the introduction of IWI. The aim of the game is to highlight the relationship between GDP and wealth of produced, human and natural capitals. The game also allows the players to understand the relationship between the wealth of all three capitals and all independent variables.

Annual growth rate and CAGR over the review period (1990–2010) of all dependent and independent variables of the game demonstrate the trend of each parameter. Correlation between trends of each capital, GDP and all independent variables can be used to understand the relationship between trends of these parameters.

We have selected 27 countries for the game, based on macroeconomic indicators and disaster parameters, out of 140 listed countries in Inclusive Wealth Report 2014. Out of these 27 countries, only Myanmar shows a negative correlation between IWI and GDP during the review period. Apart from Nigeria and Russia, 25 other selected countries show a significant and positive correlation between the wealth of produced capital and GDP. Correlation between the wealth of human capital and GDP is always significant and positive for all selected countries. However, the wealth of natural capital shows significant and negative correlation with GDP, with an exception for South Korea, Luxembourg and Italy.

The correlation between all stock variables and a country's wealth of natural capital is mostly opposite as compared to the correlation with the wealth of produced capital and IWI. Based on this alternative relationship amongst these independent variables and wealth of capitals, the countries have to balance with all stock variables of natural capital and the economic output.

Dichotomy between achieving individual SDGs and sustainability

Players of the game have to achieve both country-specific goals and global goals at the same time. However, there are two targeted global objectives in the game. First is to achieve 7.0% global GDP growth rate and the second is to achieve the Sustainable Development Goals (SDGs 4, 7 and 13). The players have to prioritize sectors to allocate funds from a country's annual budget, so that, they can manage both country level and global goals.

Correlation between GDP and wealth of natural capital is negative for most of the shortlisted countries, whereas IWI is positively correlated with GDP. This explains that the growth in produced capital surpasses the effect of decreasing natural capital and leads to a growth in both GDP and IWI. Players have to decide how to create trade-off between use of natural resources and economic growth.

Our focus is mainly on SDG 4 (quality education for all), SDG 7 (sustainable energy) and SDG 13 (climate action). We have mapped each SDG of all selected countries to the nodal ministries, both public and private investments, respective schemes and policy description. The game also allows the players to observe the direct and indirect impact of investment and policy implementation. Player actions concerning each of the three SDGs in the game can be broadly divided into three categories: direct investments, indirect investments, and regulatory or policy changes. The impact on SDGs for each shortlisted country will be based on the allocated annual budget into different sectors of the economy. Each country has a specific information matrix to understand the impact of policy implementation and the inflow of investments to schemes which are targeted towards achieving the objectives under the considered SDGs.

Country vs. global

Comparison between each country and the global scenario is an important parameter in the game to understand a country's standing globally. Global comparison of each country includes a comparison of the share of each capital in IWI and CAGR of capitals. The wealth of human capital accounted for the largest share of 62.4% out of the global IWI at an average basis, during the period 1990–2010. However, the share has declined from 64.3% in 1990 to 61.3% in 2010. Likewise, the wealth of produced capital at global perspective accounted for an average of 22.5% share, whereas the remaining of 15.1% has been accounted as the wealth of natural capital out of global IWI. Due to rise in economic growth, the wealth of produced capital at global context has increased significantly from 19.0% in 1990 to 26.6% in 2010. On the other hand, extensive use of natural resources to generate more economic output led to a noticeable decline in the share of the wealth of natural capital out of the global IWI from 16.7% in 1990 to 12.1% in 2010.

Global IWI accounted for a 1.6% CAGR over the period of 2000–2010. The growth in IWI is mainly driven by a continuous rise in the wealth of both produced (CAGR of 3.3%) and human (CAGR of 1.5%) capital over the period. However, due to continuous reduction in stocks of natural resources, the wealth of natural capital at global scenario has declined by a CAGR of 0.7% during the review period.

In the game, the players would be able to notice their respective country's position at the global scenario based on the shares and growth of each capital. Players have also to compare their respective country's economic growth with the global targeted growth rate.

Short term vs. long-term

Players are responsible to balance between short-term and long-term goals for the respective countries. It is all about the adjustment within the use of natural resources and economic output. Players have to decide whether to invest more on the country's output or production to achieve high economic growth rate after a decade as targeted for the game or minimize the extensive use of natural resources. To achieve the global and country's economic growth in a sustainable way, the players are entitled to trade-off between short-term and long-term outcomes for the country's perspective.

Future work

In this chapter, we present a game that helps operationalize IWI for policymaking. The game provides the players with a "sandbox" environment where they can test various policy formulations and the impact of their choices on the macro-indicators. The players are able to understand the dichotomy between the growth rates and sustainability, individual SDG and sustainability, short vs. long-term and an individual country and the global needs. The players can factor trade-offs that have been operationalized as game elements in order to understand the dynamics of interaction of the various constituent elements and the resulting impacts at multiple levels. In the future, it would be possible to bring in more contextual elements of climate change, gender, global trade and migration into this "game world" to help the players understand the impact of their actions. It is possible to be able to understand the role of preferences (and biases) on policies through the game as the players have to set these priorities in the game. As we conduct more game sessions, it is possible to map the role of gender, disciplinary/domain background and similar contextual elements on the player's decisions in the game. This can then be explored further to understand the deviations in the real world and the game world. It is then possible to design appropriate pedagogical responses to help policymakers deal with the complexity of the real world.

As the game does not provide a definite "winning" condition, the traditional model of a single winner and multiple "losers" is brought into question. It is possible to then test if this changed value system will affect the player behaviour in the game. The potential motivation map for policy choices will, therefore, change over a period of time during the game. With a sufficient number of game sessions, we are then able to understand if such a change is uniform across future policymakers or if there are trigger conditions that enable this change. The data generated by the game provide the future policymakers a window into potential alternatives for the chosen 27 countries. These alternatives become powerful as the game provides a year on year trajectory of this change based on human preference and bias for certain policies (modelled on the real world scenario).

MAPPING VARIABLES IN SDGS AND IWI

Table 8.5 Relationship between variables in IWI and SDGs

SDG	Parameters from SDG	Capitals in IWI	Parameters from IWI	Additional variables required
SDG 1: Poverty	Proportion of population living below the national poverty line, by sex and age	Human capital		Percentage of people below poverty line
	Proportion of total government spending on essential services (education, health and social protection)	Produced capital		Expenditure on education as % of total government expenditure (%), Investment
SDG 4: Education	Participation rate in primary schools	Human capital	Gross enrolment ratio, primary, both sexes (%), Educational attainment	
	Participation rate in secondary schools	Human capital	Gross enrolment ratio, secondary, both sexes (%)	
	Literacy rate	Human capital	Adult literacy rate, population 15+ years, both sexes (%)	

(*Continued*)

Table 8.5 (Continued)

SDG	Parameters from SDG	Capitals in IWI	Parameters from IWI	Additional variables required
SDG 7: Energy	Energy intensity measured in terms of primary energy and GDP	Natural capital	Energy required – energy intensity level of primary energy (MJ/$2011 PPP GDP)	
	Renewable energy share in the total final energy consumption	Natural capital	% of energy use – energy imports, net	
SDG 10: Economic Growth and Productive Employment	Annual growth rate of real GDP (per capita)	Produced capital	GDP growth (annual %)	
	Average hourly earnings of female and male employees, by occupation, age and persons with disabilities	Human capital	Compensation of employees – average daily wage rate	
SDG 13: Climate Change	Green House Emissions	Natural capital	CO_2 emissions (in kt)	

OBJECTIVES OF THE GAME

Table 8.6 Mapping between objectives of the game and the various game elements

Sl. No.	Objectives	Roles	Resources	Constraints	Boundaries	Ending criteria	Actions/ procedures
1	Taking policy decisions and understanding their impacts on the three capitals (IWI) and the SDGs 4, 7 and 13	X			X		X
2	To see how policy decisions of different temporal scales impact sustainability	X			X		X
3	To understand the relationship between produced capital and human capital	X	X	X			X
4	To realize the conflict between individual country-wise objectives and global objectives for achieving SDGs 4, 7 and 13		X	X			X
5	To realize the trade-offs, resources and constraints of policy operationalization and its impact on productivity and sustainability			X			X

Sl. No.	Objectives	Roles	Resources	Constraints	Boundaries	Ending criteria	Actions/ procedures
6	To understand the link and the nature of relationship that human capital shares with natural capital and produced capital and the overall impact on IWI	X					X
7	Short term vs. long-term decisions that are made and how each of them affect sustainability, specifically SDGs 4, 7 and 13 in the game			X			X
8	To understand the short-, medium- and long-term impacts of policy decisions on IWI in the game by choosing different levers attached to different capitals	X					X
9	Tracking direct investments, indirect investments and regulatory/policy changes and their impacts on SDGs 4, 7 and 13		X		X		X
10	GDP (produced capital) vs. well-being (human capital) and carbon emissions (natural capital) vs. well-being (human capital)	X	X	X			X

OBJECTIVES IN THE GAME

Table 8.7 Mapping between objectives in the game and the game elements

Sl. No.	Objectives	Roles	Resources	Constraints	Boundaries	Ending criteria	Actions/ procedures
1	Bring in 7% GDP growth for the world	X	X	X		X	X
2	Achieve SDGs 4, 7 and 13 targets for individual countries	X			X	X	X

References

Abt, C. C. (1987). *Serious games*. University Press of America. Retrieved from https://books.google.co.in/books?hl=en&lr=&id=axUs9HA-hF8C&oi=fnd&pg=PR13&dq=abt+c+serious+games&ots=dZZ48iybxN&sig=d5HZ75fcRTaAXQIBq9Rkk0iXXU8

Bots, P., & Van Daalen, E. (2007). Functional design of games to support natural resource management policy development. *Simulation & Gaming, 38*(4), 512–532.

Breuer, J., & Bente, G. (2010). Why so serious? On the relation of serious games and learning. *Journal for Computer Game Culture, 4,* 7–24.

Brewer, G. D. (1986). Methods for synthesis: Policy exercises. *Sustainable Development of the Biosphere, 17,* 455–473.

Crookall, D. (2010). Serious games, debriefing, and simulation/gaming as a discipline. *Simulation & Gaming, 41*(6), 898–920.

Dasgupta, P. (2009). The welfare economics of green national accounts, *Environmental and Resource Economics, 42*(1), 3–38.

Dasgupta, P., & Duraiappah, A. (2012). Well-being and wealth. In UNU-IHDP and UNEP (Eds.). *Inclusive wealth report 2012: Measuring progress toward sustainability.* Cambridge: Cambridge University Press.

Duke, R. D. (1982). Management under complexity: Gaming/simulation as a predecisional tool. *Simulation & Games, 13*(3), 365–373.

Duke, R. D., & Geurts, J. (2004). *Policy games for strategic management.* Rozenberg Publishers. Retrieved from https://books.google.co.in/books?hl=en&lr=&id=XGUdoR-PFx30C&oi=fnd&pg=PA11&dq=duke+games&ots=U6lFyJrtPV&sig=CVmp-k8FSSe61D6BcDjc6IbQIOs

Fischer, F., & Forester, J. (1993). *The argumentative turn in policy analysis and planning.* Duke University Press. Retrieved from https://books.google.com/books?hl=en&lr=&id=95IsUilBzdUC&oi=fnd&pg=PA1&ots=Czyr9NKJCE&sig=P8J3aBLaF0v3kGuyi7AYPusD3Qc

Haug, C., Huitema, D., & Wenzler, I. (2011). Learning through games? Evaluating the learning effect of a policy exercise on European climate policy. *Technological Forecasting and Social Change, 78*(6), 968–981.

Hoysala, O., Murthy, A., Palavalli, B. M., Subrahmanian, E., & Meijer, S. (2013). Designing energy policy through the Indian energy game. *International Simulation and Gaming Association.* Retrieved from http://docs.fieldsofview.in/public/Designing_Energy_Policy_through_the_Indian_Energy_Game_ISAGA_2013.pdf

Kolb, D. A. (2014). *Experiential learning: Experience as the source of learning and development.* FT Press. Retrieved from https://books.google.co.in/books?hl=en&lr=&id=jpbeBQAAQBAJ&oi=fnd&pg=PR7&dq=kolb+experiential+learning&ots=VmbVkUZTQg&sig=HwnQM7FZQQohYooH2yAkH0gAuU0

Mayer, I. S. (2009). The gaming of policy and the politics of gaming: A review. *Simulation & Gaming, 40*(6), 825–862.

Palavalli, B., Krishna, H., & Hoysala, O. (2011). Discovering communication Protocols for inter-agency collaboration for emergency response. In *Bonds & Bridges: Facing the challenges of the globalizing world with the use of simulation and gaming.* Warsaw.

Rittel, H. W., & Webber, M. M. (1973). Dilemmas in a general theory of planning. *Policy Sciences, 4*(2), 155–169.

Roth, A. E., & Erev, I. (1995). Learning in extensive-form games: Experimental data and simple dynamic models in the intermediate term. *Games and Economic Behavior, 8*(1), 164–212.

Stiglitz, J. E., Sen, A., & Fitoussi, J.-P. (2010). *Mismeasuring our lives: Why GDP doesn't add up: The report.* New York: New Press.

Susi, T., Johannesson, M., & Backlund, P. (2007). *Serious games: An overview.* Institutionen för kommunikation och information. Retrieved from www.diva-portal.org/smash/record.jsf?pid=diva2:2416

Wenzler, I. (1993). *Policy exercises: A new approach to policy development.* Instituut voor Toegepaste Wetenschappen.

9 The IWR and policy lessons

Shunsuke Managi

Introduction

The purpose of genuine savings and inclusive wealth clearly lies in sustainability analysis. The analysis can indicate whether the national productive base is on the increase or decrease, in accordance with intergenerational well-being. As such, proceeding from sustainability analysis to policy implication is not straightforward. Specifically, even if the shadow price of a given asset is known to be high, it does not necessarily mean that the given asset should be the focus of investment. A cost-benefit analysis, using the same set of shadow prices, should be performed to determine what kind of policy should be the means to increase social well-being (Dasgupta, 2009).

However, inclusive wealth figures on their own are not silent about policy implications. For example, if a particular component class of inclusive wealth is on a rapid decline within a relatively short period of time, the necessity for policy intervention should be reflected, perhaps even in the absence of cost-benefit analysis. In this chapter, we first discuss those implications that may arise from certain classes of capital assets. Investing in human capital, which has not been the focus of previous chapters, is something that we all agree on, but the questions of how and to what extent this investment should be made remain. As our previous edition (UNU-IHDP, 2014), there are many critical aspects that are not captured by the current exercise of human capital measurement. Health status of mothers, early childhood education, home environment, vocational training and non-cognitive development are all examples of these aspects. Among others, we highlight vocational training and child labour.

We also examine fishery resources, which is another area of contentious debate in natural capital management. Globally, it is a growing industry facing the threat of overfishing, but there are many positive sides of the industry, such as aquaculture and recent experiences of sustainable fishery and green labelling.

We next address an important area of negative capital stock, which is not previously addressed in inclusive wealth accounting, aside from carbon damage. As long as a capital-like source of pollution causes direct disutility or damage to capital stock (health capital), this source should be one of the capital assets relevant to social well-being. The World Bank has plausibly included particulate matter emission in their account of genuine savings, which we will review in our context.

Certain policy implications can also be derived for investing in technological advancements. Total factor productivity (TFP) measures all the residual contributions to social well-being, after accounting for all the relevant capital assets (Arrow et al., 2012). It is known to affect the bottom line figure of IWI adjusted (UNU-IHDP, 2014).

Finally, we also note how to put the concept and measurement into policy action. In this chapter, we address this issue from a different perspective. In particular, we suggest a new financial policy tool, where national or local governments may consider issuing financial bonds that are linked with the Inclusive Wealth Index (IWI) of their sovereignty. As the asset side of the national balance sheet is now expanded to include human and natural capital, the liability side can also increase, analogous to the corporate finance structure. Not only is this idea inspired by the proposal and recent practice of GDP-linked bonds, but it also appears to be more plausible than the original argument, in that the capital asset we assume is wider and more comprehensive from a well-being perspective.

We hope that the debates in this chapter will provide suggestions for policymakers committed to returning their regions to (more) sustainable paths.

Policy lessons for education

Education is an important contributor to human capital, and countries can increase their productivity by increasing their investment in education. Thus, investment in education provides a high rate of return to the inclusive wealth of countries, both directly through accumulating human capital and through enhancing total factor productivity adjustment.

But how can we boost investing in education? Many things come to mind, from physical infrastructure (school building, toilets), to consumables (textbook, uniform, nutritious meal), and to human capital (quantity and quality of teachers, class size). All of them can potentially be behind still the low average years of schooling shown in Figure 9.1.

The educational portion of human capital is explained in inclusive wealth accounting. However, this accounts for only a small portion of human capital. It does not

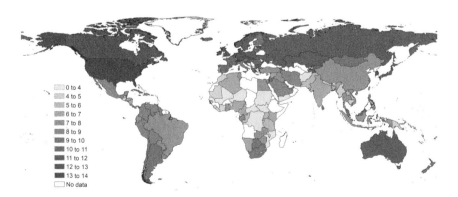

Figure 9.1 Average years of schooling from 1990 to 2014

Source: Author, using Barro and Lee (2013).

mean that the other factors are irrelevant. Indeed, it is only that we should start from the most measurable chunk. For example, what is missing can include parenting, on-the-job training, informal education/learning, adult education, healthcare, migration and others (Boarini et al., 2012).

In fact, vocational training is an important means of education to increase human capital in developing countries. Vocational training generally benefits low-income students, enabling them to become earners and contribute to the economy quicker than regular schooling. This training is also effective in reducing child labour in many developing countries and assists in human capital performance. The vocational school should benefit a special group of students, and they should have specific skills in the sector of their own interest.

Figure 9.2 shows the average proportion of vocational students in total enrolment in secondary education. The success of vocational schooling depends on the orientation of special skills and techniques, which can be managed scientifically. Many developing countries experience challenges in obtaining benefits from vocational schooling due to less efficient curriculums and management.

Investments in the education infrastructure can lead a country to improve both current welfare and future well-being by accumulating human capital. The majority of low-income countries have a child labour problem, and this problem is widespread in the developing world. In particular, child labour has been known to suppress educational attainment (e.g. Psacharopoulos, 1997). Of course, poverty is one of the driving forces leading children to perform physical labour. It can be easily imagined that a child gives up schooling when faced with its trade-off with getting paid for work.

Care should be taken, however, as many factors come in to create this problem and thus abolishing child labour altogether may not be a solution (Basu and Tzannatos, 2003). Ranjan (1999, 2001) has shown that child labour might arise in poor households with credit constraints. In a second-best world, child labour may provide the only way to finance their own school attendance, as debated in a mining case study by Maconachie and Hilson (2016). Moreover, the majority of child labour exists in the agricultural sector, typically operated by their own farms (Bhalotra and Heady, 2003).

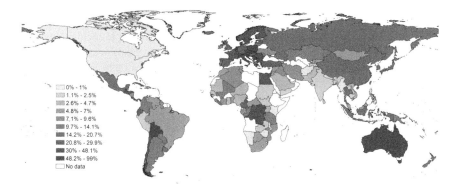

Figure 9.2 Percentage of vocational students in total secondary school enrolment

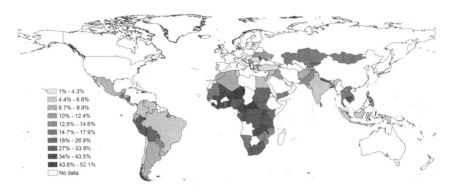

Figure 9.3 Percentage of children (aged 7–14) employed in labour

Source: Author, using Barro and Lee (2013).

Figure 9.3 shows the percentage of children (7–14 years) employed in the labour market; apparently, most of the African nations and certain Asian and Latin American countries have alarming levels of child labour. Understanding the reasons for low years of schooling and the economics of child labour can improve the education condition in low-income countries. These problems should be examined also with poverty and credit constraints in rural households. A most obvious policy lesson for those countries, therefore, is to resolve poverty, human capital investment, child labour and other market imperfection problems simultaneously.[1]

Regulating pollution and inclusion in inclusive wealth

Including the regulating ecosystem services in the inclusive wealth measure is important. They span from flood prevention at local scale to climate control at global scale. IWR 2012 and 2014 have employed carbon damage to account for climate change damage. Being a global public bad, this needs to be reckoned based on the global aggregate. A flow damage cost of a nation, regardless of how much she emits, is subtracted from IWI, to reflect true social well-being. This is a plausible move to account for negative pressure on social well-being; however, at the other end of the spatial spectrum lies local air pollution, which is yet unaddressed in inclusive wealth accounting. Local air pollution is especially relevant to policymakers at national and local scales. Regulating air pollution will benefit human health by improving the mortality rate and reducing healthcare expenses.

Among many potential sources of air pollution, the anthropogenic sources of PM2.5 are fast-growing which creates a chronic effect on human health. PM in ambient air is considered to be related to an increased risk of premature death, as well as other less severe health end-points like respiratory and cardiac emergencies (WHO, 2006), although some mechanisms remain still uncertain (Harrison and Yin, 2000). Many sources of PM2.5 are noted: for instance, transportation, energy resource usage, construction, agriculture and international trade are major emitting industries. In addition, the exposure exists at the local and international levels, implying that

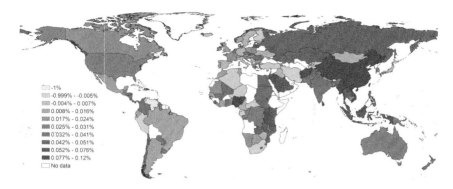

Figure 9.4 Growth of PM2.5 damages from 1990–2014 (percentage)

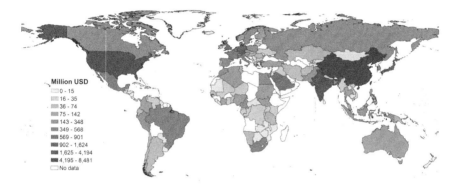

Figure 9.5 Average PM2.5 damages from 1990–2014 (million USD 2005)

PM2.5 affects more people in developing economies in Asia. For instance, China, Russia, India, Vietnam, Thailand, Indonesia and Afghanistan are encountering significant health damage due to the adverse impact of PM2.5. Figure 9.4 reports the annual average growth rate of PM2.5 damages based on the World Bank (2017) database. On the aggregate level, the intensity of damages is also very high in the United States, Japan, Brazil and the European Union (Figure 9.5), but their environmental policies seemingly significantly reduce this growth (Figure 9.4). BRICS countries also experience major damages from PM2.5 exposure.

Figure 9.6 shows the growth of PM2.5 damages in per capita terms; emerging economies are increasingly vulnerable to the exposure of damages. The average damages per capita over 25 years (1990 to 2014) are reported in Figure 9.7, where Saudi Arabia, South Africa, the United States, Japan, China and European Union countries show relatively high per capita damages, surpassing 10 USD per person.

What is distinct about ambient air pollution caused by PM is that it is transboundary (WHO, 2006; Anenberg et al., 2010), so that it should be treated as regional public bad, if not global public bad. In our inclusive wealth accounting, we adjust carbon damage as it affects human well-being as a global public bad. We therefore

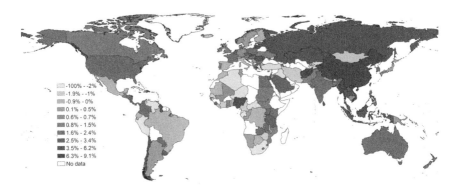

Figure 9.6 Growth of the PM2.5 damages per capita from 1990–2014 (percentage)

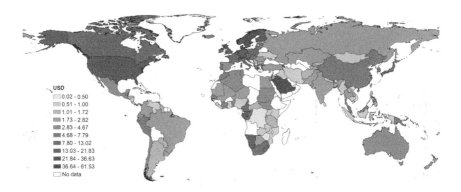

Figure 9.7 Average PM2.5 damages per capita from 1990–2014 (USD 2005)

might want to consider PM damage as another adjustment to IWI, while avoiding double counting with health capital accounts.

Fisheries policy

Fisheries are an essential part of the natural capital, which significantly contribute to the total wealth. However, the ability of a marine ecosystem to provide non-declined utility is limited by its regenerative capacity, which is currently being threatened by increasing human activities to satisfy food needs and to pursue higher economic development. The growing population of the world has led to an increase in annual global fish consumption from 9 kg/capita in 1961 to 16.5 kg/capita in 2003, and this figure is expected to increase further to 17 kg/capita in 2020 (Delgado, 2003). The increasing demand of fish consumption was followed by the industrialization of the marine fisheries sector in the first half of the 20th century through the mechanization of fishing fleets and the improvement of marketing systems, which led to increasing productivity and employment in the fisheries sector

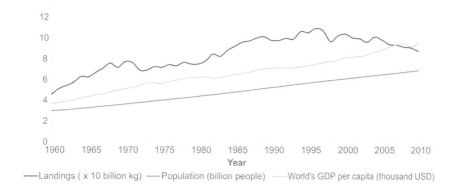

Figure 9.8 Time-series data of global marine fisheries catch, population and world GDP
per capita

(Coulthard et al., 2011). However, despite the industrialization of the marine fisheries sector and the increasing demand of consumption, the total catches of global marine fisheries eventually achieved their peak in the mid-1990s (see Figure 9.8). This finding is also followed by the increasing number of overfished and collapsed stock (Branch et al., 2011; Froese et al., 2012) and the declining mean trophic level of catch (Myers and Worm, 2003; Pauly et al., 1998; Pauly and Palomares, 2005). These factors have led to persistent debates regarding the sustainability of marine fisheries over the last two decades.

Sugiawan et al. (2017) argue that the sustainability of global marine fisheries is correlated with economic development. The researchers find a non-linear relationship between economic growth and both marine fisheries catch and estimated stock, suggesting the existence of turning points in the economy beyond which the beneficial impacts of economic growth on a marine ecosystem will be achieved. Hence, declines in resource abundance arising due to the development of the fisheries sector are only temporary. As the economy grows, the structural changes in the economy lead to more stringent environmental regulations, better fisheries management and new technologies. These changes will lead to a decline in catch levels in the short-run and stock recovery in the long-run. Similarly, by using the Ocean Health Index (OHI), a novel index to quantify and observe the health of human-marine ecosystem interactions, Halpern et al. (2012) show that, in general, developed countries have healthier oceans than developing countries. Flaaten (2013) discusses the institutional influence on the relationship between economic growth and fishing.

In terms of wealth accounting, sustainability is achieved if the capital stock of marine fisheries is non-declining over time (strong sustainability) or if the decline in marine fisheries stock can be compensated by a sufficient increase in other types of capital stock (weak sustainability). Figure 9.9 shows a comparison of capital stock of marine fisheries in 1976, 1990 and 2014 for selected countries having fish capital of more than 25 billion USD. The size of the bubble indicates the size of the population. From Figure 9.9, we can see that in general, the wealth of fisheries declines

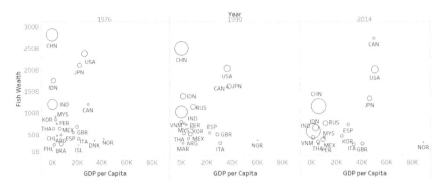

Figure 9.9 Comparison of fish stock capital for selected countries

over time as a result of continuously increasing fishing efforts, which are driven by economic development and population growth. Only a few countries, such as Canada and Spain, can maintain or increase their level of stock. From Figure 9.9, we can also see different patterns of fish stock depletion between developed and developing countries. Certain rich countries, regardless of their population, are found to have a declining rate of fish stock depletion. This finding may have resulted from the institution of better management systems and policies and the adoption of more advanced technologies. On the other hand, developing countries, which are characterized by increasing economies of scale, tend to have a steadily declining rate of fish stock depletion. In addition, we can see that the rate of stock depletion is also influenced by the size of the population. Countries that have a relatively large population, such as China, India and Indonesia, are very likely to have an increasing rate of stock depletion. However, Sugiawan et al. (2017) argue that this rapid depletion is inevitable but only occurs temporarily. The researchers argue that as the economy grows, there will be declining pressures on the marine ecosystem that will lead to stock recovery in the long-run.

From the discussion, we highlight certain important policy implications. First, the composition and technical effect of the economy, which are marked by, among others, the institution of better management systems and policies, investment in cleaner and more advanced technologies, and adoption of more stringent environmental regulations, are essential for decoupling economic growth from fish stock depletion. The immediate impact of these effects would be in reducing the volume of fish catches and discards. However, stock recovery is likely to be observed only in the long-term. These findings suggest the need to implement better fishing practices and fisheries management to achieve sustainability in the fisheries sector. Second, to maintain positive growth of total wealth, the inevitable stock depletion in the earlier stage of the economy should be compensated by a sufficient increase in other types of capital. Consequently, the constant pressure of population growth on fish stock should not only be considered a threat to sustainability but should be viewed as a potential asset, which needs to be managed to increase the productive base of an economy, that will compensate the declining level of natural capital.

TFP and social capital

TFP and sustainability implications

Arrow et al. (2004, 2012) suggested that total factor productivity (TFP) can contribute to social well-being not through three capital changes. Formally, TFP can be regarded as shadow value of time as a capital asset (UNU-IHDP and UNEP, 2012). IWR thus includes the change in TFP as an adjustment term, based on the finding that we need merely to add TFP growth to inclusive investment (Arrow et al., 2012).

A in the production function $A(t)F(K(t))$, where $K(t)$ is the vector of capital assets and $F(.)$ is the constant-returns-to-scale production function, can be interpreted to be an aggregate index of knowledge and the economy's institutions. In conventional growth accounting, $K(t)$ include produced and human capital. In a remarkable move to include natural capital in growth accounting, however, Vouvaki and Xepapadeas (2009) observe that dismissing natural capital can mislead the analyst to interpret degradation of the environment as an improvement of knowledge and institutions. Brandt et al. (2013) argued that failing to account for natural capital tends to lead to a biased estimation of productivity growth. Natural capital has also remained largely hidden to policymakers due to the limitations of traditional economic indices (Fujii and Managi, 2013; Managi et al., 2004; Johnstone et al., 2017; Kurniawan and Managi, 2017).

In this report, therefore, we calculated TFP as a residual by expanding natural capital (forest, agriculture land, fish, fossil and minerals) as an explicit factor of input into the production process. By integrating natural capital, we can understand that the same productive base of a country can lead to an increase (decrease) in aggregate output over time regarding the effective utilization of its productive resources. In particular, the frontier approach in IWR 2018 measures TFP adjustment by capturing the efficient utilization of natural capital, as well as produced and human capital, by using the Malmquist Productivity Index approach. The result shows 55 of the 140 countries – more than one-third of our sample – have negative average TFP. Increasing investments in R&D tend to be focused on areas revolving around produced and human capital, but we need to shed a new light on ways to efficiently employ natural capital and the environment in modern economy. This brings us to the question of how environmental policy actually improves productivity.

Productivity and environmental policy

Porter and van der Linde (1995) postulated an apparent link between productivity and environmental policy. According to their hypothesis, well-designed environmental regulation can provide "a free lunch" and can trigger innovation, which in turn, can decrease and offset the costs of pollution abatement and enhance competitiveness. New evidence from the OECD countries shows that the more stringent environmental policies of recent years have had no negative effect on overall productivity growth (Ambec et al., 2013). The researchers found that before tighter environmental policies came into effect, the overall productivity growth of a country slowed, possibly because firms anticipated the changes and prepared themselves for new operating conditions. However, a rebound in productivity growth soon followed, with no cumulative loss reflected in the data. Lanoie et al. (2008) also found a positive relationship between lagged regulatory stringency and productivity; innovations may take several years to develop, and capital expenditures are often delayed for a few years through normal budgetary cycles and building lags.

These results imply that more stringent environmental policies, when properly designed, can be introduced to benefit the environment with no loss of productivity. Well-designed market-based instruments, such as taxes on externalities or cap-and-trade schemes, score better in dynamic efficiency than environmental standards and effectively induce broadly defined innovation, providing firms more flexibility in the way they adapt to new environmental policy (De Serres et al., 2010). Global society is required to innovate environmental practices based on incentives for industries to perform well in their environmental management and formulate economic and environmental policies simultaneously to achieve the sustainability of the growth process.

Productivity on sectoral case

Innovations have minor importance in sustainable development issues with respect to exploiting resources for production, consumption and disposal by a better means. Thus, it has been pivotal to work toward a more advanced technological shift and shift in the progress up to this point, through the deployment of sustainable techniques and products (Hemmelskamp, 1999). Technology innovation and efficiency catch-up are driven by productivity growth. Consequently, environmentally friendly technologies, such as waste heat to electricity conversion, may lead to an improvement in productivity regarding which resources (energy) are used.

The widespread adoption of energy-saving technologies is necessary to have policy-induced impulses that help companies cope with the adoption barrier. Particularly, regarding energy efficiency, Jaffe and Stavins (1994) argued that several factors that cause energy-efficient technologies are not widely used without policy inducement. Contributing factors are a lack of information about available technologies, particularly when there are no incentives, principal/agent problems, low energy prices and high implicit discount rates. The most powerful driver to support energy efficiency is an economical aspect; if an energy efficiency project is profitable, everyone will participate in the projects. Investments in energy efficiency have many positive effects, not only an economic impact through maintaining energy security and increasing competitiveness but also environmental and health impacts by reducing GHG emissions. Arvanitis et al. (2016) proved that there is a direct positive effect of investment spending for energy-related technologies on labour productivity and indirect positive effects of energy taxes through investments in energy-related technology. Consequently, countries need to induce more investment in the energy efficiency sector.

In the agricultural sector, public policies, such as investments in research extension, education and infrastructure, and natural resource management have been the major sources of TFP growth. Chand et al. (2011) found that public investment in research has enhanced a significant source of TFP growth in most crops. The variables for natural agricultural resource management and produced capital have been important sources of TFP growth for most crops. Among natural resources, a dependable supply of irrigation revealed by the proportion of groundwater in total irrigation, in addition to the balanced use of fertilizers, has played a significant role in increasing TFP. Investments in agricultural technologies, such as drought-resistant seed varieties, soil-improving technologies and solar energy sources, are options that may increase the productivity of the agricultural sector.

These results and previous discussions provide several noteworthy contributions to policymakers. First, these findings enhance our understanding of how particular countries can measure and manage their sustainability by incorporating natural capital into TFP. Second, countries need to develop well-designed environmental regulations to trigger innovation and utilize their productive assets in a more effective manner. Third, policymakers are encouraged to support the research and development of renewable resource technologies, although their impact on social well-being is yet to be captured (but see also Chapter 3). The contribution of investment in technology is crucial to confront the dwindling natural resources and to achieve the desired productivity growth in terms of social well-being.

Policy instruments: IWI-linked bonds

In its inaugural report, IWR 2012 has proposed that inclusive wealth, rather than GDP, interest rate, unemployment or other indicators, should be "mainstreamed" to be used in economic policymaking. We believe that conventional economic indices continue to play a key role in economic policymaking, as they represent how the economy, rather than social well-being, is performing overall. Conventional aspects of the economy have many ramifications. For instance, inflation and unemployment certainly affect our short-term well-being. It is well-known that job security is an important constituent of subjective well-being and a sense of dignity. Moreover, our index of inclusive wealth pertains more to the question of whether a productive base is on the increase in the long-run, rather than short-run fluctuations. Thus, we should be humble in what our index says about the sustainability of social well-being and the productive base in the long-run.

Having acknowledged this difference in focus, we also trust that inclusive wealth should be more highlighted in economic policymaking, if not mainstreamed. Political administrations naturally tend to increase their reputations and can thus be short-sighted. For example, it is expected that current administrations have an incentive to prefer policies that cater to the current generation and leave the policy burden to be dealt with by future generations. Therefore, inclusive wealth can be a headline index in economic, as well as social and ecological, policymaking, as a sort of commitment device for sustainable development.

There could be many alternative means to operationalize the idea of making inclusive wealth a headline index, as with the interest rates of stock prices. In a recent thought experiment, Yamaguchi and Managi (2017) proposed that national governments could issue bonds that are linked to the level or the growth rate of inclusive wealth. By linking bond coupons (fixed income) to inclusive wealth, holders of this financial asset would be "in the same boat" with the trend of inclusive wealth, an indicator of sustainable well-being.

However, the main intention of this proposal is much wider than garnering focus on inclusive wealth in the policy arena. In theory, this instrument would create macro-financial markets for a previously unnoted but important portion of wealth. Kamstra and Shiller (2009) refer to human capital, which accounts for a large proportion of wealth, particularly in high-income countries, but there is no reason not to extend this discussion to natural capital. Therefore, the proposed financial vehicle can be seen as a plausible extension of the recent proposals of GDP-linked bonds (Borensztein and Mauro, 2004; Kamstra and Shiller, 2009; Barr et al., 2014).

By properly designing new bonds, governments could offer institutional and other investors opportunities to mobilize their financial resources into investments in the components of inclusive wealth: produced, human and natural capital. One way to accomplish this mobilization is to set aside the proceeds from the general budget and establish a bond revenue fund to be used for reinvestment in capital assets that comprise inclusive wealth.

In this case, the government, with the aid of the voice of citizens, is expected to craft investment strategies in capital assets. Suppose that, hopefully from the future editions of Inclusive Wealth Report, the shadow price of a forest in a given country is rising, due to aggressive deforestation and rising scarcities. Then, the national government would conduct a cost-benefit analysis, using the same shadow prices as well as cost estimates, to determine whether and how investment in the forest is justified (see, e.g., Collins et al., 2017). If the investment is indeed rationalized, then the government taps into the revenue from the proposed inclusive wealth-linked bonds for afforestation, reforestation or protection from illegal logging.

The bond of this kind can face some obstacles in practice. First, government budget deficits may increase, at least in the short-run, in a sluggish economy. GDP-linked bonds, it is argued, have an advantage of being countercyclical, by automatically suppressing interest payments when the output is not increasing. In the current proposal of IWI-linked bonds, interest payments are linked with a long-run productive base, which may conflict with the short-run trend in output. Second, unless we have a very transparent institution of measuring the shadow prices of the list of capital assets and democratically prioritizing public investments, the government may have an incentive to report (the growth rate in) inclusive wealth that is higher than the true value. This finding is particularly true of administrations facing the threat of being expelled from power. However, this mechanism may be attenuated to a certain extent due to the obligation of the government to pay IWI-linked interests.

To fix ideas, take India as an example. As Table 9.1 shows, produced, human and natural capital represented 8%, 61% and 31% of total capital of the nation in 1990, respectively. The relatively high position of natural capital in inclusive wealth is typical of developing countries, as discussed in Chapter 1. However, this position is reduced to as low as 15% in the latest figure. More fossil fuel (oil, natural gas and coal) experienced an across-the-board decline. Fisheries nearly halved, and pastureland also witnessed

Table 9.1 Inclusive wealth in India, 1990–2014

Year	1990		2014		Annual change rate	
	$billion	*Share*	*$billion*	*Share*		*Weighted*
Produced	867	7.5%	5,049	23.5%	7.62%	1.36%
Human	7,110	61.4%	13,215	61.5%	2.62%	1.61%
Natural	3,605	31.1%	3,242	15.1%	−0.44%	−0.09%
Total	11,582		21,505		2.61%	2.88%

a decline. In contrast, forest resources somewhat increased during the period. The last quarter century has also observed massive investment in infrastructure, contributing to the elevated share of produced capital in 2014 (24%). Interestingly, the relative share of human capital remained at 60%. Apparently, we could argue that the country has invested in produced capital, at the expense of certain natural capital resources.

Let us review the order of the magnitude of this financial instrument in this example. First, we study a possible bond whose interest payment is linked with the level of inclusive wealth of India. Suppose that the social discount rate is 5% per annum. Assuming, at a cost of rigour, that the NNP is the return on wealth (the latter being $21,505 billion in monetary units in 2014), we can simply estimate that the NNP in 2014 would be $1,075 billion (=$21,505 billion times 0.05). The interest payment would be a share of the corresponding NNP, which should be fixed before the issuance of the bond. Suppose that this constant share is 100 billionths of the current NNP. Then, the coupon payment would be $10.75 (=$1,075 billion/100 billion).

Second, we could also consider a potential bond that is linked to the growth rate of wealth. Table 9.1 shows that inclusive wealth has increased at a rate of 2.6% annually since 1990.[2] This growth rate can be directly used as the coupon interest rate of this possible bond. As is often the case with an emerging economy, the ten-year government bond in India is higher than its peers in developed countries, with the latest figure being approximately 6.5% as of September 2017. This comparison shows that a premium would be needed to compensate investors for taking risks in the growth of inclusive wealth; in this case, the interest payment could be based on a benchmark rate, such as short-term government debt.

Finally, comparisons with other similar initiatives are in order. The proposal of GDP-linked bonds was innovative and provocative (Shiller, 1993), but their focus is on fiscal sustainability and the inclusion of capital assets, the income of which is revealed in the GDP boundary. This focus naturally needs to be extended to sustainable development and the inclusion of income from the non-GDP boundary (Yamaguchi and Managi, 2017).

Another relevant trend in the financial market is the increasing issuance of green bonds. As case studies demonstrate (Cochu, Annica, et al., 2016), green bonds are issued for specific projects that should be green in the fields of renewable energy, energy efficiency, low carbon transport, sustainable water, and waste and pollution, some of which overlap with natural capital investments. The IWI-linked bonds have an advantage of prioritizing projects on a macro scale, based on shadow prices for a wide variety of human and natural capital. This advantage would also enable the issuer to shift investments to more needy projects when relative scarcity changes in the long-run. Moreover, interest payments are linked with nationally aggregated IWI, such that the return to bond holders decreases when wealth does not increase sufficiently. This finding also demonstrates that the risk of the decreased well-being of the future generation is shared with investors in the current generation.

Notes

1 See Fors (2012) for a survey. Islam and Choe (2013) have investigated the role of microcredit in child labour and human capital formation. Shimamura and Lastarria-Cornhiel (2010) discuss the effect of credit programme participation.

2 If consumption does not grow, this rate should be equal to the growth in green NNP.

References

Ambec, S., Cohen, M., Elgie, S., Lanoie, P. (2013). The Porter hypothesis at 20: Can environmental regulation enhance innovation and competitiveness? *Review of Environmental Economics and Policy*, *7* (1), 2–22.

Anenberg, S. C., Horowitz, L. W., Tong, D. Q., & West, J. J. (2010). An estimate of the global burden of anthropogenic ozone and fine particulate matter on premature human mortality using atmospheric modeling. *Environmental Health Perspectives*, *118*(9), 1189.

Arrow, K. J., Dasgupta, P., Goulder, L. H., Daily, G., Ehrlich, P., Heal, G., et al. (2004). Are we consuming too much? *The Journal of Economic Perspectives*, *18*(3), 147–172.

Arrow, K. J., Dasgupta, P., Goulder, L. H., Mumford, K. J., & Oleson, K. (2012). Sustainability and the measurement of wealth. *Environment and Development Economics*, *17*(3), 317–353.

Arvanitis, S., Peneder, M., Rammer, C., Stucki, T., & Wörter, M. (2016). *Development and utilization of energy-related technologies, economic performance and the role of policy instruments* (No. 419). KOF Working Papers.

Barr, D., Bush, O., & Pienkowski, A. (2014). GDP-linked bonds and sovereign default. In Stiglitz, J. E. & Heymann, D. (Eds.), *Life after debt: The origins and resolutions of debt crisis*. London, UK: Palgrave Macmillan, 246–275.

Barro, R., & Lee, J. W. (2013). A New Data Set of Educational Attainment in the World, 1950–2010. *Journal of Development Economics*, *104*, 184–198.

Basu, K., & Tzannatos, Z. (2003). The global child labor problem: What do we know and what can we do? *The World Bank Economic Review*, *17*(2), 147–173.

Bhalotra, S., & Heady, C. (2003). Child farm labor: The wealth paradox. *The World Bank Economic Review*, *17*(2), 197–227.

Boarini, R., Comola, M., Smith, C., Manchin, R., & De Keulenaer, F. (2012). What makes for a better life?: The determinants of subjective well-being in OECD countries-evidence from the Gallup World Poll. *OECD Statistics Working Papers 2012*, (3), 0_1.

Borensztein, E., & Mauro, P. (2004). The case for GDP indexed bonds. *Economic Policy*, *19*(38), 166–216.

Branch, T. A., Jensen, O. P., Ricard, D., Ye, Y., Hilborn, R. (2011). Contrasting global trends in marine fishery status obtained from catches and from stock assessments. *Conservation Biology*, *25*, 777–786.

Brandt, N., Schreyer, P., & Zipperer, V. (2013) Productivity measurement with natural capital. *OECD Economics Department Working Papers, No. 1092*. OECD Publishing. http://dx.doi.org/10.1787/5k3xnhsz0vtg-en

Chand, R., Kumar, P., & Kumar, S. (2011). Total factor productivity and contribution of research investment to agricultural growth in India.

Cochu, Annica, et al. (2016). Study on the potential of green bond finance for resource-efficient investments. *European Commission Report*.

Collins, M., Barnes, R.F., Nelson, C.J., & Moore, K.J. (2017). Forages, volume 1: an introduction to grassland agriculture. John Wiley & Sons.

Coulthard, S., Johnson, D., & McGregor, J. A., (2011). Poverty, sustainability and human wellbeing: A social wellbeing approach to the global fisheries crisis. *Global Environmental Change*, *21*, 453–463.

Dasgupta, P. (2009). The welfare economic theory of green national accounts. *Environmental and Resources Economics*. https://doi.org/10.1007/s10640-008-9223-y

Dasgupta, P. (2015). Disregarded capitals: What national accounting ignores. *Accounting and Business Research*, *45*(4), 447–464.

Delgado, C. L., (2003). *Fish to 2020: Supply and demand in changing global markets*. WorldFish, *62*.

de Serres, A., Murtin, F. & Nicoletti, G. (2010). A framework for assessing green growth policies, *OECD Economics Department Working Papers, No. 774*. OECD Publishing. doi: 10.1787/5kmfj2xvcmkf-en

Flaaten, O. (2013). Institutional quality and catch performance of fishing nations. *Marine Policy, 38*, 267–276.

Fors, H. C. (2012). Child labour: A review of recent theory and evidence with policy implications. *Journal of Economic Surveys, 26*(4), 570–593.

Froese, R., Zeller, D., Kleisner, K., & Pauly, D., (2012). What catch data can tell us about the status of global fisheries. *Marine Biology, 159*, 1283–1292.

Fujii, H., & Managi, S. (2013). Which industry is greener? An empirical study of nine industries in OECD countries. *Energy Policy, 57*, 381–388.

Grifell-Tatjé, E., & Lovell, C. K. (1995). A note on the Malmquist productivity index. *Economics Letters, 47*(2), 169–175.

Halpern, B. S., Longo, C., Hardy, D., McLeod, K. L., Samhouri, J. F., Katona, S. K., Kleisner, K., Lester, S. E., O'Leary, J., Ranelletti, M., Rosenberg, A. A., Scarborough, C., Selig, E. R., Best, B. D., Brumbaugh, D. R., Chapin, F. S., Crowder, L. B., Daly, K. L., Doney, S. C., Elfes, C., Fogarty, M. J., Gaines, S. D., Jacobsen, K. I., Karrer, L. B., Leslie, H. M., Neeley, E., Pauly, D., Polasky, S., Ris, B., St Martin, K., Stone, G. S., Sumaila, U. R., Zeller, D., (2012). An index to assess the health and benefits of the global ocean. *Nature, 488*, 615–620.

Harrison, R. M., & Yin, J. (2000). Particulate matter in the atmosphere: Which particle properties are important for its effects on health? *Science of the Total Environment, 249*(1), 85–101.

Hemmelskamp, J. (1999). The influence of environmental policy on innovative behaviour: An econometric study. *Fondazione Eni Enrico Mattei Working Paper No. 18.99*.

Islam, A., & Choe, C. (2013). Child labor and schooling responses to access to microcredit in rural Bangladesh. *Economic Inquiry, 51*(1), 46–61.

Jaffe, A.B., & Stavins, R.N. (1994). The energy-efficiency gap What does it mean? *Energy Policy, 22*, 804–810.

Johnstone, N., Managi, S., Rodríguez, M., Haščič, I., Fujii, H., & Souchier, M. (2017). Environmental policy design, innovation and efficiency gains in electricity generation, *Energy Economics, 63*, 106–115.

Kamstra, M. J., & Shiller, R. J. (2009). The case for trills: Giving the people and their pension funds a stake in the wealth of the nation (Cowles Foundation Discussion Paper No. 1717).

Kurniawan, R., & Managi, S. (2017). Sustainable development and performance measurement: Global productivity decomposition. *Sustainable development*, forthcoming.

Lanoie, P., Patry, M., & Lajeunesse, R. (2008). Environmental regulation and productivity: Testing the Porter hypothesis. *Journal of Productivity Analysis, 30*(2), 121–128.

Maconachie, R., & Hilson, G. (2016). Re-thinking the child labor "Problem" in rural sub-Saharan Africa: The case of Sierra Leone's Half Shovels. *World Development, 78*, 136–147.

Managi, S., Opaluch, J. J., Jin, D., & Grigalunas, T. A. (2004). Technological change and depletion in offshore oil and gas. *Journal of Environmental Economics and Management, 47*(2), 388–409.

Myers, R. A., & Worm, B. (2003). Rapid worldwide depletion of predatory fish communities. *Nature, 423*, 280–283.

Pauly, D., Christensen, V., Dalsgaard, J., Froese, R., & Torres, F. (1998). Fishing down marine food webs. *Science, 279*, 860–863.

Pauly, D., & Palomares, M.-L., (2005). Fishing down marine food web: It is far more pervasive than we thought. *Bulletin of Marine Science, 76*, 197–212.

Porter, M. E., & Van der Linde, C. (1995). Toward a new conception of the environment-competitiveness relationship. *Journal of Economic Perspectives, 9*(4), 97–118.

Psacharopoulos, G. (1997). Child labor versus educational attainment some evidence from Latin America. *Journal of Population Economics, 10*(4), 377–386.

Ranjan, P. (1999). An economic analysis of child labor. *Economics Letters, 64*(1), 99–105.

Ranjan, P. (2001). Credit constraints and the phenomenon of child labor. *Journal of Development Economics, 64*(1), 81–102.

Shiller, R. J. (1993). *Macro markets: Creating institutions for managing society's largest economic risks.* New York, NY: Oxford University Press.

Shimamura, Y., & Lastarria-Cornhiel, S. (2010). Credit program participation and child schooling in rural Malawi. *World Development, 38*(4), 567–580.

Sugiawan, Y., Islam, M., & Managi, S. (2017). Global marine fisheries with economic growth. *Economic Analysis and Policy, 55*, 158–168.

UNU-IHDP, & UNEP (2012). *Inclusive wealth report 2012: Measuring progress toward sustainability.* Cambridge, MA: Cambridge University Press.

UNU-IHDP (2014). *Inclusive wealth report 2014:measuring progress toward sustainability.* Cambridge University Press.

Vouvaki, D., & Xepapadeas, A. (2009). Total factor productivity growth when factors of production generate environmental externalities. *Working Paper No. 20–2009*, FEEM, Milan.

World Bank Open Data (2017). https://data.worldbank.org/

World Health Organization Regional Office for Europe (2006). *Health risks of particulate matter from long-range transboundary air pollution.* European Centre for Environment and Health, Bonn.

Yamaguchi, R., & Managi, S. (2017). New financing for sustainable development: The case for NNP-or inclusive wealth-linked bonds. *The Journal of Environment & Development, 26*(2), 214–239.

Annex

Annex 1: key statistics

Table A1.1 Key statistics of Inclusive Wealth Report 2018

Code	Country	Region	Income level	IW Growth rate	Contribution by capital PC	HC	NC
AFG	Afghanistan	South-Central Asia	Low Income	4.4%	0.1%	4.3%	0.0%
ALB	Albania	Southern Europe	Lower Middle Income	0.7%	0.6%	0.1%	0.0%
ARE	United Arab Emirates	Western Asia	High Income	3.0%	0.5%	2.8%	−0.3%
ARG	Argentina	South America	Upper Middle Income	1.4%	0.6%	0.9%	−0.1%
ARM	Armenia	Western Asia	Lower Middle Income	0.1%	0.3%	−0.2%	0.1%
AUS	Australia	Australia/ New Zealand	High Income	1.6%	1.3%	0.5%	−0.3%
AUT	Austria	Western Europe	High Income	1.7%	1.3%	0.4%	0.0%
BDI	Burundi	Eastern Africa	Low Income	2.9%	0.0%	2.8%	0.0%
BEL	Belgium	Western Europe	High Income	1.9%	1.4%	0.6%	0.0%
BEN	Benin	Western Africa	Low Income	3.3%	0.0%	3.3%	0.0%
BGD	Bangladesh	South–Central Asia	Low Income	1.8%	0.1%	1.7%	0.0%
BGR	Bulgaria	Eastern Europe	Upper Middle Income	−0.7%	0.1%	−0.7%	−0.1%
BHR	Bahrain	Western Asia	High Income	4.3%	2.5%	2.0%	−0.4%
BLZ	Belize	Central America	Lower Middle Income	0.5%	0.6%	0.3%	−0.4%
BOL	Bolivia (Plurinational State of)	South America	Lower Middle Income	0.2%	0.1%	0.5%	−0.4%
BRA	Brazil	South America	Upper Middle Income	0.7%	0.5%	0.5%	−0.3%
BRB	Barbados	Caribbean	High Income	1.0%	0.6%	0.5%	0.0%
BWA	Botswana	Southern Africa	Upper Middle Income	2.1%	0.2%	2.0%	−0.1%
CAF	Central African Republic	Middle Africa	Low Income	1.7%	0.0%	1.7%	0.0%
CAN	Canada	Northern America	High Income	0.8%	0.9%	0.4%	−0.6%
CHE	Switzerland	Western Europe	High Income	2.2%	1.8%	0.5%	0.0%
CHL	Chile	South America	Upper Middle Income	2.2%	1.6%	0.9%	−0.2%

(*Continued*)

Table A1.1 (Continued)

Code	Country	Region	Income level	IW			
				Growth rate	Contribution by capital		
					PC	HC	NC
CHN	China	Eastern Asia	Upper Middle Income	2.4%	1.4%	1.1%	−0.2%
CIV	Côte d'Ivoire	Western Africa	Lower Middle Income	2.3%	−0.1%	2.3%	0.0%
CMR	Cameroon	Middle Africa	Lower Middle Income	2.4%	0.0%	2.5%	−0.4%
COD	Democratic Republic of the Congo	Middle Africa	Low Income	−0.1%	0.0%	0.2%	−0.2%
COG	Congo	Middle Africa	Lower Middle Income	2.5%	0.1%	2.5%	−0.1%
COL	Colombia	South America	Upper Middle Income	0.2%	0.8%	0.8%	−2.1%
CRI	Costa Rica	Central America	Upper Middle Income	2.5%	1.5%	0.9%	0.3%
CUB	Cuba	Caribbean	Upper Middle Income	0.7%	0.0%	0.7%	0.0%
CYP	Cyprus	Western Asia	High Income	2.7%	1.4%	1.3%	0.0%
CZE	Czech Republic	Eastern Europe	High Income	1.3%	1.1%	0.3%	−0.1%
DEU	Germany	Western Europe	High Income	1.1%	0.9%	0.2%	0.0%
DNK	Denmark	Northern Europe	High Income	1.6%	1.4%	0.3%	−0.1%
DOM	Dominican Republic	Caribbean	Upper Middle Income	2.9%	1.5%	1.4%	0.0%
DZA	Algeria	Northern Africa	Upper Middle Income	1.5%	0.5%	1.6%	−0.7%
ECU	Ecuador	South America	Upper Middle Income	0.9%	0.6%	0.9%	−0.5%
EGY	Egypt	Northern Africa	Lower Middle Income	2.3%	0.2%	2.2%	−0.1%
ESP	Spain	Southern Europe	High Income	2.6%	1.9%	0.7%	0.0%
EST	Estonia	Northern Europe	High Income	1.0%	1.0%	−0.1%	0.0%
FIN	Finland	Northern Europe	High Income	1.4%	1.0%	0.5%	0.0%
FJI	Fiji	Melanesia	Lower Middle Income	1.3%	0.6%	0.7%	0.0%
FRA	France	Western Europe	High Income	1.9%	1.4%	0.5%	0.0%
GAB	Gabon	Middle Africa	Upper Middle Income	0.0%	0.0%	0.1%	−0.1%

Code	Country	Region	Income level	IW Growth rate	Contribution by capital PC	HC	NC
GBR	United Kingdom	Northern Europe	High Income	1.9%	1.6%	0.5%	-0.1%
GHA	Ghana	Western Africa	Lower Middle Income	2.3%	0.1%	2.1%	0.0%
GMB	Gambia	Western Africa	Low Income	2.7%	0.6%	2.5%	-0.4%
GRC	Greece	Southern Europe	High Income	1.2%	0.8%	0.5%	-0.1%
GTM	Guatemala	Central America	Lower Middle Income	2.1%	0.1%	2.0%	-0.1%
GUY	Guyana	South America	Lower Middle Income	0.6%	0.1%	0.0%	0.6%
HND	Honduras	Central America	Lower Middle Income	0.1%	0.9%	0.6%	-1.2%
HRV	Croatia	Southern Europe	High Income	1.0%	0.9%	0.1%	0.0%
HTI	Haiti	Caribbean	Low Income	1.9%	0.0%	1.8%	0.0%
HUN	Hungary	Eastern Europe	High Income	1.0%	0.7%	0.3%	0.0%
IDN	Indonesia	South-Eastern Asia	Lower Middle Income	1.4%	0.7%	1.2%	-0.4%
IND	India	South-Central Asia	Lower Middle Income	1.6%	0.0%	1.5%	0.0%
IRL	Ireland	Northern Europe	High Income	3.2%	2.5%	0.8%	-0.1%
IRN	Iran (Islamic Republic of)	South-Central Asia	Upper Middle Income	0.4%	0.3%	0.5%	-0.4%
IRQ	Iraq	Western Asia	Lower Middle Income	0.9%	0.1%	1.1%	-0.3%
ISL	Iceland	Northern Europe	High Income	0.7%	0.7%	0.3%	-0.2%
ISR	Israel	Western Asia	High Income	3.6%	2.0%	1.5%	0.0%
ITA	Italy	Southern Europe	High Income	1.5%	1.1%	0.4%	0.0%
JAM	Jamaica	Caribbean	Upper Middle Income	1.1%	0.7%	0.5%	-0.1%
JOR	Jordan	Western Asia	Upper Middle Income	4.4%	0.9%	3.4%	0.0%
JPN	Japan	Eastern Asia	High Income	1.3%	1.1%	0.3%	0.0%
KAZ	Kazakhstan	South-Central Asia	Upper Middle Income	0.5%	0.3%	0.3%	-0.1%
KEN	Kenya	Eastern Africa	Low Income	3.0%	0.1%	3.0%	0.0%
KGZ	Kyrgyzstan	South-Central Asia	Low Income	1.7%	0.1%	1.6%	0.0%

(Continued)

Table A1.1 (Continued)

Code	Country	Region	Income level	IW Growth rate	Contribution by capital		
					PC	HC	NC
KHM	Cambodia	South-Eastern Asia	Low Income	0.3%	0.2%	1.0%	−0.8%
KOR	Republic of Korea	Eastern Asia	High Income	4.2%	3.8%	0.7%	0.0%
KWT	Kuwait	Western Asia	High Income	0.3%	0.3%	0.4%	−0.4%
LAO	Lao People's Democratic Republic	South-Eastern Asia	Lower Middle Income	1.3%	0.2%	1.1%	0.0%
LBR	Liberia	Western Africa	Low Income	2.9%	0.0%	2.9%	0.0%
LKA	Sri Lanka	South-Central Asia	Lower Middle Income	1.8%	0.6%	1.4%	−0.1%
LSO	Lesotho	Southern Africa	Lower Middle Income	0.3%	0.0%	0.2%	0.0%
LTU	Lithuania	Northern Europe	Upper Middle Income	0.5%	0.5%	0.0%	0.0%
LUX	Luxembourg	Western Europe	High Income	3.4%	2.4%	1.0%	0.0%
LVA	Latvia	Northern Europe	Upper Middle Income	0.7%	0.9%	−0.4%	0.1%
MAR	Morocco	Northern Africa	Lower Middle Income	1.6%	0.2%	1.4%	0.0%
MDA	Republic of Moldova	Eastern Europe	Lower Middle Income	−0.1%	−0.4%	0.4%	−0.3%
MDV	Maldives	South-Central Asia	Upper Middle Income	3.2%	1.5%	2.1%	−0.4%
MEX	Mexico	Central America	Upper Middle Income	2.3%	1.4%	1.2%	−0.1%
MLI	Mali	Western Africa	Low Income	2.9%	0.0%	2.9%	0.0%
MLT	Malta	Southern Europe	High Income	3.0%	2.1%	1.0%	0.0%
MMR	Myanmar	South-Eastern Asia	Low Income	1.3%	0.0%	1.3%	−0.1%
MNG	Mongolia	Eastern Asia	Lower Middle Income	0.5%	0.1%	0.7%	−0.2%
MOZ	Mozambique	Eastern Africa	Low Income	2.9%	0.0%	2.9%	0.0%
MRT	Mauritania	Western Africa	Low Income	2.6%	0.0%	2.5%	0.0%
MUS	Mauritius	Eastern Africa	Upper Middle Income	2.6%	1.8%	0.9%	−0.1%
MWI	Malawi	Eastern Africa	Low Income	2.8%	0.0%	2.7%	0.0%
MYS	Malaysia	South-Eastern Asia	Upper Middle Income	2.0%	2.0%	0.8%	−0.6%
NAM	Namibia	Southern Africa	Upper Middle Income	2.2%	0.4%	1.6%	0.2%

Code	Country	Region	Income level	IW Growth rate	Contribution by capital		
					PC	HC	NC
NER	Niger	Western Africa	Low Income	3.6%	0.0%	3.6%	0.0%
NGA	Nigeria	Western Africa	Lower Middle Income	2.6%	0.0%	2.6%	0.0%
NIC	Nicaragua	Central America	Lower Middle Income	1.6%	0.2%	1.5%	−0.1%
NLD	Netherlands	Western Europe	High Income	1.7%	1.5%	0.4%	−0.1%
NOR	Norway	Northern Europe	High Income	0.8%	1.1%	0.4%	−0.7%
NPL	Nepal	South-Central Asia	Low Income	1.9%	0.0%	1.8%	−0.1%
NZL	New Zealand	Australia/ New Zealand	High Income	0.8%	0.4%	0.2%	0.2%
PAK	Pakistan	South-Central Asia	Lower Middle Income	0.8%	0.3%	1.5%	−1.1%
PAN	Panama	Central America	Upper Middle Income	2.7%	1.6%	1.0%	0.0%
PER	Peru	South America	Upper Middle Income	0.8%	0.4%	0.4%	−0.1%
PHL	Philippines	South-Eastern Asia	Lower Middle Income	2.6%	0.4%	2.2%	0.0%
PNG	Papua New Guinea	Melanesia	Lower Middle Income	2.4%	0.0%	2.3%	0.0%
POL	Poland	Eastern Europe	High Income	1.2%	1.0%	0.3%	−0.1%
PRT	Portugal	Southern Europe	High Income	2.0%	1.6%	0.5%	0.0%
PRY	Paraguay	South America	Lower Middle Income	0.8%	0.4%	0.7%	−0.3%
QAT	Qatar	Western Asia	High Income	2.0%	1.8%	0.7%	−0.8%
ROU	Romania	Eastern Europe	Upper Middle Income	0.6%	0.6%	0.1%	−0.1%
RUS	Russian Federation	Eastern Europe	Upper Middle Income	0.2%	0.1%	0.0%	0.1%
RWA	Rwanda	Eastern Africa	Low Income	2.7%	0.0%	2.6%	0.0%
SAU	Saudi Arabia	Western Asia	High Income	0.8%	0.5%	0.6%	−0.2%
SDN	Sudan (former)	Northern Africa	Lower Middle Income	2.4%	0.0%	2.5%	−0.1%
SEN	Senegal	Western Africa	Lower Middle Income	2.7%	0.0%	2.6%	0.0%
SGP	Singapore	South-Eastern Asia	High Income	5.3%	4.0%	1.5%	0.0%
SLE	Sierra Leone	Western Africa	Low Income	1.5%	0.0%	1.5%	0.0%
SLV	El Salvador	Central America	Lower Middle Income	1.7%	0.6%	1.1%	0.0%

(*Continued*)

Table A1.1 (Continued)

Code	Country	Region	Income level	IW Growth rate	Contribution by capital PC	HC	NC
SRB	Serbia	Southern Europe	Upper Middle Income	0.2%	0.2%	0.0%	0.1%
SVK	Slovakia	Eastern Europe	High Income	1.2%	0.9%	0.3%	0.0%
SVN	Slovenia	Southern Europe	High Income	1.7%	1.4%	0.3%	0.0%
SWE	Sweden	Northern Europe	High Income	1.6%	1.2%	0.5%	−0.1%
SWZ	Swaziland	Southern Africa	Lower Middle Income	2.4%	0.7%	1.6%	0.1%
SYR	Syrian Arab Republic	Western Asia	Lower Middle Income	1.6%	0.4%	1.6%	−0.3%
TGO	Togo	Western Africa	Low Income	2.9%	0.0%	2.9%	0.0%
THA	Thailand	South-Eastern Asia	Upper Middle Income	2.1%	1.3%	1.1%	−0.1%
TJK	Tajikistan	South-Central Asia	Low Income	2.2%	−0.1%	2.2%	0.0%
TTO	Trinidad and Tobago	Caribbean	High Income	−0.7%	0.0%	0.4%	−1.3%
TUN	Tunisia	Northern Africa	Upper Middle Income	2.5%	0.9%	1.8%	−0.1%
TUR	Turkey	Western Asia	Upper Middle Income	2.6%	1.7%	1.1%	−0.1%
TZA	United Republic of Tanzania	Eastern Africa	Low Income	3.1%	0.0%	3.1%	0.0%
UGA	Uganda	Eastern Africa	Low Income	3.6%	0.0%	3.6%	0.0%
UKR	Ukraine	Eastern Europe	Lower Middle Income	−0.6%	0.0%	−0.6%	0.0%
URY	Uruguay	South America	Upper Middle Income	1.0%	0.5%	0.5%	0.0%
USA	United States of America	Northern America	High Income	2.0%	1.6%	0.5%	−0.1%
VEN	Venezuela (Bolivarian Republic of)	South America	Upper Middle Income	0.1%	0.2%	0.3%	−0.3%
VNM	Viet Nam	South-Eastern Asia	Lower Middle Income	2.0%	1.0%	1.3%	−0.1%
YEM	Yemen	Western Asia	Lower Middle Income	3.4%	0.1%	3.3%	0.0%
ZAF	South Africa	Southern Africa	Upper Middle Income	1.6%	0.3%	1.4%	−0.1%
ZMB	Zambia	Eastern Africa	Lower Middle Income	3.1%	0.0%	3.1%	0.0%
ZWE	Zimbabwe	Eastern Africa	Low Income	1.2%	0.0%	1.2%	0.0%

Annex 2: methodological annex[1]

1. *Overall framework*

In this Annex, we lay out the methodology and data used for the computation of inclusive wealth shown in Chapter 1. To recap our conceptual framework, we are interested in the change of intertemporal well-being at:

$$V(t) = \int_t^\infty U(C_\tau) e^{-\delta(\tau-t)} d\tau.$$

Assuming equivalence between wealth and well-being, this is measured by wealth in practice. Denoting produced, human and natural capital as K, H and N, the change in inclusive wealth W is expressed by:

$$\frac{dW(K,H,N,t)}{dt} = p_K \frac{dK}{dt} + p_H \frac{dH}{dt} + p_N \frac{dN}{dt} + \frac{\partial V}{\partial t},$$

where p_K, p_H and p_K are the marginal shadow prices of produced, human and natural capital, respectively. They are formally defined by

$$p_K \equiv \frac{\partial V}{\partial K}, p_H \equiv \frac{\partial V}{\partial H}, p_N \equiv \frac{\partial V}{\partial N},$$

given a forecast of how produced, human and natural capitals, as well as other flow variables, evolve in the future in the economy in question. Practically, shadow prices act as a weight factor attached to each capital, resulting in the measure of wealth, or IWI:

$$IWI = p_K K + p_H H + p_N N.$$

In practice, we can use W and IWI interchangeably, although they can differ in that IWI also uses shadow prices on the margin. In addition, the unit of IWI is dollar (monetary) terms, rather than utility units. Of course, this does not affect sustainability assessment.

   Another point worth exploring is the effect of population. Aside from simple Malthusian effect (Arrow et al. 2004; Ferreira et al. 2008), wealth per capita may not represent well-being divided by current population (Arrow et al. 2003). Moreover, as expounded in Arrow et al. (2012), even if we employ well-being divided by future population, i.e. adopting dynamic average utilitarianism, inclusive wealth per capita is shown to be in line with social well-being, under simple assumptions. When these assumptions do not hold, sustainability assessment may change (Yamaguchi 2017).

2. *Produced capital*

Produced capital, also referred to as manufactured or reproducible capital, includes physical infrastructure, land, property and facilities of private firms, houses, etc. Upon calculation, we follow the method originated by Harberger (1978) and applied by

Table A2.1 Data sources and assumptions for the calculation of produced capital

Variables	Data sources/assumptions
Investment, I	United Nations Statistics Division (2013a)
Output, y	United Nations Statistics Division (2013a)
Depreciation rate, δ	4% (as taking the country average from Feenstra et al. (2013))
Capital lifetime	Indefinite

King and Levine (1994) and Feenstra et al. (2013). In particular, we employ perpetual inventory method (PIM), which is a simple summation of gross investment net of depreciation that occurs in each period. One cannot keep track of investment and depreciation indefinitely into the past, so should start from somewhere. This is called a benchmark year $t = 0$, in which the initial capital stock $K(0)$ is set. Formally, produced capital stock at t is:

$$K(t) = K(0)(1-\delta)^t + \sum_{\tau=1}^{t} I(\tau)(1-\delta)^{t-\tau},$$

where $I(t)$ and δ stand for investment at t and depreciation rate. In our computation, the initial capital stock $K(0)$ is estimated by assuming a steady state of capital-output ratio. That is, if we assume $0 = \dfrac{d}{dt}\left(\dfrac{K}{y}\right) = (I - \delta K)/K - \gamma$ where y is the economic growth rate, the steady state capital stock would be $K^{ss} = \dfrac{I}{\delta + \gamma}$.

Finally, it is worth noting that the shadow price of produced capital is unity, since national statisticians measure investment in produced capital in dollar terms, which is the unit of inclusive wealth. The dataset we employ is summarized in Table A2.1.

3. Human capital

As we mentioned in the main text of Chapter 1, we employ two approaches to human capital, and report them separately. However, both approaches have in common the education-induced human capital, so we start from that bit.

3.1. Education

Education pays off later in life as a raised lifetime income and well-being, both at personal and aggregate levels. In line with the literature on human capital, and for practical reasons, we focus on the return on formal education, but this does not mean that other non-formal education (e.g. early childhood education, vocational training) is not adequate as part of wealth. We estimate the value of human capital on the output of education production function. This is generally called income approach to human capital computation. In contrast, some other estimates use the input side of education production function, typically by educational expenditure (World Bank 2014). For a more detailed excellent review of human capital in general and a detailed account of this, see Chapters 3–4 of IWR 2014.

Table A2.2 Data sources and assumptions for the calculation of human capital

Variables	Data sources/assumptions
Educational attainment, A	Barro and Lee (2013)
Population P by age, gender, time	United Nations Population Division (2016)
Interest rate, ρ	8.5% (Klenow and Rodríguez-Clare 1997)
Discount rate, ρ	8.5%
Employment	International Labor Organization (2015); Conference Board (2016)
Compensation of employees	United Nations Statistics Division (2013a); OECD (2016); Feenstra et al. (2013); Lenzen et al. (2013); Conference Board (2016)

We estimate the value of human capital based on the idea that educational attainment yields returns to human capital. Following Arrow et al. (2012) and Klenow and Rodríguez-Clare (1997), educational attainment is proxied by the average years of total schooling per person, A, which is obtained from Barro and Lee (2013). The rate of return on education is assumed to be constant at $p = 8.5\%$. This is multiplied by the population who has had education, P_{5+edu}. Thus, the stock of human capital is:

$$H = e^{\rho A} * P_{5+edu}$$

Regarding the shadow price of one unit of human capital, it is calculated by the present value of lifetime income, which is proxied by the average compensation to employees, w, per unit of human capital times the expected working years, T. This brings us to the following formula:

$$p_H(t) = \int_0^{T(t)} w(\tau) e^{-\delta \tau} d\tau$$

The dataset we employ is summarized in Table A2.2.

3.2.   Health

The state of health affects human well-being through at least three channels: by directly contributing to well-being, raising productivity and extending life years (UNU-IHDP, 2014). We have computed the latter third value of health capital, largely because it is still challenging to account for the first and second contributions.

Health capital of an individual of age a is defined by

$$H(a) = \sum_{t=a}^{100} f(t \mid t \geq a) V(a,t),$$

where conditional density of age of death given survival to age a is

$$f(t \mid t \geq a) = \frac{f(t)}{[1 - F(a)]},$$

and

$$V(a,t) = \sum_{u=0}^{t-a} (1 - \delta)^u$$

is the discount factor. Total health capital of a country is

$$H = \sum_{a=0}^{100} H(a) P(a),$$

where $P(a)$ is the population of age a.

The shadow price of health capital is simply the value of statistical life year (VSLY). For more detailed illustration, see Arrow et al. (2012, 2013) and UNU-IHDP and UNEP (2014).

3.3. *Shadow price of human and health capital*

In the frontier approach of calculation, we determine shadow prices of education- and health-induced human capital by employing a non-parametric method. In this subsection we outline this method. Previous measurement of that portion of longevity of health capital is based on the assumption that marginal willingness to pay to reduce the risk of death is common for all the age groups. Alternatively, we use non-parametric estimation of shadow prices with inputs being capital assets.

In particular, we assume a production possibility set, P, with input vector (produced, human, health and natural capital), x, output (GDP), y, and a directional vector $g = g_y$ with $g \in \mathfrak{R}^M$. Formally,

$$P(x) = \{(x,y) : x \text{ can produce } y\}$$

$$D(x,y;g) = \max_{\beta} \{\beta : y + \beta g_y \in P(x)\}$$

D is called the distance function, which maximizes the output, controlling the coefficient, β. By solving the revenue-maximizing problem and parametrizing DDF, the shadow price of human and health capital can be derived. For details, see Färe et al. (2005) and Tamaki et al. (2017).

4. *Natural capital*

For natural capital, the current edition of IWR accounts for non-renewable resources (fossil fuel and mineral) and renewable resources (agricultural land, forest and fishery). We illustrate how we account for the five classes in turn.

4.1. Fossil fuels

Our account scope for fossil fuels is coal, natural gas and oil. For a given resource, we start from the current stock, and then trace back past stocks by using each year production. In this way, we can construct a consistent time-series dataset that reflects more recent accurate flow (extraction) variables. In other words, the corresponding stock under study in year $t - 1, S(t - 1)$ is derived from the production, $P(t)$ and the stock in year t, $S(t)$ by

$$S(t-1) = S(t) + P(t).$$

The unit shadow price of a non-renewable resource, p_S, is the price net of extraction cost, which is sometimes called rental price. Ideally, the marginal cost of extraction should be used for corresponding remaining stock, but it is known to be hard to obtain. We instead assume that the rental rate of the total price is constant, which is obtained from Narayanan et al. (2012).

4.2. Metals and minerals

The methodology for accounting for minerals is much the same as fossil fuels, the other form of non-renewable resources. For rental rates, we retrieved sectoral rental rates of different mineral industries from Narayanan et al. (2012). For other data of reserves, extraction and prices are obtained from U.S. Geological Survey (2015), which is the most authorized dataset on the subject.

4.3. Agricultural land

Agricultural land is composed of cropland and pastureland. The methodology for accounting for these two classes is much the same. For the quantity of this natural capital, permanent cropland/pastureland area data from Food and Agricultural Organization (FAO 2015a) are simply employed.

Table A2.3 Data sources and assumptions for the calculation of fossil fuels

Variables	Data sources/assumptions
S: reserve	U.S. Energy Information Administration (2015)
P: extraction	U.S. Energy Information Administration (2015)
Prices	BP (2015)
	• Coal: averaged prices from US, northwestern Europe, Japan coking, and Japan steam
	• Natural gas: averaged prices from EU, UK, US, Japan and Canada
	• Oil: averaged prices of Dubai, Brent, Nigerian Forcados and West Texas Intermediate
	• adjusted for inflation before averaging over time using the US GDP deflator
Rental rates	Narayanan et al. (2012)

Table A2.4 Data sources and assumptions for the calculation of metal and mineral resources

Variables	Data sources/assumptions
S: reserve	U.S. Geological Survey (2015)
P: Extraction	U.S. Geological Survey (2015)
Prices	U.S. Geological Survey (2015)
Rental rates	Narayanan et al. (2012)

To quantify the marginal shadow price of a unit of agricultural land, we cannot use the market price as in the case of non-renewable resources, since there does not usually exist a market for agricultural land. Instead, we compute the shadow price as the net present value of the annual flow of services per hectare that the parcel yields, in line with World Bank (2011) and past editions of IWR. More specifically, rental price per hectare of cropland for country i in year t can be expressed as:

$$RPA_{it} = \left(\frac{1}{A}\right)\sum_{k=1}^{N} R_{ik} P_{itk} Q_{itk}$$

where A, R, P and Q are the harvested area in crops, rental rate, crop price and crop quantity produced, respectively. N stands for the number of crops, which is as many as 159 ($k = 1,\ldots,159$) in the current study. t is the year of analysis, from 1990 to 2014. For the estimation of the rental rate by crop group, we mapped FAO crop classification (HS) with those sectoral rental rates provided by Narayanan et al. (2012).

Note that the above rental price corresponds to an annual flow of services; we need to capitalize it to be employed as the shadow price. Formally, the NPV of this rental price for country i in year t is written as:

$$p_{Ait} = \sum_{\tau=0}^{\infty} \frac{RPA_{it}}{(1+r)^{\tau}} = \frac{1+r}{r} RPA_{it},$$

where r is the discount rate, set at 5% per annum. Finally, to avoid unnecessary volatility in the social value of natural capital, we take the year average of this price for country i:

$$\overline{p_{Ai}} = \frac{1}{25} \sum_{t=1990}^{2014} p_{Ait}$$

which is used as the shadow price of cropland.

For the calculation of pastureland wealth, the difference from cropland lies in the fact that it is difficult to link rents to a particular amount of land involved in the production process. Thus, we opted to assume the shadow price of pastureland to be equal to cropland, which is a limitation of the current accounting.

4.4. Forest

In the current forest accounting, we follow IWR 2014 methodology. The forest wealth is composed of timber value and non-timber forest benefits (NTFB).

Table A2.5 Data sources and assumptions for the calculation of agricultural land

Variables	Data sources/assumptions
Quantity of crops produced, Q	FAO (2015a)
Price of crops produced, P	FAO (2015a)
Rental rate, R	Narayanan et al. (2012)
Harvested area in crops, A	FAO (2015a)
Discount rate, r	5%
Permanent cropland/pastureland area	FAO (2015a)

4.4.1. TIMBER

We estimate the volume of timber resources commercially available. For the quantity of this specific capital, the total forest area, excluding cultivated forest, is multiplied by timber density per area, and percentage of total volume that is commercially available. The exclusion of cultivated forest could be debatable, as it is regarded as contributing to timber and non-timber values. It is due to the fact that the activity of cultivating forest is categorized as a production activity in the System of National Accounts. In line with this reasoning, we have registered cultivated forest under produced capital in IWR 2014 and 2017.

For the computation of shadow prices, there are several steps involved, following IWR 2014. First, we followed the World Bank's (2006) method by adopting a weighted average price of two different commodities: industrial round wood and fuelwood, which are also country-specific parameters. The weight attached to the different prices is based on the quantity of the commodity manufactured, while industrial round wood and fuelwood prices are obtained from the value and quantity exported and produced, respectively. Second, we converted the annual estimated values from current to constant prices by using each country-specific gross domestic product (GDP) deflator. Third, we used information on the regional rental rates for timber estimated by Bolt et al. (2002). Such rates are assumed to be constant over time. Fourth, we then estimated the average price over the entire study period (1990 to 2014), thereby obtaining our proxy value for the shadow price of timber.

Finally, in the same manner as other resources, wealth corresponding to timber value is calculated as the product of quantity, price and average rental rate over time.

4.4.2. NON-TIMBER FOREST BENEFITS (NTFB)

Aside from provisioning services in the form of timber production, forest capital yields many ecosystem services. Following IWR 2014, we have accounted for this non-timber forest benefits in the following manner.

First, total forest area in the country under analysis excluding cultivated forest is retrieved from FAO (2015b), which we denote Q (ha). Second, fraction of the total forest area which is accessed by individuals to obtain benefits is assumed to be γ. The ecological literature has stressed that only the portion of the forest that contributes to well-being should be accounted for. For want of better assumptions, we assume γ to be 10%, following World Bank (2006).

Table A2.6 Data sources and assumptions for the calculation of forest

Variables	Data sources/assumptions
Forest stocks	FAO (2015b)
Forest stock commercially available	FAO (2006)
Wood production	FAO (2015b)
Value of wood production	FAO (2015b)
Rental rate, R	Bolt et al. (2002)

Table A2.7 Accounting of non-timber forest benefits

Select service	Temperate and boreal forests (USD/yr/ha)	Tropical forest (USD/yr/ha)
Provisioning services		
1 food	23	107
2 water	146	137
3 genetic	2	451
4 medical		475
5 raw materials		
6 ornamental		
Regulating services		
7 air quality	868	223
8 climate		
9 extreme events	0	33
10 water flows	2	14
11 waste	40	343
12 erosion	1	342
13 soil fertility	37	129
14 pollination	418	54
15 bio control	20	13
Habitat services		
16 nursery		17
17 genepool	506	396
Cultural services		
18 aesthetic		
19 recreation	27	257
20 inspiration	0	
21 spiritual		
22 cognitive	0	
Total	2,091	2,990

Source: Van der Ploeg and de Groot (2010).

Third, the unit benefit of non-timber forest to intertemporal social well-being is taken from Ecosystem Service Valuation Database (ESVD) database of van der Ploeg and de Groot (2010). We denote this by P (USD/ha/year). The average value per hectare should be different for temperate and boreal, and tropical forest, as shown in Table A2.7. Accordingly, we weighted the corresponding values by the share of each forest type in the total forest of the country. Fourth, to make this benefit into capital asset value, we take its net present value, using the discount rate of $r = 5\%$.

In short, the value of NTFB forest wealth is calculated as

$$\sum_{\tau=t}^{\infty} \frac{PQ_\tau \gamma}{(1+r)^{\tau-t}} = \frac{1+r}{r} PQ\gamma.$$

4.5. Fisheries

This edition is the first to estimate fish capital stock as part of renewable natural capital. Estimating the fish stock is a herculean task, compared to other classes of natural capital, for many reasons. They cannot be estimated based on the habitat area, unlike the case of forest or agricultural land, whose computation can be based on the area. Moreover, the sheer mobility of the resource not only makes the exercise harder, but also poses a fundamental question: to which area can a given fishery be attributed, given that a marine fishery habitat is usually not within national borders? In the current exercise, we simplify the matter by assuming that the fish stock belongs to a country where harvest arises and the resource is loaded. Of course, this is a crude treatment in many ways. In particular, just because a fishery biomass is loaded to country A does not necessarily mean that the fishery belongs to A. Having acknowledged this shortcoming, we have no alternative sound theory to allocate harvest to countries.

In renewable resource economics, or just bioeconomics in short, there is a long tradition of assuming resource dynamics. The stock is the population growth net of harvest:

$$\frac{dS_t}{dt} = G(S_t) - H_t,$$

where S_t denotes the renewable resource biomass stock; $G(S_t)$ is the growth function; H_t is the harvest. Population, whether it is renewable resource or human being, is often assumed to follow a logistic growth function:

$$G(S_t) = rS_t \left(1 - \frac{S_t}{k}\right),$$

where r and k are the parameters which represent intrinsic (relative) growth rate and carrying capacity of the resource stock, respectively. Harvest, in turn, depends on the resource abundance. A simple but empirically supported harvest production function is to assume it is proportional to the product of effort and stock, i.e.,

$$H_t = qE_t S_t,$$

where q is called catchability coefficient. E_t stands for effort put in the production process, which is often proxied by the number of vessels or fishermen working hours. Combining these two equations, we arrive at a well-known Gordon-Schaeffer model:

$$\frac{dS_t}{dt} = rS_t\left(1 - \frac{S_t}{k}\right) - qE_tS_t$$

All this means that, to estimate the fishery stock, S_t, we can resort either to harvest function, (1), or total resource dynamics, (2). World's fish stocks are commonly assessed by examining the trend in catch or harvest data. Although this catch-based assessment method has attracted a lot of criticism (see for instance Daan et al. (2011)), either due to its technical and conceptual flaws, it is still being considered as the most reliable method for assessing fish stock (Froese et al. 2012; Kleisner et al. 2013). The main reason is simply because the only data available for most fisheries are the weight of fish caught each year (Pauly et al. 2013). If effort and harvest are known data, as well as catchability coefficient q, then s_t can be estimated solely from the Schaefer production function (Yamaguchi et al. 2016).

But effort data are sparse worldly, so we cannot employ this method for inclusive wealth accounting all over the globe. Alternatively, we use the resource dynamics; however, there is no reliable data on r and k for most fish stocks. Given this constraint, we followed Martell and Froese (2013) who developed an algorithm to randomly generate feasible (r, k) pairs from a uniform distribution function. The likelihood of the generated (r, k) pairs are further evaluated by using Bernoulli distribution to ensure that the estimated stock meets the following assumptions: it has never collapsed or exceeded the carrying capacity, and that the final stock lies within the assumed range of depletion.

In a case where the values of (r, k) are not obtainable, the stocks are simply estimated according to the following rules:

- If the year under study is after the year of maximum catch, then the biomass stock is estimated as twice the catch;
- Otherwise, the biomass stock is estimated as twice maximum catch, net of catch (2 × Maximum Catch − Catch).

Time-series data of catch (tonnage and value) of each country's economic exclusive zone (EEZ) for the period of 1950–2010 are obtained from Sea Around Us Project (SAUP 2016). We only evaluate the stock that has a catch record for at least 20 years and which has a total catch in a given area of at least 1,000 tonnes over the time span.

5. *Adjustments*

As we outlined in Chapter 1, we treated three adjustments that are not covered by familiar capital assets that however contribute to social well-being change: carbon damage, oil capital gain and total factor productivity. We basically follow IWR 2014 methodology for these adjustments.

5.1. Carbon damage

Following Arrow et al. (2012), we can think of carbon damage as a mostly exogenous change in social well-being, as this does not correspond to each country's emission. As in IWR 2014, the key methodological steps can be described as follows:

1 Obtain the total global carbon emissions for the period under analysis, 1990 to 2014;
2 Derive the total global damages as a function of the emissions; and
3 Allocate the global damages to the countries according to the potential effect of global warming in their economies.

Global carbon emissions: Two sources of carbon emissions were taken into account: (i) carbon emissions stemming from fuel consumption and cement, which were obtained from the Carbon Dioxide Information Analysis Centre (Boden et al. 2011); and (ii) emissions resulting from global deforestation. In this case, we used FAO (2013) data on the changes in annual global forest land. It is further estimated that the average carbon release per hectare is equal to 100 tonnes of carbon (Lampietti and Dixon 1995).

Global carbon damages: The damages per tonne of carbon released to the atmosphere are estimated at US$50 (see Tol 2009). By multiplying the total amount of global tonnes of carbon released to the atmosphere by the price per tonne, we obtain the total global carbon damages. Note that this parameter is constant over time.

Assigning carbon damages to countries: To calculate the distribution of the damages that each region suffers, we referred to the study of Nordhaus and Boyer (2000). This study presents the distribution of damages which different regions and the global economy as a whole will suffer as a percentage of the corresponding regional and global GDP. By using country and global GDP information, we were able to reestimate regional percentage damages in terms of the total global GDP – and not related to the country GDP – as initially presented in Nordhaus and Boyer (2000). Finally, we apportioned the global damages estimated in previous steps according to this latter percentage.

5.2. Oil capital gain and loss

If oil price goes up, oil-rich nations enjoy wealth increase. This is not a gain in quantity of natural capital, but so long as countries can tap into this windfall to improve social well-being, this should be accounted for in wealth accounting. An annual increase of 3% in the rental price of oil is assumed, which corresponds to the annual average oil price increase during 1990–2014 (BP 2015). Conversely, importing countries may have fewer investment opportunities due to higher oil prices, so oil capital losses are distributed to consuming countries.

5.3. Total factor productivity

Total factor productivity of a nation is a source of resource that can be accessed even though they are tangible. We take different methods in computing TFP: for frontier analysis, we used a non-parametric analysis called Malmquist productivity index, which in turn is based on the concept of data envelopment analysis. For IWR 2014 methods, we directly use the TFP data calculated conventionally by Conference Board (2017), in line with Arrow et al. (2012) and IWR 2012 (UNU-IHDP, 2012).

For frontier analysis, let

- x_i: Inputs (produced, human and natural capital)
- y_i: Outputs (GDP)
- Distance function: $d\left(x_t, y_t\right) = \max\left\{\delta; (x_t, y_t | \delta) \in T(t)\right\}$
- Malmquist Productivity Index $M\left(\Upsilon_{it}, K_{it}, H_{it}, N_{it}, \Upsilon_{it+1}, K_{it+1}, H_{it+1}, N_{it+1}\right)$

$$= \left[\frac{d^t\left(\Upsilon_{it+1}, K_{it+1}, H_{it+1}, N_{it+1}\right)}{d^t\left(\Upsilon_{it}, K_{it}, H_{it}, N_{it}\right)} \times \frac{d^{t+1}\left(\Upsilon_{it+1}, K_{it+1}, H_{it+1}, N_{it+1}\right)}{d^{t+1}\left(\Upsilon_{it}, K_{it}, H_{it}, N_{it}\right)}\right]^{\frac{1}{2}}$$

where d is the geometric distance to the production frontier caused by production inefficiency, while the frontier denotes the best available technology from the given inputs and outputs. i refers to the country under analysis, running i from 1 up to 140 nations in our sample; Υ is the corresponding value of gross domestic product; K, H and N stand for produced, human and natural capital inputs.

Note

1 Rintaro Yamaguchi and Moinul Islam have provided excellent research assistance in preparing this methodological appendix.

References

Arrow, K., Dasgupta, P., Goulder, L. H., Daily, G., Ehrlich, P., Heal, G., . . . Walker, B. (2004). Are we consuming too much? *The Journal of Economic Perspectives, 18*(3), 147–172.

Arrow, K. J., Dasgupta, P., Goulder, L. H., Mumford, K. J., & Oleson, K. (2012). Sustainability and the measurement of wealth. *Environment and Development Economics, 17*(3), 317–353. https://doi.org/10.1017/s1355770x12000137

Arrow, K., Cropper, M., Gollier, C., Groom, B., Heal, G., Newell, R., Nordhaus, W., Pindyck, R., Pizer, W., Portney, P. (2013). Determining benefits and costs for future generations. *Science* (80). *341*, 349–350.

Arrow, K. J., Dasgupta, P., & Mäler, K. G. (2003). The genuine savings criterion and the value of population. *Economic Theory, 21*(2), 217–225.

Barro, R. J., Lee, J. W. (2013). A new data set of educational attainment in the world, 1950–2010. *Journal of Development Economics, 104*, 184–198.

Boden, T.A., Marland, G., Andres, R.J. (2011). Global, regional, and national fossil fuel CO_2 emissions. *Carbon Dioxide Inf. Anal. Center*. 36335–37831.

Bolt, K., Matete, M., & Clemens, M. (2002). Manual for calculating adjusted net savings. Environment Department, World Bank, 1–23.

BP. (2015). *Statistical Review of World Energy 2015*. Retrieved from www.bp.com/ Statistical review

Conference Board. (2016). *Total Economy Database™ (Adjusted Version)*.

Conference Board. (2017). *Total Economy Database™ (Adjusted Version)*, May 2017.

Daan, N., Gislason, H., Pope, J. G., & Rice, J. C. (2011). Apocalypse in world fisheries? The reports of their death are greatly exaggerated. *ICES Journal of Marine Science*, 68(7), 1375–1378.

FAO Statistical Yearbook (2013). http://www.fao.org/docrep/018/i3107e/i3107e00.htm

Färe, R., Grosskopf, S., Noh, D. W., & Weber, W. (2005). Characteristics of a polluting technology: Theory and practice. *Journal of Econometrics*, 126(2), 469–492.

Feenstra, R., Inklaar, R., & Timmer, M. (2013). *The Next Generation of the Penn World Table*. Retrieved from www.ggdc.net/pwt

Ferreira, S., Hamilton, K., & Vincent, J. R. (2008). Comprehensive wealth and future consumption: Accounting for population growth. *The World Bank Economic Review*, 22(2), 233–248.

Food and Agriculture Organization of the United Nations (FAO). (2015a). *FAOSTAT*. Retrieved from http://faostat3.fao.org/download/Q/QC/E.

Food and Agriculture Organization of the United Nations (FAO). (2015b). *Global Forest Resources Assessment 2015*. Retrieved from www.fao.org/forest-resources-assessment/explore-data/en/

Froese, R., Zeller, D., Kleisner, K., & Pauly, D. (2012). What catch data can tell us about the status of global fisheries. *Marine Biology*, 159(6), 1283–1292.

Harberger, A. (1978). Perspectives on capital and technology in less developed countries. In M. Artis & A. Nobay (Eds.). *Contemporary economic analysis*. London: Croom Helm.

International Labor Organization. (2015). *Key Indicators of the Labour Market (KILM) Database*. Retrieved from www.ilo.org

King, R. G. & Levine, R. (1994). Capital fundamentalism, economic development and economic growth. *Carnegie-Rochester Conference Series on Public Policy*, 40, 259–292.

Kleisner, K., Zeller, D., Froese, R., & Pauly, D. (2013). Using global catch data for inferences on the world's marine fisheries. *Fish and Fisheries*, 14(3), 293–311.

Klenow, P. & Rodríguez-Clare, A. (1997). The neoclassical revival in growth economics: Has it gone too far? In B. Bernanke & J. Rotemberg (Eds.). *NBER macroeconomics annual 1997*. Cambridge, MA: MIT Press, 73–102.

Lampietti, J. & Dixon, J. (1995). *To see the forest for the trees: A guide to non-timber forest benefits*. Washington, DC: World Bank.

Lenzen, M., Moran, D., Kanemoto, K., & Geschke, A. (2013). Building Eora: A global multi-region input-output database at high country and sector resolution. *Economic Systems Research*, 25(1), 20–49.

Martell, S. & Froese, R. (2013). A simple method for estimating MSY from catch and resilience. *Fish and Fisheries*, 14(4), 504–514.

Narayanan, B., Aguiar, A., & McDougall, R. (2012). Global trade, assistance, and production: The GTAP 8 data base. Center for Global Trade Analysis, Purdue University. Retrieved from www.gtap.agecon. purdue.edu/databases/v8/v8_doco.asp.

Nordhaus, W.D. & Boyer, J. (2000). *Warming the world: economic models of global warming*. MIT press.

OECD. (2016). *OECD National Accounts*. Retrieved from http://stats.oecd.org/

Pauly, D., Hilborn, R., & Branch, T. A. (2013). Fisheries: Does catch reflect abundance? *Nature*, 494(7437), 303–306.

SAUP. (2016). www.seaaroundus.org

Tamaki, T., Shin, K. J., Nakamura, H., Fujii, H., & Managi, S. (2017). Shadow prices and production inefficiency of mineral resources. *Economic Analysis and Policy*, forthcoming.

Tol, R. J. (2009). The economic effects of climate change. *Journal of Economic Perspectives*, 23, 29–51.

United Nations Population Division. (2016). *United Nations New York, 2017: The 2017 revision.* https://esa.un.org/unpd/wpp/publications/Files/WPP2017_KeyFindings.pdf

United Nations Statistics Division. (2012). *National Accounts Estimates of Main Aggregates.* Retrieved from http://data.un.org

United Nations Statistics Division. (2013a). *Nationals Accounts Main Aggregates Database.* Retrieved from http://unstats.un.org/unsd/snaama/Introduction.asp

United Nations Statistics Division. (2013b). *SEEA Experimental Ecosystem Accounting.*

UNU-IHDP. (2012). *Inclusive wealth report 2012: measuring progress toward sustainability.* Cambridge University Press.

UNU-IHDP. (2014). *Inclusive wealth report 2014:measuring progress toward sustainability.* Cambridge University Press.

U.S. Energy Information Administration. (2015). *International Energy Statistics.* Retrieved from www.eia.gov/countries/data.cfm

U.S. Geological Survey. (2015). *Mineral Commodity Summaries.* Retrieved from http://minerals.usgs.gov/minerals/pubs/mcs/

Van der Ploeg, S., De Groot, R.S. (2010). The TEEB Valuation Database–a searchable database of 1310 estimates of monetary values of ecosystem services. *Found. Sustain. Dev.* Wageningen, Netherlands.

World Bank. (2006). *Where is the wealth of nations?* Washington, DC: World Bank.

World Bank. (2011). *The changing wealth of nations.* Washington, DC: World Bank.

World Bank Open Data, 2014. https://data.worldbank.org/

Yamaguchi, R. (2017). Wealth and population growth under dynamic average utilitarianism. *Environment and Development Economics,* forthcoming.

Yamaguchi, R., Sato, M., & Ueta, K. (2016). Measuring regional wealth and assessing sustainable development: An application to a disaster-torn region in Japan. *Social Indicators Research, 129*(1), 365–389.

Annex 3: data

Table A3.1 Wealth (Inclusive wealth in billions of constant 2005 US$)

	Country/year	1990	1995	2000	2005	2010	2014
1	Afghanistan	177	237	283	353	422	493
2	Albania	118	116	118	125	135	141
3	Algeria	1,426	1,509	1,596	1,692	1,853	2,032
4	Argentina	2,364	2,497	2,655	2,789	3,046	3,273
5	Armenia	129	120	117	119	129	134
6	Australia	6,270	6,592	7,048	7,666	8,480	9,207
7	Austria	1,613	1,792	1,955	2,124	2,272	2,394
8	Bahrain	49	57	65	81	121	134
9	Bangladesh	9,243	10,336	11,433	12,427	13,372	14,088
10	Barbados	21	22	23	24	26	27
11	Belgium	1,770	1,946	2,142	2,352	2,609	2,803
12	Belize	17	17	18	18	19	19
13	Benin	2,085	2,496	2,918	3,418	4,013	4,504
14	Bolivia (Plurinational State of)	882	888	900	908	918	931
15	Botswana	528	581	612	684	799	877
16	Brazil	11,367	11,624	11,943	12,261	12,731	13,407
17	Bulgaria	2,425	2,273	2,172	2,108	2,097	2,056
18	Burundi	2,747	2,915	3,377	3,959	4,715	5,436
19	Cambodia	341	346	348	348	357	368
20	Cameroon	2,240	2,516	2,814	3,195	3,679	3,951
21	Canada	9,663	10,046	10,545	11,179	11,937	11,659
22	Central African Republic	681	746	806	861	951	1,024
23	Chile	779	847	937	1,036	1,170	1,315
24	China	34,176	37,795	41,374	45,731	52,592	60,253
25	Colombia	1,797	1,909	2,005	2,085	2,246	1,878
26	Congo	1,014	1,118	1,223	1,391	1,681	1,845
27	Costa Rica	112	120	132	147	168	203
28	Côte d'Ivoire	2,263	2,623	2,936	3,234	3,618	3,912
29	Croatia	370	373	385	421	463	470
30	Cuba	439	461	475	489	507	522
31	Cyprus	77	92	105	120	140	146
32	Czech Republic	1,068	1,131	1,197	1,269	1,399	1,468
33	Democratic Republic of the Congo	1,389	1,378	1,365	1,357	1,356	1,361
34	Denmark	1,168	1,244	1,367	1,492	1,629	1,707
35	Dominican Republic	223	253	299	342	398	439
36	Ecuador	538	552	564	581	610	665
37	Egypt	3,737	4,179	4,545	5,090	5,792	6,512
38	El Salvador	150	167	183	199	214	225

(*Continued*)

Table A3.1 (Continued)

	Country/year	1990	1995	2000	2005	2010	2014
39	Estonia	132	123	122	144	158	166
40	Fiji	25	27	28	29	31	34
41	Finland	1,207	1,269	1,363	1,466	1,635	1,690
42	France	9,425	10,349	11,354	12,592	13,859	14,733
43	Gabon	1,176	1,173	1,171	1,170	1,171	1,179
44	Gambia	12	13	15	17	20	23
45	Germany	17,894	19,362	20,605	21,486	22,377	23,091
46	Ghana	1,349	1,495	1,633	1,832	2,080	2,321
47	Greece	1,395	1,482	1,591	1,749	1,910	1,873
48	Guatemala	1,358	1,518	1,688	1,864	2,072	2,248
49	Guyana	208	209	209	209	210	242
50	Haiti	3,038	3,405	3,808	4,201	3,678	4,724
51	Honduras	139	137	134	136	140	142
52	Hungary	910	952	998	1,063	1,122	1,155
53	Iceland	163	165	171	180	192	193
54	India	320,231	341,430	375,521	407,938	440,219	465,400
55	Indonesia	5,429	5,769	6,137	6,542	7,035	7,497
56	Iran (Islamic Republic of)	6,169	6,242	6,353	6,533	6,792	6,867
57	Iraq	1,908	1,964	2,029	2,111	2,227	2,362
58	Ireland	595	640	766	975	1,186	1,268
59	Israel	477	600	730	826	971	1,105
60	Italy	8,332	9,010	9,758	10,727	11,582	11,917
61	Jamaica	109	119	127	134	139	142
62	Japan	26,237	29,594	32,324	34,102	35,458	36,085
63	Jordan	97	130	151	177	227	269
64	Kazakhstan	1,761	1,866	1,811	1,815	1,912	1,995
65	Kenya	2,606	2,996	3,351	3,917	4,736	5,345
66	Kuwait	2,400	2,224	2,282	2,343	2,469	2,572
67	Kyrgyzstan	149	160	175	189	208	226
68	Lao People's Democratic Republic	262	278	293	306	325	357
69	Latvia	168	164	167	177	193	197
70	Lesotho	1,011	1,057	1,043	994	1,058	1,078
71	Liberia	1,833	1,691	2,362	2,658	3,366	3,662
72	Lithuania	271	278	284	291	303	308
73	Luxembourg	100	116	137	163	194	222
74	Malawi	3,551	3,653	4,076	4,728	5,882	6,924
75	Malaysia	931	1,039	1,148	1,223	1,328	1,481
76	Maldives	9	11	12	14	17	19
77	Mali	3,695	4,174	4,787	5,611	6,580	7,417
78	Malta	21	25	30	35	40	43
79	Mauritania	1,055	1,223	1,371	1,559	1,766	1,945

	Country/year	1990	1995	2000	2005	2010	2014
80	Mauritius	33	37	43	49	55	60
81	Mexico	4,361	4,876	5,483	6,099	6,893	7,581
82	Mongolia	345	348	365	360	369	393
83	Morocco	3,146	3,444	3,727	4,011	4,330	4,596
84	Mozambique	10,425	12,809	14,617	16,216	18,475	20,599
85	Myanmar	3,120	3,371	3,623	3,843	4,049	4,226
86	Namibia	141	157	175	190	217	240
87	Nepal	2,873	3,298	3,646	3,941	4,194	4,467
88	Netherlands	2,914	3,179	3,542	3,889	4,230	4,413
89	New Zealand	2,038	2,076	2,131	2,146	2,599	2,495
90	Nicaragua	209	234	253	270	288	307
91	Niger	4,024	4,719	5,603	6,733	8,174	9,482
92	Nigeria	26,856	30,327	34,102	38,984	44,866	49,966
93	Norway	1,868	1,886	1,934	1,981	2,124	2,263
94	Pakistan	2,637	2,705	2,784	2,873	3,027	3,172
95	Panama	97	104	116	125	146	183
96	Papua New Guinea	4,247	4,823	5,473	6,165	6,835	7,452
97	Paraguay	170	176	188	192	201	205
98	Peru	1,696	1,716	1,756	1,780	1,849	2,031
99	Philippines	1,665	1,932	2,221	2,525	2,830	3,092
100	Poland	2,471	2,552	2,718	2,857	3,097	3,306
101	Portugal	804	900	1,052	1,195	1,301	1,309
102	Qatar	500	496	498	525	671	812
103	Republic of Korea	2,595	3,444	4,358	5,280	6,249	6,938
104	Republic of Moldova	129	134	132	132	133	125
105	Romania	1,415	1,420	1,451	1,468	1,562	1,618
106	Russian Federation	26,878	29,296	28,635	28,060	28,226	28,491
107	Rwanda	799	635	968	1,134	1,355	1,528
108	Saudi Arabia	6,746	7,333	7,307	7,402	7,677	8,141
109	Senegal	1,986	2,254	2,538	2,899	3,341	3,722
110	Serbia	880	882	878	889	922	920
111	Sierra Leone	4,189	3,856	3,788	4,821	5,517	5,961
112	Singapore	258	349	481	574	746	898
113	Slovakia	408	428	459	483	521	548
114	Slovenia	200	209	230	257	289	297
115	South Africa	4,121	4,449	4,788	5,074	5,609	6,058
116	Spain	4,460	5,045	5,729	6,846	7,958	8,272
117	Sri Lanka	406	447	489	511	536	626
118	Sudan (former)	6,699	8,211	9,335	10,679	11,151	11,880
119	Swaziland	27	33	38	41	44	47
120	Sweden	1,970	2,105	2,260	2,466	2,726	2,893

(*Continued*)

Table A3.1 (Continued)

	Country/year	1990	1995	2000	2005	2010	2014
121	Switzerland	2,068	2,542	2,850	3,009	3,295	3,502
122	Syrian Arab Republic	460	518	581	648	749	665
123	Tajikistan	160	182	197	218	244	268
124	Thailand	1,801	2,116	2,350	2,555	2,759	2,963
125	Togo	289	323	377	431	502	572
126	Trinidad and Tobago	173	169	167	166	158	145
127	Tunisia	251	287	323	361	415	458
128	Turkey	2,101	2,381	2,720	3,034	3,453	3,928
129	Uganda	8,879	10,463	12,130	14,883	17,941	20,789
130	Ukraine	18,805	18,568	17,495	16,637	16,481	16,308
131	United Arab Emirates	2,599	2,925	3,330	3,868	4,736	5,224
132	United Kingdom	8,276	8,973	9,996	11,079	12,166	12,962
133	United Republic of Tanzania	8,561	9,934	11,219	13,092	15,526	17,857
134	United States of America	54,549	59,962	67,699	76,021	83,540	88,166
135	Uruguay	262	277	294	300	315	333
136	Venezuela (Bolivarian Republic of)	5,599	5,602	5,584	5,567	5,654	5,749
137	Viet Nam	1,000	1,102	1,212	1,328	1,488	1,626
138	Yemen	1,864	2,288	2,678	3,118	3,663	4,120
139	Zambia	6,020	6,770	7,673	8,960	10,895	12,415
140	Zimbabwe	10,731	11,113	10,964	10,660	11,562	14,264

Table A3.2 IW per capita (Inclusive wealth per capita in thousands of constant 2005 US$)

	Country/year	1990	1995	2000	2005	2010	2014
1	Afghanistan	15	14	14	14	15	16
2	Albania	36	36	38	42	46	49
3	Algeria	55	52	51	51	51	52
4	Argentina	72	71	72	71	74	76
5	Armenia	36	37	38	39	43	44
6	Australia	367	365	368	376	385	392
7	Austria	210	226	244	258	272	280
8	Bahrain	99	101	97	93	96	98
9	Bangladesh	87	87	87	87	88	89
10	Barbados	81	82	84	89	92	94
11	Belgium	178	192	209	224	239	250

	Country/year	1990	1995	2000	2005	2010	2014
12	Belize	90	83	72	64	58	54
13	Benin	417	417	420	418	422	425
14	Bolivia (Plurinational State of)	129	117	108	100	93	88
15	Botswana	383	369	352	367	390	395
16	Brazil	76	71	68	65	64	65
17	Bulgaria	278	270	266	272	284	285
18	Burundi	489	467	499	499	498	503
19	Cambodia	38	32	29	26	25	24
20	Cameroon	186	181	177	176	179	173
21	Canada	348	342	343	346	351	328
22	Central African Republic	232	224	216	212	214	213
23	Chile	59	60	62	64	69	74
24	China	30	31	33	35	39	44
25	Colombia	52	51	50	48	49	39
26	Congo	425	411	393	397	413	409
27	Costa Rica	36	34	34	35	37	43
28	Côte d'Ivoire	186	182	178	178	180	177
29	Croatia	77	80	87	95	105	111
30	Cuba	41	42	43	43	45	46
31	Cyprus	100	108	111	116	126	127
32	Czech Republic	103	110	117	124	134	140
33	Democratic Republic of the Congo	40	33	28	24	21	18
34	Denmark	227	238	256	275	294	302
35	Dominican Republic	31	32	35	37	40	42
36	Ecuador	53	48	45	42	41	42
37	Egypt	66	67	67	68	71	73
38	El Salvador	29	30	32	33	35	37
39	Estonia	84	85	87	106	118	126
40	Fiji	34	35	35	35	36	38
41	Finland	242	248	263	280	305	309
42	France	161	174	186	199	213	222
43	Gabon	1,235	1,079	951	849	760	699
44	Gambia	13	12	12	12	12	12
45	Germany	225	237	251	261	274	285
46	Ghana	92	89	87	86	86	87
47	Greece	137	140	147	159	172	172
48	Guatemala	148	147	144	141	141	140
49	Guyana	289	288	282	282	279	317
50	Haiti	428	435	445	453	368	447
51	Honduras	28	24	21	20	19	18
52	Hungary	88	92	98	105	112	117
53	Iceland	638	616	608	608	603	591
54	India	368	355	357	357	358	359
55	Indonesia	30	29	29	29	29	29
56	Iran (Islamic Republic of)	110	103	96	93	91	88

(*Continued*)

Table A3.2 (Continued)

	Country/year	1990	1995	2000	2005	2010	2014
57	Iraq	109	97	86	78	72	67
58	Ireland	169	177	201	234	260	275
59	Israel	102	108	116	119	127	135
60	Italy	147	159	171	185	195	196
61	Jamaica	46	48	49	51	52	52
62	Japan	212	236	255	267	277	284
63	Jordan	29	30	32	33	35	36
64	Kazakhstan	108	118	122	120	117	115
65	Kenya	111	109	108	111	117	119
66	Kuwait	1,166	1,358	1,183	1,035	807	685
67	Kyrgyzstan	34	35	36	37	38	39
68	Lao People's Democratic Republic	62	57	55	53	52	53
69	Latvia	63	66	71	79	92	99
70	Lesotho	633	602	562	516	526	511
71	Liberia	872	813	817	813	850	833
72	Lithuania	73	77	81	88	98	105
73	Luxembourg	261	284	315	351	382	398
74	Malawi	377	372	364	371	398	415
75	Malaysia	51	50	49	47	47	50
76	Maldives	42	41	43	45	46	48
77	Mali	436	433	433	436	434	434
78	Malta	60	68	77	85	96	101
79	Mauritania	521	524	506	494	492	490
80	Mauritius	31	33	36	40	44	47
81	Mexico	51	52	53	56	58	60
82	Mongolia	158	152	152	143	136	135
83	Morocco	126	127	129	132	135	135
84	Mozambique	780	805	800	768	760	757
85	Myanmar	74	75	76	77	78	79
86	Namibia	100	95	92	94	99	100
87	Nepal	153	154	154	155	156	159
88	Netherlands	195	206	222	238	255	262
89	New Zealand	612	565	553	519	597	553
90	Nicaragua	50	51	50	50	50	51
91	Niger	509	504	499	499	502	496
92	Nigeria	281	280	277	279	281	281
93	Norway	440	433	431	428	434	440
94	Pakistan	25	22	20	19	18	17
95	Panama	39	38	38	38	40	47
96	Papua New Guinea	1,021	1,023	1,018	1,013	998	998
97	Paraguay	40	37	35	33	32	31
98	Peru	78	71	68	64	63	66
99	Philippines	27	28	28	29	30	31

	Country/year	1990	1995	2000	2005	2010	2014
100	Poland	65	66	71	75	81	87
101	Portugal	81	90	102	114	123	126
102	Qatar	1,050	991	840	627	380	374
103	Republic of Korea	61	76	93	110	126	138
104	Republic of Moldova	35	36	36	37	37	35
105	Romania	61	63	65	69	77	81
106	Russian Federation	181	197	195	196	198	198
107	Rwanda	110	107	121	126	132	135
108	Saudi Arabia	412	389	342	299	273	264
109	Senegal	264	259	257	257	258	254
110	Serbia	116	116	117	119	126	129
111	Sierra Leone	1,066	1,005	933	951	955	944
112	Singapore	85	99	119	135	147	164
113	Slovakia	77	80	85	90	97	101
114	Slovenia	100	105	116	128	141	144
115	South Africa	117	114	109	107	110	112
116	Spain	115	128	142	157	171	178
117	Sri Lanka	24	25	26	26	27	30
118	Sudan (former)	335	333	332	334	309	302
119	Swaziland	31	35	36	37	37	37
120	Sweden	230	238	255	273	291	298
121	Switzerland	308	361	397	405	421	428
122	Syrian Arab Republic	37	36	36	36	36	35
123	Tajikistan	30	31	32	32	32	32
124	Thailand	32	36	37	39	41	44
125	Togo	76	75	77	77	79	80
126	Trinidad and Tobago	142	135	132	128	119	107
127	Tunisia	31	32	34	36	39	42
128	Turkey	39	41	43	45	48	51
129	Uganda	511	513	511	531	541	550
130	Ukraine	362	360	356	353	359	360
131	United Arab Emirates	1,435	1,245	1,092	863	569	575
132	United Kingdom	145	155	170	183	194	201
133	United Republic of Tanzania	336	332	330	335	340	345
134	United States of America	219	225	240	257	270	276
135	Uruguay	84	86	88	90	93	97
136	Venezuela (Bolivarian Republic of)	282	252	228	208	195	187
137	Viet Nam	15	15	16	16	17	18
138	Yemen	156	150	150	152	155	157
139	Zambia	739	732	725	744	783	790
140	Zimbabwe	1,023	951	877	821	827	936

Table A3.3 IW Growth (unadjusted) (Inclusive wealth change (%) with respect to base year 1990)

	Country/year	1995	2000	2005	2010	2014
1	Afghanistan	6.0%	12.5%	18.8%	24.3%	40.7%
2	Albania	-0.4%	-0.2%	1.4%	3.3%	6.1%
3	Algeria	1.1%	2.9%	4.4%	6.8%	12.5%
4	Argentina	1.1%	3.0%	4.2%	6.5%	11.5%
5	Armenia	-1.4%	-2.4%	-2.1%	-0.1%	1.1%
6	Australia	1.0%	3.0%	5.2%	7.8%	13.7%
7	Austria	2.1%	4.9%	7.1%	8.9%	14.1%
8	Bahrain	3.0%	7.0%	13.1%	25.1%	39.7%
9	Bangladesh	2.3%	5.5%	7.7%	9.7%	15.1%
10	Barbados	0.6%	2.0%	3.9%	5.1%	8.3%
11	Belgium	1.9%	4.9%	7.4%	10.2%	16.6%
12	Belize	0.4%	1.1%	1.8%	2.4%	3.8%
13	Benin	3.7%	8.8%	13.2%	17.8%	29.3%
14	Bolivia (Plurinational State of)	0.1%	0.5%	0.7%	1.0%	1.8%
15	Botswana	1.9%	3.8%	6.7%	10.9%	18.4%
16	Brazil	0.4%	1.2%	1.9%	2.9%	5.7%
17	Bulgaria	-1.3%	-2.7%	-3.4%	-3.6%	-5.4%
18	Burundi	1.2%	5.3%	9.6%	14.5%	25.5%
19	Cambodia	0.3%	0.5%	0.5%	1.2%	2.6%
20	Cameroon	2.4%	5.9%	9.3%	13.2%	20.8%
21	Canada	0.8%	2.2%	3.7%	5.4%	6.5%
22	Central African Republic	1.8%	4.3%	6.0%	8.7%	14.5%
23	Chile	1.7%	4.7%	7.4%	10.7%	19.1%
24	China	2.0%	4.9%	7.6%	11.4%	20.8%
25	Colombia	1.2%	2.8%	3.8%	5.7%	1.5%
26	Congo	2.0%	4.8%	8.2%	13.5%	22.1%
27	Costa Rica	1.5%	4.2%	7.1%	10.8%	21.9%
28	Côte d'Ivoire	3.0%	6.7%	9.3%	12.4%	20.0%
29	Croatia	0.2%	1.0%	3.3%	5.7%	8.3%
30	Cuba	1.0%	2.0%	2.8%	3.7%	6.0%
31	Cyprus	3.7%	8.0%	11.8%	16.1%	23.8%
32	Czech Republic	1.1%	2.9%	4.4%	7.0%	11.2%
33	Democratic Republic of the Congo	-0.2%	-0.4%	-0.6%	-0.6%	-0.7%
34	Denmark	1.3%	4.0%	6.3%	8.7%	13.5%
35	Dominican Republic	2.6%	7.6%	11.3%	15.6%	25.3%
36	Ecuador	0.5%	1.2%	1.9%	3.2%	7.3%
37	Egypt	2.3%	5.0%	8.0%	11.6%	20.3%
38	El Salvador	2.1%	5.1%	7.3%	9.2%	14.4%
39	Estonia	-1.5%	-2.1%	2.1%	4.5%	7.9%
40	Fiji	2.0%	3.4%	4.1%	5.9%	10.9%
41	Finland	1.0%	3.1%	5.0%	7.9%	11.9%
42	France	1.9%	4.8%	7.5%	10.1%	16.1%
43	Gabon	-0.1%	-0.1%	-0.1%	-0.1%	0.1%

	Country/year	1995	2000	2005	2010	2014
44	Gambia	1.1%	4.7%	9.1%	13.8%	23.8%
45	Germany	1.6%	3.6%	4.7%	5.7%	8.9%
46	Ghana	2.1%	4.9%	8.0%	11.4%	19.8%
47	Greece	1.2%	3.3%	5.8%	8.2%	10.3%
48	Guatemala	2.3%	5.6%	8.2%	11.1%	18.3%
49	Guyana	0.1%	0.1%	0.1%	0.2%	5.2%
50	Haiti	2.3%	5.8%	8.4%	4.9%	15.9%
51	Honduras	−0.4%	−1.0%	−0.6%	0.2%	0.7%
52	Hungary	0.9%	2.3%	3.9%	5.4%	8.2%
53	Iceland	0.3%	1.3%	2.6%	4.2%	5.9%
54	India	1.3%	4.1%	6.2%	8.3%	13.3%
55	Indonesia	1.2%	3.1%	4.8%	6.7%	11.4%
56	Iran (Islamic Republic of)	0.2%	0.7%	1.4%	2.4%	3.6%
57	Iraq	0.6%	1.6%	2.6%	3.9%	7.4%
58	Ireland	1.5%	6.5%	13.1%	18.8%	28.7%
59	Israel	4.7%	11.2%	14.7%	19.4%	32.3%
60	Italy	1.6%	4.0%	6.5%	8.6%	12.7%
61	Jamaica	1.8%	3.8%	5.3%	6.2%	9.1%
62	Japan	2.4%	5.4%	6.8%	7.8%	11.2%
63	Jordan	6.1%	11.8%	16.4%	23.8%	40.7%
64	Kazakhstan	1.2%	0.7%	0.8%	2.1%	4.2%
65	Kenya	2.8%	6.5%	10.7%	16.1%	27.1%
66	Kuwait	−1.5%	−1.2%	−0.6%	0.7%	2.3%
67	Kyrgyzstan	1.4%	4.1%	6.1%	8.6%	14.8%
68	Lao People's Democratic Republic	1.2%	2.8%	3.9%	5.5%	10.8%
69	Latvia	−0.4%	−0.1%	1.4%	3.5%	5.4%
70	Lesotho	0.9%	0.8%	−0.4%	1.1%	2.2%
71	Liberia	−1.6%	6.5%	9.7%	16.4%	26.0%
72	Lithuania	0.5%	1.2%	1.8%	2.9%	4.4%
73	Luxembourg	3.1%	8.4%	13.2%	18.1%	30.5%
74	Malawi	0.6%	3.5%	7.4%	13.4%	24.9%
75	Malaysia	2.2%	5.4%	7.1%	9.3%	16.7%
76	Maldives	2.9%	8.0%	11.9%	17.0%	28.6%
77	Mali	2.5%	6.7%	11.0%	15.5%	26.1%
78	Malta	3.2%	8.4%	12.7%	16.6%	26.4%
79	Mauritania	3.0%	6.8%	10.3%	13.7%	22.6%
80	Mauritius	2.8%	7.3%	10.6%	14.1%	22.4%
81	Mexico	2.3%	5.9%	8.7%	12.1%	20.2%
82	Mongolia	0.2%	1.4%	1.1%	1.7%	4.4%
83	Morocco	1.8%	4.3%	6.3%	8.3%	13.5%
84	Mozambique	4.2%	8.8%	11.7%	15.4%	25.5%
85	Myanmar	1.6%	3.8%	5.4%	6.7%	10.7%
86	Namibia	2.1%	5.5%	7.7%	11.4%	19.4%
87	Nepal	2.8%	6.1%	8.2%	9.9%	15.8%

(*Continued*)

Table A3.3 (Continued)

	Country/year	1995	2000	2005	2010	2014
88	Netherlands	1.8%	5.0%	7.5%	9.8%	14.8%
89	New Zealand	0.4%	1.1%	1.3%	6.3%	7.0%
90	Nicaragua	2.3%	4.9%	6.7%	8.4%	13.7%
91	Niger	3.2%	8.6%	13.7%	19.4%	33.1%
92	Nigeria	2.5%	6.2%	9.8%	13.7%	23.0%
93	Norway	0.2%	0.9%	1.5%	3.3%	6.6%
94	Pakistan	0.5%	1.4%	2.2%	3.5%	6.4%
95	Panama	1.5%	4.5%	6.6%	10.8%	23.7%
96	Papua New Guinea	2.6%	6.5%	9.8%	12.6%	20.6%
97	Paraguay	0.7%	2.5%	3.1%	4.3%	6.4%
98	Peru	0.2%	0.9%	1.2%	2.2%	6.2%
99	Philippines	3.0%	7.5%	11.0%	14.2%	22.9%
100	Poland	0.6%	2.4%	3.7%	5.8%	10.2%
101	Portugal	2.3%	6.9%	10.4%	12.8%	17.6%
102	Qatar	-0.2%	-0.1%	1.2%	7.6%	17.5%
103	Republic of Korea	5.8%	13.8%	19.4%	24.6%	38.8%
104	Republic of Moldova	0.8%	0.6%	0.5%	0.9%	-1.0%
105	Romania	0.1%	0.6%	0.9%	2.5%	4.6%
106	Russian Federation	1.7%	1.6%	1.1%	1.2%	2.0%
107	Rwanda	-4.5%	4.9%	9.1%	14.1%	24.1%
108	Saudi Arabia	1.7%	2.0%	2.3%	3.3%	6.5%
109	Senegal	2.6%	6.3%	9.9%	13.9%	23.3%
110	Serbia	0.0%	0.0%	0.2%	1.2%	1.5%
111	Sierra Leone	-1.6%	-2.5%	3.6%	7.1%	12.5%
112	Singapore	6.2%	16.8%	22.1%	30.4%	51.5%
113	Slovakia	1.0%	3.0%	4.3%	6.3%	10.3%
114	Slovenia	0.9%	3.5%	6.5%	9.7%	14.0%
115	South Africa	1.5%	3.8%	5.3%	8.0%	13.7%
116	Spain	2.5%	6.5%	11.3%	15.6%	22.9%
117	Sri Lanka	2.0%	4.8%	6.0%	7.2%	15.5%
118	Sudan (former)	4.2%	8.7%	12.4%	13.6%	21.0%
119	Swaziland	4.4%	9.2%	11.2%	13.3%	20.6%
120	Sweden	1.3%	3.5%	5.8%	8.5%	13.7%
121	Switzerland	4.2%	8.4%	9.8%	12.4%	19.2%
122	Syrian Arab Republic	2.4%	6.0%	9.0%	13.0%	13.1%
123	Tajikistan	2.6%	5.4%	8.0%	11.1%	18.8%
124	Thailand	3.3%	6.9%	9.1%	11.3%	18.0%
125	Togo	2.3%	6.9%	10.5%	14.8%	25.6%
126	Trinidad and Tobago	-0.5%	-0.9%	-1.0%	-2.3%	-5.8%
127	Tunisia	2.7%	6.4%	9.5%	13.4%	22.1%
128	Turkey	2.5%	6.7%	9.6%	13.2%	23.2%
129	Uganda	3.3%	8.1%	13.8%	19.2%	32.8%
130	Ukraine	-0.3%	-1.8%	-3.0%	-3.2%	-4.6%
131	United Arab Emirates	2.4%	6.4%	10.5%	16.2%	26.2%

	Country/year	1995	2000	2005	2010	2014
132	United Kingdom	1.6%	4.8%	7.6%	10.1%	16.1%
133	United Republic of Tanzania	3.0%	7.0%	11.2%	16.0%	27.8%
134	United States of America	1.9%	5.5%	8.7%	11.2%	17.4%
135	Uruguay	1.1%	2.9%	3.5%	4.7%	8.3%
136	Venezuela (Bolivarian Republic of)	0.0%	−0.1%	−0.1%	0.2%	0.9%
137	Viet Nam	2.0%	4.9%	7.3%	10.4%	17.6%
138	Yemen	4.2%	9.5%	13.7%	18.4%	30.3%
139	Zambia	2.4%	6.3%	10.5%	16.0%	27.3%
140	Zimbabwe	0.7%	0.5%	−0.2%	1.9%	9.9%

Table A3.4 IW per capita growth (unadjusted) (Inclusive wealth per capita change (%) with respect to base year 1990)

	Country/year	1995	2000	2005	2010	2014
1	Afghanistan	−0.7%	−0.5%	−0.4%	0.7%	2.1%
2	Albania	0.2%	1.4%	3.6%	6.4%	10.7%
3	Algeria	−1.0%	−1.8%	−2.0%	−1.7%	−1.7%
4	Argentina	−0.2%	−0.2%	−0.3%	0.6%	1.8%
5	Armenia	0.4%	1.1%	1.9%	4.5%	6.9%
6	Australia	−0.1%	0.0%	0.6%	1.2%	2.2%
7	Austria	1.4%	3.8%	5.3%	6.6%	10.1%
8	Bahrain	0.3%	−0.6%	−1.6%	−0.9%	−0.3%
9	Bangladesh	0.0%	0.0%	−0.1%	0.3%	0.5%
10	Barbados	0.2%	1.1%	2.6%	3.3%	5.3%
11	Belgium	1.6%	4.2%	6.0%	7.8%	12.0%
12	Belize	−1.5%	−5.6%	−8.2%	−10.5%	−15.8%
13	Benin	0.0%	0.2%	0.1%	0.3%	0.6%
14	Bolivia (Plurinational State of)	−1.8%	−4.3%	−6.2%	−7.9%	−11.8%
15	Botswana	−0.7%	−2.0%	−1.1%	0.5%	1.1%
16	Brazil	−1.1%	−2.6%	−3.7%	−4.0%	−4.9%
17	Bulgaria	−0.6%	−1.1%	−0.5%	0.5%	0.8%
18	Burundi	−0.9%	0.5%	0.5%	0.5%	0.9%
19	Cambodia	−3.1%	−6.8%	−8.9%	−10.0%	−14.1%
20	Cameroon	−0.5%	−1.2%	−1.3%	−0.9%	−2.2%
21	Canada	−0.3%	−0.4%	−0.1%	0.2%	−1.9%
22	Central African Republic	−0.7%	−1.7%	−2.2%	−2.0%	−2.8%
23	Chile	0.1%	1.0%	2.1%	3.8%	7.7%
24	China	0.8%	2.1%	3.9%	6.9%	13.6%
25	Colombia	−0.6%	−1.4%	−2.1%	−1.7%	−9.2%
26	Congo	−0.7%	−1.9%	−1.7%	−0.7%	−1.2%
27	Costa Rica	−1.1%	−1.8%	−1.0%	0.6%	5.7%
28	Côte d'Ivoire	−0.4%	−1.1%	−1.0%	−0.9%	−1.7%

(*Continued*)

Table A3.4 (Continued)

	Country/year	1995	2000	2005	2010	2014
29	Croatia	0.6%	3.0%	5.2%	7.8%	12.7%
30	Cuba	0.4%	0.8%	1.2%	2.0%	3.5%
31	Cyprus	1.4%	2.6%	3.7%	6.0%	8.0%
32	Czech Republic	1.2%	3.1%	4.7%	6.6%	10.5%
33	Democratic Republic of the Congo	−3.8%	−8.0%	−11.7%	−15.2%	−22.9%
34	Denmark	0.9%	3.0%	4.9%	6.6%	10.0%
35	Dominican Republic	0.6%	3.0%	4.5%	6.7%	10.8%
36	Ecuador	−1.7%	−4.0%	−5.3%	−6.1%	−7.4%
37	Egypt	0.2%	0.1%	0.6%	1.6%	3.1%
38	El Salvador	0.9%	2.5%	4.0%	5.4%	8.8%
39	Estonia	0.3%	0.8%	5.9%	8.9%	14.5%
40	Fiji	0.8%	0.6%	1.0%	1.6%	3.9%
41	Finland	0.5%	2.1%	3.7%	5.9%	8.5%
42	France	1.5%	3.7%	5.5%	7.3%	11.2%
43	Gabon	−2.7%	−6.3%	−8.9%	−11.4%	−17.3%
44	Gambia	−1.9%	−2.7%	−2.5%	−2.4%	−3.3%
45	Germany	1.0%	2.7%	3.7%	5.0%	8.2%
46	Ghana	−0.7%	−1.5%	−1.8%	−1.9%	−2.1%
47	Greece	0.5%	1.9%	3.9%	5.9%	7.9%
48	Guatemala	−0.2%	−0.7%	−1.2%	−1.3%	−1.8%
49	Guyana	−0.1%	−0.6%	−0.7%	−0.9%	3.1%
50	Haiti	0.3%	1.0%	1.5%	−3.7%	1.5%
51	Honduras	−2.9%	−6.8%	−8.7%	−9.9%	−14.3%
52	Hungary	1.0%	2.7%	4.7%	6.3%	10.1%
53	Iceland	−0.7%	−1.2%	−1.2%	−1.4%	−2.5%
54	India	−0.7%	−0.8%	−0.8%	−0.7%	−0.8%
55	Indonesia	−0.4%	−0.8%	−0.9%	−0.7%	−0.5%
56	Iran (Islamic Republic of)	−1.2%	−3.2%	−4.0%	−4.5%	−7.2%
57	Iraq	−2.3%	−5.8%	−8.0%	−9.8%	−15.0%
58	Ireland	0.9%	4.4%	8.4%	11.3%	17.5%
59	Israel	1.1%	3.2%	3.9%	5.6%	9.5%
60	Italy	1.5%	3.9%	5.9%	7.4%	10.1%
61	Jamaica	1.1%	1.7%	2.6%	3.1%	4.5%
62	Japan	2.1%	4.7%	5.9%	6.8%	10.1%
63	Jordan	0.9%	2.4%	3.7%	4.9%	8.0%
64	Kazakhstan	1.8%	3.1%	2.7%	2.1%	2.3%
65	Kenya	−0.3%	−0.8%	−0.1%	1.4%	2.3%
66	Kuwait	3.1%	0.4%	−2.9%	−8.8%	−16.2%
67	Kyrgyzstan	0.7%	1.3%	1.9%	2.9%	4.4%
68	Lao People's Democratic Republic	−1.5%	−2.9%	−3.6%	−4.2%	−4.8%
69	Latvia	1.0%	2.9%	5.9%	9.9%	16.1%
70	Lesotho	−1.0%	−2.9%	−5.0%	−4.5%	−6.9%

	Country/year	1995	2000	2005	2010	2014
71	Liberia	−1.4%	−1.6%	−1.7%	−0.6%	−1.5%
72	Lithuania	0.9%	2.6%	4.6%	7.5%	12.8%
73	Luxembourg	1.7%	4.8%	7.7%	10.0%	15.2%
74	Malawi	−0.3%	−0.9%	−0.4%	1.4%	3.2%
75	Malaysia	−0.4%	−1.0%	−1.9%	−2.0%	−1.0%
76	Maldives	−0.2%	0.9%	1.6%	2.7%	5.0%
77	Mali	−0.1%	−0.1%	0.0%	−0.1%	−0.1%
78	Malta	2.3%	6.4%	9.0%	12.1%	18.7%
79	Mauritania	0.1%	−0.7%	−1.3%	−1.4%	−2.0%
80	Mauritius	1.6%	4.3%	6.5%	9.5%	15.5%
81	Mexico	0.3%	1.2%	2.2%	3.4%	5.9%
82	Mongolia	−0.8%	−0.9%	−2.5%	−3.6%	−5.1%
83	Morocco	0.1%	0.5%	1.1%	1.7%	2.4%
84	Mozambique	0.6%	0.7%	−0.4%	−0.6%	−1.0%
85	Myanmar	0.3%	0.6%	0.9%	1.3%	2.1%
86	Namibia	−1.0%	−1.9%	−1.6%	−0.1%	0.1%
87	Nepal	0.1%	0.0%	0.2%	0.4%	1.1%
88	Netherlands	1.1%	3.4%	5.2%	6.9%	10.3%
89	New Zealand	−1.6%	−2.5%	−4.0%	−0.6%	−3.3%
90	Nicaragua	0.1%	−0.1%	−0.1%	−0.1%	0.5%
91	Niger	−0.2%	−0.5%	−0.5%	−0.3%	−0.8%
92	Nigeria	−0.1%	−0.3%	−0.1%	0.1%	0.1%
93	Norway	−0.4%	−0.6%	−0.7%	−0.3%	0.0%
94	Pakistan	−2.1%	−4.8%	−6.5%	−7.7%	−11.2%
95	Panama	−0.5%	−0.6%	−1.0%	0.7%	6.5%
96	Papua New Guinea	0.0%	−0.1%	−0.2%	−0.6%	−0.8%
97	Paraguay	−1.7%	−3.2%	−4.8%	−5.4%	−8.1%
98	Peru	−1.7%	−3.4%	−4.6%	−5.1%	−5.5%
99	Philippines	0.6%	1.5%	2.2%	3.1%	5.1%
100	Poland	0.4%	2.3%	3.7%	5.8%	10.3%
101	Portugal	2.2%	6.1%	9.0%	11.2%	16.0%
102	Qatar	−1.2%	−5.4%	−12.1%	−22.4%	−29.1%
103	Republic of Korea	4.8%	11.2%	16.0%	20.2%	31.5%
104	Republic of Moldova	0.9%	1.0%	1.2%	1.8%	0.3%
105	Romania	0.5%	1.5%	3.1%	6.1%	10.0%
106	Russian Federation	1.7%	1.9%	1.9%	2.2%	3.0%
107	Rwanda	−0.5%	2.3%	3.4%	4.6%	7.0%
108	Saudi Arabia	−1.2%	−4.6%	−7.7%	−9.8%	−13.9%
109	Senegal	−0.4%	−0.7%	−0.7%	−0.6%	−1.4%
110	Serbia	−0.1%	0.2%	0.7%	2.2%	3.6%
111	Sierra Leone	−1.2%	−3.3%	−2.8%	−2.7%	−4.0%
112	Singapore	3.1%	9.0%	12.3%	14.7%	24.7%
113	Slovakia	0.7%	2.6%	4.0%	5.9%	9.5%
114	Slovenia	1.0%	3.7%	6.4%	9.0%	12.9%

(*Continued*)

Table A3.4 (Continued)

	Country/year	1995	2000	2005	2010	2014
115	South Africa	-0.6%	-1.8%	-2.1%	-1.4%	-1.4%
116	Spain	2.2%	5.5%	8.1%	10.5%	15.7%
117	Sri Lanka	0.8%	2.5%	2.7%	2.9%	8.2%
118	Sudan (former)	-0.1%	-0.2%	-0.1%	-2.0%	-3.4%
119	Swaziland	2.1%	3.6%	4.5%	4.5%	6.1%
120	Sweden	0.7%	2.6%	4.4%	6.0%	9.0%
121	Switzerland	3.2%	6.5%	7.1%	8.1%	11.6%
122	Syrian Arab Republic	-0.4%	-0.9%	-0.8%	-0.5%	-1.3%
123	Tajikistan	0.8%	1.4%	1.4%	1.6%	2.3%
124	Thailand	2.3%	4.2%	5.1%	6.8%	11.2%
125	Togo	-0.2%	0.3%	0.3%	0.7%	1.8%
126	Trinidad and Tobago	-1.0%	-1.9%	-2.5%	-4.3%	-9.0%
127	Tunisia	0.7%	2.3%	4.0%	6.3%	10.6%
128	Turkey	0.9%	2.5%	3.5%	5.3%	9.2%
129	Uganda	0.1%	0.0%	1.0%	1.5%	2.5%
130	Ukraine	-0.1%	-0.5%	-0.6%	-0.2%	-0.3%
131	United Arab Emirates	-2.8%	-6.6%	-11.9%	-20.7%	-26.3%
132	United Kingdom	1.4%	4.1%	6.1%	7.6%	11.5%
133	United Republic of Tanzania	-0.2%	-0.5%	-0.1%	0.3%	0.8%
134	United States of America	0.6%	2.4%	4.2%	5.4%	8.2%
135	Uruguay	0.4%	1.2%	1.7%	2.6%	5.0%
136	Venezuela (Bolivarian Republic of)	-2.2%	-5.2%	-7.3%	-8.8%	-12.7%
137	Viet Nam	0.2%	0.8%	1.6%	3.1%	5.8%
138	Yemen	-0.8%	-0.9%	-0.6%	-0.1%	0.3%
139	Zambia	-0.2%	-0.5%	0.2%	1.4%	2.2%
140	Zimbabwe	-1.5%	-3.8%	-5.4%	-5.2%	-2.9%

Table A3.5 Human capital (Human capital in billions of constant 2005 US$)

	Country/year	1990	1995	2000	2005	2010	2014
1	Afghanistan	139	200	248	316	382	451
2	Albania	73	73	74	75	75	76
3	Algeria	526	639	757	871	1,019	1,154
4	Argentina	1,009	1,116	1,222	1,336	1,455	1,559
5	Armenia	111	103	101	100	101	103
6	Australia	1,596	1,734	1,901	2,095	2,341	2,545
7	Austria	750	796	816	853	882	919
8	Bahrain	17	20	25	34	52	58
9	Bangladesh	9,128	10,212	11,285	12,243	13,128	13,778
10	Barbados	10	11	11	12	12	13
11	Belgium	890	937	988	1,045	1,124	1,191

	Country/year	1990	1995	2000	2005	2010	2014
12	Belize	1	1	2	2	2	3
13	Benin	2,037	2,449	2,872	3,372	3,965	4,453
14	Bolivia (Plurinational State of)	132	149	171	193	217	240
15	Botswana	453	504	532	600	708	776
16	Brazil	1,925	2,174	2,429	2,717	2,987	3,185
17	Bulgaria	2,296	2,147	2,045	1,964	1,920	1,887
18	Burundi	2,739	2,908	3,370	3,952	4,707	5,426
19	Cambodia	90	108	125	137	153	167
20	Cameroon	1,962	2,250	2,557	2,945	3,429	3,837
21	Canada	2,137	2,315	2,511	2,705	2,895	3,088
22	Central African Republic	467	532	594	650	742	815
23	Chile	337	380	423	465	508	545
24	China	23,086	26,012	28,448	30,647	32,811	34,371
25	Colombia	523	601	677	757	838	902
26	Congo	698	802	912	1,084	1,370	1,522
27	Costa Rica	37	43	50	56	61	66
28	Côte d'Ivoire	2,054	2,403	2,692	3,012	3,413	3,727
29	Croatia	253	254	250	260	266	263
30	Cuba	297	322	340	356	367	376
31	Cyprus	36	43	50	58	65	70
32	Czech Republic	605	636	643	645	679	692
33	Democratic Republic of the Congo	19	24	29	35	43	51
34	Denmark	572	592	615	635	655	676
35	Dominican Republic	139	158	179	200	223	241
36	Ecuador	115	134	156	177	201	221
37	Egypt	3,423	3,864	4,219	4,746	5,398	6,088
38	El Salvador	118	130	141	151	160	167
39	Estonia	81	76	77	76	77	77
40	Fiji	11	13	13	13	14	16
41	Finland	501	531	552	574	656	668
42	France	3,997	4,244	4,530	4,861	5,176	5,439
43	Gabon	11	14	16	20	23	27
44	Gambia	6	7	9	11	14	16
45	Germany	9,052	9,467	9,692	9,806	9,890	9,928
46	Ghana	1,241	1,389	1,526	1,723	1,960	2,158
47	Greece	567	623	671	718	759	763
48	Guatemala	1,207	1,368	1,534	1,705	1,908	2,071
49	Guyana	2	2	2	2	2	2
50	Haiti	3,022	3,389	3,790	4,180	3,655	4,699

(*Continued*)

Table A3.5 (Continued)

	Country/year	1990	1995	2000	2005	2010	2014
51	Honduras	17	20	24	27	31	34
52	Hungary	554	585	604	617	627	636
53	Iceland	25	27	29	32	35	37
54	India	315,760	336,737	370,475	402,271	433,257	457,110
55	Indonesia	2,145	2,472	2,793	3,145	3,533	3,851
56	Iran (Islamic Republic of)	844	961	1,124	1,303	1,489	1,655
57	Iraq	307	383	478	586	717	853
58	Ireland	268	285	313	363	419	439
59	Israel	260	315	366	408	482	536
60	Italy	3,484	3,644	3,808	4,045	4,280	4,510
61	Jamaica	42	46	50	53	56	57
62	Japan	12,310	12,931	13,528	13,987	14,505	14,688
63	Jordan	63	90	106	127	165	197
64	Kazakhstan	571	567	552	576	648	705
65	Kenya	2,526	2,913	3,262	3,822	4,624	5,208
66	Kuwait	708	554	651	745	869	966
67	Kyrgyzstan	125	135	150	164	179	195
68	Lao People's Democratic Republic	110	127	143	156	172	185
69	Latvia	114	110	108	106	102	99
70	Lesotho	1,007	1,051	1,036	986	1,050	1,069
71	Liberia	1,792	1,652	2,324	2,622	3,330	3,627
72	Lithuania	186	194	197	193	188	183
73	Luxembourg	49	55	60	66	74	84
74	Malawi	3,519	3,622	4,046	4,698	5,850	6,892
75	Malaysia	168	207	252	298	344	381
76	Maldives	5	7	8	9	11	12
77	Mali	3,614	4,092	4,704	5,528	6,497	7,355
78	Malta	15	16	17	19	20	22
79	Mauritania	1,030	1,200	1,349	1,536	1,741	1,915
80	Mauritius	23	25	28	29	31	32
81	Mexico	1,747	2,045	2,363	2,631	2,968	3,247
82	Mongolia	110	121	130	140	152	165
83	Morocco	2,947	3,228	3,484	3,730	3,980	4,186
84	Mozambique	10,148	12,536	14,347	15,947	18,087	20,200
85	Myanmar	2,864	3,130	3,398	3,631	3,838	4,000
86	Namibia	75	88	102	111	126	141
87	Nepal	2,642	3,083	3,448	3,751	3,998	4,266
88	Netherlands	1,344	1,426	1,507	1,584	1,640	1,688
89	New Zealand	217	245	264	288	308	324
90	Nicaragua	148	174	192	210	228	241
91	Niger	3,998	4,695	5,581	6,710	8,148	9,452

	Country/year	1990	1995	2000	2005	2010	2014
92	Nigeria	25,718	29,233	33,063	38,005	43,909	49,003
93	Norway	596	623	653	683	735	788
94	Pakistan	1,033	1,207	1,397	1,603	1,853	2,087
95	Panama	33	38	44	50	56	62
96	Papua New Guinea	3,912	4,497	5,155	5,853	6,529	7,032
97	Paraguay	37	43	50	58	64	70
98	Peru	211	245	278	309	343	374
99	Philippines	1,342	1,579	1,823	2,085	2,329	2,533
100	Poland	1,501	1,560	1,599	1,637	1,674	1,707
101	Portugal	341	360	392	429	458	466
102	Qatar	21	23	27	39	82	102
103	Republic of Korea	1,301	1,465	1,635	1,762	1,903	1,996
104	Republic of Moldova	87	91	93	96	98	100
105	Romania	920	933	957	947	931	940
106	Russian Federation	12,773	12,865	12,753	12,543	12,708	12,962
107	Rwanda	794	629	962	1,127	1,343	1,513
108	Saudi Arabia	452	572	695	890	1,091	1,267
109	Senegal	1,891	2,160	2,444	2,803	3,239	3,614
110	Serbia	793	794	788	787	789	783
111	Sierra Leone	4,167	3,834	3,767	4,801	5,497	5,939
112	Singapore	121	150	182	199	254	285
113	Slovakia	246	253	261	264	272	279
114	Slovenia	99	101	104	107	111	114
115	South Africa	3,163	3,491	3,807	4,050	4,459	4,801
116	Spain	1,796	1,982	2,132	2,433	2,709	2,796
117	Sri Lanka	292	331	369	385	392	449
118	Sudan (former)	6,279	7,807	8,939	10,271	10,727	11,597
119	Swaziland	14	17	20	22	25	28
120	Sweden	807	861	903	951	1,014	1,070
121	Switzerland	1,047	1,117	1,159	1,210	1,295	1,365
122	Syrian Arab Republic	336	397	464	527	618	535
123	Tajikistan	141	162	179	200	227	252
124	Thailand	1,146	1,263	1,406	1,555	1,657	1,752
125	Togo	276	311	365	420	490	558
126	Trinidad and Tobago	52	55	57	60	63	65
127	Tunisia	157	184	211	237	273	305
128	Turkey	952	1,076	1,214	1,359	1,498	1,662
129	Uganda	8,820	10,403	12,068	14,814	17,859	20,695
130	Ukraine	17,579	17,244	16,241	15,419	15,267	15,132

(*Continued*)

Table A3.5 (Continued)

	Country/year	1990	1995	2000	2005	2010	2014
131	United Arab Emirates	971	1,309	1,719	2,245	3,008	3,396
132	United Kingdom	3,960	4,117	4,323	4,548	4,848	5,129
133	United Republic of Tanzania	8,259	9,635	10,926	12,798	15,218	17,381
134	United States of America	22,901	24,852	26,787	28,289	30,118	31,265
135	Uruguay	190	200	210	214	220	225
136	Venezuela (Bolivarian Republic of)	315	367	419	478	536	587
137	Viet Nam	618	703	777	846	924	991
138	Yemen	1,758	2,185	2,575	3,016	3,529	3,981
139	Zambia	5,642	6,401	7,309	8,597	10,529	12,037
140	Zimbabwe	10,625	11,013	10,872	10,575	11,484	14,190

Table A3.6 Human capital per capita (Human capital per capita in thousands of constant 2005 US$)

	Country/year	1990	1995	2000	2005	2010	2014
1	Afghanistan	11.6	11.9	12.6	12.9	13.7	14.2
2	Albania	22.3	23.0	24.0	24.8	25.7	26.2
3	Algeria	20.3	22.1	24.3	26.2	28.3	29.6
4	Argentina	30.8	31.9	33.0	34.1	35.3	36.3
5	Armenia	31.4	31.9	32.7	33.3	34.1	34.4
6	Australia	93.5	95.9	99.3	102.7	106.3	108.4
7	Austria	97.7	100.2	101.9	103.7	105.4	107.6
8	Bahrain	33.9	35.7	37.2	39.2	41.6	42.7
9	Bangladesh	86.1	86.2	85.9	85.7	86.6	86.6
10	Barbados	39.7	41.1	40.9	42.8	43.2	45.9
11	Belgium	89.3	92.4	96.4	99.8	103.2	106.1
12	Belize	6.7	6.9	7.1	7.2	7.4	7.6
13	Benin	407.3	409.2	413.3	412.1	417.0	420.1
14	Bolivia (Plurinational State of)	19.2	19.7	20.6	21.2	21.9	22.7
15	Botswana	328.2	319.9	306.5	321.6	345.5	349.4
16	Brazil	12.8	13.4	13.8	14.4	15.0	15.5
17	Bulgaria	263.4	255.4	250.3	253.7	259.5	261.2
18	Burundi	487.9	466.1	498.0	498.1	497.5	501.7
19	Cambodia	9.9	10.1	10.3	10.3	10.7	10.9
20	Cameroon	162.5	161.5	160.6	162.4	166.5	168.5
21	Canada	76.9	78.9	81.6	83.7	85.1	86.9

	Country/year	1990	1995	2000	2005	2010	2014
22	Central African Republic	158.9	159.6	159.3	160.3	166.9	169.7
23	Chile	25.6	26.7	27.9	28.9	29.9	30.7
24	China	20.3	21.6	22.5	23.5	24.5	25.2
25	Colombia	15.3	16.1	16.8	17.5	18.2	18.9
26	Congo	292.3	294.8	293.3	309.5	336.9	337.9
27	Costa Rica	11.9	12.3	12.7	13.1	13.5	13.8
28	Côte d'Ivoire	168.8	166.9	163.0	166.1	169.5	168.2
29	Croatia	52.9	54.3	56.6	58.6	60.3	62.0
30	Cuba	28.1	29.5	30.5	31.6	32.4	33.1
31	Cyprus	46.9	49.8	52.8	56.1	59.0	61.0
32	Czech Republic	58.6	61.6	62.7	63.2	64.8	65.7
33	Democratic Republic of the Congo	0.5	0.6	0.6	0.6	0.7	0.7
34	Denmark	111.3	113.2	115.1	117.1	118.1	119.7
35	Dominican Republic	19.4	20.0	20.9	21.6	22.6	23.2
36	Ecuador	11.2	11.7	12.3	12.9	13.4	13.9
37	Egypt	60.7	61.9	61.7	63.3	65.8	68.0
38	El Salvador	22.4	23.3	24.3	25.3	26.4	27.4
39	Estonia	51.8	53.1	55.0	56.4	57.9	58.6
40	Fiji	15.3	16.8	16.3	15.8	16.5	18.1
41	Finland	100.5	104.0	106.7	109.4	122.2	122.2
42	France	68.3	71.3	74.4	76.9	79.6	81.8
43	Gabon	11.7	12.5	13.3	14.3	15.1	15.8
44	Gambia	6.5	6.8	7.2	7.6	8.0	8.4
45	Germany	114.0	115.9	117.9	118.9	120.9	122.6
46	Ghana	84.9	82.8	81.1	80.5	80.6	80.6
47	Greece	55.6	59.0	62.1	65.4	68.2	70.1
48	Guatemala	131.7	132.1	131.2	129.3	129.5	129.3
49	Guyana	2.5	2.6	2.6	2.7	2.8	2.8
50	Haiti	425.7	433.4	443.3	451.3	365.6	444.5
51	Honduras	3.5	3.6	3.8	3.9	4.1	4.2
52	Hungary	53.4	56.7	59.1	61.2	62.7	64.5
53	Iceland	99.5	101.2	103.9	107.5	110.2	112.5
54	India	362.7	350.4	351.8	351.6	352.0	353.0
55	Indonesia	11.8	12.5	13.2	13.9	14.6	15.1
56	Iran (Islamic Republic of)	15.0	15.9	17.1	18.6	20.1	21.2
57	Iraq	17.5	18.9	20.3	21.7	23.2	24.2
58	Ireland	76.3	78.9	82.3	87.4	91.9	95.1
59	Israel	55.7	56.9	58.2	58.9	63.3	65.3
60	Italy	61.4	64.1	66.9	69.8	72.2	74.2
61	Jamaica	17.8	18.7	19.5	20.2	20.7	21.1
62	Japan	99.7	103.1	106.7	109.4	113.2	115.6
63	Jordan	18.7	20.8	22.3	23.9	25.3	26.6
64	Kazakhstan	35.0	35.9	37.1	38.1	39.7	40.8

(*Continued*)

Table A3.6 (Continued)

	Country/year	1990	1995	2000	2005	2010	2014
65	Kenya	107.7	106.4	105.0	108.1	114.7	116.1
66	Kuwait	343.7	338.2	337.6	329.1	283.9	257.3
67	Kyrgyzstan	28.4	29.6	30.6	31.7	32.8	33.5
68	Lao People's Democratic Republic	25.8	26.2	26.7	27.2	27.5	27.7
69	Latvia	42.7	44.2	45.7	47.3	48.5	49.5
70	Lesotho	630.5	599.3	558.0	512.1	522.2	506.7
71	Liberia	852.3	794.3	803.6	801.8	841.4	824.9
72	Lithuania	50.4	53.4	56.2	58.2	60.7	62.4
73	Luxembourg	129.3	133.8	137.2	142.0	146.9	151.0
74	Malawi	374.1	368.7	361.5	368.5	396.1	412.8
75	Malaysia	9.3	10.0	10.8	11.5	12.2	12.8
76	Maldives	24.7	25.8	27.1	28.2	30.2	30.0
77	Mali	426.1	424.4	425.8	429.2	428.3	430.5
78	Malta	41.5	42.9	44.8	46.7	48.7	50.8
79	Mauritania	508.9	514.3	497.7	487.1	484.7	482.4
80	Mauritius	21.5	22.2	23.2	24.0	24.8	25.3
81	Mexico	20.4	21.7	23.0	24.0	25.0	25.9
82	Mongolia	50.6	52.6	54.4	55.4	56.0	56.6
83	Morocco	118.1	118.8	120.4	122.7	123.9	123.4
84	Mozambique	758.9	787.8	785.5	754.8	743.7	742.2
85	Myanmar	68.2	70.0	71.3	72.6	74.2	74.9
86	Namibia	52.7	53.0	53.5	54.9	57.5	58.7
87	Nepal	141.0	144.1	145.2	147.0	148.8	151.4
88	Netherlands	89.9	92.2	94.6	97.0	98.7	100.1
89	New Zealand	65.1	66.8	68.5	69.7	70.9	71.9
90	Nicaragua	35.6	37.7	38.2	39.0	39.7	40.0
91	Niger	505.3	501.5	497.2	497.6	500.1	494.5
92	Nigeria	269.0	269.7	269.0	272.2	275.5	276.1
93	Norway	140.5	142.9	145.3	147.8	150.4	153.5
94	Pakistan	9.6	9.8	10.1	10.4	10.9	11.3
95	Panama	13.2	13.9	14.5	15.0	15.6	16.0
96	Papua New Guinea	941.0	953.6	959.2	961.6	953.4	942.2
97	Paraguay	8.8	9.1	9.5	9.9	10.4	10.6
98	Peru	9.7	10.2	10.7	11.2	11.7	12.1
99	Philippines	21.7	22.6	23.4	24.2	25.0	25.6
100	Poland	39.4	40.4	41.8	42.9	44.0	44.9
101	Portugal	34.1	35.9	38.1	40.8	43.3	44.8
102	Qatar	43.1	44.9	45.7	46.5	46.5	46.8
103	Republic of Korea	30.4	32.5	34.8	36.6	38.5	39.6
104	Republic of Moldova	23.6	24.8	25.7	26.6	27.5	28.1
105	Romania	39.6	41.1	42.6	44.4	46.0	47.2
106	Russian Federation	86.1	86.7	87.0	87.4	89.0	90.1
107	Rwanda	109.3	106.4	119.9	125.2	130.5	133.4

	Country/year	1990	1995	2000	2005	2010	2014
108	Saudi Arabia	27.6	30.4	32.5	36.0	38.8	41.0
109	Senegal	251.7	248.0	247.9	248.7	250.0	246.3
110	Serbia	104.5	104.1	104.9	105.8	108.2	109.8
111	Sierra Leone	1,059.9	999.0	927.7	946.6	951.6	940.4
112	Singapore	39.8	42.6	45.2	46.8	50.1	52.1
113	Slovakia	46.4	47.1	48.4	49.2	50.5	51.5
114	Slovenia	49.5	50.8	52.1	53.4	54.3	55.4
115	South Africa	89.9	89.2	86.5	85.7	87.8	88.8
116	Spain	46.2	50.3	53.0	55.7	58.2	60.2
117	Sri Lanka	17.1	18.3	19.8	19.9	19.5	21.6
118	Sudan (former)	313.8	316.2	318.4	321.1	297.0	294.7
119	Swaziland	16.1	17.2	18.4	19.7	21.1	22.3
120	Sweden	94.3	97.6	101.8	105.4	108.1	110.3
121	Switzerland	156.0	158.6	161.4	162.7	165.5	166.7
122	Syrian Arab Republic	27.0	27.7	28.3	29.1	29.8	28.5
123	Tajikistan	26.6	28.0	28.9	29.4	29.9	30.3
124	Thailand	20.3	21.3	22.4	23.6	24.8	25.9
125	Togo	72.8	72.6	74.9	75.2	76.7	78.5
126	Trinidad and Tobago	42.2	43.7	45.3	46.1	47.4	48.2
127	Tunisia	19.2	20.6	22.0	23.6	25.9	27.7
128	Turkey	17.6	18.4	19.2	20.0	20.7	21.4
129	Uganda	507.3	509.6	507.9	528.3	538.8	547.7
130	Ukraine	338.8	334.8	330.3	327.3	332.8	333.6
131	United Arab Emirates	536.0	557.0	563.5	500.9	361.1	373.8
132	United Kingdom	69.2	71.0	73.4	75.3	77.2	79.4
133	United Republic of Tanzania	324.4	322.2	321.4	327.6	333.4	335.4
134	United States of America	91.7	93.3	94.9	95.7	97.4	98.0
135	Uruguay	61.0	61.9	63.1	64.4	65.2	65.9
136	Venezuela (Bolivarian Republic of)	15.9	16.5	17.1	17.9	18.5	19.1
137	Viet Nam	9.4	9.8	10.0	10.3	10.6	10.9
138	Yemen	147.0	143.1	144.7	147.1	149.6	152.0
139	Zambia	692.9	691.7	690.5	713.8	756.5	765.7
140	Zimbabwe	1,013.4	942.7	869.8	814.4	821.8	930.8

Table A3.7 Human capital growth (Human capital change (%) with respect to base year 1990)

	Country/year	1995	2000	2005	2010	2014
1	Afghanistan	7.5%	15.4%	22.7%	28.7%	47.8%
2	Albania	0.1%	0.4%	0.6%	0.6%	1.3%
3	Algeria	4.0%	9.5%	13.5%	18.0%	30.0%

(*Continued*)

Table A3.7 (Continued)

	Country/year	1995	2000	2005	2010	2014
4	Argentina	2.0%	4.9%	7.3%	9.6%	15.6%
5	Armenia	−1.5%	−2.5%	−2.5%	−2.3%	−2.4%
6	Australia	1.7%	4.5%	7.0%	10.0%	16.8%
7	Austria	1.2%	2.1%	3.3%	4.1%	7.0%
8	Bahrain	3.6%	10.2%	19.2%	32.9%	51.3%
9	Bangladesh	2.3%	5.4%	7.6%	9.5%	14.7%
10	Barbados	1.1%	1.7%	3.2%	4.0%	8.0%
11	Belgium	1.0%	2.6%	4.1%	6.0%	10.2%
12	Belize	2.5%	8.5%	13.0%	17.4%	28.5%
13	Benin	3.8%	9.0%	13.4%	18.1%	29.8%
14	Bolivia (Plurinational State of)	2.5%	6.8%	10.0%	13.3%	22.1%
15	Botswana	2.2%	4.1%	7.3%	11.8%	19.6%
16	Brazil	2.5%	6.0%	9.0%	11.6%	18.3%
17	Bulgaria	−1.3%	−2.9%	−3.8%	−4.4%	−6.3%
18	Burundi	1.2%	5.3%	9.6%	14.5%	25.6%
19	Cambodia	3.9%	8.7%	11.3%	14.4%	23.0%
20	Cameroon	2.8%	6.9%	10.7%	15.0%	25.1%
21	Canada	1.6%	4.1%	6.1%	7.9%	13.1%
22	Central African Republic	2.7%	6.2%	8.6%	12.3%	20.4%
23	Chile	2.4%	5.9%	8.4%	10.8%	17.4%
24	China	2.4%	5.4%	7.3%	9.2%	14.2%
25	Colombia	2.8%	6.7%	9.7%	12.5%	19.9%
26	Congo	2.8%	6.9%	11.7%	18.4%	29.7%
27	Costa Rica	3.2%	7.9%	10.8%	13.6%	21.2%
28	Côte d'Ivoire	3.2%	7.0%	10.0%	13.5%	22.0%
29	Croatia	0.1%	−0.2%	0.7%	1.3%	1.3%
30	Cuba	1.6%	3.4%	4.6%	5.4%	8.2%
31	Cyprus	3.4%	8.5%	12.6%	16.0%	25.1%
32	Czech Republic	1.0%	1.5%	1.6%	2.9%	4.6%
33	Democratic Republic of the Congo	4.7%	10.8%	16.4%	22.5%	38.4%
34	Denmark	0.7%	1.8%	2.6%	3.4%	5.7%
35	Dominican Republic	2.6%	6.5%	9.5%	12.6%	20.2%
36	Ecuador	3.2%	7.9%	11.4%	15.0%	24.4%
37	Egypt	2.5%	5.4%	8.5%	12.1%	21.2%
38	El Salvador	2.1%	4.6%	6.3%	7.9%	12.4%
39	Estonia	−1.2%	−1.4%	−1.5%	−1.3%	−1.7%
40	Fiji	3.1%	4.2%	3.7%	6.2%	12.8%
41	Finland	1.2%	2.5%	3.5%	6.9%	10.0%
42	France	1.2%	3.2%	5.0%	6.7%	10.8%
43	Gabon	4.1%	10.1%	15.2%	20.2%	33.6%
44	Gambia	3.9%	10.1%	16.1%	22.7%	39.0%
45	Germany	0.9%	1.7%	2.0%	2.2%	3.1%
46	Ghana	2.3%	5.3%	8.5%	12.1%	20.2%
47	Greece	1.9%	4.3%	6.1%	7.5%	10.4%

	Country/year	1995	2000	2005	2010	2014
48	Guatemala	2.5%	6.2%	9.0%	12.1%	19.7%
49	Guyana	0.7%	2.3%	2.9%	4.0%	6.0%
50	Haiti	2.3%	5.8%	8.4%	4.9%	15.8%
51	Honduras	3.5%	8.3%	12.1%	15.8%	25.5%
52	Hungary	1.1%	2.2%	2.7%	3.2%	4.7%
53	Iceland	1.3%	3.6%	5.9%	8.4%	13.2%
54	India	1.3%	4.1%	6.2%	8.2%	13.1%
55	Indonesia	2.9%	6.8%	10.0%	13.3%	21.5%
56	Iran (Islamic Republic of)	2.6%	7.4%	11.5%	15.3%	25.2%
57	Iraq	4.5%	11.7%	17.6%	23.7%	40.7%
58	Ireland	1.2%	4.0%	7.9%	11.8%	17.9%
59	Israel	4.0%	9.0%	11.9%	16.7%	27.3%
60	Italy	0.9%	2.2%	3.8%	5.3%	9.0%
61	Jamaica	1.8%	4.4%	5.9%	7.0%	10.6%
62	Japan	1.0%	2.4%	3.2%	4.2%	6.1%
63	Jordan	7.5%	14.1%	19.4%	27.4%	46.5%
64	Kazakhstan	−0.2%	−0.9%	0.2%	3.2%	7.3%
65	Kenya	2.9%	6.6%	10.9%	16.3%	27.3%
66	Kuwait	−4.8%	−2.1%	1.3%	5.3%	10.9%
67	Kyrgyzstan	1.6%	4.8%	7.0%	9.4%	16.2%
68	Lao People's Democratic Republic	3.0%	6.8%	9.2%	11.9%	19.0%
69	Latvia	−0.7%	−1.2%	−1.8%	−2.7%	−4.6%
70	Lesotho	0.9%	0.7%	−0.5%	1.0%	2.0%
71	Liberia	−1.6%	6.7%	10.0%	16.8%	26.5%
72	Lithuania	0.8%	1.4%	0.9%	0.2%	−0.6%
73	Luxembourg	2.1%	4.9%	7.5%	10.8%	19.4%
74	Malawi	0.6%	3.5%	7.5%	13.5%	25.1%
75	Malaysia	4.2%	10.6%	15.3%	19.6%	31.3%
76	Maldives	4.1%	9.5%	13.9%	19.7%	30.6%
77	Mali	2.5%	6.8%	11.2%	15.8%	26.7%
78	Malta	1.6%	3.8%	6.5%	8.3%	13.9%
79	Mauritania	3.1%	7.0%	10.5%	14.0%	23.0%
80	Mauritius	1.9%	4.9%	6.7%	8.1%	12.0%
81	Mexico	3.2%	7.8%	10.8%	14.2%	22.9%
82	Mongolia	1.8%	4.2%	6.1%	8.3%	14.3%
83	Morocco	1.8%	4.3%	6.1%	7.8%	12.4%
84	Mozambique	4.3%	9.0%	12.0%	15.5%	25.8%
85	Myanmar	1.8%	4.4%	6.1%	7.6%	11.8%
86	Namibia	3.3%	8.0%	10.5%	14.0%	23.6%
87	Nepal	3.1%	6.9%	9.2%	10.9%	17.3%
88	Netherlands	1.2%	2.9%	4.2%	5.1%	7.9%
89	New Zealand	2.5%	5.1%	7.4%	9.2%	14.3%
90	Nicaragua	3.3%	6.8%	9.2%	11.5%	17.7%
91	Niger	3.3%	8.7%	13.8%	19.5%	33.2%

(*Continued*)

Table A3.7 (Continued)

	Country/year	1995	2000	2005	2010	2014
92	Nigeria	2.6%	6.5%	10.3%	14.3%	24.0%
93	Norway	0.9%	2.3%	3.5%	5.4%	9.8%
94	Pakistan	3.2%	7.8%	11.6%	15.7%	26.4%
95	Panama	3.1%	7.7%	11.1%	14.6%	23.6%
96	Papua New Guinea	2.8%	7.1%	10.6%	13.7%	21.6%
97	Paraguay	3.2%	8.0%	11.6%	14.7%	23.4%
98	Peru	3.0%	7.1%	10.0%	12.9%	21.0%
99	Philippines	3.3%	8.0%	11.6%	14.8%	23.6%
100	Poland	0.8%	1.6%	2.2%	2.8%	4.4%
101	Portugal	1.1%	3.6%	5.9%	7.7%	11.0%
102	Qatar	1.9%	7.2%	17.3%	41.4%	70.5%
103	Republic of Korea	2.4%	5.9%	7.9%	10.0%	15.3%
104	Republic of Moldova	0.9%	1.8%	2.3%	2.9%	4.6%
105	Romania	0.3%	1.0%	0.7%	0.3%	0.7%
106	Russian Federation	0.1%	0.0%	-0.5%	-0.1%	0.5%
107	Rwanda	-4.5%	4.9%	9.2%	14.1%	24.0%
108	Saudi Arabia	4.8%	11.3%	18.4%	24.6%	41.0%
109	Senegal	2.7%	6.6%	10.3%	14.4%	24.1%
110	Serbia	0.0%	-0.1%	-0.2%	-0.1%	-0.4%
111	Sierra Leone	-1.7%	-2.5%	3.6%	7.2%	12.5%
112	Singapore	4.4%	10.7%	13.3%	20.3%	33.0%
113	Slovakia	0.6%	1.5%	1.8%	2.6%	4.3%
114	Slovenia	0.4%	1.2%	2.0%	3.0%	5.0%
115	South Africa	2.0%	4.7%	6.4%	9.0%	14.9%
116	Spain	2.0%	4.4%	7.9%	10.8%	15.9%
117	Sri Lanka	2.6%	6.1%	7.2%	7.7%	15.5%
118	Sudan (former)	4.5%	9.2%	13.1%	14.3%	22.7%
119	Swaziland	3.6%	9.0%	11.9%	16.1%	26.8%
120	Sweden	1.3%	2.9%	4.2%	5.9%	9.8%
121	Switzerland	1.3%	2.6%	3.7%	5.5%	9.2%
122	Syrian Arab Republic	3.4%	8.4%	11.9%	16.5%	16.8%
123	Tajikistan	2.8%	6.2%	9.2%	12.7%	21.4%
124	Thailand	2.0%	5.2%	7.9%	9.6%	15.2%
125	Togo	2.4%	7.3%	11.1%	15.5%	26.5%
126	Trinidad and Tobago	1.2%	2.7%	3.8%	5.1%	8.2%
127	Tunisia	3.3%	7.6%	10.8%	14.9%	24.8%
128	Turkey	2.5%	6.3%	9.3%	12.0%	20.4%
129	Uganda	3.4%	8.2%	13.8%	19.3%	32.9%
130	Ukraine	-0.4%	-2.0%	-3.2%	-3.5%	-4.9%
131	United Arab Emirates	6.2%	15.3%	23.3%	32.7%	51.8%
132	United Kingdom	0.8%	2.2%	3.5%	5.2%	9.0%
133	United Republic of Tanzania	3.1%	7.2%	11.6%	16.5%	28.2%
134	United States of America	1.6%	4.0%	5.4%	7.1%	10.9%
135	Uruguay	1.0%	2.5%	3.1%	3.8%	5.9%

	Country/year	1995	2000	2005	2010	2014
136	Venezuela (Bolivarian Republic of)	3.1%	7.4%	11.0%	14.2%	23.0%
137	Viet Nam	2.6%	5.9%	8.2%	10.6%	17.1%
138	Yemen	4.4%	10.0%	14.4%	19.0%	31.3%
139	Zambia	2.6%	6.7%	11.1%	16.9%	28.7%
140	Zimbabwe	0.7%	0.6%	-0.1%	2.0%	10.1%

Table A3.8 Human capital per capita growth (Human capital per capita change (%) with respect to base year 1990)

	Country/year	1995	2000	2005	2010	2014
1	Afghanistan	0.7%	2.1%	2.9%	4.3%	7.2%
2	Albania	0.7%	1.9%	2.8%	3.7%	5.7%
3	Algeria	1.7%	4.6%	6.6%	8.6%	13.5%
4	Argentina	0.7%	1.7%	2.6%	3.5%	5.6%
5	Armenia	0.3%	1.1%	1.5%	2.1%	3.1%
6	Australia	0.5%	1.5%	2.4%	3.2%	5.1%
7	Austria	0.5%	1.1%	1.5%	1.9%	3.3%
8	Bahrain	1.0%	2.4%	3.7%	5.2%	8.0%
9	Bangladesh	0.0%	0.0%	-0.1%	0.1%	0.2%
10	Barbados	0.7%	0.8%	1.9%	2.1%	5.0%
11	Belgium	0.7%	1.9%	2.8%	3.7%	5.9%
12	Belize	0.5%	1.3%	1.9%	2.6%	4.2%
13	Benin	0.1%	0.4%	0.3%	0.6%	1.0%
14	Bolivia (Plurinational State of)	0.5%	1.7%	2.4%	3.3%	5.7%
15	Botswana	-0.5%	-1.7%	-0.5%	1.3%	2.1%
16	Brazil	0.9%	1.9%	3.0%	4.1%	6.5%
17	Bulgaria	-0.6%	-1.3%	-0.9%	-0.4%	-0.3%
18	Burundi	-0.9%	0.5%	0.5%	0.5%	0.9%
19	Cambodia	0.4%	0.8%	0.9%	1.8%	3.0%
20	Cameroon	-0.1%	-0.3%	0.0%	0.6%	1.2%
21	Canada	0.5%	1.5%	2.1%	2.6%	4.2%
22	Central African Republic	0.1%	0.1%	0.2%	1.2%	2.2%
23	Chile	0.9%	2.1%	3.0%	3.9%	6.2%
24	China	1.2%	2.6%	3.7%	4.8%	7.4%
25	Colombia	1.0%	2.4%	3.5%	4.6%	7.3%
26	Congo	0.2%	0.1%	1.4%	3.6%	5.0%
27	Costa Rica	0.7%	1.7%	2.4%	3.2%	5.1%
28	Côte d'Ivoire	-0.2%	-0.9%	-0.4%	0.1%	-0.1%
29	Croatia	0.6%	1.7%	2.6%	3.3%	5.4%
30	Cuba	1.0%	2.1%	3.0%	3.7%	5.7%
31	Cyprus	1.2%	3.0%	4.6%	5.9%	9.2%
32	Czech Republic	1.0%	1.7%	1.9%	2.6%	3.9%

(*Continued*)

Table A3.8 (Continued)

	Country/year	1995	2000	2005	2010	2014
33	Democratic Republic of the Congo	0.9%	2.4%	3.5%	4.6%	7.3%
34	Denmark	0.3%	0.9%	1.3%	1.5%	2.5%
35	Dominican Republic	0.7%	1.9%	2.8%	3.9%	6.2%
36	Ecuador	0.9%	2.4%	3.5%	4.6%	7.3%
37	Egypt	0.4%	0.4%	1.1%	2.0%	3.8%
38	El Salvador	0.8%	2.0%	3.1%	4.2%	6.9%
39	Estonia	0.5%	1.5%	2.1%	2.8%	4.2%
40	Fiji	1.8%	1.5%	0.7%	1.9%	5.7%
41	Finland	0.7%	1.5%	2.1%	5.0%	6.7%
42	France	0.9%	2.1%	3.0%	3.9%	6.2%
43	Gabon	1.4%	3.2%	5.0%	6.6%	10.4%
44	Gambia	0.9%	2.4%	3.7%	5.2%	8.5%
45	Germany	0.3%	0.9%	1.1%	1.5%	2.5%
46	Ghana	−0.5%	−1.1%	−1.3%	−1.3%	−1.7%
47	Greece	1.2%	2.8%	4.1%	5.2%	8.0%
48	Guatemala	0.1%	−0.1%	−0.5%	−0.4%	−0.6%
49	Guyana	0.5%	1.5%	2.1%	2.8%	4.0%
50	Haiti	0.4%	1.0%	1.5%	−3.7%	1.4%
51	Honduras	0.9%	1.9%	3.0%	4.1%	6.7%
52	Hungary	1.2%	2.6%	3.5%	4.1%	6.5%
53	Iceland	0.3%	1.1%	1.9%	2.6%	4.2%
54	India	−0.7%	−0.8%	−0.8%	−0.7%	−0.9%
55	Indonesia	1.2%	2.8%	4.1%	5.5%	8.6%
56	Iran (Islamic Republic of)	1.2%	3.2%	5.5%	7.5%	12.1%
57	Iraq	1.5%	3.7%	5.5%	7.3%	11.3%
58	Ireland	0.7%	1.9%	3.5%	4.8%	7.6%
59	Israel	0.4%	1.1%	1.4%	3.2%	5.4%
60	Italy	0.9%	2.1%	3.2%	4.1%	6.5%
61	Jamaica	1.0%	2.4%	3.2%	3.9%	6.0%
62	Japan	0.7%	1.7%	2.4%	3.2%	5.1%
63	Jordan	2.2%	4.6%	6.4%	8.0%	12.5%
64	Kazakhstan	0.5%	1.5%	2.1%	3.2%	5.3%
65	Kenya	−0.2%	−0.6%	0.1%	1.6%	2.5%
66	Kuwait	−0.3%	−0.5%	−1.1%	−4.7%	−9.2%
67	Kyrgyzstan	0.9%	1.9%	2.8%	3.7%	5.7%
68	Lao People's Democratic Republic	0.3%	0.9%	1.3%	1.5%	2.3%
69	Latvia	0.7%	1.7%	2.6%	3.2%	5.1%
70	Lesotho	−1.0%	−3.0%	−5.1%	−4.6%	−7.0%
71	Liberia	−1.4%	−1.5%	−1.5%	−0.3%	−1.1%
72	Lithuania	1.2%	2.8%	3.7%	4.8%	7.4%
73	Luxembourg	0.7%	1.5%	2.4%	3.2%	5.3%
74	Malawi	−0.3%	−0.9%	−0.4%	1.4%	3.3%

	Country/year	1995	2000	2005	2010	2014
75	Malaysia	1.5%	3.9%	5.7%	7.3%	11.3%
76	Maldives	0.9%	2.3%	3.4%	5.1%	6.6%
77	Mali	−0.1%	0.0%	0.2%	0.1%	0.3%
78	Malta	0.7%	1.9%	3.0%	4.1%	7.0%
79	Mauritania	0.2%	−0.6%	−1.1%	−1.2%	−1.8%
80	Mauritius	0.7%	1.9%	2.8%	3.7%	5.7%
81	Mexico	1.2%	3.0%	4.1%	5.2%	8.3%
82	Mongolia	0.8%	1.8%	2.3%	2.6%	3.8%
83	Morocco	0.1%	0.5%	1.0%	1.2%	1.5%
84	Mozambique	0.7%	0.9%	−0.1%	−0.5%	−0.7%
85	Myanmar	0.5%	1.1%	1.6%	2.1%	3.2%
86	Namibia	0.1%	0.4%	1.0%	2.2%	3.6%
87	Nepal	0.4%	0.7%	1.1%	1.4%	2.4%
88	Netherlands	0.5%	1.3%	1.9%	2.4%	3.6%
89	New Zealand	0.5%	1.3%	1.7%	2.1%	3.3%
90	Nicaragua	1.2%	1.8%	2.3%	2.8%	4.0%
91	Niger	−0.2%	−0.4%	−0.4%	−0.3%	−0.7%
92	Nigeria	0.1%	0.0%	0.3%	0.6%	0.9%
93	Norway	0.3%	0.9%	1.3%	1.7%	3.0%
94	Pakistan	0.5%	1.3%	2.1%	3.2%	5.5%
95	Panama	1.0%	2.4%	3.2%	4.1%	6.5%
96	Papua New Guinea	0.3%	0.5%	0.5%	0.3%	0.0%
97	Paraguay	0.7%	1.9%	3.0%	4.1%	6.5%
98	Peru	1.0%	2.6%	3.7%	4.8%	7.6%
99	Philippines	0.9%	1.9%	2.8%	3.7%	5.7%
100	Poland	0.5%	1.5%	2.1%	2.8%	4.5%
101	Portugal	1.0%	2.8%	4.6%	6.1%	9.5%
102	Qatar	0.9%	1.5%	1.9%	1.9%	2.8%
103	Republic of Korea	1.4%	3.5%	4.8%	6.1%	9.2%
104	Republic of Moldova	1.0%	2.1%	3.0%	3.9%	6.0%
105	Romania	0.7%	1.8%	2.9%	3.8%	6.0%
106	Russian Federation	0.1%	0.2%	0.4%	0.8%	1.5%
107	Rwanda	−0.5%	2.3%	3.4%	4.5%	6.9%
108	Saudi Arabia	1.9%	4.1%	6.8%	8.9%	14.0%
109	Senegal	−0.3%	−0.4%	−0.3%	−0.2%	−0.7%
110	Serbia	−0.1%	0.1%	0.3%	0.9%	1.7%
111	Sierra Leone	−1.2%	−3.3%	−2.8%	−2.7%	−3.9%
112	Singapore	1.4%	3.2%	4.1%	5.9%	9.4%
113	Slovakia	0.3%	1.1%	1.5%	2.1%	3.6%
114	Slovenia	0.5%	1.3%	1.9%	2.4%	3.9%
115	South Africa	−0.1%	−0.9%	−1.2%	−0.6%	−0.4%
116	Spain	1.7%	3.5%	4.8%	5.9%	9.2%
117	Sri Lanka	1.4%	3.7%	3.9%	3.3%	8.2%
118	Sudan (former)	0.1%	0.4%	0.6%	−1.4%	−2.1%

(Continued)

Table A3.8 (Continued)

	Country/year	1995	2000	2005	2010	2014
119	Swaziland	1.4%	3.5%	5.2%	7.0%	11.5%
120	Sweden	0.7%	1.9%	2.8%	3.5%	5.4%
121	Switzerland	0.3%	0.9%	1.1%	1.5%	2.2%
122	Syrian Arab Republic	0.5%	1.3%	1.9%	2.6%	1.9%
123	Tajikistan	1.0%	2.1%	2.6%	3.0%	4.5%
124	Thailand	1.0%	2.6%	3.9%	5.2%	8.5%
125	Togo	-0.1%	0.7%	0.8%	1.3%	2.5%
126	Trinidad and Tobago	0.7%	1.8%	2.3%	3.0%	4.5%
127	Tunisia	1.4%	3.5%	5.2%	7.7%	13.0%
128	Turkey	0.9%	2.1%	3.2%	4.1%	6.7%
129	Uganda	0.1%	0.0%	1.0%	1.5%	2.6%
130	Ukraine	-0.2%	-0.6%	-0.9%	-0.4%	-0.5%
131	United Arab Emirates	0.8%	1.3%	-1.7%	-9.4%	-11.3%
132	United Kingdom	0.5%	1.5%	2.1%	2.8%	4.7%
133	United Republic of Tanzania	-0.1%	-0.2%	0.2%	0.7%	1.1%
134	United States of America	0.3%	0.9%	1.1%	1.5%	2.2%
135	Uruguay	0.3%	0.9%	1.4%	1.7%	2.6%
136	Venezuela (Bolivarian Republic of)	0.9%	1.9%	3.0%	3.9%	6.4%
137	Viet Nam	0.9%	1.7%	2.4%	3.2%	5.3%
138	Yemen	-0.5%	-0.4%	0.0%	0.4%	1.1%
139	Zambia	0.0%	-0.1%	0.7%	2.2%	3.4%
140	Zimbabwe	-1.4%	-3.7%	-5.3%	-5.1%	-2.8%

Table A3.9 Produced capital (Produced capital in billions of constant 2005 US$)

	Country/year	1990	1995	2000	2005	2010	2014
1	Afghanistan	25	25	24	24	28	31
2	Albania	25	23	24	31	41	47
3	Algeria	280	293	309	346	421	512
4	Argentina	488	533	608	634	770	915
5	Armenia	15	15	14	16	23	25
6	Australia	1,333	1,557	1,900	2,397	3,105	3,755
7	Austria	805	937	1,077	1,210	1,330	1,418
8	Bahrain	25	30	34	42	65	74
9	Bangladesh	53	66	91	130	190	259
10	Barbados	10	10	11	12	13	13
11	Belgium	875	1,004	1,148	1,300	1,478	1,605
12	Belize	1	2	2	3	3	4
13	Benin	9	11	12	15	18	21
14	Bolivia (Plurinational State of)	13	15	19	21	25	32

	Country/year	1990	1995	2000	2005	2010	2014
15	Botswana	8	13	18	25	35	47
16	Brazil	1,899	2,068	2,316	2,506	2,904	3,435
17	Bulgaria	48	46	49	66	99	114
18	Burundi	2	2	2	3	3	5
19	Cambodia	4	4	6	9	15	21
20	Cameroon	32	34	36	42	51	61
21	Canada	2,010	2,295	2,686	3,227	3,899	4,468
22	Central African Republic	4	4	4	4	4	4
23	Chile	91	129	186	248	352	465
24	China	1,537	2,365	3,831	6,445	11,534	18,000
25	Colombia	276	338	382	420	530	669
26	Congo	16	19	20	22	30	45
27	Costa Rica	23	29	37	46	60	75
28	Côte d'Ivoire	147	146	160	138	121	102
29	Croatia	94	95	110	135	170	183
30	Cuba	111	106	101	97	106	113
31	Cyprus	40	48	54	61	73	74
32	Czech Republic	383	418	483	558	659	719
33	Democratic Republic of the Congo	50	47	43	40	45	53
34	Denmark	519	583	693	809	933	997
35	Dominican Republic	47	58	84	107	140	164
36	Ecuador	88	99	106	121	145	180
37	Egypt	95	117	150	188	260	307
38	El Salvador	24	28	33	39	45	49
39	Estonia	31	31	35	46	59	68
40	Fiji	6	6	7	8	9	10
41	Finland	539	570	639	727	818	868
42	France	5,152	5,829	6,548	7,452	8,404	9,019
43	Gabon	42	42	45	47	50	55
44	Gambia	1	1	1	2	2	3
45	Germany	7,209	8,321	9,384	10,196	11,045	11,749
46	Ghana	30	32	36	43	59	84
47	Greece	579	616	693	812	940	906
48	Guatemala	42	48	59	70	82	90
49	Guyana	3	4	5	5	6	7
50	Haiti	8	9	11	15	17	20
51	Honduras	16	20	26	31	39	43
52	Hungary	288	301	332	385	437	462
53	Iceland	31	34	40	49	58	59
54	India	867	1,141	1,557	2,241	3,618	5,049
55	Indonesia	310	485	660	811	1,056	1,343
56	Iran (Islamic Republic of)	558	599	652	793	989	1,096

(*Continued*)

Table A3.9 (Continued)

	Country/year	1990	1995	2000	2005	2010	2014
57	Iraq	60	54	48	56	77	112
58	Ireland	285	320	419	580	736	799
59	Israel	203	270	349	404	475	557
60	Italy	4,493	5,021	5,594	6,326	6,941	7,072
61	Jamaica	34	40	44	49	53	54
62	Japan	13,360	16,115	18,265	19,606	20,452	20,939
63	Jordan	26	32	37	43	55	65
64	Kazakhstan	259	284	260	265	327	386
65	Kenya	34	38	44	51	69	90
66	Kuwait	86	95	107	127	192	248
67	Kyrgyzstan	9	9	9	9	11	13
68	Lao People's Democratic Republic	2	3	5	7	13	20
69	Latvia	33	32	35	47	64	73
70	Lesotho	4	5	7	7	8	9
71	Liberia	3	3	3	2	3	4
72	Lithuania	67	67	70	79	97	108
73	Luxembourg	49	60	76	96	118	136
74	Malawi	7	7	7	8	10	11
75	Malaysia	134	234	337	413	512	638
76	Maldives	1	1	1	2	4	5
77	Mali	6	7	9	11	14	16
78	Malta	7	9	12	15	19	21
79	Mauritania	5	5	5	7	10	17
80	Mauritius	7	10	14	17	22	26
81	Mexico	1,463	1,724	2,065	2,465	2,973	3,385
82	Mongolia	13	15	16	18	19	27
83	Morocco	115	135	163	204	275	335
84	Mozambique	5	6	8	11	16	33
85	Myanmar	3	3	5	9	23	51
86	Namibia	12	13	15	18	25	35
87	Nepal	9	12	16	20	26	31
88	Netherlands	1,413	1,616	1,915	2,200	2,501	2,651
89	New Zealand	213	235	275	338	401	458
90	Nicaragua	19	19	21	23	26	31
91	Niger	12	11	11	11	15	19
92	Nigeria	185	177	171	168	216	265
93	Norway	688	730	830	928	1,091	1,224
94	Pakistan	157	196	231	265	315	339
95	Panama	18	22	29	34	49	74
96	Papua New Guinea	7	8	9	11	14	22
97	Paraguay	18	23	26	27	31	36
98	Peru	153	166	192	208	272	363
99	Philippines	181	212	256	298	353	419
100	Poland	426	469	615	740	962	1,152

	Country/year	1990	1995	2000	2005	2010	2014
101	Portugal	402	477	595	703	781	784
102	Qatar	28	31	41	75	206	359
103	Republic of Korea	875	1,562	2,297	3,081	3,906	4,548
104	Republic of Moldova	36	37	32	29	28	24
105	Romania	278	278	293	330	444	495
106	Russian Federation	3,185	3,466	3,189	3,127	3,439	3,774
107	Rwanda	3	3	4	4	7	11
108	Saudi Arabia	411	462	521	639	965	1,328
109	Senegal	13	15	19	24	31	38
110	Serbia	63	62	64	71	90	101
111	Sierra Leone	2	3	2	3	4	6
112	Singapore	137	198	299	374	491	613
113	Slovakia	148	160	183	203	234	255
114	Slovenia	77	83	101	124	151	157
115	South Africa	477	497	543	613	766	895
116	Spain	2,368	2,763	3,287	4,103	4,939	5,167
117	Sri Lanka	35	42	52	64	86	113
118	Sudan (former)	6	7	14	34	61	80
119	Swaziland	11	14	16	16	16	16
120	Sweden	954	1,039	1,158	1,313	1,515	1,669
121	Switzerland	935	1,340	1,606	1,714	1,916	2,054
122	Syrian Arab Republic	43	50	57	71	89	94
123	Tajikistan	13	13	12	11	10	10
124	Thailand	310	522	635	710	829	939
125	Togo	8	7	7	7	8	10
126	Trinidad and Tobago	50	47	48	53	54	52
127	Tunisia	66	76	89	104	123	136
128	Turkey	499	664	871	1,053	1,368	1,683
129	Uganda	11	14	18	26	41	56
130	Ukraine	555	599	538	512	519	496
131	United Arab Emirates	282	318	363	427	591	743
132	United Kingdom	3,826	4,439	5,347	6,279	7,115	7,667
133	United Republic of Tanzania	12	21	28	40	66	95
134	United States of America	20,669	24,439	30,540	37,543	43,404	47,411
135	Uruguay	34	39	46	49	58	72
136	Venezuela (Bolivarian Republic of)	496	520	539	546	651	739
137	Viet Nam	24	41	76	131	227	307
138	Yemen	16	19	25	33	48	58
139	Zambia	29	25	25	29	37	50
140	Zimbabwe	3	4	4	5	5	5

Table A3.10 Produced capital per capita (Produced capital per capita in thousands of constant 2005 US$)

	Country/year	1990	1995	2000	2005	2010	2014
1	Afghanistan	2.1	1.5	1.2	1.0	1.0	1.0
2	Albania	7.8	7.3	7.9	10.4	14.1	16.2
3	Algeria	10.8	10.1	9.9	10.4	11.7	13.1
4	Argentina	14.9	15.2	16.4	16.2	18.7	21.3
5	Armenia	4.3	4.5	4.5	5.3	7.7	8.4
6	Australia	78.1	86.1	99.2	117.5	140.9	160.0
7	Austria	104.8	117.8	134.5	147.1	159.1	166.0
8	Bahrain	49.9	53.8	51.7	49.0	51.7	54.2
9	Bangladesh	0.5	0.6	0.7	0.9	1.3	1.6
10	Barbados	38.3	38.0	41.1	44.4	46.7	46.5
11	Belgium	87.8	99.1	111.9	124.1	135.7	142.9
12	Belize	7.9	9.6	10.0	10.6	10.8	10.7
13	Benin	1.9	1.8	1.8	1.8	1.8	2.0
14	Bolivia (Plurinational State of)	1.9	1.9	2.2	2.3	2.5	3.0
15	Botswana	6.0	8.0	10.4	13.6	17.3	21.4
16	Brazil	12.6	12.7	13.2	13.3	14.6	16.7
17	Bulgaria	5.5	5.4	6.0	8.6	13.3	15.7
18	Burundi	0.4	0.4	0.4	0.4	0.4	0.4
19	Cambodia	0.4	0.4	0.5	0.7	1.0	1.4
20	Cameroon	2.7	2.4	2.3	2.3	2.5	2.7
21	Canada	72.3	78.2	87.3	99.9	114.7	125.7
22	Central African Republic	1.3	1.2	1.1	1.0	0.9	0.8
23	Chile	6.9	9.1	12.3	15.4	20.7	26.2
24	China	1.4	2.0	3.0	4.9	8.6	13.2
25	Colombia	8.1	9.0	9.5	9.7	11.5	14.0
26	Congo	6.5	6.9	6.5	6.2	7.3	10.0
27	Costa Rica	7.3	8.1	9.3	10.8	13.2	15.8
28	Côte d'Ivoire	12.1	10.2	9.7	7.6	6.0	4.6
29	Croatia	19.8	20.3	24.8	30.4	38.4	43.1
30	Cuba	10.5	9.7	9.1	8.7	9.3	9.9
31	Cyprus	51.7	56.4	56.8	58.8	66.3	64.4
32	Czech Republic	37.0	40.4	47.1	54.6	62.9	68.3
33	Democratic Republic of the Congo	1.4	1.1	0.9	0.7	0.7	0.7
34	Denmark	100.9	111.4	129.8	149.3	168.3	176.7
35	Dominican Republic	6.5	7.4	9.8	11.6	14.1	15.7
36	Ecuador	8.6	8.7	8.4	8.8	9.7	11.3
37	Egypt	1.7	1.9	2.2	2.5	3.2	3.4
38	El Salvador	4.6	5.0	5.8	6.6	7.4	8.0
39	Estonia	19.6	21.9	25.2	33.7	44.5	51.9
40	Fiji	7.7	8.0	8.6	9.8	10.3	10.7
41	Finland	108.1	111.5	123.5	138.5	152.6	158.8

	Country/year	1990	1995	2000	2005	2010	2014
42	France	88.0	97.9	107.5	117.9	129.2	135.6
43	Gabon	43.8	38.9	36.8	33.8	32.1	32.5
44	Gambia	0.7	0.8	0.9	1.3	1.4	1.4
45	Germany	90.8	101.9	114.1	123.6	135.1	145.1
46	Ghana	2.0	1.9	1.9	2.0	2.4	3.1
47	Greece	56.8	58.3	64.1	73.9	84.5	83.2
48	Guatemala	4.6	4.6	5.0	5.3	5.6	5.6
49	Guyana	4.7	5.7	6.5	7.1	8.1	8.9
50	Haiti	1.2	1.2	1.3	1.6	1.8	1.9
51	Honduras	3.2	3.5	4.1	4.5	5.1	5.4
52	Hungary	27.7	29.1	32.5	38.1	43.7	46.8
53	Iceland	123.0	126.5	142.4	164.7	182.6	179.6
54	India	1.0	1.2	1.5	2.0	2.9	3.9
55	Indonesia	1.7	2.5	3.1	3.6	4.4	5.3
56	Iran (Islamic Republic of)	9.9	9.9	9.9	11.3	13.3	14.0
57	Iraq	3.4	2.7	2.0	2.1	2.5	3.2
58	Ireland	81.0	88.7	110.1	139.3	161.3	173.1
59	Israel	43.6	48.7	55.5	58.3	62.3	67.7
60	Italy	79.2	88.3	98.2	109.1	117.1	116.3
61	Jamaica	14.4	16.1	16.9	18.5	19.5	19.8
62	Japan	108.2	128.5	144.0	153.4	159.7	164.7
63	Jordan	7.8	7.5	7.8	8.0	8.4	8.7
64	Kazakhstan	15.9	18.0	17.5	17.5	20.0	22.3
65	Kenya	1.5	1.4	1.4	1.5	1.7	2.0
66	Kuwait	41.6	58.2	55.2	56.0	62.7	66.2
67	Kyrgyzstan	2.0	2.0	1.8	1.7	1.9	2.2
68	Lao People's Democratic Republic	0.5	0.7	0.9	1.3	2.1	2.9
69	Latvia	12.4	13.0	15.0	21.0	30.7	36.5
70	Lesotho	2.3	3.1	3.7	3.8	4.0	4.4
71	Liberia	1.4	1.2	0.9	0.7	0.8	0.9
72	Lithuania	18.2	18.4	19.9	23.9	31.4	36.7
73	Luxembourg	128.6	147.2	174.4	206.1	232.0	245.0
74	Malawi	0.8	0.8	0.7	0.6	0.7	0.6
75	Malaysia	7.4	11.3	14.4	16.0	18.2	21.4
76	Maldives	2.9	3.8	5.2	7.4	11.1	13.5
77	Mali	0.7	0.8	0.8	0.8	0.9	0.9
78	Malta	18.4	24.3	32.3	38.3	46.4	50.0
79	Mauritania	2.4	2.1	1.8	2.2	2.8	4.2
80	Mauritius	7.1	9.2	11.5	14.1	17.9	20.7
81	Mexico	17.1	18.3	20.1	22.5	25.1	27.0
82	Mongolia	6.1	6.5	6.9	7.3	7.0	9.2
83	Morocco	4.6	5.0	5.6	6.7	8.6	9.9
84	Mozambique	0.3	0.4	0.4	0.5	0.7	1.2

(*Continued*)

Table A3.10 (Continued)

	Country/year	1990	1995	2000	2005	2010	2014
85	Myanmar	0.1	0.1	0.1	0.2	0.4	1.0
86	Namibia	8.7	7.9	7.9	9.0	11.6	14.6
87	Nepal	0.5	0.6	0.7	0.8	1.0	1.1
88	Netherlands	94.5	104.5	120.3	134.8	150.5	157.2
89	New Zealand	63.9	64.0	71.3	81.7	92.2	101.5
90	Nicaragua	4.6	4.1	4.2	4.3	4.6	5.1
91	Niger	1.5	1.2	1.0	0.8	0.9	1.0
92	Nigeria	1.9	1.6	1.4	1.2	1.4	1.5
93	Norway	162.1	167.4	184.7	200.8	223.1	238.2
94	Pakistan	1.5	1.6	1.7	1.7	1.9	1.8
95	Panama	7.3	8.1	9.7	10.3	13.5	19.1
96	Papua New Guinea	1.8	1.7	1.7	1.8	2.1	2.9
97	Paraguay	4.3	4.8	4.8	4.7	4.9	5.5
98	Peru	7.0	6.9	7.4	7.5	9.3	11.7
99	Philippines	2.9	3.0	3.3	3.5	3.8	4.2
100	Poland	11.2	12.1	16.1	19.4	25.3	30.3
101	Portugal	40.2	47.6	57.8	67.0	73.9	75.4
102	Qatar	58.6	61.4	69.1	89.5	116.4	165.2
103	Republic of Korea	20.4	34.6	48.9	64.0	79.1	90.2
104	Republic of Moldova	9.7	10.0	8.8	8.1	7.9	6.7
105	Romania	12.0	12.3	13.0	15.5	21.9	24.9
106	Russian Federation	21.5	23.4	21.8	21.8	24.1	26.2
107	Rwanda	0.4	0.5	0.4	0.5	0.7	0.9
108	Saudi Arabia	25.1	24.5	24.4	25.8	34.4	43.0
109	Senegal	1.7	1.7	1.9	2.1	2.4	2.6
110	Serbia	8.2	8.2	8.5	9.6	12.4	14.2
111	Sierra Leone	0.6	0.7	0.6	0.5	0.6	0.9
112	Singapore	44.8	56.2	74.1	87.8	96.8	112.1
113	Slovakia	27.9	29.8	33.9	37.8	43.4	47.0
114	Slovenia	38.6	41.9	50.8	61.9	73.5	76.3
115	South Africa	13.6	12.7	12.3	13.0	15.1	16.6
116	Spain	61.0	70.1	81.6	94.0	106.0	111.2
117	Sri Lanka	2.1	2.3	2.8	3.3	4.3	5.4
118	Sudan (former)	0.3	0.3	0.5	1.1	1.7	2.0
119	Swaziland	12.2	14.7	14.9	14.9	13.6	12.5
120	Sweden	111.4	117.7	130.5	145.4	161.5	172.2
121	Switzerland	139.2	190.3	223.5	230.4	244.8	250.8
122	Syrian Arab Republic	3.4	3.5	3.5	3.9	4.3	5.0
123	Tajikistan	2.4	2.3	2.0	1.6	1.4	1.2
124	Thailand	5.5	8.8	10.1	10.8	12.4	13.9
125	Togo	2.0	1.6	1.4	1.3	1.2	1.4
126	Trinidad and Tobago	40.8	37.3	37.5	41.1	40.6	38.1
127	Tunisia	8.1	8.5	9.3	10.3	11.7	12.4
128	Turkey	9.2	11.4	13.8	15.5	18.9	21.7

	Country/year	1990	1995	2000	2005	2010	2014
129	Uganda	0.6	0.7	0.8	0.9	1.2	1.5
130	Ukraine	10.7	11.6	10.9	10.9	11.3	10.9
131	United Arab Emirates	155.7	135.2	119.0	95.2	70.9	81.7
132	United Kingdom	66.8	76.5	90.8	104.0	113.4	118.7
133	United Republic of Tanzania	0.5	0.7	0.8	1.0	1.4	1.8
134	United States of America	82.8	91.8	108.2	127.0	140.3	148.7
135	Uruguay	10.9	12.1	13.9	14.7	17.3	20.9
136	Venezuela (Bolivarian Republic of)	24.9	23.4	22.0	20.4	22.4	24.1
137	Viet Nam	0.4	0.6	1.0	1.6	2.6	3.4
138	Yemen	1.4	1.2	1.4	1.6	2.0	2.2
139	Zambia	3.5	2.7	2.3	2.4	2.7	3.2
140	Zimbabwe	0.3	0.3	0.3	0.4	0.3	0.3

Table A3.11 Produced capital growth (Produced capital change (%) with respect to base year 1990)

	Country/year	1995	2000	2005	2010	2014
1	Afghanistan	-0.5%	-1.7%	-0.8%	2.6%	6.8%
2	Albania	-1.9%	-1.2%	5.3%	12.6%	22.5%
3	Algeria	0.8%	2.5%	5.4%	10.7%	22.2%
4	Argentina	1.8%	5.6%	6.7%	12.0%	23.3%
5	Armenia	-0.8%	-2.0%	1.3%	10.8%	18.6%
6	Australia	3.2%	9.3%	15.8%	23.5%	41.2%
7	Austria	3.1%	7.6%	10.7%	13.4%	20.8%
8	Bahrain	4.1%	8.7%	14.5%	27.4%	43.9%
9	Bangladesh	4.5%	14.4%	24.9%	37.2%	69.3%
10	Barbados	0.2%	2.7%	5.1%	7.0%	9.7%
11	Belgium	2.8%	7.0%	10.4%	14.0%	22.4%
12	Belize	6.2%	13.9%	19.6%	24.0%	36.6%
13	Benin	2.2%	6.9%	11.6%	16.6%	31.3%
14	Bolivia (Plurinational State of)	2.8%	10.2%	13.1%	18.3%	35.3%
15	Botswana	8.7%	21.5%	32.1%	43.6%	78.6%
16	Brazil	1.7%	5.1%	7.2%	11.2%	21.8%
17	Bulgaria	-0.8%	0.8%	8.6%	20.0%	33.7%
18	Burundi	-0.6%	-0.3%	3.1%	8.7%	23.6%
19	Cambodia	2.4%	10.6%	23.2%	39.7%	76.0%
20	Cameroon	0.8%	2.8%	7.0%	11.7%	23.3%
21	Canada	2.7%	7.5%	12.6%	18.0%	30.5%
22	Central African Republic	1.7%	1.6%	0.9%	0.9%	0.1%
23	Chile	7.2%	19.5%	28.4%	40.1%	72.1%

(*Continued*)

Table A3.11 (Continued)

	Country/year	1995	2000	2005	2010	2014
24	China	9.0%	25.6%	43.1%	65.5%	127.1%
25	Colombia	4.1%	8.4%	11.0%	17.7%	34.2%
26	Congo	3.9%	6.8%	8.5%	17.4%	42.5%
27	Costa Rica	4.7%	12.6%	19.3%	27.5%	48.9%
28	Côte d'Ivoire	−0.1%	2.1%	−1.6%	−4.9%	−11.4%
29	Croatia	0.0%	3.8%	9.4%	15.8%	24.6%
30	Cuba	−1.0%	−2.4%	−3.2%	−1.2%	0.7%
31	Cyprus	4.0%	7.8%	11.2%	16.6%	23.3%
32	Czech Republic	1.8%	6.0%	9.9%	14.6%	23.4%
33	Democratic Republic of the Congo	−1.2%	−4.2%	−5.5%	−2.9%	1.4%
34	Denmark	2.4%	7.5%	11.8%	15.8%	24.3%
35	Dominican Republic	4.3%	15.5%	22.8%	31.3%	51.6%
36	Ecuador	2.4%	4.9%	8.3%	13.4%	27.0%
37	Egypt	4.2%	12.2%	18.6%	28.6%	47.8%
38	El Salvador	3.2%	8.8%	13.2%	17.0%	26.9%
39	Estonia	0.4%	3.4%	10.3%	17.8%	30.4%
40	Fiji	2.1%	5.5%	9.4%	12.0%	19.3%
41	Finland	1.1%	4.3%	7.7%	11.0%	17.2%
42	France	2.5%	6.2%	9.7%	13.0%	20.5%
43	Gabon	0.3%	2.1%	2.8%	4.4%	9.6%
44	Gambia	8.3%	17.4%	32.7%	41.0%	65.7%
45	Germany	2.9%	6.8%	9.1%	11.3%	17.7%
46	Ghana	1.6%	4.8%	9.6%	18.4%	41.4%
47	Greece	1.2%	4.6%	8.8%	12.9%	16.1%
48	Guatemala	2.6%	8.7%	13.7%	18.3%	29.1%
49	Guyana	3.8%	9.1%	11.5%	15.4%	25.7%
50	Haiti	2.0%	8.5%	15.1%	20.5%	34.5%
51	Honduras	4.9%	13.1%	18.6%	25.4%	40.7%
52	Hungary	0.9%	3.7%	7.5%	11.0%	17.1%
53	Iceland	1.5%	6.3%	11.7%	16.7%	23.3%
54	India	5.7%	15.8%	26.8%	42.9%	79.9%
55	Indonesia	9.4%	20.8%	27.2%	35.9%	63.1%
56	Iran (Islamic Republic of)	1.4%	4.0%	9.2%	15.4%	25.2%
57	Iraq	−2.2%	−5.7%	−2.0%	6.3%	23.0%
58	Ireland	2.4%	10.2%	19.5%	26.8%	41.1%
59	Israel	5.9%	14.5%	18.8%	23.7%	39.9%
60	Italy	2.2%	5.6%	8.9%	11.5%	16.3%
61	Jamaica	3.0%	6.3%	9.3%	11.2%	16.1%
62	Japan	3.8%	8.1%	10.1%	11.2%	16.2%
63	Jordan	4.3%	9.1%	13.0%	20.2%	35.2%
64	Kazakhstan	1.8%	0.1%	0.6%	5.9%	14.2%
65	Kenya	2.1%	6.4%	10.8%	19.0%	38.0%
66	Kuwait	2.1%	5.6%	10.3%	22.3%	42.6%

	Country/year	1995	2000	2005	2010	2014
67	Kyrgyzstan	0.8%	0.3%	0.5%	4.9%	13.1%
68	Lao People's Democratic Republic	10.7%	25.9%	38.9%	59.7%	113.7%
69	Latvia	−0.6%	1.7%	9.1%	18.0%	30.0%
70	Lesotho	8.2%	17.5%	19.3%	21.7%	36.5%
71	Liberia	−3.3%	−2.3%	−4.9%	0.7%	9.1%
72	Lithuania	−0.2%	0.8%	4.2%	9.6%	16.9%
73	Luxembourg	4.2%	11.6%	18.2%	24.4%	40.5%
74	Malawi	0.5%	0.5%	1.4%	8.9%	13.5%
75	Malaysia	11.8%	26.0%	32.5%	39.8%	68.3%
76	Maldives	9.2%	24.3%	39.5%	59.4%	105.2%
77	Mali	4.5%	10.4%	15.6%	22.8%	38.4%
78	Malta	6.6%	17.2%	24.1%	31.0%	48.5%
79	Mauritania	0.3%	0.6%	9.8%	20.6%	51.4%
80	Mauritius	6.6%	16.2%	23.5%	31.7%	51.7%
81	Mexico	3.3%	9.0%	13.9%	19.4%	32.3%
82	Mongolia	2.2%	5.3%	8.2%	9.3%	25.8%
83	Morocco	3.2%	9.1%	15.4%	24.2%	42.6%
84	Mozambique	3.7%	13.2%	22.8%	36.5%	91.4%
85	Myanmar	4.9%	18.6%	36.1%	71.2%	168.8%
86	Namibia	1.1%	5.2%	10.3%	19.9%	41.5%
87	Nepal	6.1%	15.3%	22.4%	29.9%	50.9%
88	Netherlands	2.7%	7.9%	11.7%	15.4%	23.3%
89	New Zealand	2.0%	6.6%	12.2%	17.2%	29.1%
90	Nicaragua	−0.1%	2.7%	5.2%	8.3%	17.2%
91	Niger	−1.1%	−1.9%	−0.4%	6.1%	17.7%
92	Nigeria	−0.9%	−2.0%	−2.5%	3.9%	12.7%
93	Norway	1.2%	4.8%	7.8%	12.2%	21.2%
94	Pakistan	4.6%	10.2%	14.0%	19.1%	29.3%
95	Panama	4.4%	13.1%	17.4%	28.4%	60.1%
96	Papua New Guinea	1.9%	5.8%	11.2%	18.5%	44.3%
97	Paraguay	4.5%	8.8%	10.3%	13.9%	25.1%
98	Peru	1.7%	5.8%	8.1%	15.5%	33.5%
99	Philippines	3.3%	9.1%	13.3%	18.2%	32.4%
100	Poland	1.9%	9.7%	14.8%	22.6%	39.4%
101	Portugal	3.5%	10.3%	15.0%	18.1%	25.0%
102	Qatar	2.0%	10.1%	28.0%	64.7%	134.2%
103	Republic of Korea	12.3%	27.3%	37.0%	45.3%	73.2%
104	Republic of Moldova	0.4%	−2.8%	−5.3%	−6.0%	−12.8%
105	Romania	0.0%	1.3%	4.4%	12.4%	21.2%
106	Russian Federation	1.7%	0.0%	−0.5%	1.9%	5.8%
107	Rwanda	1.2%	4.2%	10.1%	23.5%	51.9%
108	Saudi Arabia	2.4%	6.1%	11.7%	23.8%	47.8%
109	Senegal	2.9%	9.3%	15.9%	24.0%	43.3%
110	Serbia	0.0%	0.4%	3.3%	9.6%	17.4%

(*Continued*)

Table A3.11 (Continued)

	Country/year	1995	2000	2005	2010	2014
111	Sierra Leone	1.3%	−0.1%	1.7%	8.9%	31.3%
112	Singapore	7.7%	21.6%	28.7%	37.7%	64.9%
113	Slovakia	1.6%	5.5%	8.3%	12.2%	19.9%
114	Slovenia	1.5%	6.9%	12.5%	18.2%	26.8%
115	South Africa	0.8%	3.3%	6.5%	12.6%	23.3%
116	Spain	3.1%	8.5%	14.7%	20.2%	29.7%
117	Sri Lanka	3.6%	10.1%	15.8%	24.8%	47.4%
118	Sudan (former)	3.2%	24.9%	55.5%	79.3%	138.8%
119	Swaziland	6.1%	10.9%	11.9%	11.4%	14.8%
120	Sweden	1.7%	5.0%	8.3%	12.3%	20.5%
121	Switzerland	7.5%	14.5%	16.4%	19.6%	30.0%
122	Syrian Arab Republic	3.2%	7.8%	13.7%	20.3%	30.3%
123	Tajikistan	0.6%	−1.6%	−4.2%	−5.5%	−8.4%
124	Thailand	11.0%	19.7%	23.0%	27.9%	44.7%
125	Togo	−1.5%	−2.5%	−1.7%	0.5%	8.7%
126	Trinidad and Tobago	−1.2%	−1.2%	1.7%	2.0%	1.1%
127	Tunisia	2.9%	7.5%	11.8%	16.9%	27.2%
128	Turkey	5.9%	14.9%	20.5%	28.6%	49.9%
129	Uganda	4.4%	13.7%	23.9%	38.6%	72.4%
130	Ukraine	1.5%	−0.8%	−2.0%	−1.6%	−3.7%
131	United Arab Emirates	2.4%	6.5%	10.9%	20.3%	38.1%
132	United Kingdom	3.0%	8.7%	13.2%	16.8%	26.1%
133	United Republic of Tanzania	12.5%	24.3%	36.0%	53.5%	100.3%
134	United States of America	3.4%	10.3%	16.1%	20.4%	31.9%
135	Uruguay	2.8%	8.0%	9.5%	14.4%	28.2%
136	Venezuela (Bolivarian Republic of)	1.0%	2.1%	2.5%	7.1%	14.2%
137	Viet Nam	11.6%	33.9%	53.5%	76.0%	135.1%
138	Yemen	2.7%	11.1%	18.8%	31.0%	52.2%
139	Zambia	−2.4%	−3.6%	0.7%	6.9%	20.3%
140	Zimbabwe	3.3%	6.6%	9.8%	8.9%	14.0%

Table A3.12 Produced capital per capita growth (Produced capital per capita change (%) with respect to base year 1990)

	Country/year	1995	2000	2005	2010	2014
1	Afghanistan	−6.8%	−13.0%	−16.8%	−16.8%	−22.5%
2	Albania	−1.3%	0.3%	7.6%	16.1%	27.9%
3	Algeria	−1.3%	−2.2%	−1.0%	2.0%	6.7%
4	Argentina	0.4%	2.4%	2.1%	5.8%	12.6%
5	Armenia	1.1%	1.5%	5.5%	15.9%	25.2%

	Country/year	1995	2000	2005	2010	2014
6	Australia	2.0%	6.2%	10.8%	15.9%	27.0%
7	Austria	2.4%	6.4%	8.8%	11.0%	16.6%
8	Bahrain	1.5%	0.9%	−0.5%	0.9%	2.8%
9	Bangladesh	2.2%	8.4%	15.9%	25.5%	47.8%
10	Barbados	−0.2%	1.8%	3.8%	5.1%	6.7%
11	Belgium	2.4%	6.3%	9.0%	11.5%	17.6%
12	Belize	4.1%	6.3%	7.9%	8.3%	10.7%
13	Benin	−1.4%	−1.5%	−1.3%	−0.7%	2.2%
14	Bolivia (Plurinational State of)	0.8%	4.9%	5.3%	7.9%	17.2%
15	Botswana	5.9%	14.7%	22.6%	30.1%	52.4%
16	Brazil	0.1%	1.1%	1.3%	3.7%	9.7%
17	Bulgaria	−0.1%	2.4%	11.9%	25.0%	42.3%
18	Burundi	−2.7%	−4.8%	−5.4%	−4.6%	−0.7%
19	Cambodia	−1.1%	2.5%	11.7%	24.3%	47.4%
20	Cameroon	−2.0%	−4.1%	−3.4%	−2.2%	−0.2%
21	Canada	1.6%	4.8%	8.4%	12.2%	20.2%
22	Central African Republic	−0.9%	−4.3%	−7.0%	−9.0%	−15.0%
23	Chile	5.5%	15.3%	22.0%	31.4%	55.6%
24	China	7.7%	22.3%	38.2%	58.8%	113.6%
25	Colombia	2.3%	4.1%	4.7%	9.4%	20.2%
26	Congo	1.2%	−0.1%	−1.4%	2.8%	15.3%
27	Costa Rica	2.1%	6.1%	10.2%	15.9%	29.0%
28	Côte d'Ivoire	−3.5%	−5.4%	−11.0%	−16.1%	−27.5%
29	Croatia	0.5%	5.8%	11.4%	18.1%	29.7%
30	Cuba	−1.6%	−3.6%	−4.7%	−2.8%	−1.7%
31	Cyprus	1.8%	2.4%	3.3%	6.4%	7.6%
32	Czech Republic	1.8%	6.2%	10.2%	14.2%	22.7%
33	Democratic Republic of the Congo	−4.9%	−11.5%	−16.0%	−17.1%	−21.3%
34	Denmark	2.0%	6.5%	10.3%	13.6%	20.5%
35	Dominican Republic	2.4%	10.6%	15.3%	21.2%	33.9%
36	Ecuador	0.1%	−0.5%	0.6%	3.1%	9.6%
37	Egypt	2.1%	6.9%	10.4%	17.1%	26.7%
38	El Salvador	1.9%	6.0%	9.8%	13.0%	20.7%
39	Estonia	2.2%	6.4%	14.5%	22.7%	38.3%
40	Fiji	0.9%	2.7%	6.1%	7.5%	11.7%
41	Finland	0.6%	3.4%	6.4%	9.0%	13.7%
42	France	2.1%	5.1%	7.6%	10.1%	15.5%
43	Gabon	−2.3%	−4.3%	−6.2%	−7.4%	−9.5%
44	Gambia	5.1%	9.1%	18.5%	21.0%	29.4%
45	Germany	2.3%	5.9%	8.0%	10.5%	16.9%
46	Ghana	−1.1%	−1.6%	−0.4%	4.3%	15.5%
47	Greece	0.5%	3.1%	6.8%	10.4%	13.6%

(*Continued*)

Table A3.12 (Continued)

	Country/year	1995	2000	2005	2010	2014
48	Guatemala	0.1%	2.3%	3.8%	5.0%	7.1%
49	Guyana	3.6%	8.3%	10.7%	14.1%	23.3%
50	Haiti	0.0%	3.5%	7.7%	10.6%	17.8%
51	Honduras	2.2%	6.5%	9.0%	12.7%	19.7%
52	Hungary	1.0%	4.1%	8.3%	12.0%	19.1%
53	Iceland	0.6%	3.7%	7.6%	10.4%	13.4%
54	India	3.6%	10.4%	18.4%	31.1%	57.6%
55	Indonesia	7.6%	16.2%	20.3%	26.5%	45.7%
56	Iran (Islamic Republic of)	0.0%	−0.1%	3.3%	7.6%	12.2%
57	Iraq	−5.0%	−12.5%	−12.1%	−7.8%	−2.7%
58	Ireland	1.8%	8.0%	14.5%	18.8%	28.8%
59	Israel	2.3%	6.2%	7.6%	9.3%	15.8%
60	Italy	2.2%	5.5%	8.3%	10.3%	13.7%
61	Jamaica	2.3%	4.1%	6.6%	8.0%	11.2%
62	Japan	3.5%	7.4%	9.1%	10.2%	15.1%
63	Jordan	−0.8%	−0.1%	0.7%	1.8%	3.8%
64	Kazakhstan	2.5%	2.5%	2.5%	6.0%	12.1%
65	Kenya	−1.1%	−0.8%	0.0%	3.9%	11.2%
66	Kuwait	6.9%	7.3%	7.7%	10.7%	16.7%
67	Kyrgyzstan	0.0%	−2.4%	−3.5%	−0.6%	2.8%
68	Lao People's Democratic Republic	7.7%	18.8%	28.8%	45.0%	83.6%
69	Latvia	0.8%	4.7%	14.0%	25.3%	43.2%
70	Lesotho	6.2%	13.2%	13.9%	14.9%	24.4%
71	Liberia	−3.1%	−9.8%	−14.8%	−14.0%	−14.7%
72	Lithuania	0.2%	2.2%	7.0%	14.5%	26.3%
73	Luxembourg	2.8%	7.9%	12.5%	15.9%	24.0%
74	Malawi	−0.3%	−3.8%	−6.0%	−2.7%	−6.2%
75	Malaysia	9.0%	18.3%	21.5%	25.4%	42.7%
76	Maldives	5.8%	16.1%	26.6%	40.0%	67.4%
77	Mali	1.8%	3.3%	4.2%	6.2%	9.6%
78	Malta	5.7%	15.0%	20.1%	25.9%	39.5%
79	Mauritania	−2.5%	−6.5%	−1.8%	4.5%	20.9%
80	Mauritius	5.4%	12.9%	19.0%	26.3%	43.1%
81	Mexico	1.3%	4.1%	7.1%	10.1%	16.5%
82	Mongolia	1.1%	2.9%	4.3%	3.5%	14.3%
83	Morocco	1.5%	5.1%	9.8%	16.6%	28.8%
84	Mozambique	0.1%	4.7%	9.5%	17.5%	51.0%
85	Myanmar	3.6%	14.9%	30.3%	62.5%	148.1%
86	Namibia	−2.0%	−2.3%	0.9%	7.4%	18.7%
87	Nepal	3.3%	8.7%	13.4%	18.7%	31.7%
88	Netherlands	2.0%	6.2%	9.3%	12.4%	18.5%
89	New Zealand	0.0%	2.8%	6.3%	9.6%	16.7%

	Country/year	1995	2000	2005	2010	2014
90	Nicaragua	-2.2%	-2.1%	-1.4%	-0.1%	3.5%
91	Niger	-4.4%	-10.1%	-12.8%	-11.5%	-12.3%
92	Nigeria	-3.3%	-8.0%	-11.3%	-8.6%	-8.3%
93	Norway	0.6%	3.3%	5.5%	8.3%	13.7%
94	Pakistan	1.9%	3.5%	4.3%	6.2%	7.9%
95	Panama	2.2%	7.4%	9.1%	16.7%	37.9%
96	Papua New Guinea	-0.7%	-0.7%	1.1%	4.6%	18.7%
97	Paraguay	2.0%	2.7%	1.9%	3.4%	8.0%
98	Peru	-0.3%	1.4%	1.9%	7.2%	18.8%
99	Philippines	0.8%	3.0%	4.4%	6.8%	13.2%
100	Poland	1.7%	9.5%	14.8%	22.7%	39.5%
101	Portugal	3.4%	9.5%	13.6%	16.4%	23.3%
102	Qatar	0.9%	4.2%	11.2%	18.7%	41.3%
103	Republic of Korea	11.1%	24.4%	33.1%	40.3%	64.1%
104	Republic of Moldova	0.5%	-2.4%	-4.6%	-5.1%	-11.6%
105	Romania	0.5%	2.2%	6.6%	16.3%	27.6%
106	Russian Federation	1.7%	0.3%	0.4%	2.9%	6.9%
107	Rwanda	5.5%	1.7%	4.3%	13.2%	30.9%
108	Saudi Arabia	-0.5%	-0.8%	0.7%	8.1%	19.6%
109	Senegal	-0.1%	2.1%	4.8%	8.2%	14.7%
110	Serbia	-0.1%	0.6%	3.8%	10.7%	19.8%
111	Sierra Leone	1.8%	-0.9%	-4.6%	-1.0%	12.1%
112	Singapore	4.6%	13.4%	18.3%	21.2%	35.7%
113	Slovakia	1.4%	5.0%	8.0%	11.7%	19.0%
114	Slovenia	1.6%	7.1%	12.5%	17.4%	25.4%
115	South Africa	-1.3%	-2.3%	-1.1%	2.7%	6.9%
116	Spain	2.8%	7.6%	11.4%	14.8%	22.2%
117	Sri Lanka	2.4%	7.6%	12.2%	19.8%	38.1%
118	Sudan (former)	-1.1%	14.8%	38.3%	54.7%	90.6%
119	Swaziland	3.8%	5.2%	5.2%	2.7%	0.9%
120	Sweden	1.1%	4.0%	6.9%	9.7%	15.6%
121	Switzerland	6.5%	12.6%	13.4%	15.2%	21.7%
122	Syrian Arab Republic	0.3%	0.7%	3.5%	6.0%	13.7%
123	Tajikistan	-1.1%	-5.4%	-10.0%	-13.6%	-21.1%
124	Thailand	10.0%	16.6%	18.5%	22.7%	36.3%
125	Togo	-3.9%	-8.4%	-10.8%	-11.8%	-11.9%
126	Trinidad and Tobago	-1.8%	-2.1%	0.2%	-0.1%	-2.3%
127	Tunisia	1.0%	3.4%	6.2%	9.6%	15.2%
128	Turkey	4.2%	10.5%	13.8%	19.6%	32.9%
129	Uganda	1.1%	5.2%	9.9%	18.0%	33.1%
130	Ukraine	1.7%	0.6%	0.4%	1.4%	0.7%
131	United Arab Emirates	-2.8%	-6.5%	-11.6%	-17.8%	-19.3%
132	United Kingdom	2.7%	8.0%	11.7%	14.1%	21.1%
133	United Republic of Tanzania	8.9%	15.6%	22.2%	32.6%	58.1%

(*Continued*)

Table A3.12 (Continued)

	Country/year	1995	2000	2005	2010	2014
134	United States of America	2.1%	6.9%	11.3%	14.1%	21.5%
135	Uruguay	2.1%	6.3%	7.7%	12.1%	24.2%
136	Venezuela (Bolivarian Republic of)	−1.2%	−3.1%	−4.9%	−2.6%	−1.2%
137	Viet Nam	9.7%	28.6%	45.2%	64.3%	111.4%
138	Yemen	−2.2%	0.6%	3.9%	10.5%	17.2%
139	Zambia	−4.9%	−9.7%	−8.7%	−6.5%	−3.4%
140	Zimbabwe	1.1%	2.1%	4.1%	1.4%	0.6%

Table A3.13 Natural capital (Natural capital in billions of constant 2005 US$)

	Country/year	1990	1995	2000	2005	2010	2014
1	Afghanistan	12	12	12	12	12	12
2	Albania	20	19	19	19	19	19
3	Algeria	619	577	530	475	413	366
4	Argentina	867	848	825	819	820	799
5	Armenia	3	3	2	2	5	5
6	Australia	3,341	3,302	3,247	3,175	3,034	2,907
7	Austria	58	59	61	61	60	57
8	Bahrain	8	6	5	4	3	2
9	Bangladesh	62	58	56	54	54	51
10	Barbados	1	1	1	1	1	0
11	Belgium	4	5	6	6	7	6
12	Belize	14	14	13	13	13	13
13	Benin	38	36	33	32	30	30
14	Bolivia (Plurinational State of)	737	724	710	694	676	659
15	Botswana	67	64	61	59	56	54
16	Brazil	7,543	7,382	7,198	7,037	6,840	6,786
17	Bulgaria	82	80	78	78	79	56
18	Burundi	5	5	4	4	4	4
19	Cambodia	248	233	217	201	189	180
20	Cameroon	246	233	220	208	200	53
21	Canada	5,516	5,436	5,348	5,247	5,143	4,103
22	Central African Republic	211	209	208	207	205	205
23	Chile	351	338	327	323	310	305
24	China	9,552	9,417	9,094	8,640	8,247	7,882
25	Colombia	997	970	946	909	878	308
26	Congo	301	297	291	285	282	277
27	Costa Rica	52	48	45	46	47	62
28	Côte d'Ivoire	62	73	84	84	84	83
29	Croatia	23	25	25	26	26	25
30	Cuba	31	33	35	36	35	33

	Country/year	1990	1995	2000	2005	2010	2014
31	Cyprus	1	1	1	1	1	1
32	Czech Republic	81	77	71	66	61	57
33	Democratic Republic of the Congo	1,320	1,307	1,294	1,281	1,268	1,258
34	Denmark	77	69	60	49	41	34
35	Dominican Republic	37	37	36	35	35	34
36	Ecuador	335	319	301	283	264	263
37	Egypt	219	199	176	156	135	117
38	El Salvador	9	9	9	9	9	9
39	Estonia	20	15	10	22	21	21
40	Fiji	8	8	8	8	8	8
41	Finland	166	169	171	166	161	155
42	France	276	276	277	279	278	275
43	Gabon	1,123	1,117	1,109	1,103	1,098	1,098
44	Gambia	5	5	5	4	4	4
45	Germany	1,633	1,574	1,528	1,485	1,442	1,413
46	Ghana	78	74	71	66	62	79
47	Greece	249	243	228	219	212	204
48	Guatemala	109	103	95	89	81	86
49	Guyana	203	203	202	202	202	233
50	Haiti	8	7	7	6	5	5
51	Honduras	107	97	85	78	71	65
52	Hungary	69	66	63	61	58	57
53	Iceland	106	104	102	100	99	98
54	India	3,605	3,552	3,489	3,426	3,344	3,242
55	Indonesia	2,974	2,811	2,684	2,587	2,446	2,302
56	Iran (Islamic Republic of)	4,768	4,682	4,577	4,437	4,314	4,116
57	Iraq	1,541	1,528	1,504	1,470	1,434	1,397
58	Ireland	43	35	33	32	32	30
59	Israel	15	14	14	14	13	13
60	Italy	355	345	356	355	362	335
61	Jamaica	32	33	32	32	30	30
62	Japan	567	548	531	509	501	458
63	Jordan	8	8	7	7	7	7
64	Kazakhstan	930	1,015	998	973	937	904
65	Kenya	46	46	44	44	43	47
66	Kuwait	1,606	1,575	1,524	1,472	1,409	1,358
67	Kyrgyzstan	16	16	16	17	18	18
68	Lao People's Democratic Republic	150	147	145	142	140	152
69	Latvia	21	22	23	24	27	25
70	Lesotho	0	0	0	0	0	0
71	Liberia	37	36	35	34	33	32
72	Lithuania	17	17	18	18	18	17
73	Luxembourg	1	1	1	1	1	1

(*Continued*)

Table A3.13 (Continued)

	Country/year	1990	1995	2000	2005	2010	2014
74	Malawi	25	24	23	23	22	22
75	Malaysia	628	597	558	513	471	461
76	Maldives	3	3	3	3	2	2
77	Mali	75	75	74	72	69	46
78	Malta	0	0	0	0	0	0
79	Mauritania	20	18	17	15	15	13
80	Mauritius	2	2	2	2	2	2
81	Mexico	1,151	1,106	1,055	1,002	952	948
82	Mongolia	221	213	218	202	198	201
83	Morocco	84	82	79	77	75	75
84	Mozambique	272	267	262	258	371	367
85	Myanmar	253	237	220	203	188	175
86	Namibia	54	56	58	60	66	64
87	Nepal	222	202	182	170	170	170
88	Netherlands	157	138	120	105	89	75
89	New Zealand	1,609	1,595	1,592	1,520	1,889	1,713
90	Nicaragua	42	41	39	37	34	36
91	Niger	15	13	12	12	11	11
92	Nigeria	953	917	868	811	742	697
93	Norway	584	533	452	369	298	250
94	Pakistan	1,448	1,302	1,156	1,006	859	747
95	Panama	46	44	42	41	40	47
96	Papua New Guinea	327	318	309	300	292	398
97	Paraguay	115	110	112	108	106	100
98	Peru	1,332	1,305	1,287	1,263	1,234	1,294
99	Philippines	142	141	142	143	149	140
100	Poland	545	524	504	480	461	447
101	Portugal	62	63	65	63	62	58
102	Qatar	452	443	430	411	383	351
103	Republic of Korea	418	418	426	437	440	394
104	Republic of Moldova	6	6	7	7	7	1
105	Romania	218	209	201	191	188	184
106	Russian Federation	10,921	12,965	12,694	12,390	12,079	11,754
107	Rwanda	3	2	3	3	4	4
108	Saudi Arabia	5,882	6,299	6,090	5,872	5,621	5,547
109	Senegal	82	78	75	73	71	71
110	Serbia	25	26	27	30	42	36
111	Sierra Leone	20	19	19	18	16	16
112	Singapore	0	0	0	0	0	0
113	Slovakia	15	16	15	15	15	14
114	Slovenia	24	25	25	26	27	25
115	South Africa	481	461	437	410	384	363
116	Spain	295	300	309	310	310	308
117	Sri Lanka	79	73	68	62	59	63

	Country/year	1990	1995	2000	2005	2010	2014
118	Sudan (former)	413	398	381	374	363	203
119	Swaziland	2	3	3	3	3	3
120	Sweden	209	204	199	202	197	154
121	Switzerland	86	85	85	85	84	84
122	Syrian Arab Republic	81	72	60	50	42	36
123	Tajikistan	6	7	6	6	6	6
124	Thailand	345	330	309	290	274	272
125	Togo	6	5	5	4	4	4
126	Trinidad and Tobago	72	67	62	53	41	28
127	Tunisia	28	26	23	21	19	17
128	Turkey	650	640	636	622	587	583
129	Uganda	48	46	45	43	41	38
130	Ukraine	672	725	717	706	694	680
131	United Arab Emirates	1,346	1,298	1,249	1,196	1,137	1,086
132	United Kingdom	490	417	327	251	202	166
133	United Republic of Tanzania	290	278	265	253	242	380
134	United States of America	10,980	10,671	10,372	10,189	10,018	9,490
135	Uruguay	38	38	38	37	36	36
136	Venezuela (Bolivarian Republic of)	4,788	4,715	4,626	4,542	4,467	4,423
137	Viet Nam	359	358	358	350	337	328
138	Yemen	89	85	78	70	86	81
139	Zambia	349	344	339	334	329	328
140	Zimbabwe	102	95	88	81	74	68

Table A3.14 Natural capital per capita (Natural capital per capita in thousands of constant 2005 US$)

	Country/year	1990	1995	2000	2005	2010	2014
1	Afghanistan	1.0	0.7	0.6	0.5	0.4	0.4
2	Albania	6.0	6.1	6.2	6.3	6.5	6.4
3	Algeria	23.9	20.0	17.0	14.3	11.4	9.4
4	Argentina	26.5	24.2	22.3	20.9	19.9	18.6
5	Armenia	0.8	0.8	0.8	0.8	1.6	1.7
6	Australia	195.8	182.7	169.5	155.7	137.7	123.9
7	Austria	7.6	7.5	7.6	7.4	7.1	6.6
8	Bahrain	15.4	11.5	7.9	4.7	2.3	1.4
9	Bangladesh	0.6	0.5	0.4	0.4	0.4	0.3
10	Barbados	2.7	2.5	2.3	2.0	1.8	1.7
11	Belgium	0.4	0.5	0.6	0.6	0.6	0.6
12	Belize	75.6	67.0	54.4	46.1	39.6	35.6

(*Continued*)

Table A3.14 (Continued)

	Country/year	1990	1995	2000	2005	2010	2014
13	Benin	7.7	6.0	4.8	3.9	3.1	2.8
14	Bolivia (Plurinational State of)	107.5	95.7	85.1	76.1	68.2	62.4
15	Botswana	48.4	40.7	35.4	31.5	27.3	24.3
16	Brazil	50.2	45.3	40.9	37.3	34.4	32.9
17	Bulgaria	9.4	9.5	9.6	10.1	10.7	7.7
18	Burundi	1.0	0.8	0.6	0.5	0.4	0.4
19	Cambodia	27.5	21.8	17.8	15.1	13.2	11.8
20	Cameroon	20.4	16.7	13.8	11.5	9.7	2.3
21	Canada	198.5	185.2	173.8	162.4	151.2	115.4
22	Central African Republic	71.7	62.8	55.8	50.9	46.2	42.6
23	Chile	26.7	23.8	21.6	20.1	18.2	17.2
24	China	8.4	7.8	7.2	6.6	6.2	5.8
25	Colombia	29.1	25.9	23.4	21.0	19.1	6.4
26	Congo	126.0	109.0	93.6	81.4	69.3	61.5
27	Costa Rica	16.9	13.8	11.5	10.7	10.3	13.1
28	Côte d'Ivoire	5.1	5.1	5.1	4.6	4.2	3.7
29	Croatia	4.8	5.3	5.7	5.8	6.0	5.8
30	Cuba	2.9	3.0	3.1	3.2	3.1	2.9
31	Cyprus	1.7	1.5	1.4	1.4	1.2	1.1
32	Czech Republic	7.8	7.5	7.0	6.5	5.8	5.5
33	Democratic Republic of the Congo	37.7	31.0	26.9	22.8	19.2	16.8
34	Denmark	15.0	13.2	11.2	9.0	7.3	6.1
35	Dominican Republic	5.1	4.7	4.2	3.8	3.5	3.3
36	Ecuador	32.8	27.9	23.9	20.6	17.7	16.6
37	Egypt	3.9	3.2	2.6	2.1	1.6	1.3
38	El Salvador	1.6	1.6	1.5	1.5	1.5	1.5
39	Estonia	12.8	10.4	6.9	15.9	16.0	15.8
40	Fiji	11.0	10.5	10.0	9.9	9.5	9.3
41	Finland	33.4	33.0	33.1	31.6	30.1	28.4
42	France	4.7	4.6	4.5	4.4	4.3	4.1
43	Gabon	1,179.2	1,027.8	900.6	800.9	712.4	650.4
44	Gambia	6.0	4.3	3.7	3.0	2.5	2.1
45	Germany	20.6	19.3	18.6	18.0	17.6	17.4
46	Ghana	5.3	4.4	3.7	3.1	2.5	2.9
47	Greece	24.4	23.0	21.1	20.0	19.0	18.7
48	Guatemala	11.9	9.9	8.2	6.7	5.5	5.4
49	Guyana	281.9	279.3	272.7	271.8	267.7	305.3
50	Haiti	1.1	0.9	0.8	0.6	0.5	0.5
51	Honduras	21.7	17.3	13.6	11.3	9.5	8.2
52	Hungary	6.6	6.4	6.1	6.1	5.8	5.8
53	Iceland	415.4	388.3	361.9	335.5	309.9	298.5
54	India	4.1	3.7	3.3	3.0	2.7	2.5
55	Indonesia	16.4	14.3	12.7	11.4	10.1	9.0

	Country/year	1990	1995	2000	2005	2010	2014
56	Iran (Islamic Republic of)	84.9	77.6	69.5	63.3	58.1	52.7
57	Iraq	88.2	75.6	63.8	54.4	46.4	39.6
58	Ireland	12.2	9.7	8.8	7.6	6.9	6.4
59	Israel	3.1	2.6	2.3	2.0	1.8	1.5
60	Italy	6.3	6.1	6.2	6.1	6.1	5.5
61	Jamaica	13.5	13.4	12.5	12.0	11.3	11.1
62	Japan	4.6	4.4	4.2	4.0	3.9	3.6
63	Jordan	2.3	1.8	1.6	1.4	1.1	0.9
64	Kazakhstan	56.9	64.2	67.1	64.2	57.4	52.3
65	Kenya	2.0	1.7	1.4	1.2	1.1	1.1
66	Kuwait	780.1	962.1	790.0	650.1	460.5	361.8
67	Kyrgyzstan	3.6	3.6	3.3	3.2	3.4	3.1
68	Lao People's Democratic Republic	35.4	30.3	27.1	24.7	22.4	22.7
69	Latvia	7.9	8.9	9.9	10.9	12.7	12.7
70	Lesotho	0.1	0.1	0.1	0.1	0.1	0.1
71	Liberia	17.8	17.4	12.1	10.3	8.2	7.2
72	Lithuania	4.6	4.8	5.0	5.4	5.8	5.9
73	Luxembourg	3.0	3.2	3.3	3.1	2.8	2.5
74	Malawi	2.6	2.4	2.1	1.8	1.5	1.3
75	Malaysia	34.5	28.8	23.8	19.9	16.8	15.4
76	Maldives	14.2	11.6	11.0	8.9	5.3	4.8
77	Mali	8.9	7.7	6.7	5.6	4.6	2.7
78	Malta	0.6	0.5	0.4	0.4	0.5	0.4
79	Mauritania	9.9	7.8	6.3	4.9	4.0	3.3
80	Mauritius	2.2	1.9	1.7	1.4	1.3	1.3
81	Mexico	13.4	11.7	10.3	9.1	8.0	7.6
82	Mongolia	101.2	92.5	90.9	80.1	73.2	69.2
83	Morocco	3.4	3.0	2.7	2.5	2.3	2.2
84	Mozambique	20.4	16.8	14.4	12.2	15.3	13.5
85	Myanmar	6.0	5.3	4.6	4.1	3.6	3.3
86	Namibia	38.3	34.0	30.7	29.7	30.0	26.7
87	Nepal	11.8	9.4	7.7	6.7	6.3	6.0
88	Netherlands	10.5	8.9	7.6	6.4	5.3	4.4
89	New Zealand	483.1	434.2	412.7	367.8	434.3	379.8
90	Nicaragua	10.2	8.8	7.8	6.9	5.9	6.0
91	Niger	1.9	1.4	1.0	0.9	0.7	0.6
92	Nigeria	10.0	8.5	7.1	5.8	4.7	3.9
93	Norway	137.7	122.2	100.7	79.8	60.9	48.7
94	Pakistan	13.5	10.6	8.4	6.6	5.1	4.0
95	Panama	18.7	16.1	13.9	12.4	11.1	12.2
96	Papua New Guinea	78.7	67.4	57.4	49.4	42.6	53.3
97	Paraguay	27.2	23.1	21.1	18.6	17.1	15.2
98	Peru	61.0	54.3	49.7	45.7	42.0	41.8
99	Philippines	2.3	2.0	1.8	1.7	1.6	1.4

(*Continued*)

Table A3.14 (Continued)

	Country/year	1990	1995	2000	2005	2010	2014
100	Poland	14.3	13.6	13.2	12.6	12.1	11.8
101	Portugal	6.2	6.3	6.4	6.0	5.9	5.6
102	Qatar	948.7	884.2	724.9	491.3	217.1	161.7
103	Republic of Korea	9.8	9.3	9.1	9.1	8.9	7.8
104	Republic of Moldova	1.6	1.7	1.8	2.0	2.1	0.4
105	Romania	9.4	9.2	9.0	9.0	9.3	9.2
106	Russian Federation	73.6	87.4	86.6	86.3	84.6	81.7
107	Rwanda	0.4	0.4	0.3	0.3	0.4	0.4
108	Saudi Arabia	359.5	334.1	284.7	237.3	200.1	179.6
109	Senegal	10.9	9.0	7.6	6.4	5.5	4.8
110	Serbia	3.3	3.4	3.5	4.0	5.8	5.1
111	Sierra Leone	5.1	5.0	4.6	3.5	2.9	2.6
112	Singapore	0.1	0.1	0.1	0.1	0.0	0.0
113	Slovakia	2.8	2.9	2.9	2.8	2.8	2.6
114	Slovenia	12.0	12.4	12.7	13.2	13.4	12.2
115	South Africa	13.7	11.8	9.9	8.7	7.6	6.7
116	Spain	7.6	7.6	7.7	7.1	6.7	6.6
117	Sri Lanka	4.6	4.1	3.6	3.2	2.9	3.1
118	Sudan (former)	20.7	16.1	13.6	11.7	10.1	5.2
119	Swaziland	2.9	2.7	2.5	2.5	2.4	2.4
120	Sweden	24.5	23.2	22.5	22.3	21.0	15.9
121	Switzerland	12.8	12.1	11.9	11.4	10.8	10.2
122	Syrian Arab Republic	6.5	5.0	3.7	2.8	2.0	1.9
123	Tajikistan	1.2	1.1	1.1	1.0	0.9	0.8
124	Thailand	6.1	5.6	4.9	4.4	4.1	4.0
125	Togo	1.5	1.2	1.0	0.7	0.6	0.5
126	Trinidad and Tobago	58.7	53.5	48.7	41.1	30.8	20.6
127	Tunisia	3.5	2.9	2.5	2.1	1.8	1.5
128	Turkey	12.0	10.9	10.1	9.2	8.1	7.5
129	Uganda	2.8	2.3	1.9	1.5	1.2	1.0
130	Ukraine	12.9	14.1	14.6	15.0	15.1	15.0
131	United Arab Emirates	743.0	552.3	409.3	266.9	136.6	119.5
132	United Kingdom	8.6	7.2	5.5	4.2	3.2	2.6
133	United Republic of Tanzania	11.4	9.3	7.8	6.5	5.3	7.3
134	United States of America	44.0	40.1	36.8	34.5	32.4	29.8
135	Uruguay	12.3	11.8	11.3	11.2	10.7	10.5
136	Venezuela (Bolivarian Republic of)	241.1	212.5	189.0	169.7	154.1	144.1
137	Viet Nam	5.4	5.0	4.6	4.3	3.9	3.6
138	Yemen	7.4	5.6	4.4	3.4	3.6	3.1
139	Zambia	42.8	37.1	32.0	27.7	23.6	20.9
140	Zimbabwe	9.8	8.1	7.0	6.2	5.3	4.5

Table A3.15 Natural capital growth (Natural capital change (%) with respect to base year 1990)

	Country/year	1995	2000	2005	2010	2014
1	Afghanistan	-0.1%	-0.2%	-0.2%	-0.3%	-0.8%
2	Albania	-0.4%	-0.9%	-1.1%	-1.2%	-2.1%
3	Algeria	-1.4%	-3.8%	-6.4%	-9.7%	-16.1%
4	Argentina	-0.4%	-1.2%	-1.4%	-1.4%	-2.7%
5	Armenia	-1.2%	-3.0%	-4.7%	13.4%	21.7%
6	Australia	-0.2%	-0.7%	-1.3%	-2.4%	-4.5%
7	Austria	0.4%	1.0%	1.2%	0.5%	-0.9%
8	Bahrain	-3.3%	-8.9%	-14.4%	-21.1%	-36.3%
9	Bangladesh	-1.3%	-2.3%	-3.2%	-3.4%	-5.9%
10	Barbados	-1.2%	-3.2%	-6.1%	-7.5%	-12.3%
11	Belgium	2.9%	7.0%	9.5%	10.9%	13.2%
12	Belize	-0.5%	-1.3%	-2.0%	-2.6%	-4.1%
13	Benin	-1.4%	-3.4%	-4.8%	-6.2%	-8.1%
14	Bolivia (Plurinational State of)	-0.4%	-0.9%	-1.5%	-2.1%	-3.6%
15	Botswana	-0.8%	-2.1%	-3.2%	-4.3%	-6.9%
16	Brazil	-0.4%	-1.2%	-1.7%	-2.4%	-3.5%
17	Bulgaria	-0.3%	-1.0%	-1.0%	-0.8%	-12.0%
18	Burundi	-1.9%	-5.8%	-6.5%	-6.5%	-7.1%
19	Cambodia	-1.2%	-3.3%	-5.1%	-6.5%	-10.1%
20	Cameroon	-1.1%	-2.7%	-4.1%	-5.1%	-39.9%
21	Canada	-0.3%	-0.8%	-1.2%	-1.7%	-9.4%
22	Central African Republic	-0.1%	-0.3%	-0.5%	-0.7%	-0.9%
23	Chile	-0.7%	-1.7%	-2.0%	-3.1%	-4.6%
24	China	-0.3%	-1.2%	-2.5%	-3.6%	-6.2%
25	Colombia	-0.5%	-1.3%	-2.3%	-3.1%	-32.4%
26	Congo	-0.3%	-0.8%	-1.3%	-1.6%	-2.7%
27	Costa Rica	-1.5%	-3.5%	-3.3%	-2.7%	5.9%
28	Côte d'Ivoire	3.5%	7.9%	7.9%	8.1%	10.3%
29	Croatia	1.6%	2.4%	2.9%	3.4%	2.2%
30	Cuba	1.4%	2.9%	3.8%	3.3%	1.9%
31	Cyprus	-0.2%	0.2%	1.5%	-0.3%	-0.4%
32	Czech Republic	-0.9%	-3.0%	-4.9%	-6.8%	-10.7%
33	Democratic Republic of the Congo	-0.2%	-0.5%	-0.7%	-1.0%	-1.6%
34	Denmark	-2.2%	-6.2%	-10.9%	-14.8%	-23.8%
35	Dominican Republic	-0.1%	-0.5%	-1.1%	-1.4%	-2.6%
36	Ecuador	-1.0%	-2.6%	-4.1%	-5.8%	-7.7%
37	Egypt	-1.9%	-5.3%	-8.1%	-11.4%	-18.8%
38	El Salvador	0.3%	0.5%	1.5%	1.5%	2.2%
39	Estonia	-5.9%	-16.9%	1.7%	1.5%	1.1%
40	Fiji	0.4%	0.5%	0.5%	0.5%	1.1%

(*Continued*)

Table A3.15 (Continued)

	Country/year	1995	2000	2005	2010	2014
41	Finland	0.2%	0.7%	−0.1%	−0.8%	−2.3%
42	France	0.0%	0.1%	0.3%	0.2%	−0.1%
43	Gabon	−0.1%	−0.3%	−0.4%	−0.5%	−0.8%
44	Gambia	−3.5%	−4.5%	−5.4%	−5.8%	−9.3%
45	Germany	−0.7%	−1.6%	−2.4%	−3.1%	−4.7%
46	Ghana	−1.1%	−2.5%	−4.0%	−5.7%	0.2%
47	Greece	−0.5%	−2.2%	−3.1%	−4.0%	−6.4%
48	Guatemala	−1.3%	−3.3%	−5.0%	−7.1%	−7.7%
49	Guyana	0.0%	−0.1%	−0.2%	−0.2%	4.7%
50	Haiti	−1.4%	−3.6%	−5.8%	−8.4%	−13.2%
51	Honduras	−1.9%	−5.6%	−7.5%	−9.6%	−15.1%
52	Hungary	−0.9%	−2.4%	−3.0%	−4.3%	−6.3%
53	Iceland	−0.4%	−1.0%	−1.5%	−1.8%	−2.6%
54	India	−0.3%	−0.8%	−1.3%	−1.9%	−3.5%
55	Indonesia	−1.1%	−2.5%	−3.4%	−4.8%	−8.2%
56	Iran (Islamic Republic of)	−0.4%	−1.0%	−1.8%	−2.5%	−4.8%
57	Iraq	−0.2%	−0.6%	−1.2%	−1.8%	−3.2%
58	Ireland	−3.8%	−6.0%	−7.3%	−7.2%	−11.6%
59	Israel	−0.2%	−0.5%	−1.4%	−2.1%	−4.8%
60	Italy	−0.5%	0.1%	0.0%	0.5%	−1.9%
61	Jamaica	0.6%	−0.1%	−0.6%	−1.5%	−2.1%
62	Japan	−0.7%	−1.6%	−2.7%	−3.0%	−6.9%
63	Jordan	0.1%	−0.7%	−1.7%	−2.3%	−3.6%
64	Kazakhstan	1.8%	1.8%	1.1%	0.2%	−1.0%
65	Kenya	−0.2%	−1.0%	−1.4%	−1.6%	0.7%
66	Kuwait	−0.4%	−1.3%	−2.2%	−3.2%	−5.4%
67	Kyrgyzstan	0.4%	0.9%	1.2%	3.9%	4.2%
68	Lao People's Democratic Republic	−0.4%	−1.0%	−1.4%	−1.8%	0.3%
69	Latvia	1.2%	2.7%	3.8%	6.2%	6.4%
70	Lesotho	−0.1%	−0.1%	−0.2%	−0.3%	−1.8%
71	Liberia	−0.7%	−1.7%	−2.5%	−3.4%	−5.5%
72	Lithuania	0.4%	0.9%	1.5%	1.5%	0.4%
73	Luxembourg	2.2%	5.2%	5.2%	5.2%	5.8%
74	Malawi	−0.7%	−1.3%	−2.0%	−2.6%	−4.0%
75	Malaysia	−1.0%	−2.9%	−5.0%	−6.9%	−9.8%
76	Maldives	−0.8%	0.4%	−2.0%	−11.0%	−14.5%
77	Mali	−0.2%	−0.5%	−1.1%	−2.1%	−15.5%
78	Malta	−1.7%	−4.7%	−3.6%	−1.9%	−5.5%
79	Mauritania	−2.0%	−4.1%	−6.2%	−7.7%	−13.4%
80	Mauritius	−1.3%	−3.3%	−6.3%	−7.6%	−11.5%
81	Mexico	−0.8%	−2.1%	−3.4%	−4.6%	−6.3%
82	Mongolia	−0.8%	−0.4%	−2.2%	−2.7%	−3.1%
83	Morocco	−0.5%	−1.3%	−2.1%	−2.6%	−3.7%

	Country/year	1995	2000	2005	2010	2014
84	Mozambique	−0.4%	−0.9%	−1.3%	8.1%	10.4%
85	Myanmar	−1.3%	−3.4%	−5.3%	−7.1%	−11.5%
86	Namibia	0.7%	1.8%	2.7%	5.0%	5.7%
87	Nepal	−1.9%	−4.9%	−6.5%	−6.5%	−8.6%
88	Netherlands	−2.6%	−6.5%	−9.7%	−13.4%	−21.9%
89	New Zealand	−0.2%	−0.3%	−1.4%	4.1%	2.1%
90	Nicaragua	−0.7%	−1.7%	−3.2%	−5.3%	−5.2%
91	Niger	−2.3%	−5.7%	−5.5%	−6.6%	−9.0%
92	Nigeria	−0.8%	−2.3%	−3.9%	−6.1%	−9.9%
93	Norway	−1.8%	−6.2%	−10.9%	−15.5%	−24.6%
94	Pakistan	−2.1%	−5.5%	−8.7%	−12.2%	−19.8%
95	Panama	−0.9%	−2.2%	−2.9%	−3.3%	0.9%
96	Papua New Guinea	−0.6%	−1.5%	−2.1%	−2.8%	6.7%
97	Paraguay	−0.9%	−0.6%	−1.6%	−2.0%	−4.6%
98	Peru	−0.4%	−0.8%	−1.3%	−1.9%	−0.9%
99	Philippines	−0.1%	0.0%	0.1%	1.1%	−0.6%
100	Poland	−0.8%	−1.9%	−3.1%	−4.1%	−6.3%
101	Portugal	0.3%	1.4%	0.6%	0.2%	−2.1%
102	Qatar	−0.4%	−1.2%	−2.3%	−4.0%	−8.1%
103	Republic of Korea	0.0%	0.5%	1.1%	1.3%	−2.0%
104	Republic of Moldova	1.3%	3.2%	4.9%	6.3%	−36.6%
105	Romania	−0.8%	−1.9%	−3.1%	−3.6%	−5.5%
106	Russian Federation	3.5%	3.8%	3.2%	2.6%	2.5%
107	Rwanda	−3.7%	−3.1%	−1.6%	10.8%	14.0%
108	Saudi Arabia	1.4%	0.9%	0.0%	−1.1%	−1.9%
109	Senegal	−0.9%	−2.1%	−3.0%	−3.4%	−4.9%
110	Serbia	0.6%	1.6%	4.6%	14.1%	13.0%
111	Sierra Leone	−0.9%	−2.2%	−3.5%	−5.0%	−7.2%
112	Singapore	−4.7%	−7.4%	−8.6%	−10.3%	−5.7%
113	Slovakia	1.2%	1.3%	1.1%	0.8%	−1.0%
114	Slovenia	0.6%	1.4%	2.3%	3.4%	1.7%
115	South Africa	−0.8%	−2.3%	−3.9%	−5.5%	−9.0%
116	Spain	0.3%	1.2%	1.3%	1.3%	1.4%
117	Sri Lanka	−1.3%	−3.6%	−5.6%	−7.0%	−6.9%
118	Sudan (former)	−0.8%	−2.0%	−2.5%	−3.2%	−21.1%
119	Swaziland	0.9%	2.1%	3.0%	3.9%	6.5%
120	Sweden	−0.5%	−1.2%	−0.9%	−1.5%	−9.8%
121	Switzerland	−0.1%	−0.2%	−0.3%	−0.4%	−1.0%
122	Syrian Arab Republic	−2.5%	−7.3%	−11.4%	−15.2%	−23.5%
123	Tajikistan	0.5%	0.6%	0.5%	0.5%	0.5%
124	Thailand	−0.9%	−2.7%	−4.3%	−5.6%	−7.6%
125	Togo	−1.8%	−4.0%	−7.2%	−8.5%	−13.8%
126	Trinidad and Tobago	−1.3%	−3.7%	−7.2%	−13.1%	−27.0%
127	Tunisia	−1.8%	−4.7%	−7.3%	−10.0%	−15.8%

(*Continued*)

Table A3.15 (Continued)

	Country/year	1995	2000	2005	2010	2014
128	Turkey	−0.3%	−0.6%	−1.1%	−2.5%	−3.6%
129	Uganda	−0.8%	−2.0%	−3.0%	−3.9%	−7.8%
130	Ukraine	1.5%	1.6%	1.2%	0.8%	0.4%
131	United Arab Emirates	−0.7%	−1.9%	−2.9%	−4.1%	−6.9%
132	United Kingdom	−3.2%	−9.7%	−15.4%	−19.8%	−30.3%
133	United Republic of Tanzania	−0.9%	−2.2%	−3.3%	−4.4%	9.5%
134	United States of America	−0.6%	−1.4%	−1.9%	−2.3%	−4.7%
135	Uruguay	−0.2%	−0.5%	−0.8%	−1.6%	−2.1%
136	Venezuela (Bolivarian Republic of)	−0.3%	−0.9%	−1.3%	−1.7%	−2.6%
137	Viet Nam	0.0%	0.0%	−0.6%	−1.5%	−2.9%
138	Yemen	−0.9%	−3.1%	−5.9%	−0.8%	−2.9%
139	Zambia	−0.3%	−0.7%	−1.1%	−1.4%	−2.0%
140	Zimbabwe	−1.5%	−3.8%	−5.8%	−7.9%	−12.6%

Table A3.16 Natural capital per capita growth (Natural capital per capita change (%) with respect to base year 1990)

	Country/year	1995	2000	2005	2010	2014
1	Afghanistan	−6.5%	−11.7%	−16.3%	−19.2%	−28.1%
2	Albania	0.2%	0.7%	1.1%	1.8%	2.1%
3	Algeria	−3.5%	−8.2%	−12.1%	−16.8%	−26.7%
4	Argentina	−1.8%	−4.2%	−5.7%	−6.9%	−11.1%
5	Armenia	0.7%	0.5%	−0.8%	18.6%	28.6%
6	Australia	−1.4%	−3.5%	−5.6%	−8.4%	−14.1%
7	Austria	−0.3%	−0.1%	−0.5%	−1.6%	−4.4%
8	Bahrain	−5.7%	−15.4%	−25.6%	−37.5%	−54.5%
9	Bangladesh	−3.5%	−7.4%	−10.2%	−11.7%	−17.8%
10	Barbados	−1.5%	−4.1%	−7.3%	−9.2%	−14.8%
11	Belgium	2.5%	6.2%	8.1%	8.4%	8.8%
12	Belize	−2.4%	−7.9%	−11.6%	−14.9%	−22.2%
13	Benin	−4.8%	−11.0%	−15.8%	−20.1%	−28.4%
14	Bolivia (Plurinational State of)	−2.3%	−5.7%	−8.3%	−10.8%	−16.6%
15	Botswana	−3.4%	−7.5%	−10.2%	−13.3%	−20.5%
16	Brazil	−2.0%	−4.9%	−7.1%	−9.0%	−13.1%
17	Bulgaria	0.4%	0.6%	2.0%	3.3%	−6.3%
18	Burundi	−3.9%	−10.1%	−14.3%	−17.9%	−25.4%
19	Cambodia	−4.6%	−10.3%	−13.9%	−16.8%	−24.7%
20	Cameroon	−3.9%	−9.3%	−13.3%	−16.9%	−51.3%

	Country/year	1995	2000	2005	2010	2014
21	Canada	-1.4%	-3.3%	-4.9%	-6.6%	-16.5%
22	Central African Republic	-2.6%	-6.1%	-8.2%	-10.4%	-15.9%
23	Chile	-2.3%	-5.2%	-6.9%	-9.2%	-13.7%
24	China	-1.5%	-3.8%	-5.8%	-7.5%	-11.8%
25	Colombia	-2.3%	-5.3%	-7.8%	-10.0%	-39.5%
26	Congo	-2.9%	-7.2%	-10.4%	-13.9%	-21.3%
27	Costa Rica	-3.9%	-9.1%	-10.7%	-11.6%	-8.2%
28	Côte d'Ivoire	0.0%	0.0%	-2.3%	-4.7%	-9.7%
29	Croatia	2.1%	4.4%	4.8%	5.5%	6.3%
30	Cuba	0.7%	1.6%	2.2%	1.6%	-0.6%
31	Cyprus	-2.3%	-4.9%	-5.8%	-9.0%	-13.1%
32	Czech Republic	-0.9%	-2.9%	-4.6%	-7.1%	-11.3%
33	Democratic Republic of the Congo	-3.9%	-8.1%	-11.8%	-15.5%	-23.6%
34	Denmark	-2.5%	-7.1%	-12.1%	-16.4%	-26.1%
35	Dominican Republic	-2.0%	-4.8%	-7.2%	-9.0%	-13.9%
36	Ecuador	-3.2%	-7.6%	-11.0%	-14.3%	-20.3%
37	Egypt	-3.9%	-9.8%	-14.4%	-19.4%	-30.4%
38	El Salvador	-0.9%	-2.0%	-1.6%	-2.0%	-2.8%
39	Estonia	-4.2%	-14.5%	5.5%	5.7%	7.2%
40	Fiji	-0.8%	-2.2%	-2.5%	-3.6%	-5.3%
41	Finland	-0.2%	-0.2%	-1.4%	-2.6%	-5.3%
42	France	-0.4%	-0.9%	-1.6%	-2.4%	-4.3%
43	Gabon	-2.7%	-6.5%	-9.2%	-11.8%	-18.0%
44	Gambia	-6.3%	-11.2%	-15.5%	-19.2%	-29.2%
45	Germany	-1.3%	-2.5%	-3.3%	-3.8%	-5.3%
46	Ghana	-3.7%	-8.4%	-12.7%	-17.0%	-18.1%
47	Greece	-1.2%	-3.6%	-4.9%	-6.0%	-8.5%
48	Guatemala	-3.7%	-9.1%	-13.3%	-17.6%	-23.4%
49	Guyana	-0.2%	-0.8%	-0.9%	-1.3%	2.7%
50	Haiti	-3.3%	-8.0%	-11.8%	-15.9%	-24.0%
51	Honduras	-4.5%	-11.1%	-15.0%	-18.7%	-27.8%
52	Hungary	-0.8%	-2.0%	-2.3%	-3.4%	-4.7%
53	Iceland	-1.3%	-3.4%	-5.2%	-7.1%	-10.4%
54	India	-2.2%	-5.4%	-7.8%	-10.0%	-15.4%
55	Indonesia	-2.7%	-6.2%	-8.6%	-11.3%	-18.0%
56	Iran (Islamic Republic of)	-1.8%	-4.9%	-7.1%	-9.0%	-14.7%
57	Iraq	-3.0%	-7.8%	-11.4%	-14.8%	-23.4%
58	Ireland	-4.4%	-7.9%	-11.1%	-13.1%	-19.3%
59	Israel	-3.6%	-7.7%	-10.7%	-13.4%	-21.2%
60	Italy	-0.6%	0.0%	-0.5%	-0.6%	-4.1%
61	Jamaica	-0.2%	-2.0%	-3.0%	-4.4%	-6.3%
62	Japan	-1.0%	-2.3%	-3.5%	-3.9%	-7.8%

(Continued)

Table A3.16 (Continued)

	Country/year	1995	2000	2005	2010	2014
63	Jordan	−4.8%	−9.0%	−12.4%	−17.2%	−26.0%
64	Kazakhstan	2.4%	4.2%	3.1%	0.2%	−2.8%
65	Kenya	−3.3%	−7.7%	−11.0%	−14.1%	−18.9%
66	Kuwait	4.3%	0.3%	−4.5%	−12.3%	−22.6%
67	Kyrgyzstan	−0.3%	−1.8%	−2.8%	−1.6%	−5.2%
68	Lao People's Democratic Republic	−3.1%	−6.5%	−8.6%	−10.8%	−13.8%
69	Latvia	2.6%	5.8%	8.4%	12.7%	17.1%
70	Lesotho	−1.9%	−3.8%	−4.8%	−5.9%	−10.4%
71	Liberia	−0.5%	−9.2%	−12.7%	−17.5%	−26.1%
72	Lithuania	0.8%	2.3%	4.3%	6.1%	8.5%
73	Luxembourg	0.8%	1.8%	0.2%	−2.0%	−6.7%
74	Malawi	−1.6%	−5.5%	−9.2%	−12.9%	−20.7%
75	Malaysia	−3.5%	−8.8%	−12.9%	−16.5%	−23.6%
76	Maldives	−3.9%	−6.2%	−11.1%	−21.9%	−30.2%
77	Mali	−2.7%	−6.8%	−10.9%	−15.4%	−33.1%
78	Malta	−2.6%	−6.4%	−6.7%	−5.7%	−11.3%
79	Mauritania	−4.7%	−10.8%	−16.0%	−20.0%	−30.8%
80	Mauritius	−2.5%	−6.1%	−9.7%	−11.3%	−16.5%
81	Mexico	−2.7%	−6.5%	−9.2%	−12.1%	−17.5%
82	Mongolia	−1.8%	−2.7%	−5.7%	−7.8%	−11.9%
83	Morocco	−2.2%	−4.9%	−6.8%	−8.5%	−13.0%
84	Mozambique	−3.8%	−8.4%	−12.0%	−7.0%	−12.8%
85	Myanmar	−2.5%	−6.4%	−9.3%	−11.8%	−18.3%
86	Namibia	−2.4%	−5.4%	−6.1%	−5.9%	−11.4%
87	Nepal	−4.4%	−10.3%	−13.4%	−14.6%	−20.2%
88	Netherlands	−3.3%	−7.9%	−11.7%	−15.6%	−25.0%
89	New Zealand	−2.1%	−3.9%	−6.6%	−2.6%	−7.7%
90	Nicaragua	−2.8%	−6.3%	−9.3%	−12.7%	−16.3%
91	Niger	−5.5%	−13.6%	−17.3%	−22.0%	−32.2%
92	Nigeria	−3.2%	−8.2%	−12.6%	−17.3%	−26.7%
93	Norway	−2.4%	−7.5%	−12.8%	−18.4%	−29.3%
94	Pakistan	−4.6%	−11.2%	−16.4%	−21.7%	−33.1%
95	Panama	−2.9%	−7.0%	−9.8%	−12.1%	−13.1%
96	Papua New Guinea	−3.1%	−7.6%	−11.0%	−14.2%	−12.2%
97	Paraguay	−3.3%	−6.1%	−9.1%	−11.0%	−17.7%
98	Peru	−2.3%	−5.0%	−7.0%	−8.9%	−11.9%
99	Philippines	−2.4%	−5.6%	−7.8%	−8.7%	−15.0%
100	Poland	−1.0%	−2.0%	−3.1%	−4.0%	−6.3%
101	Portugal	0.2%	0.6%	−0.6%	−1.3%	−3.4%
102	Qatar	−1.4%	−6.5%	−15.2%	−30.8%	−44.6%

	Country/year	1995	2000	2005	2010	2014
103	Republic of Korea	−1.0%	−1.8%	−1.8%	−2.3%	−7.2%
104	Republic of Moldova	1.4%	3.6%	5.7%	7.2%	−35.8%
105	Romania	−0.4%	−1.1%	−1.1%	−0.3%	−0.6%
106	Russian Federation	3.5%	4.1%	4.1%	3.5%	3.5%
107	Rwanda	0.3%	−5.4%	−6.8%	1.5%	−1.8%
108	Saudi Arabia	−1.5%	−5.7%	−9.9%	−13.6%	−20.7%
109	Senegal	−3.8%	−8.5%	−12.3%	−15.7%	−23.9%
110	Serbia	0.5%	1.8%	5.1%	15.2%	15.4%
111	Sierra Leone	−0.4%	−2.9%	−9.5%	−13.7%	−20.7%
112	Singapore	−7.4%	−13.6%	−16.0%	−21.0%	−22.4%
113	Slovakia	1.0%	0.9%	0.7%	0.3%	−1.7%
114	Slovenia	0.7%	1.5%	2.3%	2.8%	0.6%
115	South Africa	−2.9%	−7.6%	−10.7%	−13.8%	−21.1%
116	Spain	0.0%	0.3%	−1.7%	−3.2%	−4.4%
117	Sri Lanka	−2.5%	−5.7%	−8.5%	−10.7%	−12.8%
118	Sudan (former)	−4.9%	−10.0%	−13.3%	−16.5%	−37.1%
119	Swaziland	−1.3%	−3.1%	−3.2%	−4.2%	−6.4%
120	Sweden	−1.1%	−2.1%	−2.2%	−3.7%	−13.5%
121	Switzerland	−1.1%	−1.9%	−2.8%	−4.2%	−7.3%
122	Syrian Arab Republic	−5.2%	−13.4%	−19.4%	−25.4%	−33.3%
123	Tajikistan	−1.2%	−3.2%	−5.6%	−8.2%	−13.5%
124	Thailand	−1.8%	−5.2%	−7.8%	−9.4%	−13.0%
125	Togo	−4.2%	−9.9%	−15.8%	−19.7%	−30.1%
126	Trinidad and Tobago	−1.9%	−4.6%	−8.6%	−14.9%	−29.5%
127	Tunisia	−3.6%	−8.4%	−11.9%	−15.6%	−23.8%
128	Turkey	−1.9%	−4.4%	−6.6%	−9.4%	−14.5%
129	Uganda	−3.9%	−9.4%	−14.0%	−18.2%	−28.8%
130	Ukraine	1.7%	3.0%	3.7%	4.0%	5.0%
131	United Arab Emirates	−5.8%	−13.8%	−22.6%	−34.5%	−45.6%
132	United Kingdom	−3.4%	−10.3%	−16.5%	−21.7%	−33.0%
133	United Republic of Tanzania	−4.0%	−9.0%	−13.1%	−17.4%	−13.6%
134	United States of America	−1.8%	−4.4%	−5.9%	−7.4%	−12.2%
135	Uruguay	−0.9%	−2.1%	−2.4%	−3.5%	−5.2%
136	Venezuela (Bolivarian Republic of)	−2.5%	−5.9%	−8.4%	−10.6%	−15.8%
137	Viet Nam	−1.7%	−4.0%	−6.0%	−8.1%	−12.7%
138	Yemen	−5.6%	−12.2%	−17.7%	−16.3%	−25.2%
139	Zambia	−2.8%	−7.0%	−10.3%	−13.8%	−21.3%
140	Zimbabwe	−3.6%	−7.9%	−10.7%	−14.3%	−22.9%

Table A3.17 Renewable resources (Renewable resources in billions of constant 2005 US$)

	Country/year	1990	1995	2000	2005	2010	2014
1	Afghanistan	9	9	9	9	9	9
2	Albania	7	7	6	6	6	6
3	Algeria	16	15	14	13	11	12
4	Argentina	807	792	777	779	790	774
5	Armenia	3	3	2	2	2	2
6	Australia	1,299	1,296	1,284	1,263	1,177	1,099
7	Austria	54	56	58	59	58	56
8	Bahrain	1	1	1	1	1	1
9	Bangladesh	57	54	53	51	50	49
10	Barbados	1	1	1	0	0	0
11	Belgium	4	5	6	6	7	6
12	Belize	14	14	13	13	13	13
13	Benin	38	36	33	32	30	30
14	Bolivia (Plurinational State of)	725	712	698	684	668	653
15	Botswana	65	62	60	57	55	53
16	Brazil	6,988	6,848	6,691	6,568	6,421	6,416
17	Bulgaria	22	24	25	28	31	10
18	Burundi	5	5	4	4	4	4
19	Cambodia	248	233	217	201	189	180
20	Cameroon	234	223	213	203	193	48
21	Canada	2,884	2,885	2,895	2,902	2,908	1,958
22	Central African Republic	211	209	208	207	205	205
23	Chile	240	231	226	230	224	225
24	China	5,369	5,407	5,283	5,085	5,081	5,120
25	Colombia	771	757	752	733	724	178
26	Congo	259	258	258	257	257	257
27	Costa Rica	52	48	45	46	47	62
28	Côte d'Ivoire	58	70	81	81	81	80
29	Croatia	20	21	22	24	25	23
30	Cuba	16	18	21	24	25	23
31	Cyprus	1	1	1	1	1	1
32	Czech Republic	0	0	0	0	0	0
33	Democratic Republic of the Congo	1,320	1,307	1,294	1,281	1,268	1,258
34	Denmark	32	28	25	24	25	23
35	Dominican Republic	35	36	35	34	34	33
36	Ecuador	183	175	166	158	150	159
37	Egypt	11	13	13	13	14	14
38	El Salvador	9	9	9	9	9	9
39	Estonia	20	15	10	22	21	21
40	Fiji	8	8	8	8	8	8
41	Finland	166	168	171	165	161	155

	Country/year	1990	1995	2000	2005	2010	2014
42	France	272	273	275	278	277	274
43	Gabon	1,072	1,072	1,071	1,071	1,071	1,075
44	Gambia	5	5	5	4	4	4
45	Germany	148	150	154	157	156	160
46	Ghana	74	70	67	64	60	77
47	Greece	169	168	159	157	155	151
48	Guatemala	107	100	94	87	80	85
49	Guyana	201	201	201	200	200	232
50	Haiti	8	7	7	6	5	5
51	Honduras	107	97	85	78	71	65
52	Hungary	26	25	24	24	23	23
53	Iceland	106	104	102	100	99	98
54	India	1,256	1,248	1,241	1,242	1,243	1,216
55	Indonesia	1,902	1,795	1,730	1,695	1,628	1,557
56	Iran (Islamic Republic of)	566	569	565	535	540	446
57	Iraq	8	8	8	8	8	8
58	Ireland	41	34	32	31	31	29
59	Israel	5	5	5	4	4	4
60	Italy	329	323	338	341	351	327
61	Jamaica	28	29	28	27	26	26
62	Japan	530	518	508	491	489	450
63	Jordan	2	3	3	2	2	2
64	Kazakhstan	12	12	12	12	12	12
65	Kenya	46	46	44	44	43	47
66	Kuwait	1	0	0	0	0	0
67	Kyrgyzstan	5	6	6	6	8	8
68	Lao People's Democratic Republic	149	146	143	141	139	151
69	Latvia	21	22	23	24	27	25
70	Lesotho	0	0	0	0	0	0
71	Liberia	37	36	35	34	33	32
72	Lithuania	17	17	17	18	18	17
73	Luxembourg	1	1	1	1	1	1
74	Malawi	25	24	23	23	22	22
75	Malaysia	322	312	299	284	274	289
76	Maldives	3	3	3	3	2	2
77	Mali	75	75	74	72	69	46
78	Malta	0	0	0	0	0	0
79	Mauritania	15	13	12	11	10	8
80	Mauritius	2	2	2	2	2	2
81	Mexico	854	843	830	819	812	839
82	Mongolia	175	167	173	158	155	160
83	Morocco	84	81	79	77	75	74

(*Continued*)

Table A3.17 (Continued)

	Country/year	1990	1995	2000	2005	2010	2014
84	Mozambique	242	237	232	228	224	221
85	Myanmar	231	216	200	186	174	161
86	Namibia	54	56	58	60	63	61
87	Nepal	222	202	182	170	170	170
88	Netherlands	35	33	33	32	32	32
89	New Zealand	1,464	1,452	1,452	1,383	1,754	1,579
90	Nicaragua	42	41	39	37	34	36
91	Niger	12	10	9	9	8	8
92	Nigeria	241	248	246	240	224	224
93	Norway	100	102	99	102	106	108
94	Pakistan	1,313	1,173	1,034	891	755	651
95	Panama	46	44	42	41	40	47
96	Papua New Guinea	311	303	296	290	282	388
97	Paraguay	115	110	112	108	106	100
98	Peru	1,240	1,218	1,205	1,186	1,165	1,234
99	Philippines	131	130	131	132	134	128
100	Poland	49	49	48	43	40	39
101	Portugal	62	63	65	63	62	58
102	Qatar	1	1	1	1	1	1
103	Republic of Korea	397	399	410	423	428	384
104	Republic of Moldova	6	6	7	7	7	1
105	Romania	170	170	171	167	170	170
106	Russian Federation	6,598	6,581	6,563	6,554	6,586	6,553
107	Rwanda	3	2	3	3	3	3
108	Saudi Arabia	1,505	2,114	2,114	2,113	2,109	2,241
109	Senegal	82	78	75	72	71	70
110	Serbia	25	26	27	30	37	33
111	Sierra Leone	20	19	19	18	16	16
112	Singapore	0	0	0	0	0	0
113	Slovakia	10	10	11	11	11	11
114	Slovenia	14	15	17	18	20	18
115	South Africa	180	183	184	183	183	184
116	Spain	254	263	275	279	281	280
117	Sri Lanka	79	73	68	62	59	63
118	Sudan (former)	352	336	320	317	313	157
119	Swaziland	1	2	2	2	2	2
120	Sweden	196	192	187	190	185	142
121	Switzerland	86	85	85	85	84	84
122	Syrian Arab Republic	11	10	9	9	9	8
123	Tajikistan	1	1	1	1	1	1
124	Thailand	251	241	228	220	220	234
125	Togo	5	5	5	4	4	3
126	Trinidad and Tobago	7	7	7	7	7	3
127	Tunisia	9	9	9	9	9	9

	Country/year	1990	1995	2000	2005	2010	2014
128	Turkey	381	378	381	373	347	349
129	Uganda	21	19	17	15	13	10
130	Ukraine	44	49	53	55	57	53
131	United Arab Emirates	2	2	2	1	1	1
132	United Kingdom	153	143	135	132	132	121
133	United Republic of Tanzania	288	275	263	251	240	378
134	United States of America	5,051	5,090	5,140	5,294	5,459	5,246
135	Uruguay	38	38	38	37	36	36
136	Venezuela (Bolivarian Republic of)	471	461	452	444	436	444
137	Viet Nam	194	196	201	201	196	196
138	Yemen	37	37	36	35	34	34
139	Zambia	340	336	332	327	322	322
140	Zimbabwe	93	86	79	72	65	60

Table A3.18 Renewable resources per capita (Renewable resources per capita in thousands of constant 2005 US$)

	Country/year	1990	1995	2000	2005	2010	2014
1	Afghanistan	0.7	0.5	0.4	0.4	0.3	0.3
2	Albania	2.0	2.1	2.1	2.1	2.2	2.2
3	Algeria	0.6	0.5	0.4	0.4	0.3	0.3
4	Argentina	24.6	22.6	21.0	19.9	19.2	18.0
5	Armenia	0.8	0.8	0.8	0.8	0.7	0.8
6	Australia	76.1	71.7	67.0	61.9	53.4	46.8
7	Austria	7.0	7.0	7.2	7.2	7.0	6.6
8	Bahrain	2.1	1.8	1.4	1.0	0.6	0.5
9	Bangladesh	0.5	0.5	0.4	0.4	0.3	0.3
10	Barbados	2.1	2.1	2.0	1.8	1.8	1.7
11	Belgium	0.4	0.5	0.6	0.6	0.6	0.6
12	Belize	75.6	67.0	54.4	46.1	39.5	35.6
13	Benin	7.7	6.0	4.8	3.9	3.1	2.8
14	Bolivia (Plurinational State of)	105.7	94.1	83.8	74.9	67.3	61.8
15	Botswana	46.9	39.4	34.4	30.6	26.7	23.8
16	Brazil	46.5	42.1	38.1	34.8	32.3	31.1
17	Bulgaria	2.6	2.8	3.0	3.6	4.1	1.4
18	Burundi	1.0	0.8	0.6	0.5	0.4	0.4
19	Cambodia	27.5	21.8	17.8	15.1	13.2	11.8
20	Cameroon	19.4	16.0	13.4	11.2	9.4	2.1
21	Canada	103.8	98.3	94.1	89.8	85.5	55.1

(*Continued*)

Table A3.18 (Continued)

	Country/year	1990	1995	2000	2005	2010	2014
22	Central African Republic	71.7	62.8	55.8	50.9	46.2	42.6
23	Chile	18.3	16.3	14.9	14.3	13.1	12.7
24	China	4.7	4.5	4.2	3.9	3.8	3.8
25	Colombia	22.5	20.2	18.6	16.9	15.8	3.7
26	Congo	108.6	95.0	82.9	73.4	63.1	57.0
27	Costa Rica	16.9	13.8	11.5	10.7	10.3	13.1
28	Côte d'Ivoire	4.8	4.9	4.9	4.5	4.0	3.6
29	Croatia	4.3	4.6	5.1	5.3	5.6	5.5
30	Cuba	1.5	1.7	1.9	2.1	2.2	2.1
31	Cyprus	1.7	1.5	1.4	1.4	1.2	1.1
32	Czech Republic	0.0	0.0	0.0	0.0	0.0	0.0
33	Democratic Republic of the Congo	37.7	31.0	26.9	22.8	19.2	16.8
34	Denmark	6.2	5.4	4.7	4.4	4.4	4.0
35	Dominican Republic	4.9	4.5	4.1	3.7	3.4	3.2
36	Ecuador	18.0	15.3	13.2	11.5	10.1	10.0
37	Egypt	0.2	0.2	0.2	0.2	0.2	0.2
38	El Salvador	1.6	1.6	1.5	1.5	1.5	1.5
39	Estonia	12.8	10.4	6.9	15.9	15.9	15.8
40	Fiji	11.0	10.5	10.0	9.9	9.5	9.3
41	Finland	33.3	32.9	33.1	31.5	30.1	28.4
42	France	4.7	4.6	4.5	4.4	4.3	4.1
43	Gabon	1,125.5	986.4	870.0	777.5	694.8	636.7
44	Gambia	6.0	4.3	3.7	3.0	2.5	2.1
45	Germany	1.9	1.8	1.9	1.9	1.9	2.0
46	Ghana	5.1	4.2	3.6	3.0	2.5	2.9
47	Greece	16.6	15.9	14.7	14.3	13.9	13.9
48	Guatemala	11.7	9.7	8.0	6.6	5.4	5.3
49	Guyana	279.5	276.9	270.3	269.5	265.5	303.1
50	Haiti	1.1	0.9	0.8	0.6	0.5	0.5
51	Honduras	21.7	17.3	13.6	11.3	9.5	8.2
52	Hungary	2.5	2.4	2.4	2.4	2.3	2.3
53	Iceland	415.4	388.3	361.9	335.5	309.9	298.5
54	India	1.4	1.3	1.2	1.1	1.0	0.9
55	Indonesia	10.5	9.1	8.2	7.5	6.7	6.1
56	Iran (Islamic Republic of)	10.1	9.4	8.6	7.6	7.3	5.7
57	Iraq	0.5	0.4	0.3	0.3	0.2	0.2
58	Ireland	11.6	9.3	8.4	7.4	6.8	6.3
59	Israel	1.0	0.8	0.7	0.6	0.5	0.5
60	Italy	5.8	5.7	5.9	5.9	5.9	5.4
61	Jamaica	11.6	11.6	10.8	10.4	9.8	9.7

	Country/year	1990	1995	2000	2005	2010	2014
62	Japan	4.3	4.1	4.0	3.8	3.8	3.5
63	Jordan	0.7	0.6	0.5	0.5	0.4	0.3
64	Kazakhstan	0.7	0.8	0.8	0.8	0.8	0.7
65	Kenya	2.0	1.7	1.4	1.2	1.1	1.1
66	Kuwait	0.3	0.3	0.2	0.2	0.1	0.1
67	Kyrgyzstan	1.2	1.3	1.2	1.2	1.5	1.3
68	Lao People's Democratic Republic	35.1	30.0	26.8	24.5	22.2	22.5
69	Latvia	7.9	8.9	9.9	10.9	12.7	12.7
70	Lesotho	0.1	0.1	0.1	0.1	0.1	0.1
71	Liberia	17.8	17.4	12.1	10.3	8.2	7.2
72	Lithuania	4.5	4.7	5.0	5.4	5.8	5.9
73	Luxembourg	3.0	3.2	3.3	3.1	2.8	2.5
74	Malawi	2.6	2.4	2.1	1.8	1.5	1.3
75	Malaysia	17.7	15.0	12.8	11.0	9.8	9.7
76	Maldives	14.2	11.6	11.0	8.9	5.3	4.8
77	Mali	8.9	7.7	6.7	5.6	4.6	2.7
78	Malta	0.6	0.5	0.4	0.4	0.5	0.4
79	Mauritania	7.4	5.7	4.6	3.5	2.7	2.1
80	Mauritius	2.2	1.9	1.7	1.4	1.3	1.3
81	Mexico	10.0	8.9	8.1	7.5	6.8	6.7
82	Mongolia	80.2	72.7	72.1	62.4	57.1	54.9
83	Morocco	3.3	3.0	2.7	2.5	2.3	2.2
84	Mozambique	18.1	14.9	12.7	10.8	9.2	8.1
85	Myanmar	5.5	4.8	4.2	3.7	3.4	3.0
86	Namibia	38.3	34.0	30.7	29.7	28.7	25.5
87	Nepal	11.8	9.4	7.7	6.7	6.3	6.0
88	Netherlands	2.4	2.1	2.0	2.0	1.9	1.9
89	New Zealand	439.5	395.4	376.4	334.5	403.2	350.2
90	Nicaragua	10.2	8.8	7.8	6.9	5.9	6.0
91	Niger	1.5	1.1	0.8	0.7	0.5	0.4
92	Nigeria	2.5	2.3	2.0	1.7	1.4	1.3
93	Norway	23.6	23.4	22.1	22.0	21.7	21.1
94	Pakistan	12.2	9.6	7.5	5.8	4.4	3.5
95	Panama	18.7	16.1	13.9	12.4	11.1	12.2
96	Papua New Guinea	74.9	64.4	55.1	47.6	41.2	52.1
97	Paraguay	27.2	23.1	21.1	18.6	17.0	15.2
98	Peru	56.8	50.7	46.5	43.0	39.7	39.8
99	Philippines	2.1	1.9	1.7	1.5	1.4	1.3
100	Poland	1.3	1.3	1.3	1.1	1.0	1.0
101	Portugal	6.2	6.3	6.4	6.0	5.8	5.5
102	Qatar	1.6	1.5	1.3	0.8	0.4	0.3

(*Continued*)

Table A3.18 (Continued)

	Country/year	1990	1995	2000	2005	2010	2014
103	Republic of Korea	9.3	8.9	8.7	8.8	8.7	7.6
104	Republic of Moldova	1.6	1.7	1.8	2.0	2.1	0.4
105	Romania	7.3	7.5	7.6	7.9	8.4	8.5
106	Russian Federation	44.5	44.3	44.8	45.7	46.1	45.6
107	Rwanda	0.4	0.4	0.3	0.3	0.3	0.2
108	Saudi Arabia	92.0	112.1	98.8	85.4	75.1	72.6
109	Senegal	10.9	9.0	7.6	6.4	5.5	4.8
110	Serbia	3.3	3.4	3.5	4.0	5.0	4.7
111	Sierra Leone	5.1	5.0	4.6	3.5	2.9	2.6
112	Singapore	0.1	0.1	0.1	0.1	0.0	0.0
113	Slovakia	1.8	1.9	2.0	2.1	2.1	2.0
114	Slovenia	7.2	7.8	8.3	9.0	9.6	8.6
115	South Africa	5.1	4.7	4.2	3.9	3.6	3.4
116	Spain	6.5	6.7	6.8	6.4	6.0	6.0
117	Sri Lanka	4.6	4.1	3.6	3.2	2.9	3.1
118	Sudan (former)	17.6	13.6	11.4	9.9	8.7	4.0
119	Swaziland	1.7	1.7	1.6	1.7	1.6	1.6
120	Sweden	22.9	21.7	21.0	21.0	19.8	14.7
121	Switzerland	12.8	12.1	11.9	11.4	10.8	10.2
122	Syrian Arab Republic	0.9	0.7	0.5	0.5	0.4	0.4
123	Tajikistan	0.3	0.3	0.2	0.2	0.2	0.2
124	Thailand	4.4	4.1	3.6	3.3	3.3	3.5
125	Togo	1.4	1.1	0.9	0.7	0.6	0.5
126	Trinidad and Tobago	6.1	5.8	5.6	5.2	5.0	2.6
127	Tunisia	1.1	1.0	0.9	0.9	0.8	0.8
128	Turkey	7.1	6.5	6.0	5.5	4.8	4.5
129	Uganda	1.2	0.9	0.7	0.5	0.4	0.3
130	Ukraine	0.9	0.9	1.1	1.2	1.2	1.2
131	United Arab Emirates	1.2	0.8	0.5	0.3	0.1	0.1
132	United Kingdom	2.7	2.5	2.3	2.2	2.1	1.9
133	United Republic of Tanzania	11.3	9.2	7.7	6.4	5.2	7.3
134	United States of America	20.2	19.1	18.2	17.9	17.6	16.4
135	Uruguay	12.3	11.8	11.3	11.2	10.7	10.5
136	Venezuela (Bolivarian Republic of)	23.7	20.8	18.5	16.6	15.0	14.5
137	Viet Nam	2.9	2.7	2.6	2.4	2.3	2.2
138	Yemen	3.1	2.4	2.1	1.7	1.4	1.3
139	Zambia	41.8	36.3	31.3	27.1	23.2	20.5
140	Zimbabwe	8.8	7.3	6.3	5.6	4.7	4.0

Table A3.19 Renewable resources growth (Renewable resources change (%) with respect to base year 1990)

	Country/year	1995	2000	2005	2010	2014
1	Afghanistan	0.0%	0.0%	0.0%	0.0%	−0.1%
2	Albania	−0.1%	−0.4%	−0.6%	−0.5%	−0.7%
3	Algeria	−1.1%	−2.6%	−4.7%	−7.4%	−8.3%
4	Argentina	−0.4%	−0.9%	−0.9%	−0.5%	−1.3%
5	Armenia	−1.2%	−3.0%	−4.7%	−7.5%	−4.0%
6	Australia	0.0%	−0.3%	−0.7%	−2.4%	−5.4%
7	Austria	0.7%	1.7%	2.3%	1.9%	1.4%
8	Bahrain	−1.0%	−3.6%	−5.2%	−7.4%	−12.3%
9	Bangladesh	−1.3%	−2.2%	−3.0%	−3.3%	−5.4%
10	Barbados	−0.3%	−0.9%	−2.7%	−3.1%	−5.4%
11	Belgium	2.9%	7.0%	9.5%	10.5%	13.2%
12	Belize	−0.5%	−1.3%	−2.0%	−2.7%	−4.1%
13	Benin	−1.4%	−3.4%	−4.8%	−6.2%	−8.1%
14	Bolivia (Plurinational State of)	−0.4%	−0.9%	−1.4%	−2.0%	−3.4%
15	Botswana	−0.8%	−2.0%	−3.1%	−4.1%	−6.5%
16	Brazil	−0.4%	−1.1%	−1.5%	−2.1%	−2.8%
17	Bulgaria	1.4%	2.7%	5.5%	8.1%	−23.9%
18	Burundi	−1.9%	−5.8%	−6.5%	−6.5%	−7.1%
19	Cambodia	−1.2%	−3.3%	−5.1%	−6.5%	−10.1%
20	Cameroon	−0.9%	−2.3%	−3.5%	−4.6%	−40.8%
21	Canada	0.0%	0.1%	0.2%	0.2%	−12.1%
22	Central African Republic	−0.1%	−0.3%	−0.5%	−0.7%	−0.9%
23	Chile	−0.8%	−1.5%	−1.1%	−1.8%	−2.1%
24	China	0.1%	−0.4%	−1.4%	−1.4%	−1.6%
25	Colombia	−0.4%	−0.6%	−1.2%	−1.6%	−38.7%
26	Congo	−0.1%	−0.1%	−0.2%	−0.2%	−0.3%
27	Costa Rica	−1.5%	−3.5%	−3.3%	−2.7%	5.9%
28	Côte d'Ivoire	3.7%	8.4%	8.5%	8.5%	11.3%
29	Croatia	0.9%	2.4%	3.7%	4.9%	4.4%
30	Cuba	3.2%	7.6%	10.9%	11.8%	14.2%
31	Cyprus	−0.2%	0.2%	1.5%	−0.3%	−0.4%
32	Czech Republic	1.0%	2.5%	2.5%	3.7%	−13.3%
33	Democratic Republic of the Congo	−0.2%	−0.5%	−0.7%	−1.0%	−1.6%
34	Denmark	−2.4%	−5.7%	−6.9%	−6.1%	−10.3%
35	Dominican Republic	0.0%	−0.3%	−0.8%	−1.0%	−2.1%
36	Ecuador	−0.9%	−2.4%	−3.7%	−4.9%	−4.6%
37	Egypt	2.9%	3.0%	4.3%	4.5%	6.9%
38	El Salvador	0.3%	0.5%	1.5%	1.5%	2.2%
39	Estonia	−5.9%	−16.9%	1.7%	1.3%	1.1%
40	Fiji	0.4%	0.5%	0.5%	0.5%	1.1%

(*Continued*)

Table A3.19 (Continued)

	Country/year	1995	2000	2005	2010	2014
41	Finland	0.2%	0.7%	−0.1%	−0.8%	−2.3%
42	France	0.0%	0.2%	0.5%	0.4%	0.2%
43	Gabon	0.0%	0.0%	0.0%	0.0%	0.1%
44	Gambia	−3.5%	−4.5%	−5.4%	−5.8%	−9.3%
45	Germany	0.3%	1.0%	1.4%	1.4%	2.6%
46	Ghana	−1.0%	−2.4%	−3.7%	−5.3%	1.2%
47	Greece	−0.1%	−1.5%	−1.9%	−2.1%	−3.6%
48	Guatemala	−1.3%	−3.3%	−4.9%	−7.0%	−7.4%
49	Guyana	0.0%	−0.1%	−0.1%	−0.2%	4.8%
50	Haiti	−1.4%	−3.6%	−5.8%	−8.4%	−13.2%
51	Honduras	−1.9%	−5.6%	−7.5%	−9.6%	−15.1%
52	Hungary	−0.6%	−1.7%	−1.5%	−3.4%	−4.5%
53	Iceland	−0.4%	−1.0%	−1.5%	−1.8%	−2.6%
54	India	−0.1%	−0.3%	−0.3%	−0.3%	−1.1%
55	Indonesia	−1.1%	−2.3%	−2.8%	−3.8%	−6.4%
56	Iran (Islamic Republic of)	0.1%	0.0%	−1.4%	−1.1%	−7.6%
57	Iraq	0.0%	−1.4%	0.2%	−1.7%	−2.0%
58	Ireland	−3.8%	−5.7%	−6.8%	−6.6%	−10.6%
59	Israel	−0.2%	−0.7%	−2.8%	−3.3%	−4.2%
60	Italy	−0.3%	0.7%	0.9%	1.7%	−0.1%
61	Jamaica	0.7%	0.1%	−0.3%	−1.4%	−1.8%
62	Japan	−0.5%	−1.1%	−1.9%	−2.0%	−5.3%
63	Jordan	1.2%	0.6%	−0.6%	−0.8%	−1.1%
64	Kazakhstan	−0.3%	−0.8%	0.5%	0.3%	0.4%
65	Kenya	−0.2%	−1.0%	−1.4%	−1.6%	0.7%
66	Kuwait	−1.9%	−3.6%	−3.6%	−4.7%	−8.7%
67	Kyrgyzstan	0.9%	2.3%	3.4%	10.4%	12.0%
68	Lao People's Democratic Republic	−0.4%	−1.0%	−1.4%	−1.8%	0.4%
69	Latvia	1.2%	2.7%	3.8%	6.2%	6.4%
70	Lesotho	−0.1%	−0.1%	−0.2%	−0.3%	−1.8%
71	Liberia	−0.7%	−1.7%	−2.5%	−3.4%	−5.5%
72	Lithuania	0.4%	1.0%	1.8%	1.8%	1.0%
73	Luxembourg	2.2%	5.2%	5.2%	5.2%	5.8%
74	Malawi	−0.7%	−1.3%	−2.0%	−2.6%	−4.0%
75	Malaysia	−0.7%	−1.8%	−3.1%	−3.9%	−3.6%
76	Maldives	−0.8%	0.4%	−2.0%	−11.0%	−14.5%
77	Mali	−0.2%	−0.5%	−1.1%	−2.1%	−15.5%
78	Malta	−1.7%	−4.7%	−3.6%	−1.9%	−5.5%
79	Mauritania	−2.4%	−4.7%	−7.3%	−10.5%	−17.6%
80	Mauritius	−1.3%	−3.3%	−6.3%	−7.6%	−11.5%
81	Mexico	−0.2%	−0.7%	−1.0%	−1.3%	−0.6%
82	Mongolia	−0.9%	−0.3%	−2.6%	−3.0%	−3.0%
83	Morocco	−0.5%	−1.3%	−2.1%	−2.6%	−3.7%

	Country/year	1995	2000	2005	2010	2014
84	Mozambique	−0.4%	−1.0%	−1.5%	−1.9%	−3.0%
85	Myanmar	−1.3%	−3.6%	−5.4%	−6.9%	−11.5%
86	Namibia	0.7%	1.8%	2.7%	3.9%	4.2%
87	Nepal	−1.9%	−4.9%	−6.5%	−6.5%	−8.6%
88	Netherlands	−1.2%	−2.0%	−2.2%	−2.2%	−3.7%
89	New Zealand	−0.2%	−0.2%	−1.4%	4.6%	2.6%
90	Nicaragua	−0.7%	−1.7%	−3.2%	−5.3%	−5.2%
91	Niger	−2.8%	−7.2%	−6.9%	−8.2%	−10.6%
92	Nigeria	0.6%	0.6%	−0.1%	−1.8%	−2.3%
93	Norway	0.4%	−0.2%	0.5%	1.5%	2.7%
94	Pakistan	−2.2%	−5.8%	−9.2%	−12.9%	−20.8%
95	Panama	−0.9%	−2.2%	−2.9%	−3.3%	0.9%
96	Papua New Guinea	−0.5%	−1.2%	−1.8%	−2.4%	7.6%
97	Paraguay	−0.9%	−0.6%	−1.6%	−2.0%	−4.6%
98	Peru	−0.4%	−0.7%	−1.1%	−1.5%	−0.2%
99	Philippines	−0.1%	0.0%	0.2%	0.7%	−0.8%
100	Poland	0.0%	−0.3%	−3.2%	−4.9%	−7.2%
101	Portugal	0.3%	1.4%	0.7%	0.0%	−2.3%
102	Qatar	−0.3%	0.1%	−1.5%	−3.6%	−3.8%
103	Republic of Korea	0.1%	0.8%	1.6%	1.9%	−1.1%
104	Republic of Moldova	1.3%	3.2%	4.9%	6.3%	−36.6%
105	Romania	0.0%	0.1%	−0.4%	0.0%	0.0%
106	Russian Federation	−0.1%	−0.1%	−0.2%	0.0%	−0.2%
107	Rwanda	−3.7%	−3.1%	−1.6%	−1.5%	−2.9%
108	Saudi Arabia	7.0%	8.9%	8.9%	8.8%	14.2%
109	Senegal	−0.9%	−2.1%	−3.0%	−3.3%	−4.8%
110	Serbia	0.6%	1.6%	4.6%	10.1%	10.1%
111	Sierra Leone	−0.9%	−2.2%	−3.5%	−5.0%	−7.2%
112	Singapore	−4.7%	−7.4%	−8.6%	−11.0%	−5.7%
113	Slovakia	0.9%	2.2%	3.3%	4.1%	4.0%
114	Slovenia	1.5%	3.7%	5.9%	8.1%	7.3%
115	South Africa	0.3%	0.6%	0.5%	0.4%	0.7%
116	Spain	0.7%	2.1%	2.5%	2.6%	3.3%
117	Sri Lanka	−1.3%	−3.6%	−5.6%	−7.0%	−6.9%
118	Sudan (former)	−0.9%	−2.3%	−2.6%	−2.9%	−23.6%
119	Swaziland	1.5%	3.6%	5.2%	6.7%	11.1%
120	Sweden	−0.5%	−1.2%	−0.9%	−1.4%	−10.1%
121	Switzerland	−0.1%	−0.2%	−0.3%	−0.4%	−1.0%
122	Syrian Arab Republic	−1.8%	−4.1%	−4.9%	−3.9%	−9.6%
123	Tajikistan	−0.1%	−0.2%	−0.3%	−0.3%	−0.4%
124	Thailand	−0.8%	−2.4%	−3.2%	−3.2%	−2.3%
125	Togo	−1.7%	−3.7%	−6.9%	−8.1%	−13.3%
126	Trinidad and Tobago	−0.5%	−1.3%	−2.2%	−2.8%	−22.5%
127	Tunisia	0.1%	−0.2%	−0.4%	−0.4%	−0.8%

(*Continued*)

Table A3.19 (Continued)

	Country/year	1995	2000	2005	2010	2014
128	Turkey	−0.2%	0.0%	−0.5%	−2.3%	−2.9%
129	Uganda	−1.9%	−4.9%	−7.7%	−10.0%	−21.0%
130	Ukraine	1.8%	4.3%	5.3%	6.2%	6.0%
131	United Arab Emirates	−2.6%	−7.1%	−12.3%	−15.0%	−20.6%
132	United Kingdom	−1.3%	−3.2%	−3.8%	−3.8%	−7.7%
133	United Republic of Tanzania	−0.9%	−2.2%	−3.3%	−4.5%	9.6%
134	United States of America	0.2%	0.4%	1.2%	2.0%	1.3%
135	Uruguay	−0.2%	−0.5%	−0.8%	−1.6%	−2.1%
136	Venezuela (Bolivarian Republic of)	−0.5%	−1.0%	−1.5%	−1.9%	−2.0%
137	Viet Nam	0.2%	0.9%	0.9%	0.2%	0.3%
138	Yemen	0.0%	−0.5%	−1.7%	−2.2%	−3.3%
139	Zambia	−0.3%	−0.6%	−1.0%	−1.3%	−1.7%
140	Zimbabwe	−1.5%	−3.9%	−6.1%	−8.4%	−13.4%

Table A3.20 Renewable resources per capita growth (Renewable resources per capita change (%) with respect to base year 1990)

	Country/year	1995	2000	2005	2010	2014
1	Afghanistan	−6.4%	−11.5%	−16.1%	−18.9%	−27.5%
2	Albania	0.5%	1.2%	1.6%	2.6%	3.7%
3	Algeria	−3.2%	−7.0%	−10.5%	−14.7%	−20.0%
4	Argentina	−1.7%	−4.0%	−5.2%	−6.1%	−9.9%
5	Armenia	0.7%	0.5%	−0.8%	−3.2%	1.4%
6	Australia	−1.2%	−3.1%	−5.0%	−8.5%	−15.0%
7	Austria	0.0%	0.7%	0.6%	−0.2%	−2.2%
8	Bahrain	−3.5%	−10.5%	−17.6%	−26.7%	−37.3%
9	Bangladesh	−3.5%	−7.3%	−9.9%	−11.5%	−17.4%
10	Barbados	−0.7%	−1.8%	−4.0%	−4.8%	−8.0%
11	Belgium	2.5%	6.2%	8.1%	8.1%	8.8%
12	Belize	−2.4%	−7.9%	−11.6%	−15.0%	−22.2%
13	Benin	−4.8%	−11.0%	−15.8%	−20.1%	−28.4%
14	Bolivia (Plurinational State of)	−2.3%	−5.7%	−8.2%	−10.7%	−16.4%
15	Botswana	−3.4%	−7.5%	−10.1%	−13.1%	−20.2%
16	Brazil	−2.0%	−4.9%	−6.9%	−8.7%	−12.5%
17	Bulgaria	2.1%	4.4%	8.7%	12.7%	−19.0%
18	Burundi	−3.9%	−10.1%	−14.3%	−17.9%	−25.4%
19	Cambodia	−4.6%	−10.3%	−13.9%	−16.8%	−24.7%
20	Cameroon	−3.7%	−8.8%	−12.8%	−16.5%	−52.1%

	Country/year	1995	2000	2005	2010	2014
21	Canada	−1.1%	−2.4%	−3.6%	−4.7%	−19.0%
22	Central African Republic	−2.6%	−6.1%	−8.2%	−10.4%	−15.9%
23	Chile	−2.3%	−5.0%	−6.0%	−7.9%	−11.5%
24	China	−1.1%	−3.0%	−4.7%	−5.3%	−7.4%
25	Colombia	−2.1%	−4.6%	−6.8%	−8.5%	−45.1%
26	Congo	−2.6%	−6.5%	−9.3%	−12.7%	−19.3%
27	Costa Rica	−3.9%	−9.1%	−10.7%	−11.6%	−8.2%
28	Côte d'Ivoire	0.2%	0.4%	−1.8%	−4.3%	−8.8%
29	Croatia	1.4%	4.4%	5.6%	6.9%	8.6%
30	Cuba	2.6%	6.2%	9.2%	10.0%	11.4%
31	Cyprus	−2.3%	−4.9%	−5.8%	−9.0%	−13.1%
32	Czech Republic	1.0%	2.7%	2.8%	3.4%	−13.8%
33	Democratic Republic of the Congo	−3.9%	−8.1%	−11.8%	−15.5%	−23.6%
34	Denmark	−2.8%	−6.6%	−8.1%	−7.9%	−13.1%
35	Dominican Republic	−1.8%	−4.5%	−6.8%	−8.7%	−13.5%
36	Ecuador	−3.1%	−7.4%	−10.6%	−13.5%	−17.7%
37	Egypt	0.9%	−1.8%	−2.9%	−4.8%	−8.4%
38	El Salvador	−0.9%	−2.0%	−1.6%	−2.0%	−2.8%
39	Estonia	−4.2%	−14.5%	5.5%	5.6%	7.2%
40	Fiji	−0.8%	−2.2%	−2.5%	−3.6%	−5.3%
41	Finland	−0.2%	−0.2%	−1.4%	−2.6%	−5.2%
42	France	−0.3%	−0.8%	−1.4%	−2.2%	−4.0%
43	Gabon	−2.6%	−6.2%	−8.8%	−11.4%	−17.3%
44	Gambia	−6.3%	−11.2%	−15.5%	−19.2%	−29.2%
45	Germany	−0.3%	0.1%	0.5%	0.6%	1.9%
46	Ghana	−3.7%	−8.3%	−12.5%	−16.6%	−17.3%
47	Greece	−0.8%	−3.0%	−3.7%	−4.2%	−5.7%
48	Guatemala	−3.7%	−9.0%	−13.2%	−17.4%	−23.2%
49	Guyana	−0.2%	−0.8%	−0.9%	−1.3%	2.7%
50	Haiti	−3.3%	−8.0%	−11.8%	−15.9%	−24.0%
51	Honduras	−4.5%	−11.1%	−15.0%	−18.7%	−27.8%
52	Hungary	−0.6%	−1.3%	−0.8%	−2.5%	−2.9%
53	Iceland	−1.3%	−3.4%	−5.2%	−7.1%	−10.4%
54	India	−2.1%	−4.9%	−6.9%	−8.5%	−13.3%
55	Indonesia	−2.8%	−6.0%	−8.1%	−10.5%	−16.4%
56	Iran (Islamic Republic of)	−1.3%	−3.9%	−6.7%	−7.8%	−17.2%
57	Iraq	−2.9%	−8.5%	−10.1%	−14.7%	−22.4%
58	Ireland	−4.3%	−7.6%	−10.7%	−12.5%	−18.4%
59	Israel	−3.7%	−7.9%	−12.0%	−14.5%	−20.7%
60	Italy	−0.4%	0.6%	0.4%	0.5%	−2.4%
61	Jamaica	0.0%	−1.8%	−2.8%	−4.3%	−5.9%

(*Continued*)

Table A3.20 (Continued)

	Country/year	1995	2000	2005	2010	2014
62	Japan	−0.8%	−1.7%	−2.7%	−2.9%	−6.2%
63	Jordan	−3.8%	−7.9%	−11.4%	−16.0%	−24.1%
64	Kazakhstan	0.3%	1.6%	2.4%	0.4%	−1.4%
65	Kenya	−3.3%	−7.7%	−11.0%	−14.1%	−18.9%
66	Kuwait	2.7%	−2.0%	−5.9%	−13.7%	−25.3%
67	Kyrgyzstan	0.2%	−0.5%	−0.7%	4.6%	1.9%
68	Lao People's Democratic Republic	−3.1%	−6.5%	−8.6%	−10.8%	−13.7%
69	Latvia	2.6%	5.8%	8.4%	12.7%	17.1%
70	Lesotho	−1.9%	−3.8%	−4.8%	−5.9%	−10.4%
71	Liberia	−0.5%	−9.2%	−12.7%	−17.5%	−26.1%
72	Lithuania	0.8%	2.4%	4.6%	6.4%	9.2%
73	Luxembourg	0.8%	1.8%	0.2%	−2.0%	−6.7%
74	Malawi	−1.6%	−5.5%	−9.2%	−13.0%	−20.7%
75	Malaysia	−3.2%	−7.8%	−11.2%	−13.8%	−18.3%
76	Maldives	−3.9%	−6.2%	−11.1%	−21.9%	−30.2%
77	Mali	−2.7%	−6.8%	−10.9%	−15.4%	−33.1%
78	Malta	−2.6%	−6.4%	−6.7%	−5.7%	−11.3%
79	Mauritania	−5.1%	−11.4%	−17.0%	−22.5%	−34.2%
80	Mauritius	−2.5%	−6.1%	−9.7%	−11.3%	−16.5%
81	Mexico	−2.2%	−5.1%	−7.0%	−9.0%	−12.5%
82	Mongolia	−1.9%	−2.6%	−6.1%	−8.1%	−11.9%
83	Morocco	−2.2%	−4.9%	−6.8%	−8.6%	−13.1%
84	Mozambique	−3.8%	−8.5%	−12.1%	−15.5%	−23.4%
85	Myanmar	−2.6%	−6.6%	−9.4%	−11.7%	−18.3%
86	Namibia	−2.4%	−5.4%	−6.1%	−6.9%	−12.6%
87	Nepal	−4.4%	−10.3%	−13.4%	−14.6%	−20.2%
88	Netherlands	−1.9%	−3.6%	−4.3%	−4.7%	−7.5%
89	New Zealand	−2.1%	−3.8%	−6.6%	−2.1%	−7.3%
90	Nicaragua	−2.8%	−6.3%	−9.3%	−12.7%	−16.3%
91	Niger	−6.0%	−14.9%	−18.5%	−23.4%	−33.4%
92	Nigeria	−1.9%	−5.5%	−9.1%	−13.6%	−20.5%
93	Norway	−0.1%	−1.6%	−1.7%	−2.1%	−3.6%
94	Pakistan	−4.7%	−11.5%	−16.9%	−22.3%	−33.9%
95	Panama	−2.9%	−7.0%	−9.8%	−12.1%	−13.1%
96	Papua New Guinea	−3.0%	−7.4%	−10.7%	−13.9%	−11.4%
97	Paraguay	−3.3%	−6.1%	−9.1%	−11.0%	−17.7%
98	Peru	−2.3%	−4.9%	−6.8%	−8.6%	−11.2%
99	Philippines	−2.4%	−5.5%	−7.7%	−9.1%	−15.2%
100	Poland	−0.3%	−0.4%	−3.2%	−4.9%	−7.1%
101	Portugal	0.2%	0.6%	−0.6%	−1.4%	−3.6%
102	Qatar	−1.3%	−5.3%	−14.4%	−30.5%	−42.0%

	Country/year	1995	2000	2005	2010	2014
103	Republic of Korea	-0.9%	-1.5%	-1.3%	-1.6%	-6.3%
104	Republic of Moldova	1.4%	3.6%	5.7%	7.2%	-35.8%
105	Romania	0.5%	0.9%	1.7%	3.4%	5.2%
106	Russian Federation	-0.1%	0.2%	0.7%	0.9%	0.8%
107	Rwanda	0.3%	-5.4%	-6.8%	-9.7%	-16.3%
108	Saudi Arabia	4.0%	1.8%	-1.8%	-4.9%	-7.6%
109	Senegal	-3.8%	-8.5%	-12.3%	-15.6%	-23.9%
110	Serbia	0.5%	1.8%	5.1%	11.1%	12.4%
111	Sierra Leone	-0.4%	-2.9%	-9.5%	-13.7%	-20.7%
112	Singapore	-7.4%	-13.6%	-16.0%	-21.6%	-22.4%
113	Slovakia	0.7%	1.8%	2.9%	3.7%	3.2%
114	Slovenia	1.6%	3.8%	5.9%	7.5%	6.1%
115	South Africa	-1.8%	-4.9%	-6.7%	-8.3%	-12.7%
116	Spain	0.4%	1.2%	-0.5%	-1.9%	-2.7%
117	Sri Lanka	-2.5%	-5.7%	-8.5%	-10.7%	-12.8%
118	Sudan (former)	-5.0%	-10.3%	-13.4%	-16.2%	-39.0%
119	Swaziland	-0.7%	-1.7%	-1.1%	-1.6%	-2.3%
120	Sweden	-1.1%	-2.1%	-2.2%	-3.6%	-13.8%
121	Switzerland	-1.1%	-1.9%	-2.8%	-4.2%	-7.3%
122	Syrian Arab Republic	-4.5%	-10.4%	-13.4%	-15.4%	-21.2%
123	Tajikistan	-1.8%	-4.0%	-6.4%	-8.8%	-14.2%
124	Thailand	-1.7%	-4.8%	-6.8%	-7.1%	-8.0%
125	Togo	-4.1%	-9.6%	-15.5%	-19.3%	-29.7%
126	Trinidad and Tobago	-1.1%	-2.2%	-3.7%	-4.8%	-25.2%
127	Tunisia	-1.7%	-4.1%	-5.4%	-6.6%	-10.2%
128	Turkey	-1.7%	-3.9%	-6.0%	-9.2%	-13.9%
129	Uganda	-5.0%	-12.0%	-18.1%	-23.4%	-39.0%
130	Ukraine	1.9%	5.8%	7.9%	9.5%	10.8%
131	United Arab Emirates	-7.5%	-18.4%	-30.0%	-41.9%	-53.6%
132	United Kingdom	-1.6%	-3.9%	-5.1%	-6.0%	-11.3%
133	United Republic of Tanzania	-4.0%	-9.0%	-13.2%	-17.4%	-13.6%
134	United States of America	-1.1%	-2.6%	-3.0%	-3.4%	-6.7%
135	Uruguay	-0.9%	-2.1%	-2.4%	-3.5%	-5.2%
136	Venezuela (Bolivarian Republic of)	-2.6%	-6.1%	-8.6%	-10.8%	-15.2%
137	Viet Nam	-1.5%	-3.1%	-4.5%	-6.4%	-9.8%
138	Yemen	-4.8%	-9.9%	-14.1%	-17.5%	-25.6%
139	Zambia	-2.8%	-6.9%	-10.2%	-13.7%	-21.1%
140	Zimbabwe	-3.6%	-8.0%	-11.0%	-14.7%	-23.5%

Table A3.21 Non-renewable resources (Non-renewable resources in billions of constant 2005 US$)

	Country/year	1990	1995	2000	2005	2010	2014
1	Afghanistan	4	4	3	3	3	3
2	Albania	13	13	13	13	12	12
3	Algeria	604	563	516	462	401	354
4	Argentina	60	56	49	40	31	24
5	Armenia	–	–	–	–	3	3
6	Australia	2,041	2,006	1,963	1,912	1,857	1,808
7	Austria	4	4	3	2	1	0
8	Bahrain	7	5	4	3	2	1
9	Bangladesh	4	4	4	3	3	3
10	Barbados	0	0	0	0	0	–
11	Belgium	–	–	–	–	0	–
12	Belize	–	–	–	–	0	–
13	Benin	–	–	–	–	–	–
14	Bolivia (Plurinational State of)	12	12	11	10	9	7
15	Botswana	2	2	2	2	1	1
16	Brazil	554	534	507	469	419	371
17	Bulgaria	59	56	53	51	48	46
18	Burundi	–	–	–	–	–	–
19	Cambodia	–	–	–	–	–	–
20	Cameroon	12	9	7	5	6	5
21	Canada	2,632	2,550	2,453	2,346	2,235	2,145
22	Central African Republic	–	–	–	–	0	0
23	Chile	111	107	101	94	86	79
24	China	4,183	4,009	3,812	3,555	3,166	2,762
25	Colombia	226	214	195	176	154	130
26	Congo	42	38	33	28	25	20
27	Costa Rica	–	–	–	–	0	–
28	Côte d'Ivoire	3	3	3	3	3	2
29	Croatia	3	4	3	2	2	1
30	Cuba	15	14	13	12	10	9
31	Cyprus	–	–	–	–	0	–
32	Czech Republic	81	77	71	66	61	57
33	Democratic Republic of the Congo	–	–	–	–	–	–
34	Denmark	45	41	35	25	16	11
35	Dominican Republic	1	1	1	1	1	1
36	Ecuador	151	144	135	125	114	104
37	Egypt	208	186	164	143	121	103
38	El Salvador	–	–	–	–	–	–
39	Estonia	–	–	–	–	0	–
40	Fiji	–	–	–	–	–	–

	Country/year	1990	1995	2000	2005	2010	2014
41	Finland	0	0	0	0	0	–
42	France	4	3	2	1	1	1
43	Gabon	51	45	38	32	27	23
44	Gambia	–	–	–	–	–	–
45	Germany	1,485	1,424	1,375	1,328	1,285	1,253
46	Ghana	4	4	3	3	2	2
47	Greece	80	74	69	62	57	52
48	Guatemala	2	2	2	2	1	1
49	Guyana	2	2	2	2	2	2
50	Haiti	–	–	–	–	–	–
51	Honduras	–	–	–	–	–	–
52	Hungary	43	41	38	37	35	34
53	Iceland	–	–	–	–	–	–
54	India	2,348	2,304	2,248	2,184	2,101	2,025
55	Indonesia	1,072	1,016	953	892	818	745
56	Iran (Islamic Republic of)	4,202	4,113	4,012	3,902	3,773	3,671
57	Iraq	1,533	1,520	1,496	1,462	1,426	1,390
58	Ireland	2	2	1	1	1	0
59	Israel	10	10	10	10	9	8
60	Italy	26	22	18	14	11	8
61	Jamaica	4	4	4	4	4	4
62	Japan	37	30	24	18	12	8
63	Jordan	5	5	5	5	5	5
64	Kazakhstan	918	1,003	987	961	925	891
65	Kenya	–	–	–	–	–	–
66	Kuwait	1,606	1,574	1,524	1,471	1,408	1,357
67	Kyrgyzstan	10	10	10	10	10	10
68	Lao People's Democratic Republic	1	1	1	1	1	1
69	Latvia	–	–	–	–	0	–
70	Lesotho	–	–	–	–	–	–
71	Liberia	–	–	–	–	–	–
72	Lithuania	0	0	0	0	0	–
73	Luxembourg	–	–	–	–	–	–
74	Malawi	–	–	–	–	0	0
75	Malaysia	306	286	259	229	197	172
76	Maldives	–	–	–	–	–	–
77	Mali	–	–	–	–	–	–
78	Malta	–	–	–	–	–	–
79	Mauritania	5	5	5	4	5	5
80	Mauritius	–	–	–	–	–	–
81	Mexico	297	263	225	183	141	109
82	Mongolia	46	46	45	45	44	42

(*Continued*)

Table A3.21 (Continued)

	Country/year	1990	1995	2000	2005	2010	2014
83	Morocco	0	0	0	0	0	0
84	Mozambique	30	30	30	30	147	146
85	Myanmar	21	21	20	18	15	14
86	Namibia	–	–	–	–	3	3
87	Nepal	0	0	0	0	0	0
88	Netherlands	122	105	88	72	56	43
89	New Zealand	145	143	140	138	135	133
90	Nicaragua	–	–	–	–	0	–
91	Niger	3	3	3	3	3	3
92	Nigeria	712	669	622	571	518	473
93	Norway	484	431	353	267	192	142
94	Pakistan	135	129	123	115	104	96
95	Panama	–	–	–	–	–	–
96	Papua New Guinea	16	14	12	11	10	9
97	Paraguay	–	–	–	–	0	–
98	Peru	91	87	82	76	69	60
99	Philippines	11	11	11	11	14	12
100	Poland	496	475	455	438	421	409
101	Portugal	0	0	0	0	1	0
102	Qatar	451	442	429	410	383	351
103	Republic of Korea	21	18	16	14	12	10
104	Republic of Moldova	–	–	–	–	–	–
105	Romania	47	38	31	24	18	13
106	Russian Federation	4,322	6,384	6,131	5,835	5,493	5,201
107	Rwanda	–	–	–	–	2	2
108	Saudi Arabia	4,378	4,185	3,977	3,759	3,512	3,305
109	Senegal	0	0	0	0	0	0
110	Serbia	–	–	–	–	6	3
111	Sierra Leone	–	–	–	–	–	–
112	Singapore	–	–	–	–	0	–
113	Slovakia	5	5	5	4	4	3
114	Slovenia	10	9	9	8	8	8
115	South Africa	301	278	253	227	200	179
116	Spain	42	37	34	31	29	28
117	Sri Lanka	–	–	–	–	–	–
118	Sudan (former)	61	61	61	57	50	45
119	Swaziland	1	1	1	1	1	1
120	Sweden	13	13	13	12	12	11
121	Switzerland	0	0	0	0	0	–
122	Syrian Arab Republic	71	62	51	41	33	28
123	Tajikistan	5	5	5	5	5	5
124	Thailand	94	89	81	69	54	38
125	Togo	0	0	0	0	0	0
126	Trinidad and Tobago	64	60	55	46	34	24

	Country/year	1990	1995	2000	2005	2010	2014
127	Tunisia	19	17	14	12	10	8
128	Turkey	269	262	255	249	241	234
129	Uganda	28	28	28	28	28	28
130	Ukraine	627	676	664	651	638	627
131	United Arab Emirates	1,344	1,296	1,247	1,195	1,136	1,085
132	United Kingdom	337	274	192	120	71	45
133	United Republic of Tanzania	2	2	2	2	2	2
134	United States of America	5,929	5,581	5,232	4,895	4,559	4,244
135	Uruguay	0	–	–	–	0	–
136	Venezuela (Bolivarian Republic of)	4,317	4,254	4,174	4,099	4,031	3,979
137	Viet Nam	165	162	157	149	142	133
138	Yemen	52	48	42	35	52	48
139	Zambia	9	8	8	7	6	6
140	Zimbabwe	10	9	9	9	8	8

Table A3.22 Non-renewable resources per capita (Non-renewable resources per capita in thousands of constant 2005 US$)

	Country/year	1990	1995	2000	2005	2010	2014
1	Afghanistan	0.3	0.2	0.2	0.1	0.1	0.1
2	Albania	4.0	4.0	4.1	4.2	4.2	4.2
3	Algeria	23.3	19.5	16.5	13.9	11.1	9.1
4	Argentina	1.8	1.6	1.3	1.0	0.7	0.6
5	Armenia	–	–	–	–	0.9	0.9
6	Australia	119.6	111.0	102.5	93.8	84.3	77.1
7	Austria	0.6	0.4	0.3	0.2	0.1	0.1
8	Bahrain	13.2	9.7	6.5	3.7	1.7	0.9
9	Bangladesh	0.0	0.0	0.0	0.0	0.0	0.0
10	Barbados	0.5	0.4	0.3	0.2	0.1	–
11	Belgium	–	–	–	–	–	–
12	Belize	–	–	–	–	0.2	–
13	Benin	–	–	–	–	–	–
14	Bolivia (Plurinational State of)	1.8	1.6	1.4	1.1	0.9	0.6
15	Botswana	1.5	1.2	1.0	0.8	0.6	0.5
16	Brazil	3.7	3.3	2.9	2.5	2.1	1.8
17	Bulgaria	6.8	6.7	6.5	6.6	6.5	6.3
18	Burundi	–	–	–	–	–	–
19	Cambodia	–	–	–	–	–	–

(*Continued*)

Table A3.22 (Continued)

	Country/year	1990	1995	2000	2005	2010	2014
20	Cameroon	1.0	0.7	0.4	0.3	0.3	0.2
21	Canada	94.7	86.9	79.7	72.6	65.7	60.4
22	Central African Republic	–	–	–	–	–	–
23	Chile	8.4	7.5	6.7	5.8	5.1	4.5
24	China	3.7	3.3	3.0	2.7	2.4	2.0
25	Colombia	6.6	5.7	4.8	4.1	3.4	2.7
26	Congo	17.4	14.0	10.7	7.9	6.2	4.5
27	Costa Rica	–	–	–	–	–	–
28	Côte d'Ivoire	0.3	0.2	0.2	0.1	0.2	0.1
29	Croatia	0.6	0.8	0.7	0.5	0.4	0.3
30	Cuba	1.4	1.3	1.2	1.1	0.9	0.8
31	Cyprus	–	–	–	–	–	–
32	Czech Republic	7.8	7.4	6.9	6.4	5.8	5.4
33	Democratic Republic of the Congo	–	–	–	–	–	–
34	Denmark	8.8	7.9	6.5	4.6	2.9	2.0
35	Dominican Republic	0.2	0.2	0.1	0.1	0.1	0.1
36	Ecuador	14.8	12.6	10.7	9.1	7.6	6.6
37	Egypt	3.7	3.0	2.4	1.9	1.5	1.2
38	El Salvador	–	–	–	–	–	–
39	Estonia	–	–	–	–	–	–
40	Fiji	–	–	–	–	–	–
41	Finland	0.1	0.0	0.0	0.0	0.0	–
42	France	0.1	0.0	0.0	0.0	0.0	0.0
43	Gabon	53.7	41.4	30.5	23.4	17.6	13.7
44	Gambia	–	–	–	–	–	–
45	Germany	18.7	17.4	16.7	16.1	15.7	15.5
46	Ghana	0.3	0.2	0.2	0.1	0.1	0.1
47	Greece	7.8	7.0	6.4	5.7	5.1	4.8
48	Guatemala	0.3	0.2	0.2	0.1	0.1	0.1
49	Guyana	2.4	2.4	2.3	2.3	2.2	2.2
50	Haiti	–	–	–	–	–	–
51	Honduras	–	–	–	–	–	–
52	Hungary	4.1	3.9	3.8	3.6	3.5	3.5
53	Iceland	–	–	–	–	–	–
54	India	2.7	2.4	2.1	1.9	1.7	1.6
55	Indonesia	5.9	5.2	4.5	3.9	3.4	2.9
56	Iran (Islamic Republic of)	74.8	68.2	60.9	55.6	50.8	47.0
57	Iraq	87.7	75.2	63.5	54.1	46.2	39.4
58	Ireland	0.6	0.4	0.3	0.2	0.1	0.1
59	Israel	2.1	1.8	1.6	1.4	1.2	1.0

	Country/year	1990	1995	2000	2005	2010	2014
60	Italy	0.5	0.4	0.3	0.2	0.2	0.1
61	Jamaica	1.9	1.8	1.6	1.6	1.5	1.4
62	Japan	0.3	0.2	0.2	0.1	0.1	0.1
63	Jordan	1.6	1.2	1.0	0.9	0.7	0.6
64	Kazakhstan	56.2	63.4	66.3	63.4	56.7	51.6
65	Kenya	–	–	–	–	–	–
66	Kuwait	779.9	961.8	789.8	649.9	460.4	361.7
67	Kyrgyzstan	2.4	2.3	2.1	2.0	1.9	1.8
68	Lao People's Democratic Republic	0.3	0.3	0.3	0.3	0.2	0.2
69	Latvia	–	–	–	–	–	–
70	Lesotho	–	–	–	–	–	–
71	Liberia	–	–	–	–	–	–
72	Lithuania	0.1	0.1	0.1	0.0	0.0	–
73	Luxembourg	–	–	–	–	–	–
74	Malawi	–	–	–	–	–	–
75	Malaysia	16.8	13.8	11.1	8.9	7.0	5.8
76	Maldives	–	–	–	–	–	–
77	Mali	–	–	–	–	–	–
78	Malta	–	–	–	–	–	–
79	Mauritania	2.5	2.1	1.7	1.4	1.4	1.2
80	Mauritius	–	–	–	–	–	–
81	Mexico	3.5	2.8	2.2	1.7	1.2	0.9
82	Mongolia	21.1	19.8	18.8	17.7	16.1	14.3
83	Morocco	0.0	0.0	0.0	0.0	0.0	0.0
84	Mozambique	2.3	1.9	1.7	1.4	6.0	5.4
85	Myanmar	0.5	0.5	0.4	0.4	0.3	0.3
86	Namibia	–	–	–	–	1.2	1.1
87	Nepal	0.0	0.0	0.0	0.0	0.0	0.0
88	Netherlands	8.2	6.8	5.5	4.4	3.4	2.6
89	New Zealand	43.6	38.8	36.3	33.3	31.1	29.6
90	Nicaragua	–	–	–	–	–	–
91	Niger	0.4	0.3	0.2	0.2	0.2	0.1
92	Nigeria	7.4	6.2	5.1	4.1	3.2	2.7
93	Norway	114.2	98.8	78.6	57.7	39.3	27.6
94	Pakistan	1.3	1.1	0.9	0.7	0.6	0.5
95	Panama	–	–	–	–	–	–
96	Papua New Guinea	3.8	3.1	2.3	1.8	1.4	1.2
97	Paraguay	–	–	–	–	0.0	–
98	Peru	4.2	3.6	3.2	2.8	2.3	1.9
99	Philippines	0.2	0.2	0.1	0.1	0.2	0.1
100	Poland	13.0	12.3	11.9	11.5	11.1	10.7
101	Portugal	0.0	0.0	0.0	0.0	0.0	0.0

(*Continued*)

Table A3.22 (Continued)

	Country/year	1990	1995	2000	2005	2010	2014
102	Qatar	947.2	882.7	723.7	490.5	216.7	161.4
103	Republic of Korea	0.5	0.4	0.3	0.3	0.2	0.2
104	Republic of Moldova	–	–	–	–	–	–
105	Romania	2.0	1.7	1.4	1.1	0.9	0.7
106	Russian Federation	29.1	43.0	41.8	40.7	38.5	36.2
107	Rwanda	–	–	–	–	0.2	0.1
108	Saudi Arabia	267.6	222.0	185.9	151.9	125.0	107.0
109	Senegal	0.1	0.0	0.0	0.0	0.0	0.0
110	Serbia	–	–	–	–	0.8	0.4
111	Sierra Leone	–	–	–	–	–	–
112	Singapore	–	–	–	–	–	–
113	Slovakia	0.9	1.0	0.9	0.8	0.7	0.6
114	Slovenia	4.8	4.6	4.4	4.1	3.8	3.6
115	South Africa	8.5	7.1	5.7	4.8	3.9	3.3
116	Spain	1.1	0.9	0.8	0.7	0.6	0.6
117	Sri Lanka	–	–	–	–	–	–
118	Sudan (former)	3.1	2.5	2.2	1.8	1.4	1.2
119	Swaziland	1.1	1.0	0.9	0.9	0.8	0.7
120	Sweden	1.5	1.5	1.4	1.3	1.3	1.2
121	Switzerland	0.0	0.0	0.0	0.0	0.0	–
122	Syrian Arab Republic	5.7	4.3	3.1	2.3	1.6	1.5
123	Tajikistan	0.9	0.9	0.8	0.7	0.7	0.6
124	Thailand	1.7	1.5	1.3	1.1	0.8	0.6
125	Togo	0.1	0.1	0.0	0.0	0.0	0.0
126	Trinidad and Tobago	52.6	47.7	43.1	35.8	25.7	18.1
127	Tunisia	2.4	1.9	1.5	1.2	0.9	0.7
128	Turkey	5.0	4.5	4.0	3.7	3.3	3.0
129	Uganda	1.6	1.4	1.2	1.0	0.8	0.7
130	Ukraine	12.1	13.1	13.5	13.8	13.9	13.8
131	United Arab Emirates	741.8	551.4	408.8	266.6	136.4	119.4
132	United Kingdom	5.9	4.7	3.3	2.0	1.1	0.7
133	United Republic of Tanzania	0.1	0.1	0.1	0.1	0.1	0.0
134	United States of America	23.8	21.0	18.5	16.6	14.7	13.3
135	Uruguay	–	–	–	–	–	–
136	Venezuela (Bolivarian Republic of)	217.4	191.7	170.5	153.1	139.0	129.6
137	Viet Nam	2.5	2.3	2.0	1.8	1.6	1.5
138	Yemen	4.3	3.1	2.4	1.7	2.2	1.8
139	Zambia	1.0	0.9	0.7	0.6	0.5	0.4
140	Zimbabwe	0.9	0.8	0.7	0.7	0.6	0.5

Table A3.23 Non-renewable resources growth (Non-renewable resources change (%) with respect to base year 1990)

	Country/year	1995	2000	2005	2010	2014
1	Afghanistan	−0.3%	−0.8%	−0.8%	−1.2%	−2.7%
2	Albania	−0.6%	−1.1%	−1.4%	−1.6%	−2.9%
3	Algeria	−1.4%	−3.8%	−6.5%	−9.7%	−16.3%
4	Argentina	−1.6%	−5.1%	−9.7%	−15.5%	−26.1%
5	Armenia	−	−	−	−	−
6	Australia	−0.4%	−1.0%	−1.6%	−2.3%	−4.0%
7	Austria	−3.7%	−10.2%	−17.9%	−26.6%	−51.7%
8	Bahrain	−3.6%	−9.9%	−16.2%	−24.1%	−42.3%
9	Bangladesh	−1.1%	−3.4%	−6.6%	−5.4%	−13.6%
10	Barbados	−4.9%	−14.3%	−24.4%	−38.8%	−100.0%
11	Belgium	−	−	−	−	−
12	Belize	−	−	−	−	−
13	Benin	−	−	−	−	−
14	Bolivia (Plurinational State of)	−0.8%	−2.0%	−4.1%	−8.3%	−17.8%
15	Botswana	−1.7%	−4.5%	−7.5%	−10.8%	−18.6%
16	Brazil	−0.7%	−2.2%	−4.1%	−6.8%	−12.5%
17	Bulgaria	−1.0%	−2.5%	−3.8%	−4.9%	−8.2%
18	Burundi	−	−	−	−	−
19	Cambodia	−	−	−	−	−
20	Cameroon	−5.4%	−13.6%	−19.1%	−15.5%	−25.2%
21	Canada	−0.6%	−1.8%	−2.8%	−4.0%	−6.6%
22	Central African Republic	−	−	−	−	−
23	Chile	−0.7%	−2.2%	−4.0%	−6.1%	−10.5%
24	China	−0.8%	−2.3%	−4.0%	−6.7%	−12.9%
25	Colombia	−1.1%	−3.7%	−6.1%	−9.1%	−16.9%
26	Congo	−1.7%	−5.5%	−9.6%	−11.8%	−21.4%
27	Costa Rica	−	−	−	−	−
28	Côte d'Ivoire	−0.3%	−2.7%	−5.3%	−1.3%	−12.1%
29	Croatia	6.3%	2.1%	−3.7%	−9.9%	−19.2%
30	Cuba	−0.7%	−2.8%	−5.6%	−8.8%	−15.4%
31	Cyprus	−	−	−	−	−
32	Czech Republic	−0.9%	−3.0%	−4.9%	−6.8%	−10.7%
33	Democratic Republic of the Congo	−	−	−	−	−
34	Denmark	−2.0%	−6.6%	−14.1%	−23.0%	−37.0%
35	Dominican Republic	−2.9%	−7.4%	−10.9%	−12.6%	−18.7%
36	Ecuador	−1.0%	−2.8%	−4.7%	−6.9%	−11.7%
37	Egypt	−2.2%	−5.8%	−9.0%	−12.6%	−20.8%
38	El Salvador	−	−	−	−	−
39	Estonia	−	−	−	−	−
40	Fiji	−	−	−	−	−

(*Continued*)

Table A3.23 (Continued)

	Country/year	1995	2000	2005	2010	2014
41	Finland	-3.7%	-11.8%	-21.5%	-25.0%	-100.0%
42	France	-6.1%	-14.4%	-21.2%	-25.9%	-40.7%
43	Gabon	-2.5%	-7.4%	-10.9%	-14.6%	-23.2%
44	Gambia	-	-	-	-	-
45	Germany	-0.8%	-1.9%	-2.8%	-3.6%	-5.5%
46	Ghana	-1.4%	-4.9%	-8.6%	-13.9%	-23.4%
47	Greece	-1.4%	-3.6%	-5.9%	-8.2%	-13.0%
48	Guatemala	-0.9%	-4.8%	-9.8%	-15.1%	-24.7%
49	Guyana	-0.2%	-0.6%	-0.9%	-1.1%	-1.8%
50	Haiti	-	-	-	-	-
51	Honduras	-	-	-	-	-
52	Hungary	-1.1%	-2.8%	-3.9%	-4.9%	-7.3%
53	Iceland	-	-	-	-	-
54	India	-0.4%	-1.1%	-1.8%	-2.7%	-4.8%
55	Indonesia	-1.1%	-2.9%	-4.5%	-6.5%	-11.4%
56	Iran (Islamic Republic of)	-0.4%	-1.1%	-1.8%	-2.7%	-4.4%
57	Iraq	-0.2%	-0.6%	-1.2%	-1.8%	-3.2%
58	Ireland	-5.0%	-12.3%	-18.5%	-25.1%	-39.3%
59	Israel	-0.1%	-0.4%	-0.7%	-1.6%	-5.1%
60	Italy	-3.3%	-9.0%	-14.0%	-20.0%	-32.2%
61	Jamaica	-0.5%	-1.3%	-2.1%	-2.5%	-4.3%
62	Japan	-4.1%	-10.5%	-16.6%	-24.2%	-40.2%
63	Jordan	-0.5%	-1.4%	-2.2%	-3.0%	-4.8%
64	Kazakhstan	1.8%	1.8%	1.1%	0.2%	-1.0%
65	Kenya	-	-	-	-	-
66	Kuwait	-0.4%	-1.3%	-2.2%	-3.2%	-5.4%
67	Kyrgyzstan	0.2%	0.1%	0.0%	-0.1%	-0.4%
68	Lao People's Democratic Republic	0.0%	0.0%	-0.1%	-0.2%	-0.5%
69	Latvia	-	-	-	-	-
70	Lesotho	-	-	-	-	-
71	Liberia	-	-	-	-	-
72	Lithuania	-0.9%	-6.7%	-21.7%	-36.7%	-100.0%
73	Luxembourg	-	-	-	-	-
74	Malawi	-	-	-	-	-
75	Malaysia	-1.4%	-4.1%	-7.0%	-10.5%	-17.5%
76	Maldives	-	-	-	-	-
77	Mali	-	-	-	-	-
78	Malta	-	-	-	-	-
79	Mauritania	-0.8%	-2.1%	-3.2%	-0.5%	-2.6%
80	Mauritius	-	-	-	-	-
81	Mexico	-2.4%	-6.7%	-11.4%	-17.0%	-28.3%
82	Mongolia	-0.2%	-0.5%	-0.8%	-1.3%	-3.3%

	Country/year	1995	2000	2005	2010	2014
83	Morocco	−0.7%	−2.3%	−4.1%	21.8%	27.8%
84	Mozambique	0.0%	0.0%	0.0%	48.4%	68.9%
85	Myanmar	−0.3%	−1.0%	−4.2%	−8.9%	−11.8%
86	Namibia	–	–	–	–	–
87	Nepal	−0.2%	−1.5%	−2.6%	−4.2%	−7.0%
88	Netherlands	−3.1%	−7.9%	−12.3%	−17.6%	−29.1%
89	New Zealand	−0.4%	−0.9%	−1.3%	−1.7%	−2.8%
90	Nicaragua	–	–	–	–	–
91	Niger	−0.1%	−0.1%	−0.2%	−0.3%	−2.6%
92	Nigeria	−1.2%	−3.3%	−5.4%	−7.7%	−12.8%
93	Norway	−2.3%	−7.6%	−13.8%	−20.6%	−33.6%
94	Pakistan	−0.8%	−2.3%	−3.9%	−6.1%	−10.8%
95	Panama	–	–	–	–	–
96	Papua New Guinea	−1.9%	−6.1%	−9.0%	−11.5%	−17.1%
97	Paraguay	–	–	–	–	–
98	Peru	−1.0%	−2.6%	−4.4%	−6.9%	−12.9%
99	Philippines	−0.3%	−0.8%	−1.4%	6.2%	1.7%
100	Poland	−0.9%	−2.1%	−3.1%	−4.0%	−6.3%
101	Portugal	−4.1%	−9.4%	−10.1%	61.1%	86.5%
102	Qatar	−0.4%	−1.2%	−2.3%	−4.0%	−8.1%
103	Republic of Korea	−3.1%	−7.2%	−10.3%	−13.8%	−23.1%
104	Republic of Moldova	–	–	–	–	–
105	Romania	−4.2%	−10.2%	−15.6%	−21.7%	−34.4%
106	Russian Federation	8.1%	9.1%	7.8%	6.2%	6.4%
107	Rwanda	–	–	–	–	–
108	Saudi Arabia	−0.9%	−2.4%	−3.7%	−5.4%	−8.9%
109	Senegal	−2.2%	−5.6%	−8.6%	−9.6%	−15.4%
110	Serbia	–	–	–	–	–
111	Sierra Leone	–	–	–	–	–
112	Singapore	–	–	–	–	–
113	Slovakia	1.9%	−0.6%	−3.8%	−7.1%	−12.7%
114	Slovenia	−0.9%	−2.4%	−3.7%	−5.1%	−8.0%
115	South Africa	−1.5%	−4.2%	−6.8%	−9.6%	−15.9%
116	Spain	−2.2%	−5.1%	−7.2%	−8.5%	−11.9%
117	Sri Lanka	–	–	–	–	–
118	Sudan (former)	0.0%	−0.1%	−1.9%	−5.1%	−9.5%
119	Swaziland	−0.1%	−0.4%	−0.7%	−0.9%	−1.4%
120	Sweden	−0.5%	−1.4%	−2.1%	−2.6%	−4.9%
121	Switzerland	0.0%	0.0%	0.0%	16.7%	−100.0%
122	Syrian Arab Republic	−2.6%	−7.7%	−12.6%	−17.4%	−26.1%
123	Tajikistan	0.7%	0.8%	0.8%	0.7%	0.7%
124	Thailand	−1.1%	−3.8%	−7.3%	−13.1%	−26.2%
125	Togo	−3.8%	−9.7%	−13.0%	−15.4%	−23.2%
126	Trinidad and Tobago	−1.4%	−4.0%	−7.8%	−14.6%	−27.5%

(*Continued*)

Table A3.23 (Continued)

	Country/year	1995	2000	2005	2010	2014
127	Tunisia	-2.7%	-7.0%	-11.1%	-15.8%	-25.2%
128	Turkey	-0.5%	-1.3%	-2.0%	-2.8%	-4.5%
129	Uganda	0.0%	0.0%	0.0%	0.0%	0.0%
130	Ukraine	1.5%	1.4%	0.9%	0.4%	0.0%
131	United Arab Emirates	-0.7%	-1.9%	-2.9%	-4.1%	-6.9%
132	United Kingdom	-4.1%	-13.1%	-22.8%	-32.3%	-48.7%
133	United Republic of Tanzania	0.0%	0.0%	-0.1%	-0.1%	-0.1%
134	United States of America	-1.2%	-3.1%	-4.7%	-6.4%	-10.5%
135	Uruguay	–	–	–	–	–
136	Venezuela (Bolivarian Republic of)	-0.3%	-0.8%	-1.3%	-1.7%	-2.7%
137	Viet Nam	-0.3%	-1.1%	-2.5%	-3.7%	-7.0%
138	Yemen	-1.5%	-5.1%	-9.3%	0.2%	-2.5%
139	Zambia	-1.3%	-2.8%	-4.3%	-6.9%	-12.7%
140	Zimbabwe	-1.0%	-2.3%	-3.2%	-3.7%	-6.0%

Table A3.24 Non-renewable resources per capita growth (Non-renewable resources per capita change (%) with respect to base year 1990)

	Country/year	1995	2000	2005	2010	2014
1	Afghanistan	-6.7%	-12.2%	-16.8%	-19.9%	-29.5%
2	Albania	0.0%	0.5%	0.8%	1.4%	1.4%
3	Algeria	-3.5%	-8.2%	-12.1%	-16.9%	-26.9%
4	Argentina	-2.9%	-8.0%	-13.7%	-20.2%	-32.5%
5	Armenia	–	–	–	–	–
6	Australia	-1.5%	-3.8%	-5.9%	-8.4%	-13.6%
7	Austria	-4.4%	-11.2%	-19.3%	-28.2%	-53.4%
8	Bahrain	-6.1%	-16.3%	-27.1%	-39.9%	-58.8%
9	Bangladesh	-3.3%	-8.4%	-13.4%	-13.5%	-24.6%
10	Barbados	-5.2%	-15.1%	-25.4%	-39.8%	-100.0%
11	Belgium	–	–	–	–	–
12	Belize	–	–	–	–	–
13	Benin	–	–	–	–	–
14	Bolivia (Plurinational State of)	-2.7%	-6.6%	-10.7%	-16.4%	-28.8%
15	Botswana	-4.3%	-9.9%	-14.2%	-19.2%	-30.5%
16	Brazil	-2.3%	-6.0%	-9.3%	-13.0%	-21.3%
17	Bulgaria	-0.3%	-1.0%	-0.9%	-0.9%	-2.3%
18	Burundi	–	–	–	–	–
19	Cambodia	–	–	–	–	–

	Country/year	1995	2000	2005	2010	2014
20	Cameroon	−8.1%	−19.4%	−26.9%	−26.1%	−39.5%
21	Canada	−1.7%	−4.2%	−6.4%	−8.7%	−13.9%
22	Central African Republic	−	−	−	−	−
23	Chile	−2.2%	−5.7%	−8.8%	−12.0%	−19.0%
24	China	−2.0%	−4.9%	−7.3%	−10.5%	−18.1%
25	Colombia	−2.9%	−7.6%	−11.5%	−15.5%	−25.6%
26	Congo	−4.3%	−11.6%	−17.9%	−22.8%	−36.4%
27	Costa Rica	−	−	−	−	−
28	Côte d'Ivoire	−3.6%	−9.9%	−14.3%	−13.0%	−28.0%
29	Croatia	6.8%	4.1%	−1.9%	−8.1%	−15.9%
30	Cuba	−1.3%	−4.0%	−7.0%	−10.3%	−17.4%
31	Cyprus	−	−	−	−	−
32	Czech Republic	−0.9%	−2.9%	−4.6%	−7.1%	−11.3%
33	Democratic Republic of the Congo	−	−	−	−	−
34	Denmark	−2.3%	−7.5%	−15.2%	−24.4%	−38.9%
35	Dominican Republic	−4.7%	−11.3%	−16.3%	−19.3%	−28.2%
36	Ecuador	−3.2%	−7.9%	−11.5%	−15.4%	−23.8%
37	Egypt	−4.2%	−10.3%	−15.2%	−20.4%	−32.1%
38	El Salvador	−	−	−	−	−
39	Estonia	−	−	−	−	−
40	Fiji	−	−	−	−	−
41	Finland	−4.2%	−12.6%	−22.4%	−26.4%	−100.0%
42	France	−6.5%	−15.2%	−22.7%	−27.8%	−43.2%
43	Gabon	−5.1%	−13.1%	−18.8%	−24.3%	−36.6%
44	Gambia	−	−	−	−	−
45	Germany	−1.4%	−2.8%	−3.7%	−4.2%	−6.1%
46	Ghana	−4.0%	−10.8%	−16.9%	−24.2%	−37.4%
47	Greece	−2.1%	−5.0%	−7.7%	−10.2%	−14.9%
48	Guatemala	−3.3%	−10.4%	−17.6%	−24.6%	−37.5%
49	Guyana	−0.4%	−1.4%	−1.6%	−2.2%	−3.7%
50	Haiti	−	−	−	−	−
51	Honduras	−	−	−	−	−
52	Hungary	−1.0%	−2.4%	−3.2%	−4.0%	−5.8%
53	Iceland	−	−	−	−	−
54	India	−2.3%	−5.7%	−8.3%	−10.8%	−16.6%
55	Indonesia	−2.7%	−6.5%	−9.6%	−13.0%	−20.9%
56	Iran (Islamic Republic of)	−1.8%	−5.0%	−7.1%	−9.2%	−14.4%
57	Iraq	−3.0%	−7.8%	−11.4%	−14.8%	−23.4%
58	Ireland	−5.5%	−14.0%	−21.8%	−29.8%	−44.6%
59	Israel	−3.5%	−7.6%	−10.1%	−13.0%	−21.5%
60	Italy	−3.3%	−9.1%	−14.4%	−20.9%	−33.7%

(*Continued*)

Table A3.24 (Continued)

	Country/year	1995	2000	2005	2010	2014
61	Jamaica	−1.2%	−3.3%	−4.5%	−5.3%	−8.3%
62	Japan	−4.4%	−11.1%	−17.3%	−24.9%	−40.8%
63	Jordan	−5.4%	−9.6%	−12.9%	−17.8%	−26.9%
64	Kazakhstan	2.5%	4.2%	3.1%	0.2%	−2.8%
65	Kenya	−	−	−	−	−
66	Kuwait	4.3%	0.3%	−4.5%	−12.3%	−22.6%
67	Kyrgyzstan	−0.6%	−2.6%	−4.0%	−5.4%	−9.4%
68	Lao People's Democratic Republic	−2.6%	−5.6%	−7.3%	−9.4%	−14.5%
69	Latvia	−	−	−	−	−
70	Lesotho	−	−	−	−	−
71	Liberia	−	−	−	−	−
72	Lithuania	−0.5%	−5.4%	−19.6%	−33.8%	−100.0%
73	Luxembourg	−	−	−	−	−
74	Malawi	−	−	−	−	−
75	Malaysia	−3.9%	−10.0%	−14.8%	−19.7%	−30.1%
76	Maldives	−	−	−	−	−
77	Mali	−	−	−	−	−
78	Malta	−	−	−	−	−
79	Mauritania	−3.6%	−9.1%	−13.4%	−13.8%	−22.2%
80	Mauritius	−	−	−	−	−
81	Mexico	−4.3%	−10.9%	−16.7%	−23.5%	−36.9%
82	Mongolia	−1.2%	−2.8%	−4.3%	−6.5%	−12.1%
83	Morocco	−2.4%	−5.9%	−8.7%	14.3%	15.3%
84	Mozambique	−3.4%	−7.5%	−10.8%	27.8%	33.3%
85	Myanmar	−1.5%	−4.1%	−8.3%	−13.5%	−18.6%
86	Namibia	−	−	−	−	−
87	Nepal	−2.8%	−7.2%	−9.8%	−12.4%	−18.8%
88	Netherlands	−3.7%	−9.3%	−14.2%	−19.7%	−31.9%
89	New Zealand	−2.3%	−4.5%	−6.5%	−8.1%	−12.1%
90	Nicaragua	−	−	−	−	−
91	Niger	−3.4%	−8.5%	−12.7%	−16.8%	−27.4%
92	Nigeria	−3.7%	−9.2%	−13.9%	−18.7%	−29.0%
93	Norway	−2.8%	−8.9%	−15.7%	−23.4%	−37.7%
94	Pakistan	−3.4%	−8.2%	−12.0%	−16.3%	−25.5%
95	Panama	−	−	−	−	−
96	Papua New Guinea	−4.3%	−11.9%	−17.3%	−21.9%	−31.8%
97	Paraguay	−	−	−	−	−
98	Peru	−2.9%	−6.7%	−9.8%	−13.5%	−22.5%
99	Philippines	−2.7%	−6.3%	−9.2%	−4.1%	−13.0%
100	Poland	−1.1%	−2.2%	−3.1%	−4.0%	−6.2%
101	Portugal	−4.2%	−10.1%	−11.2%	58.8%	84.0%
102	Qatar	−1.4%	−6.5%	−15.2%	−30.8%	−44.6%

	Country/year	1995	2000	2005	2010	2014
103	Republic of Korea	−4.1%	−9.3%	−12.9%	−16.8%	−27.2%
104	Republic of Moldova	−	−	−	−	−
105	Romania	−3.8%	−9.5%	−13.8%	−19.0%	−31.0%
106	Russian Federation	8.1%	9.4%	8.7%	7.2%	7.5%
107	Rwanda	−	−	−	−	−
108	Saudi Arabia	−3.7%	−8.7%	−13.2%	−17.3%	−26.3%
109	Senegal	−5.1%	−11.8%	−17.4%	−21.1%	−32.3%
110	Serbia	−	−	−	−	−
111	Sierra Leone	−	−	−	−	−
112	Singapore	−	−	−	−	−
113	Slovakia	1.7%	−1.0%	−4.2%	−7.5%	−13.4%
114	Slovenia	−0.8%	−2.3%	−3.7%	−5.6%	−8.9%
115	South Africa	−3.6%	−9.4%	−13.4%	−17.6%	−27.1%
116	Spain	−2.5%	−5.9%	−9.8%	−12.6%	−17.1%
117	Sri Lanka	−	−	−	−	−
118	Sudan (former)	−4.1%	−8.2%	−12.7%	−18.1%	−27.8%
119	Swaziland	−2.3%	−5.5%	−6.7%	−8.6%	−13.3%
120	Sweden	−1.1%	−2.3%	−3.4%	−4.8%	−8.8%
121	Switzerland	−0.9%	−1.7%	−2.5%	12.3%	−100.0%
122	Syrian Arab Republic	−5.3%	−13.8%	−20.4%	−27.3%	−35.6%
123	Tajikistan	−1.0%	−3.0%	−5.4%	−8.0%	−13.3%
124	Thailand	−2.0%	−6.2%	−10.8%	−16.6%	−30.5%
125	Togo	−6.1%	−15.2%	−21.0%	−25.8%	−37.8%
126	Trinidad and Tobago	−1.9%	−4.9%	−9.2%	−16.4%	−30.0%
127	Tunisia	−4.5%	−10.6%	−15.6%	−21.1%	−32.3%
128	Turkey	−2.1%	−5.2%	−7.4%	−9.6%	−15.3%
129	Uganda	−3.2%	−7.5%	−11.3%	−14.9%	−22.8%
130	Ukraine	1.7%	2.8%	3.4%	3.5%	4.6%
131	United Arab Emirates	−5.8%	−13.8%	−22.6%	−34.5%	−45.6%
132	United Kingdom	−4.3%	−13.7%	−23.8%	−33.8%	−50.7%
133	United Republic of Tanzania	−3.2%	−7.0%	−10.2%	−13.6%	−21.2%
134	United States of America	−2.5%	−6.0%	−8.6%	−11.2%	−17.6%
135	Uruguay	−	−	−	−	−
136	Venezuela (Bolivarian Republic of)	−2.5%	−5.9%	−8.4%	−10.6%	−15.8%
137	Viet Nam	−2.0%	−5.0%	−7.7%	−10.1%	−16.3%
138	Yemen	−6.2%	−14.0%	−20.8%	−15.4%	−24.9%
139	Zambia	−3.7%	−9.0%	−13.3%	−18.6%	−29.9%
140	Zimbabwe	−3.1%	−6.5%	−8.2%	−10.4%	−17.1%

Table A3.25 Agriculture land (Agriculture land in billions of constant 2005 US$)

	Country/year	1990	1995	2000	2005	2010	2014
1	Afghanistan	–	–	–	–	–	–
2	Albania	–	–	–	–	–	–
3	Algeria	–	–	–	–	–	–
4	Argentina	206	206	207	222	238	239
5	Armenia	–	–	–	–	–	–
6	Australia	644	642	632	617	553	558
7	Austria	22	21	21	20	20	19
8	Bahrain	–	–	–	–	–	–
9	Bangladesh	27	25	25	25	24	24
10	Barbados	0	0	0	0	0	0
11	Belgium	–	–	–	–	–	–
12	Belize	1	1	1	1	1	1
13	Benin	–	–	–	–	–	–
14	Bolivia (Plurinational State of)	55	57	58	57	58	58
15	Botswana	5	5	5	4	4	4
16	Brazil	307	328	332	346	347	358
17	Bulgaria	6	6	5	5	5	5
18	Burundi	4	4	4	3	4	3
19	Cambodia	23	24	25	28	29	30
20	Cameroon	11	11	11	11	12	12
21	Canada	63	63	63	62	58	59
22	Central African Republic	–	–	–	–	–	–
23	Chile	122	117	116	122	121	121
24	China	3,961	4,095	4,088	4,053	4,030	4,039
25	Colombia	65	58	59	47	44	40
26	Congo	34	34	34	34	34	34
27	Costa Rica	28	25	23	22	22	21
28	Côte d'Ivoire	14	14	14	15	15	15
29	Croatia	–	–	–	–	–	–
30	Cuba	–	–	–	–	–	–
31	Cyprus	0	0	0	0	0	0
32	Czech Republic	–	–	–	–	–	–
33	Democratic Republic of the Congo	–	–	–	–	–	–
34	Denmark	6	6	5	6	5	5
35	Dominican Republic	16	16	15	15	15	14
36	Ecuador	15	16	16	15	15	14
37	Egypt	8	10	10	11	12	12
38	El Salvador	5	5	5	6	5	6
39	Estonia	–	–	–	–	–	–
40	Fiji	2	2	2	2	2	2
41	Finland	15	14	14	14	14	14
42	France	154	152	150	149	145	144
43	Gabon	–	–	–	–	–	–

	Country/year	1990	1995	2000	2005	2010	2014
44	Gambia	0	0	0	0	0	0
45	Germany	68	66	65	65	63	63
46	Ghana	21	22	24	25	26	27
47	Greece	138	137	128	125	123	119
48	Guatemala	–	–	–	–	–	–
49	Guyana	20	20	19	19	19	19
50	Haiti	–	–	–	–	–	–
51	Honduras	10	10	9	9	10	9
52	Hungary	23	22	21	21	19	19
53	Iceland	87	87	86	86	86	86
54	India	698	697	697	693	691	691
55	Indonesia	329	313	344	378	405	424
56	Iran (Islamic Republic of)	89	93	91	69	67	65
57	Iraq	5	5	4	5	4	4
58	Ireland	29	22	22	22	23	22
59	Israel	4	4	4	4	4	4
60	Italy	181	164	168	158	154	146
61	Jamaica	24	25	24	24	22	22
62	Japan	239	229	221	197	193	180
63	Jordan	2	2	2	2	2	2
64	Kazakhstan	–	–	–	–	–	–
65	Kenya	22	23	22	23	23	23
66	Kuwait	–	–	–	–	–	–
67	Kyrgyzstan	–	–	–	–	–	–
68	Lao People's Democratic Republic	11	11	12	13	15	15
69	Latvia	–	–	–	–	–	–
70	Lesotho	–	–	–	–	–	–
71	Liberia	–	–	–	–	–	–
72	Lithuania	–	–	–	–	–	–
73	Luxembourg	–	–	–	–	–	–
74	Malawi	6	6	6	7	8	8
75	Malaysia	34	35	34	35	37	37
76	Maldives	0	0	0	0	0	0
77	Mali	12	13	14	15	15	16
78	Malta	0	0	0	0	0	0
79	Mauritania	–	–	–	–	–	–
80	Mauritius	1	1	1	1	1	1
81	Mexico	473	478	478	479	480	481
82	Mongolia	90	85	94	81	81	81
83	Morocco	31	31	31	30	30	30
84	Mozambique	45	45	45	46	47	47
85	Myanmar	–	–	–	–	–	–
86	Namibia	0	0	0	0	0	0
87	Nepal	10	10	10	10	10	10

(*Continued*)

Table A3.25 (Continued)

	Country/year	1990	1995	2000	2005	2010	2014
88	Netherlands	23	22	22	22	21	21
89	New Zealand	101	93	96	73	71	63
90	Nicaragua	9	10	11	11	11	12
91	Niger	2	2	3	3	3	3
92	Nigeria	151	168	175	178	172	181
93	Norway	11	13	12	12	11	12
94	Pakistan	98	100	102	100	98	100
95	Panama	9	9	9	9	9	9
96	Papua New Guinea	–	–	–	–	–	–
97	Paraguay	26	25	31	31	33	34
98	Peru	111	112	118	118	122	125
99	Philippines	49	48	49	50	53	54
100	Poland	42	42	41	36	33	32
101	Portugal	37	37	38	36	33	34
102	Qatar	0	0	0	0	0	0
103	Republic of Korea	242	228	219	209	197	190
104	Republic of Moldova	–	–	–	–	–	–
105	Romania	77	78	78	74	74	72
106	Russian Federation	–	–	–	–	–	–
107	Rwanda	2	2	2	2	2	2
108	Saudi Arabia	1,497	2,106	2,106	2,105	2,102	2,234
109	Senegal	3	3	3	3	3	3
110	Serbia	–	–	–	–	–	–
111	Sierra Leone	–	–	–	–	–	–
112	Singapore	0	0	0	0	0	0
113	Slovakia	–	–	–	–	–	–
114	Slovenia	–	–	–	–	–	–
115	South Africa	126	128	129	128	128	128
116	Spain	136	133	133	130	123	121
117	Sri Lanka	11	11	11	12	13	13
118	Sudan (former)	–	–	–	–	–	–
119	Swaziland	–	–	–	–	–	–
120	Sweden	10	10	10	10	9	9
121	Switzerland	68	67	67	66	65	65
122	Syrian Arab Republic	–	–	–	–	–	–
123	Tajikistan	–	–	–	–	–	–
124	Thailand	76	75	71	70	75	73
125	Togo	1	1	2	1	2	2
126	Trinidad and Tobago	1	1	1	1	1	1
127	Tunisia	5	6	6	6	6	6
128	Turkey	177	176	180	183	174	175
129	Uganda	–	–	–	–	–	–
130	Ukraine	–	–	–	–	–	–
131	United Arab Emirates	–	–	–	–	–	–

Country/year	1990	1995	2000	2005	2010	2014
132 United Kingdom	96	92	90	89	91	90
133 United Republic of Tanzania	24	25	26	27	28	29
134 United States of America	1,385	1,363	1,344	1,336	1,325	1,312
135 Uruguay	32	32	32	32	31	31
136 Venezuela (Bolivarian Republic of)	218	216	216	215	215	215
137 Viet Nam	36	38	47	53	57	61
138 Yemen	29	29	29	29	29	29
139 Zambia	21	21	23	23	23	24
140 Zimbabwe	–	–	–	–	–	–

Table A3.26 Agriculture land per capita (Agriculture land per capita in thousands of constant 2005 US$)

Country/year	1990	1995	2000	2005	2010	2014
1 Afghanistan	–	–	–	–	–	–
2 Albania	–	–	–	–	–	–
3 Algeria	–	–	–	–	–	–
4 Argentina	6.3	5.9	5.6	5.7	5.8	5.6
5 Armenia	–	–	–	–	–	–
6 Australia	37.7	35.5	33.0	30.3	25.1	23.8
7 Austria	2.8	2.7	2.6	2.5	2.4	2.3
8 Bahrain	–	–	–	–	–	–
9 Bangladesh	0.3	0.2	0.2	0.2	0.2	0.1
10 Barbados	1.3	1.3	1.2	1.1	1.0	0.9
11 Belgium	–	–	–	–	–	–
12 Belize	3.1	3.3	2.8	2.5	2.3	2.1
13 Benin	–	–	–	–	–	–
14 Bolivia (Plurinational State of)	8.0	7.5	6.9	6.3	5.8	5.5
15 Botswana	3.3	2.9	2.6	2.4	2.2	2.0
16 Brazil	2.0	2.0	1.9	1.8	1.7	1.7
17 Bulgaria	0.7	0.7	0.6	0.6	0.6	0.6
18 Burundi	0.7	0.6	0.5	0.4	0.4	0.3
19 Cambodia	2.5	2.2	2.0	2.1	2.0	2.0
20 Cameroon	0.9	0.8	0.7	0.6	0.6	0.5
21 Canada	2.3	2.1	2.0	1.9	1.7	1.7
22 Central African Republic	–	–	–	–	–	–
23 Chile	9.3	8.3	7.6	7.6	7.1	6.8
24 China	3.5	3.4	3.2	3.1	3.0	3.0
25 Colombia	1.9	1.5	1.5	1.1	1.0	0.8
26 Congo	14.3	12.5	11.0	9.8	8.4	7.6
27 Costa Rica	9.1	7.1	5.7	5.2	4.9	4.3
28 Côte d'Ivoire	1.1	1.0	0.9	0.8	0.7	0.7
29 Croatia	–	–	–	–	–	–

(Continued)

Table A3.26 (Continued)

	Country/year	1990	1995	2000	2005	2010	2014
30	Cuba	–	–	–	–	–	–
31	Cyprus	0.5	0.4	0.3	0.4	0.2	0.2
32	Czech Republic	–	–	–	–	–	–
33	Democratic Republic of the Congo	–	–	–	–	–	–
34	Denmark	1.1	1.1	1.0	1.0	1.0	1.0
35	Dominican Republic	2.2	2.0	1.8	1.6	1.5	1.4
36	Ecuador	1.5	1.4	1.3	1.1	1.0	0.9
37	Egypt	0.1	0.2	0.2	0.1	0.1	0.1
38	El Salvador	1.0	0.9	0.9	0.9	0.9	0.9
39	Estonia	–	–	–	–	–	–
40	Fiji	3.0	3.0	2.8	2.8	2.6	2.5
41	Finland	3.0	2.8	2.7	2.7	2.7	2.6
42	France	2.6	2.5	2.5	2.4	2.2	2.2
43	Gabon	–	–	–	–	–	–
44	Gambia	0.0	0.0	0.0	0.0	0.1	0.1
45	Germany	0.9	0.8	0.8	0.8	0.8	0.8
46	Ghana	1.4	1.3	1.3	1.2	1.1	1.0
47	Greece	13.6	13.0	11.8	11.4	11.0	10.9
48	Guatemala	–	–	–	–	–	–
49	Guyana	27.1	26.9	25.9	25.5	25.1	24.6
50	Haiti	–	–	–	–	–	–
51	Honduras	2.0	1.9	1.4	1.4	1.3	1.2
52	Hungary	2.2	2.1	2.1	2.1	1.9	1.9
53	Iceland	341.4	324.9	307.4	290.2	269.7	261.2
54	India	0.8	0.7	0.7	0.6	0.6	0.5
55	Indonesia	1.8	1.6	1.6	1.7	1.7	1.7
56	Iran (Islamic Republic of)	1.6	1.5	1.4	1.0	0.9	0.8
57	Iraq	0.3	0.2	0.2	0.2	0.1	0.1
58	Ireland	8.1	6.2	5.9	5.2	5.1	4.7
59	Israel	0.9	0.7	0.6	0.5	0.5	0.4
60	Italy	3.2	2.9	2.9	2.7	2.6	2.4
61	Jamaica	10.1	10.1	9.4	8.9	8.3	8.3
62	Japan	1.9	1.8	1.7	1.5	1.5	1.4
63	Jordan	0.6	0.5	0.5	0.4	0.3	0.3
64	Kazakhstan	–	–	–	–	–	–
65	Kenya	1.0	0.8	0.7	0.6	0.6	0.5
66	Kuwait	–	–	–	–	–	–
67	Kyrgyzstan	–	–	–	–	–	–
68	Lao People's Democratic Republic	2.6	2.3	2.2	2.3	2.3	2.3
69	Latvia	–	–	–	–	–	–
70	Lesotho	–	–	–	–	–	–
71	Liberia	–	–	–	–	–	–
72	Lithuania	–	–	–	–	–	–
73	Luxembourg	–	–	–	–	–	–

	Country/year	1990	1995	2000	2005	2010	2014
74	Malawi	0.6	0.6	0.6	0.6	0.5	0.5
75	Malaysia	1.8	1.7	1.5	1.4	1.3	1.2
76	Maldives	0.1	0.1	0.1	0.1	0.1	0.1
77	Mali	1.4	1.3	1.3	1.1	1.0	0.9
78	Malta	0.4	0.3	0.3	0.3	0.3	0.2
79	Mauritania	–	–	–	–	–	–
80	Mauritius	1.1	1.0	0.9	0.8	0.8	0.7
81	Mexico	5.5	5.1	4.7	4.4	4.0	3.8
82	Mongolia	41.2	37.0	39.0	32.2	30.0	27.7
83	Morocco	1.2	1.1	1.1	1.0	0.9	0.9
84	Mozambique	3.4	2.8	2.5	2.2	1.9	1.7
85	Myanmar	–	–	–	–	–	–
86	Namibia	0.1	0.1	0.1	0.1	0.1	0.1
87	Nepal	0.5	0.5	0.4	0.4	0.4	0.4
88	Netherlands	1.5	1.4	1.4	1.3	1.3	1.2
89	New Zealand	30.2	25.4	24.9	17.6	16.3	14.0
90	Nicaragua	2.1	2.1	2.2	2.1	1.9	1.9
91	Niger	0.3	0.3	0.2	0.2	0.2	0.2
92	Nigeria	1.6	1.5	1.4	1.3	1.1	1.0
93	Norway	2.6	2.9	2.6	2.5	2.3	2.2
94	Pakistan	0.9	0.8	0.7	0.7	0.6	0.5
95	Panama	3.5	3.2	3.0	2.7	2.5	2.4
96	Papua New Guinea	–	–	–	–	–	–
97	Paraguay	6.2	5.3	5.9	5.3	5.2	5.2
98	Peru	5.1	4.6	4.6	4.3	4.2	4.0
99	Philippines	0.8	0.7	0.6	0.6	0.6	0.5
100	Poland	1.1	1.1	1.1	0.9	0.9	0.8
101	Portugal	3.7	3.7	3.7	3.4	3.1	3.2
102	Qatar	0.8	0.8	0.7	0.5	0.2	0.2
103	Republic of Korea	5.6	5.0	4.7	4.3	4.0	3.8
104	Republic of Moldova	–	–	–	–	–	–
105	Romania	3.3	3.4	3.5	3.5	3.7	3.6
106	Russian Federation	–	–	–	–	–	–
107	Rwanda	0.3	0.3	0.2	0.2	0.2	0.2
108	Saudi Arabia	91.5	111.7	98.5	85.1	74.8	72.3
109	Senegal	0.4	0.3	0.3	0.3	0.2	0.2
110	Serbia	–	–	–	–	–	–
111	Sierra Leone	–	–	–	–	–	–
112	Singapore	0.0	0.0	0.0	0.0	0.0	0.0
113	Slovakia	–	–	–	–	–	–
114	Slovenia	–	–	–	–	–	–
115	South Africa	3.6	3.3	2.9	2.7	2.5	2.4
116	Spain	3.5	3.4	3.3	3.0	2.6	2.6

(*Continued*)

Table A3.26 (Continued)

	Country/year	1990	1995	2000	2005	2010	2014
117	Sri Lanka	0.7	0.6	0.6	0.6	0.6	0.6
118	Sudan (former)	–	–	–	–	–	–
119	Swaziland	–	–	–	–	–	–
120	Sweden	1.2	1.1	1.1	1.1	1.0	0.9
121	Switzerland	10.2	9.6	9.3	8.9	8.4	7.9
122	Syrian Arab Republic	–	–	–	–	–	–
123	Tajikistan	–	–	–	–	–	–
124	Thailand	1.3	1.3	1.1	1.1	1.1	1.1
125	Togo	0.4	0.3	0.3	0.3	0.3	0.2
126	Trinidad and Tobago	0.8	0.8	0.7	0.5	0.5	0.4
127	Tunisia	0.6	0.6	0.6	0.6	0.6	0.6
128	Turkey	3.3	3.0	2.8	2.7	2.4	2.3
129	Uganda	–	–	–	–	–	–
130	Ukraine	–	–	–	–	–	–
131	United Arab Emirates	–	–	–	–	–	–
132	United Kingdom	1.7	1.6	1.5	1.5	1.4	1.4
133	United Republic of Tanzania	0.9	0.8	0.8	0.7	0.6	0.6
134	United States of America	5.5	5.1	4.8	4.5	4.3	4.1
135	Uruguay	10.4	10.0	9.8	9.7	9.3	9.2
136	Venezuela (Bolivarian Republic of)	11.0	9.7	8.8	8.0	7.4	7.0
137	Viet Nam	0.5	0.5	0.6	0.6	0.7	0.7
138	Yemen	2.4	1.9	1.6	1.4	1.2	1.1
139	Zambia	2.6	2.3	2.1	1.9	1.7	1.5
140	Zimbabwe	–	–	–	–	–	–

Table A3.27 Agriculture land growth (Agriculture land change (%) with respect to base year 1990)

	Country/year	1995	2000	2005	2010	2014
1	Afghanistan	–	–	–	–	–
2	Albania	–	–	–	–	–
3	Algeria	–	–	–	–	–
4	Argentina	0.1%	0.2%	1.9%	3.7%	5.2%
5	Armenia	–	–	–	–	–
6	Australia	0.0%	–0.5%	–1.1%	–3.8%	–4.7%
7	Austria	–0.4%	–0.9%	–1.8%	–2.3%	–3.7%
8	Bahrain	–	–	–	–	–
9	Bangladesh	–2.0%	–2.5%	–2.7%	–2.9%	–4.6%
10	Barbados	0.0%	–1.3%	–4.2%	–5.7%	–9.4%
11	Belgium	–	–	–	–	–
12	Belize	3.0%	4.3%	4.8%	5.7%	8.7%
13	Benin	–	–	–	–	–
14	Bolivia (Plurinational State of)	0.6%	1.2%	1.0%	1.2%	2.1%
15	Botswana	–0.1%	–0.1%	–0.2%	–0.2%	–0.2%

	Country/year	1995	2000	2005	2010	2014
16	Brazil	1.4%	2.0%	3.0%	3.1%	5.3%
17	Bulgaria	0.0%	−2.4%	−3.8%	−4.8%	−8.1%
18	Burundi	−0.7%	−3.0%	−3.6%	−3.5%	−5.6%
19	Cambodia	0.5%	1.7%	4.7%	6.1%	9.6%
20	Cameroon	0.0%	0.0%	0.1%	1.4%	1.4%
21	Canada	0.1%	−0.1%	−0.1%	−1.7%	−1.7%
22	Central African Republic	–	–	–	–	–
23	Chile	−0.7%	−1.3%	0.0%	−0.2%	−0.3%
24	China	0.7%	0.8%	0.6%	0.4%	0.7%
25	Colombia	−2.4%	−2.4%	−7.8%	−9.5%	−15.0%
26	Congo	0.0%	0.0%	0.1%	0.1%	0.2%
27	Costa Rica	−2.3%	−5.5%	−5.9%	−5.7%	−9.9%
28	Côte d'Ivoire	0.9%	0.9%	1.6%	2.1%	3.2%
29	Croatia	–	–	–	–	–
30	Cuba	–	–	–	–	–
31	Cyprus	−2.3%	−3.1%	1.0%	−8.2%	−9.0%
32	Czech Republic	–	–	–	–	–
33	Democratic Republic of the Congo	–	–	–	–	–
34	Denmark	−0.4%	−1.3%	−0.7%	−1.5%	−2.1%
35	Dominican Republic	0.2%	−0.3%	−1.3%	−1.5%	−2.6%
36	Ecuador	0.7%	0.7%	−1.1%	−1.1%	−2.3%
37	Egypt	4.4%	5.6%	7.4%	8.5%	13.1%
38	El Salvador	0.6%	1.6%	2.6%	2.1%	4.1%
39	Estonia	–	–	–	–	–
40	Fiji	1.4%	1.1%	1.1%	0.9%	1.3%
41	Finland	−1.3%	−1.9%	−1.3%	−1.1%	−2.2%
42	France	−0.3%	−0.6%	−0.9%	−1.4%	−2.1%
43	Gabon	–	–	–	–	–
44	Gambia	−0.2%	10.4%	14.5%	24.1%	33.7%
45	Germany	−0.8%	−1.4%	−1.4%	−1.9%	−2.6%
46	Ghana	0.8%	3.4%	4.6%	5.5%	9.1%
47	Greece	−0.1%	−1.9%	−2.4%	−2.9%	−5.0%
48	Guatemala	–	–	–	–	–
49	Guyana	0.0%	−0.3%	−0.8%	−0.8%	−1.3%
50	Haiti	–	–	–	–	–
51	Honduras	0.9%	−3.0%	−1.3%	−0.7%	−2.2%
52	Hungary	−0.9%	−2.5%	−2.4%	−4.7%	−6.0%
53	Iceland	0.0%	−0.2%	−0.3%	−0.4%	−0.6%
54	India	−0.1%	−0.1%	−0.2%	−0.3%	−0.4%
55	Indonesia	−1.0%	1.1%	3.6%	5.4%	8.9%
56	Iran (Islamic Republic of)	0.9%	0.6%	−6.2%	−6.8%	−9.8%
57	Iraq	−0.3%	−2.6%	0.4%	−2.9%	−3.2%
58	Ireland	−4.9%	−6.0%	−6.6%	−5.2%	−8.8%
59	Israel	−0.2%	−0.6%	−2.9%	−3.4%	−4.6%

(*Continued*)

Table A3.27 (Continued)

	Country/year	1995	2000	2005	2010	2014
60	Italy	−1.9%	−1.8%	−3.3%	−4.0%	−6.8%
61	Jamaica	0.9%	0.2%	−0.5%	−1.7%	−2.3%
62	Japan	−0.9%	−2.0%	−4.7%	−5.2%	−9.0%
63	Jordan	1.4%	0.7%	−0.7%	−0.9%	−1.3%
64	Kazakhstan	−	−	−	−	−
65	Kenya	0.3%	−0.1%	0.2%	0.5%	0.8%
66	Kuwait	−	−	−	−	−
67	Kyrgyzstan	−	−	−	−	−
68	Lao People's Democratic Republic	0.5%	2.1%	4.6%	7.5%	11.5%
69	Latvia	−	−	−	−	−
70	Lesotho	−	−	−	−	−
71	Liberia	−	−	−	−	−
72	Lithuania	−	−	−	−	−
73	Luxembourg	−	−	−	−	−
74	Malawi	0.3%	2.9%	5.3%	7.7%	11.3%
75	Malaysia	0.6%	0.6%	1.1%	2.2%	3.3%
76	Maldives	0.0%	3.0%	3.0%	−0.3%	2.6%
77	Mali	2.0%	4.7%	5.9%	6.3%	10.6%
78	Malta	−3.3%	−8.8%	−8.0%	−5.6%	−12.1%
79	Mauritania	−	−	−	−	−
80	Mauritius	−1.3%	−2.3%	−3.6%	−4.8%	−8.1%
81	Mexico	0.2%	0.3%	0.3%	0.4%	0.6%
82	Mongolia	−1.2%	0.9%	−2.5%	−2.5%	−3.6%
83	Morocco	0.3%	0.3%	−0.3%	−0.3%	−0.3%
84	Mozambique	0.1%	0.2%	0.8%	1.2%	1.7%
85	Myanmar	−	−	−	−	−
86	Namibia	4.4%	5.5%	5.5%	5.1%	8.8%
87	Nepal	0.2%	0.6%	0.3%	−0.1%	0.1%
88	Netherlands	−0.4%	−0.6%	−0.9%	−1.7%	−2.4%
89	New Zealand	−1.5%	−1.2%	−7.8%	−8.4%	−14.3%
90	Nicaragua	2.5%	6.3%	7.2%	5.7%	10.9%
91	Niger	0.0%	1.1%	6.9%	6.9%	10.9%
92	Nigeria	2.1%	3.7%	4.2%	3.3%	6.3%
93	Norway	2.9%	1.6%	1.5%	0.8%	1.3%
94	Pakistan	0.5%	1.0%	0.5%	0.0%	0.9%
95	Panama	0.1%	1.2%	1.2%	1.6%	2.4%
96	Papua New Guinea	−	−	−	−	−
97	Paraguay	−0.8%	4.3%	3.8%	5.5%	8.8%
98	Peru	0.0%	1.4%	1.6%	2.4%	3.8%
99	Philippines	−0.2%	0.2%	0.5%	2.1%	3.2%
100	Poland	−0.2%	−0.5%	−4.1%	−6.4%	−8.9%
101	Portugal	0.2%	1.0%	−0.8%	−2.7%	−2.8%
102	Qatar	1.3%	2.0%	1.3%	2.2%	3.2%
103	Republic of Korea	−1.2%	−2.5%	−3.6%	−5.0%	−7.7%
104	Republic of Moldova	−	−	−	−	−

	Country/year	1995	2000	2005	2010	2014
105	Romania	0.0%	0.1%	-1.0%	-1.1%	-2.4%
106	Russian Federation	–	–	–	–	–
107	Rwanda	-4.6%	-2.9%	-1.3%	-1.0%	-1.0%
108	Saudi Arabia	7.1%	8.9%	8.9%	8.9%	14.3%
109	Senegal	-0.2%	-0.4%	-0.6%	-0.6%	-1.0%
110	Serbia	–	–	–	–	–
111	Sierra Leone	–	–	–	–	–
112	Singapore	-9.7%	-12.0%	-21.5%	-22.0%	-34.7%
113	Slovakia	–	–	–	–	–
114	Slovenia	–	–	–	–	–
115	South Africa	0.4%	0.7%	0.5%	0.3%	0.6%
116	Spain	-0.5%	-0.6%	-1.1%	-2.5%	-3.8%
117	Sri Lanka	-0.1%	0.1%	1.8%	2.9%	4.1%
118	Sudan (former)	–	–	–	–	–
119	Swaziland	–	–	–	–	–
120	Sweden	-0.9%	-2.0%	-1.5%	-2.5%	-4.0%
121	Switzerland	-0.3%	-0.6%	-0.9%	-1.1%	-1.8%
122	Syrian Arab Republic	–	–	–	–	–
123	Tajikistan	–	–	–	–	–
124	Thailand	-0.2%	-1.9%	-2.1%	-0.4%	-1.5%
125	Togo	0.7%	3.3%	0.5%	3.5%	5.3%
126	Trinidad and Tobago	-0.3%	-3.4%	-8.5%	-8.5%	-15.6%
127	Tunisia	1.6%	2.5%	3.3%	3.8%	5.4%
128	Turkey	-0.1%	0.5%	1.0%	-0.4%	-0.4%
129	Uganda	–	–	–	–	–
130	Ukraine	–	–	–	–	–
131	United Arab Emirates	–	–	–	–	–
132	United Kingdom	-0.9%	-1.7%	-1.8%	-1.4%	-2.1%
133	United Republic of Tanzania	0.7%	1.5%	2.5%	4.0%	6.5%
134	United States of America	-0.3%	-0.7%	-0.9%	-1.1%	-1.8%
135	Uruguay	0.0%	0.1%	-0.1%	-0.8%	-1.0%
136	Venezuela (Bolivarian Republic of)	-0.2%	-0.3%	-0.3%	-0.3%	-0.5%
137	Viet Nam	1.0%	6.9%	10.6%	12.5%	19.7%
138	Yemen	0.1%	0.0%	-0.1%	0.0%	-0.2%
139	Zambia	0.6%	2.0%	2.3%	3.0%	5.0%
140	Zimbabwe	–	–	–	–	–

Table A3.28 Agriculture land per capita growth (Agriculture land per capita change (%) with respect to base year 1990)

	Country/year	1995	2000	2005	2010	2014
1	Afghanistan	–	–	–	–	–
2	Albania	–	–	–	–	–
3	Algeria	–	–	–	–	–

(*Continued*)

Table A3.28 (Continued)

	Country/year	1995	2000	2005	2010	2014
4	Argentina	−1.3%	−2.9%	−2.5%	−2.1%	−3.9%
5	Armenia	–	–	–	–	–
6	Australia	−1.2%	−3.3%	−5.4%	−9.7%	−14.3%
7	Austria	−1.1%	−2.0%	−3.5%	−4.4%	−7.1%
8	Bahrain	–	–	–	–	–
9	Bangladesh	−4.2%	−7.5%	−9.7%	−11.2%	−16.7%
10	Barbados	−0.3%	−2.2%	−5.4%	−7.4%	−12.0%
11	Belgium	–	–	–	–	–
12	Belize	1.0%	−2.7%	−5.5%	−7.7%	−11.8%
13	Benin	–	–	–	–	–
14	Bolivia (Plurinational State of)	−1.3%	−3.7%	−5.9%	−7.7%	−11.6%
15	Botswana	−2.7%	−5.7%	−7.4%	−9.5%	−14.9%
16	Brazil	−0.2%	−1.9%	−2.6%	−3.8%	−5.2%
17	Bulgaria	0.7%	−0.8%	−0.9%	−0.8%	−2.1%
18	Burundi	−2.8%	−7.4%	−11.6%	−15.3%	−24.1%
19	Cambodia	−2.9%	−5.7%	−5.0%	−5.5%	−8.2%
20	Cameroon	−2.8%	−6.7%	−9.6%	−11.3%	−18.0%
21	Canada	−1.0%	−2.6%	−3.8%	−6.5%	−9.5%
22	Central African Republic	–	–	–	–	–
23	Chile	−2.2%	−4.7%	−5.0%	−6.5%	−9.8%
24	China	−0.5%	−1.9%	−2.9%	−3.6%	−5.3%
25	Colombia	−4.1%	−6.3%	−13.0%	−15.9%	−23.9%
26	Congo	−2.6%	−6.4%	−9.1%	−12.4%	−18.9%
27	Costa Rica	−4.8%	−10.9%	−13.1%	−14.4%	−21.9%
28	Côte d'Ivoire	−2.4%	−6.6%	−8.0%	−9.9%	−15.5%
29	Croatia	–	–	–	–	–
30	Cuba	–	–	–	–	–
31	Cyprus	−4.4%	−8.0%	−6.3%	−16.2%	−20.6%
32	Czech Republic	–	–	–	–	–
33	Democratic Republic of the Congo	–	–	–	–	–
34	Denmark	−0.8%	−2.2%	−2.0%	−3.3%	−5.1%
35	Dominican Republic	−1.6%	−4.6%	−7.3%	−9.1%	−13.9%
36	Ecuador	−1.6%	−4.5%	−8.2%	−10.1%	−15.7%
37	Egypt	2.3%	0.6%	0.0%	−1.2%	−3.1%
38	El Salvador	−0.6%	−1.0%	−0.5%	−1.4%	−1.0%
39	Estonia	–	–	–	–	–
40	Fiji	0.2%	−1.6%	−1.9%	−3.2%	−5.1%
41	Finland	−1.8%	−2.8%	−2.5%	−2.9%	−5.1%
42	France	−0.6%	−1.6%	−2.7%	−4.0%	−6.2%
43	Gabon	–	–	–	–	–
44	Gambia	−3.2%	2.6%	2.3%	6.4%	4.3%
45	Germany	−1.3%	−2.2%	−2.3%	−2.6%	−3.2%
46	Ghana	−1.9%	−2.9%	−4.9%	−7.1%	−10.8%
47	Greece	−0.8%	−3.3%	−4.2%	−5.0%	−7.0%
48	Guatemala	–	–	–	–	–

	Country/year	1995	2000	2005	2010	2014
49	Guyana	-0.2%	-1.1%	-1.5%	-1.9%	-3.2%
50	Haiti	–	–	–	–	–
51	Honduras	-1.7%	-8.7%	-9.3%	-10.7%	-16.8%
52	Hungary	-0.8%	-2.1%	-1.8%	-3.8%	-4.4%
53	Iceland	-1.0%	-2.6%	-4.0%	-5.7%	-8.5%
54	India	-2.0%	-4.7%	-6.8%	-8.5%	-12.7%
55	Indonesia	-2.6%	-2.7%	-2.0%	-1.9%	-2.7%
56	Iran (Islamic Republic of)	-0.6%	-3.4%	-11.3%	-13.1%	-19.2%
57	Iraq	-3.1%	-9.6%	-9.9%	-15.7%	-23.4%
58	Ireland	-5.4%	-7.8%	-10.4%	-11.2%	-16.8%
59	Israel	-3.6%	-7.7%	-12.1%	-14.6%	-21.0%
60	Italy	-1.9%	-1.9%	-3.8%	-5.0%	-9.0%
61	Jamaica	0.1%	-1.8%	-3.0%	-4.6%	-6.4%
62	Japan	-1.2%	-2.6%	-5.5%	-6.1%	-9.8%
63	Jordan	-3.6%	-7.8%	-11.5%	-16.1%	-24.2%
64	Kazakhstan	–	–	–	–	–
65	Kenya	-2.7%	-6.9%	-9.6%	-12.2%	-18.8%
66	Kuwait	–	–	–	–	–
67	Kyrgyzstan	–	–	–	–	–
68	Lao People's Democratic Republic	-2.2%	-3.6%	-3.0%	-2.4%	-4.2%
69	Latvia	–	–	–	–	–
70	Lesotho	–	–	–	–	–
71	Liberia	–	–	–	–	–
72	Lithuania	–	–	–	–	–
73	Luxembourg	–	–	–	–	–
74	Malawi	-0.6%	-1.5%	-2.4%	-3.7%	-8.1%
75	Malaysia	-2.0%	-5.5%	-7.4%	-8.3%	-12.4%
76	Maldives	-3.1%	-3.8%	-6.5%	-12.5%	-16.3%
77	Mali	-0.6%	-2.0%	-4.6%	-8.1%	-12.4%
78	Malta	-4.2%	-10.5%	-11.0%	-9.2%	-17.5%
79	Mauritania	–	–	–	–	–
80	Mauritius	-2.4%	-5.1%	-7.1%	-8.7%	-13.3%
81	Mexico	-1.7%	-4.2%	-5.7%	-7.5%	-11.5%
82	Mongolia	-2.2%	-1.4%	-6.0%	-7.6%	-12.4%
83	Morocco	-1.4%	-3.4%	-5.1%	-6.4%	-10.0%
84	Mozambique	-3.3%	-7.3%	-10.1%	-12.9%	-19.7%
85	Myanmar	–	–	–	–	–
86	Namibia	1.2%	-2.0%	-3.6%	-5.8%	-8.8%
87	Nepal	-2.4%	-5.1%	-7.1%	-8.7%	-12.6%
88	Netherlands	-1.1%	-2.2%	-3.0%	-4.3%	-6.3%
89	New Zealand	-3.5%	-4.8%	-12.6%	-14.3%	-22.6%
90	Nicaragua	0.3%	1.3%	0.4%	-2.5%	-2.1%
91	Niger	-3.3%	-7.3%	-6.4%	-10.7%	-17.3%
92	Nigeria	-0.4%	-2.6%	-5.2%	-9.1%	-13.5%
93	Norway	2.4%	0.2%	-0.7%	-2.8%	-5.0%

(*Continued*)

Table A3.28 (Continued)

	Country/year	1995	2000	2005	2010	2014
94	Pakistan	−2.1%	−5.1%	−8.0%	−10.8%	−15.8%
95	Panama	−2.0%	−3.8%	−6.0%	−7.6%	−11.8%
96	Papua New Guinea	–	–	–	–	–
97	Paraguay	−3.2%	−1.5%	−4.1%	−4.3%	−6.1%
98	Peru	−1.9%	−2.8%	−4.2%	−4.9%	−7.6%
99	Philippines	−2.6%	−5.4%	−7.5%	−7.8%	−11.8%
100	Poland	−0.4%	−0.6%	−4.1%	−6.3%	−8.8%
101	Portugal	0.1%	0.3%	−2.0%	−4.1%	−4.1%
102	Qatar	0.3%	−3.5%	−12.0%	−26.4%	−37.7%
103	Republic of Korea	−2.2%	−4.7%	−6.4%	−8.3%	−12.6%
104	Republic of Moldova	–	–	–	–	–
105	Romania	0.5%	1.0%	1.1%	2.4%	2.7%
106	Russian Federation	–	–	–	–	–
107	Rwanda	−0.6%	−5.3%	−6.5%	−9.3%	−14.6%
108	Saudi Arabia	4.1%	1.9%	−1.8%	−4.9%	−7.5%
109	Senegal	−3.1%	−7.0%	−10.2%	−13.3%	−20.8%
110	Serbia	–	–	–	–	–
111	Sierra Leone	–	–	–	–	–
112	Singapore	−12.3%	−17.9%	−27.8%	−31.4%	−46.3%
113	Slovakia	–	–	–	–	–
114	Slovenia	–	–	–	–	–
115	South Africa	−1.7%	−4.8%	−6.7%	−8.4%	−12.8%
116	Spain	−0.8%	−1.5%	−3.9%	−6.8%	−9.4%
117	Sri Lanka	−1.2%	−2.1%	−1.4%	−1.3%	−2.5%
118	Sudan (former)	–	–	–	–	–
119	Swaziland	–	–	–	–	–
120	Sweden	−1.5%	−2.8%	−2.8%	−4.7%	−7.9%
121	Switzerland	−1.2%	−2.3%	−3.4%	−4.8%	−8.1%
122	Syrian Arab Republic	–	–	–	–	–
123	Tajikistan	–	–	–	–	–
124	Thailand	−1.1%	−4.3%	−5.8%	−4.4%	−7.3%
125	Togo	−1.8%	−3.0%	−8.8%	−9.2%	−14.7%
126	Trinidad and Tobago	−0.8%	−4.3%	−9.8%	−10.4%	−18.4%
127	Tunisia	−0.3%	−1.5%	−2.0%	−2.7%	−4.6%
128	Turkey	−1.7%	−3.4%	−4.6%	−7.4%	−11.7%
129	Uganda	–	–	–	–	–
130	Ukraine	–	–	–	–	–
131	United Arab Emirates	–	–	–	–	–
132	United Kingdom	−1.2%	−2.4%	−3.1%	−3.6%	−6.0%
133	United Republic of Tanzania	−2.5%	−5.6%	−7.9%	−10.1%	−15.9%
134	United States of America	−1.6%	−3.7%	−5.0%	−6.3%	−9.5%
135	Uruguay	−0.7%	−1.6%	−1.8%	−2.8%	−4.1%
136	Venezuela (Bolivarian Republic of)	−2.4%	−5.3%	−7.5%	−9.3%	−13.9%
137	Viet Nam	−0.7%	2.6%	4.6%	5.0%	7.6%
138	Yemen	−4.7%	−9.4%	−12.7%	−15.7%	−23.1%
139	Zambia	−1.9%	−4.5%	−7.3%	−9.9%	−15.7%
140	Zimbabwe	–	–	–	–	–

Table A3.29 Forest resources (Forest resources in billions of constant 2005 US$)

	Country/year	1990	1995	2000	2005	2010	2014
1	Afghanistan	9	9	9	9	9	9
2	Albania	6	6	6	6	6	6
3	Algeria	10	9	9	8	8	9
4	Argentina	560	552	544	536	537	524
5	Armenia	3	3	2	2	2	2
6	Australia	642	642	643	637	616	534
7	Austria	32	35	37	39	39	37
8	Bahrain	0	0	–	0	0	0
9	Bangladesh	16	15	15	15	15	15
10	Barbados	0	0	0	0	0	0
11	Belgium	4	4	5	5	6	5
12	Belize	13	13	13	12	12	12
13	Benin	37	35	32	31	29	29
14	Bolivia (Plurinational State of)	670	655	641	626	610	594
15	Botswana	60	58	55	53	50	48
16	Brazil	6,662	6,501	6,341	6,205	6,057	6,042
17	Bulgaria	16	18	19	22	26	5
18	Burundi	1	1	1	1	1	1
19	Cambodia	196	185	173	160	150	142
20	Cameroon	221	211	201	191	181	36
21	Canada	2,662	2,643	2,624	2,606	2,593	1,627
22	Central African Republic	211	209	208	207	205	205
23	Chile	85	86	86	87	86	88
24	China	1,159	1,089	1,019	887	923	966
25	Colombia	703	697	691	684	677	135
26	Congo	224	223	222	221	220	220
27	Costa Rica	22	21	21	22	23	40
28	Côte d'Ivoire	42	53	64	64	64	64
29	Croatia	19	20	21	22	23	22
30	Cuba	14	17	20	22	23	22
31	Cyprus	1	1	1	1	1	1
32	Czech Republic	0	0	0	0	0	0
33	Democratic Republic of the Congo	1,320	1,307	1,294	1,281	1,268	1,258
34	Denmark	1	1	1	2	2	1
35	Dominican Republic	18	18	18	18	18	18
36	Ecuador	163	155	147	139	131	141
37	Egypt	–	–	–	–	–	–
38	El Salvador	2	2	1	1	1	1
39	Estonia	19	14	9	21	21	20
40	Fiji	4	4	4	4	4	4
41	Finland	150	153	156	150	146	140
42	France	106	109	113	119	122	121
43	Gabon	1,070	1,070	1,070	1,070	1,070	1,073
44	Gambia	2	2	2	2	2	2

(Continued)

Table A3.29 (Continued)

	Country/year	1990	1995	2000	2005	2010	2014
45	Germany	74	78	83	85	86	89
46	Ghana	45	41	37	33	29	46
47	Greece	23	24	25	26	27	28
48	Guatemala	106	99	93	87	79	84
49	Guyana	180	180	180	180	180	212
50	Haiti	7	6	6	5	5	4
51	Honduras	96	86	75	68	61	56
52	Hungary	3	3	3	3	3	3
53	Iceland	0	0	0	0	0	0
54	India	456	460	465	477	488	468
55	Indonesia	1,435	1,357	1,279	1,227	1,147	1,067
56	Iran (Islamic Republic of)	465	466	467	460	467	375
57	Iraq	3	3	3	3	3	3
58	Ireland	1	1	1	1	1	1
59	Israel	0	0	0	0	0	0
60	Italy	119	131	144	157	169	154
61	Jamaica	2	2	2	2	2	2
62	Japan	130	138	145	155	155	137
63	Jordan	0	0	0	0	0	0
64	Kazakhstan	12	12	12	12	12	12
65	Kenya	24	23	22	21	20	24
66	Kuwait	–	–	–	–	–	–
67	Kyrgyzstan	5	6	6	6	8	8
68	Lao People's Democratic Republic	138	135	131	128	124	135
69	Latvia	20	21	22	23	26	24
70	Lesotho	0	0	0	0	0	0
71	Liberia	36	35	34	33	32	31
72	Lithuania	16	17	17	18	18	17
73	Luxembourg	1	1	1	1	1	1
74	Malawi	19	18	17	16	14	14
75	Malaysia	216	211	207	198	191	209
76	Maldives	0	0	0	0	0	0
77	Mali	64	62	60	57	54	30
78	Malta	0	0	0	0	0	0
79	Mauritania	2	2	1	1	1	1
80	Mauritius	0	0	0	0	0	0
81	Mexico	330	319	309	297	290	319
82	Mongolia	85	82	79	76	73	79
83	Morocco	23	23	23	24	24	25
84	Mozambique	193	189	184	179	174	171
85	Myanmar	192	180	169	160	152	141
86	Namibia	38	36	34	33	31	30
87	Nepal	212	192	171	159	159	159
88	Netherlands	–	–	–	–	–	–

Country/year	1990	1995	2000	2005	2010	2014
89 New Zealand	1,339	1,339	1,339	1,295	1,669	1,505
90 Nicaragua	32	30	27	25	22	23
91 Niger	9	8	6	6	5	5
92 Nigeria	81	72	64	56	48	39
93 Norway	53	54	55	58	62	65
94 Pakistan	1,197	1,057	917	779	646	541
95 Panama	35	33	31	30	29	36
96 Papua New Guinea	306	299	292	285	278	385
97 Paraguay	88	85	81	77	73	66
98 Peru	1,054	1,044	1,034	1,026	1,011	1,081
99 Philippines	58	60	61	64	65	60
100 Poland	4	5	5	5	6	6
101 Portugal	15	15	16	15	15	11
102 Qatar	–	–	–	–	–	–
103 Republic of Korea	90	113	136	162	182	148
104 Republic of Moldova	6	6	7	7	7	1
105 Romania	93	93	93	93	96	98
106 Russian Federation	6,485	6,479	6,473	6,466	6,498	6,478
107 Rwanda	1	1	1	1	1	1
108 Saudi Arabia	6	6	6	6	6	6
109 Senegal	59	57	55	53	51	51
110 Serbia	25	26	27	30	37	33
111 Sierra Leone	18	17	16	15	15	14
112 Singapore	0	0	0	0	0	0
113 Slovakia	10	10	11	11	11	11
114 Slovenia	14	15	17	18	20	18
115 South Africa	38	38	37	37	37	37
116 Spain	64	73	82	84	88	86
117 Sri Lanka	56	52	47	43	40	45
118 Sudan (former)	352	336	320	317	313	157
119 Swaziland	1	2	2	2	2	2
120 Sweden	181	178	174	176	172	130
121 Switzerland	18	18	19	19	19	19
122 Syrian Arab Republic	1	1	1	1	1	0
123 Tajikistan	1	1	1	1	1	1
124 Thailand	122	119	116	112	109	129
125 Togo	3	2	2	1	1	1
126 Trinidad and Tobago	6	6	5	5	5	2
127 Tunisia	2	1	1	1	1	1
128 Turkey	188	188	188	178	163	164
129 Uganda	21	19	17	15	13	10
130 Ukraine	43	47	51	53	55	51
131 United Arab Emirates	–	–	–	–	–	–
132 United Kingdom	7	8	8	8	9	2

(*Continued*)

Table A3.29 (Continued)

Country/year	1990	1995	2000	2005	2010	2014
133 United Republic of Tanzania	261	248	235	222	209	347
134 United States of America	3,463	3,529	3,596	3,759	3,934	3,734
135 Uruguay	3	3	3	3	3	3
136 Venezuela (Bolivarian Republic of)	244	237	230	224	217	226
137 Viet Nam	80	85	90	93	91	92
138 Yemen	2	2	2	2	2	2
139 Zambia	319	314	309	304	299	298
140 Zimbabwe	93	86	79	72	65	60

Table A3.30 Forest resources per capita (Forest resources per capita in thousands of constant 2005 US$)

Country/year	1990	1995	2000	2005	2010	2014
1 Afghanistan	0.7	0.5	0.4	0.4	0.3	0.3
2 Albania	1.9	2.0	2.0	2.1	2.2	2.2
3 Algeria	0.4	0.3	0.3	0.3	0.2	0.2
4 Argentina	17.1	15.8	14.7	13.7	13.0	12.2
5 Armenia	0.8	0.8	0.8	0.8	0.7	0.8
6 Australia	37.6	35.5	33.6	31.2	28.0	22.8
7 Austria	4.2	4.4	4.6	4.7	4.6	4.3
8 Bahrain	0.0	0.0	–	0.0	0.0	0.0
9 Bangladesh	0.1	0.1	0.1	0.1	0.1	0.1
10 Barbados	0.1	0.1	0.1	0.1	0.1	0.1
11 Belgium	0.4	0.4	0.5	0.5	0.5	0.5
12 Belize	71.0	62.4	50.6	42.7	36.3	32.7
13 Benin	7.4	5.8	4.7	3.8	3.1	2.8
14 Bolivia (Plurinational State of)	97.7	86.6	76.9	68.7	61.5	56.3
15 Botswana	43.6	36.6	31.8	28.2	24.5	21.8
16 Brazil	44.3	39.9	36.1	32.9	30.5	29.3
17 Bulgaria	1.9	2.1	2.4	2.9	3.5	0.7
18 Burundi	0.3	0.2	0.1	0.1	0.1	0.1
19 Cambodia	21.8	17.3	14.2	12.0	10.5	9.3
20 Cameroon	18.3	15.2	12.6	10.5	8.8	1.6
21 Canada	95.8	90.0	85.3	80.6	76.2	45.8
22 Central African Republic	71.7	62.8	55.8	50.9	46.2	42.6
23 Chile	6.4	6.0	5.7	5.4	5.0	4.9
24 China	1.0	0.9	0.8	0.7	0.7	0.7
25 Colombia	20.5	18.6	17.1	15.8	14.8	2.8
26 Congo	93.7	81.8	71.4	63.1	54.2	48.9
27 Costa Rica	7.0	6.1	5.3	5.1	5.0	8.4
28 Côte d'Ivoire	3.5	3.7	3.9	3.5	3.2	2.9
29 Croatia	4.0	4.3	4.8	5.0	5.3	5.2
30 Cuba	1.3	1.5	1.8	2.0	2.0	1.9

	Country/year	1990	1995	2000	2005	2010	2014
31	Cyprus	1.3	1.2	1.1	1.0	1.0	0.9
32	Czech Republic	0.0	0.0	0.0	0.0	0.0	0.0
33	Democratic Republic of the Congo	37.7	31.0	26.9	22.8	19.2	16.8
34	Denmark	0.2	0.2	0.2	0.3	0.3	0.3
35	Dominican Republic	2.6	2.3	2.1	2.0	1.8	1.7
36	Ecuador	16.0	13.5	11.6	10.1	8.8	8.9
37	Egypt	–	–	–	–	–	–
38	El Salvador	0.3	0.3	0.3	0.2	0.2	0.2
39	Estonia	12.4	9.9	6.4	15.4	15.5	15.4
40	Fiji	4.9	4.6	4.4	4.3	4.1	4.0
41	Finland	30.1	30.0	30.2	28.7	27.2	25.7
42	France	1.8	1.8	1.9	1.9	1.9	1.8
43	Gabon	1,123.1	984.4	868.4	776.3	693.6	635.8
44	Gambia	2.4	2.1	1.9	1.6	1.4	1.2
45	Germany	0.9	1.0	1.0	1.0	1.1	1.1
46	Ghana	3.1	2.4	2.0	1.5	1.2	1.7
47	Greece	2.2	2.3	2.3	2.4	2.4	2.6
48	Guatemala	11.6	9.6	7.9	6.6	5.4	5.3
49	Guyana	250.3	248.1	242.9	242.8	239.3	277.6
50	Haiti	0.9	0.8	0.7	0.6	0.5	0.4
51	Honduras	19.6	15.3	12.1	9.9	8.2	7.0
52	Hungary	0.3	0.3	0.3	0.3	0.3	0.3
53	Iceland	0.1	0.1	0.1	0.1	0.1	0.1
54	India	0.5	0.5	0.4	0.4	0.4	0.4
55	Indonesia	7.9	6.9	6.0	5.4	4.7	4.2
56	Iran (Islamic Republic of)	8.3	7.7	7.1	6.6	6.3	4.8
57	Iraq	0.2	0.2	0.1	0.1	0.1	0.1
58	Ireland	0.2	0.2	0.2	0.2	0.1	0.1
59	Israel	0.1	0.1	0.0	0.0	0.0	0.0
60	Italy	2.1	2.3	2.5	2.7	2.9	2.5
61	Jamaica	0.9	0.8	0.8	0.8	0.7	0.7
62	Japan	1.1	1.1	1.1	1.2	1.2	1.1
63	Jordan	0.1	0.1	0.1	0.1	0.1	0.0
64	Kazakhstan	0.7	0.8	0.8	0.8	0.8	0.7
65	Kenya	1.0	0.8	0.7	0.6	0.5	0.5
66	Kuwait	–	–	–	–	–	–
67	Kyrgyzstan	1.2	1.3	1.2	1.2	1.5	1.3
68	Lao People's Democratic Republic	32.5	27.7	24.6	22.2	19.8	20.2
69	Latvia	7.4	8.5	9.4	10.4	12.2	12.1
70	Lesotho	0.1	0.1	0.1	0.1	0.1	0.1
71	Liberia	17.2	16.8	11.7	10.0	8.0	7.0
72	Lithuania	4.4	4.6	4.9	5.3	5.7	5.8
73	Luxembourg	3.0	3.2	3.3	3.1	2.8	2.5
74	Malawi	2.0	1.8	1.5	1.2	1.0	0.8

(Continued)

Table A3.30 (Continued)

Country/year	1990	1995	2000	2005	2010	2014
75 Malaysia	11.9	10.2	8.8	7.7	6.8	7.0
76 Maldives	0.0	0.0	0.0	0.0	0.0	0.0
77 Mali	7.5	6.4	5.4	4.5	3.6	1.7
78 Malta	0.0	0.0	0.0	0.0	0.0	0.0
79 Mauritania	0.9	0.7	0.5	0.4	0.3	0.2
80 Mauritius	0.4	0.4	0.3	0.3	0.3	0.3
81 Mexico	3.9	3.4	3.0	2.7	2.4	2.5
82 Mongolia	38.9	35.7	33.0	30.2	27.0	27.2
83 Morocco	0.9	0.9	0.8	0.8	0.7	0.7
84 Mozambique	14.5	11.8	10.1	8.5	7.2	6.3
85 Myanmar	4.6	4.0	3.5	3.2	2.9	2.6
86 Namibia	26.6	21.8	18.2	16.2	14.3	12.5
87 Nepal	11.3	9.0	7.2	6.3	5.9	5.7
88 Netherlands	–	–	–	–	–	–
89 New Zealand	402.1	364.5	347.0	313.2	383.6	333.6
90 Nicaragua	7.8	6.5	5.4	4.6	3.9	3.9
91 Niger	1.2	0.8	0.6	0.4	0.3	0.3
92 Nigeria	0.8	0.7	0.5	0.4	0.3	0.2
93 Norway	12.4	12.3	12.2	12.6	12.6	12.7
94 Pakistan	11.1	8.6	6.6	5.1	3.8	2.9
95 Panama	14.1	11.9	10.1	9.0	8.1	9.4
96 Papua New Guinea	73.5	63.3	54.3	46.8	40.6	51.6
97 Paraguay	21.0	17.8	15.2	13.3	11.8	10.0
98 Peru	48.3	43.4	39.9	37.2	34.4	34.9
99 Philippines	0.9	0.9	0.8	0.7	0.7	0.6
100 Poland	0.1	0.1	0.1	0.1	0.2	0.2
101 Portugal	1.5	1.5	1.5	1.5	1.4	1.0
102 Qatar	–	–	–	–	–	–
103 Republic of Korea	2.1	2.5	2.9	3.4	3.7	2.9
104 Republic of Moldova	1.6	1.7	1.8	2.0	2.1	0.4
105 Romania	4.0	4.1	4.1	4.4	4.7	4.9
106 Russian Federation	43.7	43.7	44.2	45.1	45.5	45.0
107 Rwanda	0.1	0.1	0.1	0.1	0.1	0.1
108 Saudi Arabia	0.4	0.3	0.3	0.2	0.2	0.2
109 Senegal	7.8	6.5	5.6	4.7	4.0	3.5
110 Serbia	3.3	3.4	3.5	4.0	5.0	4.7
111 Sierra Leone	4.5	4.4	4.0	3.0	2.5	2.3
112 Singapore	0.0	0.0	0.0	0.0	0.0	0.0
113 Slovakia	1.8	1.9	2.0	2.1	2.1	2.0
114 Slovenia	7.2	7.8	8.3	9.0	9.6	8.6
115 South Africa	1.1	1.0	0.8	0.8	0.7	0.7
116 Spain	1.7	1.9	2.0	1.9	1.9	1.8
117 Sri Lanka	3.3	2.9	2.5	2.2	2.0	2.2
118 Sudan (former)	17.6	13.6	11.4	9.9	8.7	4.0

	Country/year	1990	1995	2000	2005	2010	2014
119	Swaziland	1.7	1.7	1.6	1.7	1.6	1.6
120	Sweden	21.2	20.1	19.6	19.5	18.4	13.4
121	Switzerland	2.6	2.6	2.6	2.5	2.4	2.3
122	Syrian Arab Republic	0.1	0.1	0.1	0.0	0.0	0.0
123	Tajikistan	0.3	0.3	0.2	0.2	0.2	0.2
124	Thailand	2.2	2.0	1.9	1.7	1.6	1.9
125	Togo	0.7	0.5	0.4	0.3	0.2	0.1
126	Trinidad and Tobago	4.6	4.4	4.3	4.1	3.9	1.6
127	Tunisia	0.2	0.2	0.1	0.1	0.1	0.1
128	Turkey	3.5	3.2	3.0	2.6	2.3	2.1
129	Uganda	1.2	0.9	0.7	0.5	0.4	0.3
130	Ukraine	0.8	0.9	1.0	1.1	1.2	1.1
131	United Arab Emirates	–	–	–	–	–	–
132	United Kingdom	0.1	0.1	0.1	0.1	0.1	0.0
133	United Republic of Tanzania	10.2	8.3	6.9	5.7	4.6	6.7
134	United States of America	13.9	13.3	12.7	12.7	12.7	11.7
135	Uruguay	1.0	1.0	1.0	1.0	1.0	1.0
136	Venezuela (Bolivarian Republic of)	12.3	10.7	9.4	8.4	7.5	7.4
137	Viet Nam	1.2	1.2	1.2	1.1	1.0	1.0
138	Yemen	0.2	0.2	0.1	0.1	0.1	0.1
139	Zambia	39.2	33.9	29.2	25.2	21.5	19.0
140	Zimbabwe	8.8	7.3	6.3	5.6	4.7	4.0

Table A3.31 Forest growth (Forest change (%) with respect to base year 1990)

	Country/year	1995	2000	2005	2010	2014
1	Afghanistan	0.0%	0.0%	0.0%	0.0%	-0.1%
2	Albania	0.0%	0.0%	-0.1%	0.1%	0.2%
3	Algeria	-0.7%	-1.9%	-3.3%	-4.8%	-2.2%
4	Argentina	-0.3%	-0.7%	-1.1%	-1.1%	-2.2%
5	Armenia	-1.2%	-3.0%	-4.7%	-7.5%	-4.0%
6	Australia	0.0%	0.0%	-0.2%	-1.0%	-6.0%
7	Austria	1.4%	3.4%	4.8%	4.5%	4.5%
8	Bahrain	-12.9%	–	-15.6%	0.3%	-41.3%
9	Bangladesh	-0.4%	-0.9%	-1.5%	-0.8%	-1.9%
10	Barbados	0.0%	0.0%	-0.1%	-0.1%	-7.0%
11	Belgium	3.1%	7.4%	9.9%	10.7%	13.1%
12	Belize	-0.6%	-1.5%	-2.4%	-3.2%	-4.7%
13	Benin	-1.3%	-3.2%	-4.4%	-5.7%	-7.6%
14	Bolivia (Plurinational State of)	-0.4%	-1.1%	-1.7%	-2.3%	-3.9%
15	Botswana	-0.8%	-2.2%	-3.3%	-4.5%	-7.0%
16	Brazil	-0.5%	-1.2%	-1.8%	-2.4%	-3.2%
17	Bulgaria	1.8%	4.4%	8.3%	11.8%	-32.1%
18	Burundi	-5.4%	-15.4%	-16.5%	-17.2%	-11.9%

(*Continued*)

Table A3.31 (Continued)

	Country/year	1995	2000	2005	2010	2014
19	Cambodia	-1.2%	-3.0%	-4.9%	-6.4%	-10.2%
20	Cameroon	-0.9%	-2.3%	-3.6%	-4.9%	-45.3%
21	Canada	-0.1%	-0.4%	-0.5%	-0.7%	-15.1%
22	Central African Republic	-0.1%	-0.3%	-0.5%	-0.7%	-0.9%
23	Chile	0.2%	0.5%	0.6%	0.3%	1.2%
24	China	-1.2%	-3.2%	-6.5%	-5.5%	-5.9%
25	Colombia	-0.2%	-0.5%	-0.7%	-0.9%	-42.2%
26	Congo	-0.1%	-0.2%	-0.3%	-0.4%	-0.5%
27	Costa Rica	-0.4%	-1.0%	0.1%	1.2%	22.5%
28	Côte d'Ivoire	4.8%	11.2%	11.2%	11.1%	14.7%
29	Croatia	1.1%	2.7%	4.0%	5.3%	5.0%
30	Cuba	3.8%	9.0%	12.7%	13.7%	16.7%
31	Cyprus	0.5%	1.4%	1.7%	2.2%	2.5%
32	Czech Republic	1.0%	2.5%	2.5%	3.7%	-13.3%
33	Democratic Republic of the Congo	-0.2%	-0.5%	-0.7%	-1.0%	-1.6%
34	Denmark	1.2%	2.9%	9.6%	8.8%	10.4%
35	Dominican Republic	0.0%	0.0%	-0.1%	-0.4%	-1.2%
36	Ecuador	-1.0%	-2.6%	-3.9%	-5.2%	-4.7%
37	Egypt	–	–	–	–	–
38	El Salvador	-1.3%	-3.4%	-5.3%	-7.2%	-11.6%
39	Estonia	-6.1%	-17.6%	1.8%	1.5%	1.3%
40	Fiji	-0.1%	-0.3%	-0.5%	-0.7%	-0.1%
41	Finland	0.4%	1.0%	0.0%	-0.7%	-2.2%
42	France	0.7%	1.8%	3.0%	3.7%	4.6%
43	Gabon	0.0%	0.0%	0.0%	0.0%	0.1%
44	Gambia	0.4%	1.1%	1.6%	2.1%	3.2%
45	Germany	1.2%	2.8%	3.7%	3.9%	6.6%
46	Ghana	-1.9%	-4.8%	-7.5%	-10.4%	0.5%
47	Greece	0.9%	2.2%	3.2%	4.3%	7.0%
48	Guatemala	-1.3%	-3.3%	-4.9%	-7.0%	-7.3%
49	Guyana	0.0%	0.0%	0.0%	0.0%	5.6%
50	Haiti	-1.5%	-3.8%	-5.9%	-8.4%	-13.2%
51	Honduras	-2.2%	-5.8%	-8.1%	-10.6%	-16.7%
52	Hungary	1.6%	4.0%	5.4%	5.6%	6.2%
53	Iceland	-0.8%	-2.0%	-2.1%	-1.7%	31.7%
54	India	0.2%	0.5%	1.2%	1.7%	0.9%
55	Indonesia	-1.1%	-2.8%	-3.9%	-5.5%	-9.4%
56	Iran (Islamic Republic of)	0.0%	0.1%	-0.3%	0.1%	-6.9%
57	Iraq	0.2%	0.4%	0.7%	0.7%	0.9%
58	Ireland	-1.0%	-2.6%	-3.4%	-5.2%	-9.9%
59	Israel	-0.2%	-0.5%	0.3%	-0.1%	3.7%
60	Italy	2.1%	5.0%	7.2%	9.3%	9.2%
61	Jamaica	-0.2%	-0.5%	-0.6%	-1.1%	-1.1%
62	Japan	1.2%	2.8%	4.5%	4.6%	1.7%
63	Jordan	0.0%	0.0%	0.0%	0.0%	-0.1%

	Country/year	1995	2000	2005	2010	2014
64	Kazakhstan	-0.3%	-0.8%	0.5%	0.3%	0.4%
65	Kenya	-0.8%	-1.9%	-3.0%	-3.9%	0.6%
66	Kuwait	–	–	–	–	–
67	Kyrgyzstan	0.9%	2.3%	3.4%	10.4%	12.0%
68	Lao People's Democratic Republic	-0.5%	-1.2%	-1.9%	-2.6%	-0.6%
69	Latvia	1.2%	3.0%	4.1%	6.6%	6.9%
70	Lesotho	-0.1%	-0.1%	-0.2%	-0.3%	-1.8%
71	Liberia	-0.6%	-1.6%	-2.4%	-3.2%	-5.1%
72	Lithuania	0.5%	1.1%	2.0%	2.0%	1.4%
73	Luxembourg	2.2%	5.2%	5.2%	5.2%	5.8%
74	Malawi	-1.1%	-2.7%	-4.6%	-6.5%	-9.9%
75	Malaysia	-0.4%	-1.1%	-2.1%	-3.1%	-1.1%
76	Maldives	0.0%	0.0%	0.0%	0.0%	-41.5%
77	Mali	-0.6%	-1.5%	-2.6%	-4.0%	-22.5%
78	Malta	0.0%	0.0%	0.0%	0.0%	-41.5%
79	Mauritania	-2.7%	-7.2%	-11.6%	-14.3%	-21.0%
80	Mauritius	-0.1%	-0.4%	-2.6%	-2.8%	-3.7%
81	Mexico	-0.6%	-1.6%	-2.5%	-3.1%	-1.1%
82	Mongolia	-0.7%	-1.7%	-2.7%	-3.6%	-2.4%
83	Morocco	0.0%	0.1%	0.6%	0.4%	2.1%
84	Mozambique	-0.5%	-1.3%	-2.0%	-2.6%	-4.1%
85	Myanmar	-1.2%	-3.1%	-4.4%	-5.6%	-9.6%
86	Namibia	-0.8%	-2.2%	-3.3%	-4.5%	-7.2%
87	Nepal	-2.0%	-5.2%	-6.8%	-6.8%	-9.0%
88	Netherlands	–	–	–	–	–
89	New Zealand	0.0%	0.0%	-0.8%	5.7%	4.0%
90	Nicaragua	-1.6%	-4.1%	-6.4%	-9.0%	-10.3%
91	Niger	-3.6%	-9.7%	-11.7%	-13.7%	-18.3%
92	Nigeria	-2.1%	-5.4%	-8.6%	-12.1%	-21.2%
93	Norway	0.4%	1.0%	2.6%	4.1%	7.5%
94	Pakistan	-2.5%	-6.4%	-10.2%	-14.3%	-23.2%
95	Panama	-1.2%	-3.1%	-3.7%	-4.2%	1.5%
96	Papua New Guinea	-0.5%	-1.1%	-1.7%	-2.3%	8.0%
97	Paraguay	-0.9%	-2.2%	-3.4%	-4.6%	-9.5%
98	Peru	-0.2%	-0.5%	-0.7%	-1.0%	0.9%
99	Philippines	0.5%	1.4%	2.4%	3.0%	1.2%
100	Poland	2.1%	5.1%	7.7%	9.8%	12.2%
101	Portugal	0.9%	2.1%	1.4%	1.3%	-9.7%
102	Qatar	–	–	–	–	–
103	Republic of Korea	4.6%	10.8%	15.8%	19.2%	17.9%
104	Republic of Moldova	1.3%	3.2%	4.9%	6.3%	-36.6%
105	Romania	0.0%	0.0%	0.1%	0.8%	1.9%
106	Russian Federation	0.0%	0.0%	-0.1%	0.1%	0.0%
107	Rwanda	-1.4%	-3.5%	-2.5%	-2.8%	-8.7%
108	Saudi Arabia	0.0%	0.0%	0.0%	0.0%	0.0%

(*Continued*)

Table A3.31 (Continued)

	Country/year	1995	2000	2005	2010	2014
109	Senegal	−0.6%	−1.5%	−2.5%	−3.2%	−4.6%
110	Serbia	0.6%	1.6%	4.6%	10.1%	10.1%
111	Sierra Leone	−0.9%	−2.4%	−3.5%	−4.7%	−6.7%
112	Singapore	0.0%	0.0%	0.0%	0.0%	80.6%
113	Slovakia	0.9%	2.2%	3.3%	4.1%	4.0%
114	Slovenia	1.5%	3.7%	5.9%	8.2%	7.3%
115	South Africa	−0.1%	−0.3%	−0.4%	−0.5%	−0.6%
116	Spain	2.7%	6.4%	6.8%	8.1%	10.0%
117	Sri Lanka	−1.6%	−4.2%	−6.5%	−8.3%	−7.1%
118	Sudan (former)	−0.9%	−2.3%	−2.6%	−2.9%	−23.6%
119	Swaziland	1.5%	3.6%	5.2%	6.7%	11.1%
120	Sweden	−0.4%	−1.1%	−0.7%	−1.3%	−10.5%
121	Switzerland	0.5%	1.4%	1.7%	2.1%	2.3%
122	Syrian Arab Republic	0.0%	0.1%	0.0%	0.0%	−41.5%
123	Tajikistan	−0.1%	−0.2%	−0.3%	−0.3%	−0.4%
124	Thailand	−0.4%	−1.1%	−2.0%	−2.8%	1.9%
125	Togo	−3.4%	−9.1%	−14.8%	−22.0%	−37.3%
126	Trinidad and Tobago	−0.3%	−0.9%	−1.4%	−2.2%	−28.1%
127	Tunisia	−0.9%	−2.4%	−2.4%	−2.5%	−3.5%
128	Turkey	0.0%	−0.1%	−1.4%	−3.6%	−4.4%
129	Uganda	−1.9%	−4.9%	−7.7%	−10.0%	−21.0%
130	Ukraine	1.9%	4.5%	5.6%	6.5%	6.3%
131	United Arab Emirates	−	−	−	−	−
132	United Kingdom	0.2%	0.5%	2.1%	4.0%	−38.4%
133	United Republic of Tanzania	−1.0%	−2.6%	−3.9%	−5.3%	10.0%
134	United States of America	0.4%	0.9%	2.1%	3.2%	2.5%
135	Uruguay	0.4%	0.9%	1.3%	1.8%	2.4%
136	Venezuela (Bolivarian Republic of)	−0.6%	−1.4%	−2.1%	−2.9%	−2.5%
137	Viet Nam	1.2%	3.0%	3.8%	3.2%	4.8%
138	Yemen	0.0%	0.0%	0.0%	0.0%	0.0%
139	Zambia	−0.3%	−0.8%	−1.2%	−1.6%	−2.2%
140	Zimbabwe	−1.5%	−3.9%	−6.1%	−8.4%	−13.4%

Table A3.32 Forest per capita growth (Forest per capita change (%) with respect to base year 1990)

	Country/year	1995	2000	2005	2010	2014
1	Afghanistan	−6.4%	−11.5%	−16.1%	−18.9%	−27.5%
2	Albania	0.6%	1.5%	2.1%	3.1%	4.5%
3	Algeria	−2.9%	−6.3%	−9.2%	−12.3%	−14.6%
4	Argentina	−1.6%	−3.8%	−5.4%	−6.6%	−10.7%
5	Armenia	0.7%	0.5%	−0.8%	−3.2%	1.4%
6	Australia	−1.1%	−2.8%	−4.5%	−7.1%	−15.4%
7	Austria	0.7%	2.3%	3.0%	2.3%	0.8%

	Country/year	1995	2000	2005	2010	2014
8	Bahrain	−15.1%	–	−26.6%	−20.6%	−58.1%
9	Bangladesh	−2.6%	−6.1%	−8.6%	−9.3%	−14.3%
10	Barbados	−0.3%	−0.9%	−1.3%	−1.9%	−9.6%
11	Belgium	2.7%	6.6%	8.5%	8.3%	8.7%
12	Belize	−2.6%	−8.1%	−11.9%	−15.4%	−22.7%
13	Benin	−4.7%	−10.9%	−15.5%	−19.7%	−28.0%
14	Bolivia (Plurinational State of)	−2.4%	−5.8%	−8.4%	−10.9%	−16.8%
15	Botswana	−3.5%	−7.6%	−10.3%	−13.4%	−20.7%
16	Brazil	−2.1%	−5.0%	−7.2%	−8.9%	−12.9%
17	Bulgaria	2.6%	6.1%	11.6%	16.5%	−27.7%
18	Burundi	−7.4%	−19.2%	−23.4%	−27.3%	−29.2%
19	Cambodia	−4.5%	−10.1%	−13.8%	−16.7%	−24.7%
20	Cameroon	−3.7%	−8.9%	−12.9%	−16.8%	−55.7%
21	Canada	−1.2%	−2.9%	−4.2%	−5.5%	−21.8%
22	Central African Republic	−2.6%	−6.1%	−8.2%	−10.4%	−15.9%
23	Chile	−1.3%	−3.0%	−4.4%	−6.0%	−8.5%
24	China	−2.4%	−5.7%	−9.7%	−9.3%	−11.5%
25	Colombia	−1.9%	−4.5%	−6.3%	−7.9%	−48.3%
26	Congo	−2.7%	−6.6%	−9.4%	−12.8%	−19.5%
27	Costa Rica	−2.9%	−6.7%	−7.5%	−8.1%	6.1%
28	Côte d'Ivoire	1.3%	3.0%	0.6%	−2.1%	−6.1%
29	Croatia	1.6%	4.7%	5.9%	7.4%	9.3%
30	Cuba	3.2%	7.7%	11.0%	11.8%	13.9%
31	Cyprus	−1.6%	−3.8%	−5.6%	−6.7%	−10.6%
32	Czech Republic	1.0%	2.7%	2.8%	3.4%	−13.8%
33	Democratic Republic of the Congo	−3.9%	−8.1%	−11.8%	−15.5%	−23.6%
34	Denmark	0.8%	2.0%	8.2%	6.8%	7.0%
35	Dominican Republic	−1.9%	−4.3%	−6.2%	−8.0%	−12.7%
36	Ecuador	−3.2%	−7.6%	−10.7%	−13.8%	−17.7%
37	Egypt	–	–	–	–	–
38	El Salvador	−2.6%	−5.8%	−8.2%	−10.4%	−16.0%
39	Estonia	−4.4%	−15.2%	5.6%	5.7%	7.5%
40	Fiji	−1.4%	−3.0%	−3.4%	−4.7%	−6.4%
41	Finland	−0.1%	0.1%	−1.2%	−2.5%	−5.2%
42	France	0.4%	0.8%	1.0%	1.0%	0.2%
43	Gabon	−2.6%	−6.2%	−8.8%	−11.4%	−17.3%
44	Gambia	−2.5%	−6.1%	−9.2%	−12.4%	−19.4%
45	Germany	0.6%	2.0%	2.7%	3.1%	5.9%
46	Ghana	−4.5%	−10.6%	−15.9%	−21.1%	−17.8%
47	Greece	0.2%	0.7%	1.3%	2.1%	4.6%
48	Guatemala	−3.7%	−9.0%	−13.2%	−17.4%	−23.1%
49	Guyana	−0.2%	−0.7%	−0.8%	−1.1%	3.5%
50	Haiti	−3.4%	−8.1%	−11.9%	−15.9%	−24.0%
51	Honduras	−4.8%	−11.4%	−15.6%	−19.6%	−29.1%
52	Hungary	1.7%	4.4%	6.1%	6.6%	8.0%

(*Continued*)

Table A3.32 (Continued)

	Country/year	1995	2000	2005	2010	2014
53	Iceland	-1.7%	-4.3%	-5.8%	-7.0%	21.2%
54	India	-1.8%	-4.2%	-5.5%	-6.7%	-11.6%
55	Indonesia	-2.7%	-6.5%	-9.0%	-12.0%	-19.1%
56	Iran (Islamic Republic of)	-1.4%	-3.8%	-5.7%	-6.6%	-16.6%
57	Iraq	-2.7%	-6.8%	-9.7%	-12.7%	-20.2%
58	Ireland	-1.6%	-4.6%	-7.4%	-11.2%	-17.8%
59	Israel	-3.6%	-7.7%	-9.2%	-11.7%	-14.2%
60	Italy	2.0%	4.9%	6.6%	8.1%	6.7%
61	Jamaica	-0.9%	-2.4%	-3.0%	-4.0%	-5.3%
62	Japan	0.9%	2.2%	3.6%	3.6%	0.7%
63	Jordan	-4.9%	-8.4%	-11.0%	-15.3%	-23.3%
64	Kazakhstan	0.3%	1.6%	2.4%	0.4%	-1.4%
65	Kenya	-3.8%	-8.6%	-12.5%	-16.1%	-18.9%
66	Kuwait	–	–	–	–	–
67	Kyrgyzstan	0.2%	-0.5%	-0.7%	4.6%	1.9%
68	Lao People's Democratic Republic	-3.1%	-6.7%	-9.1%	-11.6%	-14.6%
69	Latvia	2.6%	6.1%	8.7%	13.1%	17.7%
70	Lesotho	-1.9%	-3.8%	-4.8%	-5.9%	-10.4%
71	Liberia	-0.4%	-9.1%	-12.6%	-17.4%	-25.8%
72	Lithuania	0.8%	2.5%	4.8%	6.7%	9.5%
73	Luxembourg	0.8%	1.8%	0.2%	-2.0%	-6.7%
74	Malawi	-1.9%	-6.9%	-11.6%	-16.5%	-25.5%
75	Malaysia	-3.0%	-7.1%	-10.3%	-13.1%	-16.2%
76	Maldives	-3.1%	-6.6%	-9.2%	-12.2%	-52.3%
77	Mali	-3.1%	-7.8%	-12.2%	-17.0%	-38.6%
78	Malta	-0.9%	-1.8%	-3.2%	-3.9%	-45.1%
79	Mauritania	-5.5%	-13.8%	-20.9%	-25.8%	-36.9%
80	Mauritius	-1.3%	-3.2%	-6.2%	-6.7%	-9.1%
81	Mexico	-2.6%	-6.0%	-8.4%	-10.7%	-12.9%
82	Mongolia	-1.7%	-4.0%	-6.2%	-8.7%	-11.3%
83	Morocco	-1.6%	-3.5%	-4.3%	-5.8%	-7.8%
84	Mozambique	-3.9%	-8.7%	-12.6%	-16.1%	-24.3%
85	Myanmar	-2.5%	-6.2%	-8.4%	-10.4%	-16.6%
86	Namibia	-3.9%	-9.1%	-11.6%	-14.4%	-22.2%
87	Nepal	-4.5%	-10.6%	-13.8%	-14.9%	-20.6%
88	Netherlands	–	–	–	–	–
89	New Zealand	-1.9%	-3.6%	-6.1%	-1.2%	-6.0%
90	Nicaragua	-3.7%	-8.6%	-12.3%	-16.1%	-20.8%
91	Niger	-6.8%	-17.3%	-22.7%	-28.0%	-39.1%
92	Nigeria	-4.5%	-11.2%	-16.8%	-22.6%	-35.9%
93	Norway	-0.1%	-0.4%	0.4%	0.5%	0.9%
94	Pakistan	-5.0%	-12.1%	-17.8%	-23.5%	-35.9%
95	Panama	-3.2%	-7.9%	-10.5%	-12.9%	-12.6%
96	Papua New Guinea	-2.9%	-7.3%	-10.7%	-13.8%	-11.1%

	Country/year	1995	2000	2005	2010	2014
97	Paraguay	−3.3%	−7.7%	−10.8%	−13.4%	−21.8%
98	Peru	−2.1%	−4.7%	−6.3%	−8.1%	−10.2%
99	Philippines	−1.8%	−4.3%	−5.7%	−6.9%	−13.5%
100	Poland	1.9%	5.0%	7.6%	9.9%	12.3%
101	Portugal	0.8%	1.4%	0.1%	−0.2%	−10.9%
102	Qatar	–	–	–	–	–
103	Republic of Korea	3.6%	8.3%	12.5%	15.1%	11.6%
104	Republic of Moldova	1.4%	3.6%	5.7%	7.2%	−35.8%
105	Romania	0.4%	0.8%	2.2%	4.3%	7.3%
106	Russian Federation	0.0%	0.2%	0.8%	1.0%	1.0%
107	Rwanda	2.8%	−5.8%	−7.7%	−10.9%	−21.3%
108	Saudi Arabia	−2.8%	−6.5%	−9.8%	−12.6%	−19.1%
109	Senegal	−3.5%	−8.0%	−11.9%	−15.6%	−23.7%
110	Serbia	0.5%	1.8%	5.1%	11.1%	12.4%
111	Sierra Leone	−0.5%	−3.2%	−9.5%	−13.4%	−20.3%
112	Singapore	−2.9%	−6.7%	−8.1%	−12.0%	48.6%
113	Slovakia	0.7%	1.8%	2.9%	3.7%	3.2%
114	Slovenia	1.6%	3.8%	5.9%	7.5%	6.2%
115	South Africa	−2.2%	−5.7%	−7.5%	−9.2%	−13.8%
116	Spain	2.4%	5.4%	3.7%	3.3%	3.6%
117	Sri Lanka	−2.7%	−6.3%	−9.4%	−12.0%	−13.0%
118	Sudan (former)	−5.0%	−10.3%	−13.4%	−16.2%	−39.0%
119	Swaziland	−0.7%	−1.7%	−1.1%	−1.6%	−2.3%
120	Sweden	−1.0%	−2.0%	−2.0%	−3.5%	−14.2%
121	Switzerland	−0.4%	−0.3%	−0.8%	−1.7%	−4.3%
122	Syrian Arab Republic	−2.7%	−6.5%	−9.0%	−12.0%	−49.0%
123	Tajikistan	−1.8%	−4.0%	−6.4%	−8.8%	−14.2%
124	Thailand	−1.4%	−3.6%	−5.6%	−6.7%	−4.0%
125	Togo	−5.7%	−14.6%	−22.7%	−31.5%	−49.2%
126	Trinidad and Tobago	−0.9%	−1.8%	−2.9%	−4.2%	−30.5%
127	Tunisia	−2.8%	−6.2%	−7.3%	−8.6%	−12.7%
128	Turkey	−1.6%	−4.0%	−6.8%	−10.4%	−15.3%
129	Uganda	−5.0%	−12.0%	−18.1%	−23.4%	−39.0%
130	Ukraine	2.0%	5.9%	8.2%	9.8%	11.2%
131	United Arab Emirates	–	–	–	–	–
132	United Kingdom	−0.1%	−0.2%	0.7%	1.6%	−40.9%
133	United Republic of Tanzania	−4.1%	−9.4%	−13.7%	−18.2%	−13.2%
134	United States of America	−0.9%	−2.1%	−2.1%	−2.1%	−5.5%
135	Uruguay	−0.4%	−0.7%	−0.4%	−0.2%	−0.8%
136	Venezuela (Bolivarian Republic of)	−2.7%	−6.4%	−9.2%	−11.7%	−15.6%
137	Viet Nam	−0.5%	−1.1%	−1.8%	−3.6%	−5.7%
138	Yemen	−4.8%	−9.5%	−12.6%	−15.6%	−23.0%
139	Zambia	−2.8%	−7.1%	−10.4%	−14.0%	−21.5%
140	Zimbabwe	−3.6%	−8.0%	−11.0%	−14.7%	−23.5%

Table A3.33 Fishery (Fishery in billions of constant 2005 US$)

	Country/year	1990	1995	2000	2005	2010	2014
1	Afghanistan	–	–	–	–	–	–
2	Albania	0.3	0.2	0.2	0.1	0.1	0.1
3	Algeria	6.0	5.5	5.1	4.4	3.6	3.0
4	Argentina	40.7	34.0	25.5	20.9	15.1	11.4
5	Armenia	–	–	–	–	–	–
6	Australia	13.5	11.4	9.7	8.5	7.9	7.0
7	Austria	–	–	–	–	–	–
8	Bahrain	1.1	1.0	0.9	0.9	0.8	0.7
9	Bangladesh	14.4	13.6	12.6	11.6	10.8	10.1
10	Barbados	0.2	0.2	0.2	0.2	0.2	0.2
11	Belgium	0.7	0.8	0.9	1.0	1.0	1.1
12	Belize	0.3	0.3	0.3	0.3	0.3	0.3
13	Benin	1.5	1.2	1.0	0.8	0.7	0.7
14	Bolivia (Plurinational State of)	–	–	–	–	–	–
15	Botswana	–	–	–	–	–	–
16	Brazil	19.5	18.7	18.6	17.7	16.8	15.6
17	Bulgaria	0.2	0.2	0.2	0.2	0.2	0.2
18	Burundi	–	–	–	–	–	–
19	Cambodia	28.8	24.8	19.2	13.4	9.7	7.8
20	Cameroon	1.5	1.2	1.0	0.7	0.7	0.6
21	Canada	159.5	179.5	208.4	233.6	256.9	271.7
22	Central African Republic	–	–	–	–	–	–
23	Chile	34.0	28.4	24.1	21.1	17.3	17.0
24	China	249.3	223.2	175.1	145.3	127.5	114.5
25	Colombia	2.4	1.9	1.9	2.1	2.3	2.2
26	Congo	1.4	1.5	1.8	2.0	2.1	2.1
27	Costa Rica	2.3	2.1	1.9	1.7	1.7	1.5
28	Côte d'Ivoire	2.6	2.3	2.2	2.1	2.0	1.9
29	Croatia	1.3	1.1	1.1	1.2	1.1	1.1
30	Cuba	1.9	1.7	1.5	1.4	1.5	1.4
31	Cyprus	–	–	–	–	–	–
32	Czech Republic	–	–	–	–	–	–
33	Democratic Republic of the Congo	–	–	–	–	–	–
34	Denmark	24.9	21.3	18.4	16.6	17.7	16.0
35	Dominican Republic	1.6	1.4	1.4	1.3	1.3	1.3
36	Ecuador	4.9	4.4	3.9	3.9	4.1	3.6
37	Egypt	2.9	2.7	2.3	2.2	1.9	1.7
38	El Salvador	1.9	2.0	1.9	2.2	2.4	2.3
39	Estonia	0.7	0.7	0.6	0.6	0.6	0.6
40	Fiji	2.2	2.2	2.3	2.3	2.4	2.4
41	Finland	0.9	0.8	0.7	0.7	0.6	0.6
42	France	12.9	11.9	11.3	10.6	9.9	9.1
43	Gabon	2.3	2.2	1.9	1.7	1.8	1.5

	Country/year	1990	1995	2000	2005	2010	2014
44	Gambia	3.3	2.3	2.2	2.0	1.8	1.6
45	Germany	5.9	6.3	6.6	6.8	7.0	7.2
46	Ghana	8.3	7.7	6.6	5.7	4.6	4.0
47	Greece	8.0	7.0	6.1	5.7	5.3	4.8
48	Guatemala	1.2	1.1	0.9	0.8	0.8	0.7
49	Guyana	1.5	1.4	1.1	0.9	0.8	0.7
50	Haiti	0.8	0.8	0.7	0.7	0.6	0.5
51	Honduras	0.7	0.6	0.5	0.4	0.4	0.3
52	Hungary	–	–	–	–	–	–
53	Iceland	18.8	16.9	15.3	13.4	12.8	12.2
54	India	101.9	91.0	79.2	71.5	63.9	57.6
55	Indonesia	137.8	124.7	107.4	90.4	76.6	65.6
56	Iran (Islamic Republic of)	11.5	9.8	7.3	6.4	6.2	5.2
57	Iraq	0.2	0.3	0.2	0.1	0.1	0.1
58	Ireland	11.3	10.5	9.0	8.2	7.2	6.8
59	Israel	0.2	0.2	0.2	0.2	0.2	0.2
60	Italy	29.5	27.6	26.2	26.3	28.0	26.9
61	Jamaica	1.7	1.7	1.8	1.9	1.9	1.9
62	Japan	161.3	152.0	141.6	139.7	141.0	133.1
63	Jordan	0.0	0.0	0.0	0.0	0.0	0.0
64	Kazakhstan	–	–	–	–	–	–
65	Kenya	0.4	0.4	0.4	0.4	0.4	0.4
66	Kuwait	0.5	0.5	0.5	0.5	0.4	0.4
67	Kyrgyzstan	–	–	–	–	–	–
68	Lao People's Democratic Republic	–	–	–	–	–	–
69	Latvia	1.2	1.1	1.0	1.1	1.1	1.1
70	Lesotho	–	–	–	–	–	–
71	Liberia	1.3	1.1	1.0	1.0	0.9	0.8
72	Lithuania	0.4	0.3	0.3	0.3	0.2	0.2
73	Luxembourg	–	–	–	–	–	–
74	Malawi	–	–	–	–	–	–
75	Malaysia	72.3	65.6	58.1	50.6	47.0	42.8
76	Maldives	3.1	2.9	3.1	2.8	1.9	1.9
77	Mali	–	–	–	–	–	–
78	Malta	0.1	0.1	0.1	0.1	0.1	0.1
79	Mauritania	13.1	11.7	11.0	10.0	8.6	7.5
80	Mauritius	0.7	0.6	0.5	0.4	0.3	0.3
81	Mexico	50.9	46.5	43.1	42.0	41.3	38.4
82	Mongolia	–	–	–	–	–	–
83	Morocco	29.7	27.0	25.0	22.6	21.2	19.4
84	Mozambique	3.7	3.3	3.1	3.0	3.1	3.0
85	Myanmar	39.8	36.2	31.0	25.3	21.6	19.3
86	Namibia	16.4	20.0	23.7	27.2	31.6	31.1
87	Nepal	–	–	–	–	–	–

(*Continued*)

Table A3.33 (Continued)

Country/year	1990	1995	2000	2005	2010	2014
88 Netherlands	12.7	11.0	10.4	10.5	11.2	10.5
89 New Zealand	24.1	20.5	17.5	15.2	14.2	11.7
90 Nicaragua	1.3	1.3	1.1	1.0	1.0	0.9
91 Niger	–	–	–	–	–	–
92 Nigeria	9.1	8.1	7.0	5.6	4.4	3.6
93 Norway	36.2	35.5	32.4	31.8	32.7	31.4
94 Pakistan	18.7	16.4	14.4	12.3	10.9	9.8
95 Panama	2.7	2.7	2.5	2.0	1.9	1.8
96 Papua New Guinea	5.9	4.8	4.5	4.7	4.3	3.5
97 Paraguay	–	–	–	–	–	–
98 Peru	74.8	62.5	53.4	42.0	31.9	27.8
99 Philippines	23.7	22.3	20.3	18.1	15.6	13.8
100 Poland	2.3	2.3	1.7	1.5	1.3	1.2
101 Portugal	10.6	10.6	11.3	12.5	13.6	13.2
102 Qatar	0.3	0.3	0.3	0.3	0.2	0.2
103 Republic of Korea	64.6	58.5	55.0	52.0	49.0	46.2
104 Republic of Moldova	–	–	–	–	–	–
105 Romania	–	–	–	–	–	–
106 Russian Federation	113.4	101.8	89.5	87.8	87.6	75.2
107 Rwanda	–	–	–	–	–	–
108 Saudi Arabia	2.2	1.8	1.5	1.5	1.5	1.3
109 Senegal	20.0	18.3	17.1	16.4	17.0	16.6
110 Serbia	–	–	–	–	–	–
111 Sierra Leone	2.5	2.4	2.4	2.1	1.8	1.7
112 Singapore	0.2	0.2	0.2	0.2	0.2	0.2
113 Slovakia	–	–	–	–	–	–
114 Slovenia	0.0	0.0	0.0	0.0	0.0	0.0
115 South Africa	16.2	16.9	17.7	17.9	18.4	18.3
116 Spain	53.3	56.9	60.1	65.6	70.6	73.0
117 Sri Lanka	11.0	10.4	9.3	7.3	6.5	5.7
118 Sudan (former)	0.1	0.1	0.1	0.1	0.1	0.1
119 Swaziland	–	–	–	–	–	–
120 Sweden	4.4	4.1	3.5	3.4	3.5	3.3
121 Switzerland	–	–	–	–	–	–
122 Syrian Arab Republic	9.8	8.9	8.2	7.9	8.2	7.7
123 Tajikistan	–	–	–	–	–	–
124 Thailand	53.2	46.6	41.2	38.3	36.4	32.6
125 Togo	1.1	1.0	1.0	1.1	1.1	1.1
126 Trinidad and Tobago	0.8	0.7	0.8	0.8	0.8	0.8
127 Tunisia	2.3	2.0	1.8	1.6	1.4	1.3
128 Turkey	15.8	14.1	12.7	11.6	10.5	9.5
129 Uganda	–	–	–	–	–	–
130 Ukraine	1.8	1.8	1.8	1.8	1.7	1.6
131 United Arab Emirates	2.2	1.9	1.6	1.3	1.1	1.1
132 United Kingdom	49.9	44.2	37.6	34.0	31.9	28.9

Country/year	1990	1995	2000	2005	2010	2014
133 United Republic of Tanzania	2.5	2.3	2.1	1.9	1.8	1.6
134 United States of America	202.6	197.6	199.4	198.7	199.9	199.6
135 Uruguay	2.9	2.4	2.0	1.7	1.4	1.2
136 Venezuela (Bolivarian Republic of)	9.2	7.8	6.2	4.6	3.6	3.1
137 Viet Nam	78.5	73.8	64.7	55.4	48.2	42.5
138 Yemen	6.3	6.0	5.5	4.0	3.1	2.8
139 Zambia	–	–	–	–	–	–
140 Zimbabwe	–	–	–	–	–	–

Table A3.34 Fishery per capita (Fishery per capita in thousands of constant 2005 US$)

	Country/year	1990	1995	2000	2005	2010	2014
1	Afghanistan	–	–	–	–	–	–
2	Albania	0.1	0.1	0.1	0.0	0.0	0.0
3	Algeria	0.2	0.2	0.2	0.1	0.1	0.1
4	Argentina	1.2	1.0	0.7	0.5	0.4	0.3
5	Armenia	–	–	–	–	–	–
6	Australia	0.8	0.6	0.5	0.4	0.4	0.3
7	Austria	–	–	–	–	–	–
8	Bahrain	2.1	1.8	1.4	1.0	0.6	0.5
9	Bangladesh	0.1	0.1	0.1	0.1	0.1	0.1
10	Barbados	0.7	0.6	0.6	0.6	0.7	0.7
11	Belgium	0.1	0.1	0.1	0.1	0.1	0.1
12	Belize	1.5	1.3	1.1	1.0	0.9	0.7
13	Benin	0.3	0.2	0.1	0.1	0.1	0.1
14	Bolivia (Plurinational State of)	–	–	–	–	–	–
15	Botswana	–	–	–	–	–	–
16	Brazil	0.1	0.1	0.1	0.1	0.1	0.1
17	Bulgaria	0.0	0.0	0.0	0.0	0.0	0.0
18	Burundi	–	–	–	–	–	–
19	Cambodia	3.2	2.3	1.6	1.0	0.7	0.5
20	Cameroon	0.1	0.1	0.1	0.0	0.0	0.0
21	Canada	5.7	6.1	6.8	7.2	7.6	7.6
22	Central African Republic	–	–	–	–	–	–
23	Chile	2.6	2.0	1.6	1.3	1.0	1.0
24	China	0.2	0.2	0.1	0.1	0.1	0.1
25	Colombia	0.1	0.0	0.0	0.0	0.1	0.0
26	Congo	0.6	0.6	0.6	0.6	0.5	0.5
27	Costa Rica	0.7	0.6	0.5	0.4	0.4	0.3
28	Côte d'Ivoire	0.2	0.2	0.1	0.1	0.1	0.1
29	Croatia	0.3	0.2	0.3	0.3	0.3	0.2
30	Cuba	0.2	0.2	0.1	0.1	0.1	0.1
31	Cyprus	–	–	–	–	–	–

(*Continued*)

Table A3.34 (Continued)

	Country/year	1990	1995	2000	2005	2010	2014
32	Czech Republic	–	–	–	–	–	–
33	Democratic Republic of the Congo	–	–	–	–	–	–
34	Denmark	4.8	4.1	3.4	3.1	3.2	2.8
35	Dominican Republic	0.2	0.2	0.2	0.1	0.1	0.1
36	Ecuador	0.5	0.4	0.3	0.3	0.3	0.2
37	Egypt	0.1	0.0	0.0	0.0	0.0	0.0
38	El Salvador	0.4	0.3	0.3	0.4	0.4	0.4
39	Estonia	0.5	0.5	0.5	0.5	0.5	0.5
40	Fiji	3.0	2.9	2.9	2.9	2.8	2.7
41	Finland	0.2	0.2	0.1	0.1	0.1	0.1
42	France	0.2	0.2	0.2	0.2	0.2	0.1
43	Gabon	2.4	2.0	1.6	1.2	1.1	0.9
44	Gambia	3.5	2.2	1.8	1.4	1.1	0.8
45	Germany	0.1	0.1	0.1	0.1	0.1	0.1
46	Ghana	0.6	0.5	0.4	0.3	0.2	0.1
47	Greece	0.8	0.7	0.6	0.5	0.5	0.4
48	Guatemala	0.1	0.1	0.1	0.1	0.1	0.0
49	Guyana	2.0	1.9	1.5	1.2	1.0	0.9
50	Haiti	0.1	0.1	0.1	0.1	0.1	0.0
51	Honduras	0.1	0.1	0.1	0.1	0.0	0.0
52	Hungary	–	–	–	–	–	–
53	Iceland	73.9	63.3	54.4	45.1	40.2	37.1
54	India	0.1	0.1	0.1	0.1	0.1	0.0
55	Indonesia	0.8	0.6	0.5	0.4	0.3	0.3
56	Iran (Islamic Republic of)	0.2	0.2	0.1	0.1	0.1	0.1
57	Iraq	0.0	0.0	0.0	0.0	0.0	0.0
58	Ireland	3.2	2.9	2.4	2.0	1.6	1.5
59	Israel	0.0	0.0	0.0	0.0	0.0	0.0
60	Italy	0.5	0.5	0.5	0.5	0.5	0.4
61	Jamaica	0.7	0.7	0.7	0.7	0.7	0.7
62	Japan	1.3	1.2	1.1	1.1	1.1	1.0
63	Jordan	0.0	0.0	0.0	0.0	0.0	0.0
64	Kazakhstan	–	–	–	–	–	–
65	Kenya	0.0	0.0	0.0	0.0	0.0	0.0
66	Kuwait	0.3	0.3	0.2	0.2	0.1	0.1
67	Kyrgyzstan	–	–	–	–	–	–
68	Lao People's Democratic Republic	–	–	–	–	–	–
69	Latvia	0.4	0.5	0.4	0.5	0.5	0.5
70	Lesotho	–	–	–	–	–	–
71	Liberia	0.6	0.5	0.4	0.3	0.2	0.2
72	Lithuania	0.1	0.1	0.1	0.1	0.1	0.1
73	Luxembourg	–	–	–	–	–	–
74	Malawi	–	–	–	–	–	–
75	Malaysia	4.0	3.2	2.5	2.0	1.7	1.4

	Country/year	1990	1995	2000	2005	2010	2014
76	Maldives	14.1	11.5	10.9	8.8	5.2	4.8
77	Mali	–	–	–	–	–	–
78	Malta	0.2	0.2	0.2	0.2	0.2	0.2
79	Mauritania	6.5	5.0	4.1	3.2	2.4	1.9
80	Mauritius	0.7	0.6	0.4	0.3	0.3	0.2
81	Mexico	0.6	0.5	0.4	0.4	0.3	0.3
82	Mongolia	–	–	–	–	–	–
83	Morocco	1.2	1.0	0.9	0.7	0.7	0.6
84	Mozambique	0.3	0.2	0.2	0.1	0.1	0.1
85	Myanmar	0.9	0.8	0.7	0.5	0.4	0.4
86	Namibia	11.6	12.1	12.5	13.4	14.4	13.0
87	Nepal	–	–	–	–	–	–
88	Netherlands	0.8	0.7	0.7	0.6	0.7	0.6
89	New Zealand	7.2	5.6	4.5	3.7	3.3	2.6
90	Nicaragua	0.3	0.3	0.2	0.2	0.2	0.2
91	Niger	–	–	–	–	–	–
92	Nigeria	0.1	0.1	0.1	0.0	0.0	0.0
93	Norway	8.5	8.1	7.2	6.9	6.7	6.1
94	Pakistan	0.2	0.1	0.1	0.1	0.1	0.1
95	Panama	1.1	1.0	0.8	0.6	0.5	0.5
96	Papua New Guinea	1.4	1.0	0.8	0.8	0.6	0.5
97	Paraguay	–	–	–	–	–	–
98	Peru	3.4	2.6	2.1	1.5	1.1	0.9
99	Philippines	0.4	0.3	0.3	0.2	0.2	0.1
100	Poland	0.1	0.1	0.0	0.0	0.0	0.0
101	Portugal	1.1	1.1	1.1	1.2	1.3	1.3
102	Qatar	0.7	0.6	0.5	0.3	0.1	0.1
103	Republic of Korea	1.5	1.3	1.2	1.1	1.0	0.9
104	Republic of Moldova	–	–	–	–	–	–
105	Romania	–	–	–	–	–	–
106	Russian Federation	0.8	0.7	0.6	0.6	0.6	0.5
107	Rwanda	–	–	–	–	–	–
108	Saudi Arabia	0.1	0.1	0.1	0.1	0.1	0.0
109	Senegal	2.7	2.1	1.7	1.5	1.3	1.1
110	Serbia	–	–	–	–	–	–
111	Sierra Leone	0.6	0.6	0.6	0.4	0.3	0.3
112	Singapore	0.1	0.1	0.0	0.0	0.0	0.0
113	Slovakia	–	–	–	–	–	–
114	Slovenia	0.0	0.0	0.0	0.0	0.0	0.0
115	South Africa	0.5	0.4	0.4	0.4	0.4	0.3
116	Spain	1.4	1.4	1.5	1.5	1.5	1.6
117	Sri Lanka	0.6	0.6	0.5	0.4	0.3	0.3
118	Sudan (former)	0.0	0.0	0.0	0.0	0.0	0.0
119	Swaziland	–	–	–	–	–	–

(*Continued*)

Table A3.34 (Continued)

	Country/year	1990	1995	2000	2005	2010	2014
120	Sweden	0.5	0.5	0.4	0.4	0.4	0.3
121	Switzerland	–	–	–	–	–	–
122	Syrian Arab Republic	0.8	0.6	0.5	0.4	0.4	0.4
123	Tajikistan	–	–	–	–	–	–
124	Thailand	0.9	0.8	0.7	0.6	0.5	0.5
125	Togo	0.3	0.2	0.2	0.2	0.2	0.2
126	Trinidad and Tobago	0.7	0.6	0.6	0.6	0.6	0.6
127	Tunisia	0.3	0.2	0.2	0.2	0.1	0.1
128	Turkey	0.3	0.2	0.2	0.2	0.1	0.1
129	Uganda	–	–	–	–	–	–
130	Ukraine	0.0	0.0	0.0	0.0	0.0	0.0
131	United Arab Emirates	1.2	0.8	0.5	0.3	0.1	0.1
132	United Kingdom	0.9	0.8	0.6	0.6	0.5	0.4
133	United Republic of Tanzania	0.1	0.1	0.1	0.0	0.0	0.0
134	United States of America	0.8	0.7	0.7	0.7	0.6	0.6
135	Uruguay	0.9	0.8	0.6	0.5	0.4	0.3
136	Venezuela (Bolivarian Republic of)	0.5	0.3	0.3	0.2	0.1	0.1
137	Viet Nam	1.2	1.0	0.8	0.7	0.6	0.5
138	Yemen	0.5	0.4	0.3	0.2	0.1	0.1
139	Zambia	–	–	–	–	–	–
140	Zimbabwe	–	–	–	–	–	–

Table A3.35 Fishery growth (Fishery change (%) with respect to base year 1990)

	Country/year	1995	2000	2005	2010	2014
1	Afghanistan	–	–	–	–	–
2	Albania	-2.7%	-10.4%	-14.9%	-15.4%	-24.4%
3	Algeria	-1.7%	-3.8%	-7.1%	-12.1%	-20.3%
4	Argentina	-3.5%	-11.0%	-15.3%	-21.9%	-34.6%
5	Armenia	–	–	–	–	–
6	Australia	-3.5%	-7.9%	-11.0%	-12.5%	-19.7%
7	Austria	–	–	–	–	–
8	Bahrain	-1.0%	-3.6%	-5.2%	-7.4%	-12.3%
9	Bangladesh	-1.1%	-3.1%	-5.1%	-6.9%	-11.1%
10	Barbados	-1.0%	-0.4%	-0.6%	1.0%	1.9%
11	Belgium	1.7%	4.8%	7.3%	9.5%	13.6%
12	Belize	-1.0%	-1.8%	-1.6%	-1.3%	-3.5%
13	Benin	-4.3%	-9.2%	-15.2%	-18.8%	-23.6%
14	Bolivia (Plurinational State of)	–	–	–	–	–
15	Botswana	–	–	–	–	–
16	Brazil	-0.8%	-1.2%	-2.3%	-3.6%	-7.1%
17	Bulgaria	3.0%	3.8%	4.1%	4.3%	5.2%
18	Burundi	–	–	–	–	–
19	Cambodia	-3.0%	-9.6%	-17.4%	-23.8%	-35.2%

	Country/year	1995	2000	2005	2010	2014
20	Cameroon	−4.0%	−9.8%	−17.5%	−18.2%	−26.9%
21	Canada	2.4%	6.9%	10.0%	12.7%	19.4%
22	Central African Republic	−	−	−	−	−
23	Chile	−3.5%	−8.2%	−11.2%	−15.5%	−20.6%
24	China	−2.2%	−8.4%	−12.6%	−15.4%	−22.8%
25	Colombia	−4.8%	−5.7%	−3.6%	−0.7%	−2.2%
26	Congo	2.3%	6.6%	9.5%	11.5%	14.8%
27	Costa Rica	−1.9%	−4.7%	−7.0%	−6.9%	−12.9%
28	Côte d'Ivoire	−1.8%	−4.2%	−5.3%	−5.6%	−10.0%
29	Croatia	−2.4%	−2.9%	−1.6%	−2.5%	−5.7%
30	Cuba	−1.9%	−5.8%	−6.8%	−5.2%	−8.9%
31	Cyprus	−	−	−	−	−
32	Czech Republic	−	−	−	−	−
33	Democratic Republic of the Congo	−	−	−	−	−
34	Denmark	−3.1%	−7.2%	−9.5%	−8.2%	−13.7%
35	Dominican Republic	−2.2%	−3.4%	−4.4%	−4.6%	−7.1%
36	Ecuador	−2.3%	−6.0%	−5.8%	−4.4%	−10.1%
37	Egypt	−1.9%	−5.7%	−6.8%	−10.5%	−17.0%
38	El Salvador	1.0%	1.2%	3.9%	6.3%	7.9%
39	Estonia	−0.7%	−3.2%	−3.2%	−3.1%	−5.5%
40	Fiji	0.3%	1.2%	1.4%	2.0%	2.9%
41	Finland	−1.8%	−6.3%	−6.9%	−8.1%	−12.7%
42	France	−1.7%	−3.3%	−4.9%	−6.5%	−10.9%
43	Gabon	−0.9%	−3.7%	−6.7%	−6.2%	−12.2%
44	Gambia	−6.5%	−9.2%	−11.6%	−13.2%	−21.3%
45	Germany	1.3%	2.7%	3.6%	4.5%	6.8%
46	Ghana	−1.5%	−5.6%	−8.9%	−13.5%	−21.8%
47	Greece	−2.7%	−6.5%	−8.1%	−10.0%	−15.5%
48	Guatemala	−1.9%	−7.0%	−10.0%	−10.7%	−17.8%
49	Guyana	−1.1%	−7.1%	−11.6%	−14.5%	−22.1%
50	Haiti	−0.8%	−2.2%	−4.8%	−8.6%	−13.1%
51	Honduras	−3.1%	−9.4%	−13.6%	−15.5%	−23.9%
52	Hungary	−	−	−	−	−
53	Iceland	−2.1%	−5.1%	−8.2%	−9.2%	−13.6%
54	India	−2.2%	−6.1%	−8.5%	−11.0%	−17.3%
55	Indonesia	−2.0%	−6.1%	−10.0%	−13.7%	−21.9%
56	Iran (Islamic Republic of)	−3.2%	−10.7%	−13.7%	−14.3%	−23.1%
57	Iraq	2.2%	−4.4%	−11.2%	−17.0%	−24.2%
58	Ireland	−1.3%	−5.3%	−7.7%	−10.6%	−15.6%
59	Israel	−1.1%	−3.8%	−6.3%	−6.2%	−8.7%
60	Italy	−1.4%	−3.0%	−2.9%	−1.3%	−3.0%
61	Jamaica	0.1%	0.7%	1.8%	2.8%	4.0%
62	Japan	−1.2%	−3.2%	−3.5%	−3.3%	−6.2%
63	Jordan	0.1%	−0.1%	−0.4%	−1.1%	−2.0%
64	Kazakhstan	−	−	−	−	−

(*Continued*)

	Country/year	1995	2000	2005	2010	2014
65	Kenya	-0.6%	0.2%	1.4%	1.6%	-0.2%
66	Kuwait	-1.9%	-3.6%	-3.6%	-4.7%	-8.7%
67	Kyrgyzstan	–	–	–	–	–
68	Lao People's Democratic Republic	–	–	–	–	–
69	Latvia	-0.3%	-2.5%	-2.1%	-1.0%	-3.2%
70	Lesotho	–	–	–	–	–
71	Liberia	-2.6%	-5.8%	-7.3%	-9.8%	-16.2%
72	Lithuania	-0.6%	-5.6%	-7.8%	-9.5%	-17.0%
73	Luxembourg	–	–	–	–	–
74	Malawi	–	–	–	–	–
75	Malaysia	-1.9%	-5.3%	-8.5%	-10.2%	-16.1%
76	Maldives	-0.8%	0.3%	-2.1%	-11.2%	-14.6%
77	Mali	–	–	–	–	–
78	Malta	2.0%	4.1%	5.7%	6.2%	8.3%
79	Mauritania	-2.3%	-4.4%	-6.7%	-10.0%	-17.1%
80	Mauritius	-2.1%	-7.2%	-14.3%	-16.8%	-24.4%
81	Mexico	-1.8%	-4.1%	-4.7%	-5.1%	-8.9%
82	Mongolia	–	–	–	–	–
83	Morocco	-1.8%	-4.1%	-6.6%	-8.1%	-13.2%
84	Mozambique	-2.1%	-4.4%	-5.1%	-3.9%	-6.5%
85	Myanmar	-1.9%	-6.1%	-10.7%	-14.2%	-21.5%
86	Namibia	4.0%	9.5%	13.4%	17.7%	23.7%
87	Nepal	–	–	–	–	–
88	Netherlands	-2.8%	-4.7%	-4.7%	-3.1%	-6.2%
89	New Zealand	-3.2%	-7.7%	-10.9%	-12.4%	-21.5%
90	Nicaragua	0.0%	-3.7%	-6.6%	-7.0%	-11.0%
91	Niger	–	–	–	–	–
92	Nigeria	-2.2%	-6.4%	-11.4%	-16.8%	-26.8%
93	Norway	-0.4%	-2.8%	-3.2%	-2.5%	-4.7%
94	Pakistan	-2.5%	-6.2%	-9.8%	-12.6%	-19.4%
95	Panama	-0.5%	-2.0%	-7.4%	-8.6%	-12.5%
96	Papua New Guinea	-4.0%	-6.8%	-5.7%	-7.8%	-16.1%
97	Paraguay	–	–	–	–	–
98	Peru	-3.5%	-8.1%	-13.5%	-19.2%	-28.1%
99	Philippines	-1.3%	-3.8%	-6.5%	-9.9%	-16.4%
100	Poland	-0.6%	-7.0%	-10.7%	-13.1%	-20.3%
101	Portugal	0.0%	1.7%	4.3%	6.5%	7.7%
102	Qatar	-2.2%	-2.3%	-4.9%	-11.9%	-13.3%
103	Republic of Korea	-2.0%	-3.9%	-5.3%	-6.7%	-10.6%
104	Republic of Moldova	–	–	–	–	–
105	Romania	–	–	–	–	–
106	Russian Federation	-2.1%	-5.7%	-6.2%	-6.2%	-12.8%
107	Rwanda	–	–	–	–	–
108	Saudi Arabia	-3.3%	-8.4%	-8.4%	-9.2%	-16.2%
109	Senegal	-1.8%	-3.9%	-4.8%	-4.0%	-6.0%

	Country/year	1995	2000	2005	2010	2014
110	Serbia	–	–	–	–	–
111	Sierra Leone	–0.6%	–0.6%	–3.4%	–7.3%	–10.9%
112	Singapore	–3.8%	–6.7%	–6.6%	–9.4%	–11.2%
113	Slovakia	–	–	–	–	–
114	Slovenia	–3.4%	–9.1%	–14.1%	–17.3%	–24.9%
115	South Africa	0.9%	2.3%	2.5%	3.3%	4.2%
116	Spain	1.3%	3.0%	5.3%	7.3%	11.0%
117	Sri Lanka	–1.1%	–4.1%	–9.8%	–12.5%	–19.8%
118	Sudan (former)	–0.3%	–1.5%	–3.8%	–6.2%	–6.5%
119	Swaziland	–	–	–	–	–
120	Sweden	–1.4%	–5.6%	–6.3%	–5.5%	–9.4%
121	Switzerland	–	–	–	–	–
122	Syrian Arab Republic	–2.0%	–4.5%	–5.3%	–4.3%	–7.8%
123	Tajikistan	–	–	–	–	–
124	Thailand	–2.6%	–6.2%	–7.9%	–9.1%	–15.1%
125	Togo	–0.9%	–1.1%	–0.5%	0.7%	0.6%
126	Trinidad and Tobago	–2.3%	–1.7%	–1.3%	–0.5%	–2.3%
127	Tunisia	–2.7%	–6.0%	–9.0%	–10.8%	–16.7%
128	Turkey	–2.3%	–5.3%	–7.4%	–9.7%	–15.7%
129	Uganda	–	–	–	–	–
130	Ukraine	0.0%	0.3%	–0.7%	–1.3%	–3.8%
131	United Arab Emirates	–2.6%	–7.1%	–12.3%	–15.0%	–20.6%
132	United Kingdom	–2.4%	–6.8%	–9.2%	–10.6%	–16.7%
133	United Republic of Tanzania	–1.5%	–3.8%	–6.0%	–8.2%	–13.5%
134	United States of America	–0.5%	–0.4%	–0.5%	–0.3%	–0.5%
135	Uruguay	–3.5%	–9.4%	–12.0%	–17.0%	–25.6%
136	Venezuela (Bolivarian Republic of)	–3.4%	–9.4%	–16.0%	–20.8%	–30.7%
137	Viet Nam	–1.2%	–4.7%	–8.3%	–11.5%	–18.5%
138	Yemen	–0.7%	–3.4%	–10.8%	–15.8%	–23.7%
139	Zambia	–	–	–	–	–
140	Zimbabwe	–	–	–	–	–

Table A3.36 Fishery per capita growth (Fishery per capita change (%) with respect to base year 1990)

	Country/year	1995	2000	2005	2010	2014
1	Afghanistan	–	–	–	–	–
2	Albania	–2.1%	–9.0%	–13.0%	–12.8%	–21.2%
3	Algeria	–3.8%	–8.2%	–12.7%	–19.0%	–30.4%
4	Argentina	–4.8%	–13.7%	–19.0%	–26.3%	–40.3%
5	Armenia	–	–	–	–	–
6	Australia	–4.6%	–10.5%	–14.8%	–17.9%	–27.8%
7	Austria	–	–	–	–	–
8	Bahrain	–3.5%	–10.5%	–17.6%	–26.7%	–37.3%

(*Continued*)

Table A3.36 (Continued)

	Country/year	1995	2000	2005	2010	2014
9	Bangladesh	-3.3%	-8.2%	-11.9%	-14.9%	-22.4%
10	Barbados	-1.4%	-1.3%	-1.9%	-0.8%	-0.9%
11	Belgium	1.4%	4.1%	6.0%	7.0%	9.2%
12	Belize	-2.9%	-8.3%	-11.3%	-13.8%	-21.8%
13	Benin	-7.6%	-16.3%	-25.0%	-30.9%	-40.5%
14	Bolivia (Plurinational State of)	-	-	-	-	-
15	Botswana	-	-	-	-	-
16	Brazil	-2.4%	-5.0%	-7.7%	-10.1%	-16.4%
17	Bulgaria	3.7%	5.5%	7.3%	8.7%	12.0%
18	Burundi	-	-	-	-	-
19	Cambodia	-6.2%	-16.2%	-25.1%	-32.2%	-45.7%
20	Cameroon	-6.7%	-15.9%	-25.5%	-28.5%	-40.8%
21	Canada	1.3%	4.2%	5.9%	7.1%	10.0%
22	Central African Republic	-	-	-	-	-
23	Chile	-5.0%	-11.5%	-15.6%	-20.8%	-28.2%
24	China	-3.3%	-10.9%	-15.6%	-18.8%	-27.4%
25	Colombia	-6.4%	-9.5%	-9.1%	-7.7%	-12.4%
26	Congo	-0.3%	-0.2%	-0.5%	-2.4%	-7.1%
27	Costa Rica	-4.3%	-10.2%	-14.1%	-15.4%	-24.5%
28	Côte d'Ivoire	-5.1%	-11.2%	-14.3%	-16.8%	-26.3%
29	Croatia	-1.9%	-1.0%	0.2%	-0.5%	-1.9%
30	Cuba	-2.5%	-6.9%	-8.2%	-6.8%	-11.1%
31	Cyprus	-	-	-	-	-
32	Czech Republic	-	-	-	-	-
33	Democratic Republic of the Congo	-	-	-	-	-
34	Denmark	-3.4%	-8.1%	-10.7%	-9.9%	-16.3%
35	Dominican Republic	-4.0%	-7.6%	-10.2%	-11.9%	-17.9%
36	Ecuador	-4.5%	-10.9%	-12.5%	-13.1%	-22.4%
37	Egypt	-3.8%	-10.1%	-13.2%	-18.5%	-28.9%
38	El Salvador	-0.3%	-1.4%	0.7%	2.6%	2.6%
39	Estonia	1.1%	-0.4%	0.4%	0.9%	0.2%
40	Fiji	-1.0%	-1.5%	-1.6%	-2.1%	-3.6%
41	Finland	-2.3%	-7.2%	-8.1%	-9.7%	-15.3%
42	France	-2.1%	-4.2%	-6.7%	-9.0%	-14.6%
43	Gabon	-3.5%	-9.7%	-15.0%	-16.8%	-27.5%
44	Gambia	-9.3%	-15.6%	-21.1%	-25.5%	-38.5%
45	Germany	0.7%	1.8%	2.7%	3.7%	6.1%
46	Ghana	-4.1%	-11.3%	-17.1%	-23.8%	-36.1%
47	Greece	-3.4%	-7.9%	-9.8%	-11.9%	-17.3%
48	Guatemala	-4.3%	-12.5%	-17.9%	-20.7%	-31.8%
49	Guyana	-1.3%	-7.8%	-12.3%	-15.5%	-23.6%
50	Haiti	-2.7%	-6.6%	-11.0%	-16.1%	-23.9%
51	Honduras	-5.6%	-14.7%	-20.6%	-24.0%	-35.2%
52	Hungary	-	-	-	-	-
53	Iceland	-3.1%	-7.4%	-11.6%	-14.1%	-20.5%

	Country/year	1995	2000	2005	2010	2014
54	India	−4.1%	−10.5%	−14.5%	−18.4%	−27.6%
55	Indonesia	−3.6%	−9.6%	−14.9%	−19.6%	−30.2%
56	Iran (Islamic Republic of)	−4.6%	−14.1%	−18.4%	−20.1%	−31.1%
57	Iraq	−0.7%	−11.3%	−20.4%	−28.0%	−40.0%
58	Ireland	−1.8%	−7.2%	−11.5%	−16.3%	−23.0%
59	Israel	−4.5%	−10.8%	−15.1%	−17.0%	−24.4%
60	Italy	−1.4%	−3.1%	−3.4%	−2.4%	−5.2%
61	Jamaica	−0.6%	−1.3%	−0.7%	−0.2%	−0.4%
62	Japan	−1.5%	−3.8%	−4.4%	−4.2%	−7.1%
63	Jordan	−4.8%	−8.5%	−11.3%	−16.2%	−24.7%
64	Kazakhstan	−	−	−	−	−
65	Kenya	−3.7%	−6.6%	−8.5%	−11.3%	−19.6%
66	Kuwait	2.7%	−2.0%	−5.9%	−13.7%	−25.3%
67	Kyrgyzstan	−	−	−	−	−
68	Lao People's Democratic Republic	−	−	−	−	−
69	Latvia	1.1%	0.4%	2.2%	5.1%	6.7%
70	Lesotho	−	−	−	−	−
71	Liberia	−2.4%	−13.0%	−17.0%	−23.0%	−34.4%
72	Lithuania	−0.2%	−4.3%	−5.3%	−5.4%	−10.3%
73	Luxembourg	−	−	−	−	−
74	Malawi	−	−	−	−	−
75	Malaysia	−4.4%	−11.1%	−16.2%	−19.4%	−28.9%
76	Maldives	−3.9%	−6.3%	−11.1%	−22.0%	−30.3%
77	Mali	−	−	−	−	−
78	Malta	1.1%	2.2%	2.3%	2.1%	1.7%
79	Mauritania	−5.1%	−11.1%	−16.5%	−22.0%	−33.8%
80	Mauritius	−3.2%	−9.8%	−17.4%	−20.2%	−28.6%
81	Mexico	−3.7%	−8.4%	−10.4%	−12.5%	−19.8%
82	Mongolia	−	−	−	−	−
83	Morocco	−3.5%	−7.6%	−11.1%	−13.7%	−21.6%
84	Mozambique	−5.4%	−11.5%	−15.4%	−17.3%	−26.2%
85	Myanmar	−3.1%	−9.0%	−14.5%	−18.5%	−27.5%
86	Namibia	0.8%	1.8%	3.6%	5.5%	3.7%
87	Nepal	−	−	−	−	−
88	Netherlands	−3.4%	−6.2%	−6.8%	−5.6%	−9.9%
89	New Zealand	−5.1%	−11.1%	−15.6%	−18.0%	−29.1%
90	Nicaragua	−2.1%	−8.2%	−12.5%	−14.3%	−21.4%
91	Niger	−	−	−	−	−
92	Nigeria	−4.7%	−12.1%	−19.4%	−26.8%	−40.4%
93	Norway	−0.9%	−4.1%	−5.3%	−5.9%	−10.6%
94	Pakistan	−5.0%	−11.9%	−17.5%	−22.0%	−32.7%
95	Panama	−2.5%	−6.9%	−13.9%	−16.9%	−24.6%
96	Papua New Guinea	−6.4%	−12.6%	−14.2%	−18.6%	−31.0%

(*Continued*)

Table A3.36 (Continued)

Country/year	1995	2000	2005	2010	2014
97 Paraguay	–	–	–	–	–
98 Peru	–5.4%	–12.0%	–18.4%	–25.0%	–36.0%
99 Philippines	–3.6%	–9.2%	–13.9%	–18.6%	–28.5%
100 Poland	–0.9%	–7.1%	–10.7%	–13.1%	–20.2%
101 Portugal	–0.1%	0.9%	3.0%	4.9%	6.2%
102 Qatar	–3.2%	–7.5%	–17.4%	–36.5%	–47.7%
103 Republic of Korea	–3.0%	–6.1%	–8.0%	–10.0%	–15.3%
104 Republic of Moldova	–	–	–	–	–
105 Romania	–	–	–	–	–
106 Russian Federation	–2.1%	–5.5%	–5.4%	–5.4%	–11.9%
107 Rwanda	–	–	–	–	–
108 Saudi Arabia	–6.0%	–14.3%	–17.4%	–20.7%	–32.2%
109 Senegal	–4.7%	–10.2%	–14.0%	–16.2%	–24.8%
110 Serbia	–	–	–	–	–
111 Sierra Leone	–0.1%	–1.4%	–9.4%	–15.8%	–23.9%
112 Singapore	–6.6%	–13.0%	–14.1%	–20.3%	–26.9%
113 Slovakia	–	–	–	–	–
114 Slovenia	–3.4%	–9.0%	–14.1%	–17.8%	–25.7%
115 South Africa	–1.2%	–3.2%	–4.8%	–5.7%	–9.7%
116 Spain	1.0%	2.1%	2.3%	2.5%	4.6%
117 Sri Lanka	–2.3%	–6.2%	–12.6%	–16.0%	–24.9%
118 Sudan (former)	–4.4%	–9.5%	–14.5%	–19.1%	–25.4%
119 Swaziland	–	–	–	–	–
120 Sweden	–2.0%	–6.5%	–7.6%	–7.6%	–13.1%
121 Switzerland	–	–	–	–	–
122 Syrian Arab Republic	–4.7%	–10.8%	–13.8%	–15.7%	–19.6%
123 Tajikistan	–	–	–	–	–
124 Thailand	–3.5%	–8.6%	–11.4%	–12.8%	–20.0%
125 Togo	–3.4%	–7.2%	–9.7%	–11.7%	–18.5%
126 Trinidad and Tobago	–2.8%	–2.6%	–2.8%	–2.5%	–5.6%
127 Tunisia	–4.5%	–9.6%	–13.6%	–16.4%	–24.6%
128 Turkey	–3.8%	–8.9%	–12.6%	–16.1%	–25.3%
129 Uganda	–	–	–	–	–
130 Ukraine	0.2%	1.6%	1.7%	1.8%	0.6%
131 United Arab Emirates	–7.5%	–18.4%	–30.0%	–41.9%	–53.6%
132 United Kingdom	–2.7%	–7.5%	–10.4%	–12.6%	–20.0%
133 United Republic of Tanzania	–4.6%	–10.5%	–15.5%	–20.7%	–31.8%
134 United States of America	–1.8%	–3.4%	–4.6%	–5.5%	–8.3%
135 Uruguay	–4.2%	–10.9%	–13.5%	–18.7%	–27.9%
136 Venezuela (Bolivarian Republic of)	–5.5%	–14.0%	–22.1%	–28.0%	–40.1%
137 Viet Nam	–2.9%	–8.5%	–13.3%	–17.4%	–26.7%
138 Yemen	–5.4%	–12.5%	–22.0%	–28.9%	–41.2%
139 Zambia	–	–	–	–	–
140 Zimbabwe	–	–	–	–	–

Table A3.37 Fossil fuels (Fossil fuels in billions of constant 2005 US$)

	Country/year	1990	1995	2000	2005	2010	2014
1	Afghanistan	3.6	3.5	3.5	3.5	3.4	3.3
2	Albania	13.2	12.8	12.7	12.5	12.4	12.1
3	Algeria	594.3	553.3	506.6	452.5	391.8	344.8
4	Argentina	60.2	55.5	48.8	40.0	30.7	24.3
5	Armenia	–	–	–	–	2.6	2.6
6	Australia	1,780.8	1,749.7	1,713.3	1,670.6	1,625.0	1,583.7
7	Austria	4.3	3.6	2.8	2.0	1.2	0.5
8	Bahrain	6.6	5.5	4.3	3.2	2.2	1.3
9	Bangladesh	4.2	4.0	3.7	3.2	3.4	2.7
10	Barbados	0.1	0.1	0.1	0.0	0.0	–
11	Belgium	–	–	–	–	0.1	–
12	Belize	–	–	–	–	0.1	–
13	Benin	–	–	–	–	–	–
14	Bolivia (Plurinational State of)	9.6	9.3	9.0	8.2	6.9	5.4
15	Botswana	1.2	1.1	1.1	1.0	0.9	0.8
16	Brazil	426.7	410.2	387.2	354.8	311.6	270.1
17	Bulgaria	59.2	56.3	53.4	50.8	48.4	45.8
18	Burundi	–	–	–	–	–	–
19	Cambodia	–	–	–	–	–	–
20	Cameroon	12.2	9.2	6.8	5.2	6.2	5.1
21	Canada	2,587.9	2,509.8	2,415.9	2,312.3	2,204.9	2,115.9
22	Central African Republic	–	–	–	–	–	–
23	Chile	20.6	20.0	19.6	19.3	18.9	18.6
24	China	3,988.3	3,821.9	3,632.2	3,385.5	3,019.4	2,644.2
25	Colombia	224.1	211.6	192.8	174.2	153.2	129.0
26	Congo	41.6	38.1	33.1	27.7	25.1	20.2
27	Costa Rica						
28	Côte d'Ivoire	3.2	3.2	2.9	2.6	3.0	2.2
29	Croatia	2.7	3.6	2.9	2.3	1.8	1.4
30	Cuba	9.0	8.6	7.8	6.6	5.4	4.3
31	Cyprus	–	–	–	–	–	–
32	Czech Republic	80.6	76.9	71.2	65.8	60.8	57.3
33	Democratic Republic of the Congo	–	–	–	–	–	–
34	Denmark	45.5	41.2	34.6	24.7	16.0	11.4
35	Dominican Republic	–	–	–	–	–	–
36	Ecuador	151.5	143.9	135.0	125.0	113.6	104.2
37	Egypt	202.7	180.5	158.1	137.6	116.2	98.3
38	El Salvador	–	–	–	–	–	–
39	Estonia	–	–	–	–	0.1	–
40	Fiji	–	–	–	–	–	–
41	Finland	0.3	0.2	0.2	0.1	0.1	–
42	France	3.5	2.6	1.9	1.4	1.1	0.7
43	Gabon	51.1	44.9	37.6	32.2	27.1	23.1

(*Continued*)

Table A3.37 (Continued)

Country/year	1990	1995	2000	2005	2010	2014
44 Gambia	–	–	–	–	–	–
45 Germany	1,485.4	1,424.0	1,374.6	1,327.8	1,285.4	1,253.1
46 Ghana	–	–	–	–	–	0.1
47 Greece	79.2	73.9	68.2	61.9	56.1	52.0
48 Guatemala	2.3	2.2	1.9	1.5	1.2	1.0
49 Guyana	–	–	–	–	–	–
50 Haiti	–	–	–	–	–	–
51 Honduras	–	–	–	–	–	–
52 Hungary	43.0	40.6	38.4	36.6	35.2	34.2
53 Iceland	–	–	–	–	–	–
54 India	2,197.5	2,154.0	2,100.5	2,038.2	1,960.1	1,887.8
55 Indonesia	1,043.6	989.1	928.5	869.9	799.3	728.9
56 Iran (Islamic Republic of)	4,190.3	4,101.4	4,001.1	3,891.1	3,762.7	3,660.5
57 Iraq	1,532.8	1,519.5	1,495.8	1,461.5	1,426.0	1,389.6
58 Ireland	1.1	0.8	0.5	0.4	0.4	0.3
59 Israel	9.0	9.0	9.0	8.9	8.7	7.9
60 Italy	26.1	22.1	17.9	14.3	10.7	8.1
61 Jamaica	–	–	–	–	0.0	–
62 Japan	36.3	29.4	23.2	17.5	11.9	7.7
63 Jordan	0.5	0.5	0.4	0.3	0.3	0.2
64 Kazakhstan	901.2	986.3	970.9	945.9	911.4	878.8
65 Kenya	–	–	–	–	–	–
66 Kuwait	1,605.6	1,574.5	1,523.9	1,471.1	1,408.4	1,357.4
67 Kyrgyzstan	10.4	10.5	10.4	10.4	10.3	10.3
68 Lao People's Democratic Republic	1.5	1.5	1.5	1.4	1.4	1.4
69 Latvia	–	–	–	–	–	–
70 Lesotho	–	–	–	–	–	–
71 Liberia	–	–	–	–	–	–
72 Lithuania	0.3	0.3	0.2	0.1	0.0	–
73 Luxembourg	–	–	–	–	–	–
74 Malawi	–	–	–	–	–	–
75 Malaysia	306.1	285.5	258.8	228.6	196.7	171.9
76 Maldives	–	–	–	–	–	–
77 Mali	–	–	–	–	–	–
78 Malta	–	–	–	–	–	–
79 Mauritania	–	–	–	–	0.7	0.6
80 Mauritius	–	–	–	–	–	–
81 Mexico	270.7	237.9	201.2	161.1	120.2	90.8
82 Mongolia	46.0	45.5	45.1	44.7	43.7	41.7
83 Morocco	0.2	0.2	0.2	0.1	0.4	0.4
84 Mozambique	30.3	30.3	30.3	30.3	146.9	145.9
85 Myanmar	21.1	20.8	20.2	17.7	14.5	14.5
86 Namibia	–	–	–	–	2.7	2.7
87 Nepal	–	–	–	–	–	–

Country/year	1990	1995	2000	2005	2010	2014
88 Netherlands	122.0	104.5	87.9	72.3	56.4	43.5
89 New Zealand	145.1	142.5	139.9	137.6	135.3	133.4
90 Nicaragua	–	–	–	–	–	–
91 Niger	2.8	2.8	2.8	2.8	2.8	2.6
92 Nigeria	712.0	668.9	621.9	571.3	517.7	472.6
93 Norway	484.3	430.8	353.1	266.9	192.0	142.0
94 Pakistan	134.6	129.1	122.6	114.9	104.4	95.6
95 Panama	–	–	–	–	–	–
96 Papua New Guinea	12.8	11.7	10.0	8.9	8.1	7.7
97 Paraguay	–	–	–	–	–	–
98 Peru	47.5	44.6	41.8	39.5	35.9	30.6
99 Philippines	6.3	6.1	6.0	5.9	10.0	9.0
100 Poland	485.3	464.7	446.0	428.8	413.3	401.0
101 Portugal	–	–	–	–	0.5	0.4
102 Qatar	451.3	442.3	429.5	410.5	382.7	350.6
103 Republic of Korea	21.5	18.4	15.9	13.9	11.9	9.7
104 Republic of Moldova	–	–	–	–	–	–
105 Romania	47.4	38.2	30.8	24.1	17.8	13.4
106 Russian Federation	4,182.8	6,248.4	6,000.0	5,709.2	5,372.1	5,084.0
107 Rwanda	–	–	–	–	1.6	1.6
108 Saudi Arabia	4,377.7	4,184.8	3,976.8	3,759.5	3,511.8	3,305.3
109 Senegal	–	–	–	–	–	–
110 Serbia	–	–	–	–	5.6	2.7
111 Sierra Leone	–	–	–	–	–	–
112 Singapore	–	–	–	–	–	–
113 Slovakia	4.9	5.4	4.8	4.2	3.6	3.2
114 Slovenia	9.7	9.2	8.8	8.3	7.8	7.5
115 South Africa	261.9	244.1	222.5	199.6	175.8	156.6
116 Spain	41.7	37.2	33.9	31.0	29.1	28.4
117 Sri Lanka	–	–	–	–	–	–
118 Sudan (former)	61.4	61.4	61.1	57.0	49.8	45.5
119 Swaziland	1.0	1.0	1.0	1.0	0.9	0.9
120 Sweden	–	–	–	–	0.1	0.0
121 Switzerland	0.0	0.0	0.0	0.0	0.0	–
122 Syrian Arab Republic	64.6	55.8	45.2	35.3	27.0	22.6
123 Tajikistan	4.9	5.1	5.0	5.0	5.0	5.0
124 Thailand	93.9	88.8	80.5	69.1	53.5	37.7
125 Togo	–	–	–	–	–	–
126 Trinidad and Tobago	64.3	59.9	54.7	46.5	34.2	24.5
127 Tunisia	18.2	15.9	13.7	11.4	9.2	7.7
128 Turkey	269.1	262.5	255.0	248.7	240.6	234.4
129 Uganda	27.8	27.8	27.8	27.8	27.8	27.8
130 Ukraine	604.8	654.8	643.2	631.0	618.6	609.1
131 United Arab Emirates	1,343.8	1,296.0	1,246.9	1,195.0	1,136.3	1,084.5

(*Continued*)

Table A3.37 (Continued)

Country/year	1990	1995	2000	2005	2010	2014
132 United Kingdom	336.7	273.6	191.8	119.8	70.9	45.4
133 United Republic of Tanzania	2.3	2.3	2.3	2.3	2.3	2.3
134 United States of America	5,843.9	5,502.4	5,160.5	4,829.0	4,497.7	4,187.2
135 Uruguay	–	–	–	–	–	–
136 Venezuela (Bolivarian Republic of)	4,300.1	4,237.3	4,157.6	4,082.7	4,015.7	3,963.6
137 Viet Nam	164.6	162.3	157.4	148.8	137.8	128.8
138 Yemen	51.6	47.9	41.9	34.9	52.0	47.8
139 Zambia	0.8	0.7	0.7	0.7	0.7	0.7
140 Zimbabwe	9.7	9.3	8.9	8.6	8.4	8.1

Table A3.38 Fossil fuel per capita (Fossil fuel per capita in thousands of constant 2005 US$)

	Country/year	1990	1995	2000	2005	2010	2014
1	Afghanistan	0.3	0.2	0.2	0.1	0.1	0.1
2	Albania	4.0	4.0	4.1	4.2	4.2	4.2
3	Algeria	22.9	19.1	16.2	13.6	10.9	8.9
4	Argentina	1.8	1.6	1.3	1.0	0.7	0.6
5	Armenia	–	–	–	–	0.9	0.9
6	Australia	104.4	96.8	89.5	81.9	73.8	67.5
7	Austria	0.6	0.4	0.3	0.2	0.1	0.1
8	Bahrain	13.2	9.7	6.5	3.7	1.7	0.9
9	Bangladesh	0.0	0.0	0.0	0.0	0.0	0.0
10	Barbados	0.5	0.4	0.3	0.2	0.1	–
11	Belgium	–	–	–	–	0.0	–
12	Belize	–	–	–	–	0.2	–
13	Benin	–	–	–	–	–	–
14	Bolivia (Plurinational State of)	1.4	1.2	1.1	0.9	0.7	0.5
15	Botswana	0.9	0.7	0.6	0.5	0.4	0.3
16	Brazil	2.8	2.5	2.2	1.9	1.6	1.3
17	Bulgaria	6.8	6.7	6.5	6.6	6.5	6.3
18	Burundi	–	–	–	–	–	–
19	Cambodia	–	–	–	–	–	–
20	Cameroon	1.0	0.7	0.4	0.3	0.3	0.2
21	Canada	93.1	85.5	78.5	71.6	64.8	59.5
22	Central African Republic	–	–	–	–	0.0	0.0
23	Chile	1.6	1.4	1.3	1.2	1.1	1.0
24	China	3.5	3.2	2.9	2.6	2.3	1.9
25	Colombia	6.5	5.7	4.8	4.0	3.3	2.7
26	Congo	17.4	14.0	10.7	7.9	6.2	4.5
27	Costa Rica	–	–	–	–	0.0	–
28	Côte d'Ivoire	0.3	0.2	0.2	0.1	0.2	0.1
29	Croatia	0.6	0.8	0.7	0.5	0.4	0.3

	Country/year	1990	1995	2000	2005	2010	2014
30	Cuba	0.9	0.8	0.7	0.6	0.5	0.4
31	Cyprus	–	–	–	–	0.0	–
32	Czech Republic	7.8	7.4	6.9	6.4	5.8	5.4
33	Democratic Republic of the Congo	–	–	–	–	–	–
34	Denmark	8.8	7.9	6.5	4.6	2.9	2.0
35	Dominican Republic	–	–	–	–	–	–
36	Ecuador	14.8	12.6	10.7	9.1	7.6	6.6
37	Egypt	3.6	2.9	2.3	1.8	1.4	1.1
38	El Salvador	–	–	–	–	–	–
39	Estonia	–	–	–	–	0.1	–
40	Fiji	–	–	–	–	–	–
41	Finland	0.1	0.0	0.0	0.0	0.0	–
42	France	0.1	0.0	0.0	0.0	0.0	0.0
43	Gabon	53.7	41.4	30.5	23.4	17.6	13.7
44	Gambia	–	–	–	–	–	–
45	Germany	18.7	17.4	16.7	16.1	15.7	15.5
46	Ghana	–	–	–	–	–	0.0
47	Greece	7.8	7.0	6.3	5.6	5.0	4.8
48	Guatemala	0.3	0.2	0.2	0.1	0.1	0.1
49	Guyana	–	–	–	–	–	–
50	Haiti	–	–	–	–	–	–
51	Honduras	–	–	–	–	–	–
52	Hungary	4.1	3.9	3.8	3.6	3.5	3.5
53	Iceland	–	–	–	–	–	–
54	India	2.5	2.2	2.0	1.8	1.6	1.5
55	Indonesia	5.8	5.0	4.4	3.8	3.3	2.9
56	Iran (Islamic Republic of)	74.6	68.0	60.8	55.5	50.7	46.8
57	Iraq	87.7	75.2	63.5	54.1	46.2	39.4
58	Ireland	0.3	0.2	0.1	0.1	0.1	0.1
59	Israel	1.9	1.6	1.4	1.3	1.1	1.0
60	Italy	0.5	0.4	0.3	0.2	0.2	0.1
61	Jamaica	–	–	–	–	0.0	–
62	Japan	0.3	0.2	0.2	0.1	0.1	0.1
63	Jordan	0.2	0.1	0.1	0.1	0.0	0.0
64	Kazakhstan	55.1	62.4	65.2	62.4	55.8	50.8
65	Kenya	–	–	–	–	–	–
66	Kuwait	779.9	961.8	789.8	649.9	460.4	361.7
67	Kyrgyzstan	2.4	2.3	2.1	2.0	1.9	1.8
68	Lao People's Democratic Republic	0.3	0.3	0.3	0.3	0.2	0.2
69	Latvia	–	–	–	–	0.0	–
70	Lesotho	–	–	–	–	–	–
71	Liberia	–	–	–	–	–	–
72	Lithuania	0.1	0.1	0.1	0.0	0.0	–
73	Luxembourg	–	–	–	–	–	–

(*Continued*)

Table A3.38 (Continued)

Country/year	1990	1995	2000	2005	2010	2014
74 Malawi	–	–	–	–	0.0	0.0
75 Malaysia	16.8	13.8	11.0	8.9	7.0	5.7
76 Maldives	–	–	–	–	–	–
77 Mali	–	–	–	–	–	–
78 Malta	–	–	–	–	–	–
79 Mauritania	–	–	–	–	0.2	0.2
80 Mauritius	–	–	–	–	–	–
81 Mexico	3.2	2.5	2.0	1.5	1.0	0.7
82 Mongolia	21.1	19.8	18.8	17.7	16.1	14.3
83 Morocco	0.0	0.0	0.0	0.0	0.0	0.0
84 Mozambique	2.3	1.9	1.7	1.4	6.0	5.4
85 Myanmar	0.5	0.5	0.4	0.4	0.3	0.3
86 Namibia	–	–	–	–	1.2	1.1
87 Nepal	0.0	0.0	0.0	0.0	0.0	0.0
88 Netherlands	8.2	6.8	5.5	4.4	3.4	2.6
89 New Zealand	43.6	38.8	36.3	33.3	31.1	29.6
90 Nicaragua	–	–	–	–	0.0	–
91 Niger	0.4	0.3	0.2	0.2	0.2	0.1
92 Nigeria	7.4	6.2	5.1	4.1	3.2	2.7
93 Norway	114.2	98.8	78.6	57.7	39.3	27.6
94 Pakistan	1.3	1.1	0.9	0.7	0.6	0.5
95 Panama	–	–	–	–	–	–
96 Papua New Guinea	3.1	2.5	1.9	1.5	1.2	1.0
97 Paraguay	–	–	–	–	0.0	–
98 Peru	2.2	1.9	1.6	1.4	1.2	1.0
99 Philippines	0.1	0.1	0.1	0.1	0.1	0.1
100 Poland	12.7	12.0	11.7	11.2	10.9	10.5
101 Portugal	–	–	–	–	0.0	0.0
102 Qatar	947.2	882.7	723.7	490.5	216.7	161.4
103 Republic of Korea	0.5	0.4	0.3	0.3	0.2	0.2
104 Republic of Moldova	–	–	–	–	–	–
105 Romania	2.0	1.7	1.4	1.1	0.9	0.7
106 Russian Federation	28.2	42.1	40.9	39.8	37.6	35.4
107 Rwanda	–	–	–	–	0.2	0.1
108 Saudi Arabia	267.6	222.0	185.9	151.9	125.0	107.0
109 Senegal	–	–	–	–	0.0	–
110 Serbia	–	–	–	–	0.8	0.4
111 Sierra Leone	–	–	–	–	–	–
112 Singapore	–	–	–	–	0.0	–
113 Slovakia	0.9	1.0	0.9	0.8	0.7	0.6
114 Slovenia	4.8	4.6	4.4	4.1	3.8	3.6
115 South Africa	7.4	6.2	5.1	4.2	3.5	2.9
116 Spain	1.1	0.9	0.8	0.7	0.6	0.6
117 Sri Lanka	–	–	–	–	–	–
118 Sudan (former)	3.1	2.5	2.2	1.8	1.4	1.2

	Country/year	1990	1995	2000	2005	2010	2014
119	Swaziland	1.1	1.0	0.9	0.9	0.8	0.7
120	Sweden	–	–	–	–	0.0	0.0
121	Switzerland	0.0	0.0	0.0	0.0	0.0	–
122	Syrian Arab Republic	5.2	3.9	2.8	1.9	1.3	1.2
123	Tajikistan	0.9	0.9	0.8	0.7	0.7	0.6
124	Thailand	1.7	1.5	1.3	1.0	0.8	0.6
125	Togo	–	–	–	–	–	–
126	Trinidad and Tobago	52.6	47.7	43.1	35.8	25.7	18.1
127	Tunisia	2.2	1.8	1.4	1.1	0.9	0.7
128	Turkey	5.0	4.5	4.0	3.7	3.3	3.0
129	Uganda	1.6	1.4	1.2	1.0	0.8	0.7
130	Ukraine	11.7	12.7	13.1	13.4	13.5	13.4
131	United Arab Emirates	741.8	551.4	408.8	266.6	136.4	119.4
132	United Kingdom	5.9	4.7	3.3	2.0	1.1	0.7
133	United Republic of Tanzania	0.1	0.1	0.1	0.1	0.1	0.0
134	United States of America	23.4	20.7	18.3	16.3	14.5	13.1
135	Uruguay	–	–	–	–	–	–
136	Venezuela (Bolivarian Republic of)	216.5	191.0	169.8	152.5	138.5	129.1
137	Viet Nam	2.5	2.3	2.0	1.8	1.6	1.4
138	Yemen	4.3	3.1	2.4	1.7	2.2	1.8
139	Zambia	0.1	0.1	0.1	0.1	0.1	0.0
140	Zimbabwe	0.9	0.8	0.7	0.7	0.6	0.5

Table A3.39 Fossil fuel growth (Fossil fuel change (%) with respect to base year 1990)

	Country/year	1995	2000	2005	2010	2014
1	Afghanistan	-0.3%	-0.8%	-0.8%	-1.2%	-2.7%
2	Albania	-0.6%	-1.1%	-1.4%	-1.6%	-2.9%
3	Algeria	-1.4%	-3.9%	-6.6%	-9.9%	-16.6%
4	Argentina	-1.6%	-5.1%	-9.7%	-15.5%	-26.1%
5	Armenia	–	–	–	–	–
6	Australia	-0.4%	-1.0%	-1.6%	-2.3%	-3.8%
7	Austria	-3.7%	-10.2%	-17.9%	-26.6%	-51.7%
8	Bahrain	-3.6%	-9.9%	-16.2%	-24.1%	-42.3%
9	Bangladesh	-1.1%	-3.4%	-6.6%	-5.4%	-13.6%
10	Barbados	-4.9%	-14.3%	-24.4%	-38.8%	-100.0%
11	Belgium	–	–	–	–	–
12	Belize	–	–	–	–	–
13	Benin	–	–	–	–	–
14	Bolivia (Plurinational State of)	-0.6%	-1.6%	-3.8%	-7.9%	-17.3%
15	Botswana	-1.4%	-3.6%	-5.7%	-7.9%	-14.0%
16	Brazil	-0.8%	-2.4%	-4.5%	-7.6%	-14.1%
17	Bulgaria	-1.0%	-2.5%	-3.8%	-4.9%	-8.2%

(*Continued*)

Table A3.39 (Continued)

	Country/year	1995	2000	2005	2010	2014
18	Burundi	–	–	–	–	–
19	Cambodia	–	–	–	–	–
20	Cameroon	–5.4%	–13.6%	–19.1%	–15.5%	–25.2%
21	Canada	–0.6%	–1.7%	–2.8%	–3.9%	–6.5%
22	Central African Republic	–	–	–	–	–
23	Chile	–0.5%	–1.2%	–1.6%	–2.1%	–3.4%
24	China	–0.8%	–2.3%	–4.0%	–6.7%	–12.8%
25	Colombia	–1.1%	–3.7%	–6.1%	–9.1%	–16.8%
26	Congo	–1.7%	–5.5%	–9.6%	–11.8%	–21.4%
27	Costa Rica	–	–	–	–	–
28	Côte d'Ivoire	–0.3%	–2.7%	–5.3%	–1.3%	–12.1%
29	Croatia	6.3%	2.1%	–3.7%	–9.9%	–19.2%
30	Cuba	–0.9%	–3.5%	–7.3%	–12.1%	–21.7%
31	Cyprus	–	–	–	–	–
32	Czech Republic	–0.9%	–3.0%	–4.9%	–6.8%	–10.7%
33	Democratic Republic of the Congo	–	–	–	–	–
34	Denmark	–2.0%	–6.6%	–14.1%	–23.0%	–37.0%
35	Dominican Republic	–	–	–	–	–
36	Ecuador	–1.0%	–2.8%	–4.7%	–6.9%	–11.7%
37	Egypt	–2.3%	–6.0%	–9.2%	–13.0%	–21.4%
38	El Salvador	–	–	–	–	–
39	Estonia	–	–	–	–	–
40	Fiji	–	–	–	–	–
41	Finland	–3.7%	–11.8%	–21.5%	–25.0%	–100.0%
42	France	–6.1%	–14.4%	–21.2%	–25.9%	–40.7%
43	Gabon	–2.5%	–7.4%	–10.9%	–14.6%	–23.2%
44	Gambia	–	–	–	–	–
45	Germany	–0.8%	–1.9%	–2.8%	–3.6%	–5.5%
46	Ghana	–	–	–	–	–
47	Greece	–1.4%	–3.7%	–6.0%	–8.3%	–13.1%
48	Guatemala	–0.9%	–4.8%	–9.8%	–15.1%	–24.7%
49	Guyana	–	–	–	–	–
50	Haiti	–	–	–	–	–
51	Honduras	–	–	–	–	–
52	Hungary	–1.1%	–2.8%	–3.9%	–4.9%	–7.3%
53	Iceland	–	–	–	–	–
54	India	–0.4%	–1.1%	–1.9%	–2.8%	–4.9%
55	Indonesia	–1.1%	–2.9%	–4.4%	–6.5%	–11.3%
56	Iran (Islamic Republic of)	–0.4%	–1.1%	–1.8%	–2.7%	–4.4%
57	Iraq	–0.2%	–0.6%	–1.2%	–1.8%	–3.2%
58	Ireland	–7.3%	–17.9%	–22.4%	–24.8%	–34.7%
59	Israel	0.0%	0.0%	–0.2%	–0.9%	–4.3%
60	Italy	–3.3%	–9.0%	–14.0%	–20.0%	–32.2%
61	Jamaica	–	–	–	–	–
62	Japan	–4.2%	–10.5%	–16.6%	–24.3%	–40.4%

	Country/year	1995	2000	2005	2010	2014
63	Jordan	−2.0%	−5.9%	−10.0%	−13.9%	−21.3%
64	Kazakhstan	1.8%	1.9%	1.2%	0.3%	−0.8%
65	Kenya	−	−	−	−	−
66	Kuwait	−0.4%	−1.3%	−2.2%	−3.2%	−5.4%
67	Kyrgyzstan	0.2%	0.1%	0.0%	−0.1%	−0.4%
68	Lao People's Democratic Republic	0.0%	0.0%	−0.1%	−0.2%	−0.5%
69	Latvia	−	−	−	−	−
70	Lesotho	−	−	−	−	−
71	Liberia	−	−	−	−	−
72	Lithuania	−0.9%	−6.7%	−21.7%	−36.7%	−100.0%
73	Luxembourg	−	−	−	−	−
74	Malawi	−	−	−	−	−
75	Malaysia	−1.4%	−4.1%	−7.0%	−10.5%	−17.5%
76	Maldives	−	−	−	−	−
77	Mali	−	−	−	−	−
78	Malta	−	−	−	−	−
79	Mauritania	−	−	−	−	−
80	Mauritius	−	−	−	−	−
81	Mexico	−2.5%	−7.2%	−12.2%	−18.4%	−30.5%
82	Mongolia	−0.2%	−0.5%	−0.8%	−1.3%	−3.3%
83	Morocco	−0.7%	−2.3%	−4.1%	21.8%	27.8%
84	Mozambique	0.0%	0.0%	0.0%	48.4%	68.9%
85	Myanmar	−0.3%	−1.0%	−4.2%	−8.9%	−11.8%
86	Namibia	−	−	−	−	−
87	Nepal	−0.2%	−1.5%	−2.6%	−4.2%	−7.0%
88	Netherlands	−3.1%	−7.9%	−12.3%	−17.6%	−29.1%
89	New Zealand	−0.4%	−0.9%	−1.3%	−1.7%	−2.8%
90	Nicaragua	−	−	−	−	−
91	Niger	−0.1%	−0.1%	−0.2%	−0.3%	−2.6%
92	Nigeria	−1.2%	−3.3%	−5.4%	−7.7%	−12.8%
93	Norway	−2.3%	−7.6%	−13.8%	−20.6%	−33.6%
94	Pakistan	−0.8%	−2.3%	−3.9%	−6.1%	−10.8%
95	Panama	−	−	−	−	−
96	Papua New Guinea	−1.8%	−6.0%	−8.8%	−10.8%	−15.7%
97	Paraguay	−	−	−	−	−
98	Peru	−1.3%	−3.1%	−4.5%	−6.8%	−13.6%
99	Philippines	−0.4%	−0.8%	−1.6%	12.6%	12.9%
100	Poland	−0.9%	−2.1%	−3.0%	−3.9%	−6.2%
101	Portugal	−	−	−	−	−
102	Qatar	−0.4%	−1.2%	−2.3%	−4.0%	−8.1%
103	Republic of Korea	−3.1%	−7.2%	−10.3%	−13.8%	−23.1%
104	Republic of Moldova	−	−	−	−	−
105	Romania	−4.2%	−10.2%	−15.6%	−21.7%	−34.4%
106	Russian Federation	8.4%	9.4%	8.1%	6.5%	6.7%

(*Continued*)

Table A3.39 (Continued)

Country/year	1995	2000	2005	2010	2014
107 Rwanda	–	–	–	–	–
108 Saudi Arabia	-0.9%	-2.4%	-3.7%	-5.4%	-8.9%
109 Senegal	–	–	–	–	–
110 Serbia	–	–	–	–	–
111 Sierra Leone	–	–	–	–	–
112 Singapore	–	–	–	–	–
113 Slovakia	1.9%	-0.6%	-3.8%	-7.1%	-12.7%
114 Slovenia	-0.9%	-2.4%	-3.7%	-5.1%	-8.0%
115 South Africa	-1.4%	-4.0%	-6.6%	-9.5%	-15.8%
116 Spain	-2.2%	-5.1%	-7.2%	-8.5%	-11.9%
117 Sri Lanka	–	–	–	–	–
118 Sudan (former)	0.0%	-0.1%	-1.9%	-5.1%	-9.5%
119 Swaziland	-0.1%	-0.4%	-0.7%	-0.9%	-1.4%
120 Sweden	–	–	–	–	–
121 Switzerland	0.0%	0.0%	0.0%	16.7%	-100.0%
122 Syrian Arab Republic	-2.9%	-8.6%	-14.0%	-19.6%	-29.6%
123 Tajikistan	0.7%	0.8%	0.8%	0.7%	0.7%
124 Thailand	-1.1%	-3.8%	-7.4%	-13.1%	-26.2%
125 Togo	–	–	–	–	–
126 Trinidad and Tobago	-1.4%	-4.0%	-7.8%	-14.6%	-27.5%
127 Tunisia	-2.7%	-7.0%	-11.0%	-15.7%	-25.0%
128 Turkey	-0.5%	-1.3%	-2.0%	-2.8%	-4.5%
129 Uganda	0.0%	0.0%	0.0%	0.0%	0.0%
130 Ukraine	1.6%	1.5%	1.1%	0.6%	0.2%
131 United Arab Emirates	-0.7%	-1.9%	-2.9%	-4.1%	-6.9%
132 United Kingdom	-4.1%	-13.1%	-22.8%	-32.3%	-48.7%
133 United Republic of Tanzania	0.0%	0.0%	-0.1%	-0.1%	-0.1%
134 United States of America	-1.2%	-3.1%	-4.7%	-6.3%	-10.5%
135 Uruguay	–	–	–	–	–
136 Venezuela (Bolivarian Republic of)	-0.3%	-0.8%	-1.3%	-1.7%	-2.7%
137 Viet Nam	-0.3%	-1.1%	-2.5%	-4.3%	-7.8%
138 Yemen	-1.5%	-5.1%	-9.3%	0.2%	-2.5%
139 Zambia	-0.6%	-1.1%	-1.4%	-1.5%	-2.3%
140 Zimbabwe	-1.0%	-2.3%	-3.2%	-3.7%	-6.0%

Table A3.40 Fossil fuel per capita growth (Fossil fuel per capita change (%) with respect to base year 1990)

Country/year	1995	2000	2005	2010	2014
1 Afghanistan	-6.7%	-12.2%	-16.8%	-19.9%	-29.5%
2 Albania	0.0%	0.5%	0.8%	1.4%	1.4%
3 Algeria	-3.6%	-8.3%	-12.2%	-17.0%	-27.2%
4 Argentina	-2.9%	-8.0%	-13.7%	-20.2%	-32.5%
5 Armenia	–	–	–	–	–

	Country/year	1995	2000	2005	2010	2014
6	Australia	−1.5%	−3.8%	−5.9%	−8.3%	−13.5%
7	Austria	−4.4%	−11.2%	−19.3%	−28.2%	−53.4%
8	Bahrain	−6.1%	−16.3%	−27.1%	−39.9%	−58.8%
9	Bangladesh	−3.3%	−8.4%	−13.4%	−13.5%	−24.6%
10	Barbados	−5.2%	−15.1%	−25.4%	−39.8%	−100.0%
11	Belgium	−	−	−	−	−
12	Belize	−	−	−	−	−
13	Benin	−	−	−	−	−
14	Bolivia (Plurinational State of)	−2.6%	−6.3%	−10.4%	−16.0%	−28.4%
15	Botswana	−4.0%	−9.0%	−12.5%	−16.5%	−26.6%
16	Brazil	−2.3%	−6.1%	−9.7%	−13.8%	−22.7%
17	Bulgaria	−0.3%	−1.0%	−0.9%	−0.9%	−2.3%
18	Burundi	−	−	−	−	−
19	Cambodia	−	−	−	−	−
20	Cameroon	−8.1%	−19.4%	−26.9%	−26.1%	−39.5%
21	Canada	−1.7%	−4.2%	−6.4%	−8.7%	−13.9%
22	Central African Republic	−	−	−	−	−
23	Chile	−2.0%	−4.7%	−6.5%	−8.2%	−12.6%
24	China	−2.0%	−4.9%	−7.3%	−10.5%	−18.0%
25	Colombia	−2.9%	−7.6%	−11.4%	−15.5%	−25.6%
26	Congo	−4.3%	−11.6%	−17.9%	−22.8%	−36.4%
27	Costa Rica	−	−	−	−	−
28	Côte d'Ivoire	−3.6%	−9.9%	−14.3%	−13.0%	−28.0%
29	Croatia	6.8%	4.1%	−1.9%	−8.1%	−15.9%
30	Cuba	−1.5%	−4.7%	−8.7%	−13.5%	−23.6%
31	Cyprus	−	−	−	−	−
32	Czech Republic	−0.9%	−2.9%	−4.6%	−7.1%	−11.3%
33	Democratic Republic of the Congo	−	−	−	−	−
34	Denmark	−2.3%	−7.5%	−15.2%	−24.4%	−38.9%
35	Dominican Republic	−	−	−	−	−
36	Ecuador	−3.2%	−7.9%	−11.5%	−15.4%	−23.8%
37	Egypt	−4.3%	−10.4%	−15.4%	−20.8%	−32.7%
38	El Salvador	−	−	−	−	−
39	Estonia	−	−	−	−	−
40	Fiji	−	−	−	−	−
41	Finland	−4.2%	−12.6%	−22.4%	−26.4%	−100.0%
42	France	−6.5%	−15.2%	−22.7%	−27.8%	−43.2%
43	Gabon	−5.1%	−13.1%	−18.8%	−24.3%	−36.6%
44	Gambia	−	−	−	−	−
45	Germany	−1.4%	−2.8%	−3.7%	−4.2%	−6.1%
46	Ghana	−	−	−	−	−
47	Greece	−2.1%	−5.0%	−7.7%	−10.2%	−15.0%
48	Guatemala	−3.3%	−10.4%	−17.6%	−24.6%	−37.5%
49	Guyana	−	−	−	−	−
50	Haiti	−	−	−	−	−

(*Continued*)

Table A3.40 (Continued)

	Country/year	1995	2000	2005	2010	2014
51	Honduras	–	–	–	–	–
52	Hungary	–1.0%	–2.4%	–3.2%	–4.0%	–5.8%
53	Iceland	–	–	–	–	–
54	India	–2.3%	–5.7%	–8.3%	–10.9%	–16.7%
55	Indonesia	–2.7%	–6.5%	–9.6%	–12.9%	–20.7%
56	Iran (Islamic Republic of)	–1.8%	–5.0%	–7.1%	–9.2%	–14.4%
57	Iraq	–3.0%	–7.8%	–11.4%	–14.8%	–23.4%
58	Ireland	–7.8%	–19.5%	–25.6%	–29.6%	–40.4%
59	Israel	–3.4%	–7.3%	–9.6%	–12.4%	–20.8%
60	Italy	–3.3%	–9.1%	–14.4%	–20.9%	–33.7%
61	Jamaica	–	–	–	–	–
62	Japan	–4.4%	–11.1%	–17.3%	–25.0%	–40.9%
63	Jordan	–6.8%	–13.8%	–19.9%	–27.1%	–39.5%
64	Kazakhstan	2.5%	4.3%	3.2%	0.3%	–2.7%
65	Kenya	–	–	–	–	–
66	Kuwait	4.3%	0.3%	–4.5%	–12.3%	–22.6%
67	Kyrgyzstan	–0.6%	–2.6%	–4.0%	–5.4%	–9.4%
68	Lao People's Democratic Republic	–2.6%	–5.6%	–7.3%	–9.4%	–14.5%
69	Latvia	–	–	–	–	–
70	Lesotho	–	–	–	–	–
71	Liberia	–	–	–	–	–
72	Lithuania	–0.5%	–5.4%	–19.6%	–33.8%	–100.0%
73	Luxembourg	–	–	–	–	–
74	Malawi	–	–	–	–	–
75	Malaysia	–3.9%	–10.0%	–14.8%	–19.7%	–30.1%
76	Maldives	–	–	–	–	–
77	Mali	–	–	–	–	–
78	Malta	–	–	–	–	–
79	Mauritania	–	–	–	–	–
80	Mauritius	–	–	–	–	–
81	Mexico	–4.4%	–11.3%	–17.5%	–24.8%	–38.8%
82	Mongolia	–1.2%	–2.8%	–4.3%	–6.5%	–12.1%
83	Morocco	–2.4%	–5.9%	–8.7%	14.3%	15.3%
84	Mozambique	–3.4%	–7.5%	–10.8%	27.8%	33.3%
85	Myanmar	–1.5%	–4.1%	–8.3%	–13.5%	–18.6%
86	Namibia	–	–	–	–	–
87	Nepal	–2.8%	–7.2%	–9.8%	–12.4%	–18.8%
88	Netherlands	–3.7%	–9.3%	–14.2%	–19.7%	–31.9%
89	New Zealand	–2.3%	–4.5%	–6.5%	–8.1%	–12.1%
90	Nicaragua	–	–	–	–	–
91	Niger	–3.4%	–8.5%	–12.7%	–16.8%	–27.4%
92	Nigeria	–3.7%	–9.2%	–13.9%	–18.7%	–29.0%
93	Norway	–2.8%	–8.9%	–15.7%	–23.4%	–37.7%
94	Pakistan	–3.4%	–8.2%	–12.0%	–16.3%	–25.5%
95	Panama	–	–	–	–	–

	Country/year	1995	2000	2005	2010	2014
96	Papua New Guinea	−4.2%	−11.9%	−17.1%	−21.3%	−30.7%
97	Paraguay	−	−	−	−	−
98	Peru	−3.2%	−7.2%	−10.0%	−13.5%	−23.1%
99	Philippines	−2.7%	−6.4%	−9.3%	1.7%	−3.5%
100	Poland	−1.1%	−2.2%	−3.1%	−3.9%	−6.1%
101	Portugal	−	−	−	−	−
102	Qatar	−1.4%	−6.5%	−15.2%	−30.8%	−44.6%
103	Republic of Korea	−4.1%	−9.3%	−12.9%	−16.8%	−27.2%
104	Republic of Moldova	−	−	−	−	−
105	Romania	−3.8%	−9.5%	−13.8%	−19.0%	−31.0%
106	Russian Federation	8.3%	9.8%	9.0%	7.5%	7.8%
107	Rwanda	−	−	−	−	−
108	Saudi Arabia	−3.7%	−8.7%	−13.2%	−17.3%	−26.3%
109	Senegal	−	−	−	−	−
110	Serbia	−	−	−	−	−
111	Sierra Leone	−	−	−	−	−
112	Singapore	−	−	−	−	−
113	Slovakia	1.7%	−1.0%	−4.2%	−7.5%	−13.4%
114	Slovenia	−0.8%	−2.3%	−3.7%	−5.6%	−8.9%
115	South Africa	−3.5%	−9.2%	−13.2%	−17.4%	−27.0%
116	Spain	−2.5%	−5.9%	−9.8%	−12.6%	−17.1%
117	Sri Lanka	−	−	−	−	−
118	Sudan (former)	−4.1%	−8.2%	−12.7%	−18.1%	−27.8%
119	Swaziland	−2.3%	−5.5%	−6.7%	−8.6%	−13.3%
120	Sweden	−	−	−	−	−
121	Switzerland	−0.9%	−1.7%	−2.5%	12.3%	−
122	Syrian Arab Republic	−5.6%	−14.6%	−21.7%	−29.2%	−38.6%
123	Tajikistan	−1.0%	−3.0%	−5.4%	−8.0%	−13.3%
124	Thailand	−2.0%	−6.2%	−10.8%	−16.6%	−30.5%
125	Togo	−	−	−	−	−
126	Trinidad and Tobago	−1.9%	−4.9%	−9.2%	−16.4%	−30.0%
127	Tunisia	−4.5%	−10.6%	−15.5%	−20.9%	−32.1%
128	Turkey	−2.1%	−5.2%	−7.4%	−9.6%	−15.3%
129	Uganda	−3.2%	−7.5%	−11.3%	−14.9%	−22.8%
130	Ukraine	1.7%	2.9%	3.5%	3.7%	4.8%
131	United Arab Emirates	−5.8%	−13.8%	−22.6%	−34.5%	−45.6%
132	United Kingdom	−4.3%	−13.7%	−23.8%	−33.8%	−50.7%
133	United Republic of Tanzania	−3.2%	−7.0%	−10.2%	−13.6%	−21.2%
134	United States of America	−2.5%	−6.0%	−8.6%	−11.2%	−17.5%
135	Uruguay	−	−	−	−	−
136	Venezuela (Bolivarian Republic of)	−2.5%	−5.9%	−8.4%	−10.6%	−15.8%
137	Viet Nam	−2.0%	−5.0%	−7.7%	−10.7%	−17.1%
138	Yemen	−6.2%	−14.0%	−20.8%	−15.4%	−24.9%
139	Zambia	−3.1%	−7.4%	−10.6%	−13.8%	−21.5%
140	Zimbabwe	−3.1%	−6.5%	−8.2%	−10.4%	−17.1%

Table A3.41 Minerals (Minerals in billions of constant 2005 US$)

	Country/year	1990	1995	2000	2005	2010	2014
1	Afghanistan	–	–	–	–	–	–
2	Albania	–	–	–	–	–	–
3	Algeria	9.4	9.4	9.4	9.4	9.3	9.3
4	Argentina	–	–	–	–	–	–
5	Armenia	–	–	–	–	–	–
6	Australia	260.7	255.8	249.5	241.6	232.1	224.7
7	Austria	–	–	–	–	–	–
8	Bahrain	–	–	–	–	–	–
9	Bangladesh	–	–	–	–	–	–
10	Barbados	–	–	–	–	–	–
11	Belgium	–	–	–	–	–	–
12	Belize	–	–	–	–	–	–
13	Benin	–	–	–	–	–	–
14	Bolivia (Plurinational State of)	2.6	2.5	2.3	2.1	1.7	1.4
15	Botswana	0.9	0.8	0.7	0.6	0.5	0.4
16	Brazil	127.7	123.8	119.6	114.4	107.0	100.8
17	Bulgaria	–	–	–	–	–	–
18	Burundi	–	–	–	–	–	–
19	Cambodia	–	–	–	–	–	–
20	Cameroon	–	–	–	–	–	–
21	Canada	44.4	40.5	36.6	33.2	30.1	29.3
22	Central African Republic	–	–	–	–	–	–
23	Chile	90.2	87.0	81.5	74.6	67.2	60.9
24	China	194.6	187.6	179.4	169.2	147.0	118.1
25	Colombia	2.2	2.1	1.9	1.6	1.3	1.0
26	Congo	–	–	–	–	–	–
27	Costa Rica	–	–	–	–	–	–
28	Côte d'Ivoire	–	–	–	–	–	–
29	Croatia	–	–	–	–	–	–
30	Cuba	6.0	5.9	5.6	5.3	5.0	4.8
31	Cyprus	–	–	–	–	–	–
32	Czech Republic	–	–	–	–	–	–
33	Democratic Republic of the Congo	–	–	–	–	–	–
34	Denmark	–	–	–	–	–	–
35	Dominican Republic	1.4	1.2	1.1	0.9	0.8	0.8
36	Ecuador	–	–	–	–	–	–
37	Egypt	5.4	5.4	5.4	5.3	5.3	5.2
38	El Salvador	–	–	–	–	–	–
39	Estonia	–	–	–	–	–	–
40	Fiji	–	–	–	–	–	–
41	Finland	–	–	–	–	–	–
42	France	–	–	–	–	–	–
43	Gabon	–	–	–	–	–	–
44	Gambia	–	–	–	–	–	–
45	Germany	–	–	–	–	–	–
46	Ghana	3.9	3.6	3.1	2.7	2.1	1.6
47	Greece	0.6	0.6	0.6	0.5	0.5	0.5

	Country/year	1990	1995	2000	2005	2010	2014
48	Guatemala	–	–	–	–	–	–
49	Guyana	1.8	1.7	1.7	1.7	1.7	1.7
50	Haiti	–	–	–	–	–	–
51	Honduras	–	–	–	–	–	–
52	Hungary	–	–	–	–	–	–
53	Iceland	–	–	–	–	–	–
54	India	151.0	149.6	148.0	145.3	140.8	137.4
55	Indonesia	28.5	27.2	24.9	21.7	18.6	16.1
56	Iran (Islamic Republic of)	11.6	11.5	11.4	11.0	10.4	10.1
57	Iraq	–	–	–	–	–	–
58	Ireland	0.9	0.8	0.7	0.5	0.3	0.1
59	Israel	0.9	0.9	0.8	0.7	0.6	0.6
60	Italy	–	–	–	–	–	–
61	Jamaica	4.5	4.4	4.3	4.1	4.0	3.9
62	Japan	0.4	0.3	0.3	0.2	0.2	0.2
63	Jordan	4.7	4.7	4.6	4.5	4.4	4.3
64	Kazakhstan	17.1	16.5	15.8	14.7	13.5	12.5
65	Kenya	–	–	–	–	–	–
66	Kuwait	–	–	–	–	–	–
67	Kyrgyzstan	–	–	–	–	–	–
68	Lao People's Democratic Republic	–	–	–	–	–	–
69	Latvia	–	–	–	–	–	–
70	Lesotho	–	–	–	–	–	–
71	Liberia	–	–	–	–	–	–
72	Lithuania	–	–	–	–	–	–
73	Luxembourg	–	–	–	–	–	–
74	Malawi	–	–	–	–	–	–
75	Malaysia	0.2	0.2	0.2	0.2	0.2	0.2
76	Maldives	–	–	–	–	–	–
77	Mali	–	–	–	–	–	–
78	Malta	–	–	–	–	–	–
79	Mauritania	5.0	4.8	4.6	4.4	4.2	4.0
80	Mauritius	–	–	–	–	–	–
81	Mexico	26.2	25.1	23.7	22.3	20.5	18.5
82	Mongolia	–	–	–	–	–	–
83	Morocco	–	–	–	–	–	–
84	Mozambique	–	–	–	–	–	–
85	Myanmar	–	–	–	–	–	–
86	Namibia	–	–	–	–	–	–
87	Nepal	–	–	–	–	–	–
88	Netherlands	–	–	–	–	–	–
89	New Zealand	–	–	–	–	–	–
90	Nicaragua	–	–	–	–	–	–
91	Niger	–	–	–	–	–	–
92	Nigeria	–	–	–	–	–	–
93	Norway	–	–	–	–	–	–
94	Pakistan	–	–	–	–	–	–

(*Continued*)

Table A3.41 (Continued)

Country/year	1990	1995	2000	2005	2010	2014
95 Panama	–	–	–	–	–	–
96 Papua New Guinea	3.1	2.7	2.4	2.0	1.6	1.4
97 Paraguay	–	–	–	–	–	–
98 Peru	43.7	42.3	40.2	36.8	32.8	29.7
99 Philippines	5.0	4.9	4.8	4.7	4.2	2.8
100 Poland	10.6	10.1	9.4	8.7	8.0	7.5
101 Portugal	0.1	0.1	0.1	0.0	0.0	0.0
102 Qatar	–	–	–	–	–	–
103 Republic of Korea	–	–	–	–	–	–
104 Republic of Moldova	–	–	–	–	–	–
105 Romania	–	–	–	–	–	–
106 Russian Federation	139.4	135.3	131.2	126.3	121.2	116.9
107 Rwanda	–	–	–	–	–	–
108 Saudi Arabia	–	–	–	–	–	–
109 Senegal	0.4	0.3	0.3	0.3	0.3	0.2
110 Serbia	–	–	–	–	–	–
111 Sierra Leone	–	–	–	–	–	–
112 Singapore	–	–	–	–	–	–
113 Slovakia	–	–	–	–	–	–
114 Slovenia	–	–	–	–	–	–
115 South Africa	38.8	34.2	30.4	27.1	24.6	22.5
116 Spain	–	–	–	–	–	–
117 Sri Lanka	–	–	–	–	–	–
118 Sudan (former)	–	–	–	–	–	–
119 Swaziland	–	–	–	–	–	–
120 Sweden	13.3	12.9	12.5	12.2	11.8	11.4
121 Switzerland	–	–	–	–	–	–
122 Syrian Arab Republic	6.1	6.1	6.0	6.0	5.9	5.9
123 Tajikistan	–	–	–	–	–	–
124 Thailand	0.2	0.1	0.1	0.1	0.1	0.1
125 Togo	0.3	0.3	0.2	0.2	0.2	0.1
126 Trinidad and Tobago	–	–	–	–	–	–
127 Tunisia	1.1	1.0	0.8	0.7	0.5	0.4
128 Turkey	–	–	–	–	–	–
129 Uganda	–	–	–	–	–	–
130 Ukraine	22.5	21.7	20.9	20.1	19.0	18.2
131 United Arab Emirates	–	–	–	–	–	–
132 United Kingdom	–	–	–	–	–	–
133 United Republic of Tanzania	–	–	–	–	–	–
134 United States of America	85.2	78.5	71.6	66.1	61.1	57.1
135 Uruguay	–	–	–	–	–	–
136 Venezuela (Bolivarian Republic of)	17.0	16.6	16.3	15.9	15.5	15.3
137 Viet Nam	–	–	–	–	3.8	3.8
138 Yemen	–	–	–	–	–	–
139 Zambia	7.8	7.3	6.9	6.4	5.7	5.0
140 Zimbabwe	–	–	–	–	–	–

Table A3.42 Minerals per capita (Minerals per capita in thousands of constant 2005 US$)

	Country/year	1990	1995	2000	2005	2010	2014
1	Afghanistan	–	–	–	–	–	–
2	Albania	–	–	–	–	–	–
3	Algeria	0.4	0.3	0.3	0.3	0.3	0.2
4	Argentina	–	–	–	–	–	–
5	Armenia	–	–	–	–	–	–
6	Australia	15.3	14.2	13.0	11.8	10.5	9.6
7	Austria	–	–	–	–	–	–
8	Bahrain	–	–	–	–	–	–
9	Bangladesh	–	–	–	–	–	–
10	Barbados	–	–	–	–	–	–
11	Belgium	–	–	–	–	–	–
12	Belize	–	–	–	–	–	–
13	Benin	–	–	–	–	–	–
14	Bolivia (Plurinational State of)	0.4	0.3	0.3	0.2	0.2	0.1
15	Botswana	0.6	0.5	0.4	0.3	0.2	0.2
16	Brazil	0.8	0.8	0.7	0.6	0.5	0.5
17	Bulgaria	–	–	–	–	–	–
18	Burundi	–	–	–	–	–	–
19	Cambodia	–	–	–	–	–	–
20	Cameroon	–	–	–	–	–	–
21	Canada	1.6	1.4	1.2	1.0	0.9	0.8
22	Central African Republic	–	–	–	–	–	–
23	Chile	6.9	6.1	5.4	4.6	3.9	3.4
24	China	0.2	0.2	0.1	0.1	0.1	0.1
25	Colombia	0.1	0.1	0.0	0.0	0.0	0.0
26	Congo	–	–	–	–	–	–
27	Costa Rica	–	–	–	–	–	–
28	Côte d'Ivoire	–	–	–	–	–	–
29	Croatia	–	–	–	–	–	–
30	Cuba	0.6	0.5	0.5	0.5	0.4	0.4
31	Cyprus	–	–	–	–	–	–
32	Czech Republic	–	–	–	–	–	–
33	Democratic Republic of the Congo	–	–	–	–	–	–
34	Denmark	–	–	–	–	–	–
35	Dominican Republic	0.2	0.2	0.1	0.1	0.1	0.1
36	Ecuador	–	–	–	–	–	–
37	Egypt	0.1	0.1	0.1	0.1	0.1	0.1
38	El Salvador	–	–	–	–	–	–
39	Estonia	–	–	–	–	–	–
40	Fiji	–	–	–	–	–	–
41	Finland	–	–	–	–	–	–
42	France	–	–	–	–	–	–
43	Gabon	–	–	–	–	–	–
44	Gambia	–	–	–	–	–	–

(*Continued*)

Table A3.42 (Continued)

	Country/year	1990	1995	2000	2005	2010	2014
45	Germany	–	–	–	–	–	–
46	Ghana	0.3	0.2	0.2	0.1	0.1	0.1
47	Greece	0.1	0.1	0.1	0.0	0.0	0.0
48	Guatemala	–	–	–	–	–	–
49	Guyana	2.4	2.4	2.3	2.3	2.2	2.2
50	Haiti	–	–	–	–	–	–
51	Honduras	–	–	–	–	–	–
52	Hungary	–	–	–	–	–	–
53	Iceland	–	–	–	–	–	–
54	India	0.2	0.2	0.1	0.1	0.1	0.1
55	Indonesia	0.2	0.1	0.1	0.1	0.1	0.1
56	Iran (Islamic Republic of)	0.2	0.2	0.2	0.2	0.1	0.1
57	Iraq	–	–	–	–	–	–
58	Ireland	0.3	0.2	0.2	0.1	0.1	0.0
59	Israel	0.2	0.2	0.1	0.1	0.1	0.1
60	Italy	–	–	–	–	–	–
61	Jamaica	1.9	1.8	1.6	1.6	1.5	1.4
62	Japan	0.0	0.0	0.0	0.0	0.0	0.0
63	Jordan	1.4	1.1	1.0	0.8	0.7	0.6
64	Kazakhstan	1.0	1.0	1.1	1.0	0.8	0.7
65	Kenya	–	–	–	–	–	–
66	Kuwait	–	–	–	–	–	–
67	Kyrgyzstan	–	–	–	–	–	–
68	Lao People's Democratic Republic	–	–	–	–	–	–
69	Latvia	–	–	–	–	–	–
70	Lesotho	–	–	–	–	–	–
71	Liberia	–	–	–	–	–	–
72	Lithuania	–	–	–	–	–	–
73	Luxembourg	–	–	–	–	–	–
74	Malawi	–	–	–	–	–	–
75	Malaysia	0.0	0.0	0.0	0.0	0.0	0.0
76	Maldives	–	–	–	–	–	–
77	Mali	–	–	–	–	–	–
78	Malta	–	–	–	–	–	–
79	Mauritania	2.5	2.1	1.7	1.4	1.2	1.0
80	Mauritius	–	–	–	–	–	–
81	Mexico	0.3	0.3	0.2	0.2	0.2	0.1
82	Mongolia	–	–	–	–	–	–
83	Morocco	–	–	–	–	–	–
84	Mozambique	–	–	–	–	–	–
85	Myanmar	–	–	–	–	–	–
86	Namibia	–	–	–	–	–	–
87	Nepal	–	–	–	–	–	–
88	Netherlands	–	–	–	–	–	–
89	New Zealand	–	–	–	–	–	–

	Country/year	1990	1995	2000	2005	2010	2014
90	Nicaragua	–	–	–	–	–	–
91	Niger	–	–	–	–	–	–
92	Nigeria	–	–	–	–	–	–
93	Norway	–	–	–	–	–	–
94	Pakistan	–	–	–	–	–	–
95	Panama	–	–	–	–	–	–
96	Papua New Guinea	0.7	0.6	0.4	0.3	0.2	0.2
97	Paraguay	–	–	–	–	–	–
98	Peru	2.0	1.8	1.6	1.3	1.1	1.0
99	Philippines	0.1	0.1	0.1	0.1	0.0	0.0
100	Poland	0.3	0.3	0.2	0.2	0.2	0.2
101	Portugal	0.0	0.0	0.0	0.0	0.0	0.0
102	Qatar	–	–	–	–	–	–
103	Republic of Korea	–	–	–	–	–	–
104	Republic of Moldova	–	–	–	–	–	–
105	Romania	–	–	–	–	–	–
106	Russian Federation	0.9	0.9	0.9	0.9	0.8	0.8
107	Rwanda	–	–	–	–	–	–
108	Saudi Arabia	–	–	–	–	–	–
109	Senegal	0.1	0.0	0.0	0.0	0.0	0.0
110	Serbia	–	–	–	–	–	–
111	Sierra Leone	–	–	–	–	–	–
112	Singapore	–	–	–	–	–	–
113	Slovakia	–	–	–	–	–	–
114	Slovenia	–	–	–	–	–	–
115	South Africa	1.1	0.9	0.7	0.6	0.5	0.4
116	Spain	–	–	–	–	–	–
117	Sri Lanka	–	–	–	–	–	–
118	Sudan (former)	–	–	–	–	–	–
119	Swaziland	–	–	–	–	–	–
120	Sweden	1.5	1.5	1.4	1.3	1.3	1.2
121	Switzerland	–	–	–	–	–	–
122	Syrian Arab Republic	0.5	0.4	0.4	0.3	0.3	0.3
123	Tajikistan	–	–	–	–	–	–
124	Thailand	0.0	0.0	0.0	0.0	0.0	0.0
125	Togo	0.1	0.1	0.0	0.0	0.0	0.0
126	Trinidad and Tobago	–	–	–	–	–	–
127	Tunisia	0.1	0.1	0.1	0.1	0.0	0.0
128	Turkey	–	–	–	–	–	–
129	Uganda	–	–	–	–	–	–
130	Ukraine	0.4	0.4	0.4	0.4	0.4	0.4
131	United Arab Emirates	–	–	–	–	–	–
132	United Kingdom	–	–	–	–	–	–
133	United Republic of Tanzania	–	–	–	–	–	–
134	United States of America	0.3	0.3	0.3	0.2	0.2	0.2

(Continued)

Table A3.42 (Continued)

	Country/year	1990	1995	2000	2005	2010	2014
135	Uruguay	–	–	–	–	–	–
136	Venezuela (Bolivarian Republic of)	0.9	0.8	0.7	0.6	0.5	0.5
137	Viet Nam	–	–	–	–	0.0	0.0
138	Yemen	–	–	–	–	–	–
139	Zambia	1.0	0.8	0.7	0.5	0.4	0.3
140	Zimbabwe	–	–	–	–	–	–

Table A3.43 Minerals growth (Minerals change (%) with respect to base year 1990)

	Country/year	1995	2000	2005	2010	2014
1	Afghanistan	–	–	–	–	–
2	Albania	–	–	–	–	–
3	Algeria	0.0%	–0.1%	–0.2%	–0.2%	–0.4%
4	Argentina	–	–	–	–	–
5	Armenia	–	–	–	–	–
6	Australia	–0.4%	–1.1%	–1.9%	–2.9%	–4.8%
7	Austria	–	–	–	–	–
8	Bahrain	–	–	–	–	–
9	Bangladesh	–	–	–	–	–
10	Barbados	–	–	–	–	–
11	Belgium	–	–	–	–	–
12	Belize	–	–	–	–	–
13	Benin	–	–	–	–	–
14	Bolivia (Plurinational State of)	–1.3%	–3.5%	–5.5%	–9.8%	–19.6%
15	Botswana	–2.1%	–5.9%	–10.1%	–15.3%	–26.0%
16	Brazil	–0.6%	–1.6%	–2.7%	–4.3%	–7.6%
17	Bulgaria	–	–	–	–	–
18	Burundi	–	–	–	–	–
19	Cambodia	–	–	–	–	–
20	Cameroon	–	–	–	–	–
21	Canada	–1.8%	–4.7%	–7.0%	–9.3%	–13.0%
22	Central African Republic	–	–	–	–	–
23	Chile	–0.7%	–2.5%	–4.6%	–7.1%	–12.3%
24	China	–0.7%	–2.0%	–3.4%	–6.8%	–15.3%
25	Colombia	–1.1%	–3.5%	–7.9%	–12.0%	–22.4%
26	Congo	–	–	–	–	–
27	Costa Rica	–	–	–	–	–
28	Côte d'Ivoire	–	–	–	–	–
29	Croatia	–	–	–	–	–
30	Cuba	–0.5%	–1.7%	–3.1%	–4.5%	–7.4%

	Country/year	1995	2000	2005	2010	2014
31	Cyprus	–	–	–	–	–
32	Czech Republic	–	–	–	–	–
33	Democratic Republic of the Congo	–	–	–	–	–
34	Denmark	–	–	–	–	–
35	Dominican Republic	–2.9%	–7.4%	–10.9%	–12.6%	–18.7%
36	Ecuador	–	–	–	–	–
37	Egypt	0.0%	–0.1%	–0.3%	–0.6%	–1.4%
38	El Salvador	–	–	–	–	–
39	Estonia	–	–	–	–	–
40	Fiji	–	–	–	–	–
41	Finland	–	–	–	–	–
42	France	–	–	–	–	–
43	Gabon	–	–	–	–	–
44	Gambia	–	–	–	–	–
45	Germany	–	–	–	–	–
46	Ghana	–1.4%	–4.9%	–8.6%	–13.9%	–25.0%
47	Greece	–0.8%	–1.7%	–2.8%	–3.8%	–5.9%
48	Guatemala	–	–	–	–	–
49	Guyana	–0.2%	–0.6%	–0.9%	–1.1%	–1.8%
50	Haiti	–	–	–	–	–
51	Honduras	–	–	–	–	–
52	Hungary	–	–	–	–	–
53	Iceland	–	–	–	–	–
54	India	–0.2%	–0.5%	–1.0%	–1.7%	–3.1%
55	Indonesia	–0.9%	–3.3%	–6.6%	–10.1%	–17.3%
56	Iran (Islamic Republic of)	–0.2%	–0.6%	–1.4%	–2.8%	–4.7%
57	Iraq	–	–	–	–	–
58	Ireland	–2.5%	–6.7%	–14.4%	–25.4%	–45.9%
59	Israel	–1.3%	–3.8%	–6.3%	–8.5%	–13.9%
60	Italy	–	–	–	–	–
61	Jamaica	–0.5%	–1.3%	–2.1%	–2.8%	–4.3%
62	Japan	–2.9%	–7.6%	–11.8%	–16.6%	–26.9%
63	Jordan	–0.3%	–0.9%	–1.5%	–2.0%	–3.3%
64	Kazakhstan	–0.8%	–2.1%	–3.7%	–5.8%	–9.9%
65	Kenya	–	–	–	–	–
66	Kuwait	–	–	–	–	–
67	Kyrgyzstan	–	–	–	–	–
68	Lao People's Democratic Republic	–	–	–	–	–
69	Latvia	–	–	–	–	–
70	Lesotho	–	–	–	–	–
71	Liberia	–	–	–	–	–
72	Lithuania	–	–	–	–	–

(*Continued*)

Table A3.43 (Continued)

	Country/year	1995	2000	2005	2010	2014
73	Luxembourg	–	–	–	–	–
74	Malawi	–	–	–	–	–
75	Malaysia	–3.2%	–6.3%	–7.8%	–8.8%	–13.3%
76	Maldives	–	–	–	–	–
77	Mali	–	–	–	–	–
78	Malta	–	–	–	–	–
79	Mauritania	–0.8%	–2.1%	–3.2%	–4.4%	–7.2%
80	Mauritius	–	–	–	–	–
81	Mexico	–0.9%	–2.5%	–4.0%	–5.9%	–11.0%
82	Mongolia	–	–	–	–	–
83	Morocco	–	–	–	–	–
84	Mozambique	–	–	–	–	–
85	Myanmar	–	–	–	–	–
86	Namibia	–	–	–	–	–
87	Nepal	–	–	–	–	–
88	Netherlands	–	–	–	–	–
89	New Zealand	–	–	–	–	–
90	Nicaragua	–	–	–	–	–
91	Niger	–	–	–	–	–
92	Nigeria	–	–	–	–	–
93	Norway	–	–	–	–	–
94	Pakistan	–	–	–	–	–
95	Panama	–	–	–	–	–
96	Papua New Guinea	–2.4%	–6.2%	–10.2%	–14.6%	–23.6%
97	Paraguay	–	–	–	–	–
98	Peru	–0.6%	–2.1%	–4.2%	–6.9%	–12.0%
99	Philippines	–0.2%	–0.7%	–1.2%	–4.0%	–17.3%
100	Poland	–1.0%	–2.9%	–4.9%	–6.8%	–10.9%
101	Portugal	–4.1%	–9.4%	–10.1%	–10.1%	–13.4%
102	Qatar	–	–	–	–	–
103	Republic of Korea	–	–	–	–	–
104	Republic of Moldova	–	–	–	–	–
105	Romania	–	–	–	–	–
106	Russian Federation	–0.6%	–1.5%	–2.4%	–3.4%	–5.7%
107	Rwanda	–	–	–	–	–
108	Saudi Arabia	–	–	–	–	–
109	Senegal	–2.2%	–5.6%	–8.6%	–10.2%	–15.4%
110	Serbia	–	–	–	–	–
111	Sierra Leone	–	–	–	–	–
112	Singapore	–	–	–	–	–
113	Slovakia	–	–	–	–	–
114	Slovenia	–	–	–	–	–
115	South Africa	–2.5%	–5.9%	–8.5%	–10.8%	–16.6%
116	Spain	–	–	–	–	–

	Country/year	1995	2000	2005	2010	2014
117	Sri Lanka	–	–	–	–	–
118	Sudan (former)	–	–	–	–	–
119	Swaziland	–	–	–	–	–
120	Sweden	–0.5%	–1.4%	–2.1%	–2.9%	–5.0%
121	Switzerland	–	–	–	–	–
122	Syrian Arab Republic	–0.1%	–0.2%	–0.4%	–0.7%	–1.0%
123	Tajikistan	–	–	–	–	–
124	Thailand	–2.8%	–4.5%	–5.3%	–5.4%	–7.3%
125	Togo	–3.8%	–9.7%	–13.0%	–15.4%	–23.2%
126	Trinidad and Tobago	–	–	–	–	–
127	Tunisia	–2.4%	–7.2%	–12.3%	–18.3%	–27.8%
128	Turkey	–	–	–	–	–
129	Uganda	–	–	–	–	–
130	Ukraine	–0.8%	–1.8%	–2.9%	–4.1%	–6.9%
131	United Arab Emirates	–	–	–	–	–
132	United Kingdom	–	–	–	–	–
133	United Republic of Tanzania	–	–	–	–	–
134	United States of America	–1.6%	–4.3%	–6.1%	–7.9%	–12.5%
135	Uruguay	–	–	–	–	–
136	Venezuela (Bolivarian Republic of)	–0.5%	–1.1%	–1.7%	–2.3%	–3.5%
137	Viet Nam	–	–	–	–	–
138	Yemen	–	–	–	–	–
139	Zambia	–1.3%	–3.0%	–4.7%	–7.5%	–13.8%
140	Zimbabwe	–	–	–	–	–

Table A3.44 Minerals per capita growth (Minerals per capita change (%) with respect to base year 1990)

	Country/year	1995	2000	2005	2010	2014
1	Afghanistan	–	–	–	–	–
2	Albania	–	–	–	–	–
3	Algeria	–2.2%	–4.6%	–6.2%	–8.1%	–13.1%
4	Argentina	–	–	–	–	–
5	Armenia	–	–	–	–	–
6	Australia	–1.5%	–3.9%	–6.2%	–8.9%	–14.4%
7	Austria	–	–	–	–	–
8	Bahrain	–	–	–	–	–
9	Bangladesh	–	–	–	–	–
10	Barbados	–	–	–	–	–
11	Belgium	–	–	–	–	–
12	Belize	–	–	–	–	–

(*Continued*)

Table A3.44 (Continued)

	Country/year	1995	2000	2005	2010	2014
13	Benin	–	–	–	–	–
14	Bolivia (Plurinational State of)	–3.3%	–8.1%	–12.0%	–17.7%	–30.3%
15	Botswana	–4.7%	–11.2%	–16.6%	–23.3%	–36.9%
16	Brazil	–2.2%	–5.4%	–8.0%	–10.7%	–16.8%
17	Bulgaria	–	–	–	–	–
18	Burundi	–	–	–	–	–
19	Cambodia	–	–	–	–	–
20	Cameroon	–	–	–	–	–
21	Canada	–2.9%	–7.1%	–10.4%	–13.7%	–19.8%
22	Central African Republic	–	–	–	–	–
23	Chile	–2.2%	–5.9%	–9.3%	–12.9%	–20.6%
24	China	–1.9%	–4.6%	–6.7%	–10.5%	–20.4%
25	Colombia	–2.8%	–7.4%	–13.1%	–18.2%	–30.6%
26	Congo	–	–	–	–	–
27	Costa Rica	–	–	–	–	–
28	Côte d'Ivoire	–	–	–	–	–
29	Croatia	–	–	–	–	–
30	Cuba	–1.1%	–2.9%	–4.6%	–6.1%	–9.6%
31	Cyprus	–	–	–	–	–
32	Czech Republic	–	–	–	–	–
33	Democratic Republic of the Congo	–	–	–	–	–
34	Denmark	–	–	–	–	–
35	Dominican Republic	–4.7%	–11.3%	–16.3%	–19.3%	–28.2%
36	Ecuador	–	–	–	–	–
37	Egypt	–2.0%	–4.8%	–7.2%	–9.5%	–15.5%
38	El Salvador	–	–	–	–	–
39	Estonia	–	–	–	–	–
40	Fiji	–	–	–	–	–
41	Finland	–	–	–	–	–
42	France	–	–	–	–	–
43	Gabon	–	–	–	–	–
44	Gambia	–	–	–	–	–
45	Germany	–	–	–	–	–
46	Ghana	–4.0%	–10.8%	–16.9%	–24.2%	–38.7%
47	Greece	–1.4%	–3.2%	–4.6%	–5.8%	–8.0%
48	Guatemala	–	–	–	–	–
49	Guyana	–0.4%	–1.4%	–1.6%	–2.2%	–3.7%
50	Haiti	–	–	–	–	–
51	Honduras	–	–	–	–	–
52	Hungary	–	–	–	–	–
53	Iceland	–	–	–	–	–
54	India	–2.1%	–5.1%	–7.5%	–9.9%	–15.1%

	Country/year	1995	2000	2005	2010	2014
55	Indonesia	–2.5%	–7.0%	–11.6%	–16.3%	–26.1%
56	Iran (Islamic Republic of)	–1.6%	–4.5%	–6.7%	–9.3%	–14.7%
57	Iraq	–	–	–	–	–
58	Ireland	–3.0%	–8.5%	–17.9%	–30.1%	–50.6%
59	Israel	–4.7%	–10.7%	–15.1%	–19.1%	–28.8%
60	Italy	–	–	–	–	–
61	Jamaica	–1.2%	–3.3%	–4.5%	–5.6%	–8.3%
62	Japan	–3.2%	–8.2%	–12.6%	–17.4%	–27.6%
63	Jordan	–5.2%	–9.2%	–12.2%	–17.0%	–25.8%
64	Kazakhstan	–0.1%	0.3%	–1.8%	–5.8%	–11.6%
65	Kenya	–	–	–	–	–
66	Kuwait	–	–	–	–	–
67	Kyrgyzstan	–	–	–	–	–
68	Lao People's Democratic Republic	–	–	–	–	–
69	Latvia	–	–	–	–	–
70	Lesotho	–	–	–	–	–
71	Liberia	–	–	–	–	–
72	Lithuania	–	–	–	–	–
73	Luxembourg	–	–	–	–	–
74	Malawi	–	–	–	–	–
75	Malaysia	–5.7%	–12.0%	–15.5%	–18.2%	–26.5%
76	Maldives	–	–	–	–	–
77	Mali	–	–	–	–	–
78	Malta	–	–	–	–	–
79	Mauritania	–3.6%	–9.1%	–13.4%	–17.2%	–25.8%
80	Mauritius	–	–	–	–	–
81	Mexico	–2.8%	–6.8%	–9.7%	–13.3%	–21.6%
82	Mongolia	–	–	–	–	–
83	Morocco	–	–	–	–	–
84	Mozambique	–	–	–	–	–
85	Myanmar	–	–	–	–	–
86	Namibia	–	–	–	–	–
87	Nepal	–	–	–	–	–
88	Netherlands	–	–	–	–	–
89	New Zealand	–	–	–	–	–
90	Nicaragua	–	–	–	–	–
91	Niger	–	–	–	–	–
92	Nigeria	–	–	–	–	–
93	Norway	–	–	–	–	–
94	Pakistan	–	–	–	–	–
95	Panama	–	–	–	–	–
96	Papua New Guinea	–4.8%	–12.0%	–18.4%	–24.7%	–37.1%
97	Paraguay	–	–	–	–	–
98	Peru	–2.5%	–6.2%	–9.6%	–13.6%	–21.7%

(*Continued*)

Table A3.44 (Continued)

	Country/year	1995	2000	2005	2010	2014
99	Philippines	−2.6%	−6.2%	−9.0%	−13.2%	−29.3%
100	Poland	−1.3%	−3.0%	−4.9%	−6.7%	−10.8%
101	Portugal	−4.2%	−10.1%	−11.2%	−11.4%	−14.6%
102	Qatar	−	−	−	−	−
103	Republic of Korea	−	−	−	−	−
104	Republic of Moldova	−	−	−	−	−
105	Romania	−	−	−	−	−
106	Russian Federation	−0.6%	−1.2%	−1.6%	−2.5%	−4.7%
107	Rwanda	−	−	−	−	−
108	Saudi Arabia	−	−	−	−	−
109	Senegal	−5.1%	−11.8%	−17.4%	−21.6%	−32.3%
110	Serbia	−	−	−	−	−
111	Sierra Leone	−	−	−	−	−
112	Singapore	−	−	−	−	−
113	Slovakia	−	−	−	−	−
114	Slovenia	−	−	−	−	−
115	South Africa	−4.5%	−11.0%	−15.0%	−18.6%	−27.7%
116	Spain	−	−	−	−	−
117	Sri Lanka	−	−	−	−	−
118	Sudan (former)	−	−	−	−	−
119	Swaziland	−	−	−	−	−
120	Sweden	−1.1%	−2.3%	−3.4%	−5.1%	−8.8%
121	Switzerland	−	−	−	−	−
122	Syrian Arab Republic	−2.8%	−6.8%	−9.4%	−12.5%	−13.7%
123	Tajikistan	−	−	−	−	−
124	Thailand	−3.7%	−6.9%	−8.8%	−9.2%	−12.7%
125	Togo	−6.1%	−15.2%	−21.0%	−25.8%	−37.8%
126	Trinidad and Tobago	−	−	−	−	−
127	Tunisia	−4.2%	−10.8%	−16.7%	−23.4%	−34.7%
128	Turkey	−	−	−	−	−
129	Uganda	−	−	−	−	−
130	Ukraine	−0.7%	−0.5%	−0.5%	−1.1%	−2.6%
131	United Arab Emirates	−	−	−	−	−
132	United Kingdom	−	−	−	−	−
133	United Republic of Tanzania	−	−	−	−	−
134	United States of America	−2.9%	−7.2%	−10.0%	−12.8%	−19.3%
135	Uruguay	−	−	−	−	−
136	Venezuela (Bolivarian Republic of)	−2.6%	−6.1%	−8.8%	−11.1%	−16.5%
137	Viet Nam	−	−	−	−	−
138	Yemen	−	−	−	−	−
139	Zambia	−3.8%	−9.2%	−13.5%	−19.1%	−30.8%
140	Zimbabwe	−	−	−	−	−

Table A3.45 IWI adjusted (Average growth rate in percentage from 1990–1995)

	Country/year	Average growth rate in percentage from 1990–1995						
		Growth IW	Growth population	Growth IW per capita (unadjusted)	Growth of carbon damages	Growth of oil capital gains	Growth of TFP	Growth IW per capita (adjusted)
1	Afghanistan	6.0%	6.8%	-0.7%	-0.1%	0.1%	-1.0%	-1.7%
2	Albania	-0.4%	-0.6%	0.2%	-0.1%	0.1%	0.9%	1.1%
3	Algeria	1.1%	2.2%	-1.0%	-0.1%	-0.9%	-1.1%	-3.2%
4	Argentina	1.1%	1.3%	-0.2%	-0.1%	0.4%	4.2%	4.2%
5	Armenia	-1.4%	-1.9%	0.4%	0.0%	0.3%	-9.3%	-8.6%
6	Australia	1.0%	1.2%	-0.1%	0.0%	0.2%	0.7%	0.8%
7	Austria	2.1%	0.7%	1.4%	-0.3%	0.3%	0.2%	1.6%
8	Bahrain	3.0%	2.6%	0.3%	-0.3%	0.1%	1.6%	1.7%
9	Bangladesh	2.3%	2.2%	0.0%	0.0%	0.0%	0.2%	0.2%
10	Barbados	0.6%	0.3%	0.2%	-0.2%	0.7%	-1.2%	-0.4%
11	Belgium	1.9%	0.3%	1.6%	-0.3%	0.5%	-0.9%	1.0%
12	Belize	0.4%	2.0%	-1.5%	-0.1%	0.2%	1.7%	0.3%
13	Benin	3.7%	3.7%	0.0%	0.0%	0.0%	3.3%	3.3%
14	Bolivia (Plurinational State of)	0.1%	2.0%	-1.8%	0.0%	0.1%	1.3%	-0.5%
15	Botswana	1.9%	2.7%	-0.7%	0.0%	0.0%	-2.0%	-2.7%
16	Brazil	0.4%	1.6%	-1.1%	-0.1%	0.1%	1.4%	0.3%
17	Bulgaria	-1.3%	-0.7%	-0.6%	0.0%	0.1%	-1.7%	-2.2%
18	Burundi	1.2%	2.1%	-0.9%	0.0%	0.0%	-1.2%	-2.1%
19	Cambodia	0.3%	3.5%	-3.1%	0.0%	0.0%	3.7%	0.5%
20	Cameroon	2.4%	2.9%	-0.5%	0.0%	0.0%	-1.8%	-2.3%

(Continued)

Table A3.45 (Continued)

	Country/year	Average growth rate in percentage from 1990–1995							
		Growth IW	Growth population	Growth IW per capita (unadjusted)	Growth of carbon damages	Growth of oil capital gains	Growth of TFP	Growth IW per capita (adjusted)
21	Canada	0.8%	1.1%	-0.3%	0.0%	-0.9%	-0.5%	-1.7%
22	Central African Republic	1.8%	2.6%	-0.7%	0.0%	0.0%	0.1%	-0.7%
23	Chile	1.7%	1.6%	0.1%	-0.1%	0.4%	2.3%	2.7%
24	China	2.0%	1.2%	0.8%	0.0%	0.1%	4.5%	5.3%
25	Colombia	1.2%	1.8%	-0.6%	-0.1%	0.0%	0.8%	0.2%
26	Congo	2.0%	2.7%	-0.7%	0.0%	-0.2%	-3.1%	-4.0%
27	Costa Rica	1.5%	2.5%	-1.1%	-0.2%	0.4%	1.6%	0.8%
28	Côte d'Ivoire	3.0%	3.4%	-0.4%	0.0%	0.0%	1.7%	1.2%
29	Croatia	0.2%	-0.5%	0.6%	0.0%	0.2%	-5.6%	-4.9%
30	Cuba	1.0%	0.6%	0.4%	-0.1%	0.8%	-5.9%	-4.8%
31	Cyprus	3.7%	2.2%	1.4%	-0.3%	0.9%	1.7%	3.8%
32	Czech Republic	1.1%	0.0%	1.2%	0.0%	0.1%	-2.1%	-0.8%
33	Democratic Republic of the Congo	-0.2%	3.8%	-3.8%	0.0%	0.0%	-11.1%	-14.9%
34	Denmark	1.3%	0.4%	0.9%	-0.3%	0.1%	0.5%	1.2%
35	Dominican Republic	2.6%	1.9%	0.6%	-0.1%	0.5%	1.1%	2.1%
36	Ecuador	0.5%	2.3%	-1.7%	-0.1%	-1.1%	1.0%	-1.9%
37	Egypt	2.3%	2.1%	0.2%	0.0%	0.0%	1.2%	1.4%
38	El Salvador	2.1%	1.3%	0.9%	-0.1%	0.3%	3.0%	4.0%
39	Estonia	-1.5%	-1.7%	0.3%	0.0%	0.3%	-6.7%	-6.2%
40	Fiji	2.0%	1.3%	0.8%	-0.1%	0.5%	-0.2%	0.9%
41	Finland	1.0%	0.5%	0.5%	-0.2%	0.4%	-1.4%	-0.7%

42	France	1.9%	0.3%	1.5%	-0.3%	0.4%	0.1%	1.7%
43	Gabon	-0.1%	2.7%	-2.7%	0.0%	-0.2%	-0.9%	-3.7%
44	Gambia	1.1%	3.1%	-1.9%	-0.1%	0.2%	-5.0%	-6.7%
45	Germany	1.6%	0.6%	1.0%	-0.2%	0.2%	-0.3%	0.8%
46	Ghana	2.1%	2.8%	-0.7%	0.0%	0.0%	2.9%	2.2%
47	Greece	1.2%	0.7%	0.5%	-0.2%	0.4%	-0.2%	0.6%
48	Guatemala	2.3%	2.5%	-0.2%	0.0%	0.0%	2.2%	1.9%
49	Guyana	0.1%	0.2%	-0.1%	0.0%	0.1%	6.3%	6.2%
50	Haiti	2.3%	2.0%	0.3%	0.0%	0.0%	-3.9%	-3.5%
51	Honduras	-0.4%	2.7%	-2.9%	-0.1%	0.2%	0.1%	-2.7%
52	Hungary	0.9%	-0.1%	1.0%	0.0%	0.3%	-3.2%	-1.9%
53	Iceland	0.3%	1.0%	-0.7%	-0.1%	0.2%	-0.9%	-1.5%
54	India	1.3%	2.0%	-0.7%	0.0%	0.0%	0.9%	0.2%
55	Indonesia	1.2%	1.7%	-0.4%	-0.1%	0.1%	-0.9%	-1.3%
56	Iran (Islamic Republic of)	0.2%	1.4%	-1.2%	0.0%	-1.8%	1.6%	-1.5%
57	Iraq	0.6%	3.0%	-2.3%	0.0%	-3.6%	-1.6%	-7.5%
58	Ireland	1.5%	0.5%	0.9%	-0.4%	0.3%	2.8%	3.7%
59	Israel	4.7%	3.5%	1.1%	0.1%	0.8%	1.4%	3.3%
60	Italy	1.6%	0.0%	1.5%	-0.3%	0.4%	0.5%	2.1%
61	Jamaica	1.8%	0.7%	1.1%	-0.1%	0.9%	0.4%	2.3%
62	Japan	2.4%	0.3%	2.1%	0.0%	0.4%	-0.6%	1.9%
63	Jordan	6.1%	5.2%	0.9%	-0.2%	1.4%	1.9%	4.1%
64	Kazakhstan	1.2%	-0.7%	1.8%	0.0%	-0.9%	-10.6%	-9.7%
65	Kenya	2.8%	3.1%	-0.3%	0.0%	0.0%	-0.3%	-0.6%
66	Kuwait	-1.5%	-4.5%	3.1%	0.0%	-3.6%	14.8%	14.3%
67	Kyrgyzstan	1.4%	0.8%	0.7%	0.0%	0.2%	-13.2%	-12.4%
68	Lao People's Democratic Republic	1.2%	2.7%	-1.5%	0.0%	0.0%	-3.4%	-4.9%

(Continued)

Table A3.45 (Continued)

Country/year	Average growth rate in percentage from 1990–1995						
	Growth IW	Growth population	Growth IW per capita (unadjusted)	Growth of carbon damages	Growth of oil capital gains	Growth of TFP	Growth IW per capita (adjusted)
69 Latvia	-0.4%	-1.4%	1.0%	0.0%	0.3%	-11.6%	-10.4%
70 Lesotho	0.9%	1.9%	-1.0%	0.0%	0.0%	-3.8%	-4.8%
71 Liberia	-1.6%	-0.2%	-1.4%	0.0%	0.0%	-19.8%	-21.1%
72 Lithuania	0.5%	-0.4%	0.9%	0.0%	0.3%	-9.7%	-8.5%
73 Luxembourg	3.1%	1.4%	1.7%	-0.5%	0.7%	0.6%	2.6%
74 Malawi	0.6%	0.9%	-0.3%	0.0%	0.0%	1.4%	1.1%
75 Malaysia	2.2%	2.6%	-0.4%	-0.2%	-0.1%	0.8%	0.2%
76 Maldives	2.9%	3.2%	-0.2%	-0.2%	0.2%	-1.6%	-1.9%
77 Mali	2.5%	2.6%	-0.1%	0.0%	0.0%	1.7%	1.6%
78 Malta	3.2%	0.9%	2.3%	-0.3%	1.1%	0.4%	3.4%
79 Mauritania	3.0%	2.9%	0.1%	0.0%	0.0%	2.7%	2.9%
80 Mauritius	2.8%	1.2%	1.6%	-0.2%	0.8%	-1.6%	0.7%
81 Mexico	2.3%	2.0%	0.3%	-0.2%	0.6%	-1.6%	-0.9%
82 Mongolia	0.2%	1.0%	-0.8%	0.0%	0.1%	-4.5%	-5.3%
83 Morocco	1.8%	1.7%	0.1%	0.0%	0.1%	-2.0%	-1.8%
84 Mozambique	4.2%	3.5%	0.6%	0.0%	0.0%	0.8%	1.4%
85 Myanmar	1.6%	1.3%	0.3%	0.0%	0.0%	3.0%	3.3%
86 Namibia	2.1%	3.2%	-1.0%	0.0%	0.1%	3.8%	2.9%
87 Nepal	2.8%	2.7%	0.1%	0.0%	0.0%	2.4%	2.5%
88 Netherlands	1.8%	0.7%	1.1%	-0.3%	0.5%	0.4%	1.7%
89 New Zealand	0.4%	2.0%	-1.6%	0.0%	0.1%	1.6%	0.1%
90 Nicaragua	2.3%	2.2%	0.1%	0.0%	0.1%	1.9%	2.1%
91 Niger	3.2%	3.4%	-0.2%	0.0%	0.0%	2.8%	2.6%
92 Nigeria	2.5%	2.5%	-0.1%	0.0%	-0.1%	2.0%	1.8%
93 Norway	0.2%	0.5%	-0.4%	-0.2%	-0.8%	2.8%	1.4%
94 Pakistan	0.5%	2.6%	-2.1%	-0.1%	0.2%	0.2%	-1.8%
95 Panama	1.5%	2.1%	-0.5%	-0.1%	1.4%	1.6%	2.4%

96	Papua New Guinea	2.6%	2.6%	0.0%	0.0%	0.0%	6.3%	6.3%
97	Paraguay	0.7%	2.5%	-1.7%	0.0%	0.2%	-0.5%	-2.1%
98	Peru	0.2%	1.9%	-1.7%	0.0%	0.1%	3.6%	1.9%
99	Philippines	3.0%	2.4%	0.6%	-0.1%	0.3%	-1.0%	-0.2%
100	Poland	0.6%	0.3%	0.4%	0.0%	0.2%	0.5%	1.1%
101	Portugal	2.3%	0.1%	2.2%	-0.3%	0.6%	0.1%	2.5%
102	Qatar	-0.2%	1.0%	-1.2%	-0.1%	-3.8%	0.8%	-4.3%
103	Republic of Korea	5.8%	1.0%	4.8%	-0.4%	1.1%	-0.7%	4.8%
104	Republic of Moldova	0.8%	-0.1%	0.9%	0.0%	0.4%	-16.1%	-14.8%
105	Romania	0.1%	-0.5%	0.5%	0.0%	0.3%	-1.8%	-1.0%
106	Russian Federation	1.7%	0.0%	1.7%	0.0%	-0.2%	-10.5%	-8.9%
107	Rwanda	-4.5%	-4.0%	-0.5%	0.0%	0.0%	-5.2%	-5.7%
108	Saudi Arabia	1.7%	2.9%	-1.2%	0.0%	-3.2%	1.2%	-3.2%
109	Senegal	2.6%	3.0%	-0.4%	0.0%	0.0%	-0.6%	-1.0%
110	Serbia	0.0%	0.1%	-0.1%	0.0%	0.0%	-12.3%	-12.4%
111	Sierra Leone	-1.6%	-0.5%	-1.2%	0.0%	0.0%	-5.5%	-6.7%
112	Singapore	6.2%	3.0%	3.1%	0.1%	3.2%	4.9%	11.3%
113	Slovakia	1.0%	0.2%	0.7%	0.0%	0.1%	-2.6%	-1.8%
114	Slovenia	0.9%	-0.1%	1.0%	-0.1%	0.2%	-1.6%	-0.5%
115	South Africa	1.5%	2.1%	-0.6%	-0.1%	0.2%	0.1%	-0.3%
116	Spain	2.5%	0.3%	2.2%	-0.3%	0.5%	-0.3%	2.1%
117	Sri Lanka	2.0%	1.1%	0.8%	-0.1%	0.2%	2.3%	3.2%
118	Sudan (former)	4.2%	4.3%	-0.1%	0.0%	0.0%	2.4%	2.2%
119	Swaziland	4.4%	2.2%	2.1%	-0.2%	0.2%	-1.8%	0.3%
120	Sweden	1.3%	0.6%	0.7%	-0.3%	0.3%	-0.6%	0.1%
121	Switzerland	4.2%	1.0%	3.2%	-0.3%	0.3%	-5.1%	-1.9%
122	Syrian Arab Republic	2.4%	2.9%	-0.4%	0.0%	0.8%	5.0%	5.4%

(*Continued*)

Table A3.45 (Continued)

	Country/year	Average growth rate in percentage from 1990–1995						
		Growth IW	Growth population	Growth IW per capita (unadjusted)	Growth of carbon damages	Growth of oil capital gains	Growth of TFP	Growth IW per capita (adjusted)
123	Tajikistan	2.6%	1.8%	0.8%	0.0%	0.1%	-17.8%	-16.9%
124	Thailand	3.3%	0.9%	2.3%	-0.1%	0.4%	-1.6%	1.1%
125	Togo	2.3%	2.5%	-0.2%	0.0%	0.0%	1.5%	1.3%
126	Trinidad and Tobago	-0.5%	0.5%	-1.0%	-0.1%	-0.4%	2.0%	0.4%
127	Tunisia	2.7%	1.9%	0.7%	-0.1%	0.3%	1.1%	2.0%
128	Turkey	2.5%	1.6%	0.9%	-0.2%	0.4%	-1.2%	-0.1%
129	Uganda	3.3%	3.3%	0.1%	0.0%	0.0%	4.6%	4.6%
130	Ukraine	-0.3%	-0.1%	-0.1%	0.0%	0.0%	-14.9%	-15.0%
131	United Arab Emirates	2.4%	5.3%	-2.8%	-0.1%	-2.6%	1.8%	-3.7%
132	United Kingdom	1.6%	0.3%	1.4%	-0.4%	0.3%	-0.6%	0.7%
133	United Republic of Tanzania	3.0%	3.3%	-0.2%	0.0%	0.0%	-1.7%	-2.0%
134	United States of America	1.9%	1.3%	0.6%	-0.1%	0.5%	-0.2%	0.8%
135	Uruguay	1.1%	0.7%	0.4%	-0.1%	0.2%	1.4%	1.9%
136	Venezuela (Bolivarian Republic of)	0.0%	2.2%	-2.2%	0.0%	-3.8%	1.4%	-4.6%
137	Viet Nam	2.0%	1.7%	0.2%	-0.1%	-0.2%	-1.4%	-1.5%
138	Yemen	4.2%	5.0%	-0.8%	0.0%	-0.1%	3.7%	2.8%
139	Zambia	2.4%	2.6%	-0.2%	0.0%	0.0%	0.8%	0.6%
140	Zimbabwe	0.7%	2.2%	-1.5%	0.0%	0.0%	0.2%	-1.2%

Table A3.46 IWI adjusted (Average growth rate in percentage from 1995–2000)

	Country/year	Average growth rate in percentage from 1995–2000							
		Growth IW	Growth population	Growth IW per capita (unadjusted)	Growth of carbon damages	Growth of oil capital gains	Growth of TFP	Growth IW per capita (adjusted)
1	Afghanistan	12.5%	13.0%	-0.5%	-0.1%	0.1%	-4.3%	-4.7%
2	Albania	-0.2%	-1.5%	1.4%	-0.1%	0.1%	4.6%	5.9%
3	Algeria	2.9%	4.7%	-1.8%	-0.1%	-1.4%	2.0%	-1.2%
4	Argentina	3.0%	3.2%	-0.2%	-0.2%	0.5%	0.4%	0.5%
5	Armenia	-2.4%	-3.5%	1.1%	-0.1%	0.5%	6.0%	7.6%
6	Australia	3.0%	2.9%	0.0%	0.0%	0.2%	0.7%	1.0%
7	Austria	4.9%	1.1%	3.8%	-0.4%	0.3%	1.4%	5.2%
8	Bahrain	7.0%	7.7%	-0.6%	-0.4%	0.1%	0.6%	-0.3%
9	Bangladesh	5.5%	5.5%	0.0%	0.0%	0.0%	-0.6%	-0.7%
10	Barbados	2.0%	0.9%	1.1%	-0.3%	0.9%	1.5%	3.2%
11	Belgium	4.9%	0.7%	4.2%	-0.4%	0.7%	0.6%	5.1%
12	Belize	1.1%	7.2%	-5.6%	-0.1%	0.4%	3.4%	-2.0%
13	Benin	8.8%	8.6%	0.2%	0.0%	0.0%	3.0%	3.2%
14	Bolivia (Plurinational State of)	0.5%	5.0%	-4.3%	0.0%	0.1%	-1.5%	-5.7%
15	Botswana	3.8%	5.9%	-2.0%	0.0%	0.0%	-1.0%	-3.1%
16	Brazil	1.2%	4.0%	-2.6%	-0.1%	0.2%	0.2%	-2.4%
17	Bulgaria	-2.7%	-1.6%	-1.1%	0.0%	0.1%	-2.7%	-3.8%
18	Burundi	5.3%	4.8%	0.5%	0.0%	0.0%	-0.8%	-0.3%
19	Cambodia	0.5%	7.9%	-6.8%	0.0%	0.1%	1.3%	-5.4%
20	Cameroon	5.9%	7.2%	-1.2%	0.0%	0.0%	3.4%	2.1%
21	Canada	2.2%	2.6%	-0.4%	0.0%	-1.5%	1.5%	-0.3%

(Continued)

Table A3.46 (Continued)

	Country/year	Average growth rate in percentage from 1995–2000						
		Growth IW	Growth population	Growth IW per capita (unadjusted)	Growth of carbon damages	Growth of oil capital gains	Growth of TFP	Growth IW per capita (adjusted)
22	Central African Republic	4.3%	6.1%	-1.7%	0.0%	0.0%	1.9%	0.2%
23	Chile	4.7%	3.7%	1.0%	-0.2%	0.7%	-1.8%	-0.3%
24	China	4.9%	2.7%	2.1%	0.0%	0.1%	-0.6%	1.6%
25	Colombia	2.8%	4.2%	-1.4%	-0.1%	0.0%	-1.1%	-2.6%
26	Congo	4.8%	6.8%	-1.9%	0.0%	-0.3%	1.0%	-1.2%
27	Costa Rica	4.2%	6.1%	-1.8%	-0.2%	0.6%	0.7%	-0.6%
28	Côte d'Ivoire	6.7%	7.9%	-1.1%	0.0%	0.0%	1.4%	0.3%
29	Croatia	1.0%	-1.9%	3.0%	-0.1%	0.5%	0.5%	3.9%
30	Cuba	2.0%	1.2%	0.8%	-0.1%	0.9%	5.5%	7.0%
31	Cyprus	8.0%	5.3%	2.6%	-0.4%	1.3%	1.5%	5.0%
32	Czech Republic	2.9%	-0.2%	3.1%	-0.1%	0.4%	-0.2%	3.2%
33	Democratic Republic of the Congo	-0.4%	8.3%	-8.0%	0.0%	0.0%	-7.1%	-15.1%
34	Denmark	4.0%	1.0%	3.0%	-0.4%	0.2%	0.2%	3.0%
35	Dominican Republic	7.6%	4.5%	3.0%	-0.2%	0.8%	-0.1%	3.5%
36	Ecuador	1.2%	5.4%	-4.0%	-0.1%	-1.8%	0.1%	-5.8%
37	Egypt	5.0%	4.9%	0.1%	0.0%	0.0%	1.1%	1.2%
38	El Salvador	5.1%	2.6%	2.5%	-0.1%	0.5%	-0.5%	2.3%
39	Estonia	-2.1%	-2.9%	0.8%	0.0%	0.4%	4.4%	5.6%
40	Fiji	3.4%	2.7%	0.6%	-0.1%	0.6%	0.4%	1.6%
41	Finland	3.1%	0.9%	2.1%	-0.3%	0.4%	3.1%	5.3%
42	France	4.8%	1.0%	3.7%	-0.4%	0.5%	1.3%	5.0%
43	Gabon	-0.1%	6.6%	-6.3%	0.0%	-0.3%	-3.6%	-10.2%

44	Gambia	4.7%	7.6%	-2.7%	-0.1%	0.3%	-0.3%	-2.8%
45	Germany	3.6%	0.9%	2.7%	-0.3%	0.4%	0.0%	2.8%
46	Ghana	4.9%	6.5%	-1.5%	0.0%	0.0%	3.0%	1.5%
47	Greece	3.3%	1.5%	1.9%	-0.3%	0.6%	1.6%	3.7%
48	Guatemala	5.6%	6.3%	-0.7%	0.0%	0.1%	0.8%	0.2%
49	Guyana	0.1%	0.8%	-0.6%	0.0%	0.1%	1.7%	1.1%
50	Haiti	5.8%	4.8%	1.0%	0.0%	0.0%	-1.5%	-0.5%
51	Honduras	-1.0%	6.2%	-6.8%	-0.1%	0.4%	-0.2%	-6.7%
52	Hungary	2.3%	-0.4%	2.7%	-0.1%	0.3%	1.1%	4.1%
53	Iceland	1.3%	2.5%	-1.2%	-0.2%	0.2%	3.3%	2.2%
54	India	4.1%	4.9%	-0.8%	0.0%	0.0%	1.1%	0.4%
55	Indonesia	3.1%	3.9%	-0.8%	-0.1%	0.1%	-4.6%	-5.4%
56	Iran (Islamic Republic of)	0.7%	4.1%	-3.2%	0.0%	-2.9%	2.0%	-4.1%
57	Iraq	1.6%	7.8%	-5.8%	0.0%	-5.8%	28.0%	16.4%
58	Ireland	6.5%	2.0%	4.4%	-0.5%	0.5%	6.5%	10.9%
59	Israel	11.2%	7.8%	3.2%	0.1%	1.1%	0.8%	5.1%
60	Italy	4.0%	0.1%	3.9%	-0.4%	0.5%	0.8%	4.8%
61	Jamaica	3.8%	2.0%	1.7%	-0.1%	1.3%	-1.8%	1.1%
62	Japan	5.4%	0.7%	4.7%	-0.1%	0.5%	-0.9%	4.2%
63	Jordan	11.8%	9.2%	2.4%	-0.2%	2.1%	0.5%	4.8%
64	Kazakhstan	0.7%	-2.3%	3.1%	0.0%	-1.5%	4.0%	5.5%
65	Kenya	6.5%	7.3%	-0.8%	0.0%	0.0%	-0.5%	-1.2%
66	Kuwait	-1.2%	-1.6%	0.4%	0.0%	-5.5%	0.1%	-5.1%
67	Kyrgyzstan	4.1%	2.8%	1.3%	0.0%	0.2%	6.1%	7.5%
68	Lao People's Democratic Republic	2.8%	5.9%	-2.9%	0.0%	0.0%	-1.8%	-4.7%
69	Latvia	-0.1%	-2.9%	2.9%	0.0%	0.5%	3.3%	6.6%

(*Continued*)

Table A3.46 (Continued)

| Country/year | Average growth rate in percentage from 1995–2000 | | | | | | |
	Growth IW	Growth population	Growth IW per capita (unadjusted)	Growth of carbon damages	Growth of oil capital gains	Growth of TFP	Growth IW per capita (adjusted)
70	Lesotho	0.8%	3.8%	-2.9%	0.0%	0.0%	-1.1%	-4.0%
71	Liberia	6.5%	8.3%	-1.6%	0.0%	0.0%	37.2%	35.5%
72	Lithuania	1.2%	-1.4%	2.6%	0.0%	0.5%	3.9%	7.0%
73	Luxembourg	8.4%	3.4%	4.8%	-0.6%	0.9%	2.4%	7.5%
74	Malawi	3.5%	4.4%	-0.9%	0.0%	0.0%	3.9%	3.1%
75	Malaysia	5.4%	6.5%	-1.0%	-0.2%	0.1%	-0.6%	-1.8%
76	Maldives	8.0%	7.0%	0.9%	-0.2%	0.5%	0.7%	1.9%
77	Mali	6.7%	6.8%	-0.1%	0.0%	0.0%	1.4%	1.3%
78	Malta	8.4%	1.9%	6.4%	-0.5%	1.8%	0.3%	8.0%
79	Mauritania	6.8%	7.6%	-0.7%	0.0%	0.0%	4.5%	3.8%
80	Mauritius	7.3%	2.9%	4.3%	-0.2%	1.1%	0.0%	5.2%
81	Mexico	5.9%	4.7%	1.2%	-0.2%	0.7%	2.1%	3.7%
82	Mongolia	1.4%	2.4%	-0.9%	0.0%	0.1%	0.8%	-0.1%
83	Morocco	4.3%	3.8%	0.5%	0.0%	0.1%	0.5%	1.1%
84	Mozambique	8.8%	8.1%	0.7%	0.0%	0.0%	5.8%	6.5%
85	Myanmar	3.8%	3.2%	0.6%	0.0%	0.0%	2.0%	2.6%
86	Namibia	5.5%	7.6%	-1.9%	-0.1%	0.2%	1.0%	-0.9%
87	Nepal	6.1%	6.1%	0.0%	0.0%	0.0%	1.4%	1.4%
88	Netherlands	5.0%	1.6%	3.4%	-0.4%	0.6%	1.9%	5.4%
89	New Zealand	1.1%	3.7%	-2.5%	0.0%	0.1%	0.8%	-1.6%
90	Nicaragua	4.9%	4.9%	-0.1%	-0.1%	0.2%	3.2%	3.3%
91	Niger	8.6%	9.1%	-0.5%	0.0%	0.0%	4.0%	3.5%
92	Nigeria	6.2%	6.5%	-0.3%	0.0%	-0.2%	3.8%	3.3%

93	Norway	0.9%	1.4%	-0.6%	-0.3%	-1.1%	2.0%	0.1%
94	Pakistan	1.4%	6.5%	-4.8%	-0.1%	0.3%	0.3%	-4.3%
95	Panama	4.5%	5.2%	-0.6%	-0.2%	1.8%	-0.1%	0.8%
96	Papua New Guinea	6.5%	6.6%	-0.1%	0.0%	0.0%	-1.8%	-1.9%
97	Paraguay	2.5%	5.9%	-3.2%	-0.1%	0.3%	-2.3%	-5.2%
98	Peru	0.9%	4.4%	-3.4%	-0.1%	0.1%	0.6%	-2.7%
99	Philippines	7.5%	5.9%	1.5%	-0.1%	0.5%	0.1%	1.9%
100	Poland	2.4%	0.1%	2.3%	-0.1%	0.3%	0.4%	3.0%
101	Portugal	6.9%	0.8%	6.1%	-0.4%	0.8%	1.3%	7.8%
102	Qatar	-0.1%	5.6%	-5.4%	-0.1%	-5.9%	7.3%	-4.2%
103	Republic of Korea	13.8%	2.3%	11.2%	-0.5%	1.8%	0.5%	13.0%
104	Republic of Moldova	0.6%	-0.4%	1.0%	0.0%	0.3%	0.1%	1.4%
105	Romania	0.6%	-0.8%	1.5%	0.0%	0.3%	-1.1%	0.6%
106	Russian Federation	1.6%	-0.3%	1.9%	0.0%	-0.3%	3.3%	4.9%
107	Rwanda	4.9%	2.5%	2.3%	0.0%	0.0%	8.5%	10.8%
108	Saudi Arabia	2.0%	5.9%	-4.6%	-0.1%	-4.9%	-0.7%	-10.3%
109	Senegal	6.3%	7.0%	-0.7%	0.0%	0.0%	1.9%	1.3%
110	Serbia	0.0%	-0.2%	0.2%	0.0%	0.0%	1.2%	1.3%
111	Sierra Leone	-2.5%	0.8%	-3.3%	0.0%	0.0%	-8.8%	-12.1%
112	Singapore	16.8%	7.2%	9.0%	0.1%	5.2%	6.0%	20.2%
113	Slovakia	3.0%	0.4%	2.6%	-0.1%	0.4%	1.5%	4.4%
114	Slovenia	3.5%	-0.1%	3.7%	-0.1%	0.6%	1.3%	5.5%
115	South Africa	3.8%	5.7%	-1.8%	-0.1%	0.2%	1.3%	-0.4%
116	Spain	6.5%	0.9%	5.5%	-0.4%	0.6%	2.1%	7.8%
117	Sri Lanka	4.8%	2.2%	2.5%	-0.1%	0.3%	1.6%	4.3%
118	Sudan (former)	8.7%	8.8%	-0.2%	0.0%	-0.1%	-2.0%	-2.3%
119	Swaziland	9.2%	5.4%	3.6%	-0.3%	0.3%	0.5%	4.1%

(*Continued*)

Table A3.46 (Continued)

| | Country/year | Average growth rate in percentage from 1995–2000 | | | | | | |
		Growth IW	Growth population	Growth IW per capita (unadjusted)	Growth of carbon damages	Growth of oil capital gains	Growth of TFP	Growth IW per capita (adjusted)
120	Sweden	3.5%	0.9%	2.6%	-0.4%	0.4%	2.1%	4.7%
121	Switzerland	8.4%	1.7%	6.5%	-0.4%	0.3%	0.5%	6.9%
122	Syrian Arab Republic	6.0%	7.1%	-0.9%	-0.1%	1.1%	1.1%	1.2%
123	Tajikistan	5.4%	4.0%	1.4%	0.0%	0.2%	2.3%	3.9%
124	Thailand	6.9%	2.6%	4.2%	-0.1%	0.8%	-2.8%	2.1%
125	Togo	6.9%	6.5%	0.3%	0.0%	0.0%	3.0%	3.4%
126	Trinidad and Tobago	-0.9%	0.9%	-1.9%	-0.1%	-0.6%	7.2%	4.6%
127	Tunisia	6.4%	4.0%	2.3%	-0.1%	0.3%	2.7%	5.1%
128	Turkey	6.7%	4.0%	2.5%	-0.3%	0.6%	-0.3%	2.6%
129	Uganda	8.1%	8.1%	0.0%	0.0%	0.0%	2.4%	2.3%
130	Ukraine	-1.8%	-1.3%	-0.5%	0.0%	0.0%	0.0%	-0.4%
131	United Arab Emirates	6.4%	13.9%	-6.6%	-0.1%	-4.0%	3.9%	-6.8%
132	United Kingdom	4.8%	0.7%	4.1%	-0.5%	0.3%	0.3%	4.2%
133	United Republic of Tanzania	7.0%	7.5%	-0.5%	0.0%	0.0%	1.3%	0.9%
134	United States of America	5.5%	3.1%	2.4%	-0.1%	0.6%	0.6%	3.4%
135	Uruguay	2.9%	1.7%	1.2%	-0.1%	0.3%	-0.8%	0.6%
136	Venezuela (Bolivarian Republic of)	-0.1%	5.4%	-5.2%	0.0%	-6.0%	0.0%	-11.2%
137	Viet Nam	4.9%	4.1%	0.8%	-0.1%	-0.3%	-4.2%	-3.8%
138	Yemen	9.5%	10.4%	-0.9%	0.0%	-0.1%	4.0%	3.0%
139	Zambia	6.3%	6.8%	-0.5%	0.0%	0.0%	3.6%	3.1%
140	Zimbabwe	0.5%	4.5%	-3.8%	0.0%	0.0%	-0.5%	-4.3%

Table A3.47 IWI adjusted (Average growth rate in percentage from 2000–2005)

Country/year	Average growth rate in percentage from 2000–2005						
	Growth IW	Growth population	Growth IW per capita (unadjusted)	Growth of carbon damages	Growth of oil capital gains	Growth of TFP	Growth IW per capita (adjusted)
1 Afghanistan	18.8%	19.2%	-0.4%	-0.1%	0.0%	15.3%	14.8%
2 Albania	1.4%	-2.2%	3.6%	-0.1%	0.1%	1.3%	5.0%
3 Algeria	4.4%	6.4%	-2.0%	-0.1%	-1.6%	3.3%	-0.4%
4 Argentina	4.2%	4.6%	-0.3%	-0.2%	0.4%	1.5%	1.4%
5 Armenia	-2.1%	-4.0%	1.9%	-0.1%	0.5%	9.8%	12.3%
6 Australia	5.2%	4.6%	0.6%	0.0%	0.2%	-0.3%	0.5%
7 Austria	7.1%	1.7%	5.3%	-0.4%	0.3%	0.3%	5.5%
8 Bahrain	13.1%	15.0%	-1.6%	-0.4%	0.1%	0.1%	-1.7%
9 Bangladesh	7.7%	7.8%	-0.1%	0.0%	0.0%	-0.9%	-0.9%
10 Barbados	3.9%	1.3%	2.6%	-0.3%	0.8%	-0.6%	2.4%
11 Belgium	7.4%	1.3%	6.0%	-0.4%	0.7%	-0.5%	5.7%
12 Belize	1.8%	10.9%	-8.2%	-0.1%	0.7%	3.1%	-4.5%
13 Benin	13.2%	13.1%	0.1%	0.0%	0.0%	1.7%	1.8%
14 Bolivia (Plurinational State of)	0.7%	7.4%	-6.2%	0.0%	0.1%	0.9%	-5.2%
15 Botswana	6.7%	7.8%	-1.1%	0.0%	0.0%	-2.2%	-3.3%
16 Brazil	1.9%	5.8%	-3.7%	-0.1%	0.1%	1.5%	-2.2%
17 Bulgaria	-3.4%	-2.9%	-0.5%	0.0%	0.1%	0.9%	0.5%
18 Burundi	9.6%	9.0%	0.5%	0.0%	0.0%	-0.1%	0.4%
19 Cambodia	0.5%	10.3%	-8.9%	0.0%	0.1%	0.7%	-8.1%
20 Cameroon	9.3%	10.7%	-1.3%	0.0%	0.0%	1.1%	-0.2%
21 Canada	3.7%	3.8%	-0.1%	0.0%	-2.0%	-0.3%	-2.4%
22 Central African Republic	6.0%	8.4%	-2.2%	0.0%	0.0%	-0.5%	-2.7%

(Continued)

Table A3.47 (Continued)

Country/year		Average growth rate in percentage from 2000–2005						
		Growth IW	Growth population	Growth IW per capita (unadjusted)	Growth of carbon damages	Growth of oil capital gains	Growth of TFP	Growth IW per capita (adjusted)
23	Chile	7.4%	5.2%	2.1%	-0.2%	0.6%	-0.3%	2.1%
24	China	7.6%	3.5%	3.9%	0.0%	0.1%	0.1%	4.2%
25	Colombia	3.8%	6.0%	-2.1%	-0.1%	-0.1%	2.0%	-0.3%
26	Congo	8.2%	10.1%	-1.7%	0.0%	-0.3%	2.5%	0.5%
27	Costa Rica	7.1%	8.2%	-1.0%	-0.2%	0.7%	0.0%	-0.6%
28	Côte d'Ivoire	9.3%	10.5%	-1.0%	0.0%	0.0%	2.7%	1.6%
29	Croatia	3.3%	-1.8%	5.2%	-0.1%	0.4%	0.4%	5.9%
30	Cuba	2.8%	1.6%	1.2%	-0.1%	0.8%	5.6%	7.5%
31	Cyprus	11.8%	7.7%	3.7%	-0.4%	1.2%	1.0%	5.6%
32	Czech Republic	4.4%	-0.3%	4.7%	-0.1%	0.3%	1.6%	6.5%
33	Democratic Republic of the Congo	-0.6%	12.5%	-11.7%	0.0%	0.0%	5.0%	-6.7%
34	Denmark	6.3%	1.3%	4.9%	-0.4%	0.1%	-1.4%	3.2%
35	Dominican Republic	11.3%	6.5%	4.5%	-0.2%	0.9%	-1.0%	4.2%
36	Ecuador	1.9%	7.7%	-5.3%	-0.1%	-2.2%	2.8%	-4.8%
37	Egypt	8.0%	7.4%	0.6%	0.0%	0.0%	0.3%	0.8%
38	El Salvador	7.3%	3.2%	4.0%	-0.1%	0.5%	-0.7%	3.6%
39	Estonia	2.1%	-3.6%	5.9%	0.0%	0.3%	1.7%	7.8%
40	Fiji	4.1%	3.1%	1.0%	-0.2%	0.9%	0.0%	1.8%
41	Finland	5.0%	1.3%	3.7%	-0.3%	0.3%	0.3%	4.0%
42	France	7.5%	1.9%	5.5%	-0.5%	0.4%	0.0%	5.4%
43	Gabon	-0.1%	9.7%	-8.9%	0.0%	-0.3%	-2.6%	-11.8%
44	Gambia	9.1%	12.0%	-2.5%	-0.1%	0.3%	-5.1%	-7.4%
45	Germany	4.7%	0.9%	3.7%	-0.3%	0.3%	-0.8%	2.8%

46	Ghana	8.0%	10.0%	-1.8%	0.0%	0.1%	2.5%	0.7%
47	Greece	5.8%	1.9%	3.9%	-0.3%	0.5%	1.0%	5.1%
48	Guatemala	8.2%	9.5%	-1.2%	0.0%	0.1%	0.3%	-0.9%
49	Guyana	0.1%	0.8%	-0.7%	0.0%	0.1%	0.2%	-0.4%
50	Haiti	8.4%	6.9%	1.5%	0.0%	0.0%	-4.3%	-2.8%
51	Honduras	-0.6%	8.8%	-8.7%	-0.1%	0.5%	2.0%	-6.3%
52	Hungary	3.9%	-0.7%	4.7%	-0.1%	0.3%	1.4%	6.3%
53	Iceland	2.6%	3.9%	-1.2%	-0.2%	0.2%	1.6%	0.4%
54	India	6.2%	7.1%	-0.8%	0.0%	0.0%	1.7%	0.9%
55	Indonesia	4.8%	5.7%	-0.9%	-0.1%	0.2%	1.0%	0.2%
56	Iran (Islamic Republic of)	1.4%	5.7%	-4.0%	0.0%	-3.7%	2.4%	-5.4%
57	Iraq	2.6%	11.5%	-8.0%	0.0%	-7.4%	1.2%	-14.3%
58	Ireland	13.1%	4.3%	8.4%	-0.6%	0.6%	1.5%	9.9%
59	Israel	14.7%	10.4%	3.9%	0.1%	1.0%	-0.6%	4.3%
60	Italy	6.5%	0.5%	5.9%	-0.4%	0.4%	-0.4%	5.5%
61	Jamaica	5.3%	2.6%	2.6%	-0.1%	1.2%	-0.4%	3.3%
62	Japan	6.8%	0.9%	5.9%	-0.1%	0.4%	0.2%	6.4%
63	Jordan	16.4%	12.3%	3.7%	-0.2%	2.0%	3.5%	9.0%
64	Kazakhstan	0.8%	-1.9%	2.7%	0.0%	-2.0%	10.1%	10.8%
65	Kenya	10.7%	10.8%	-0.1%	0.0%	0.0%	1.0%	0.9%
66	Kuwait	-0.6%	2.4%	-2.9%	0.0%	-6.8%	4.6%	-5.2%
67	Kyrgyzstan	6.1%	4.1%	1.9%	0.0%	0.1%	3.6%	5.6%
68	Lao People's Democratic Republic	3.9%	7.8%	-3.6%	0.0%	0.0%	-1.2%	-4.8%
69	Latvia	1.4%	-4.2%	5.9%	0.0%	0.3%	2.9%	9.1%
70	Lesotho	-0.4%	4.8%	-5.0%	0.0%	0.0%	1.6%	-3.3%
71	Liberia	9.7%	11.7%	-1.7%	0.0%	0.0%	6.4%	4.7%
72	Lithuania	1.8%	-2.6%	4.6%	0.0%	0.4%	5.0%	9.9%

(Continued)

Table A3.47 (Continued)

	Country/year	Average growth rate in percentage from 2000–2005							
		Growth IW	Growth population	Growth IW per capita (unadjusted)	Growth of carbon damages	Growth of oil capital gains	Growth of TFP	Growth IW per capita (adjusted)
73	Luxembourg	13.2%	5.1%	7.7%	-0.7%	1.0%	-0.4%	7.7%
74	Malawi	7.4%	7.9%	-0.4%	0.0%	0.0%	2.9%	2.5%
75	Malaysia	7.1%	9.1%	-1.9%	-0.2%	-0.1%	1.5%	-0.7%
76	Maldives	11.9%	10.2%	1.6%	-0.2%	1.0%	-1.6%	0.8%
77	Mali	11.0%	11.0%	0.0%	0.0%	0.0%	3.7%	3.7%
78	Malta	12.7%	3.3%	9.0%	-0.5%	1.5%	-2.8%	7.3%
79	Mauritania	10.3%	11.7%	-1.3%	0.0%	0.0%	0.4%	-0.9%
80	Mauritius	10.6%	3.8%	6.5%	-0.2%	1.2%	-1.3%	6.2%
81	Mexico	8.7%	6.4%	2.2%	-0.2%	0.6%	-1.3%	1.3%
82	Mongolia	1.1%	3.7%	-2.5%	0.0%	0.1%	4.4%	1.9%
83	Morocco	6.3%	5.1%	1.1%	0.0%	0.1%	0.7%	2.0%
84	Mozambique	11.7%	12.1%	-0.4%	0.0%	0.0%	2.1%	1.8%
85	Myanmar	5.4%	4.4%	0.9%	0.0%	0.0%	1.9%	2.8%
86	Namibia	7.7%	9.4%	-1.6%	-0.1%	0.2%	0.4%	-1.0%
87	Nepal	8.2%	8.0%	0.2%	0.0%	0.0%	0.3%	0.5%
88	Netherlands	7.5%	2.2%	5.2%	-0.4%	0.6%	-0.9%	4.3%
89	New Zealand	1.3%	5.6%	-4.0%	0.0%	0.1%	1.4%	-2.5%
90	Nicaragua	6.7%	6.7%	-0.1%	-0.1%	0.2%	1.6%	1.7%
91	Niger	13.7%	14.3%	-0.5%	0.0%	0.0%	3.5%	3.0%
92	Nigeria	9.8%	9.9%	-0.1%	0.0%	-0.2%	10.9%	10.6%
93	Norway	1.5%	2.2%	-0.7%	-0.3%	-1.0%	0.4%	-1.6%
94	Pakistan	2.2%	9.3%	-6.5%	-0.1%	0.2%	2.9%	-3.4%

95	Panama	6.6%	7.7%	-1.0%	-0.2%	1.5%	1.7%	2.0%
96	Papua New Guinea	9.8%	10.0%	-0.2%	0.0%	0.0%	-1.4%	-1.6%
97	Paraguay	3.1%	8.3%	-4.8%	-0.1%	0.3%	4.7%	0.1%
98	Peru	1.2%	6.1%	-4.6%	-0.1%	0.1%	3.0%	-1.6%
99	Philippines	11.0%	8.6%	2.2%	-0.1%	0.4%	1.7%	4.2%
100	Poland	3.7%	0.0%	3.7%	-0.1%	0.3%	-0.1%	3.8%
101	Portugal	10.4%	1.3%	9.0%	-0.5%	0.8%	-1.1%	8.2%
102	Qatar	1.2%	15.1%	-12.1%	-0.1%	-7.2%	0.3%	-19.1%
103	Republic of Korea	19.4%	2.9%	16.0%	-0.5%	1.5%	2.5%	19.5%
104	Republic of Moldova	0.5%	-0.7%	1.2%	0.0%	0.2%	9.2%	10.6%
105	Romania	0.9%	-2.1%	3.1%	0.0%	0.2%	3.7%	7.0%
106	Russian Federation	1.1%	-0.8%	1.9%	0.0%	-0.4%	6.6%	8.1%
107	Rwanda	9.1%	5.5%	3.4%	0.0%	0.0%	4.1%	7.5%
108	Saudi Arabia	2.3%	10.9%	-7.7%	-0.1%	-6.0%	0.0%	-13.8%
109	Senegal	9.9%	10.7%	-0.7%	0.0%	0.0%	1.4%	0.7%
110	Serbia	0.2%	-0.5%	0.7%	0.0%	0.0%	3.9%	4.6%
111	Sierra Leone	3.6%	6.6%	-2.8%	0.0%	0.0%	13.1%	10.2%
112	Singapore	22.1%	8.8%	12.3%	0.1%	5.4%	5.1%	22.9%
113	Slovakia	4.3%	0.3%	4.0%	-0.1%	0.3%	2.9%	7.1%
114	Slovenia	6.5%	0.0%	6.4%	-0.1%	0.5%	0.1%	6.9%
115	South Africa	5.3%	7.6%	-2.1%	-0.1%	0.2%	1.8%	-0.3%
116	Spain	11.3%	3.0%	8.1%	-0.5%	0.6%	0.4%	8.6%
117	Sri Lanka	6.0%	3.2%	2.7%	-0.1%	0.3%	0.6%	3.5%
118	Sudan (former)	12.4%	12.4%	-0.1%	0.0%	-0.1%	-5.4%	-5.6%
119	Swaziland	11.2%	6.4%	4.5%	-0.3%	0.2%	1.6%	6.1%
120	Sweden	5.8%	1.3%	4.4%	-0.4%	0.3%	0.5%	4.8%

(*Continued*)

Table A3.47 (Continued)

Country/year	Average growth rate in percentage from 2000–2005						
	Growth IW	Growth population	Growth IW per capita (unadjusted)	Growth of carbon damages	Growth of oil capital gains	Growth of TFP	Growth IW per capita (adjusted)
121 Switzerland	9.8%	2.6%	7.1%	-0.4%	0.2%	0.5%	7.4%
122 Syrian Arab Republic	9.0%	9.9%	-0.8%	-0.1%	1.0%	1.0%	1.2%
123 Tajikistan	8.0%	6.5%	1.4%	0.0%	0.3%	11.8%	13.5%
124 Thailand	9.1%	3.9%	5.1%	-0.1%	0.7%	3.4%	9.0%
125 Togo	10.5%	10.2%	0.3%	0.0%	0.1%	1.1%	1.4%
126 Trinidad and Tobago	-1.0%	1.5%	-2.5%	-0.1%	-0.7%	6.4%	3.2%
127 Tunisia	9.5%	5.3%	4.0%	-0.1%	0.3%	1.4%	5.4%
128 Turkey	9.6%	5.9%	3.5%	-0.3%	0.5%	1.1%	4.9%
129 Uganda	13.8%	12.7%	1.0%	0.0%	0.0%	2.4%	3.4%
130 Ukraine	-3.0%	-2.4%	-0.6%	0.0%	0.0%	8.7%	8.0%
131 United Arab Emirates	10.5%	25.4%	-11.9%	-0.1%	-5.0%	2.4%	-14.6%
132 United Kingdom	7.6%	1.3%	6.1%	-0.5%	0.2%	-0.1%	5.7%
133 United Republic of Tanzania	11.2%	11.3%	-0.1%	0.0%	0.0%	1.9%	1.8%
134 United States of America	8.7%	4.3%	4.2%	-0.1%	0.5%	-1.1%	3.5%
135 Uruguay	3.5%	1.7%	1.7%	-0.1%	0.3%	-0.5%	1.5%
136 Venezuela (Bolivarian Republic of)	-0.1%	7.7%	-7.3%	0.0%	-7.6%	2.8%	-12.1%
137 Viet Nam	7.3%	5.7%	1.6%	-0.1%	-0.3%	-2.6%	-1.4%
138 Yemen	13.7%	14.4%	-0.6%	0.0%	-0.1%	2.1%	1.4%
139 Zambia	10.5%	10.3%	0.2%	0.0%	0.0%	3.2%	3.4%
140 Zimbabwe	-0.2%	5.5%	-5.4%	0.0%	0.0%	-5.1%	-10.4%

Table A3.48 IWI adjusted (Average growth rate in percentage from 2005–2010)

	Country/year	Average growth rate in percentage from 2005–2010						
		Growth IW	Growth population	Growth IW per capita (unadjusted)	Growth of carbon damages	Growth of oil capital gains	Growth of TFP	Growth IW per capita (adjusted)
1	Afghanistan	24.3%	23.4%	0.7%	-0.2%	0.1%	3.6%	4.2%
2	Albania	3.3%	-3.0%	6.4%	-0.3%	0.0%	2.1%	8.2%
3	Algeria	6.8%	8.6%	-1.7%	-0.3%	-1.8%	1.3%	-2.5%
4	Argentina	6.5%	5.9%	0.6%	-0.5%	0.3%	2.2%	2.6%
5	Armenia	-0.1%	-4.4%	4.5%	-0.2%	0.5%	2.4%	7.1%
6	Australia	7.8%	6.6%	1.2%	0.1%	0.1%	0.3%	1.8%
7	Austria	8.9%	2.2%	6.6%	-1.2%	0.2%	0.7%	6.4%
8	Bahrain	25.1%	26.3%	-0.9%	-1.3%	0.3%	0.7%	-1.3%
9	Bangladesh	9.7%	9.4%	0.3%	0.0%	0.0%	-0.4%	-0.1%
10	Barbados	5.1%	1.8%	3.3%	-1.0%	0.5%	0.1%	3.0%
11	Belgium	10.2%	2.3%	7.8%	-1.3%	0.5%	-0.3%	6.7%
12	Belize	2.4%	14.4%	-10.5%	-0.2%	0.4%	2.7%	-7.6%
13	Benin	17.8%	17.4%	0.3%	0.0%	0.0%	2.7%	3.0%
14	Bolivia (Plurinational State of)	1.0%	9.7%	-7.9%	-0.1%	0.1%	0.4%	-7.5%
15	Botswana	10.9%	10.4%	0.5%	-0.2%	0.0%	-1.5%	-1.1%
16	Brazil	2.9%	7.2%	-4.0%	-0.4%	0.0%	1.1%	-3.3%
17	Bulgaria	-3.6%	-4.0%	0.5%	0.0%	0.1%	-1.1%	-0.6%
18	Burundi	14.5%	13.9%	0.5%	0.0%	0.0%	-0.4%	0.0%
19	Cambodia	1.2%	12.4%	-10.0%	-0.1%	0.1%	1.8%	-8.1%
20	Cameroon	13.2%	14.3%	-0.9%	-0.1%	0.0%	0.9%	-0.1%
21	Canada	5.4%	5.2%	0.2%	0.1%	-2.7%	0.2%	-2.2%
22	Central African Republic	8.7%	10.9%	-2.0%	0.0%	0.0%	0.7%	-1.3%

(Continued)

Table A3.48 (Continued)

	Country/year	Average growth rate in percentage from 2005–2010							
		Growth IW	Growth population	Growth IW per capita (unadjusted)	Growth of carbon damages	Growth of oil capital gains	Growth of TFP	Growth IW per capita (adjusted)
23	Chile	10.7%	6.7%	3.8%	-0.6%	0.5%	0.0%	3.7%
24	China	11.4%	4.2%	6.9%	0.0%	0.1%	1.4%	8.4%
25	Colombia	5.7%	7.6%	-1.7%	-0.3%	-0.2%	0.8%	-1.5%
26	Congo	13.5%	14.2%	-0.7%	-0.1%	-0.3%	0.2%	-0.9%
27	Costa Rica	10.8%	10.1%	0.6%	-0.7%	0.5%	1.0%	1.5%
28	Côte d'Ivoire	12.4%	13.4%	-0.9%	-0.1%	0.0%	2.0%	1.1%
29	Croatia	5.7%	-2.0%	7.8%	-0.2%	0.3%	-1.5%	6.5%
30	Cuba	3.7%	1.7%	2.0%	-0.4%	0.4%	2.3%	4.3%
31	Cyprus	16.1%	9.5%	6.0%	-1.2%	1.0%	1.4%	7.1%
32	Czech Republic	7.0%	0.3%	6.6%	-0.2%	0.3%	0.0%	6.7%
33	Democratic Republic of the Congo	-0.6%	17.2%	-15.2%	-0.1%	0.0%	-3.8%	-19.0%
34	Denmark	8.7%	1.9%	6.6%	-1.3%	0.0%	-0.2%	5.1%
35	Dominican Republic	15.6%	8.3%	6.7%	-0.6%	0.7%	0.3%	7.1%
36	Ecuador	3.2%	10.0%	-6.1%	-0.3%	-2.7%	1.3%	-7.8%
37	Egypt	11.6%	9.8%	1.6%	-0.1%	-0.1%	0.9%	2.3%
38	El Salvador	9.2%	3.5%	5.4%	-0.4%	0.4%	0.6%	6.0%
39	Estonia	4.5%	-4.0%	8.9%	-0.1%	0.3%	0.0%	8.9%
40	Fiji	5.9%	4.2%	1.6%	-0.5%	0.8%	0.0%	2.0%
41	Finland	7.9%	1.8%	5.9%	-1.0%	0.2%	0.7%	5.9%
42	France	10.1%	2.7%	7.3%	-1.4%	0.3%	0.5%	6.6%
43	Gabon	-0.1%	12.8%	-11.4%	0.0%	-0.3%	-2.6%	-14.4%
44	Gambia	13.8%	16.6%	-2.4%	-0.4%	0.3%	-3.5%	-6.0%

45	Germany	5.7%	0.7%	5.0%	-1.0%	0.2%	-0.2%	4.0%
46	Ghana	11.4%	13.5%	-1.9%	-0.1%	0.0%	2.6%	0.7%
47	Greece	8.2%	2.2%	5.9%	-1.0%	0.4%	0.9%	6.2%
48	Guatemala	11.1%	12.6%	-1.3%	-0.1%	0.1%	1.1%	-0.2%
49	Guyana	0.2%	1.1%	-0.9%	0.0%	0.1%	2.8%	1.9%
50	Haiti	4.9%	8.9%	-3.7%	0.0%	0.0%	-3.0%	-6.8%
51	Honduras	0.2%	11.2%	-9.9%	-0.4%	0.4%	0.8%	-9.0%
52	Hungary	5.4%	-0.9%	6.3%	-0.2%	0.2%	-0.1%	6.2%
53	Iceland	4.2%	5.7%	-1.4%	-0.6%	0.1%	1.1%	-0.7%
54	India	8.3%	9.0%	-0.7%	0.0%	0.0%	1.3%	0.6%
55	Indonesia	6.7%	7.4%	-0.7%	-0.3%	0.1%	-1.3%	-2.2%
56	Iran (Islamic Republic of)	2.4%	7.2%	-4.5%	-0.1%	-4.7%	2.0%	-7.3%
57	Iraq	3.9%	15.3%	-9.8%	-0.1%	-9.5%	8.6%	-10.8%
58	Ireland	18.8%	6.7%	11.3%	-1.7%	0.4%	3.4%	13.4%
59	Israel	19.4%	13.1%	5.6%	0.2%	0.7%	0.7%	7.2%
60	Italy	8.6%	1.1%	7.4%	-1.3%	0.2%	0.3%	6.6%
61	Jamaica	6.2%	3.0%	3.1%	-0.4%	0.9%	-0.5%	3.0%
62	Japan	7.8%	0.9%	6.8%	-0.2%	0.2%	-0.4%	6.5%
63	Jordan	23.8%	18.0%	4.9%	-0.7%	1.4%	2.1%	7.7%
64	Kazakhstan	2.1%	0.0%	2.1%	-0.1%	-2.5%	1.6%	1.1%
65	Kenya	16.1%	14.5%	1.4%	-0.1%	0.0%	0.2%	1.5%
66	Kuwait	0.7%	10.4%	-8.8%	-0.1%	-8.4%	6.1%	-11.3%
67	Kyrgyzstan	8.6%	5.5%	2.9%	-0.1%	0.2%	-1.1%	1.9%
68	Lao People's Democratic Republic	5.5%	10.2%	-4.2%	-0.1%	0.0%	-2.1%	-6.4%
69	Latvia	3.5%	-5.8%	9.9%	-0.1%	0.3%	-1.5%	8.6%
70	Lesotho	1.1%	5.9%	-4.5%	0.0%	0.0%	-0.7%	-5.3%
71	Liberia	16.4%	17.1%	-0.6%	0.0%	0.0%	8.1%	7.5%
72	Lithuania	2.9%	-4.3%	7.5%	-0.1%	0.3%	-0.1%	7.6%

(Continued)

Table A3.48 (Continued)

Country/year	Average growth rate in percentage from 2005–2010						
	Growth IW	Growth population	Growth IW per capita (unadjusted)	Growth of carbon damages	Growth of oil capital gains	Growth of TFP	Growth IW per capita (adjusted)
73 Luxembourg	18.1%	7.3%	10.0%	-2.1%	0.8%	0.9%	9.6%
74 Malawi	13.4%	11.9%	1.4%	0.0%	0.0%	2.9%	4.3%
75 Malaysia	9.3%	11.5%	-2.0%	-0.7%	-0.3%	0.7%	-2.3%
76 Maldives	17.0%	13.9%	2.7%	-0.7%	0.8%	-0.3%	2.5%
77 Mali	15.5%	15.6%	-0.1%	0.0%	0.0%	2.2%	2.1%
78 Malta	16.6%	4.0%	12.1%	-1.5%	1.5%	-0.9%	11.3%
79 Mauritania	13.7%	15.4%	-1.4%	0.0%	0.0%	3.1%	1.6%
80 Mauritius	14.1%	4.2%	9.5%	-0.7%	0.9%	-0.9%	8.7%
81 Mexico	12.1%	8.5%	3.4%	-0.7%	0.4%	-0.2%	2.8%
82 Mongolia	1.7%	5.6%	-3.6%	0.0%	0.1%	0.3%	-3.4%
83 Morocco	8.3%	6.5%	1.7%	-0.1%	0.1%	0.0%	1.6%
84 Mozambique	15.4%	16.1%	-0.6%	0.0%	0.0%	3.0%	2.3%
85 Myanmar	6.7%	5.3%	1.3%	0.0%	0.0%	2.1%	3.4%
86 Namibia	11.4%	11.6%	-0.1%	-0.2%	0.2%	1.8%	1.6%
87 Nepal	9.9%	9.4%	0.4%	0.0%	0.0%	1.3%	1.7%
88 Netherlands	9.8%	2.7%	6.9%	-1.4%	0.4%	0.5%	6.5%
89 New Zealand	6.3%	6.9%	-0.6%	0.0%	0.1%	1.1%	0.6%
90 Nicaragua	8.4%	8.5%	-0.1%	-0.2%	0.2%	2.2%	2.1%
91 Niger	19.4%	19.8%	-0.3%	0.0%	0.0%	3.4%	3.1%
92 Nigeria	13.7%	13.6%	0.1%	-0.1%	-0.3%	5.4%	5.1%
93 Norway	3.3%	3.6%	-0.3%	-1.0%	-0.9%	1.6%	-0.6%
94 Pakistan	3.5%	12.1%	-7.7%	-0.2%	0.1%	1.3%	-6.5%

95	Panama	10.8%	10.0%	0.7%	-0.6%	1.1%	1.3%	2.4%
96	Papua New Guinea	12.6%	13.3%	-0.6%	0.0%	0.0%	1.0%	0.4%
97	Paraguay	4.3%	10.2%	-5.4%	-0.2%	0.2%	0.8%	-4.5%
98	Peru	2.2%	7.7%	-5.1%	-0.2%	0.0%	2.5%	-2.8%
99	Philippines	14.2%	10.7%	3.1%	-0.3%	0.2%	0.4%	3.4%
100	Poland	5.8%	0.0%	5.8%	-0.2%	0.3%	0.4%	6.3%
101	Portugal	12.8%	1.4%	11.2%	-1.4%	0.5%	0.1%	10.3%
102	Qatar	7.6%	38.7%	-22.4%	-0.4%	-8.5%	3.3%	-28.1%
103	Republic of Korea	24.6%	3.6%	20.2%	-1.6%	1.1%	0.8%	20.5%
104	Republic of Moldova	0.9%	-0.9%	1.8%	0.0%	0.2%	-1.8%	0.1%
105	Romania	2.5%	-3.3%	6.1%	-0.1%	0.1%	0.5%	6.5%
106	Russian Federation	1.2%	-0.9%	2.2%	0.0%	-0.5%	0.3%	2.0%
107	Rwanda	14.1%	9.1%	4.6%	0.0%	0.0%	2.5%	7.1%
108	Saudi Arabia	3.3%	14.5%	-9.8%	-0.2%	-7.4%	-0.2%	-17.5%
109	Senegal	13.9%	14.6%	-0.6%	0.0%	0.0%	0.7%	0.1%
110	Serbia	1.2%	-1.0%	2.2%	0.0%	0.1%	-2.3%	-0.1%
111	Sierra Leone	7.1%	10.1%	-2.7%	0.0%	0.0%	-0.3%	-3.0%
112	Singapore	30.4%	13.6%	14.7%	0.4%	4.8%	5.4%	25.3%
113	Slovakia	6.3%	0.4%	5.9%	-0.2%	0.3%	0.9%	6.8%
114	Slovenia	9.7%	0.6%	9.0%	-0.3%	0.4%	0.0%	9.1%
115	South Africa	8.0%	9.6%	-1.4%	-0.2%	0.2%	1.1%	-0.4%
116	Spain	15.6%	4.6%	10.5%	-1.4%	0.4%	0.7%	10.2%
117	Sri Lanka	7.2%	4.2%	2.9%	-0.3%	0.3%	1.6%	4.4%
118	Sudan (former)	13.6%	15.9%	-2.0%	0.0%	-0.1%	-1.7%	-3.8%
119	Swaziland	13.3%	8.4%	4.5%	-1.0%	0.2%	0.3%	4.0%
120	Sweden	8.5%	2.3%	6.0%	-1.1%	0.2%	0.7%	5.8%
121	Switzerland	12.4%	3.9%	8.1%	-1.2%	0.2%	-1.2%	5.9%
122	Syrian Arab Republic	13.0%	13.6%	-0.5%	-0.2%	0.8%	2.3%	2.4%

(*Continued*)

Table A3.48 (Continued)

| Country/year | Average growth rate in percentage from 2005–2010 | | | | | | |
	Growth IW	Growth population	Growth IW per capita (unadjusted)	Growth of carbon damages	Growth of oil capital gains	Growth of TFP	Growth IW per capita (adjusted)
123 Tajikistan	11.1%	9.4%	1.6%	−0.1%	0.2%	−0.7%	1.0%
124 Thailand	11.3%	4.2%	6.8%	−0.4%	0.6%	−0.2%	6.8%
125 Togo	14.8%	14.0%	0.7%	−0.1%	0.1%	1.9%	2.6%
126 Trinidad and Tobago	−2.3%	2.1%	−4.3%	−0.4%	−0.7%	5.7%	0.2%
127 Tunisia	13.4%	6.6%	6.3%	−0.5%	0.1%	1.8%	7.7%
128 Turkey	13.2%	7.6%	5.3%	−0.8%	0.4%	−0.1%	4.7%
129 Uganda	19.2%	17.5%	1.5%	0.0%	0.0%	3.0%	4.4%
130 Ukraine	−3.2%	−3.0%	−0.2%	0.0%	0.0%	−1.5%	−1.7%
131 United Arab Emirates	16.2%	46.4%	−20.7%	−0.3%	−6.2%	2.9%	−24.2%
132 United Kingdom	10.1%	2.3%	7.6%	−1.7%	0.1%	−0.1%	5.9%
133 United Republic of Tanzania	16.0%	15.7%	0.3%	0.0%	0.0%	0.2%	0.5%
134 United States of America	11.2%	5.5%	5.4%	−0.2%	0.3%	−0.3%	5.2%
135 Uruguay	4.7%	2.1%	2.6%	−0.3%	0.2%	0.1%	2.6%
136 Venezuela (Bolivarian Republic of)	0.2%	9.9%	−8.8%	−0.1%	−9.6%	1.7%	−16.8%
137 Viet Nam	10.4%	7.1%	3.1%	−0.3%	−0.3%	−2.7%	−0.2%
138 Yemen	18.4%	18.5%	−0.1%	0.0%	−0.2%	3.1%	2.8%
139 Zambia	16.0%	14.3%	1.4%	0.0%	0.0%	2.6%	4.1%
140 Zimbabwe	1.9%	7.4%	−5.2%	0.0%	0.0%	−1.8%	−7.0%

Table A3.49 IWI adjusted (Average growth rate in percentage from 2010–2014)

	Country/year	Average growth rate in percentage from 2010–2014							
		Growth IW	Growth population	Growth IW per capita (unadjusted)	Growth of carbon damages	Growth of oil capital gains	Growth of TFP	Growth IW per capita (adjusted)
1	Afghanistan	40.7%	37.9%	2.1%	-0.1%	0.1%	5.0%	7.1%
2	Albania	6.1%	-4.2%	10.7%	-0.2%	-0.3%	-0.6%	9.7%
3	Algeria	12.5%	14.5%	-1.7%	-0.1%	-2.1%	-1.4%	-5.3%
4	Argentina	11.5%	9.5%	1.8%	-0.2%	0.1%	-0.7%	1.0%
5	Armenia	1.1%	-5.3%	6.9%	-0.1%	0.0%	2.2%	9.0%
6	Australia	13.7%	11.2%	2.2%	0.0%	0.0%	-0.8%	1.4%
7	Austria	14.1%	3.6%	10.1%	-0.5%	0.1%	-0.5%	9.1%
8	Bahrain	39.7%	40.0%	-0.3%	-0.6%	-0.3%	0.9%	-0.2%
9	Bangladesh	15.1%	14.5%	0.5%	0.0%	0.0%	0.3%	0.8%
10	Barbados	8.3%	2.9%	5.3%	-0.4%	0.2%	0.1%	5.1%
11	Belgium	16.6%	4.1%	12.0%	-0.6%	0.1%	-1.2%	10.4%
12	Belize	3.8%	23.3%	-15.8%	-0.1%	0.1%	0.8%	-15.0%
13	Benin	29.3%	28.4%	0.6%	0.0%	0.0%	2.2%	2.9%
14	Bolivia (Plurinational State of)	1.8%	15.5%	-11.8%	0.0%	0.0%	0.3%	-11.5%
15	Botswana	18.4%	17.2%	1.1%	-0.1%	0.0%	-0.7%	0.3%
16	Brazil	5.7%	11.1%	-4.9%	-0.2%	-0.2%	-1.9%	-7.1%
17	Bulgaria	-5.4%	-6.1%	0.8%	0.0%	0.0%	-1.9%	-1.2%
18	Burundi	25.5%	24.4%	0.9%	0.0%	0.0%	3.3%	4.2%
19	Cambodia	2.6%	19.4%	-14.1%	0.0%	0.0%	-0.8%	-14.9%
20	Cameroon	20.8%	23.6%	-2.2%	0.0%	0.0%	3.2%	0.9%
21	Canada	6.5%	8.5%	-1.9%	0.0%	-3.9%	-0.1%	-5.9%

(Continued)

Table A3.49 (Continued)

	Country/year	Average growth rate in percentage from 2010–2014						
		Growth IW	Growth population	Growth IW per capita (unadjusted)	Growth of carbon damages	Growth of oil capital gains	Growth of TFP	Growth IW per capita (adjusted)
22	Central African Republic	14.5%	17.8%	-2.8%	0.0%	0.0%	-7.5%	-10.3%
23	Chile	19.1%	10.6%	7.7%	-0.3%	0.2%	-1.5%	6.1%
24	China	20.8%	6.3%	13.6%	0.0%	0.0%	-0.7%	12.9%
25	Colombia	1.5%	11.7%	-9.2%	-0.1%	-0.3%	0.7%	-8.9%
26	Congo	22.1%	23.6%	-1.2%	0.0%	-0.4%	-4.1%	-5.8%
27	Costa Rica	21.9%	15.4%	5.7%	-0.3%	0.2%	-1.3%	4.3%
28	Côte d'Ivoire	20.0%	22.1%	-1.7%	0.0%	0.0%	9.3%	7.6%
29	Croatia	8.3%	-3.9%	12.7%	-0.1%	0.0%	-2.3%	10.4%
30	Cuba	6.0%	2.5%	3.5%	-0.2%	0.1%	1.3%	4.7%
31	Cyprus	23.8%	14.6%	8.0%	-0.5%	0.3%	-3.1%	4.7%
32	Czech Republic	11.2%	0.6%	10.5%	-0.1%	0.1%	-1.3%	9.2%
33	Democratic Republic of the Congo	-0.7%	28.9%	-22.9%	0.0%	0.0%	3.8%	-19.2%
34	Denmark	13.5%	3.2%	10.0%	-0.6%	-0.1%	-1.0%	8.2%
35	Dominican Republic	25.3%	13.1%	10.8%	-0.3%	0.2%	0.9%	11.6%
36	Ecuador	7.3%	15.9%	-7.4%	-0.1%	-3.8%	0.2%	-11.1%
37	Egypt	20.3%	16.7%	3.1%	-0.1%	-0.2%	-0.7%	2.1%
38	El Salvador	14.4%	5.2%	8.8%	-0.2%	0.1%	0.0%	8.8%
39	Estonia	7.9%	-5.7%	14.5%	-0.1%	0.1%	1.5%	16.0%
40	Fiji	10.9%	6.8%	3.9%	-0.2%	0.2%	1.3%	5.1%
41	Finland	11.9%	3.1%	8.5%	-0.4%	0.1%	-1.4%	6.8%
42	France	16.1%	4.4%	11.2%	-0.6%	0.1%	-0.9%	9.7%

43	Gabon	0.1%	21.0%	-17.3%	0.0%	-0.4%	3.1%	-14.7%
44	Gambia	23.8%	28.1%	-3.3%	-0.2%	0.1%	-1.6%	-5.0%
45	Germany	8.9%	0.6%	8.2%	-0.5%	0.1%	0.2%	7.9%
46	Ghana	19.8%	22.3%	-2.1%	0.0%	0.0%	0.2%	-1.8%
47	Greece	10.3%	2.2%	7.9%	-0.4%	0.1%	-4.0%	3.6%
48	Guatemala	18.3%	20.5%	-1.8%	-0.1%	0.0%	1.4%	-0.5%
49	Guyana	5.2%	2.0%	3.1%	0.0%	0.0%	2.6%	5.7%
50	Haiti	15.9%	14.2%	1.5%	0.0%	0.0%	1.7%	3.1%
51	Honduras	0.7%	17.5%	-14.3%	-0.2%	0.1%	0.5%	-13.9%
52	Hungary	8.2%	-1.7%	10.1%	-0.1%	0.1%	0.2%	10.3%
53	Iceland	5.9%	8.7%	-2.5%	-0.3%	0.0%	1.9%	-0.9%
54	India	13.3%	14.2%	-0.8%	0.0%	0.0%	0.4%	-0.4%
55	Indonesia	11.4%	11.9%	-0.5%	-0.1%	-0.1%	0.2%	-0.5%
56	Iran (Islamic Republic of)	3.6%	11.6%	-7.2%	-0.1%	-6.6%	-2.7%	-16.5%
57	Iraq	7.4%	26.4%	-15.0%	0.0%	-13.1%	-2.4%	-30.6%
58	Ireland	28.7%	9.5%	17.5%	-0.8%	0.1%	0.3%	17.1%
59	Israel	32.3%	20.8%	9.5%	0.1%	0.2%	-0.4%	9.5%
60	Italy	12.7%	2.3%	10.1%	-0.6%	0.0%	-1.7%	7.9%
61	Jamaica	9.1%	4.4%	4.5%	-0.2%	0.2%	0.0%	4.5%
62	Japan	11.2%	1.0%	10.1%	-0.1%	0.1%	0.2%	10.3%
63	Jordan	40.7%	30.2%	8.0%	-0.3%	0.6%	-0.7%	7.6%
64	Kazakhstan	4.2%	1.9%	2.3%	-0.1%	-3.3%	1.6%	0.6%
65	Kenya	27.1%	24.1%	2.3%	0.0%	0.0%	-0.5%	1.8%
66	Kuwait	2.3%	22.2%	-16.2%	-0.1%	-11.4%	-2.1%	-29.7%
67	Kyrgyzstan	14.8%	9.9%	4.4%	0.0%	0.1%	0.8%	5.3%
68	Lao People's Democratic Republic	10.8%	16.3%	-4.8%	0.0%	0.0%	-1.5%	-6.2%
69	Latvia	5.4%	-9.2%	16.1%	-0.1%	0.1%	1.8%	17.9%

(Continued)

Table A3.49 (Continued)

	Country/year	Average growth rate in percentage from 2010–2014						
		Growth IW	Growth population	Growth IW per capita (unadjusted)	Growth of carbon damages	Growth of oil capital gains	Growth of TFP	Growth IW per capita (adjusted)
70	Lesotho	2.2%	9.7%	-6.9%	0.0%	0.0%	0.6%	-6.3%
71	Liberia	26.0%	27.9%	-1.5%	0.0%	0.0%	2.4%	0.9%
72	Lithuania	4.4%	-7.4%	12.8%	-0.1%	0.1%	2.4%	15.2%
73	Luxembourg	30.5%	13.4%	15.2%	-0.9%	0.2%	-1.1%	13.4%
74	Malawi	24.9%	21.1%	3.2%	0.0%	0.0%	2.7%	5.9%
75	Malaysia	16.7%	18.0%	-1.0%	-0.3%	-0.8%	0.8%	-1.4%
76	Maldives	28.6%	22.5%	5.0%	-0.3%	0.3%	2.2%	7.1%
77	Mali	26.1%	26.3%	-0.1%	0.0%	0.0%	3.1%	3.0%
78	Malta	26.4%	6.5%	18.7%	-0.7%	0.8%	0.1%	18.9%
79	Mauritania	22.6%	25.2%	-2.0%	0.0%	0.0%	-3.4%	-5.5%
80	Mauritius	22.4%	6.0%	15.5%	-0.3%	0.3%	0.1%	15.5%
81	Mexico	20.2%	13.6%	5.9%	-0.3%	0.0%	-0.1%	5.4%
82	Mongolia	4.4%	10.0%	-5.1%	0.0%	0.0%	4.2%	-0.9%
83	Morocco	13.5%	10.8%	2.4%	0.0%	0.0%	-0.3%	2.2%
84	Mozambique	25.5%	26.7%	-1.0%	0.0%	0.0%	-6.2%	-7.1%
85	Myanmar	10.7%	8.4%	2.1%	0.0%	0.0%	-5.0%	-2.8%
86	Namibia	19.4%	19.3%	0.1%	-0.1%	0.1%	-2.8%	-2.7%
87	Nepal	15.8%	14.6%	1.1%	0.0%	0.0%	1.1%	2.3%
88	Netherlands	14.8%	4.1%	10.3%	-0.6%	0.1%	-1.1%	8.8%
89	New Zealand	7.0%	10.6%	-3.3%	0.0%	0.0%	-0.7%	-4.0%
90	Nicaragua	13.7%	13.2%	0.5%	-0.1%	0.1%	1.3%	1.7%

91	Niger	33.1%	34.2%	-0.8%	0.0%	0.0%	1.5%	0.7%
92	Nigeria	23.0%	22.9%	0.1%	0.0%	-0.3%	2.0%	1.7%
93	Norway	6.6%	6.6%	0.0%	-0.4%	-0.8%	-0.7%	-2.0%
94	Pakistan	6.4%	19.8%	-11.2%	-0.1%	0.0%	2.2%	-9.1%
95	Panama	23.7%	16.1%	6.5%	-0.3%	0.6%	-0.6%	6.2%
96	Papua New Guinea	20.6%	21.5%	-0.8%	0.0%	0.0%	-1.5%	-2.2%
97	Paraguay	6.4%	15.9%	-8.1%	-0.1%	0.1%	1.8%	-6.4%
98	Peru	6.2%	12.4%	-5.5%	-0.1%	0.0%	-1.8%	-7.4%
99	Philippines	22.9%	17.0%	5.1%	-0.2%	0.1%	1.6%	6.6%
100	Poland	10.2%	-0.1%	10.3%	-0.1%	0.1%	-0.6%	9.7%
101	Portugal	17.6%	1.4%	16.0%	-0.7%	0.1%	-1.6%	13.9%
102	Qatar	17.5%	65.8%	-29.1%	-0.2%	-10.8%	-0.3%	-40.4%
103	Republic of Korea	38.8%	5.6%	31.5%	-0.7%	0.4%	1.9%	33.0%
104	Republic of Moldova	-1.0%	-1.3%	0.3%	0.0%	0.1%	16.7%	17.0%
105	Romania	4.6%	-5.0%	10.0%	0.0%	0.0%	0.1%	10.0%
106	Russian Federation	2.0%	-1.0%	3.0%	0.0%	-0.7%	0.3%	2.6%
107	Rwanda	24.1%	16.0%	7.0%	0.0%	0.0%	-1.3%	5.7%
108	Saudi Arabia	6.5%	23.6%	-13.9%	-0.1%	-9.8%	-2.4%	-26.2%
109	Senegal	23.3%	25.0%	-1.4%	0.0%	0.0%	-0.9%	-2.3%
110	Serbia	1.5%	-2.0%	3.6%	0.0%	0.0%	-2.4%	1.3%
111	Sierra Leone	12.5%	17.1%	-4.0%	0.0%	0.0%	3.1%	-0.8%
112	Singapore	51.5%	21.5%	24.7%	0.2%	2.0%	-1.6%	25.2%
113	Slovakia	10.3%	0.7%	9.5%	-0.1%	0.1%	0.2%	9.8%
114	Slovenia	14.0%	1.1%	12.9%	-0.1%	0.1%	-1.0%	11.9%
115	South Africa	13.7%	15.4%	-1.4%	-0.1%	0.1%	-1.5%	-3.0%
116	Spain	22.9%	6.2%	15.7%	-0.7%	0.1%	-2.1%	13.1%
117	Sri Lanka	15.5%	6.7%	8.2%	-0.2%	0.1%	0.2%	8.4%
118	Sudan (former)	21.0%	25.3%	-3.4%	0.0%	-0.1%	-3.2%	-6.7%

(*Continued*)

Table A3.49 (Continued)

Country/year	Average growth rate in percentage from 2010–2014						
	Growth IW	Growth population	Growth IW per capita (unadjusted)	Growth of carbon damages	Growth of oil capital gains	Growth of TFP	Growth IW per capita (adjusted)
119 Swaziland	20.6%	13.7%	6.1%	−0.4%	0.1%	2.5%	8.2%
120 Sweden	13.7%	4.2%	9.0%	−0.5%	0.1%	−0.6%	7.9%
121 Switzerland	19.2%	6.8%	11.6%	−0.6%	0.0%	0.0%	11.0%
122 Syrian Arab Republic	13.1%	14.7%	−1.3%	−0.1%	0.0%	−18.0%	−19.5%
123 Tajikistan	18.8%	16.1%	2.3%	0.0%	0.0%	6.6%	8.8%
124 Thailand	18.0%	6.2%	11.2%	−0.2%	0.2%	0.3%	11.5%
125 Togo	25.6%	23.4%	1.8%	0.0%	0.0%	0.8%	2.5%
126 Trinidad and Tobago	−5.8%	3.5%	−9.0%	−0.2%	−0.9%	3.0%	−7.1%
127 Tunisia	22.1%	10.5%	10.6%	−0.2%	−0.3%	−0.1%	10.0%
128 Turkey	23.2%	12.8%	9.2%	−0.4%	0.1%	0.0%	8.9%
129 Uganda	32.8%	29.5%	2.5%	0.0%	−0.1%	−0.7%	1.7%
130 Ukraine	−4.6%	−4.4%	−0.3%	0.0%	0.0%	0.7%	0.4%
131 United Arab Emirates	26.2%	71.2%	−26.3%	−0.1%	−8.4%	−0.4%	−35.2%
132 United Kingdom	16.1%	4.1%	11.5%	−0.8%	0.0%	0.2%	11.0%
133 United Republic of Tanzania	27.8%	26.7%	0.8%	0.0%	0.0%	−1.9%	−1.0%
134 United States of America	17.4%	8.5%	8.2%	−0.1%	0.0%	0.0%	8.0%
135 Uruguay	8.3%	3.2%	5.0%	−0.1%	0.1%	−0.3%	4.6%
136 Venezuela (Bolivarian Republic of)	0.9%	15.6%	−12.7%	0.0%	−13.3%	−1.3%	−27.4%
137 Viet Nam	17.6%	11.2%	5.8%	−0.1%	−0.7%	−1.4%	3.6%
138 Yemen	30.3%	29.8%	0.3%	0.0%	−0.3%	−5.8%	−5.8%
139 Zambia	27.3%	24.5%	2.2%	0.0%	0.0%	−0.6%	1.6%
140 Zimbabwe	9.9%	13.3%	−2.9%	0.0%	0.0%	6.0%	3.1%

Table A3.50 GDP (GDP billion of constant 2005 US$)

	Country/year	1990	1995	2000	2005	2010	2014
1	Afghanistan	5.7	4.5	3.5	6.6	10.4	13.6
2	Albania	5.3	4.7	6.1	8.1	10.4	11.2
3	Algeria	66.8	67.6	80.1	103.2	117.0	132.8
4	Argentina	133.5	177.8	201.9	222.9	294.4	332.5
5	Armenia	4.0	2.1	2.7	4.9	5.9	7.1
6	Australia	453.9	532.8	642.9	762.1	870.4	975.0
7	Austria	223.1	249.0	288.9	314.6	335.5	349.9
8	Bahrain	7.8	9.9	12.4	16.0	20.9	24.4
9	Bangladesh	27.9	34.3	44.2	57.6	77.3	98.6
10	Barbados	3.3	3.2	3.7	3.9	4.1	4.1
11	Belgium	283.7	307.0	354.1	387.4	415.0	428.9
12	Belize	0.5	0.6	0.9	1.1	1.3	1.4
13	Benin	2.4	3.1	4.0	4.8	5.8	7.1
14	Bolivia (Plurinational State of)	5.7	6.9	8.2	9.5	12.0	14.9
15	Botswana	5.2	6.5	8.3	9.9	12.4	15.8
16	Brazil	606.1	704.4	778.1	892.1	1,108.5	1,206.1
17	Bulgaria	28.0	24.6	22.5	29.8	34.7	36.3
18	Burundi	1.2	1.1	1.0	1.1	2.1	3.0
19	Cambodia	2.1	2.9	4.0	6.3	8.7	11.5
20	Cameroon	11.7	11.0	13.8	16.6	19.1	23.3
21	Canada	774.6	842.8	1,026.9	1,164.2	1,240.1	1,359.8
22	Central African Republic	1.2	1.3	1.4	1.4	1.7	1.1
23	Chile	53.1	80.5	98.7	123.1	147.9	175.3
24	China	533.7	953.5	1,438.7	2,291.4	3,903.8	5,320.2
25	Colombia	94.5	117.2	122.7	146.6	183.0	222.6
26	Congo	4.3	4.4	5.0	6.1	7.9	9.3
27	Costa Rica	9.8	12.8	16.3	20.0	25.0	29.4
28	Côte d'Ivoire	13.4	14.5	17.1	17.1	19.6	24.6
29	Croatia	42.5	30.8	36.5	45.4	46.5	44.7
30	Cuba	38.5	26.7	33.4	42.6	55.4	61.1
31	Cyprus	10.1	13.0	15.8	18.8	21.3	19.1
32	Czech Republic	106.8	102.7	112.2	136.0	153.3	157.2
33	Democratic Republic of the Congo	17.7	12.1	9.9	12.0	15.7	21.3
34	Denmark	190.0	213.3	247.4	264.6	265.1	270.7
35	Dominican Republic	16.7	21.5	30.0	35.7	48.3	57.3
36	Ecuador	25.9	30.6	32.8	41.5	49.0	60.6
37	Egypt	48.6	61.0	78.7	94.5	127.5	138.5
38	El Salvador	9.7	13.1	15.2	17.1	18.3	19.8
39	Estonia	10.6	7.4	9.9	14.0	13.8	16.3
40	Fiji	2.2	2.5	2.8	3.1	3.2	3.7
41	Finland	143.6	140.4	179.9	204.4	212.9	212.0

(*Continued*)

Table A3.50 (Continued)

	Country/year	1990	1995	2000	2005	2010	2014
42	France	1,650.0	1,758.9	2,030.0	2,203.6	2,289.8	2,361.3
43	Gabon	7.9	9.2	9.1	9.6	10.1	12.7
44	Gambia	0.4	0.4	0.5	0.6	0.8	0.8
45	Germany	2,286.9	2,529.4	2,781.3	2,861.3	3,042.4	3,226.7
46	Ghana	8.7	10.7	13.3	17.2	23.2	32.2
47	Greece	160.9	171.2	205.3	247.8	243.7	200.0
48	Guatemala	15.7	19.3	23.4	27.2	32.6	37.7
49	Guyana	0.8	1.1	1.3	1.3	1.6	1.9
50	Haiti	4.3	3.8	4.3	4.2	4.3	5.0
51	Honduras	5.6	6.7	7.8	9.8	11.6	13.3
52	Hungary	88.6	78.6	91.2	112.5	111.4	117.7
53	Iceland	10.5	10.7	13.6	16.7	17.8	19.5
54	India	344.2	442.4	586.3	821.0	1,223.9	1,573.0
55	Indonesia	159.8	233.0	241.6	304.4	402.4	502.2
56	Iran (Islamic Republic of)	122.6	141.6	168.2	219.8	279.1	276.7
57	Iraq	24.5	12.1	35.4	36.3	48.2	60.7
58	Ireland	81.0	101.2	163.5	211.4	219.8	241.0
59	Israel	71.2	98.7	128.4	142.8	176.6	202.1
60	Italy	1,501.7	1,602.2	1,768.8	1,853.5	1,825.0	1,745.0
61	Jamaica	9.0	10.4	10.4	11.2	11.0	11.2
62	Japan	3,851.3	4,132.2	4,308.1	4,571.9	4,651.1	4,780.9
63	Jordan	5.8	7.9	9.2	12.6	17.0	19.0
64	Kazakhstan	50.2	30.8	34.9	57.1	77.3	96.2
65	Kenya	14.9	16.1	17.9	21.5	27.4	33.9
66	Kuwait	30.6	48.6	54.7	80.8	85.6	99.6
67	Kyrgyzstan	3.1	1.6	2.0	2.5	3.1	3.7
68	Lao People's Democratic Republic	1.1	1.5	2.0	2.7	4.0	5.4
69	Latvia	17.9	8.9	11.4	16.9	16.5	19.2
70	Lesotho	0.8	1.0	1.2	1.4	1.8	2.1
71	Liberia	0.4	0.1	0.5	0.6	1.1	1.5
72	Lithuania	24.9	14.4	18.1	26.1	27.7	32.6
73	Luxembourg	19.6	23.7	32.0	37.0	41.8	46.1
74	Malawi	2.5	2.6	3.1	3.7	5.2	5.9
75	Malaysia	57.3	90.1	113.9	143.5	178.7	220.5
76	Maldives	0.4	0.6	0.9	1.1	1.7	2.3
77	Mali	2.7	3.4	4.0	5.5	7.0	7.8
78	Malta	3.4	4.5	5.8	6.4	7.1	7.9
79	Mauritania	1.3	1.5	1.7	2.2	2.8	3.5
80	Mauritius	3.3	4.2	5.5	6.5	8.2	9.4
81	Mexico	560.2	604.4	788.2	864.8	952.0	1,067.0
82	Mongolia	2.1	1.9	2.1	2.9	4.0	6.3
83	Morocco	38.8	40.7	49.1	62.5	79.4	92.3
84	Mozambique	2.5	2.9	5.0	7.7	11.1	14.6

	Country/year	1990	1995	2000	2005	2010	2014
85	Myanmar	3.3	4.4	6.5	11.9	20.3	27.1
86	Namibia	3.9	5.0	5.9	7.3	9.0	10.9
87	Nepal	4.3	5.5	7.0	8.3	10.3	12.2
88	Netherlands	458.5	513.5	634.9	678.5	722.8	730.8
89	New Zealand	69.8	81.7	94.1	114.7	120.8	133.6
90	Nicaragua	3.9	4.2	5.4	6.3	7.2	8.7
91	Niger	2.1	2.3	2.7	3.4	4.3	5.5
92	Nigeria	87.8	94.2	109.8	180.5	249.7	306.0
93	Norway	193.0	231.8	276.9	308.7	323.3	346.2
94	Pakistan	62.7	78.6	92.3	117.7	139.2	163.0
95	Panama	7.6	10.0	12.5	15.5	22.0	30.3
96	Papua New Guinea	2.8	4.2	4.4	4.9	6.5	8.8
97	Paraguay	5.7	6.8	6.7	8.7	11.1	13.7
98	Peru	42.1	54.3	61.7	76.1	106.2	129.7
99	Philippines	62.1	69.1	82.4	103.1	131.1	165.1
100	Poland	181.6	202.2	261.3	304.4	383.3	427.7
101	Portugal	142.2	154.7	189.0	197.3	203.4	191.2
102	Qatar	15.8	17.7	30.1	44.5	101.9	137.9
103	Republic of Korea	364.3	545.7	712.8	898.1	1,098.7	1,238.7
104	Republic of Moldova	6.1	2.4	2.1	3.0	3.5	4.2
105	Romania	85.0	76.3	75.4	99.7	115.1	124.6
106	Russian Federation	844.2	524.1	567.4	764.0	909.3	999.6
107	Rwanda	1.6	1.1	1.7	2.6	3.8	5.1
108	Saudi Arabia	209.1	248.6	269.8	328.5	374.9	462.0
109	Senegal	5.1	5.5	6.9	8.7	10.4	11.9
110	Serbia	38.1	18.2	19.4	26.3	29.9	30.3
111	Sierra Leone	2.0	1.5	0.9	1.7	2.1	3.3
112	Singapore	50.4	76.3	100.4	127.4	176.5	208.3
113	Slovakia	35.2	32.2	38.3	48.8	61.6	66.9
114	Slovenia	25.5	24.7	30.5	36.3	39.6	39.5
115	South Africa	178.3	186.2	213.6	257.8	300.3	328.7
116	Spain	744.0	801.8	979.5	1,157.2	1,219.9	1,172.1
117	Sri Lanka	12.0	15.7	20.0	24.4	33.3	44.1
118	Sudan (former)	14.2	17.9	25.3	35.2	35.9	37.3
119	Swaziland	2.0	2.4	2.8	3.2	3.6	4.1
120	Sweden	276.7	286.7	341.7	389.0	420.9	446.4
121	Switzerland	335.8	338.0	378.4	407.5	454.9	485.6
122	Syrian Arab Republic	12.6	18.6	22.2	28.4	36.1	19.8
123	Tajikistan	3.8	1.5	1.5	2.3	3.2	4.0
124	Thailand	93.0	139.8	145.0	189.3	227.4	255.2
125	Togo	1.8	1.8	2.0	2.1	2.5	3.0
126	Trinidad and Tobago	7.0	7.5	10.8	16.0	18.7	19.7
127	Tunisia	16.4	19.9	26.0	32.3	40.2	42.9
128	Turkey	269.7	315.9	386.6	483.0	565.1	673.1

(*Continued*)

Table A3.50 (Continued)

	Country/year	1990	1995	2000	2005	2010	2014
129	Uganda	3.9	5.6	7.6	11.0	16.3	19.6
130	Ukraine	142.8	68.2	61.7	89.2	93.8	92.4
131	United Arab Emirates	81.9	101.6	139.2	180.6	203.4	249.6
132	United Kingdom	1,656.0	1,797.8	2,105.5	2,418.9	2,466.8	2,676.5
133	United Republic of Tanzania	8.6	10.5	12.9	18.1	24.3	31.6
134	United States of America	8,228.6	9,359.5	11,553.3	13,093.7	13,599.3	14,682.7
135	Uruguay	12.7	15.5	17.2	17.4	23.2	27.4
136	Venezuela (Bolivarian Republic of)	104.3	123.6	128.3	145.5	174.6	186.9
137	Viet Nam	19.5	29.0	40.6	57.6	78.3	97.8
138	Yemen	7.5	9.8	14.7	19.0	23.6	21.6
139	Zambia	5.3	5.2	6.2	8.3	12.6	16.2
140	Zimbabwe	7.4	7.8	7.7	6.2	9.6	12.8

Table A3.51 GDP per capita (GDP per capita in thousands of constant 2005 US$)

	Country/year	1990	1995	2000	2005	2010	2014
1	Afghanistan	0.5	0.3	0.2	0.3	0.4	0.4
2	Albania	1.6	1.5	2.0	2.7	3.6	3.9
3	Algeria	2.6	2.3	2.6	3.1	3.2	3.4
4	Argentina	4.1	5.1	5.4	5.7	7.1	7.7
5	Armenia	1.1	0.7	0.9	1.6	2.0	2.4
6	Australia	26.6	29.5	33.6	37.4	39.5	41.6
7	Austria	29.1	31.3	36.1	38.2	40.1	41.0
8	Bahrain	15.7	17.5	18.6	18.4	16.6	17.9
9	Bangladesh	0.3	0.3	0.3	0.4	0.5	0.6
10	Barbados	12.8	12.0	13.7	14.2	14.5	14.5
11	Belgium	28.5	30.3	34.5	37.0	38.1	38.2
12	Belize	2.8	3.1	3.5	3.9	3.9	4.0
13	Benin	0.5	0.5	0.6	0.6	0.6	0.7
14	Bolivia (Plurinational State of)	0.8	0.9	1.0	1.0	1.2	1.4
15	Botswana	3.7	4.1	4.8	5.3	6.1	7.1
16	Brazil	4.0	4.3	4.4	4.7	5.6	5.9
17	Bulgaria	3.2	2.9	2.8	3.9	4.7	5.0
18	Burundi	0.2	0.2	0.2	0.1	0.2	0.3
19	Cambodia	0.2	0.3	0.3	0.5	0.6	0.7
20	Cameroon	1.0	0.8	0.9	0.9	0.9	1.0
21	Canada	27.9	28.7	33.4	36.0	36.5	38.3

	Country/year	1990	1995	2000	2005	2010	2014
22	Central African Republic	0.4	0.4	0.4	0.3	0.4	0.2
23	Chile	4.0	5.7	6.5	7.6	8.7	9.9
24	China	0.5	0.8	1.1	1.8	2.9	3.9
25	Colombia	2.8	3.1	3.0	3.4	4.0	4.7
26	Congo	1.8	1.6	1.6	1.7	1.9	2.1
27	Costa Rica	3.2	3.7	4.2	4.7	5.5	6.2
28	Côte d'Ivoire	1.1	1.0	1.0	0.9	1.0	1.1
29	Croatia	8.9	6.6	8.2	10.2	10.5	10.5
30	Cuba	3.6	2.5	3.0	3.8	4.9	5.4
31	Cyprus	13.2	15.2	16.7	18.3	19.3	16.6
32	Czech Republic	10.3	9.9	10.9	13.3	14.6	14.9
33	Democratic Republic of the Congo	0.5	0.3	0.2	0.2	0.2	0.3
34	Denmark	37.0	40.8	46.3	48.8	47.8	48.0
35	Dominican Republic	2.3	2.7	3.5	3.9	4.9	5.5
36	Ecuador	2.5	2.7	2.6	3.0	3.3	3.8
37	Egypt	0.9	1.0	1.2	1.3	1.6	1.5
38	El Salvador	1.8	2.3	2.6	2.9	3.0	3.2
39	Estonia	6.7	5.1	7.1	10.3	10.3	12.4
40	Fiji	3.1	3.2	3.4	3.8	3.8	4.1
41	Finland	28.8	27.5	34.8	39.0	39.7	38.8
42	France	28.2	29.5	33.3	34.9	35.2	35.5
43	Gabon	8.3	8.4	7.4	7.0	6.6	7.5
44	Gambia	0.4	0.4	0.4	0.4	0.5	0.4
45	Germany	28.8	31.0	33.8	34.7	37.2	39.8
46	Ghana	0.6	0.6	0.7	0.8	1.0	1.2
47	Greece	15.8	16.2	19.0	22.6	21.9	18.4
48	Guatemala	1.7	1.9	2.0	2.1	2.2	2.4
49	Guyana	1.1	1.5	1.7	1.8	2.1	2.5
50	Haiti	0.6	0.5	0.5	0.4	0.4	0.5
51	Honduras	1.1	1.2	1.2	1.4	1.6	1.7
52	Hungary	8.5	7.6	8.9	11.2	11.1	11.9
53	Iceland	41.4	39.9	48.5	56.4	56.0	59.4
54	India	0.4	0.5	0.6	0.7	1.0	1.2
55	Indonesia	0.9	1.2	1.1	1.3	1.7	2.0
56	Iran (Islamic Republic of)	2.2	2.3	2.6	3.1	3.8	3.5
57	Iraq	1.4	0.6	1.5	1.3	1.6	1.7
58	Ireland	23.0	28.1	43.0	50.8	48.2	52.2
59	Israel	15.3	17.8	20.4	20.6	23.2	24.6
60	Italy	26.5	28.2	31.1	32.0	30.8	28.7
61	Jamaica	3.8	4.2	4.0	4.3	4.1	4.1
62	Japan	31.2	33.0	34.0	35.8	36.3	37.6

(*Continued*)

Table A3.51 (Continued)

	Country/year	1990	1995	2000	2005	2010	2014
63	Jordan	1.7	1.8	1.9	2.4	2.6	2.6
64	Kazakhstan	3.1	1.9	2.3	3.8	4.7	5.6
65	Kenya	0.6	0.6	0.6	0.6	0.7	0.8
66	Kuwait	14.9	29.7	28.4	35.7	28.0	26.5
67	Kyrgyzstan	0.7	0.3	0.4	0.5	0.6	0.6
68	Lao People's Democratic Republic	0.3	0.3	0.4	0.5	0.6	0.8
69	Latvia	6.7	3.6	4.8	7.5	7.9	9.7
70	Lesotho	0.5	0.6	0.6	0.7	0.9	1.0
71	Liberia	0.2	0.1	0.2	0.2	0.3	0.3
72	Lithuania	6.7	4.0	5.2	7.9	8.9	11.1
73	Luxembourg	51.2	58.1	73.3	79.5	82.4	82.9
74	Malawi	0.3	0.3	0.3	0.3	0.4	0.4
75	Malaysia	3.1	4.3	4.9	5.6	6.4	7.4
76	Maldives	1.9	2.3	3.0	3.5	4.6	5.8
77	Mali	0.3	0.3	0.4	0.4	0.5	0.5
78	Malta	9.7	12.1	15.1	15.8	17.0	18.4
79	Mauritania	0.6	0.6	0.6	0.7	0.8	0.9
80	Mauritius	3.1	3.7	4.6	5.3	6.5	7.4
81	Mexico	6.5	6.4	7.7	7.9	8.0	8.5
82	Mongolia	1.0	0.8	0.9	1.2	1.5	2.2
83	Morocco	1.6	1.5	1.7	2.1	2.5	2.7
84	Mozambique	0.2	0.2	0.3	0.4	0.5	0.5
85	Myanmar	0.1	0.1	0.1	0.2	0.4	0.5
86	Namibia	2.8	3.0	3.1	3.6	4.1	4.5
87	Nepal	0.2	0.3	0.3	0.3	0.4	0.4
88	Netherlands	30.7	33.2	39.9	41.6	43.5	43.3
89	New Zealand	21.0	22.2	24.4	27.8	27.8	29.6
90	Nicaragua	0.9	0.9	1.1	1.2	1.2	1.5
91	Niger	0.3	0.2	0.2	0.2	0.3	0.3
92	Nigeria	0.9	0.9	0.9	1.3	1.6	1.7
93	Norway	45.5	53.2	61.7	66.8	66.1	67.4
94	Pakistan	0.6	0.6	0.7	0.8	0.8	0.9
95	Panama	3.1	3.6	4.1	4.7	6.1	7.8
96	Papua New Guinea	0.7	0.9	0.8	0.8	0.9	1.2
97	Paraguay	1.4	1.4	1.3	1.5	1.8	2.1
98	Peru	1.9	2.3	2.4	2.8	3.6	4.2
99	Philippines	1.0	1.0	1.1	1.2	1.4	1.7
100	Poland	4.8	5.2	6.8	8.0	10.1	11.3
101	Portugal	14.2	15.4	18.4	18.8	19.2	18.4

	Country/year	1990	1995	2000	2005	2010	2014
102	Qatar	33.1	35.3	50.7	53.2	57.7	63.5
103	Republic of Korea	8.5	12.1	15.2	18.7	22.2	24.6
104	Republic of Moldova	1.7	0.7	0.6	0.8	1.0	1.2
105	Romania	3.7	3.4	3.4	4.7	5.7	6.3
106	Russian Federation	5.7	3.5	3.9	5.3	6.4	7.0
107	Rwanda	0.2	0.2	0.2	0.3	0.4	0.4
108	Saudi Arabia	12.8	13.2	12.6	13.3	13.3	15.0
109	Senegal	0.7	0.6	0.7	0.8	0.8	0.8
110	Serbia	5.0	2.4	2.6	3.5	4.1	4.2
111	Sierra Leone	0.5	0.4	0.2	0.3	0.4	0.5
112	Singapore	16.6	21.7	24.9	29.9	34.8	38.1
113	Slovakia	6.6	6.0	7.1	9.1	11.4	12.3
114	Slovenia	12.7	12.4	15.3	18.2	19.3	19.2
115	South Africa	5.1	4.8	4.9	5.5	5.9	6.1
116	Spain	19.2	20.4	24.3	26.5	26.2	25.2
117	Sri Lanka	0.7	0.9	1.1	1.3	1.7	2.1
118	Sudan (former)	0.7	0.7	0.9	1.1	1.0	0.9
119	Swaziland	2.4	2.5	2.6	2.9	3.0	3.2
120	Sweden	32.3	32.5	38.5	43.1	44.9	46.0
121	Switzerland	50.0	48.0	52.7	54.8	58.1	59.3
122	Syrian Arab Republic	1.0	1.3	1.4	1.6	1.7	1.1
123	Tajikistan	0.7	0.3	0.2	0.3	0.4	0.5
124	Thailand	1.6	2.4	2.3	2.9	3.4	3.8
125	Togo	0.5	0.4	0.4	0.4	0.4	0.4
126	Trinidad and Tobago	5.7	6.0	8.5	12.3	14.1	14.5
127	Tunisia	2.0	2.2	2.7	3.2	3.8	3.9
128	Turkey	5.0	5.4	6.1	7.1	7.8	8.7
129	Uganda	0.2	0.3	0.3	0.4	0.5	0.5
130	Ukraine	2.8	1.3	1.3	1.9	2.0	2.0
131	United Arab Emirates	45.2	43.2	45.6	40.3	24.4	27.5
132	United Kingdom	28.9	31.0	35.8	40.0	39.3	41.4
133	United Republic of Tanzania	0.3	0.4	0.4	0.5	0.5	0.6
134	United States of America	33.0	35.1	40.9	44.3	44.0	46.0
135	Uruguay	4.1	4.8	5.2	5.2	6.9	8.0
136	Venezuela (Bolivarian Republic of)	5.3	5.6	5.2	5.4	6.0	6.1
137	Viet Nam	0.3	0.4	0.5	0.7	0.9	1.1
138	Yemen	0.6	0.6	0.8	0.9	1.0	0.8
139	Zambia	0.7	0.6	0.6	0.7	0.9	1.0
140	Zimbabwe	0.7	0.7	0.6	0.5	0.7	0.8

Table A3.52 GDP growth (GDP change (%) with respect to base year 1990)

	Country/year	1995	2000	2005	2010	2014
1	Afghanistan	−4.6%	−11.6%	3.7%	16.1%	33.5%
2	Albania	−2.1%	3.6%	11.3%	18.5%	28.6%
3	Algeria	0.3%	4.7%	11.5%	15.0%	25.8%
4	Argentina	5.9%	10.9%	13.7%	21.9%	35.5%
5	Armenia	−12.0%	−9.3%	5.2%	10.3%	21.2%
6	Australia	3.3%	9.1%	13.8%	17.7%	29.0%
7	Austria	2.2%	6.7%	9.0%	10.7%	16.2%
8	Bahrain	4.9%	12.4%	19.7%	28.0%	46.3%
9	Bangladesh	4.2%	12.2%	19.9%	29.1%	52.4%
10	Barbados	−0.9%	2.7%	4.0%	5.1%	7.2%
11	Belgium	1.6%	5.7%	8.1%	10.0%	14.8%
12	Belize	4.3%	13.4%	21.1%	24.9%	39.5%
13	Benin	5.0%	13.0%	18.6%	24.3%	43.1%
14	Bolivia (Plurinational State of)	4.1%	9.7%	13.9%	20.5%	38.0%
15	Botswana	4.6%	12.7%	17.8%	24.5%	45.1%
16	Brazil	3.1%	6.4%	10.1%	16.3%	25.8%
17	Bulgaria	−2.6%	−5.4%	1.6%	5.5%	9.0%
18	Burundi	−2.1%	−4.1%	−2.0%	15.0%	34.9%
19	Cambodia	6.5%	17.9%	31.8%	42.9%	76.6%
20	Cameroon	−1.3%	4.3%	9.1%	13.1%	25.8%
21	Canada	1.7%	7.3%	10.7%	12.5%	20.6%
22	Central African Republic	1.9%	5.1%	4.5%	8.9%	−1.6%
23	Chile	8.7%	16.8%	23.4%	29.2%	48.9%
24	China	12.3%	28.1%	43.9%	64.5%	115.2%
25	Colombia	4.4%	6.8%	11.6%	18.0%	33.1%
26	Congo	0.4%	3.6%	8.9%	16.1%	29.2%
27	Costa Rica	5.5%	13.5%	19.3%	26.3%	44.1%
28	Côte d'Ivoire	1.6%	6.2%	6.2%	10.0%	22.4%
29	Croatia	−6.2%	−3.8%	1.6%	2.2%	1.7%
30	Cuba	−7.1%	−3.5%	2.6%	9.5%	16.6%
31	Cyprus	5.2%	11.8%	16.9%	20.5%	23.7%
32	Czech Republic	−0.8%	1.2%	6.2%	9.5%	13.8%
33	Democratic Republic of the Congo	−7.3%	−13.4%	−9.3%	−2.9%	6.4%
34	Denmark	2.3%	6.8%	8.6%	8.7%	12.5%
35	Dominican Republic	5.2%	15.8%	20.9%	30.5%	50.9%
36	Ecuador	3.4%	6.1%	12.5%	17.3%	32.8%
37	Egypt	4.7%	12.8%	18.1%	27.3%	41.8%
38	El Salvador	6.2%	11.9%	15.2%	17.3%	26.9%
39	Estonia	−6.9%	−1.6%	7.2%	6.7%	15.4%
40	Fiji	2.1%	5.3%	8.5%	9.5%	17.8%
41	Finland	−0.4%	5.8%	9.2%	10.3%	13.9%
42	France	1.3%	5.3%	7.5%	8.5%	12.7%
43	Gabon	3.1%	3.8%	5.0%	6.5%	17.2%
44	Gambia	2.3%	8.4%	12.9%	19.5%	30.1%

	Country/year	1995	2000	2005	2010	2014
45	Germany	2.0%	5.0%	5.8%	7.4%	12.2%
46	Ghana	4.3%	11.2%	18.5%	27.7%	54.6%
47	Greece	1.2%	6.3%	11.4%	10.9%	7.5%
48	Guatemala	4.3%	10.6%	14.8%	20.1%	34.1%
49	Guyana	7.1%	12.7%	13.7%	19.4%	33.9%
50	Haiti	−2.5%	0.0%	−0.7%	0.2%	5.5%
51	Honduras	3.5%	8.4%	14.8%	20.0%	33.4%
52	Hungary	−2.4%	0.7%	6.2%	5.9%	9.9%
53	Iceland	0.3%	6.7%	12.3%	14.0%	22.7%
54	India	5.1%	14.2%	24.3%	37.3%	66.0%
55	Indonesia	7.8%	10.9%	17.5%	26.0%	46.5%
56	Iran (Islamic Republic of)	2.9%	8.2%	15.7%	22.8%	31.2%
57	Iraq	−13.2%	9.6%	10.3%	18.5%	35.4%
58	Ireland	4.6%	19.2%	27.1%	28.4%	43.8%
59	Israel	6.8%	15.9%	19.0%	25.5%	41.6%
60	Italy	1.3%	4.2%	5.4%	5.0%	5.1%
61	Jamaica	3.0%	3.6%	5.7%	5.0%	7.6%
62	Japan	1.4%	2.8%	4.4%	4.8%	7.5%
63	Jordan	6.2%	12.2%	21.2%	30.7%	48.3%
64	Kazakhstan	−9.3%	−8.7%	3.3%	11.4%	24.2%
65	Kenya	1.6%	4.6%	9.6%	16.4%	31.4%
66	Kuwait	9.7%	15.6%	27.5%	29.3%	48.2%
67	Kyrgyzstan	−12.7%	−9.7%	−5.4%	−0.1%	6.5%
68	Lao People's Democratic Republic	6.2%	16.2%	25.4%	38.1%	70.1%
69	Latvia	−13.1%	−10.6%	−1.4%	−2.0%	2.5%
70	Lesotho	4.1%	10.3%	14.3%	21.8%	37.5%
71	Liberia	−22.5%	6.7%	9.8%	27.4%	51.5%
72	Lithuania	−10.3%	−7.6%	1.3%	2.7%	9.4%
73	Luxembourg	4.0%	13.1%	17.3%	20.9%	33.1%
74	Malawi	1.2%	6.2%	10.3%	20.6%	33.5%
75	Malaysia	9.5%	18.7%	25.8%	32.9%	56.7%
76	Maldives	6.8%	19.9%	28.2%	42.4%	77.8%
77	Mali	4.5%	10.5%	19.4%	26.8%	42.6%
78	Malta	5.5%	13.8%	16.7%	19.7%	31.7%
79	Mauritania	3.2%	7.9%	14.1%	21.4%	39.3%
80	Mauritius	4.8%	13.4%	18.3%	25.2%	41.3%
81	Mexico	1.5%	8.9%	11.5%	14.2%	24.0%
82	Mongolia	−2.8%	−0.1%	8.1%	16.9%	43.5%
83	Morocco	0.9%	6.0%	12.7%	19.6%	33.5%
84	Mozambique	3.3%	19.3%	32.7%	45.1%	80.2%
85	Myanmar	5.8%	18.6%	38.0%	57.5%	1019%
86	Namibia	5.0%	10.9%	16.7%	23.1%	40.7%
87	Nepal	5.2%	13.0%	17.9%	24.6%	42.1%
88	Netherlands	2.3%	8.5%	10.3%	12.1%	16.8%
89	New Zealand	3.2%	7.8%	13.2%	14.7%	24.1%

(*Continued*)

Table A3.52 (Continued)

	Country/year	1995	2000	2005	2010	2014
90	Nicaragua	1.8%	8.7%	13.0%	16.5%	31.1%
91	Niger	1.5%	6.0%	12.0%	19.3%	37.3%
92	Nigeria	1.4%	5.8%	19.7%	29.9%	51.6%
93	Norway	3.7%	9.4%	12.5%	13.8%	21.5%
94	Pakistan	4.6%	10.1%	17.1%	22.1%	37.5%
95	Panama	5.5%	13.1%	19.3%	30.2%	58.3%
96	Papua New Guinea	8.6%	11.9%	14.9%	23.5%	46.9%
97	Paraguay	3.4%	4.0%	11.1%	18.1%	33.6%
98	Peru	5.2%	10.1%	16.0%	26.0%	45.5%
99	Philippines	2.2%	7.3%	13.5%	20.5%	38.5%
100	Poland	2.2%	9.5%	13.8%	20.5%	33.1%
101	Portugal	1.7%	7.4%	8.5%	9.4%	10.4%
102	Qatar	2.3%	17.5%	29.6%	59.4%	106.0%
103	Republic of Korea	8.4%	18.3%	25.3%	31.8%	50.4%
104	Republic of Moldova	−17.0%	−23.2%	−16.3%	−13.0%	−11.4%
105	Romania	−2.1%	−3.0%	4.1%	7.9%	13.6%
106	Russian Federation	−9.1%	−9.5%	−2.5%	1.9%	5.8%
107	Rwanda	−8.5%	1.5%	11.9%	23.6%	45.3%
108	Saudi Arabia	3.5%	6.6%	11.9%	15.7%	30.2%
109	Senegal	1.4%	7.8%	14.2%	19.2%	32.4%
110	Serbia	−13.7%	−15.5%	−8.9%	−5.8%	−7.4%
111	Sierra Leone	−5.0%	−17.9%	−4.7%	1.6%	18.7%
112	Singapore	8.6%	18.8%	26.1%	36.8%	60.4%
113	Slovakia	−1.8%	2.1%	8.5%	15.0%	23.8%
114	Slovenia	−0.6%	4.6%	9.3%	11.7%	15.8%
115	South Africa	0.9%	4.6%	9.6%	13.9%	22.6%
116	Spain	1.5%	7.1%	11.7%	13.2%	16.4%
117	Sri Lanka	5.5%	13.6%	19.4%	29.0%	54.2%
118	Sudan (former)	4.8%	15.5%	25.5%	26.1%	38.0%
119	Swaziland	3.4%	8.5%	12.0%	15.6%	25.9%
120	Sweden	0.7%	5.4%	8.9%	11.1%	17.3%
121	Switzerland	0.1%	3.0%	5.0%	7.9%	13.1%
122	Syrian Arab Republic	8.1%	15.3%	22.6%	30.2%	16.4%
123	Tajikistan	−17.6%	−21.4%	−11.8%	−4.6%	1.5%
124	Thailand	8.5%	11.8%	19.5%	25.1%	40.0%
125	Togo	−0.3%	2.3%	3.8%	7.9%	18.9%
126	Trinidad and Tobago	1.4%	11.4%	22.8%	27.8%	40.9%
127	Tunisia	3.9%	12.2%	18.4%	25.1%	37.7%
128	Turkey	3.2%	9.4%	15.7%	20.3%	35.6%
129	Uganda	7.5%	18.3%	29.6%	43.1%	71.2%
130	Ukraine	−13.7%	−18.9%	−11.1%	−10.0%	−13.5%
131	United Arab Emirates	4.4%	14.2%	21.9%	25.5%	45.0%
132	United Kingdom	1.7%	6.2%	9.9%	10.5%	17.4%
133	United Republic of Tanzania	4.0%	10.6%	20.4%	29.6%	54.3%
134	United States of America	2.6%	8.9%	12.3%	13.4%	21.3%

	Country/year	1995	2000	2005	2010	2014
135	Uruguay	4.1%	8.0%	8.2%	16.4%	29.4%
136	Venezuela (Bolivarian Republic of)	3.4%	5.3%	8.7%	13.7%	21.4%
137	Viet Nam	8.2%	20.0%	31.0%	41.5%	71.1%
138	Yemen	5.5%	18.2%	26.1%	33.0%	42.1%
139	Zambia	-0.7%	3.7%	11.8%	24.1%	44.7%
140	Zimbabwe	1.2%	1.3%	-4.1%	6.7%	20.1%

Table A3.53 GDP per capita growth (GDP per capita change (%) with respect to base year 1990)

	Country/year	1995	2000	2005	2010	2014
1	Afghanistan	-10.6%	-21.8%	-13.0%	-5.9%	-3.2%
2	Albania	-1.5%	5.2%	13.7%	22.1%	34.2%
3	Algeria	-1.9%	-0.1%	4.7%	5.9%	9.8%
4	Argentina	4.5%	7.5%	8.7%	15.0%	23.8%
5	Armenia	-10.3%	-6.0%	9.6%	15.4%	28.0%
6	Australia	2.1%	6.0%	8.9%	10.4%	16.0%
7	Austria	1.5%	5.6%	7.1%	8.4%	12.1%
8	Bahrain	2.2%	4.4%	4.1%	1.4%	4.5%
9	Bangladesh	2.0%	6.4%	11.3%	18.0%	33.1%
10	Barbados	-1.2%	1.7%	2.7%	3.2%	4.3%
11	Belgium	1.3%	5.0%	6.8%	7.6%	10.3%
12	Belize	2.3%	5.9%	9.3%	9.2%	13.1%
13	Benin	1.3%	4.1%	4.8%	5.8%	11.4%
14	Bolivia (Plurinational State of)	2.1%	4.4%	6.1%	9.9%	19.5%
15	Botswana	1.8%	6.4%	9.3%	12.8%	23.8%
16	Brazil	1.4%	2.4%	4.1%	8.5%	13.2%
17	Bulgaria	-1.9%	-3.8%	4.6%	9.9%	16.1%
18	Burundi	-4.2%	-8.5%	-10.1%	1.0%	8.4%
19	Cambodia	2.9%	9.3%	19.5%	27.2%	47.9%
20	Cameroon	-4.0%	-2.7%	-1.4%	-1.0%	1.8%
21	Canada	0.6%	4.6%	6.6%	7.0%	11.1%
22	Central African Republic	-0.6%	-1.0%	-3.6%	-1.8%	-16.4%
23	Chile	7.0%	12.7%	17.3%	21.1%	34.7%
24	China	11.0%	24.8%	39.0%	57.8%	102.4%
25	Colombia	2.6%	2.5%	5.3%	9.7%	19.1%
26	Congo	-2.2%	-3.0%	-1.1%	1.7%	4.5%
27	Costa Rica	2.8%	7.0%	10.3%	14.7%	24.8%
28	Côte d'Ivoire	-1.8%	-1.6%	-3.8%	-3.0%	0.2%
29	Croatia	-5.8%	-1.9%	3.5%	4.3%	5.8%
30	Cuba	-7.6%	-4.7%	1.0%	7.7%	13.8%
31	Cyprus	2.9%	6.1%	8.5%	10.0%	7.9%
32	Czech Republic	-0.8%	1.4%	6.6%	9.1%	13.1%

(*Continued*)

Table A3.53 (Continued)

	Country/year	1995	2000	2005	2010	2014
33	Democratic Republic of the Congo	−10.7%	−20.0%	−19.4%	−17.2%	−17.4%
34	Denmark	2.0%	5.8%	7.2%	6.6%	9.1%
35	Dominican Republic	3.2%	10.8%	13.6%	20.4%	33.4%
36	Ecuador	1.1%	0.6%	4.5%	6.7%	14.6%
37	Egypt	2.6%	7.5%	10.0%	15.9%	21.5%
38	El Salvador	4.9%	9.1%	11.7%	13.2%	20.7%
39	Estonia	−5.3%	1.3%	11.2%	11.2%	22.4%
40	Fiji	0.8%	2.5%	5.3%	5.1%	10.3%
41	Finland	−0.9%	4.8%	7.9%	8.4%	10.5%
42	France	0.9%	4.3%	5.5%	5.7%	8.0%
43	Gabon	0.4%	−2.7%	−4.2%	−5.6%	−3.2%
44	Gambia	−0.7%	0.7%	0.8%	2.5%	1.5%
45	Germany	1.5%	4.1%	4.8%	6.6%	11.4%
46	Ghana	1.5%	4.4%	7.8%	12.4%	26.4%
47	Greece	0.5%	4.8%	9.3%	8.6%	5.2%
48	Guatemala	1.7%	4.1%	4.8%	6.6%	11.3%
49	Guyana	6.9%	11.8%	12.8%	18.1%	31.3%
50	Haiti	−4.3%	−4.5%	−7.1%	−8.0%	−7.6%
51	Honduras	0.9%	2.1%	5.4%	7.9%	13.5%
52	Hungary	−2.3%	1.1%	6.9%	6.9%	11.8%
53	Iceland	−0.7%	4.1%	8.1%	7.9%	12.8%
54	India	3.1%	8.9%	16.1%	25.9%	45.4%
55	Indonesia	6.1%	6.7%	11.2%	17.3%	30.8%
56	Iran (Islamic Republic of)	1.5%	4.0%	9.5%	14.6%	17.5%
57	Iraq	−15.7%	1.7%	−1.0%	2.8%	7.1%
58	Ireland	4.0%	16.9%	21.9%	20.3%	31.3%
59	Israel	3.1%	7.5%	7.8%	11.0%	17.2%
60	Italy	1.3%	4.1%	4.8%	3.8%	2.7%
61	Jamaica	2.2%	1.6%	3.0%	2.0%	3.0%
62	Japan	1.1%	2.2%	3.5%	3.9%	6.4%
63	Jordan	1.0%	2.8%	8.0%	10.8%	13.9%
64	Kazakhstan	−8.7%	−6.5%	5.3%	11.4%	21.9%
65	Kenya	−1.5%	−2.5%	−1.1%	1.7%	5.9%
66	Kuwait	14.8%	17.5%	24.5%	17.1%	21.3%
67	Kyrgyzstan	−13.4%	−12.1%	−9.1%	−5.3%	−3.1%
68	Lao People's Democratic Republic	3.4%	9.7%	16.3%	25.3%	46.2%
69	Latvia	−11.9%	−8.0%	3.0%	4.1%	12.9%
70	Lesotho	2.2%	6.3%	9.1%	15.0%	25.3%
71	Liberia	−22.3%	−1.5%	−1.6%	8.7%	18.5%
72	Lithuania	−10.0%	−6.3%	4.0%	7.4%	18.2%
73	Luxembourg	2.6%	9.4%	11.6%	12.6%	17.4%
74	Malawi	0.3%	1.6%	2.2%	7.8%	10.3%
75	Malaysia	6.7%	11.5%	15.3%	19.2%	32.8%
76	Maldives	3.5%	12.1%	16.4%	25.0%	45.1%
77	Mali	1.9%	3.4%	7.6%	9.7%	12.9%

	Country/year	1995	2000	2005	2010	2014
78	Malta	4.5%	11.7%	13.0%	15.1%	23.7%
79	Mauritania	0.3%	0.2%	2.1%	5.2%	11.3%
80	Mauritius	3.6%	10.3%	14.0%	20.1%	33.3%
81	Mexico	-0.4%	4.0%	4.8%	5.2%	9.1%
82	Mongolia	-3.8%	-2.4%	4.2%	10.7%	30.5%
83	Morocco	-0.8%	2.2%	7.2%	12.3%	20.5%
84	Mozambique	-0.3%	10.3%	18.3%	24.9%	42.2%
85	Myanmar	4.5%	14.9%	32.1%	49.5%	86.3%
86	Namibia	1.7%	3.1%	6.6%	10.3%	18.0%
87	Nepal	2.4%	6.5%	9.2%	13.9%	24.0%
88	Netherlands	1.6%	6.8%	7.9%	9.1%	12.2%
89	New Zealand	1.2%	3.9%	7.3%	7.3%	12.2%
90	Nicaragua	-0.4%	3.6%	5.9%	7.4%	15.8%
91	Niger	-1.9%	-2.9%	-2.0%	-0.5%	2.3%
92	Nigeria	-1.1%	-0.7%	8.9%	14.3%	23.4%
93	Norway	3.2%	7.9%	10.1%	9.8%	14.0%
94	Pakistan	1.9%	3.4%	7.1%	8.9%	14.8%
95	Panama	3.4%	7.5%	10.8%	18.3%	36.4%
96	Papua New Guinea	5.9%	4.9%	4.5%	9.0%	20.9%
97	Paraguay	0.9%	-1.8%	2.6%	7.2%	15.4%
98	Peru	3.2%	5.4%	9.3%	17.0%	29.5%
99	Philippines	-0.3%	1.3%	4.5%	8.9%	18.4%
100	Poland	1.9%	9.4%	13.7%	20.6%	33.2%
101	Portugal	1.6%	6.6%	7.2%	7.8%	8.9%
102	Qatar	1.3%	11.2%	12.6%	14.9%	24.2%
103	Republic of Korea	7.3%	15.6%	21.7%	27.2%	42.5%
104	Republic of Moldova	-16.9%	-22.9%	-15.8%	-12.2%	-10.3%
105	Romania	-1.7%	-2.2%	6.3%	11.6%	19.5%
106	Russian Federation	-9.1%	-9.2%	-1.7%	2.8%	6.9%
107	Rwanda	-4.7%	-1.0%	6.0%	13.3%	25.2%
108	Saudi Arabia	0.6%	-0.3%	0.9%	1.1%	5.4%
109	Senegal	-1.5%	0.8%	3.2%	4.0%	5.9%
110	Serbia	-13.8%	-15.3%	-8.5%	-4.9%	-5.5%
111	Sierra Leone	-4.5%	-18.6%	-10.5%	-7.7%	1.3%
112	Singapore	5.5%	10.8%	15.9%	20.4%	32.0%
113	Slovakia	-2.0%	1.7%	8.1%	14.5%	22.9%
114	Slovenia	-0.5%	4.7%	9.3%	11.0%	14.6%
115	South Africa	-1.2%	-1.1%	1.9%	3.9%	6.3%
116	Spain	1.2%	6.2%	8.5%	8.1%	9.6%
117	Sri Lanka	4.3%	11.2%	15.7%	23.8%	44.5%
118	Sudan (former)	0.5%	6.1%	11.6%	8.8%	10.2%
119	Swaziland	1.2%	2.9%	5.3%	6.6%	10.7%
120	Sweden	0.1%	4.5%	7.4%	8.5%	12.5%
121	Switzerland	-0.8%	1.3%	2.3%	3.8%	5.9%

(*Continued*)

Table A3.53 (Continued)

	Country/year	1995	2000	2005	2010	2014
122	Syrian Arab Republic	5.1%	7.7%	11.6%	14.6%	1.5%
123	Tajikistan	-19.0%	-24.4%	-17.2%	-12.8%	-12.6%
124	Thailand	7.5%	8.9%	15.0%	20.0%	31.9%
125	Togo	-2.7%	-3.9%	-5.7%	-5.3%	-3.7%
126	Trinidad and Tobago	0.9%	10.4%	21.0%	25.1%	36.2%
127	Tunisia	1.9%	7.9%	12.4%	17.3%	24.7%
128	Turkey	1.6%	5.2%	9.3%	11.8%	20.2%
129	Uganda	4.1%	9.4%	15.0%	21.7%	32.2%
130	Ukraine	-13.6%	-17.8%	-8.9%	-7.1%	-9.6%
131	United Arab Emirates	-0.9%	0.2%	-2.8%	-14.3%	-15.3%
132	United Kingdom	1.4%	5.4%	8.5%	8.0%	12.7%
133	United Republic of Tanzania	0.7%	2.9%	8.2%	12.0%	21.7%
134	United States of America	1.3%	5.6%	7.7%	7.5%	11.8%
135	Uruguay	3.3%	6.2%	6.4%	14.0%	25.4%
136	Venezuela (Bolivarian Republic of)	1.2%	-0.1%	0.9%	3.5%	5.0%
137	Viet Nam	6.3%	15.3%	24.0%	32.1%	53.9%
138	Yemen	0.4%	7.0%	10.2%	12.2%	9.4%
139	Zambia	-3.2%	-2.9%	1.4%	8.5%	16.2%
140	Zimbabwe	-1.0%	-3.1%	-9.1%	-0.6%	6.0%

Table A3.54 Country classification by region

Africa	Asia	Europe
Eastern Africa	**Eastern Asia**	**Eastern Europe**
Burundi	China	Bulgaria
Kenya	Japan	Czech Republic
Malawi	Mongolia	Hungary
Mauritius	Republic of Korea	Poland
Mozambique	**South–Central Asia**	Republic of Moldova
Rwanda	Afghanistan	Romania
Uganda	Bangladesh	Russian Federation
United Republic of Tanzania	India	Slovakia
Zambia	Iran (Islamic Republic of)	Ukraine
Zimbabwe	Kazakhstan	**Northern Europe**
Middle Africa	Kyrgyzstan	Denmark
Cameroon	Maldives	Estonia
Central African Republic	Nepal	Finland
Congo	Pakistan	Iceland
Democratic Republic of the Congo	Sri Lanka	Ireland
Gabon	Tajikistan	Latvia

Africa	*Asia*	*Europe*
Northern Africa	**South-Eastern Asia**	Lithuania
Algeria	Cambodia	Norway
Egypt	Indonesia	Sweden
Morocco	Lao People's Democratic Republic	United Kingdom
Sudan (former)	Malaysia	**Southern Europe**
Tunisia	Myanmar	Albania
Southern Africa	Philippines	Croatia
Botswana	Singapore	Greece
Lesotho	Thailand	Italy
Namibia	Vietnam	Malta
South Africa	**Western Asia**	Portugal
Swaziland	Armenia	Serbia
Western Africa	Bahrain	Slovenia
Benin	Cyprus	Spain
Côte d'Ivoire	Iraq	**Western Europe**
Gambia	Israel	Austria
Ghana	Jordan	Belgium
Liberia	Kuwait	France
Mali	Qatar	Germany
Mauritania	Saudi Arabia	Luxembourg
Niger	Syrian Arab Republic	Netherlands
Nigeria	Turkey	Switzerland
Senegal	United Arab Emirates	
Sierra Leone	Yemen	
Latin America and Caribbean	**Northern America**	**Oceania**
Caribbean	**Northern America**	**Australia/New Zealand**
Barbados	Canada	Australia
Cuba	United States of America	New Zealand
Dominican Republic		**Melanesia**
Haiti		Fiji
Jamaica		Papua New Guinea
Trinidad and Tobago		
Central America		
Belize		
Costa Rica		
El Salvador		
Guatemala		
Honduras		
Mexico		
Nicaragua		
Panama		
South America		
Argentina		
Bolivia (Plurinational State of)		

(Continued)

Table A3.54 (Continued)

Africa	Asia	Europe
Northern Africa	**South-Eastern Asia**	Lithuania
Algeria	Cambodia	Norway
Egypt	Indonesia	Sweden
Morocco	Lao People's Democratic Republic	United Kingdom
Sudan (former)	Malaysia	**Southern Europe**
Tunisia	Myanmar	Albania
Southern Africa	Philippines	Croatia
Botswana	Singapore	Greece
Lesotho	Thailand	Italy
Namibia	Vietnam	Malta
South Africa	**Western Asia**	Portugal
Swaziland	Armenia	Serbia
Western Africa	Bahrain	Slovenia
Benin	Cyprus	Spain
Côte d'Ivoire	Iraq	**Western Europe**
Gambia	Israel	Austria
Ghana	Jordan	Belgium
Liberia	Kuwait	France
Mali	Qatar	Germany
Mauritania	Saudi Arabia	Luxembourg
Niger	Syrian Arab Republic	Netherlands
Nigeria	Turkey	Switzerland
Senegal	United Arab Emirates	
Sierra Leone	Yemen	
Brazil		
Chile		
Colombia		
Ecuador		
Guyana		
Paraguay		
Peru		
Uruguay		
Venezuela (Bolivarian Republic of)		

Table A3.55 Country classification by income

	Country	Income group
1	Afghanistan	Low Income
2	Albania	Lower Middle Income
3	Algeria	Upper Middle Income
4	Argentina	Upper Middle Income

Table A3.55 (Continued)

	Country	Income group
5	Armenia	Lower Middle Income
6	Australia	High Income
7	Austria	High Income
8	Bahrain	High Income
9	Bangladesh	Low Income
10	Barbados	High Income
11	Belgium	High Income
12	Belize	Lower Middle Income
13	Benin	Low Income
14	Bolivia (Plurinational State of)	Lower Middle Income
15	Botswana	Upper Middle Income
16	Brazil	Upper Middle Income
17	Bulgaria	Upper Middle Income
18	Burundi	Low Income
19	Cambodia	Low Income
20	Cameroon	Lower Middle Income
21	Canada	High Income
22	Central African Republic	Low Income
23	Chile	Upper Middle Income
24	China	Upper Middle Income
25	Colombia	Upper Middle Income
26	Congo	Lower Middle Income
27	Costa Rica	Upper Middle Income
28	Côte d'Ivoire	Lower Middle Income
29	Croatia	High Income
30	Cuba	Upper Middle Income
31	Cyprus	High Income
32	Czech Republic	High Income
33	Democratic Republic of the Congo	Low Income
34	Denmark	High Income
35	Dominican Republic	Upper Middle Income
36	Ecuador	Upper Middle Income
37	Egypt	Lower Middle Income
38	El Salvador	Lower Middle Income
39	Estonia	High Income
40	Fiji	Lower Middle Income
41	Finland	High Income
42	France	High Income
43	Gabon	Upper Middle Income
44	Gambia	Low Income
45	Germany	High Income
46	Ghana	Lower Middle Income
47	Greece	High Income
48	Guatemala	Lower Middle Income

(*Continued*)

Table A3.55 (Continued)

	Country	Income group
49	Guyana	Lower Middle Income
50	Haiti	Low Income
51	Honduras	Lower Middle Income
52	Hungary	High Income
53	Iceland	High Income
54	India	Lower Middle Income
55	Indonesia	Lower Middle Income
56	Iran (Islamic Republic of)	Upper Middle Income
57	Iraq	Lower Middle Income
58	Ireland	High Income
59	Israel	High Income
60	Italy	High Income
61	Jamaica	Upper Middle Income
62	Japan	High Income
63	Jordan	Upper Middle Income
64	Kazakhstan	Upper Middle Income
65	Kenya	Low Income
66	Kuwait	High Income
67	Kyrgyzstan	Low Income
68	Lao People's Democratic Republic	Lower Middle Income
69	Latvia	Upper Middle Income
70	Lesotho	Lower Middle Income
71	Liberia	Low Income
72	Lithuania	Upper Middle Income
73	Luxembourg	High Income
74	Malawi	Low Income
75	Malaysia	Upper Middle Income
76	Maldives	Upper Middle Income
77	Mali	Low Income
78	Malta	High Income
79	Mauritania	Low Income
80	Mauritius	Upper Middle Income
81	Mexico	Upper Middle Income
82	Mongolia	Lower Middle Income
83	Morocco	Lower Middle Income
84	Mozambique	Low Income
85	Myanmar	Low Income
86	Namibia	Upper Middle Income
87	Nepal	Low Income
88	Netherlands	High Income
89	New Zealand	High Income
90	Nicaragua	Lower Middle Income
91	Niger	Low Income
92	Nigeria	Lower Middle Income
93	Norway	High Income
94	Pakistan	Lower Middle Income

	Country	Income group
95	Panama	Upper Middle Income
96	Papua New Guinea	Lower Middle Income
97	Paraguay	Lower Middle Income
98	Peru	Upper Middle Income
99	Philippines	Lower Middle Income
100	Poland	High Income
101	Portugal	High Income
102	Qatar	High Income
103	Republic of Korea	High Income
104	Republic of Moldova	Lower Middle Income
105	Romania	Upper Middle Income
106	Russian Federation	Upper Middle Income
107	Rwanda	Low Income
108	Saudi Arabia	High Income
109	Senegal	Lower Middle Income
110	Serbia	Upper Middle Income
111	Sierra Leone	Low Income
112	Singapore	High Income
113	Slovakia	High Income
114	Slovenia	High Income
115	South Africa	Upper Middle Income
116	Spain	High Income
117	Sri Lanka	Lower Middle Income
118	Sudan (former)	Lower Middle Income
119	Swaziland	Lower Middle Income
120	Sweden	High Income
121	Switzerland	High Income
122	Syrian Arab Republic	Lower Middle Income
123	Tajikistan	Low Income
124	Thailand	Upper Middle Income
125	Togo	Low Income
126	Trinidad and Tobago	High Income
127	Tunisia	Upper Middle Income
128	Turkey	Upper Middle Income
129	Uganda	Low Income
130	Ukraine	Lower Middle Income
131	United Arab Emirates	High Income
132	United Kingdom	High Income
133	United Republic of Tanzania	Low Income
134	United States of America	High Income
135	Uruguay	Upper Middle Income
136	Venezuela (Bolivarian Republic of)	Upper Middle Income
137	Viet Nam	Lower Middle Income
138	Yemen	Lower Middle Income
139	Zambia	Lower Middle Income
140	Zimbabwe	Low Income

Index

Note: Page numbers in *italic* indicate a figure and page numbers in **bold** indicate a table on the corresponding page.

For Product Safety Concerns and Information please contact our EU
representative GPSR@taylorandfrancis.com Taylor & Francis Verlag GmbH,
Kaufingerstraße 24, 80331 München, Germany

Printed and bound by CPI Group (UK) Ltd, Croydon, CR0 4YY
01/05/2025
01858355-0011